Barry P. Goettl   Henry M. Halff
Carol L. Redfield   Valerie J. Shute (Eds.)

Intelligent
Tutoring Systems

4th International Conference, ITS '98
San Antonio, Texas, USA, August 16-19, 1998
Proceedings

Springer

Series Editors

Gerhard Goos, Karlsruhe University, Germany
Juris Hartmanis, Cornell University, NY, USA
Jan van Leeuwen, Utrecht University, The Netherlands

Volume Editors

Barry P. Goettl
Valerie J. Shute
Air Force Research Laboratory
1880 Carswell Avenue, Lackland, AFB, TX 78236-5507, USA
E-mail: {bgoettl,vshute}@colab.brooks.af.mil

Henry M. Halff
Mei Technology Corporation
8930 Fourwinds Drive, #450, San Antonio, TX 78239, USA
E-mail: henry@meitx.com

Carol L. Redfield
Computer Science Department, St. Mary's University
1 Camino Santa Maria, San Antonio, TX 78228-8524, USA
E-mail: credfield@stmarytx.edu

Cataloging-in-Publication data applied for

Die Deutsche Bibliothek - CIP-Einheitsaufnahme

Intelligent tutoring systems : 4th international conference ;
proceedings / ITS '98, San Antonio, Texas, USA, August 16 - 19,
1998. Barry P. Goettl ... (ed.). - Berlin ; Heidelberg ; New York ;
Barcelona ; Budapest ; Hong Kong ; London ; Milan ; Paris ;
Singapore ; Tokyo : Springer, 1998
    (Lecture notes in computer science ; Vol. 1452)
    ISBN 3-540-64770-8

CR Subject Classification (1991): K.3, I.2, D.2, H.5, J.1

ISSN 0302-9743
ISBN 3-540-64770-8 Springer-Verlag Berlin Heidelberg New York

© Springer-Verlag Berlin Heidelberg 1998
Printed in Germany

Typesetting: Camera-ready by author
SPIN 10638198   06/3142 – 5 4 3 2 1 0   Printed on acid-free paper

Lecture Notes in Computer Science

Edited by G. Goos, J. Hartmanis and J. van Leeuwen

Springer
Berlin
Heidelberg
New York
Barcelona
Budapest
Hong Kong
London
Milan
Paris
Singapore
Tokyo

Preface

The first International Conference on Intelligent Tutoring Systems (ITS) was held ten years ago in Montreal (ITS '88). It was so well-received by the international community that the organizers decided to do it again in Montreal four years later, in 1992, and then again in 1996. ITS '98 differs from the previous ones in that this is the first time the conference has been held outside of Montreal, and it's only been two years (not four) since the last one.

One interesting aspect of the ITS conferences is that they are not explicitly bound to some organization (e.g., IEEE or AACE). Rather, the founder of these conferences, Claude Frasson, started them as a means to congregate researchers actively involved in the ITS field and provide a forum for presentation and debate of the most currently challenging issues. Thus the unifying theme is science. This year's "hot topics" differ from those in the earlier ITS conferences as they reflect ever-changing trends in ITS research. A few of the issues being examined at ITS '98 include: Web-based tutoring systems, deploying ITS in the real world, tutoring and authoring tools, architectures, and knowledge structure and representation.

In addition to representing a wide range of topics, ITS '98 is bringing together researchers from all over the world - Australia, Brazil, Canada, England, France, Germany, Italy, Japan, Netherlands, Philippines, Portugal, Scotland, Spain, United States, Yugoslavia, and Texas (it's a country, right?). Overall, ITS '98 embodies 60 paper presentations, 25 poster sessions, 5 panels, and over 10 exhibits. Moreover, we've scheduled 4 workshops by well - known researchers (for August 16), 5 invited presentations from ITS notables (occurring throughout the conference), and various bonus activities, all with a special San Antonio flavor. Some of these include a bus tour of the city, the welcoming reception at the conference hotel, and a river barge ride along the San Antonio River (beside the world-renowned Riverwalk). Attendees may also visit the TRAIN Lab (home to a lot of ITS research) and attend the conference banquet, consisting of a Mariachi band, margaritas, and a huge Tex/Mex buffet.

The logistics involved with organizing a conference of this kind are nontrivial (for those who have not had the pleasure to do so before). However, we've been able to expedite large parts of the process by maximally exploiting computer technology – electronically handling advertising, submission and receipt of papers, registration, and so on. Many people have contributed to making the conference and proceedings reach fruition. First, we thank Claude Frasson for allowing us to host this conference. Second, we gratefully acknowledge the considerable contributions by the program chairs, Henry Halff and Barry Goettl, as well as the entire program committee. Third, we are indebted to the local organizing committee and production volunteers for their tireless efforts. Finally, we thank the different supporting organizations (AAAI, International AIED, SIGART and SIGCUE) as well as the sponsors of the conference (AFRL, Mei Technology, St. Mary's University, Galaxy Scientific, Command Technologies, and University of Texas at San Antonio).

If you are attending the conference, you'll find countless sources of stimulation. In addition to learning about the state of the art in ITS research, be sure to allot some time to cruise the Riverwalk, visit the Alamo (right across the street from the hotel), perhaps even venture into the Hill Country, visit Sea World, or cross the border into Mexico. Whatever your interests, the hotel office at the conference will be open and staffed much of the four days. Please feel free to stop in with any questions. A hot time is guaranteed!

<table>
<tr><td></td><td>Carol Redfield</td></tr>
<tr><td>San Antonio, Texas</td><td>Val Shute</td></tr>
<tr><td>May, 1998</td><td>ITS '98 Conference Chairs</td></tr>
</table>

Conference Chairs
Carol Redfield (St. Mary's University, USA)
Valerie Shute (Air Force Research Laboratory, USA)

Program Committee Chairs
Henry Halff (Mei Technology Corp., USA)
Barry Goettl (Air Force Research Laboratory, USA)

Program Committee
Esma Aimeur (Université de Montréal, Canada)
Michael Baker (Université Lumiere Lyon, France)
Ben du Boulay (University of Sussex, UK)
Paul Brna (University of Leeds, UK)
Peter Brusilovsky (Carnegie Mellon University, USA)
Stephano Cerri (University of Milano, Italy)
Albert Corbett (Carnegie Mellon University, USA)
Sharon Derry (University of Wisconsin-Madison, USA)
Isabel Fernandez de Castro (UPV/EHU, Spain)
Claude Frasson (Université de Montréal, Canada)
Guy Gouardères (Université de Pau, France)
Monique Grandbastien (Université de Nancy, France)
Jim Greer (University of Saskatchewan, Canada)
Ellen Hall (Air Force Research Laboratory, USA)
Daniele Herin (LIRMM, Université Monpellier, France)
Martin Ippel (Air Force Research Laboratory, via Leiden Univ., The Netherlands)
Lewis Johnson (University of Southern California, USA)
Sandra Katz (University of Pittsburgh, USA)
Ken Koedinger (Carnegie Mellon University, USA)
Pat Kyllonen (Air Force Research Laboratory, USA)
Susanne Lajoie (McGill University, Canada)
Alan Lesgold (Learning Research and Development Center, USA)
Looi Chee-Kit (Information Technology Institute, Japan)
Riichiro Mizoguchi (Osaka University, Japan)
Claus Moebus (University of Oldenburg, Germany)
Jean Francois Nicaud (Université de Nantes, France)
Gilbert Paquette, Teleuniversité, Canada)
Vimla Patel (McGill University, Canada)
Valery Petrushin (Andersen Consulting, USA)
Carol Redfield (St. Mary's University, USA)
Brian Reiser (Northwestern University, USA)
Kurt Rowley (Command Technologies, USA)
Valerie Shute (Air Force Research Laboratory, USA)
Daniel Suthers (Learning Research and Development Center, USA)
Lisa Torreano (Air Force Research Laboratory, USA)

Greg Trafton (Naval Research Laboratory, USA)
Kurt VanLehn (Learning Research and Development Center, USA)
Julita Vassileva (University of Saskatchewan, Canada)
Bev Woolf (University of Massachusetts, USA)
Barbara White (University of California-Berkeley, USA)

ITS Steering Committee
Stephano Cerri (University of Milano, Italy)
Claude Frasson (Université de Montréal, Canada)
Gilles Gauthier (Université de Québec à Montréal, Canada)
Guy Gouardères (Université de Pau, France)
Marc Kaltenbach (Bishop's University, Canada)
Judith Kay (University of Sydney, Australia)
Alan Lesgold (Learning Research and Development Center, USA)
Vimla Patel (McGill University, Canada)
Elliot Soloway (University of Michigan, USA)
Daniel Suthers (Learning Research and Development Center, USA)
Beverly Woolf (University of Massachusetts, USA)

Panels Chair
Pat Kyllonen (Air Force Research Laboratory, USA)

Exhibits Chairs
Kurt Rowley (Command Technologies, USA)
Donna Locke (Galaxy Scientific, USA)

Workshops Chair
Cathy Connolly (Galaxy Scientific, USA)

Publicity Chairs
Kevin Kline (Galaxy Scientific, USA)
Cathy Connolly (Galaxy Scientific, USA)

Conference Treasurer & Local Arrangements
Carol Redfield (St. Mary's University, USA)

Registration Chair
Doug Hall (St. Mary's University, USA)

Production Volunteer Coordinator
Tom Bylander (University of Texas at San Antonio, USA)

Webpage Design
Val Shute (Air Force Research Laboratory, USA)

Art and Brochure Coordinators
Denise Morelen
Lisa Torreano

External Reviewers

M.A. Alberti	R. Hill	V. Prince
L. Alem	T. Hirashima	D. Py
V. Aleven	K. Hook	H.C. Quek
A. Arruarte-Lasa	P. Hsieh	A. Ram
R. Azevedo	R. Hubscher	S. Ritter
M. Baron	M. Ikeda	J. Sandberg
J. Beck	M. Joab	J. Self
B. Bell	A. Kashihara	M. Sharples
M.-F. Canut	D. Kaufman	K. Sinitsa
P. Chan	A. Kushniruk	M. Stern
D. Christinaz	J.-M. Labat	B. Tirre
P.J. Coppock	P. Leroux	S. Trickett
C. Dede	J. Lester	L. Trilling
E. Delozanne	R. Lucklin	Y. Tsybenko
C. Desmoulins	C. Mallen	M. Urretavizcaya
A. Diaz de Llarraza	T. Mengelle	K. van Putten
H. Dufort	D. Metzler	F. Verdejo
C. Eliot	A. Munro	M. Vivet
E. Gibson	T. Murray	B. Wenzel
J. Girard	J. Nanard	K. Williams
L. Gugerty	M. Nanard	R. Willis
H. Halff	H. Narayanan	R. Winkels
C. Hall	T. Nodenot	L.H. Wong
H. Hamburger	F. Pachet	D. Wortham
N. Heffernan	H. Pain	

Table of Contents

Invited Presentations

Architectures for ITS

Design and Interface Issues

Tutoring and Authoring Tools

Collaborative Learning

Knowledge Structure and Representation

Teaching and Learning Strategies

Applications of ITS

Student Modeling

Educational Agents

Deploying ITS

Web-Based ITS

Poster Papers

Panels 616

Workshops 621

Exhibits 625

Authors Index 627

Instructional Applications of ACT: Past, Present, and Future

John R. Anderson

Carnegie Mellon University, Pennsylvania, USA
ja0s+@andrew.cmu.edu

ACT is a cognitive architecture which addresses how procedural and declarative knowledge is acquired and strengthened with practice. As originally described in 1983 it modeled human cognition at the multi-second temporal grain size. I will review how this theory and the technology of model tracing led to a generation of cognitive tutors. These tutors were based on extensive cognitive task analyses of programming tasks and mathematical problem solving. They tracked and tutored students as they solved problems in conventional computer interfaces. This technology has evolved to the point where it is used successfully to teach high school mathematics in many schools around the world.

While successful, these tutors are limited by their inability to be aware of student state changes, particularly at sub-second level. The new ACT-R architecture (developed with Christian Lebiere) now can model tasks at this temporal grain size. I will review research from my laboratory addressing the potential of the new architecture for education. Kevin Gluck has research showing how tracking of eye movements can provide more information about student state. I will review a class of tasks (dynamic, time-pressured) where important learning is taking place at this temporal grain size. Frank Lee has shown that the same ACT-R cognitive task analysis applies to these tasks as the academic topics of mathematical problem solving. However, for these tasks much of the competence resides in optimally scheduling cognitive actions and attending to the right portions of complex information displays. A version of ACT-R developed by Mike Byrne (called ACT-R/PM) has the potential modeling for high-density sensing information (tracking of eye movement, speech recognition). Dario Salvucci has developed algorithms for using such data to do real-time model tracing at the sub-second level. I will also discuss the potential of providing instructional intervention in response to the model's interpretation of the student based on such high-density sensing data including face identification.

Teaching Expertise and Learning Environments

Monique Grandbastien

LORIA, Université Henri Poincaré – Nancy, France
Monique.Grandbastien@loria.fr

To design efficient, flexible and user-adaptable learning environments, we need to embed a great deal of knowledge into them. In the field of ITS, people often classify this knowledge into four categories: domain, tutoring, student and interface, based on the ITS architecture popular in the eighties. This talk emphasizes the teacher's knowledge, which encompasses all the expertise of the teacher or of the trainer. Thus it is broader than that which is usually called tutoring knowledge.

The necessary updating of professional skills, the existing dissatisfaction with many educational systems and the aspiration for personal development call for more individualized education and training. Network and Web technologies are now available to provide education and training nearly everywhere at any time. Teacher's knowledge is now the core problem for the design of the needed environments, thus it is crucial to make this teacher's knowledge more explicit for improving the performances and flexibility of computer-based learning environments.

Teachers' knowledge is embedded in many existing prototypes, but most implementations are still beginning from scratch instead of building on existing material; few papers are really comparing their proposal with previous ones, mainly because there is no common framework for such comparisons.

Research in Artificial Intelligence has often been experimental; models and architectures mostly come from close observation and analysis of working prototypes. This has been, and continues to be true in the field of ITS. So the first part of the talk is devoted to the analysis of teacher's knowledge in several existing prototypes:

- Where is teachers' knowledge hidden?
- How is it acquired, how is it represented?
- What are its effects on the performances of the prototype?
- What kinds of architectures have been used, with what benefits and problems?

I start with some well known systems such as NEOMYCIN and GUIDON, then describe in more detail some prototypes that were built by our research team during the past ten years. I focus on the benefits of having practitioners on the design teams in order to provide us with their teaching expertise. I provide references to similar research projects that were conducted in France under the umbrella of a program funded by the French National Scientific Research Center and in programs funded by the European Union.

In the second part of the talk, my aim is to provide a framework for organizing the extensive but very unordered data that is available on teacher's knowledge. I organize this knowledge into categories according to different viewpoints. Based on this framework, I discuss the acquisition and modelisation problem; in my view commonly shared ontologies in the domain have not yet been sufficiently developed. Finally, I propose more suitable architectures for reflecting teacher's knowledge, moving from the traditional, but old "four modules model" to more up-to-date proposals such as agent models and parameterized environments.

Finally, I note that much has been accomplished, but the context is rapidly changing, especially in terms of communication and cooperation. Thus major research initiatives need to be undertaken to face these new challenges. Our task becomes LARGER, not SMALLER.

Hanging by Two Threads: The Evolution of Intelligent Tutoring Systems Research

John Self

University of Leeds, England
jas@cbl.leeds.ac.uk

This paper will present a view that, although the continual development of new information and communication technologies means that it is always dawn for ITS designers, what holds the ITS field together as a coherent, significant research activity are two threads which have been important from the beginning of ITS research and which will become increasingly so. These threads are (1) the recognition that tutors (human or otherwise) should 'care' about learners and (2) the realisation that ITS research is uniquely placed to add scientific precision to the educational process.

A notion that "ITSs care about learners" risks being dismissed as a political slogan but I believe that it captures the fundamental difference between ITSs and the many other kinds of computer-based learning system. A computer-based learning system which is not an ITS is designed to react in pre-specified ways when a learner uses it. Of course, the designer 'cares' to make this interaction as effective as possible but the system itself does not care, in the sense of performing on-line reasoning about, the learner and what he or she is doing. Rather paradoxically, such designers have been able to claim the high moral ground from ITS designers by emphasising their own concern to develop learner-oriented constructivist environments - in contrast to ITS designers who are portrayed as developing "Ve haf vays of making you learn" systems which are somewhat unsympathetic to learners. From the beginning, however, ITS designers, while recognising the need for pre-design and for supporting exploratory learning, have also emphasised that (as with human tutors) it is necessary to adapt dynamically to learning interactions. The ITS field, with its work on student modelling, was the first to recognise the need for user modelling to support system-user interactions.

The second thread is one for which I coined the phrase "computational mathetics" in order to make the process explicit when it is, in fact, an inevitable but usually implicit part of any ITS endeavour. In order to implement any kind of computer-based learning system we have to try to make computationally precise what are otherwise relatively vague theoretical concepts in education and psychology. Academically, this is the contribution that ITS research can make. So, rather like the relation between 'computational linguistics' and 'linguistics', 'computational mathetics' involves the development of computational formalisms for 'mathetics', that is (or would be, if it existed), the study of learning and teaching. Once the aims of computational mathetics are accepted as worthwhile then we can be proactive in applying the rich formalisms already available in computer science and artificial intelligence to describe learning and teaching processes. Eventually, one may hope that the design of some aspects of ITSs may be derived directly from these computational formalisms. Meanwhile, computational mathetics will continue to evolve as a side-effect of ITS design and will, rather than the ITSs themselves, be its main contribution, in due course.

These two threads will be illustrated by a series of past, present and future projects concerned with: procedural student models, concept teaching, guided discovery learning, collaborative learning, cognitive diagnosis, student modelling shells, metacognitive architectures, and process models of learning.

My Knowledge of Knowledge

Valerie J. Shute

Air Force Research Lab, Texas, USA
vshute@colab.brooks.af.mil

Intelligent tutoring systems contain a lot of knowledge; they have to know what to teach, as well as when and how to teach it, tailored for each learner. The general goal of my talk is to discuss two programs that I've been working on recently in terms of how they work in concert to acquire and manage all this knowledge required by any ITS.

The first program is called DNA (Decompose, Network, Assess). It provides the blueprint for instruction, obtaining curriculum elements directly from the responses and actions of multiple subject-matter experts who answer structured queries posed by the computer (Shute, Torreano, & Willis, in press). The second program is called SMART (Student Modeling Approach for Responsive Tutoring), a student modeling paradigm that assesses performance on each curriculum element by way of a series of regression equations based on the level of assistance the computer gives each person, per element (Shute, 1995). On the basis of the relationship between the computed, probabilistic value and the current mastery criterion, SMART decides what to instruct next (i.e., present a different version of same curriculum element, remediate that element, or present the next element for that particular learner). This decision is further informed on the basis of the knowledge structure provided by DNA. Thus, DNA relates to the "what" to teach, while SMART addresses the "when" and "how" to teach it.

DNA works by successively decomposing the expert's knowledge into primitives, then allowing the expert to network these elements via relational information to synthesize a knowledge structure. This hierarchical knowledge structure constitutes the curriculum for instruction. DNA was expressly designed to work together with SMART to make ITS development more principled and automated, as well as to render computerized instructional programs intelligent. A critical feature of both DNA and SMART is the notion that the elements making up the knowledge structure have different "flavors" that interrelate in particular ways, each with its own simple-to-complex continuum. These knowledge types include symbolic, procedural, and conceptual knowledge.

This knowledge-type distinction is important for several reasons. First, the questions used by DNA to elicit the knowledge types vary in accord with what is being captured. For instance, to elicit procedural knowledge, the computer queries the expert for progressively more detailed step-by-step information, while conceptual knowledge elicitation focuses more on probing for relational information among concepts. Second, the three knowledge types have unique ways in which they are instructed as well as assessed. This is an important characteristic of SMART, which handles the instruction and assessment of curriculum elements. I'll provide a lot of examples of the different types of knowledge, as well as examples of different instructional techniques and assessment probes. Finally, I'll describe our attempts to create a hybrid representational scheme that embodies the range of knowledge types. This allows one to represent both procedural and semantic/conceptual knowledge within a common network structure.

In summary, my contention is that individuals possess qualitatively different types of knowledge, and there are optimal ways to elicit, instruct, and assess them. Concluding with a (loose) analogy, when you go out fishing and want to lure many fish to your line, use the appropriate bait. That is, some types of fish are attracted to squirmy worms, while others go after shiny, moving objects. It is thus critical, for effective fishing, to match bait to the type of fish you're after.

Cognitive Tools to Support Discovery Learning

Wouter R. van Joolingen

University of Twente, The Netherlands
joolingen@edte.utwente.nl

Discovery learning is seen as a promising way of learning for several reasons, the main being that the active involvement of the learner with the domain would result in a better knowledge base. Because learners can design their own experiments in the domain and infer the rules of the domain themselves they are actually *constructing* their knowledge will understand the domain at a higher level than when the necessary information is just presented by a teacher. In practice, it is very hard to find solid evidence for this hypothesis. For instance, when learners are confronted with a simulation of a physics domain, and are asked to discover themselves which physical laws can explain the phenomena that can be observed, many learners will not reach a satisfactory result. The reason for this is not necessarily that the idea of discovery learning is not a good idea at all, but it indicates that learners need more than just the domain to learn about it.

In research on scientific discovery learning, it has been found that in order for this type of learning to be successful, learners need to posses a number of discovery skills, including *hypothesis generation, experiment design, prediction*, and *data analysis*. In addition, regulative skills like *planning* and *monitoring* are needed for successful discovery learning. Apart from being supportive for learning about the domain at hand, these skills are usually also seen as a learning goal in itself, as they are needed in a complex information society. Lack of these skills can result in ineffective discovery behavior, like designing inconclusive experiments, confirmation bias and drawing incorrect conclusions from data.

The approach discussed in this presentation is to support learners in performing the mentioned discovery skills with cognitive tools. Cognitive tools are defined as instruments included in a learning environment allowing learners to make cognitive processes, like discovery skills, and their results explicit. Cognitive tools therefore can play a supportive role in discovering a domain. Central themes that will be discussed in this presentation are:

How cognitive tools can be designed, starting from a theory on discovery learning. A design theory for cognitive tools is necessary to be able to offer genuine support for discovery learning. It will be discussed how a dual search space model of discovery can lead to the choice and design of cognitive tools.

Characteristics of cognitive tools in terms of their impact on the learning process. Cognitive tools have intended and unintended effect on discovery learning processes. They influence the way discovery processes are carried out and the learner's freedom.

The integration of cognitive tools in a simulation environment. It will be discussed why integration is important and how this integration can be effectuated in a simulation-based learning environment.

In the presentation a number of examples of cognitive tools will be presented and discussed, as they appear in the SIMQUEST authoring environment for simulation-based discovery learning, as well as in other discovery environments.

Using a Learning Agent with a Student Model

Joseph E. Beck and Beverly Park Woolf

Center for Knowledge Communication
Department of Computer Science
University of Massachusetts
Amherst, MA 01003
U.S.A.
{beck,bev}@cs.umass.edu

Abstract. In this paper we describe the application of machine learning to the problem of constructing a student model for an intelligent tutoring system. The proposed system learns on a per student basis how long an individual student requires to solve the problem presented by the tutor. This model of relative problem difficulty is learned within a "two-phase" learning algorithm. First, data from the entire student population are used to train a neural network. Second, the system learns how to modify the neural network's output to better fit each individual student's performance. Both components of the model proved useful in improving its accuracy. This model of time to solve a problem is used by the tutor to control the complexity of problems presented to the student.

1   Introduction

MFD (Mixed numbers, Fractions, and Decimals) is an intelligent tutoring system (ITS) that teaches arithmetic to fifth and sixth graders. This system adapts its instruction to meet the needs of each learner by intelligently selecting a topic on which the student should work, providing hints that match the student's level of ability, and dynamically constructing problems that are appropriate for the student [2].

The system represents the domain as a topic network. A topic refers to a large unit of knowledge, such as "subtract fractions" or "multiply whole numbers." Each topic has a list of pretopics; before the student can work on a topic, all of its pretopics must be passed. In addition, the system knows a topic's subskills, which are all of the individual steps that must be performed to solve a problem of a given topic.

For example, in the problem $\frac{1}{3} + \frac{1}{2}$ the topic is "add fraction." This topic has subskills of finding the least common multiple, converting the operands to equivalent denominators, simplifying the result, and making the fraction proper. However, it is not necessarily true that all subskills will have to be applied to solve a particular problem. In this case, the student will not have to simplify her answer or make the result proper.

In this paper, we describe an analysis of an evaluation of MFD that took place in Winter 1996 and Spring 1997. The machine learning techniques described here were added post hoc, and have been applied to the data gathered during the evaluation. We are working to incorporate these mechanisms into the next version of the tutor.

Currently, the MFD tutor adjusts problem difficulty via a complex, but ad hoc mechanism [2]. The system rates a problem's complexity on an absolute scale, builds problems that are at a "good" level of difficulty for each student and require the student to apply skills in which she needs more practice. Rather than controlling the problem's complexity directly, the new system will construct problems that require a certain amount of time for the student to solve. This is important, since if a problem takes too long to solve, the learner may become frustrated and lose confidence in her math abilities. MFD determines if the student is not making sufficient progress on the current problem, and if so generates an easier problem which she can handle.

For example, a student who is very confident in her abilities or very proficient could be given problems that take a considerable amount of time to solve. A student who has poor math skills, or who has low self-confidence in her math skills may become frustrated or give up if a problem requires too much time to solve. This student should be given gradually more difficult problems. Since one of the goals of the MFD system is to increase girls' confidence in mathematics [3], the tutor periodically presents the student with questionnaires [5] to rate a student's self-confidence. So it is certainly possible to add a measure of self-confidence to the system's student model.

Predicting the amount of time students require to solve a problem is difficult. First, the overall skill level of the student must be accounted for. If two students are given identical problems, the more skilled student will solve the problem more quickly than the less skilled student. Second, problems vary in difficulty; a student can solve $\frac{1}{3} + \frac{1}{3}$ much more quickly than she could solve $\frac{10}{11} + \frac{7}{12}$. Third, there are considerable individual differences in how quickly students solve problems, and these differences are not a component of most student models. For example, some students navigate the keyboard more quickly than others, some students have the multiplication tables memorized while others must use pencil and paper, etc. Any of these factors can impact the time required to solve a problem. Finally, the time required to solve a problem is a noisy variable. That is, if a student is given the same problem twice, she may take very different amounts of time to solve it. A small mistake at the beginning of the problem solving process can drastically impact the time required to solve a problem.

For these reasons, we are using a machine learning (ML) agent to predict the amount of time students require to solve a problem. We are using function approximators due to their being robust with respect to noisy data [6]. Additionally, with a learning agent, it is unnecessary to specify *a priori* how the prediction task should be accomplished; the learning agent is provided with the data and allowed to construct its own theories.

2 Related work

ML techniques have been applied to the construction of student models. Chiu and Webb [4] used C4.5, a decision tree algorithm, to construct a set of rules for determining if a student had a particular misconception. Results of this architecture were mixed: the learning agent was capable of successfully classifying student misconceptions but had difficulties deciding between multiple possible "bugs" in the student's knowledge.

ML has also been used to select which high level teaching action to perform next. Quafafou et al. [7] built a prototype system *NeTutor*. This system constructed tables of rules that would learn which types of interactions (guided, discovery learning, examples, etc.) enabled each student to learn best.

Prior work applying ML techniques to ITS have concentrated on learning features that are already a part of student models. We use the flexibility of machine learning to include other data that is not traditionally used, such as problem difficulty and student beliefs about their abilities. ML allows us to use this knowledge without knowing ahead of time how it is to be used.

3   Methodology

The MFD tutor has been used in three fifth and sixth grade classrooms in suburban and urban settings. Students enjoyed working with the system, and girls' self-confidence in their math ability increased as a result of using it [3].

3.1   Data collected

While the grade school students were using the tutor, the system gathered a variety of data: the tutor's belief of the student's ability at solving the topic and her average score in the required subskills (range of [1...7]), the student's estimates of her ability at the topic and its required subskills (integers in the range [1...7]), data about the problem type (addition or subtraction), the problem's estimated level of difficulty (derived from the domain model, range of [0...7]), and the student's gender.

The system only considers the student's ability on subskills that are related to the current problem. For example, in $\frac{1}{2} - \frac{1}{3}$, students would have to find a least common multiple of 2 and 3, and then convert $\frac{1}{3}$ and $\frac{1}{2}$ into fractions with equivalent denominators. However, students would not have to convert the answer to proper form or simplify the answer, so these subskills would be unused.

The learning algorithm is given the student's self-assessments of her abilities. The system periodically asked the student to evaluate her proficiency in various domain topics. Averaged across all students, there was no linear relationship between their self-assessment and their actual performance. However, on a per student basis, students misestimated their abilities in a fairly systematic way. For more information see [1].

After the student solved the problem, the time required was stored. Fifty students used the tutor, and solved 1781 problems involving fractions. We used these data to train a learning agent that learns a "population student model" of how long it takes students to solve a problem. So our task is given a student, her student model, and the problem to be solved, predict how long it will take her to solve the problem.

3.2   Learning architecture

There are two ML components in our system. The population student model (PSM) is based on data from the entire population of users. The second component operates on a per student basis, and adapts the PSM to better predict each student's performance.

The population student model takes as input characteristics of the student, as well as information about the problem to be solved, and outputs the expected time (in seconds) the student will need to solve that problem. This information is gathered for every student using the system. It is important to note that this population model is also a student model, since its predictions are dependent upon the student model. Therefore, the predictions will differ for each student. The rationale of training a learning agent with many different students is that it provides a larger set of datapoints. A tutor will interact with each student to only a limited extent. However, by combining all of the tutor's interactions with each student, a significant amount of training data can be gathered.

Even though this population model considers the student's abilities in making its prediction, its accuracy can still be improved by refining its predictions to better match those of the individual students. For example, in our task, some students could have the same level of ability (as reported by the tutor), yet one may navigate the keyboard more quickly, or one may think faster than another. These differences are not accounted for by our student model, so the learning agent cannot distinguish between these two students. When trying to predict a student's performance, for any interesting task *some* information will be missing (otherwise we would have a perfect cognitive model). This missing information ensures there is some room to improve our model. We therefore add a second stage of learning to the system that learns how to fine-tune the PSM's predictions to better match the student's actual performance.

4 Population student model

We use a neural network with the backpropagation learning algorithm[1] to learn the PSM. The choice of which machine learning architecture to use depends heavily on the amount of data available. As the training set grows larger, neural networks become better options as learning algorithms due to their ability to learn a variety of functions.

Our network uses 25 input units, 4 hidden units, and 1 output unit. These numbers were discovered via trial and error, as network design is still poorly understood.

4.1 Input units

The neural network uses the data listed in Section 3.1 as inputs.

Input encoding Neural network inputs typically range from 0 to 1 (inclusive). However, many of our network's inputs fall outside of this range. One option is to normalize the inputs so they fall between 0 and 1. For example, if a value x ranges from 1 to 7, the network would be given $\frac{x-1}{6}$ as input.

The other option is to discretize the input. For example, if x ranges from 1 to 7, a set of 7 input units could be created. If x was 1, the first input would be set to 1, and the other six would be 0. If x was 5, the fifth input unit would be set to 1, while the others would be 0. This requires many input units if x can be large. Another scheme is to consider ranges of x. For example, if x is 1 or 2, then input unit 1 is activated, if x is 3, 4, or 5, then input unit 2 is activated, if x is 6 or 7 then input unit 3 is activated. This is a "one-hot" encoding scheme, since for each feature, only one input unit can be active at a time. We discretized the inputs into ranges since that procedure frequently

---

[1] We thank Jeff Shufelt for making his neural network package publicly available.

works better than normalizing the inputs. This is why our network has 25 input units for relatively few (7) actual inputs.

Intelligent features An important characteristic of our choice of inputs is that the system does not learn things about any specific component of the domain model such "adding fractions." The inputs are phrased in terms of the student's proficiency in the topic being tested. For example, consider a student given the problem $\frac{1}{4} + \frac{1}{4}$, and whose proficiencies at adding fractions and its subskills are given in Table 1.

Table 1. Sample topic and subskill proficiencies

Skill	Proficiency Rating
add fractions	0.6
find the least common multiple	0.3
make equivalent fraction	0.4
simplify	0.1
make fractions proper	0.3

The neural network's inputs are phrased in terms of "problem's topic" and "subskills required". To predict the time required to solve this problem, one input to the network is the proficiency of this topic (which is 0.6). Another input is the average proficiency of the *required* subskills. Since in our example, the only subskill the student must perform is simplification, that is the only subskill considered, and the value of that input will be 0.1.

Constructing features for the neural network in this manner is very powerful. The learning agent does not have to consider additional details. In this example, the student's ability at subtracting whole numbers is unlikely to be useful, so this knowledge is not provided to the learning agent as this would slow down the learning process.

An additional benefit is the ML agent can better generalize what it does learn. In this case, the network will probably learn that if the student has a low proficiency on the subskills necessary to solve the problem, she will require a long time to solve it. This theory can be applied to a variety of topics. So if the system were to encounter a student attempting to solve a subtract mixed numbers problems, and the student had low proficiencies on the needed subskills, the ML agent could conclude the student will require significant time to solve the problem.

Restricting what the learning agent can consider is a form of bias, and can potentially enhance the agent's learning speed and generalization ability. However, there is the potential drawback that this bias causes the agent to ignore some information that is actually useful. Unfortunately, this tradeoff is all too frequent in machine learning.

4.2   Target value

The neural network is learning to predict how long students will require to solve a problem. Since time to solve a problem is recorded in seconds, it must be normalized to fall in the range [0...1]. We have decided to discard trials taking longer than 5 minutes, so 300 seconds is the normalizing constant. Thus the target value is $\frac{time}{300.0}$. This resulted in discarding approximately 5% of the dataset. Discarding these outliers is beneficial, as some of these datapoints do not reflect the actual time students spent solving the problem. For instance, some students may have left their computer for a few minutes, or saved the problem and returned to use the tutor the next day, etc.

4.3   Network constants

There are several learning parameters that must be determined to train a neural network. First, there is η, which controls how rapidly the network's weights are adjusted. A high value of η results in rapid initial learning, but the network's performance will soon plateau or possibly become worse. Small values result in slower initial learning, but the system can potentially attain superior performance.

Second is the network's *momentum*. With a high momentum, once a network starts to adjust its internal weights in a certain direction, it has a tendency to continue doing so. This speeds its learning, as the network increases its internal weights more rapidly, and is less likely to backtrack and decrease weights that have been increased. However, a high momentum may cause a network to be too "hasty" in its learning and spend considerable time undoing poor early actions.

4.4   Accuracy of PSM

To test the accuracy of the PSM, a k-fold cross-validation technique was used. The trimmed dataset consisted of 1587 datapoints, obtained from the logfiles of 50 students. To test the neural network's accuracy for each student, the network was trained on 49 students' data and then tested with the remaining student's data. This procedure was done for each of the students (reinitializing the network between each run).

The model's error was calculated on a per student basis by squaring the difference between the neural network's predicted time and the actual time the student required. Table 2 contains sample data generated for testing purposes. These data demonstrate a student who solves problems more quickly than the model anticipates. The error rate for the PSM was compared to another function that simply guessed the average time required to solve a problem (approximately 98 seconds). If our ML-agent cannot outperform another agent that simply guesses the average time, there is little point in using it. Indeed, this evaluation procedure helped uncover several bugs in our implementation.

Setting η to 0.001, momentum to 0.0, and training the network 2,000 times produced the best model fit, and had 33% less squared error than simply guessing the average (i.e. the neural network accounted for 33% of the variance). For our initial work, we were concerned with speed of learning, so we set both η and momentum to 0.4. Running the network for 10 iterations produced a fairly good model fit, on the order of 25% variance

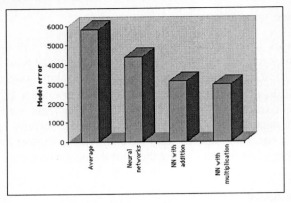

Fig. 1. Error for each model type.

accounted for. The first two entries in Figure 1 shows the sum-squared error produced by each model.

In theory, it is possible to improve the network's accuracy by altering the number of hidden units or allowing it to train longer. We experimented with having more hidden units, but performance did not improve significantly. It is unlikely that training the network for longer will produce appreciable gains, as most of our simulation runs plateaued at roughly the same level of performance.

5   Adapting the PSM to Individuals

The data indicate our model does not perfectly predict student behavior, and there is substantial room to improve its performance. Changing the network architecture or training for more iterations has been ruled out. One option is to augment the network's inputs. As mentioned previously, an ITS' student model does not contain much of the information that determines how quickly students solve problems. It is certainly possible to measure such things as typing ability, speed at multiplying simple numbers, etc. and to derive a speed estimate. However, it may be more efficient for the system to learn how to tweak the outputs of the neural network to better account for each student's performance. Since this adjusting is on a per student basis, relatively few datapoints will be available. Therefore, this "adjustment function" should be fairly simple to learn. The PSM is learned off-line from an entire population of data. However, the adjustment function can be learned on-line while students are using the ITS.

We feel it is necessary to adjust the PSM to individuals to minimize frustration. If a student spends a large amount of time on a problem, it is likely she will become frustrated and not consider that her slowness is due to problems using the keyboard or difficulty remembering the multiplication tables. In the future, MFD will be more interactive, and this model will determine how much scaffolding the student will be given.

5.1   Adjustment functions

We selected two simple operations to modify the neural networks predictions: adding a constant factor to its output, and multiplying its output by a constant factor. Either of these operations can account for students who solve problems more quickly/slowly than their student models would otherwise indicate. These adjustments were not applied simultaneously; we tested each independently.

Table 2. Error in the neural network's predictions of a sample student's performance

	Times										Total
Actual times	10	35	30	50	10	40	25	35	20	40	295
Predicted times	20	50	40	30	25	55	10	70	15	70	385
Error	100	225	100	400	225	225	225	625	25	900	3050

The formula for the additive constant is $\frac{\text{total time} - \text{predicted time}}{\text{number of cases}}$, and for the multiplicative constant it is $\frac{\text{total time}}{\text{predicted time}}$.

For the data in Table 2, the multiplication factor used for correction is $\frac{295-385}{10} = -9$. So each of the neural network's estimates would be lowered by 9 seconds for this student. Table 3 shows the result of this procedure, and its effect upon the error. To correct for the overestimation, the multiplicative factor is $\frac{295}{385} = 0.77$. So, the neural network's outputs would would be multiplied by 0.77. Table 4 shows the result of this process. The error has been reduced from 3050 to 1786.

Table 3. Sample error when adjusted by an additive constant.

	Times										Total
Predicted	20	50	40	30	25	55	10	70	15	70	385
With additive constant	11	41	31	21	16	46	1	61	6	61	295
Actual	10	35	30	50	10	40	25	35	20	40	295
$Error_{add}$	1	36	1	841	36	36	196	676	196	441	2460

This example demonstrates that substantial reductions in the error rate are possible. The additive factor reduced error from 3050 to 2460, a reduction of 20%. The multiplicative factor reduced error from 3050 to 1786, a reduction of 41%. These factors are not learned "on the fly", since they are calculated based on all of the observed instances, but serve to illustrate that fairly simple adjustments to the PSM can have a profound impact on its accuracy. It would be straightforward to alter these functions to work on-line.

5.2   Analysis of individualized models

Figure 1 shows that the multiplicative and additive factors both improve model fit. The leftmost element in the graph shows the error that remains when using a model that

Table 4. Sample error when adjusted by a multiplicative factor.

	Times										Total
Predicted	20	50	40	30	25	55	10	70	15	70	385
With multiplicative constant	15	39	31	23	19	42	8	52	12	54	297
Actual	10	35	30	50	10	40	25	35	20	40	295
$Error_{multiply}$	25	16	1	729	81	4	289	381	64	196	1786

always predicts students will take the average amount of time to solve a problem (98 seconds). The next element is the error from the PSM, which is the neural network described in Section 4.

The final two elements in the graph are the results of adjusting the neural networks output using the simple adjustment functions described in Section 5.1. A perfect model would have 0 error.

Each additional feature of the model reduces error, which provides support for our hypothesis of multiple layers of machine learning. The multiplication adjustment outperformed adding a number to the neural network by a slight amount, but overall both functions are comparable. Roughly 30% of the variance left from the PSM was accounted for by the adjustment functions. However, even the best combined models account for about 50% of the variance, and thus have significant room for improvement.

We have also constructed a PSM using linear regression. This accounted for approximately 22% of the variance on this dataset [1]. The current results are superior in three ways: (1) The linear method was not tested with a cross-validation, but was trained and tested using all datapoints. This overestimates its accuracy. (2) The NN is more flexible in what it can represent, and with additional data is likely to outperform regression by a larger margin. (3) The NN accounts for more variance than the regression model, especially if it is trained for a long time.

6   Conclusions and future work

Our two-phase learning architecture accounts for roughly 50% of the variance in the amount of time students require to solve a problem. The neural network PSM outperforms simply guessing the average and regression based techniques, and the neural network with adjustment function outperformed the basic PSM. Therefore both components of the ML architecture are useful. The PSM is powerful because data can be collected from every user of the system, and broad generalizations about student performance can be drawn. The adjustment functions are beneficial since they capture information about the students that is not stored in the student model.

We have shown that our simple adjustment functions, learned on a per student basis, are capable of improving the performance of the network. However, there is considerable room to improve our learning architecture's performance. A next step in our research is to explore adding additional data to the student model that may explain why some students solve problems more quickly/slowly than others. Additionally, perhaps our adjustment functions are too simple. A linear regression model uses both addition and multiplication, and may be more accurate than our functions. Prior work with regression models showed they are not powerful enough to learn information from a population of students, but were a good choice for learning about individuals [1].

Our plan is to use this model of time to solve a problem in the next version of the MFD tutor. Details such as a "good" length of time for a student to spend on a problem, and how this depends on her self-confidence and abilities are still unknown. Perhaps another learning agent could be added to the tutor that would observe the students and determine the optimal problem length. Eventually however, system designers must make some decisions themselves.

Although applied to the domain of simple arithmetic, this learning architecture should be applicable to a variety of skill-based domains. Most procedural skills are decomposable into components, and if the tutor can rate the student on these component skills, it is straightforward to use our learning architecture.

An open question is how well a PSM transfers to other populations, i.e. would a model built from students in an urban school work in a rural school system? We will deploy future versions of MFD to a larger variety of school systems both to test this hypothesis, and to gather more data to permit us to construct a stronger PSM.

Acknowledgements

We acknowledge the contributions of Dave Hart and Carole Beal with designing and conducting the evaluation studies, and the assistance of Mia Stern in the design and construction of the MFD system. This work is supported through the National Science foundation, under contract HRD-95555737. Any opinions, findings, and conclusions or recommendations expressed in this material are those of the authors and do not necessarily reflect the views of the National Science Foundation.

References

1. Beck, J. and Stern, M. and Woolf, B.P.: Cooperative Student Models. In: Proceedings of the Eighth World Conference on Artificial Intelligence in Education. (1997) 127–134
2. Beck, J. and Stern, M. and Woolf, B.P.: Using the Student Model to Control Problem Difficulty. In: Proceedings of the Seventh International Conference on User Modeling. (1997) 277–288
3. Beck, J. and Woolf, B.P. and Beale, C.: Improving a student's self confidence. Submitted to the Fifteenth National Conference on Artificial Intelligence (1998)
4. Chiu, B and Webb G.: Using C4.5 as an Induction Engine for Agent Modelling: An Experiment of Optimisation. Machine learning for user modeling workshop at the Seventh International Conference on User Modeling (1997)
5. Eccles, J.S. and Wigfield, A. and Harold, R.D. and Blumenfeld, P. Age and gender differences in children's self and task perceptions during elementary school. Child Development. Vol. 64. (1995) 830–847
6. Mitchell, T.: Machine Learning. McGraw Hill Text (1997)
7. Quafafou, M. and Mekaouche, A. and Nwana, H.S.: Multiviews Learning and Intelligent Tutoring Systems. In: Proceedings of Seventh World Conference on Artificial Intelligence in Education (1995)

Model-Based Explanations in Simulation-Based Training

Tariq M Khan, Stephen J Paul, Keith E Brown, R Roy Leitch

Department of Computing and Electrical Engineering, Heriot-Watt University
Edinburgh EH14 4AS
{tari,ceesjp,keb,leitch@cee.hw.ac.uk}

Abstract. A simulation based training application is described that uses a dedicated machine expert for generating explanations. The expert considers the problems the user is having with specific tasks, and by examining a normative model of problem solving, it determines an appropriate response, which involves generating many kinds of knowledge from a space of domain models. By using multiple domain models, the training system extends current approaches to simulation based training and machine generated explanations to produce a flexible learning environment for experienced plant operators and new trainees.

1 Introduction

This paper reports an approach to tailoring information provided by simulations and several additional knowledge based models to fit the pedagogic goals set by an instructional system. Evidence for the existence of many different *kinds* of domain model [1] suggests it is insufficient to adapt only one type of model to represent learning. Models containing different kinds of knowledge evolve as learning occurs in the user, so a training system must support changes in the *form* of knowledge as well as changes in *amount* of knowledge. A *multiple models* view of learning admits multiple partial models of knowledge that describe the plant or expertise and differ in several fundamental dimensions. Details of the interactions between modelling dimensions are given in [2] [3]. To support this multiple models approach to learning the training system must engage the user in activities which demand different types of knowledge, and provide explanations that clarify ambiguous, confusing or erroneous occurrences. The role of explanations is to compensate for any apparent discontinuities in the user's mental model(s). Importantly, explanations must address the kind of knowledge being communicated, such as correlative associations, causal relations and temporal sequences, and reconcile these with the user's goals.

A model based training system is described that uses an explanation expert for deciding what information is relevant for a situation and where to get it. One of its most interesting characteristics is the use of multiple domain models organised by a theoretical framework to represent the traditional Expert Module in intelligent training systems architectures. This feature is a common thread in several related projects originating with an architecture design in ITSIE [4], continuing as an implementation in MOBIT [5][6][7], and now being extended with additional functions in EXTRAS (Brite/Euram BE 95-1245), which itself will be extensively evaluated in a new project TEST. Here we concentrate on the developments achieved in EXTRAS particularly the new explanation facilities, which are absent in the earlier project. Some early results are reported in [3][8][9], which describe the theoretical basis of multiple models based explanation. Here we present other aspects of the theoretical model of explanation and a description of a demonstration prototype training system built around it.

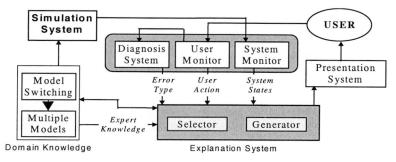

Fig. 1. Architecture of Training System

2. The EXTRAS Architecture

Figure 1 shows a conceptual description of the EXTRAS architecture, which is focused around the components that interact with the explanation component. EXTRAS is designed to provide pedagogical and advisory support through this explanation component. The primary method for support is explanations that are chosen to stimulate the user into constructing a particular type of mental model. By placing demands on the user for certain types of knowledge, e.g., a rule, the intention is that the user's attention is then focused on that particular piece of knowledge, and subsequent interactions with the explanation system will centre on clarifying it.

The explanation system is implemented as a subsystem of the EXTRAS toolkit, which includes a multiple models architecture for the domain expert and comprises several levels of knowledge. Operational models of expertise (procedural knowledge) and structural models of the plant (declarative knowledge) are described and used for providing the content of explanations. Each element of knowledge is captured as a *knowledge filler,* so that multiple kinds of knowledge can be provided in a single explanation by combining several knowledge fillers. This is explained more in [3]. The domain models are also used to evaluate the user's actions from a comparison with the expert action. Any errors are classified as being of a particular type of *deviation* following the scheme presented in [10]. A prototype diagnosis system determines the cause of error, which is given as a classification over four options [5][7].This information is used by a set of rules to decide which explanation to give. Below we describe the interaction between the explanation system and the domain models.

The knowledge fillers used in explanations at the moment are: task goal—the target state for the system to be put in to; expert action—the recommended operation to perform; user action—the action performed by the trainee; error type—a classification of any errors committed by the trainee; expert rule—a production rule justifying why an action should be performed in terms of its relation to the task goal; causal realtion—another rule that reveals the causal basis of a state change following an action; basic law—a fundamental equation or principle that indicates the scinetific basis of a causal realtionship.

An explanation is created by piecing together several knowledge fillers and arranging them in a template. For instance, an explanation can be generated from the following fillers: user action, error type and expert action:

- user action: pressed electric load set point
- error type: ommission of step
- expert action   press electric load down button

These fillers will be arranged into an explanation: *The error is* ommission of step *in the procedure. you* pressed electric load set point *instead of* electric load down button. Here, the knowledge fillers are generated from different sources. Error type and user action are determined from the user monitor, whereas the expert action is found from the domain expert. In some circumstances the expert action can be retrieved from a database of prestored procedures, indexed by the task goal they achieve. Other times, the recommended action is determined by running a rule based expert to choose a new subgoal, which is used then to select a new procedure. In general, a filler is satisfied either by retrieval from a database or through expert reasoning. The process of generating explanations is fairly constant, beginning with selection of knowledge fillers to include in a template, followed by retrieval of knowledge. More details are provided later.

3 Explanation Process

Figure 2 illustrates the interaction between the explanation and domain experts. Each has a distinct role to play in providing explanations. When a request for help is monitored, the explanation expert's role is to service that request by determining what information is needed, and what kind of knowledge representation can provide it. The domain expert's role is to provide this information: either from its knowledge bases and database, or by executing one or more of its models to generate new results.

There are three sources of requests for either for specific or general help:

- the user asks for specific pieces of information
- the user experiences a problem and decides himself to ask for (general) help
- the user monitor identifies an error and calls the explanation subsystem

3.1 Source of Requests

Different users will make different request. For example, an experienced operator who is using the system as a decision support tool will have a better idea than a trainee of the kind of information that should contribute to solving the problem. Consequently, the operator can take greater responsibility for selecting the information and knowledge to be generated or retrieved from the domain expert. In this situation the explanation expert is dormant other than passing on the user's requests to the domain expert. In contrast, a trainee who has less understanding of the significance of information must rely on delegating responsibility for information request to the explanation expert whenever he or she experiences difficulties and needs general help. The third request type involves the training system monitoring the user's actions (or inaction) and comparing this with a desired "expert" action. If an error is signalled then a request for assistance is made by the user monitor.

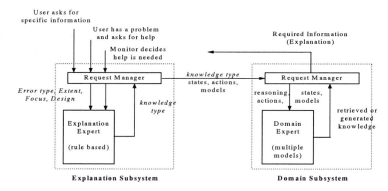

Fig. 2. Information flow between explanation expert and domain expert

3.2 Types of Request

There are four types of requests available to the user and the explanation system: states, actions, models and reasoning. Reasoning is performed when the request cannot be serviced from stored data so fresh results are needed.

3.2.1 System States

These include the qualitative evaluation or quantitative value of a parameter, component or system; and can be any of past, present, and future. For example, Water Temperature is 96 deg C, Steam Pressure is Abnormal, Boiler is in Normal condition are valid responses to requests for states. A request can also have two levels of precision—exact, which is a precise numerical value, or interval, which is a less precise range of values that share a common consequence for each value.

- **past**—these indicate previous states achieved by the component or system, or previous values for parameters. They can be determined from a time series or retrieval from a database.
- **present**—these give the current values of parameters and any evaluations of those values to give current states of components and systems. They are taken from a dedicated system monitor, which accesses the plant simulator.
- **future**—these give possible and/or likely states and values that *might occur* if certain actions are taken. They are determined from running a simulation of the plant from a given start state, with a specific action, to some time into the future.
- **goal**—these are values of parameters or states that should be the target to achieve. They are determined from expert reasoning by evoking a rule-based expert, which identifies a suitable target future state.

3.2.2 Operator Actions

These include mental and physical operational and planning actions, and can be any of: actions that were, could be or should be performed on the plant to control it (operational), as well as actions intended to reason out a solution prior to executing any controls on the plant, i.e., planning. For example, Press Electrical Load Set Point Lower button, Valve B was opened, retrieve temperature values for last hour from database, are all valid responses to requests for actions.

- **past**—these are actions taken by the user or other users prior to the current state being achieved, and they are retrieved from a log.
- **present**—this is the latest action taken by the user and is given by a dedicated monitor, which observes the user operating the simulator.
- **future**—these are actions recommended for completing a task, and are determined from expert reasoning. The rule based domain expert selects a target goal state (as above) then a standard operating procedure is retrieved from a database, which is designed to achieve that goal state.
- **planning**—these are actions taken prior to operating the plant and are recommended actions. They are determined from an analysis of the task using a normative model of problem solving, which contains a general plan that is instantiated with different specific values in different problem situations.

3.2.3 System and Expertise Models

These include any elements of knowledge stored in databases and knowledge bases, and can be any of procedures, association, and equations. Whereas requests of the first two types are the results of applying a knowledge representation, this request type seeks the knowledge representation itself. For example, press valve_hm set point raise button, wait until value increases by 10% and release; IF increase flow_hm + FIC_hm on manual THEN increase valve_hm set point 10%; voltage = current × resistance are valid responses to requests for models.

A request can be for any model, e.g., procedure, rule, principle, at different levels of precision and for different scopes. Additionally, a set of equations, rules, etc. chained together can be retrieved to give justification to reasoning performed by the expert or the user.

- **Model**—these are individual rules or procedures, or sets of equations for particular components or systems, and are retrieved from a database.
- **Executed Model**—a set of rules connected through chaining with specific values, and are determined from expert reasoning.

3.2.4 Reasoning

This involves executing one or more of the available models, and can be any of simulating with mathematical equations, chaining rule-based experts, and running a sequence of actions on the plant (procedure).

- **expert reasoning**—this involves rule based reasoning, and can include several kinds of rules, e.g., diagnostic, and operational. Each kind of rule is located in a separate knowledge base, and executing it produces different results, e.g., a cause of a problem (diagnostic), or a goal state and a recommended expert action for achieving it (operational).
- **execution**—this involves running known procedures and producing their effects on the plant simulation. The product of reasoning is a newly achieved system state.
- **simulation**—this involves running either equations models with exact values (quantitative) or intervals (qualitative), using appropriate equation models. Alternatively, a rule based simulation can be used as an approximation using causal rules. The product of reasoning is a newly reached system state.

3.3 Response Modes

There are two response modes available to deal with the requests:

- when the user asks for *specific* information this request is passed directly to the domain expert request manager. Here a suitable process is performed to provide the information—this is discussed later.
- when *general* help is needed, the explanation expert is called to suggest a tailored response. This involves identifying specific pieces of information that should be presented to the user.

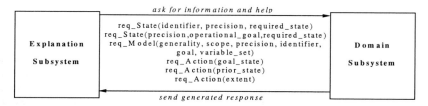

Fig. 3. Messages for the different request types

3.4 Messages

There are two messages between the explanation system and the domain system. These are: (1) requests from the explanation subsystem for information, and (2) responses from the domain subsystem. Each of these message classes has several instances shown in Figure 3 that are based on the descriptions of requests and responses set out in section 3.2. Each request has a certain form that includes a list of parameters, which identify the kind of knowledge needed in return, e.g., identifier(name of component), precision (exact or interval), operational_goal(target goal of expert reasoning), variable_set(list of parameters identifying a sought after equation).

During interaction between the explanation manager and the explanation selection components, the Explanation Manager initiates the Selector, which responds by returning a structure containing its chosen knowledge fillers and corresponding textual templates. Figure 4 shows the communication between the Selector and the other components in the system. The Selector is a management component that oversees co-operation between the Explanation Expert, which chooses the knowledge to be presented, the User Monitor, which provides information about the user's actions, and the Action Converter, which converts the user's actions into a suitable form for the Explanation Expert to use (i.e., as a value for extent).

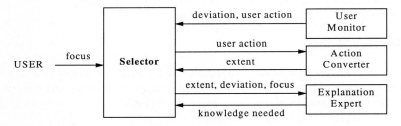

Fig. 4. Communication between Selector and other components

The focus is meant to be provided by a diagnosis component, however, there is no suitable component available yet. Therefore, focus is determined by the user indicating from a menu, responding to a direct question about his or her problem solving activity (e.g., I was trying to find the temperature display) or alternatively, a default value for focus is taken. In the demonstration system, where focus is derived has little bearing on the quality of explanations chosen as a result.

During generation of an explanation, the Generator component is responsible for retrieving the knowledge and text identified by the Selector. It returns a structure containing the retrieved knowledge and text. In order to retrieve knowledge, the Generator communicates with the User Monitor and the Domain Expert.The Generator acts as a manager to co-ordinate the retrieval or generation of information and knowledge.

The Domain Expert is responsible for deciding where to get the knowledge requested by the Explanation Expert. It can either retrieve it from a database or it must perform some reasoning to determine it. When reasoning is required, the Domain Expert must use one or more of its available multiple models and simulations. Which it uses, is a matter for model switching.

4 Domain Expert

The Domain Manager receives requests from the explanation component and controls where the knowledge is retrieved. Besides the domain models and database, information can be got from the simulation through the System Monitor, or from the user through the User Monitor. The process of choosing the appropriate source is called model switching. In the training mode, model switching is controlled by the explanation component. It decides what information is needed, and which kind of knowledge representation can provide it. An appropriate message is sent. During decision support, an independent model switching strategy is needed to guide the use of multiple models in problem solving. This aspect of the training system is under development.

The function of the domain knowledge subsystem is to construct models of the system as needed to support on-line decision making, off-line training, and to provide results and knowledge for explanations. According to the multiple models methodology [2] adopted in EXTRAS, an application domain can be segregated on the basis of *scope* into system, subsystems and components. Within the same scope, models having different *resolutions* can be created by taking into account a different number of parameters. The resolution of a model is high if the number of parameters considered in the model is comparatively high, and is low if the number of parameters considered is less. Further, knowledge of theoretical principles for the domain are best represented using groups of mathematical equations; heuristics behind the operation of the system, subsystems and components are best represented as sets of IF-THEN rules; and operating procedures are best represented using a procedural form, e.g., Petri-nets. By adopting the various representational formalisms (equations, rules and procedures), models having different *generality* can be created. Equation models are considered to be the most general form of knowledge representation and procedures the least general as they are specific to situations. The efficiency of a knowledge representation can be maximised by adopting the appropriate representational formalism.

Besides scope, resolution and generality, the methodology proposes *precision*, which allows precise, less-precise or least-precise behaviours to be generated from the models using precise, less-precise or least-precise values for parameters with suitable quantity spaces. The separation of knowledge and its encoding using the various representational formalisms produces a cubical framework, which is useful for organising the multiple models.

5 Related Research

Some research on related ideas in the generation of explanations is briefly discussed next, although further discussion is found in [3]. Pilkington *et al* [11] examined dialogue between people to determine a protocol for designing communication, potentially between a training system and a user; however, they do not examine dialogue from the perspective of its knowledge content (other than causal explanations). Rather, the analysis is of dialogue strategies in which learner and training system adopt different roles (enquirer/responder). Cawsey [12] presents a way to generate natural language explanations using techniques from planning. The aim was to enable the explanation system to vary its content, so knowing how content can change is crucial. We present a new structure analysis scheme based on modelling dimensions that develops a more discriminating classification of knowledge than Cawsey's. Chandrasekaran *et al* [13] offer a classification that identifies three types of explanation: (1) why decisions were made; (2) how elements of knowledge relate; and (3) what control strategy applied, which we also address. The multiple models approach, however, allows greater flexibility in moving among the various levels of knowledge (compiled, structural). Early work in explanation generation, e.g. SOPHIE, attempted to construct an explanation generation system from qualitative models. However that work was limited to the principles level of explanations only. QUEST [14], also employed multiple models but concentrated on causal models mostly, and did not examine the full range of available models.

Our work extends current assumptions of explanation generation by reducing explanation content to identifiable elements of knowledge, and constructing explanations by switching between multiple domain models to satisfy the demands of different situations. The works cited above have similar motivations to our own research, but none has examined both how to describe the contents of an explanation in terms of different kinds of knowledge, and how to relate these descriptions to different situations encountered during training, learning and problem solving.

6 Conclusion

We presented the EXTRAS training and explanation system, which applies multiple models to the generation of explanations in simulation based training. The novelty of EXTRAS is to produce explanations for a variety of situations by considering which of the many domain models is best suited. It then switches from the currently used model to the most suitable one. In order to accommodate this strategy, the domain knowledge subsystem must be separated into a space of models, each of which contains different knowledge in a suitable representation.

At the moment the ideas presented here have been implemented as a demonstration prototype from which four full applications are being developed. These are planned to be fully functioning systems for use in the process industries, such as power generation. A further project (ESPRIT EP25364:TEST) has begun to evaluate these ideas by building and deploying a simulation based training system for domestic wiring regulations.

7 References

1. Rassmussen,J. Skills, Rules, and Knowledge; Signals, Signs, and Symbols, and other Distinctions in Human Performance Models, IEEE Transactions on Systems, Man and Cybernetics, Vol SMC-13 No.3 (1983) 257-266.
2. Leitch *et al*, Modelling Choices in Intelligent Systems, AISB Quarterly No 93 (1995) 54-60.

3. Khan,T.M., Brown, K.E., Leitch, R.R. Leitch, Didactic and Informational Explanation in Simulations with Multiple Models, Proceedings of AI-ED 1997, pp:355-362.
4. J Sime and R Leitch, A learning environment based on multiple qualitative models, proceedings of ITS'92. Montreal, Canada.Itsie from ITS'92
5. J.E.M. Mitchell, J. Liddle, K. Brown and R. Leitch, Integrating Simulations into Intelligent Training Systems, EuroAI-ed '96, Lisbon, September 1996. pp. 80-87.
6. J. Liddle, R. Leitch, K. Brown. Generic Approaches to Developing Practical Intelligent Industrial Training Systems, Proceedings of Third International Conference, ITS '96, Montreal, Canada, pp 512-520 (1996).
7. J.E.M. Mitchell, K. Brown, R. Leitch and P.J.P. Slater. MOBIT: Pragmatic Diagnosis for Industrial Training. pp99-112. The Intelligent Systems Integration Program:Proceedings of Expert System 96, Cambridge, UK (1996).
8. T.M. Khan, K.E. Brown, R.R. Leitch, EXTRAS: a multiple models based learning environment,   submitted to Workshop 1, AI-ED (1997).
9. T.M. Khan, M Ravindranathan, K.E. Brown, R.R. Leitch, EXTRAS: a toolkit for simulation based training, International Conference on Cognitive Systems (ICCS '97) (1997), India.
10. E. Hollnagel, Human Reliability Analysis Context and Control, Academic Press, (1993).
11. R. Pilkington and C. Mallen, Dialogue Games to Support Reasoning and Reflection in Diagnostic Tasks, EuroAI-ed '96, Lisbon, September (1996), pp. 213-219.
12. A. Cawsey, Planning Interactive Explanations, International Journal of Man-Machine Studies 38 (1993) 169-199.
13. B. Chandrasekaran, M.C. Tanner and J.R. Josephson, Explaining Control Strategies in Problem Solving, IEEE Expert Spring (1989) 9-24.
14. B.Y. White, and J.R. Frederiksen (1986) ACM SIGART, no.93, pp34-37.

Acknowledgement

The work described in this paper has been undertaken in Brite/Euram III Project BE-1245 (EXTRAS: Explanation in On-line Help and Off-line Training Based on Continuous Simulation) by the following partners: GEC Marconi S3I R&D, CISE, ENEL, Heriot-Watt University, Iberdrola, KCL, LABEIN, TECNATOM, United Paper Mills. The authors wish to acknowledge the contribution of all members of the project team to the ideas presented in this paper, whilst taking full responsibility for the way they are expressed.

Towards an Intelligent Tutoring System for Situation Awareness Training in Complex, Dynamic Environments

Ellen J. Bass

Search Technology
4960 Peachtree Industrial Blvd., Suite 230
Norcross, GA 30071-1580
ellen@searchtech.com

Abstract: Some accidents in complex systems have been attributed to a lack of situation awareness. Despite increased use of automation and improvements in display design, accidents of these types have not been eliminated. One option is to train operators to acquire and to maintain situation awareness. This paper describes an instructional design, human-computer interface, and the computational architecture for implementing an intelligent tutoring system for training situation awareness. The system furnishes detailed guidance in the early practice stages of training and provides performance feedback in the reinforcement stages of training. The system includes a debriefing capability to structure the review after performance and aid in the evaluation of student performance.

1 Introduction

Accidents in complex systems have been attributed to a lack of situation awareness (SA). Despite increased use of automation and improvements in display design, accidents of these types have not been eliminated. One option is to train operators to acquire and maintain SA.

In complex, real-time domains, where resources are scarce and expensive and there is a need for training of critical skills, intelligent tutoring systems (ITSs) provide a potentially cost-effective way to enhance SA training. However, relatively little work has addressed ITSs for real-time operations [6],[7].

This paper expands upon an approach to training SA skills in real-time operations [2],[4]. Knowledge-based state, expert, instructional, and student models and an instructional human-computer interface (HCI) are integrated with a domain simulation. The design provides for SA skills training in a dynamic, interactive environment. Students can receive feedback during practice about deviations between the actual and the expected system state. Such guided practice with feedback in an authentic environment is critical for transfer to actual operations [19]. An empirical evaluation of the approach has yet to be accomplished.

1.1 What is Situation Awareness?

The impact of SA on operators in complex systems is recognized, but no one theory for SA has emerged. The behaviors that the theory should account for are [14]:
- Considering and selecting goals dynamically,
- Attending to the critical cues at the appropriate times to determine if the plans generated and executed to achieve the chosen goals are effective, and
- Predicting future states of the system to support goal creation and abandonment.

SA is a state of knowledge which relates the elements of a dynamic environment to the operator's goals. Although separate from the processes of decision-making and performance, SA is intricately associated with them. Endsley characterized this state of knowledge in terms of the operator's perception of the elements within the environment, the comprehension of the elements' meanings, and the projection of their status into the future [10]. SA is enhanced by operators' internal long-term memory structures that enable processing large amounts of information. The importance of mental models has been advocated by many (e.g., [17]) and relates to the discovery that less effective operators lack sensitivity to contextual factors, indicating a failure to recognize significant prototypical situations (c.f., [13]).

2 An Approach for SA Training

The challenge is to train operators to acquire and maintain accurate SA in order to improve total system performance. Training should focus on timely, critical, information seeking and processing behaviors and on developing appropriate mental models. Training in an authentic environment is necessary [19]. In such situated environments, students learn necessary skills, conditions for their application, and skill selection strategies -- that is, operational skills [7].

During SA training, the student's attention should be focused on each of the situational components at the appropriate time in order to identify the relationship between the situation and the current goal: a form of *structured cueing* [21]. By exploiting the role of feedback, an ITS employing a structured cueing paradigm can show students how to assess and interpret the current system state and other environmental features relative to the operational goals. Simultaneously, students build the mental representations for acquiring and maintaining SA in the future.

An alternative for providing structured cueing in a training environment is via scaffolding: support helping the student to complete tasks otherwise not possible and to achieve proficiency in target skills [8]. To be effective, scaffolding must be able to fade. The phases of demonstration, scaffolding, and fading are like apprenticeship where the master gradually introduces skills and allows the apprentice more independence as skills are mastered. For teaching cognitive skills, this process is called *cognitive apprenticeship* [8]. Due to the tacit nature of cognitive processes, their articulation is necessary.   Providing mechanisms for reflecting upon performance is advocated.

Unfortunately, ITSs for real-time operations are rare (c.f., [7]). The approach to SA training discussed here is to demonstrate SA, coach during practice, and fade as the student learns. Detailed guidance is supplied in early practice stages of training and performance feedback in the reinforcement stages. A debriefing capability is included to structure the review after performance and to help with evaluation.

Decision making includes cue detection and interpretation plus action planning and evaluation [10],[14].   Experts, using cues in the controlled system and the environment, recognize the situation, determine or prioritize the current goals, create expectations about the future system state, and choose a course of action to make the future system state meet the current goals. At a minimum, to train the SA skills to support this process, an ITS must identify when the state of the controlled system fails to meet expectations. It must provide aiding feedback when the student demonstrates a potential loss of SA by allowing the controlled system's state to fail to meet expectations. In these situations, the ITS should also support learning cue detection and interpretation, action planning and prioritizing, and evaluation skills.

To meet the objectives of SA training, the ITS requires a proactive guidance capability. The ITS should provide preparatory guidance about what to pay attention to next. Instead of waiting until a problem occurs, the ITS must prepare the student for upcoming situations and on which cues to focus. This capability teaches the less experienced student how to "stay ahead" of the controlled system.

The ITS must be able to explain its process in a pedagogically sound manner. By implementing the concepts from cognitive apprenticeship [8] and lessons from the feedback literature, the ITS must present the appropriate information to the student during practice and during post-practice debrief. During practice, the ITS provides advice about what important cues within the current context are not as expected. During debrief, the ITS provides details about why the cues are important, how to recognize the current context, and what to expect in that context.

To support reflection on the student's performance and to aid with debriefing, the ITS should summarize the set of SA problems encountered during performance. This summary helps with reviewing progress and identifying additional training. During performance, the ITS can track discrepancies between performance and associated evaluation criteria.   This capability supports debriefing and provides input for determining the student's proficiency.

In order to provide a mechanism for adapting feedback within and across training sessions, the ITS must support student modeling [23]. By augmenting the same mechanisms that summarize student performance, the architecture can determine the student's current capability level.

3 Instructional Design And Human-Computer Interface

To understand what the student experiences during training, this section describes the approach to instructional design and the HCI. Training for complex, real-time systems entails a combination of reading, lecture, simulator practice and practice in the operational environment. For example, instructor pilots (IPs) train pilots in ground school, coach them during simulated missions and missions in the actual aircraft, debrief them after practice, compare student performance to evaluation criteria, and select additional practice activities. This approach initially supports the training in the practice-debriefing-evaluation-practice cycle in simulated missions.

3.1 Practice

By the time students reach simulator training for a particular skill set, they know declaratively what to do but must operationalize the knowledge to be effective. Therefore the ITS emulates the following instructor activities during practice:
* *Coaching* as the student performs,
* *Scaffolding* of the student's performance until he can perform the procedures solo,
* *Guiding* SA skills by pointing out the relevant cues, and
* *Fading* away as the student masters the skills.

The real-time coaching interface alerts the student to discrepancies between actual and expected system states (a divergence that could lead to adverse consequences). This type of feedback is the "error signal" [1].

Because multiple discrepancies may occur, higher priority messages should be addressed before lower priority ones. In the ITS HCI, the coaching messages are presented with an associated severity level to denote how serious the failed expectation is. A taxonomy for alert severity level in aviation systems includes [16]:
* Warning (i.e., requires immediate operator awareness and action);
* Caution (i.e., requires immediate awareness and subsequent corrective action);
* Advisory (i.e., requires awareness and may require subsequent or future action).
Used in this way, the severity level encodes a priority order for operator action.

The coaching display contains a list of current aiding feedback sorted by severity level. The warning messages are displayed at the top of the list, followed by cautions and then advisories. There are no "reserved" locations for messages of each type. If there are no messages of a particular level, the messages of the next type are displayed higher up in the list. If the problem is resolved, either through corrective action or a change in goals, the coaching message is removed from the display and the remaining messages scroll upward.

Aiding feedback is color-coded according to the severity level. Warning messages are displayed in red; cautions in yellow; advisories in white. To draw attention to newly displayed information, messages are initially highlighted in reverse video. Also, newly displayed warnings and cautions have associated aural tones.

When problems are occurring, scaffolding is an infrastructure of support that helps the student to complete a task and to achieve proficiency in target skills that would otherwise not be possible. In this case, the ITS helps students notice problems they are not finding on their own. As a student masters skills and does not allow expectation failures to occur, the scaffolding fades away. Also as discrepancies are corrected, the ITS removes feedback (only actual current discrepancies are displayed). Thus the ITS naturally fades support based on student performance.

Because planning is a vital SA skill [10], the ITS coaches what to attend to by providing prompts *before* important events. These prompts encourage preparation for upcoming events. These messages are displayed in green below the others.

Cognitive apprenticeship requires articulation of the expert process. Therefore the coaching interface provides detailed explanatory information for aiding feedback. The content of the explanation includes the following:

- Deviation (description of deviation),
- Deviation cues (how to tell that a deviation has occurred),
- Consequence (future result if the deviation is left uncorrected),
- Severity level (a measure of the priority),
- Corrective action (action to take to return to the expected state), and
- Evaluation criteria (if applicable) to assess student performance.

The ITS points out where to find the deviation cues in the operational environment, thus indicating the source for maintaining better SA. In aviation, for example, such cues include aircraft generated visual information found in the cockpit (e.g., flight instruments and status lights). These cues involve aural inputs such as verbal communications. Motion related cues include pitch, roll, and yaw and tactile cues such as continuous feedback from the aircraft control stick and discrete pressure from switches. Along with cues from the controlled system, there are external cues. In aviation, examples include the horizon, landmarks, and other aircraft.

Consequence information lets the student know what the effect of the action (or inaction) is, while the severity level provides the notion of priority. When there are multiple deviations, higher priority ones should be addressed before lower ones.

The corrective action information is complex. When training high performance skills, feedback should identify the source of error and help to eliminate poor strategies [18]. Burton and Brown [5] include strategy feedback in their ITS to keep the student from completely missing concepts. They warn that if such strategy feedback is presented, it should be obviously superior to what the student has done. Lesgold [15] is skeptical because he found that advice for using a better strategy was rejected by his users. Degani and Wiener [9] lend credence to Lesgold's skepticism as they describe the difference between specified procedures (i.e., a progression of sub-tasks and actions to ensure that the primary task is executed in a logical, efficient, and error resistant manner) and practices (i.e., what the operator actually does) which are not always the same. They also explain how techniques (i.e., the methods used to accomplish procedures) leave room for individualism. This issue is addressed in the ITS by providing additional context information with the corrective action information and with the ability to include multiple techniques.

The evaluation criteria identify the performance level that the student must achieve in order to be qualified to perform the task in the operational environment.

The HCI provides the opportunity for a large amount of coaching messages. The ITS's HCI therefore provides the capability to enable or disable certain information:

- Show only evaluation criteria coaching messages: The idea here is that students may only want to see coaching messages that describe deviations based on performance evaluation criteria. Other aiding feedback may distract the student.
- Filter preparatory guidance messages: The student may decide that he no longer wants the preparatory guidance messages.

The ITS can adaptively fade preparatory guidance for students highly rated for particular curriculum items. Proficiency is derived from the performance evaluation criteria (see section 3.3) logged during the simulated missions. This capability addresses Schneider's [18] warning from studying high performance skills: training techniques for initial skill acquisition may not be useful for later skill development. Different intervention strategies work for higher prior knowledge learners [12].

3.2 Debriefing

It is not desirable to present all information about problems during performance. Training should support the student in developing the knowledge structures that are necessary for skilled performance [20]. However, providing too much information during performance may be distracting. Feedback laden instruction might interfere with learning processes as continuous, detailed feedback may supplant the self-reflective processes a student would apply to the problem [24]. That is in part why instructors debrief after practice. By elaborating the deviation data collected during performance with cue information, consequences, and corrective actions, the debriefing capability provides an opportunity for the student to reflect on his performance and to develop required knowledge structures. Also, when an aiding message first appears on the coaching interface, the ITS uses a process called "snapshot" to save the state of the aircraft and its environment. To understand the context surrounding a problem, the student can request its snapshot.

The deviation data are classified by multiple criteria: time of onset for the failed expectation, severity, type of deviation, context within which the expectation failed, and type of skill with which the deviation is associated [2]. The data can be viewed in many ways, thus providing the ability for pedagogically motivated sequencing strategies based on the content of the feedback. For example, the instructor can select a chronological approach (i.e., discuss errors as they occurred). Alternatively, the instructor can select a "focus" or a "threaded" strategy based on the concept that the most recently presented idea should be discussed again to reiterate the point [15]. Here the instructor organizes the debrief by action characteristics or the nature of the criticism. The instructor can use a "breadth" strategy, the concept that the least recently discussed idea should be selected next because it will prevent two interdependent errors from blocking each other [5]. Another approach is to use the prerequisite skill strategy based on multiple dimensions (e.g., lesson objectives) [5], where the instructor debriefs each skill separately.

Detailed information is available for every deviation including cue detection and interpretation, action planning and consequence information. Cue detection and interpretation information is available for recognizing relevant contexts.

3.3 Evaluation

Instructors use evaluation criteria to evaluate student performance. Failure to meet certain criteria leads the instructor to assign a particular rating or qualification level to the student. The evaluation criteria applicable to a particular simulated mission and any failures to meet them are available for display during the debriefing.

The ITS is designed to capture violations of performance criteria based on USAF requirements. The USAF uses three categories of qualification levels that are associated with different performance criteria [22]:

1. Qualified (Q) criteria: The student has demonstrated the desired performance and knowledge of procedures within the tolerances specified in the grading criteria.
2. Qualified with training required (Q-) criteria: The student's performance is safe but additional training is required. The performance is discussed in the debriefing and may lead to a re-evaluation of that curriculum item.
3. Unqualified (U) criteria: Performance at the U level is unsafe and requires a re-evaluation of the item and may require repeating the entire mission.

3.4 Additional Practice

The ITS saves state information when expectations fail. The student can repeat the scenario from the saved state, thus practicing newly acquired knowledge and skills. This combination approach (i.e., graphic instruction with context, plus extra practice) should engage the student and lead to higher learning outcomes. The ITS provides a summary of the skills with which the student is having difficulty to help define where to focus future training.

4 The ITS Architecture

The ITS architecture is based on a knowledge-based prototype aiding system: Hazard Monitor (HM) [11]. By enhancing the operator's problem recognition and identification process, HM is designed to reduce the rate of preventable accidents regardless of the source of the problem.

HM helps to reduce preventable accidents by alerting the human operator to discrepancies between actual and expected system states -- a divergence that could lead to adverse consequences. Discrepancies are assessed as failed expectations in a situation within the context of goal-oriented activity. For example, during the approach to an airport, one expectation is for the aircraft landing gear to be down and locked. Defining expectations in this way allows the aiding message to be both timely and context-dependent. Because the discrepancies have associated levels (e.g., warning, caution, advisory), HM also provides the ability to organize them for presentation purposes. In this way, the operator can focus on the highest priority notifications first.

The aid HM requires several enhancements to become an ITS:

- It requires a proactive capability. HM is a reactive aid. It waits until there is a failed expectation before it provides feedback.
- HM must be able to explain its process in a pedagogically sound manner.
- To support reflection on the student's performance and to aid with debriefing, HM must summarize the encountered set of SA problems.
- In order to provide a mechanism for adapting feedback within and across simulated missions, the architecture must be able to support student modeling.

A high-level overview of the ITS architecture is shown in Figure 1. The major components of the ITS include the curriculum, state model, expert model, instructional model, instructional interface, and a student model [3]. The domain simulation is included in the figure for completeness. The simulation represents the host environment with which the ITS is integrated. It periodically provides the controlled system and environmental state data as the student practices.

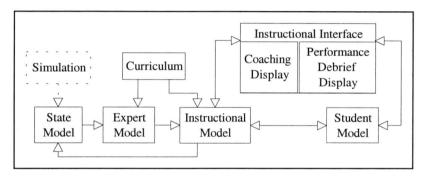

Fig. 1. ITS architecture

The state model stores and processes the simulator data. Low-level communication components in the state model are designed to make interfacing the ITS with a range of data sources practical and straight forward.

The curriculum component specifies the training objective, performance evaluation criteria, and other knowledge bases to use for training. This component is a data file used by both the expert model and the instructional model.

The expert model instantiates a normative model of monitoring and related SA skills. For training SA skills, this expert knowledge is augmented with tutoring knowledge and provides detailed information related to aiding feedback and preparatory guidance available on the instructional interface. The expert model also monitors for violations of performance evaluation criteria.

The instructional model processes the deviations detected by the expert model and presents them in a timely and context sensitive manner to the student through the instructional interface. The instructional model processes preparatory guidance messages, invokes state model snapshots to support debriefing, and logs aiding feedback to support student modeling and debriefing.

The student model stores the aiding feedback history built by the instructional model. It also maintains an evaluation history (violations of performance criteria) and a model of the student's proficiency (used to fade preparatory guidance).

The instructional interface consists of two sub-systems:

1. During practice, the coaching interface displays aiding feedback and preparatory guidance information. Detailed explanatory information is presented in a separate window when the student selects aiding feedback on the display.
2. The performance debriefing interface can be used to analyze the results of the simulated mission [2].

5 Acknowledgments

This work was supported in part by USAF contract F41624-97-C-5027.

References

1. Bangert-Drowns, R.L., Kulik, C.C., Kulik, J.A & Morgan, M. (1991). The instructional effect of feedback in test-like events. *Review of Educational Research*, 61(2), 213-238.
2. Bass, E.J., Ernst-Fortin, S.T., & Duncan, P.C. (In press). An intelligent debriefing tool for situation awareness training. In *Proceedings of the 11th International Florida Artificial Intelligence Research Society (FLAIRS) Conference*, May 17-20, 1998, Sanibel Island, FL.
3. Bass, E.J., Ernst-Fortin, S.T., Duncan, P.C., & Small, R.L. (1997). *Training and aiding situation awareness: A context based approach*. (Final Report under US Air Force contract # F41624-97-C-5027). Norcross, GA: Search Technology, Inc.
4. Bass, E.J., Zenyuh, J.P., Small, R.L., & Fortin, S.T. (1996). A context-based approach to training situation awareness. In *Proceedings of the Third Annual Symposium on Human Interaction with Complex Systems*. Los Alamitos, CA: IEEE Computer Society Press, 89-95.
5. Burton, R.R. & Brown, J.S. (1982). An investigation of computer coaching for informal learning activities. In D. H. Sleeman and J. S. Brown (Eds.), *Intelligent Tutoring Systems* (pp.79-98). , London: Academic Press.
6. Chappell, A.R., Crowther, E.G., Mitchell, C.M. & Govindaraj, T. (1997). The VNAV tutor: Addressing a mode awareness difficulty for pilots of glass cockpit aircraft. *IEEE Transactions on Systems, Man and Cybernetics*, 27(3), 372-385.
7. Chu, R.W., Mitchell, C.M., & Jones, P.M. (1995). Using the operator function model and OFMspert as the basis for an intelligent tutoring system: Towards a tutor/aid paradigm for operators of supervisory control systems. *IEEE Transactions on Systems, Man And Cybernetics*, 25(7), 937-955.
8. Collins, A., Brown, J.S., & Newman, S. (1989). Cognitive apprenticeship: Teaching the crafts of reading, writing, and mathematics. In L. B. Resnick (Ed.), *Knowing, Learning, and Instruction: Essays in honor of Robert Glaser* (pp. 454-494). Hillsdale, NJ: LEA.

9. Degani, A. & Wiener, E.L. (1997). Procedures in complex systems: The airline cockpit. *IEEE Transactions on Systems, Man and Cybernetics*, 27(3), 302-312.

10. Endsley, M.R. (1995). Toward a theory of situation awareness in dynamic systems. *Human Factors*, 37(1), 32-64.

11. Ernst-Fortin, S.T., Small, R.L., Bass, E.J. & Hogans, Jr., J. (1997). *An adaptive cockpit hazard monitoring system*. (Final Report under US Air Force contract #F33615-95-C-3611). Norcross, GA: Search Technology, Inc.

12. Fischer, P.M. & Mandl, H. (1988). Improvement in the acquisition of knowledge by informing feedback. In H. Mandl and A. Lesgold (Eds.), *Learning issues for intelligent tutoring systems* (pp. 187-241). New York: Springer-Verlag.

13. Fischer, U., Orasanu, J., & Montalvo, M. (1993). Efficient decision strategies on the flight deck. In R. S. Jensen and D. Neumeister (Eds.), *Proceedings of the Seventh International Symposium on Aviation Psychology*. Columbus, OH: Ohio State University Press, 238-243.

14. Klein, G.A. (1989). Recognition-primed decisions. In W. B. Rouse (Ed.), *Advances in man-machine systems research*, 5 (pp. 47-92), Greenwich, CT: JAI.

15. Lesgold, A. (1994). Ideas about feedback and their implications for intelligent coached apprenticeship. *Machine Mediated Learning, 4*(1), 67-80.

16. Randle, R.J., Larsen, W.E., & Williams, D.H. (1980). *Some human factors issues in the development and evaluation of cockpit alerting and warning systems*. NASA Reference Publication 1055. Moffett Field, CA: NASA Ames Research Center.

17. Rouse, W.B., & Morris, N.M. (1985). *On looking into the black box: Prospects and limits in the search for mental models* (DTIC AD-A159080). Atlanta, GA: Georgia Institute of Technology, Center for Human-Machine Systems Research.

18. Schneider, W. (1985). Training high-performance skills: Fallacies and guidelines. *Human Factors*, 27(3), 285-300.

19. Shrestha, L.B., Prince, C., Baker, D.P. & Salas, E. (1995). Understanding situation awareness: Concepts, methods, and training. In W. B. Rouse (Ed.), *Human/Technology Interaction in Complex Systems*, 7 (pp. 45-83). Greenwich, CT: JAI Press.

20. Stout, R.J., Salas, E., & Kraiger, K. (1997). The role of trainee knowledge structures in aviation team environments. *The International Journal of Aviation Psychology*, 7(3), 235-250.

21. Stout, R.J., Cannon-Bowers, J.A. & Salas, E. (In preparation). Team situational awareness. Cue-recognition training. To appear in D. J. Garland and M. R. Endsley (Eds.), *Situation Awareness Analysis and Measurement*. Mahwah, NJ: LEA.

22. USAF (1995). *Flying Operations, Aircrew Standardization/Evaluation Program: Air Force Instruction 11-408/ACC Sup 1*, November 1, 1995.

23. VanLehn, K. (1988). Student Modeling. In M. C. Polson and J. J. Richardson (Eds.), *Foundations of intelligent tutoring systems* (pp. 55-78). Hillsdale, NJ: LEA.

24. Wilson, B. & Cole, P. (1991). A review of cognitive teaching models. *Educational Technology Research and Development*, 39(4), 47-64.

Embedded Training for Complex Information Systems

Brant A. Cheikes, Marty Geier, Rob Hyland, Frank Linton,
Linda Rodi, and Hans-Peter Schaefer

The MITRE Corporation
202 Burlington Road, M/S K302
Bedford, MA 01730-1420 USA
bcheikes@mitre.org

Abstract. One solution to providing affordable operator training in the workplace is to augment applications with intelligent *embedded training systems*. Intelligent embedded training is highly interactive: trainees practice problem-solving tasks on the prime application with guidance and feedback from the training system. We group the necessary assistance mechanisms into three layers: (1) an *application interface* layer, (2) an *action interpretation* layer, and (3) a *training services* layer. We discuss these layers, their interactions, and our prototype implementation of each one.

1. Introduction

Workers today perform ever-larger portions of their jobs with the help of complex, specialized information systems. These systems are growing in power and scope as they automate tasks previously handled by trained staff. The systems are upgraded regularly and may be widely deployed around the world. In the military, shortages of well-trained operators are becoming common due to declining budgets, frequent personnel rotations, promotions, and attrition. Classroom instruction at central training facilities is becoming increasingly impractical and unaffordable.

One means of providing affordable operator training in the workplace is to augment applications with *embedded training systems* (ETS), task-specific training tools that operate in the same computing environment as the prime application. ETSs aim to bring users quickly up to basic proficiency in system operation. After initial training, ETSs remain available for refresher training.

We are developing ETSs that employ *intelligent computer-assisted instruction* (ICAI) techniques [13]. Training provided by an ICAI-based ETS (IETS) is highly interactive: trainees practice problem-solving tasks on the prime application with guidance and feedback from the training system. The training component tailors its services to individual needs and maintains an appropriate level of challenge, keeping students working at the edge of their competence.

1.1 Related Research

ICAI systems described in the literature tend to be self-contained software artifacts designed from the ground up to address a chosen instructional task. The system described here differs from other ICAI efforts by using a pre-existing, external application (the "prime application") as a tool to provide training. Moreover, the use of the tool to perform job tasks constitutes the subject matter to be learned.

The most closely related effort is described in Ritter and Koedinger's article on tutoring agents [12]. They describe how to add tutoring components to Microsoft's Excel spreadsheet and Geometer's Sketchpad construction tool to create systems that teach algebra problem-solving and geometric construction, respectively. Neither system is an IETS since use of the tools is incidental to the subject matter.

Lentini *et al.* describe an ICAI system that teaches users how to operate a "spreadsheet application"—a pre-programmed spreadsheet meant to support a particular task such as creating a cash-flow report [7]. Unlike our system, Lentini *et al.*'s tutoring component is implemented within the spreadsheet tool; moreover, their research focuses on automatically extracting tutoring knowledge from the contents (formulae) of the spreadsheet application.

IETSs may also be compared with *intelligent help systems* (IHS). Such systems support users while they perform tasks with a software application (e.g., the Macsyma advisor [5]). IHSs differ from IETSs in that they focus on *assisting* rather than *training* users. While IHS assistance might help a user overcome an impasse, the user may be no better able to solve the problem unassisted the next time they encounter it. Moreover, IHSs are typically designed as integral parts of the software application. Giroux *et al.* have described an architecture for IHSs in which the help component operates as an external module [6].

1.2 Overview

This paper presents results of our work to date developing IETSs for military information systems. We limit our focus to techniques for *within-exercise support*, i.e., coaching and feedback offered during problem-solving exercises. Our IETS prototype currently offers task-related hints on demand. When the trainee requests a hint, the IETS identifies what it believes to be the trainee's current problem-solving goal, and recommends the next step to take towards that goal. The system states the user's current goal in job-specific terms, and states the next step either in job-specific terms (cf. H1), or in terms of user-interface (UI) gestures if the next step corresponds to an action on the interface (cf. H2).

H1: *Your current goal:* Perform a surface-to-air threat assessment.
     To do that, you should next: Locate all surface-to-air missile launchers in the area of interest.

H2: *Your current goal:* Locate all surface-to-air missile launchers in the area of interest.
     To do that, you should next: Select "Find Platforms" from the "Search" menu in the "System View" window.

Implementing within-exercise support presents three technical challenges. First, the IETS requires special access to the prime application in order to monitor and guide users while they work on exercises. Second, the IETS must infer users' task-related plans and goals incrementally from reports of their actions on the prime application's UI. Third, the IETS must select appropriate instructional interventions based on its changing model of the user's plans and goals. We group the necessary mechanisms into three information-processing "layers". The next section presents an overview of these layers and discusses their interactions. Sections 3 through 5 present details of our current implementation of each layer. Section 6 presents our conclusions.

2. Layers of Processing Required for Within-Exercise Support

Processing in our IETS occurs in three layers (Fig. 1): (1) the *application interface* layer, (2) the *action interpretation* layer, and (3) the *training services* layer. Labeled arrows indicate the source and type of communication between the layers.

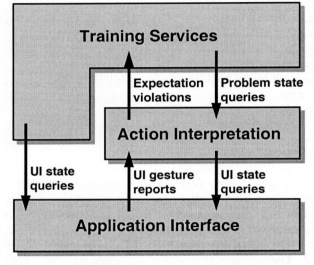

2.1 Application Interface Layer: Overview

Off-the-shelf software applications (e.g., word processors and spread-

Fig. 1. IETS processing layers

sheets) need to be *observable*, *inspectable* and *scriptable* if they are to be used to support learning [12]. A software tool is *observable* if it is able to report all actions taken by the user. Software is *inspectable* when it is able to respond to requests for information about its internal state. *Scriptable* software can execute commands from an external application as if they were initiated by the user. To interoperate with an IETS, the prime application must likewise be observable, inspectable and scriptable.

The elements that provide observing, inspecting and scripting services comprise a distinct software layer, which we call the *application interface* layer. In [12], the interface layer is part of the prime application. This approach allows communication between the "tutor" and the "tool" to be conducted in the language of the tool. For example, a spreadsheet tool might report user actions in terms of operations like "inserting a row" and "updating a cell".

Building the interface layer into an application requires a substantial amount of engineering labor. This work gets done only if a compelling business need exists. Even when such a need exists, the lack of standards in this area promotes interfaces which differ greatly across both tools and vendors. (See [11] for an IEEE-sponsored project to develop standards for educational technology.) Our approach is to move the application interface layer *outside* the prime application. Following this approach, communication between the "tool" and the "tutor" is conducted in terms of user-interface gestures and states. This detailed level of description has the advantage of enabling our IETS to provide guidance down to suggesting user-interface actions.

2.2 Action Interpretation Layer: Overview

The action interpretation layer maintains two models: a model of the trainee's problem-solving process during an exercise, and a model of "expert" problem-solving behavior. Each UI gesture is reported to the interpretation layer by the interface layer, causing the interpretation layer to (a) update its model of the trainee's solution, and (b) note any deviations from the expected "expert" solution process. The interpretation layer may occasionally ask the interface layer for the value of one of the prime application's state variables. The model created by the interpretation layer may be accessed by the training services layer as needed to support guidance and feedback. The interpretation layer may alert the training services layer if it notices that the user is deviating from the desired solution path.

Norman's "stages of user activity" model characterizes the process of operating a computer-human interface as a cycle of planning, acting, evaluating results, and replanning [10]. Most of this work takes place in the user's mind; only the user's UI gestures are observable. The key question to be addressed in designing the action-interpretation mechanisms is: How much of the user's mental model of the task must be reconstructed in order to support intelligent coaching? Since *instructional strategy* seems to be the principal driver of requirements for action interpretation, we turn our attention to the training services layer.

2.3 Training Services Layer: Overview

The training services layer implements the IETS's instructional strategy. Informing the decision-making processes at this level is the system's interpretation of its observations of user actions. Inspection of the prime application may occasionally be needed to help select the form and content of instructional interventions. Training-service mechanisms may also respond to notifications from the action interpretation layer sent to it when the user veers from an interpretable course of action.

Norman [10] (cf. also [1, 4]) identifies two conceptual "gulfs" to explain why users have difficulty operating UIs. The *gulf of execution* arises from the difference between the user's conception of the steps required to achieve a goal, and the actions allowed by the system. The *gulf of evaluation* arises from the difference between the system's presentation of its internal state, and the user's conception of the expected results of his actions. Both gulfs derive from the difficulties that users encounter in translating between the the concepts and operations that they use to describe their tasks (the *task language*) and the concepts and operations understood by the system (the *core language*). The training services that an IETS provides should help users bridge these gulfs.

Our work on training services has thus far focused on techniques to help users bridge the gulf of execution. We have implemented one service: hints on request. These hints help users locate their "place" in the problem-solving process, and suggest the next problem-solving step to take. Implementing this service has helped us to identify design requirements for the action interpretation layer. Specifically, we have found that the action-interpretation model must be hierarchical, and explicitly relate task-language concepts and actions to core-language concepts and actions. That is, the upper levels of the model should be expressed in task-language terms, the leaves in core-language terms; each path from root to leaf should contain a transition from task-language representation to core-language representation.

3. Application Interface Layer: Implementation

An embedded training system must be able to observe, inspect, and script the prime application in order to employ ICAI techniques. We have developed a tool that provides the needed access without requiring modifications to the prime application. This section describes our implementation of this tool, called WOSIT (Widget Observation, Scripting and Inspection Tool).

3.1 Overview

WOSIT is a Unix application that runs independently of both the prime application and the IETS. It forms the interface layer of our prototype IETS, and works by modifying the windowing environment in which the prime application operates. The version of WOSIT described here works with any Unix application built with the X-Windows "Motif" widget set. The only requirement for using WOSIT is that the prime application must be *dynamically linked* with the X-Windows libraries.

By modifying the windowing environment, WOSIT gains access to all the X-Windows functions that the prime application itself can perform. WOSIT can intercept widget state-change notifications, query widget state, and even generate widget actions (e.g., button clicks) as though performed by the user. WOSIT and the IETS communicate with each other over network sockets. Each time WOSIT notices that a UI widget has undergone a significant state change, it sends a descriptive message to the connected IETS. A sequence of WOSIT reports is shown in Fig. 2.

As the figure illustrates, WOSIT uses symbolic labels to refer to windows and widgets. (Whenever possible, WOSIT uses the text from windows and widgets for their label.) To enable us to build behavior models from its output, WOSIT ensures that these labels are constant across invocations of the prime application and unique within each window.

3.2 Technical approach

Three technologies enable non-intrusive observing, inspecting and scripting of X/Motif applications: The InterClient Exchange (ICE) library, X-Windows hooks,

```
menu_select_item("State Tools","View;Open...");
scroll_drag("Select File",dirscroll,VSCROLL,9);
scroll_drag("Select File",filescroll,VSCROLL,6);
list_select_item("Select File",dirlist,"training");
list_select_item("Select File",filelist,"t2.view");
button_press("Select File","OK");
```

Fig. 2. WOSIT message stream

and the Remote Access Protocol (RAP). ICE and the necessary hooks have been part of the standard X11 package since Release 6.1. RAP was developed at Georgia Institute of Technology. Fig. 3 illustrates how these elements are combined.

The ICE library enables programs to communicate across address spaces. Functions to send and receive data, and to open and close connections are all standardized within the ICE library. The X-Windows hooks provide the means for a software component within the same address space as a client program to subscribe to widget-level changes in the client. RAP provides the "bridge" enabling widget notifications to be passed across address spaces from the prime application to WOSIT. RAP was originally developed at Georgia Tech as part of the the Mercator research project [8, 9]. It was later revised and publically released by Will Walker at Digital Equipment Corporation. RAP provides a standard set of procedures to send and receive widget information using X-Windows hooks. It comes in two parts: a client-side library and an agent-side library. The client-side library resides in the prime application's address space, interfacing with the X-Windows hooks and sending data via ICE to the agent-side library. The agent-side library resides in WOSIT's address space, acting as a buffer between the WOSIT application and the RAP client library. The WOSIT application processes messages coming from the prime application via RAP, and provides a socket-based reporting and query interface to the IETS.

3.3 Status

Our implementation of WOSIT has been tested under both SunOS 4.1.3 and Solaris 2.5. We are currently investigating designs suitable for the Windows 95/NT environments. We intend to make WOSIT freely available; for information on how to obtain WOSIT, contact the first author.

4. Action Interpretation Layer: Implementation

The action interpretation layer receives a stream of reports from the interface layer (cf. Fig. 2) describing the trainee's actions on the prime application's UI. This section describes how the interpretation layer processes this input to build and maintain a hierarchical model of the trainee's problem-solving process.

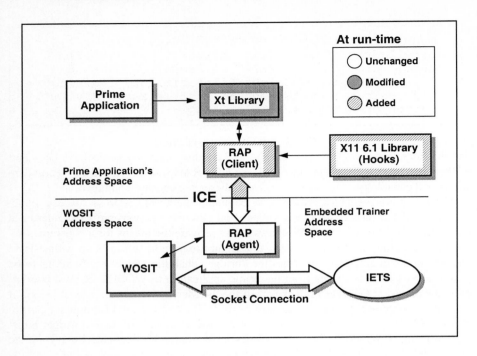

Fig. 3. WOSIT architecture

4.1 Overview

Embedded training is a structured process consisting of presentation-oriented learning activities and interactive problem-solving exercises. Exercises are used to reinforce the concepts and methods conveyed by the presentations. Consequently, the action interpretation mechanisms can begin with strong expectations about the problem-solving process the trainee will follow.

In our current implementation, the system attempts to match action reports against an *expectation model* representing the student's anticipated problem-solving process. (The expectation model can be thought of as representing expert problem-solving behavior.) When an interactive exercise begins, the interpretation layer is initialized with an expression defining the top-level task for the trainee to perform. This expression is encoded in a task description language of our own design. Consulting a library of declaratively-encoded models of problem solving in the domain, the interpretation layer builds the expectation model by extending the root-task expression to form a tree. The leaves of the expectation model are patterns representing expected actions on the prime application's UI. Fig. 4 illustrates an expectation model.

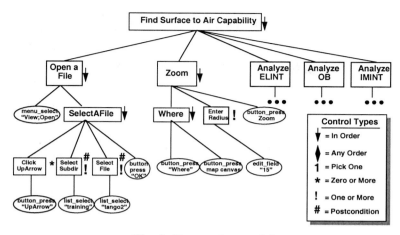

Fig. 4. Expectation model

4.2 Action interpretation method

Our action interpretation procedure is inspired by Generic Task (GT) theory [2, 3]. GT analyzes complex problems into simpler units, called *generic tasks*, each of which solves a specific portion of the given problem.

Our action interpretation layer implements two generic tasks: *hierarchical classification* and *routine recognition* [3]. Hierarchical classification (HC) is the process of traversing a classification hierarchy to find the most specific node that can plausibly describe the input data. (Input data in our case consists of UI-gesture reports.) At each node, the algorithm determines whether the node is plausible in the current context. If plausible, the node establishes; if implausible, the node rejects. If a node establishes, the traversal continues by attempting to refine into more detail by establishing any or all of the node's children. If a node is rejected, its entire subtree is ignored. Nodes which neither establish nor reject may be suspended for future use. The traversal strategy can be depth first, breadth first, or explored in parallel.

HC requires two forms of knowledge: a classification hierarchy (a taxonomy of relevant physical or conceptual objects) and establish/reject knowledge for every node. Establish/reject knowledge must be associated with each node in order to determine relevance to the current case. This knowledge must produce one of three values per node: *establish*, *reject*, or *suspend*. The expectation model for an exercise serves as the classification hierarchy.

The traversal procedure for the hierarchy is established at each node. Only seven control types are needed to describe the possible orders in which nodes are processed: *InOrder, AnyOrder, ZeroOrMore, OneOrMore, PickOne, InOrderTask*, and *BasicMatch*. Either alone or composed, these control types are sufficient to represent the space of possible paths (which map into sequences of UI gestures) through the expected solution space for exercises with the prime application. The control types permit multiple solution paths as well as for interleaving of subtasks.

Unexpected student actions, called *violations*, are currently defined as tasks that violate the order, number, or constraints on steps in the expectation model. A thorough discussion of unexpected-action handling is beyond the scope of this paper. At present, the action interpretation mechanisms we have implemented are able to recognize unexpected trainee behavior, but we do not yet have any training services that can respond to this information.

4.3 Summary

We have implemented an action-interpretation layer that processes UI-gesture reports and maps trainee actions to the model of expert problem-solving behavior. Initially, this model encodes the IETS's *expectation* of the solution process that the trainee will follow. The expectation model uses seven control constructs to represent legitimate variations that may be observed. These constructs allow IETS developers to model one or more expert problem-solving approaches, and allow the interpretation component to recognize tasks that are being pursued in parallel. As the trainee works through the exercise, the system revises and annotates the model by recording the actual process followed, flagging any unexpected actions. This model is used by the training services layer to provide guidance and feedback.

5. Training Services Layer: Implementation

During interactive exercises, the IETS maintains a UI on the trainee workstation that enables students to access training services. At present, services are provided only when the student requests them by clicking the IETS's 'hint' button.

Hints are constructed using natural-language patterns attached to the nodes of the expectation model maintained by the action interpretation layer. When the student requests a hint, the hint-generation mechanism inspects the expectation model and determines the trainee's current goal and the next uncompleted step towards that goal. Hints are produced by filling in a simple natural-language template.

6. Conclusions

IETSs have the potential to provide high-quality, cost-effective operator training at or near operators' workplaces. We have identified three "layers" of information processing required for an IETS to provide intelligent coaching and feedback to users while they perform interactive exercises with the prime application. The principal contributions of this work are (1) a freely available, general-purpose tool (WOSIT) that enables an IETS to non-intrusively observe, inspect and script Unix/X-Windows applications, and (2) an expectation-driven approach to action interpretation.

7. Acknowledgments

This research has been supported by the MITRE Technology Program.

References

1. G. D. Abowd and R. Beale. Users, systems and interfaces: A unifying framework for interaction. In D. Diaper and N. Hammond, editors, *HCI'91: People and Computers VI*, Cambridge University Press, Cambridge, 1991, pages 73-87.

2. B. Chandrasekaran. Towards a Taxonomy of Problem Solving Types. *AI Magazine*, 4(1): 1983, pp. 9-17.

3. B. Chandrasekaran and T. R. Johnson. Generic Tasks And Task Structures: History, Critique and New Directions. In J. M. David, J. P. Krivine, and R. Simmons, editors, *Second Generation Expert Systems*, Springer-Verlag, 1993, pp. 239-280.

4. A. Dix, J. Finlay, G. Abowd and R. Beale. *Human-Computer Interaction*. Prentice Hall, New York, 1993.

5. M. R. Genesereth. The role of plans in automated consultation. In *Proceedings of the 6th International Joint Conference on Artificial Intelligence*, pp. 311–319. Tokyo, August 1979.

6. S. Giroux, G. Paquette, F. Pachet and J. Girard. EpiTalk—A Platform for Epiphyte Advisor Systems Dedicated to Both Individual and Collaborative Learning. In C. Frasson, G. Gauthier, and A. Lesgold, editors, *Intelligent Tutoring Systems—Third International Conference*, pp. 363–371. Montreal, June 1996.

7. M. Lentini, D. Nardi and A. Simonetta. Automatic Generation of Tutors for Spreadsheet Applications. In *Proceedings of AI-ED 95—World Conference on Artificial Intelligence in Education*, pp. 91–98. Washington DC, August 1995.

8. Mercator Project Home Page.
   See http://www.cc.gatech.edu/gvu/multimedia/mercator/mercator.html

9. E. D. Mynatt and W. K. Edwards. *The Mercator Environment: A Nonvisual Interface to the X Window System*. Technical Report GIT-GVU-92-05, Georgia Institute of Technology, February, 1992.

10. D. A. Norman. *The Psychology of Everyday Things.* Basic Books, 1988.

11. P1484 Home Page. See http://www.manta.ieee.org/P1484.

12. S. Ritter and K. R. Koedinger. Towards Lightweight Tutoring Agents. In *Proceedings of AI-ED 95—World Conference on Artificial Intelligence in Education*, pp. 91–98. Washington DC, August 1995.

13. W. Regian, R. Seidel, J. Schuler, and P. Radtke. *Functional Area Analysis of Intelligent Computer-Assisted Instruction*. Training and Personnel Systems Science and Technology Evaluation and Management Committee, 1996.
   See http://www.brooks.af.mil/AL/HR/ICAI/litlfaa.htm.

Macro-Definitions, a Basic Component for Interoperability between ILEs at the Knowledge Level : Application to Geometry

Marilyne Macrelle, Cyrille Desmoulins

LORIA & Université Henri Poincaré,
B.P.239, F-54506 Vandoeuvre-lès-Nancy cedex, France
Marilyne.Macrelle@loria.fr, Cyrille.Desmoulins@loria.fr

Abstract. Within a given domain, a significant number of Interactive Learning Environments (ILEs) have been developed during the last decade, but they can not interoperate because of incompatible hardware, operating systems or knowledge representations. Our research aims at defining principles and models for interoperation between ILEs. In this paper we focus on the knowledge level. Our goal is to present a general framework for domain knowledge translation, using what we call macro-definitions. They allow us to specify a general translator for a given domain. After analysing principles used in ad hoc approaches, we provide a formal definition of the macro-definition concept and we demonstrate that it meets our goals. We illustrate the ease of the implementation of this concept with the example of interoperation between two ILEs in the geometry domain, TALC and MENTONIEZH.

1. Introduction

A significant number of Interactive Learning Environments (ILEs) have been developed in the last decade. However, a given ILE offers only a few of the many features (simulation, solving, diagnostic and explanation tools) that are possible. Thus teachers are not able to use all the available features since these features are incorporated in different, incompatible systems. Indeed, there are many obstacles for the joint use of several ILEs, *i.e.* the diversity of computers and operating systems, the specific knowledge representation used for each ILE, ... Significant expertise and effort is required to implement a single ILE. Thus it would be very difficult to integrate several ILEs into a single unit.

Our research aims at defining principles and models for interoperation between existing or future ILEs, rather than trying to integrate them into a single unit. Thus our goal was to build a platform allowing this interoperation, useful for end-users (teacher and learner) as well as for ILE researchers. Geometry was chosen as the application domain of a first version of this platform because of the large variety of ILEs available in this domain (Cabri-Geometry [9], Geometer's Sketchpad [7]) and because of our experience in this domain (CALQUES [1], TALC [2]).

To make ILEs interoperate means to provide a way of sharing information and to enable them to send mutual requests. Thus our first objective is to define principles and models allowing information sharing between ILEs at the knowledge level.

The current approach aimed at providing a joint use of two ILEs is based on the client-server model. For example, Ritter & Koedinger [14] focused on providing help and tutoring information. They defined a general method to plug-in a tutor (client) into a given tool (server). More specifically, geometry systems like CABRI-DEFI [6], TELE-CABRI [15] and TALC have been built using a server version of Cabri-Geometry. At the geometry knowledge level, this led to the translation of the client ILE language into the server ILE language. For each ILE, a specific translator was developed inside the client.

Our approach is to define what we call "macro-definitions" which provide a simple and elegant way to implement a general translator for a given domain.

2. Interoperation on the Knowledge Level, from Specific Solutions to Macro-Definitions

In order that the user can use several ILE features for the same exercise, ILEs first need to be able to share the domain knowledge. Until now this was carried out in two ways: either «by hand» by the teacher, or by specific translators between the two ILEs languages. In this section, starting from the analysis of the principles used in these two processes and of the constraints which make the translation possible, we define macro-definitions as a way of generalising these principles and constraints.

2.1 «By Hand» Use of Several ILEs

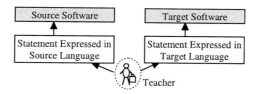

Fig. 1. The Teacher Expresses the Statement Independently in two Different Languages

At present the context where each ILE has its own knowledge representation is the most frequent. Thus, a teacher, who wants to express the same statement in several ILEs, needs to express a different statement for the particular language of each ILE. To simplify the situation, let us consider that the teacher uses both a source ILE whose knowledge representation language is SL - source language - and a target ILE whose knowledge representation language is TL - target language - (see Fig. 1).

Example 1. The teacher wants to express the following geometry statement:

Let (A B C D) be a parallelogram, L1 a line passing through B and orthogonal to the segment B C, L2 a line passing through D and orthogonal to the segment A D. Prove that the lines L1 and L2 are parallel

Let us suppose that he uses the two ILEs, MENTONIEZH and TALC (see Section 4). MENTONIEZH is formally defined using the language HDL (source language). TALC is formally defined using the language CDL (target language).

The teacher must translate this statement into the two languages HDL and CDL. Table 1 gives this translation and the semantics of each CDL sentence. In this example, both languages express the statement without any loss of information.

Fig. 2.

Table 1. Translation of the Statement in HDL and CDL

Statement	HDL	CDL	CDL Semantics
let (A B C D) a parallelogram	Parallelogram (A, B, C, D)	[A B] // [C D], [B C] // [A D]	The segment [A B] and the segment [C D] are parallel The segment [B C] and the segment [A D] are parallel
L1 a line passing through B and orthogonal to the segment B C	Belongs-line(B, L1) Orthogonal(L1,B,C)	B ∈ L1, L1 ⊥ [B C]	The point B belongs to the line L1 The line L1 is orthogonal to the line passing through B and C.
L2 a line passing through D and orthogonal to the segment A D.	Belongs-line(D, L2) Orthogonal(L2,A, D)	D ∈ L2, L2 ⊥ [A D]	The point D belongs to the line L2 The line L2 is orthogonal to the line passing through A and D.
Prove that L1 and L2 are parallel	Parallel(L1, L2)	L1 // L2	L1 is parallel to L2

This method solves the previous problem, but it forces the teacher to understand several different languages and to express several times the same knowledge. The only advantage is that it relies only on the teacher's skills and goodwill and thus does not require any specific software extension.

2.2 Specific Translator Principles at the Knowledge Level

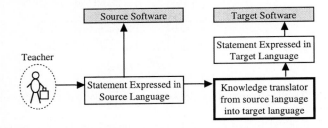

Fig. 3. Use of a Specific Translator

In order to avoid the teacher expressing several times the same knowledge, the usual approach (for example in CABRI-DEFI [6]) is to automatically translate the source language into the target one (assuming it is possible). A translator transforms the statement expressed in source language into the target language. (see Fig. 3).

This method solves the previous problem, but now the problem is that the designer needs to implement a specific translator for each pairs of ILEs.

2.3 Translatability Constraints

In order to avoid the designer having to implement a specific translator for each pairs of ILEs, we need to define a general approach for automatic knowledge translation.

Obviously, the choice of source language or target language cannot be made randomly and depends on constraints we call « translatability constraints».

Definition 1. Translatability A source language is translatable into an target language if the source language domain is covered by the target language domain and, in addition, the knowledge granularity is thinner (see Definition 4) in the target language than in the source language.

Definition 2. Covering A source language is covered by an target language if any concept expressed in the source language can be expressed in the target language.

Definition 3. Sentence A language sentence is the minimal component of a statement in this language.

Example 2. In the HDL language, `equal(A,B,A,C)` is a sentence, in the CDL language `|A B|=|A C|` is a sentence but none of the sentence elements `B|`, `A`, `B`, `« | »` have meaning as separate entities; they are only meaningful in the context of the specific sentence.

Definition 4. Granularity. A target language, covering a source language, has a thinner granularity than a source language if any information expressed with only one sentence in source language can be broken up into parts, each expressed by a sentence of target language.

Example 3. A target language expressing point, segment, orthogonal, parallel by a sentence has a thinner granularity than an source language expressing triangle, rectangle, triangle-rectangle, parallelogram by a sentence.

If a pair of languages respects this translatability constraint then, for any sentence of the source language, a statement in the target language which represents the same knowledge can be found.

2.4 Macro-Definitions

A general way to implement an automatic target language translator is to use what we call macro-definitions. Thus the specification of a macro-definition expresses that a single source language sentence can be replaced by a list of target language sentences (see Example 4). The translatability allows us to provide such a macro-definition expressed in target language for each sentence in the source language. We call macro-definition language the macro-language.

Example 4. Let us define the following macro-definition :
`parallelogram(P1,P2,P3,P4)` **←** `[P1 P2] // [P4 P3], [P1 P4] // [P2 P3]`
where the part before the symbol **←** is expressed in HDL and the rest is expressed in CDL.

From the user point of view, the context is either the same or better than the context of Section 2.2, *i.e.* he only needs to express once the statement of his exercise for both ILEs (see Fig. 4). The context is even richer, because the teacher can now express his own macro-definitions, which enables him to enrich the two languages (source an target) or even to develop the macro-definitions allowing automated translation.

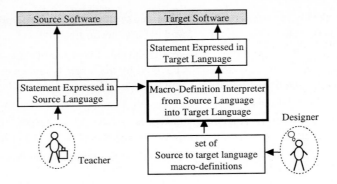

Fig. 4. Use of a Macro-Definition Interpreter.

From the designer's point of view, there is no need to define a specific translator for each application. He only needs to define the macro-definitions expressed in the macro-language of the target ILE. Instead of defining a specific translator for each pairs of ILEs, he only defines a macro-language for each ILE.

3. Formalisation of Macro-Definitions

3.1 Syntax

The syntax of a macro-language is defined as follows using the BNF grammar formalism:

Macro-Set ::= Macro-Declaration *macro-set-terminator* | Macro-Declaration Macro-Set
Macro-Declaration ::= Macro-Head *macro-constructor* Macro-Tail *macro-terminator*
Macro-Head ::= *Source-Language-Sentence*
Macro-Tail ::= Sentence | Sentence *target-language-separator* Macro-Tail
Sentence ::= *Target-Language-Sentence* | Macro-Use

This grammar states that a macro-declaration is consists of a left part named macro-head, a right part named macro-tail, separated by a macro-constructor and ending with a macro-terminator. The macro-head is a source language sentence, the macro-tail is a target language sentence or a use of a macro-definition. The formal syntax of Macro-use is not defined here but it is usually the same as the Source-Language-Sentence. In Example 4, the *Source-Language-Sentence* is HDL, the *Target-Language-Sentence* is CDL, the *target-language-separator* (CDL sentence separator) is the comma and the *macro-constructor* is the symbol "←".

Example 5. In the following set of macro-definitions
```
triangle(P1,P2,P3) ← not (P3 ∈ (P1 P2)), seg1 = [P1, P2],
    seg2 = [P2, P3], seg3 = [P1, P3].
isosceles(A, B, C) ← triangle(A, B, C), |A B| = |A C|.
```
the first part of the tail of the second macro-definition is a macro-use of the first macro-definition and the second part is expressed in CDL.

Indeed, this grammar is a meta-grammar since the way it is instantiated depends on the selection of both the source and target languages (see [10] and [3]).

3.2 Semantics

The semantics rules are the following:

Rule 1: Each macro-tail uses only macro-use defined earlier in the order of the macro-set.

Rule 2: Two different tails can not refer to the same head.

Rule 3: Each formal head parameter is used in the tail.

Rule 4: The formal parameter types in a macro-declaration and the effective corresponding parameter types are the same.

Within a macro-declaration, the *macro-constructor* symbol expresses that a head is replaced by a tail. This translation is performed by substituting, in a statement expressed in the source language, the head by the tail for each corresponding macro-use, and substituting the formal parameters by the actual values in the macro-tail. Thus macro-definitions can be considered as rewriting rules or as logical implications. This substitution process is also quite similar to the way the C pre-processor operates with the #define statements [8].

This definition of the macro-definition concept permits each statement of the first language, using the macro-definition of a macro-set, to be translated into a statement in the second language, via the principle of successive substitutions.

4. Illustration in Geometry with TALC and MENTONIEZH

4.1 TALC and MENTONIEZH for Interoperability at the Knowledge Level

As the two ILEs TALC and MENTONIEZH are both programmed in the same language, PrologII [12], it was only necessary to reprogram the interface parts of one of the two ILEs (the non-graphic interface of MENTONIEZH in this case) to make these ILEs interoperate on the same computer (Macintosh), operating system (Mac-OS) and programming language (PrologII+) level. Only the knowledge level remained different.

The aim of TALC is to check the correctness of a student figure with respect to a teacher statement. To provide the students with tools for constructing a figure, TALC interoperates with Cabri-géomètre using the Mac-OS inter-application communication primitives, named Apple-events, (using a "server" version of Cabri-Geometry [16]). The knowledge level interoperability is implemented by a specific translator, as described in §1.2. It translates a Cabri-Geometry statement directly into the TALC internal language LDL (Logical Description Language [4]).

MENTONIEZH is an ILE which helps the learner to find and justify a geometrical proof. An exercise statement is composed of two parts: first the hypothesis statement and secondly the statement of the property to prove. MENTONIEZH is programmed on a PC using DOS. MENTONIEZH does not provide any geometric construction and verification interface. These operations are currently written on paper (the learner constructs the figures on a sheet and the teacher possibly checks it).

Thus, it would be very beneficial for TALC and MENTONIEZH to interoperate, since this would allow one to take advantage of these ILEs complementary features.

4.2 How TALC and MENTONIEZH fit the translation constraints

The CDL language (Classroom Description Language) the teacher uses to express a geometric figure is similar to that used in geometry text books. A CDL statement allows one to express objects (point, line, ray, circle and distance) and relations between objects (for example *belongs*, *is parallel* and *is equal*). CDL is a declarative language where each sentence expresses a property on objects, themselves expressed by terms (like [A,B] to express a segment) or by identifiers (see example 1).

The HDL language (Hypothesis Description Language) the teacher uses to express a geometric proof theorem statement allows him to express the hypotheses of the theorem and the property to prove. A HDL statement permits to express basic objects (point, line, circle) and composed objects (triangle, rectangle, right-angle triangle, parallelogram, ...) and relations between them (*belongs, is parallel, non-crossed tetragon*, ...). HDL is also a declarative language where each sentence is a property predicate whose parameters are identifiers expressing basic objects (see Example 1).

TALC and MENTONIEZH Compliance with the Translation Constraints

The only reason CDL does not cover HDL is because the property "non-crossed tetragon" (expressing that none of its opposite sides cuts the other) cannot be expressed in CDL. Without this property, CDL covers HDL (see Section 2.3)

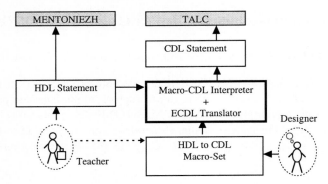

Fig. 5. Use of a Macro-Definition Interpreter for HDL to CDL translation

CDL granularity is thinner than that of HDL (CDL expresses components like point, line and circle; and HDL expresses figures like triangle, rectangle and parallelogram). Thus HDL is translatable into CDL and for each HDL sentence it is possible to express with a CDL statement the same knowledge. We can then define a macro-definition language for CDL, called Macro-CDL. The language using macro-use of these macro-definitions is called ECDL (Extended CDL). We can use a set of Macro-CDL macro-definition for HDL to translate HDL into CDL (see Fig. 5).

4.3 Macro-CDL Definitions for HDL

For a given HDL sentence (*i.e.* a predicate and its arguments), we need to define the appropriate macro-CDL statement. Each of the 26 HDL predicate corresponds to at least one Macro-CDL definitions. Table 2 gives some examples of MacroCDL for HDL (see [10] for the complete set).

If several macro-definitions are possible, the teacher has to choose between them. For example, he may chose the most general macro-definition, or he may use current lesson objects or he may use macro-definitions referring to the learner knowledge.

Table 2 Examples of Macro-CDL Macro-definitions for HDL

HDL predicate (macro-head) or intermediate macro-definition	Semantic	Macro-tail
3-non-aligned(P1,P2,P3)	P1,P2 and P3 are not aligned	not(P3 ∈ (P1 P2)
triangle(P1,P2,P3)	(P1 P2 P3) is a triangle	3-not-aligned(P1,P2,P3), s1= [P1 P2], s2 = [P2 P3], s3 = [P3 P1].
trirect(P1,P2,P3)	P1 P2 P3 is a right-angle triangle in P1	triangle(P1,P2,P3), (P1 P2) ⊥ (P1 P3).

The « non-crossed(P1, P2, P3, P4) » HDL predicate is not translatable in CDL. To geometrically express that a tetragon A B C D is non-crossed we can either directly express that none of its opposite sides cuts the other or express that C and D are in the same half-plane whose border is the line (A B). These two solutions are impossible with CDL, the former because a didactic constraint prevents the expression of disjunction, the latter because the half-plane object does not exist in CDL. Another solution is to request external knowledge, for example analytic geometry or a student visual verification.

As MENTONIEZH itself uses this last method for this predicate and because the other methods require modification to TALC, we chose to express it by the following macro-definition :

```
Non-crossed(A,B,C,D)  ← not(C ∈ (A B)), not(D ∈ (B C)), not(A ∈ (D C)),
   not (B ∈ (D A)).
```

Thus we suppose that this knowledge, which is generally implicit in geometry statements, is also implicitly used by the learner.

4.4 Implementation

As explained in Section 4.1, an early version of MENTONIEZH was implemented in PROLOGII+ to allow interoperability at the computer, system and software level and to focus only on the knowledge level.

Our goal is to allow the learner to construct with TALC a figure corresponding to the MENTONIEZH hypothesis. After TALC confirms that the figure is correct, the learner can now use MENTONIEZH to help him develop a geometrical proof of the required property. Thus the interaction between TALC and MENTONIEZH is of the form " one then the other ", via a knowledge transfer.

To meet this goal, we defined a Macro-CDL interpreter. It takes as input a file containing Macro-CDL macro-definitions for HDL and a statement in HDL (*i.e.* in

ECDL) and produces a corresponding statement in CDL. The CDL statement is transferred to TALC and the HDL statement to MENTONIEZH, as shown in Fig. 5. .The Macro-CDL interpreter fits the definition of Section 3, i.e. for each macro-definition in the macro-definitions file order, it successively replaces each use of this macro-definition in the file containing the HDL statement. For this aim, the interpreter is classically built in sequence by a lexical analyser, a parser and a semantic translator respecting the rules defined in section 3.2.

Thus this method requires little implementation work. This implementation allowed us to translate each statement given in [13] (about 40 statements).

With this Macro-CDL implementation, interoperation between TALC and another system whose language is translatable in CDL can be achieved without the designer needing to modify TALC. It will simply be performed by the definition of appropriate macro-definitions in a text file.

Thus we obtained a first prototype of a platform, using the same computer, the same operating systems, and the same programming language.

5. Conclusion

In order to demonstrate that the concept of macro-definition is a possible solution to the interoperability issue on the knowledge level, we provide a formal definition of the translatability constraints and of macro-definition syntax and semantics. We then demonstrate the feasibility of our approach by implementing the macro-definition concept in geometry between two languages, HDL and CDL. The declarative semantics of these two language permits us to merge translation with a simple concatenation. Thus, an implementation of a macro-definition language for other domains can easily and quickly be implemented when the two constraints of translatability and of availability of a merging algorithm are verified.

Concerning the knowledge level in general, other kinds of knowledge information besides domain knowledge may interoperate [10]. To characterise them, we plan to use the concept of observable-events [5] and our research team's model of knowledge representation for interaction in ITS's' [17] For example, such knowledge information could be teaching knowledge, rule-based knowledge (definitions, theorems, axioms), and student knowledge.

Our ultimate goal is to build a platform allowing interoperation between geometry ILEs and providing common services (learner model features, curriculum manager, knowledge coherence checker, ...), especially in the case of distributed data, assuming that ILEs cooperate remotely. Our approach is to construct it via a «middleware» (or « broker »), such as CORBA [11], allowing ILEs to mutually send requests using communication and synchronisation protocols.

Acknowledgements

Thanks to Dominique Py for her work with us on the Macintosh version of MENTONIEZH and to Robert Aiken for useful comments on the final version.

References

1. Bernat, P.: *CALQUES2*. Topiques Editions, Nancy (France) (1994)
2. Desmoulins, C.: *On the didactic contract in an ITS for teaching geometry*. In *Proceeding of the 7th International PEG Conference*. Edimbourg. (1993)
3. Desmoulins, C. and Macrelle, M.: *Interopérer via des macro-définitions pour partager des connaissances, Application aux EIAH de géométrie*. In *IC'98*. Nancy. LORIA (1998) 12
4. Desmoulins, C. and Trilling, L.: *Translation of a figure specification into a logical formula in a system for teaching geometry*. In *Proceeding of the 6th International PEG Conference*. Genova (Italy). CNR (1991) 292-303
5. Dubourg, X.: *Modélisation de l'Interaction en EIAO, une Approche Événementielle pour la Réalisation du Système REPÈRE*. Ph. D. Thesis. Caen University, Caen (France) (1995) 48-56
6. Giorgiutti, I. and Baullac, Y.: *Interaction micromonde/tuteur en géométrie, le cas de Cabri-géomètre et de DEFI*. Proceeding of EIAO'91. Les Éditions de l'École Normale Supérieure de Cachan. (1991) 11-18
7. Jackiw, N.: *The Geometer's Sketchpad*. Key curriculum Press (1995)
8. Kernighan, B. and Ritchie, D.: *The C Programming Language*. Prentice Hall, Upper Saddle River (NJ) (1988)
9. Laborde, J.-M. and Bellemain, F.: *Cabri-Geometry II, Software and User Handbook*. Texas Instruments Inc., Dallas (Texas) (1994)
10. Macrelle: *HDL to CDL Macro-Definition Set*. LORIA (www.loria.fr), Nancy (France) (1998)
11. Orfali, R., *et al.*: *Instant CORBA*. Wiley Computer Publishing, New York (1997)
12. PrologIA: *PrologII+, Reference Manual*. PrologIA, Marseille (1995)
13. Py, D.: *Geometry problem solving with Mentoniezh*. Computers in Education. 20(1) (1993) 141-146
14. Ritter, S. and Koedinger, K.R.: *An Architecture for Plug-in Tutor Agents*. Journal of Artificial Intelligence in Education. 7(3/4) (1996) 315-347
15. Tahri, S.: *Modélisation de l'interaction didactique : un tuteur hybride sur Cabri-géomètre*. Ph. D. Thesis. Joseph Fourier University, Grenoble (1993) 226
16. Tessier, S. and Laborde, J.-M.: *Descriptions des Événements Apple Acceptés par Cabri-géomètre*. IMAG, Grenoble (1994)
17. Van Labeke, N., *et al.*: *Designing Adaptable Educational Software: a Case-study for Spatial Geometry*. In *Proceedings of ED-MEDIA'98*. Freiburg, Germany. (to appear) (1998)

Modeling the Knowledge-Based Components of a Learning Environment within the Task/Method Paradigm

Christophe CHOQUET, Frédéric DANNA,
Pierre TCHOUNIKINE, and Francky TRICHET

IRIN – Université de Nantes & École Centrale de Nantes
2, rue de la Houssinière – BP 92208 – F-44322 Nantes Cedex 03, France
{choquet|danna|tchou|trichet}@irin.univ-nantes.fr

Abstract. We show that the Task/Method paradigm is adapted for modeling the problem-solving method that the teacher wants to communicate to the student as well as the pedagogical strategies that have to be put into practice for managing the interaction with the student.

1   Introduction

Constructing an educational system that focuses on teaching a problem-solving method requires the construction of different knowledge-bases (KBs). First, as the system must be able to perform on its own the problem-solving method, this method must be modeled and implemented. Second, interacting with the student on the basis of a particular solving context can also be viewed as a specific problem-solving task.

In this paper, we argue in favour of modeling each of the KBs of the ITS with the Task/Method (T&M) paradigm [3], and of operationalising within a reflective architecture [4] both the KB that solves the domain exercises and the KB that manages the system-student interaction. From the point of view of problem-solving exercises, a T&M model allows an abstract modeling of the teacher's problem-solving method, representing knowledge at different levels of abstraction (e.g. [1]), presenting and accepting variants of the "ideal" problem-solving. From the point of view of the management of the system-student interaction, a T&M modeling allows an opportunistic behaviour of the system. The operationalisation of these different kinds of knowledge within an architecture that proposes reflective capabilities enables the construction of modules that analyse the problem-solving state, and provides the pedagogical module with the information that is needed to define the most pertinent interaction.

In the remainder of this paper, we develop these different points with examples from the Emma system. Emma is an educational system (under construction) that aims at training students in the practice of linear programming as a technique to solve concrete problems. Emma is a support tool; this characteristic has been set by the teacher. For this reason, Emma's KBs are constructed on the hypotheses that the system and the student share the same vocabulary and that the student is already familiarised with the problem-solving method proposed by the system.

2   Modeling the Domain Knowledge

In Emma, a typical problem describes a company that must face a command with constraints that it cannot manage. We will consider a company which has to produce and deliver two kinds of steel manufactured pieces in such quantities and delay that it cannot achieve it. The company needs to optimise the production in order to minimise the loss. The domain expert has to (1) identify the type of problem, (2) formalise the mathematical situation, (3) solve the problem (select and apply the method that enables the solving of the considered linear programming problem), and (4) analyse the coherence of the results.

2.1   Modeling the "Ideal" Problem-Solving Method

While elaborating a model within the T&M paradigm, one has to explicit what activities have to be achieved for solving the problem, as well as how the activities can be achieved, from the analysis of the problem up to the submission of a solution. This leads to define how tasks and methods should be described to model the expected behaviour, and to construct the T&M knowledge-base in a process guided by the adopted definitions.

In Emma, an *activity*[1] is an aspect of the problem-solving method that teachers can identify when they present their reasoning process. Examples are "Formalisation of the mathematical situation" or "Resolution of a linear programming system". An activity is defined by a name, pre-conditions (when it is pertinent from the point of view of the problem-solving method), an activation context (when it is pertinent from the point of view of mathematical constraints), resources (what knowledge is required to achieve the activity), post-conditions (what strategic aspect has been obtained afterwards) and methods (the methods that can reach the goal underlying the activity).

A *method* is a possible means for achieving an activity. A *decomposition method* splits an activity into multiple sub-activities, whereas an *operational method* defines what process effectively achieves an activity. An activity can often be achieved by different methods. Figure 1 presents an extract of Emma's activities and methods.

Activities and methods are manipulated by mechanisms that perform the dynamic selection of the most pertinent tasks and methods according to the current state of the solving process. Such a selection is done by comparing the selection criteria of a task and/or a method with a set of valued facts denoting the current state of the solving context. Theses facts and their relations (e.g. "Is a", "Imply" or "Exclude") are modeled within a *domain graph* [2]. With each

---

[1] In Emma's expert model, a *task* has been renamed an *activity* in order to respect the teacher's vocabulary.

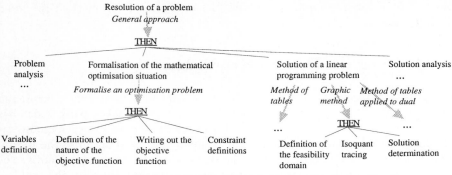

Text in plain denotes activities. Text in *italics* denotes methods.

Fig. 1. Extract of the T&M knowledge-base that models the expert knowledge

activity is associated knowledge that is used to interpret the results produced by the activity. This *interpretation knowledge* is composed of relations from the domain graph.

2.2   From an "Ideal" Solving Model to a Model of the Correct Solving Processes

As Emma is a support system, we have to use the problem-solving method taught in class as a reference. Nevertheless, some slightly different variants of the global solving process can be viewed as correct, even if they are not exactly the "ideal" one. In order to allow the system to follow slightly different versions from the expert problem-solving process, we have defined three possible status for an interpretation. An interpretation is *necessary* if the relation must be considered when the activity is finished (the resolution cannot go on if it is not considered). An interpretation is *advised* if the teacher usually considers the relation when the activity is finished (it is not necessary at this state of the solving process, but it is more efficient to consider it here). An interpretation is *possible* if the relation can be considered when the activity is over (it is mathematically possible to consider the interpretation at this state of the solving, but it is not usually done here).

For example, let us suppose that the terms of the problem have already been analysed (it is certain that it is an optimisation problem), and that the variables of the problem have been defined. In this context, the activity to be achieved next is to define the nature of the objective function (cf. fig. 1).

Figure 2 shows the representation of the activities "Definition of the nature of the objective function" and "Writing out the objective function". In order to explain how the system can decide whether a solving step is correct, we will take four examples of student's behaviour at the same step, the "definition of the nature of the objective function".

```
Name:                  Definition-nature-objective-function
Pre-conditions:        ((variables,defined))
Activation-context:    ((optimisation-problem,certain))
Resources:             (list-of-variables)
Post-conditions:       ((objective-function-nature,defined))
Methods:               (Define-nature-objective-function)
Interpretations:
    necessary-interpretations  (status, (variable-cost, (true,false))
                               (status, (variable-recipes, (true,false))
                               ((variable-cost,true) and (variable-recipes,true)) imply (maximise-the-margins,true) ...
    advised-interpretations    ((maximise-the-margins,true) or (maximise-the-recipes,true)) imply (maximisation,true))  ..
    possible-interpretations   (status, (objective-function, (defined,undefined)))
                               (status, (objective-function-linear, (true,false)))

Name:                  Writing-out-objective-function
Pre-conditions:        ((variables,defined), (objective-function-nature,defined))
Activation-context:    ((optimisation-problem,certain))
Resources:             (list-of-variables)
Post-conditions:       (objective-function,defined)
Methods:               (Write-objective-function)
Interpretations:
    necessary-interpretations  (status, (objective-function-linear, (true,false)))
```

Fig. 2. Example of encoding of activities

The "not enough" student: The student has not considered some necessary interpretations. For instance, he states that both the cost and the recipes are variable but does not say that the objective function is to maximise the margins. The solving process cannot be pursued because defining the nature of the objective function is a *sine qua none* condition for writing out the objective function.

The "just enough" student: The student considers all the necessary interpretations, but considers neither the advised nor the possible interpretations. The solving process can be pursued, but the student will have to consider these possible and advised interpretations further during the solving.

The "system-like" student: The student considers both necessary and advised interpretations. The solving process can be pursued. Moreover, the student has achieved the activity in the way close to the problem-solving method that is taught in class.

The "exhaustive" student: The student considers, in addition to all the necessary and advised interpretations, possible interpretations that allow him to cut across some activities. For instance, let us assume that the student has considered the possible interpretations of the activity "Definition of the nature of the objective function". In this context, he has written out the objective function (`objective-function,defined`), and he has stated that the function is linear (`objective-function-linear,true`). The postconditions of the activity "Write out the objective function" are satisfied, and all the necessary interpretations have been considered. Therefore, this activity has no longer to be achieved.

3   Management of the Interaction with the Student

In Emma, the student has to repeat the following steps until a solution is found:
(1) select the most relevant activity to be performed next according to the current

state of the solving; (2) select the most pertinent method to carry out the selected activity; (3) produce a set of results required to reach the objective of the selected activity (by the way of the selected method). After any of these three steps, the system can make comments on the student's actions.

Figure 3 presents three kinds of interaction we want our system to be able to manage. Note that we do not advocate that this is an exhaustive list.

Excerpt 1

L: The production cost is variable. The recipes are fixed. This is a maximisation kind of problem.

S: It's true that the production cost is variable, and you're right to say that it is a maximisation kind of problem. Now, why do you think it's a maximisation kind of problem?

L: It's a maximisation kind of problem because we have to maximise the margins.

S: It is true that we have to maximise the margins. Moreover, your justification is correct. But why do you say that we have to maximise the margins?

L: because the production cost is variable

S: You're right but this is not sufficient to state that the objective is to maximise the margins. You must add that the recipes are variable, which is true (and not false, as you said) for this exercise.

Excerpt 2

L: This is a maximisation kind of problem.

S: It's true that it is a maximisation kind of problem. Now, why do you think it's a maximisation kind of problem?

L: It's a maximisation kind of problem because we have to maximise the margins.

S: The production cost and the recipes are variable. So, you are right to say that the objective is to maximise the margins.

Excerpt 3

L: I am certain that this is an optimisation problem. The production cost is variable. The recipes are fixed.

S: It's true that this is an optimisation problem. But why do you say that?

L: because it's a maximisation kind of problem

S: Do you think that the objective is to maximise the margins or to minimise the production cost?

L: I think the objective is to minimise the production cost.

S: You're wrong. When one has to minimise the production cost, this is not a maximisation kind of problem. You were right to say that when the production cost is variable and the recipes are fixed, the objective is to minimise their cost. However, according to the terms of the exercise, the recipes are not fixed (as you have said) but variable. These two mistakes together lead you to fortunately give a correct answer.

L stands for "Learner", S for "System".

Fig. 3. Examples of interactions

3.1   Diagnosis of the Student's Answers

In this paper, we do not consider the student's choices of the activities and methods. The diagnosis is simplified to a classification of the results that the student produces for an activity. Three types of results are distinguished: correct, incorrect, and missing results. A student's result is *correct* (resp. *incorrect*) when its value is in accordance (resp. in contradiction) with the one expected in the domain graph. A result is *missing* when expected by the system but not produced by the student. A correct result can be *anticipated* when the student has not explicited some of the inference steps related to necessary interpretations.

For instance, let us consider that the student has already analysed the terms of the exercise, and is currently defining the type of the objective function (cf. fig. 1). Let us suppose that he produces the following results for the current activity: "the production cost is variable, the recipes are fixed and this is a maximisation kind of problem". At this point, the diagnosis is: "it is *correct* to state that the production cost is variable, and stating that this is maximisation kind of problem is *correct but anticipated* since the student has *omitted* to say that the objective is to maximise the margins; moreover, it is *incorrect* that the recipes are fixed".

3.2   Kinds of Interaction

The dynamic adaptation of the interaction is enabled by detecting special situations during the student's solving. With each kind of situation some knowledge is associated that will be used to build the interactions. When no special situation is detected, default interactions are used.

The *default interaction* consists in making comments on correct, then incorrect, and then omitted results. Other kinds of interactions can be thought of, which would be modeled and implemented in the same way. The one we have chosen seems to be of pedagogical interest since treating correct or incorrect results generally conducts to leaving out some omissions. The first excerpt of interactions provides an instance of the proposed default interaction. Asking the student why he thinks that it is a maximisation kind of problem leads him to explicit the reasoning process he has followed (following a backward chaining reasoning). In doing this, the origin of the mistake will finally be pointed out.

Up to now, we have modeled two kinds of *special situations*. These situations can be detected at different levels of interaction.

Fine-grained level interactions aim, for only one interaction step, at dynamically customising the default management of the session. The fine-grained interaction we describe in this paper consists in making comments upon some missing results before dealing with any other ones, when the student is considered as mastering these omitted results. For instance, within the second extract of interaction, the student first justifies the fact that it is a maximisation kind of problem because the objective is to maximise the margins. At this point, the default interaction would lead the system to ask the student why he thinks the objective is to maximise the margins. The fine-grained interaction we propose allows the student (if he masters the recognition of the nature of the production cost and recipes) not to justify his results. The pedagogical relevance of this fine-grained interaction relies on an optimistic analysis of the student's knowledge.

The identification of *remarkable configurations* aims at allowing a dynamic customisation of the default management of the session by treating several consecutive interaction steps as a unit. The remarkable configuration we consider in this paper is characterised by the following situation: the student infers some correct results from partially incorrect ones, and there exists more than one erroneous reasoning path underlying this mistake. The diagnosis has then to be refined in order to determine the erroneous paths the student has followed. The last excerpt of interactions shows an example of this remarkable situation. The dialogue starts with a default interaction which aims at diagnosing why the student has recognised an optimisation problem. Further, when the student states a maximisation kind of problem, the diagnoser identifies two mistakes which characterise the considered remarkable situation. The first mistake, "fixed recipes", is directly diagnosed because of the terms of the exercise. The second one is related to the reasoning path followed by the student. Two incorrect paths are possible: the first one consists in (step 1) inferring that "the objective is to maximise the margins" because "the production cost is variable" and "the recipes are fixed", and (step 2) concluding that "this is a maximisation kind of problem"; the second path consists in (step 1) inferring that "the objective is to minimise the production cost" because "this cost is variable" and "the recipes are fixed", and (step 2) concluding that "this is a maximisation kind of problem". In the former case, the first reasoning step is incorrect; in the latter, the second step is incorrect. Asking the student what he thinks about the objective (maximising the margins *vs* minimising the production cost) enables the diagnoser to state where precisely the mistake occurs. The pedagogical relevance of this remarkable configuration is to detect that the diagnosis has to be refined, and to put into evidence the contradiction in the student's reasoning (in the example, a minimisation instead of a maximisation kind of problem).

3.3   Modeling the Management of the Interactions within the T&M Paradigm

While managing the interaction with the student, the system can either act independently of the student's behaviour, observe the student's behaviour, or react according to the student's behaviour. Let us suppose (1) that the system has already initialised the interaction by proposing the first exercise to the student, and (2) that the student has given a first set of results for which the system has elaborated a diagnosis. At this point, the aim is to influence the student.

In order to influence the student, one can make comments on a diagnosis, explain the current situation of solving in order to deal with the student's misunderstanding, or present the student with a more adapted exercise. These different possibilities are modeled by the way of methods associated with the task "Influence the student". One of these methods is dynamically selected according to the problem-solving context.

In order to make comments on a diagnosis, a strategy for interacting (i.e., defining an order for dealing with all the diagnosed results of the student) is first selected and then applied. This is modeled as presented in fig. 4 by way of the method "Make comments on a diagnosis" which describes a sequential control over a sub-task decomposition ("Select a strategy for interacting" and then "Comment on the results"). The method associated with the first task ("Select a strategy for interacting") explicits the standard way for interacting. In practical terms, it sorts the diagnosed results according to their respective nature. The only method associated with the second task ("Comment on the results") defines an iterative control. It states that the current objective is to make comments on a set of results while a result that is not yet commented exists. At this point, one can make comments on a set of results related to a remarkable configuration and/or make comments on all the results not yet commented according to the adopted strategy.

When a remarkable situation is detected (cf. the third excerpt), a predefined interaction is performed and all the results related to the detected remarkable

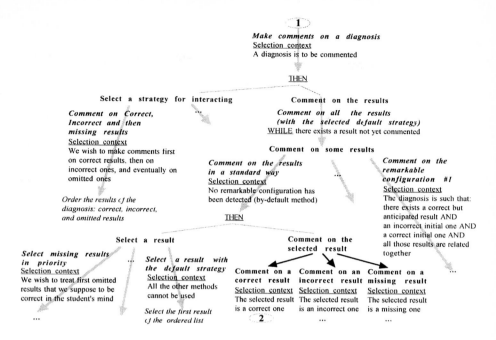

Fig. 4. T&M decomposition for making comments on a diagnosis

situation are considered as being treated. When no remarkable situation is detected, the comments on the student's results are given in a standard way (cf. fig. 4). In this case, a result that has not yet been commented has to be chosen, and comments on it have to be given to the student. The fine-grained adaptive capabilities of our system are made possible through the task "Select a result": at this point, some results can be punctually preferred to other ones according to some pedagogical criteria (for example, the one we have used in the second excerpt of interaction).

Once a result is chosen, comments have to be made according to its nature: correct, incorrect or omitted. To model this aspect, we have used the notion of *prototypic task*. A prototypic task is dynamically instantiated, at run-time, by an effective task. Let us assume that the system is currently treating a correct result; that is, the prototypic task "Comment on the selected result" has been instantiated by the effective task "Comment on a correct result" (cf. fig. 4). At this point, if the result that is currently being commented on has been introduced by the student in order to justify another one given previously, we consider that the current interaction should take into account this history. Taking such a history into account allows linking two (or more) interactions (in other words, also making comments on the inference steps that underly the produced results). To do so, each method possesses an "Interaction context" slot (cf. fig. 5).

Within this approach, the interaction we obtain for the first excerpt is the following one: "It is true that the objective is to maximise the margins. Moreover, it is true that when the objective is to maximise the margins then this is a maximisation kind of problem.". This list of sentences is computed by selecting the method "Confirm the answer and the underlying reasoning step" (because there exists a context of interaction related to the justification of the previous result "this is a maximisation kind of problem"). This method splits into three sub-tasks. The first one aims at communicating to the student that he is right for the current result. The second task aims at recalling the context of interaction. In our case, the method that is applied for doing so is to "Highlight a correct reasoning step" because (1) the inference step that he has used to justify his result is correct (satisfaction of the Selection context criterion), and (2) the result that the student is justifying is correct but anticipated (satisfaction of the Interaction context criterion). Finally, the third task aims at refining the diagnosis since we have decided that the student has to explicit each of his reasoning steps, and that he has omitted some of them (the current result, "the objective is to maximise the margins", is anticipated).

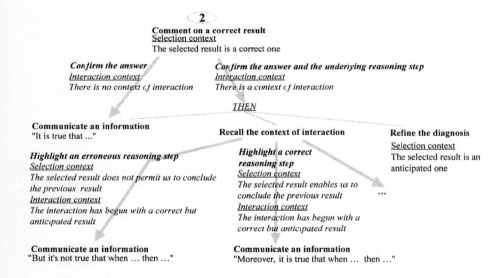

Fig. 5. The T&M decomposition for making comments on a correct result

4   Discussion

We have used the same Task/Method paradigm for modeling the pedagogical module, expert model, and diagnoser. In doing this, the whole system is endowed with reflective capabilities that allow it to dynamically analyse parts of its knowledge-bases in order to manage the interaction. This is the case when the system has to trigger the domain expert model in order to be able to select between the possible methods. That is, the system can detect that some information is required in order to select between a task or a method, and can dynamically launch the reflective modules that will retrieve this information. An example of this reflective process may occur when the task "Comment on some results" (cf. fig. 4) is being performed: for a remarkable configuration to be detected, one must determine whether the correct but anticipated result is a logical conclusion that can follow from the correct and incorrect initial results.

The problem-solving model has been implemented, and the interaction model is currently under implementation. In both cases we use the DSTM framework [5]. An important advantage of the T&M paradigm is that the designers explicitly state the pedagogical knowledge. As DSTM flexibility allows a strict structural correspondence between the implementation and the model, this results in a KB in which the pedagogical expertise is explicitly represented. This greatly simplifies any subsequent modification of the KB and leads to a KB that makes sense both for the designers and the teachers.

The pedagogical relevance of the interactions provided by our system has been confirmed from a theoretical point of view by the pedagogical expert of our team. In order to carry out an experimentation with students in real situation, we are currently refining the implementation of the current version of the tasks and methods that manage the interactions (the selection mechanisms being directly provided by the DSTM framework). We believe that such an experimentation will bring to light new remarkable situations and/or new fine-grained level interactions.

References

[1] E. Aïmeur and C. Frasson. Eliciting the learning context in cooperative tutoring systems. In *Working notes of the IJICAI-95 workshop on modelling context in knowledge representation and reasoning*, LAFORIA report 95/11, France, pages 1–11, 1995.

[2] C. Choquet, P. Tchounikine, and F. Trichet. Training strategies and knowledge acquisition: using the same reflective tools for different purposes. In *8th International Portuguese Conference on Artificial Intelligence (EPIA'97)*, LNAI, Coimbra, Portugal, 1997. Springer-Verlag.

[3] J.M. David, J.P. Krivine, and R. Simmons. *Second Generation Expert Systems*. Springer-Verlag, 1993.

[4] M. Reinders, E. Vinkhuyzen, A. Voss, H. Akkermans, J. Balder, B. Bartsch-Sporl, B. Bredeweg, U. Drouven, F. van Harmelen, W. Karbach, Z. Karsen, G. Schreiber, and B. Wielinga. A conceptual modelling framework for Knowledge-Level Reflection. *AI Communications*, 4(2-3):74–87, 1991.

[5] F. Trichet and P. Tchounikine. Reusing a Flexible Task-Method Framework to Prototype a Knowledge Based System. In *9th International Conference on Software Engineering and Knowledge Engineering (SEKE'97)*, pages 192–199, Madrid, Spain, 1997.

Deconstructing a Computer-Based Tutor: Striving for Better Learning Efficiency in Stat Lady

Kevin A. Gluck[1], Valerie J. Shute[2], John R. Anderson[1], and Marsha C. Lovett[1]

[1]Department of Psychology, Carnegie Mellon University, Pittsburgh, PA 15217, USA
{kgluck, ja, lovett}@cmu.edu
[2]Air Force Research Laboratory/HEJT, 1880 Carswell Avenue, Lackland AFB, TX 78236, USA
vshute@colab.brooks.af.mil

Abstract. This paper is a prospective report of an ongoing design project involving a computer-based tutoring system called Stat Lady (Shute & Gluck, 1994). Previous studies have shown considerable improvement on curriculum objectives as a result of interation with the tutor. The goal now is to try to improve on learning efficiency, defined as knowledge gain per unit of time. The question we will be asking in this study is: What can we peel away from the tutor to make it a more efficient teaching tool, without having a negative impact on curriculum learning? Additionally, as we remove pieces of the tutor, what effect (if any) will that have on the subjective enjoyment of the learning experience? The study in progress investigates these issues in a 2x2 factorial design varying the presence or absence of contextualized instruction and problem solving across the presence or absence of certain interface features that were an integral part of the original tutor.

Introduction

„That with psychological attention to human performance airplanes became more flyable encourages us to believe that with psychological attention to human performance computers can become more usable."

Card, Moran, and Newell (1983, p. 9)

Card, Moran, and Newell (1983) penned those hopeful words more than 15 years ago in the introductory chapter to their book on the application of information-processing psychology to the study of human-computer interaction. In the twelfth chapter of their text, Card et al. outline a framework for applying psychology in this important domain, characterizing it as an open design process, such that the computer program is regularly redefined all along the way. They write, „Thus, design proceeds in a complex, iterative fashion in which various parts of the design are incrementally generated, evaluated, and integrated" (p. 406).

Koedinger and Anderson (in press) express a similar opinion in their forthcoming paper on principled design of cognitive tutors. They note that, „It should be the natural expectation of the field that no Interactive Learning Environment will be fully effective in its intial implementations and that early demonstrations of limitations have a positive, not a negative, bearing on the value of the final system." This is to be expected, of course, because of the combinatorial complexity at the intersection of the characteristics of human users, potential variations in the characteristics of computer-based instructional systems, and differences in the pedagogical requirements of different domains.

This paper is a prospective[1] report of a design project involving a computer-based tutoring system called Stat Lady (Shute & Gluck, 1994), which teaches introductory descriptive statistics. In contrast to ITS intended for classroom deployment, Stat Lady was originally developed strictly as a tool for student modeling research in the Armstrong Laboratory TRAIN facility. Satisfyingly, however, and despite the fact that its *raison d'etre* is to be a piece of basic research software, it has been demonstrated that Stat Lady results in a good deal of curriculum-related learning on the part of those who work through it, and laboratory subjects report actually enjoying the experience (Shute, 1995). The question currently under investigation is this: What can we peel away from the tutor to make it a more efficient teaching tool, without having a negative impact on curriculum learning? Additionally, as we remove pieces of the tutor, what effect (if any) will that have on the subjective enjoyment of the learning experience? Participants in previous studies have reported that they enjoyed learning from the tutor. If altering it destroys the positive affective reaction to the experience, thereby decreasing student interest in pursuing future opportunities to learn about the domain (or in learning about a different domain from a new Stat Lady instructional module), then any gain in learning efficiency could ultimately be overshadowed by losses in motivation.

1.1 The Research Goal

Implicit in the above description of our current research question is that the goal is to increase *learning efficiency*, specifically by improving on the speed with which learners can use the tutor. Learning efficiency, defined as the amount of knowledge acquired per unit of time, is of paramount concern in the educational and training communities. There are two ways to improve on learning efficiency. One can either find a way to get students to (a) learn more - without increasing their time investment, or get them to (b) learn faster - without decreasing their learning.

---

[1]As of the due date for ITS '98 conference submissions, we are in the process of redesigning the tutor. Subjects will be run in the coming months, and the data will be ready for presentation by August.

The goal of increasing learning efficiency is the driving motivation behind a great deal of research in education and related fields. The ITS community is one of those fields. In this particular project, we are attempting (b) rather than (a). The primary reason for this is that Gluck, Lovett, Anderson, and Shute (1998) recently completed a study investigating how people use Stat Lady and how interaction with the tutor changes with practice. Through the analysis of concurrent verbal protocols (see Ericsson & Simon, 1993) collected as participants learned from Stat Lady, as well as conclusions derived from post-participation interviews, it became apparent that we were in a position to consider potentially fruitful approaches to redesigning the Stat Lady tutor, with the goal of increasing the speed of use of the system. Additionally, the verbal protocol participants turned out to be „good" subjects, who learned the material quickly and provided very few opportunities to study „problem" areas in the way the curriculum was taught. A final factor that influenced our choice of strategies for improving learning efficiency is that large-scale studies (N > 100) indicate that average posttest scores are already satisfactorily high (Shute, 1995), and since the tutor is currently used strictly as a laboratory research tool, there is no outside pressure - from school districts, for instance - to try to raise posttest scores. Thus, with little to say on improving the curriculum itself, but some well-developed ideas regarding how to speed people through the current curriculum more quickly, we have decided to adopt the latter approach in our search for better learning efficiency.

2   Overview of the Stat Lady Tutor

Stat Lady is the name of a series of computerized learning environments teaching topics in introductory statistics (e.g., probability, descriptive statistics). This paper is proposing to modify one of the modules from descriptive statistics, namely "Data Organization and Plotting" (see Shute, 1995 for more detail than we are able to provide here). The design of all the Stat Lady programs reflects the theoretical postulates that learning is a constructive process, enhanced by experiential involvement with the subject matter that is situated in real-world examples and problems. The general goal of Stat Lady is thus to enhance the acquisition of statistical knowledge and skills by making the learning experience both memorable and meaningful. To accomplish this, each module was created to be a hands-on learning environment where learners actively engage in various on-line activities. Some of the features of the Stat Lady modules include: (a) a humorous and experiential interface; (b) an organized set of curriculum objectives; (c) a pool of whimsical, „real-world" problem sets (Scenarios); and (d) a three-level feedback design, including both auditory and text feedback.

Stat Lady takes a mastery learning approach to teaching, and learning is self-paced. That is, a relevant concept or rule is presented, and then a problem is posed for students to solve in order to demonstrate comprehension (mastery) of each curriculum element. Further, the program is sensitive to (and thus addresses) errors that are recognized by the system's "bug" library. As mentioned, the particular Stat Lady curriculum relevant to this paper is descriptive statistics, assembled from the results of a cognitive task analysis performed by two subject matter experts (for validity and reliability), and consisting of 77 curriculum objectives. These were arrayed hierarchically, from simple to more complex concepts and skills, and then divided into five separate instruction Sections.

Students receive instruction and solve problems (Scenarios) within each Section, and Stat Lady provides specific feedback about each topic under investigation. More specifically, the program begins by identifying a particular topic for instruction from the list of curriculum objectives. After presenting the selected topic in broad strokes, Stat Lady quickly illustrates it with a real-life, humorous example to enhance memorability. Following instruction, learners have to apply the concept or skill in the solution of related problems. For problems that require data manipulation, they obtain their own unique data set from the Number Factory (an activity that's analogous to data collection), where they set their own parameters, such as the sample size and minimum and maximum values. If the learner successfully solves the problem on the first attempt, he or she is congratulated with positive auditory and textual feedback, and then moves on to the next problem or topic for instruction.[2] If a student is having difficulty (e.g., enters one or more incorrect responses), each response is followed by the increasingly explicit feedback (and encouragement), mentioned above. The system also allows learners to engage in elective "extracurricular" activities, such as viewing items in the on-line Dictionary and Formula Bank, playing around in the Number Factory, or using the Grab-a-Graph tool.

3 Proposed Changes

We have already mentioned two of the three sources of information from which we were able to draw implications about redesign of the tutor: verbal protocols and informal post-participation interviews. A third source of insight was the development of a production system model that reproduces the sort of adaptive changes in low-level interaction with the tutor (i.e., information-seeking behaviors) that we saw in the protocol subjects. The model was developed in ACT-R (Anderson & Lebiere, 1998), a cognitive theory of learning implemented in a simulation environment. Formal modeling of this sort forces one to make explicit the assumptions one has about goal structures and specific problem-solving paths. The assumption we made in this model was that our protocol subjects were satisfying the goal of figuring out which next action was appropriate at that point in the scenario (either by reading the directions off the screen or retrieving the next action from memory, based on past experience), and then executing that action. This seems like a reasonable interpretation of the behavior of the protocol subjects, largely because we know that they had, for the most

---

[2]There is an intelligent student modeling component (SMART - Shute, 1995), which tracks learner performance and can be relied upon to make decisions regarding which curriculum objectives need to be taught, when the student has mastered a particular topic, and so on. However, that capacity was disabled in the Gluck et al. (1998) study, as well as in this current proposal, so we do not describe it in detail.

part, already satisfied the other likely goal that someone using a computer-based tutor would have - which is to learn the curriculum. Thus, our underlying assumption is that someone learning from an ITS will be in the process of satisfying one of two goals at any point in the interaction: 1) learn the curriculum, or 2) figure out what action to take next (which may be done in service of learning a curriculum-related procedure).

The process of redesigning the tutor can be undertaken with respect to these goals. That is, we can make the assumption that any component of the tutor that is not critical for the successful completion of those two goals can be removed. This is essentially the approach taken here - to remove or modify a number of different features that were originally built into the system, and then examine the effect that removing them has on learning efficiency. These include changes to feedback sound files, the deletion of feedback text, the removal of the Number Factory, and the removal of references to problem Context. Next we'll describe each of these modifications in more detail.

3.1   Feedback Sound Files

Stat Lady offers both auditory and text feedback regarding performance on curriculum-related problems. Both the positive and negative feedback are designed such that a sound file plays first, then the text feedback appears. While the sound file is playing, the interface is "disabled," leaving the user incapacitated with respect to the tutor until it is done. The feedback sound files are selected randomly from a pool of options, and they range in length from about 250 ms to more than 8 s. It is the longer sound files that really become an issue. We observed repeatedly while running the protocol subjects that they would grow weary of waiting for the feedback sound files to finish playing, so that they could move on with the tutor. Since the hang-up really is with the length of the sound files, the modification to the tutor in this case is to replace them all with standard short (250 ms) sounds that represent positive and negative feedback. We measured the average length of the positive sound files to be 2.93 s and the negative sounds to be 2.29 s. Thus, each time a feedback sound plays, it would be 2-2.5 s faster than in the original version of the tutor. How much of an impact would this have on efficiency? We estimate that this simple manipulation alone will result in approximately a 7% decrease in tutor completion time.

3.2   Feedback Text

In the current design of the tutor, after the feedback sound file plays, feedback text appears on the screen. These are simple statements like, "Yes, that's correct!" or "Sorry, that is incorrect." If we take "learn the curriculum" and "figure out what to do next" as the two most likely goals while learning from Stat Lady (or just about any tutoring system, for that matter), then we see that the text we've been calling positive and negative feedback text achieves neither of these. There is no information about the curriculum or the next step. Due to the fact that subjects get the sound file feedback before the text, and therefore already know whether they were correct or incorrect, these messages are also redundant. Thus, they have very little information value, with respect to the likely goals of students using the tutor. It turns out that this interpretation is supported by the results of the protocol analysis, in that our subjects read a relatively low (and declining) proportion of positive feedback text as they solved problems in the scenarios. Figure 2 shows these data (Pos. Feedback) and also provides comparison data on reading behaviors for other

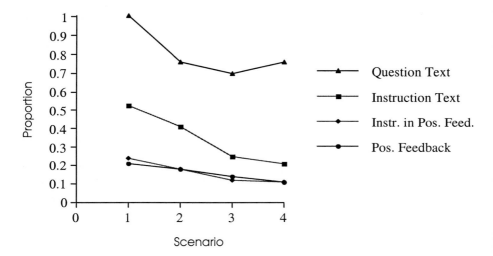

Fig. 2. Verbalization rates for four text types, averaged across scenarios in Sections 1 and 3 of the Stat Lady tutor. „Question Text" refers to the questions which appear in the scenarios to test learner ability on the curriculum objectives. „Instruction Text" contains information about what to do next and/or curriculum-relevant declarations. „Instr. in Pos. Feed." is instruction text that appears in the feedback window. „Pos. Feedback" is text that indicates whether the learner's response was correct or not.

types of text. Given the low information value of the positive feedback text, we are removing it from the tutor altogether. It seems like a theoretically and empirically justifiable change, but the impact on tutor time will be minimal. The estimate is about a 1/2% decrease in completion time as a result of this manipulation.

3.3 Number Factory

The Number Factory, which is designed as a metaphor for the process of collecting data, is an activity that is required at the beginning of each Scenario. The learner first reads the Context Statement, then goes off to the Number Factory to acquire data that will address the problem presented. Although it is an integral part of the original Stat Lady, it is not explicitly related to any curriculum objectives. There is no pretest or posttest assessment of the learner's skill in using the Number Factory, and there are not currently any data which bear on the issue of whether subjects come to associate „going to the Number Factory" with actually conducting studies. Additionally, instructing students in the use of the Number Factory and visiting it at the beginning of every Scenario is a fairly time consuming process. It adds several minutes to the length of the instructional portion of Section 1 and requires approximately 45 s extra in every scenario. A natural alternative to visiting the Number Factory is to simply provide students with the data they need at the beginning of each scenario. Including the one-time savings associated with removing that portion of the instruction in Section 1, we estimate another 5% decrease in tutor completion time resulting from the removal of the Number Factory.

3.4 Situated Contexts

In reflecting on the various components of the tutor which add time, perhaps unnecessarily, to its completion, it becomes apparent that subjects spend an awful lot of time reading about "real-world" situations. As a result of the current excitement in educational circles regarding the benefits of situated learning (e.g., Lave, 1988), an effort was made in the original design of the Stat Lady tutor to situate the problem solving, both during instruction and during the Scenarios, in real-world contexts. References to context are pervasive throughout the tutor. They come up not only in the Context that appears at the beginning of each scenario, but also in the instruction sections, in questions during the scenario, and in feedback text. This is considerable additional reading time, and it remains an empirical question whether all this situated context actually has a positive impact on learning. A new version of Stat Lady that did not include the situated contexts in the instruction sections and the Scenarios could be used to test out that hypothesis. Regardless of the effect on learning, completion time is certainly going to drop as a result of this manipulation. A decrease in the neighborhood of 10% would not be unreasonable.

4 The Plan

We see the aforementioned changes to the Stat Lady tutor as developing along two dimensions. On the one dimension is the issue of Context: present or absent. This dimension is interesting with respect to learning efficiency, in that we predict faster progress through the tutor via elimination of the Context, and it has the added attraction of being relevant to one of the hottest debates in contemporary education research (see Anderson, Reder, & Simon, 1996, and the reply by Greeno, 1997). On the other dimension lies the proposed removal of various Features (feedback, Number Factory) which, quite frankly, are largely responsible for providing Stat Lady with a special personality all her own.

Both the Features and the Context manipulations serve the function of „structural" redesign (Card, Moran, & Newell, 1983, Chapter 12) and merit evaluation. By crossing the two manipulations, we arrive at a 2x2 factorial design, with one factor being the presence or absence of Context, and the other being Features vs. No Features (more accurately, „fewer features"). Thus, this study involves comparisons of learning efficiency (outcome divided by time) across the following four conditions: 1) Stat Lady - Classic, 2) Stat Lady - NoContext, 3) Stat Lady - NoFeatures, 4) Stat Lady - NoContext *and* NoFeatures (super sleek new version). Table 1 summarizes our predicted time savings for each of these conditions.

Table 1. Predicted Time Savings (% Decrease) in the Four Conditions

Condition	Decrease in Completion Time
Stat Lady - Classic	Baseline
Stat Lady - NoContext	10.0%
Stat Lady - NoFeatures	12.5%
Stat Lady - NoContext *and* NoFeatures	22.5%

Outcome, the numerator in our learning efficiency computation, is perhaps better expressed as learning gain. It is the amount of improvement from the pretest to the posttest.

We mentioned briefly in the introductory paragraphs the issue of motivation. Ideally it is the case that any given learning experience is not only effective, but also enjoyable and rewarding. We acknowledge the possibility that either or both of the dimensions along which the tutor will change for this assessment could result in a significantly less enjoyable experience for the participants. Those data would be important, so we will include after the posttest an Affective Response Survey which queries the participants on the subjective experience of learning from the tutor.

5 Prospective Conclusions

The time savings predictions are based on performance data from previous studies. Since both manipulations essentially involve removing pieces of the tutor, we feel that it is safe to assume that their effect will be a decrease in tutor completion time, although the exact size of the effect remains to be seen. Few people would be surprised by this prediction. The real unknowns are what the impact of the modifications will be on learning outcome (posttest performance) and the subjective experience of the participants. The results are not at all obvious with respect to these two measures.

As one might anticipate, we do not expect these manipulations to have a negative impact on learning. If that were the case, it would be like shooting ourselves in the proverbial foot. Others might disagree, however, and quite possibly for good reason. Recent cognitive tutoring data, for instance, actually suggest some benefit is to be had in providing textual descriptions of problem-solving contexts similar to those in Stat Lady. One example of this is Koedinger and MacLaren's (1997) finding that students perform better solving a class of algebra word problems than they do on the analogous symbolic equations. Another relevant result is that greater emphasis on word problem solving in algebra instruction leads not only to greater posttest performance on word problem solving (no surprise there), but also to greater posttest performance on basic skills (Koedinger, Anderson, Hadley, & Mark, 1997). Perhaps it is the case, then, that posttest scores will be lower in a decontextualized, non-situated instructional environment. This is likely the prediction that the hardline situativists would make, but what if posttest scores do not go down? It will be interesting to consider the implications of such a result, if indeed that is what we find. We'll see what the data tell us.

It is worth noting that the pretest and posttest have contextualized problems. Thus, all students will be tested on contextualized problems and we will be seeing how the presence or absence of context during learning affects this transfer (to new cover stories for the Context group and to newly context-enriched problems for the NoContext group).

Finally, we consider the effects of our manipulations on subjective experience. Although there are a few exceptions (e.g., Simon, 1979), motivations and emotions and their interaction with learning are topics that have been largely ignored in cognitive psychology. In fact, Aubé (1997) recently commented on the need for better theories, and models based on those theories, of the interaction between emotional motivation and learning. If those models already existed, we might be able to generate some reasonable predictions of the effect our proposed modifications will have on subjective reactions to the new versions of Stat Lady. As it stands, however, we will again have to wait and see what sort of story unfolds in the data. We look forward to sharing that story at ITS '98.

References

1. Anderson, J. R., & Lebiere, C. (1998). The atomic components of thought. Hillsdale, NJ: Erlbaum.
2. Anderson, J. R., Reder, L.M., & Simon, H. A. (1996). Situated learning and education. Educational Researcher, 25(4), 5-11.
3. Aubé, M. (1997). Toward computational models of motivation: A much needed foundation for social sciences and education. Journal of Artificial Intelligence in Education, 8(1), 43-75.
4. Card, S. K., Moran, T. P., & Newell, A. (1983). The psychology of human-computer interaction. Hillsdale, NJ: Erlbaum.
5. Ericsson, K. A., & Simon, H. A. (1993). Protocol analysis: Verbal reports as data (revised edition). Cambridge, MA: MIT Press.
6. Gluck, K. A., Lovett, M. C., Anderson, J. R., & Shute, V. J. (1998). Learning about the learning environment: Adaptive behaviors and instruction. Unpublished manuscript.
7. Greeno, J. G. (1997). On claims that answer the wrong questions. Educational Researcher, 26(1), 5-17.
8. Koedinger, K. R., & Anderson, J. R. (in press). Illustrating principled design: The early evolution of a cognitive tutor for algebra symbolization. Interactive Learning Environments.
9. Koedinger, K. R., Anderson, J.R., Hadley, W.H., & Mark, M. A. (1997). Intelligent tutoring goes to school in the big city. International Journal of Artificial Intelligence in Education, 8, 30-43.
10. Koedinger, K.R., & MacLaren, B. A. (1997). Implicit strategies and errors in an improved model of early algebra problem solving. In Proceedings of the Nineteenth Annual Conference of the Cognitive Science Society. Hillsdale, NJ: Erlbaum.
11. Lave, J. (1988). Cognition in practice. Cambridge, UK: Cambridge University Press.
12. Shute, V. J. (1995). SMART: Student Modeling Approach for Responsive Tutoring. User Modeling and User-Adapted Interaction, 5, 1-44.
13. Shute, V. J., & Gluck, K. A. (1994). Stat Lady Descriptive Statistics Tutor: Data Organization and Plotting Module. [Unpublished computer program]. Brooks AFB, TX: Armstrong Laboratory.
14. Simon, H. A. (1979). Motivational and emotional controls of cognition. In Models of thought, Vol. 1. (pp. 29-38). New Haven: Yale University Press.

Habitable 3D Learning Environments for Situated Learning

William H. Bares   Luke S. Zettlemoyer   James C. Lester
(**whbares@eos.ncsu.edu**)   (**lszettle@eos.ncsu.edu**)   (**lester@eos.ncsu.edu**)

Multimedia Laboratory
Department of Computer Science
North Carolina State University
Raleigh, NC 27695-7534 USA

Abstract. The growing emphasis on learner-centered education focuses on intrinsically motivated learning via engaging problem-solving activities. *Habitable 3D learning environments*, in which learners guide avatars through virtual worlds for role-based problem solving, hold great promise for situated learning. We have been investigating habitable learning environments by iteratively designing, implementing, and evaluating them. In the Situated Avatar-Based Immersive Learning (SAIL) framework for habitable 3D learning environments, learners navigate avatars through virtual worlds as they solve problems by manipulating artifacts. The SAIL framework has been used to implement CPU CITY, a 3D learning environment testbed for the domain of computer architecture. A visually compelling virtual cityscape of computer components, CPU CITY presents learners with goal advertisements that focus their attention on salient problem-solving sub-tasks. The CPU CITY testbed has produced prototypes that have been evaluated. Pilot studies suggest that habitable learning environments offer a promising new paradigm for educational applications.

1 Introduction

A recent growing emphasis on learner-centered education has yielded a veritable revolution in educational theory and practice. Current theories of learning and pedagogy revolve around constructivism, which emphasizes the learner's knowledge construction process [12]. Perhaps most central among the tenets of constructivism is that learners should be engaged in active exploration, they should be intrinsically motivated, and they should develop an understanding of a domain through challenging and enjoyable problem-solving activities. Considerable work in the ITS community has addressed situated learning in microworlds [2, 5, 7, 15], but has only recently begun to explore techniques for situated learning in 3D environments [13].

Engaging 3D learning environments in which learners guide avatars through virtual worlds hold great promise for learner-centered education. By enabling learners to participate in immersive experiences, 3D learning environments could help students develop a deep, *experiential* understanding of highly complex biological, electronic, or mechanical systems. If 3D learning environments could enable learners to perform tasks typically performed by components of the system considered, qualitative improvements in learning might be possible. For example, learners could study computer architecture in a virtual computer where they might direct data from RAM memory to the hard disk. Properly designed, 3D learning environments that blur the distinction between education and entertainment could produce learning experiences that are intrinsically motivating and solidly grounded in problem solving.

Our laboratory has been investigating this question by iteratively designing, implementing, and evaluating 3D learning environments. Out of this work has emerged the Situated Avatar-Based Immersive Learning (SAIL) framework for *habitable* 3D learning environments. In habitable learning environments, learners steer avatars through 3D virtual worlds as they manipulate artifacts in the course of problem solving. Environments designed in the SAIL framework facilitate situated learning by providing learners with:

- *Habitable virtual worlds*: Inviting 3D virtual navigable worlds which represent the intended spatial mental model of the system being studied, house manipulable artifacts whose functionalities mimic those in the system.
- *Lifelike avatars*: Inhabiting the virtual worlds are learner-guided avatars capable of navigating the environments and manipulating artifacts within them; learners direct their avatar's behaviors.
- *Dynamic goal advertisements*: By tracking learners' problem-solving activities with a task model, learning environments allow investigative flexibility while at the same time assisting learners by presenting context-sensitive problem-solving goal reminders.

The SAIL framework has been used to implement CPU CITY (Fig. 1), a 3D learning environment testbed for the domain of computer architecture. CPU CITY provides learners with a virtual computer housing a CPU, RAM, and a hard disk. To develop an understanding of the activities comprising a computation, learners direct an avatar named Whizlo (Fig. 1) to pick up, transport, and insert data packets into registers. The environment presents the learners with goal advertisements that assist them in focusing their attention on the current sub-task. Pilot studies of the CPU CITY testbed indicate that habitable learning environments offer a new paradigm for educational software that can offer significant potential for situated learning.

Fig. 1. The CPU CITY Learning Environment

2 Facilitating Situated Learning

Over the course of the past few decades, many educators and learning theorists have shifted from an emphasis on rote learning and behaviorist response-strengthening to constructivist learning that emphasizes knowledge construction [10]. In large part because of its emphasis on the learner's active role as he or she acquires new concepts and procedures [12], constructivism has made considerable gains relative to more didactic approaches. A particularly appealing form of constructivist learning is situated learning, which is characterized by intrinsic motivation, situated problem solving, and role-based immersivity.

Intrinsic motivation: Learning should be fun, and a critical feature of many enjoyable experiences is motivation. Two forms of motivation have been identified by cognitive scientists: *extrinsically motivating factors*, which are external to the learner, e.g. a reward system, and *intrinsically motivating factors*, which come from within and are usually characterized by playful learning. In the classic study of intrinsic motivation in computer games [9], it was found that (1) three key components of intrinsic motivation are challenge, fantasy, and curiosity, and (2) regarding curiosity, both sensory and cognitive factors are critical.

Situated problem solving: Previous learning theories tended to emphasize rote memorization. In contrast, situated learning involves *situated* problem-solving episodes [14]: these goal-directed activities take place in concrete contexts in which learning occurs as a by-product of solving problems. For example, rather than learning algebra through abstract symbol manipulation, learners could design a space station, requiring them to formulate and solve equations.

Role-based immersivity: Recent years have seen a growing interest in story-telling software that enables users to design stories, create storytellers, and actively participate in plots, perhaps taking on the role of one or more of the characters [4,16]. A hallmark of situated learning is that the learner takes on an active role in a virtual world that simulates the system being studied. For example, when learning about a computer's fetch-execute cycle, learners could *become* the machine by taking on the role of a courier whose task is to gather data values, perform computations, and store the results in RAM. The central features of situated learning point towards a new form of educational software that could provide intrinsic motivation, support situated problem solving, and facilitate role-based immersivity.

3 Situated Avatar-Based Immersive Learning Environments

To create a new paradigm for educational software that can foster situated learning, we have been iteratively designing learning environment technologies whose evaluations suggest that they offer intrinsic motivation, situated problem solving, and role-based immersivity. Out of this work has emerged the Situated Avatar-Based Immersive Learning (SAIL) framework for *habitable* 3D learning environments.

For example, in a computer architecture learning environment, they might be asked to guide the avatar as it fetches data from RAM and performs calculations in the CPU. A learner's joystick inputs are interpreted by a world monitor which passes them to an avatar director, a point-of-view composer, and a task modeler (Fig. 2). Learners issue *navigation directives* and *manipulation directives* to the avatar director. For example, in the course of solving problems, the learner might direct the avatar to pick up an object, carry an object from one location to another, or insert an object into a receptacle. The task modeler tracks the learner's current goal and calls on the point-of-view composer and cinematography system to compose camera shots to view the avatar and salient objects of the current goal in a way that they are clearly visible [1]. The task modeler uses goal advertisements to give reminders about the purpose of the current sub-task, as well as offering advice about how it should be carried out.

Observations of learners interacting with these environments indicate that three families of design decisions are critical: designing the components and layout of the virtual worlds to create engaging universes that maximize clarity, consistency, and pedagogical value; designing avatars that are lifelike; and designing goal advertisements and a mechanism for presenting them.

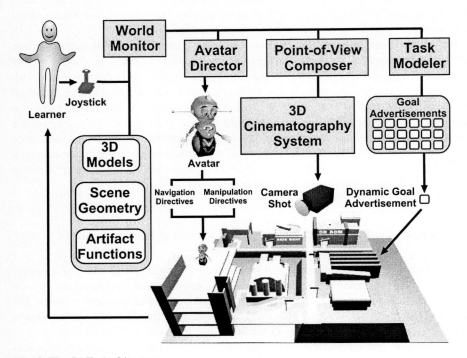

Fig. 2. The SAIL Architecture

3.1 Habitable Virtual Worlds

A 3D learning environment's virtual world must define an "information landscape" [3] that clearly communicates the central features of the system to be investigated. To help learners acquire a spatial mental model that reflects reality and a process-based mental model of its functionalities, virtual worlds can be constructed with the following techniques:

Architectural Abstraction: By creating virtual worlds around metaphors that communicate the essential structures and functions of the system, designers can facilitate situated learning. They can provide visual mnemonic devices where important spatial relationships between components are suggested by their layout, and redundant cues such as appearance and labeling assist in their identification. For example, the CPU CITY learning environment testbed is a stylized rendition of an actual computer cast as a colorful cityscape. The memory and I/O buses on which data travel are roadways and road signs identify relevant locations.

Spatial and Temporal Scaling: Virtual worlds can take advantage of an animator's ability to scale space and time. By increasing or decreasing the spatial scale, architectural structures can be designed to help learners' acquire a spatial mental model that is on a human scale, even if the physical system being studied is not. For example, the spatial scale of the CPU CITY virtual world was expanded to enable learners to navigate components of approximately human size. Temporal scaling can be equally effective for creating experiences that occur on a human time scale. Through temporal dilation, computations requiring only milliseconds are stretched out to minutes in CPU CITY to provide time for learners to reflect on them.

3. 2 Lifelike Avatars

Because direct experience seems to act as an exceptionally strong catalyst for learning, providing a learner with an avatar — a physical embodiment of the learner in the 3D world — appears promising from an educational perspective. In addition to the direct pedagogical benefits, lifelike avatars offer significant motivational promise. For much the same reasons that lifelike animated pedagogical agents have proven so successful [8], lifelike avatars seem to emotionally engage the learners who direct them. To achieve this effect, designers can create avatars that are visually compelling by exploiting the behavior cannon of animation [6]. For example, Whizlo (Figure 1), an eager, bright-eyed robot, was given a unicycle-like wheel to scoot through CPU CITY. While idle he is kept alive with a slight rocking motion as he awaits the learner's next directive.

3.3 Dynamic Goal Advertisements

SAIL environments are intended to foster exploratory freedom, one of the hallmarks of situated learning, by allowing learners to explore the virtual world at will. Increased freedom leads to the design challenge of assisting learners to cope with this flexibility by modeling their problem-solving activities and offering guidance. Ideally operating in a guided discovery mode, the environments should enable learners to pursue paths in a curiosity-driven fashion while at the same time providing support. Achieving this delicate balance entails addressing two issues: first, how to dynamically model learners problem-solving activities, and second, how to present support in a contextually appropriate manner.

SAIL environments address the first issue by maintaining a *procedural task model* and traversing it as learners perform their tasks. In contrast to more complex approaches to task modeling such as task-action grammars (TAGs) [11], procedural task models are comparatively simple. They represent tasks as a network of goals and the temporal constraints between them. Each goal has transition condition(s), which when satisfied, lead to a successor goal. For example, in CPU CITY, the goal to pick up an object is satisfied when the learner directs the avatar near the object and picks it up by pushing the joystick action button. While task networks lack the expressiveness and flexibility of elaborate TAGS, they are considerably easier to construct and have proven effective for determining when and which goal advertisements to present for procedural tasks with well-ordered goals.

SAIL environments address the issue of presenting context-sensitive support by adopting a multi-tiered goal advertisement approach. Experience with learners interacting with CPU CITY suggest that at least two forms of assistance are useful:

- *Conceptual goal advertisements*: One of the most important types of support provided by SAIL environments is helping learners bridge the gap between high-level concepts and the immediate sub-task being performed. For example, one of the conceptual goal advertisements presented as learners interact with CPU CITY suggests, "Deposit address of A: Place the address of A into the address input port. RAM will then immediately return the numeric value of A. You can think of the address of A like the library call number for a book. The value of A is like the book shelved at that spot in the library."
- *Operational goal advertisements*: To help learners keep the immediate problem-solving goal in focus, operational goal advertisements present explicit, typically abbreviated, suggestions about the course of action to take. For example, one of CPU CITY's operational goal advertisements suggests, "Walk over to control unit and pick up the address of B packet."

SAIL systems use the current state of the traversal of the task model to index into a library of goal advertisements that are linked by intentional indices to the procedural task network. When a new goal is activated, the relevant conceptual goal advertisement is presented by both text and digitized speech. After the learner clicks the action button to acknowledge that he or she has assimilated the message, the advertisement is removed. Then a corresponding operational advertisement appears at the bottom of the screen to offer a concise reminder about the current goal.

4 The CPU City Testbed

The SAIL framework for habitable learning environments has been implemented in CPU CITY, a testbed for the domain of computer architecture. CPU CITY is implemented in 55,000 lines of C++ and uses OpenGL for 3D rendering. Its task model consists of 26 goal states, its goal advertisement library contains over 40 advertisements, and its virtual world houses more than 50 3D models. A fundamental design decision was to target cost-effective platforms likely to be available in the classroom in the near future. To this end, the CPU CITY environment currently runs on a 333 MHz Pentium II with a Permedia2 3D graphics accelerator and 128 MB memory at 15 frames/second in a 640x480 full-screen window. CPU CITY provides learners with joystick control, which they use to steer Whizlo through CPU CITY and pickup and deposit objects being carried.

Consider the following example from an ongoing learning session in which the learner has just deposited the value of the first operand, A, whose value is 250, into CPU register #1 to continue the process of computing the subtraction of B from A. Verbal praise is given by Whizlo to applaud the student for having achieved this goal. The learner is reminded that in order to fetch the second operand, B, he/she must first obtain the address of that value from the CPU control unit. The learner scoots Whizlo to the control unit and grabs the address of B packet. Next, the learner directs Whizlo to exit the CPU, scurry along the CPU-memory bus pathway to enter the RAM, and positions him in front of the RAM address input port. After hitting the action button to deposit the address packet, the learner is told with a goal advertisement that the value of the second number has been swapped-out to disk since it had not been recently used. Therefore, the learner must retrieve the address packet from the RAM input port and transport it to the hard disk where the value of B can be found in virtual memory. There the learner must obtain the value of B, return it to the CPU for computation, and lastly, store the result value C into RAM.

5 Pilot Studies and Design Implications

To investigate learners' interactions with habitable learning environments, we have conducted a series of informal pilot studies with more than 30 subjects ranging in age from 11 to 53. Approximately one-third of the subjects were female and two-thirds were male. Objectives were to evaluate learner response to immersive problem solving by directing an avatar from the third person point of view with the assistance of task-sensitive goal advertisements. Four conclusions have emerged:

1. Habitable learning environments offer significant promise for true situated learning. Observing learners of different ages interact with CPU CITY suggests that the combination of learner-directed lifelike avatars, engaging 3D virtual worlds, and immersive role-based problem solving has significant potential.

2. Virtual worlds should be inviting and their structure and function should mirror the system being studied at a "learnable" level of abstraction. The architectural components of virtual worlds should mirror their real-world counterparts' structure and functionalities with pedagogically appropriate abstractions. Taking advantage of straightforward metaphors and exploiting time and space scaling may benefit learners considerably.

3. Avatars should be visually compelling, provide manipulative functionalities, and exhibit personality. Lifelike characters that can interact in interesting ways with the environment (more so than our prototype learning environments have provided to date) and can perform actions that intrigue the learner may play a central motivational role.

4. Goal advertisements — both conceptual and operational — are critical for effective learning. The immersive effects of a well-designed role-playing task in a compelling environment are very strong. In the absence of goal advertisements, learners may become so engrossed that they may fixate on the immediate sub-task and fail to make conceptual connections. Goal advertisements are one means for bridging the critical gap from concepts to the specific tasks the learner performs.

6 Conclusions

Habitable learning environments offer significant potential for fostering true situated learning. By directing lifelike avatars to perform problem-solving tasks in intriguing 3D virtual worlds, learners can be intrinsically motivated, perform situated problem solving, and be actively immersed in a role-based learning experience. By leveraging powerful graphics technologies, learners can interact with what may become a new paradigm for education software in the not too distant future. This work represents a step towards learning environments that support situated learning. It raises many more questions than it answers about learning and the role that technologies can play in nurturing it. We look forward to addressing these issues in our future work.

Acknowledgements

Thanks to: the design team (Tim Buie, Mike Cuales, and Rob Gray), led by Patrick FitzGerald, for the modeling of the CPU CITY testbed; Francis Fong, for his work on the animation tools; Dennis Rodriguez and JoЗl Gr—goire for their work on the task modeling; and Charles Callaway and Stuart Towns, for comments on earlier drafts of this paper. Support for this work is provided by a grant from the National Science Foundation (Faculty Early Career Development Award IRI-9701503), the North Carolina State University IntelliMedia Initiative, and an industrial gift from Novell.

References

1. Bares, W.H., Zettlemoyer, L.S., Rodriguez, D.W., and Lester, J.C.   Task-Sensitive Cinematography Interfaces for Interactive 3D Learning Environments. In *Proceedings of IUI '98*, San Francisco CA (1998) 81-88
2. Burton, R.R. and Brown, J.S.   An Investigation of Computer Coaching for Informal Learning Activities. In D. Sleeman and J.S. Brown, editors, *Intelligent Tutoring Systems*. Academic Press (1982) 79-98
3. Davenport, G. Seeking Dynamic, Adaptive Story Environments.   In *IEEE Multimedia* (Fall 1994) 9-13
4. Hayes-Roth, B., and Van Gent, R. Story-Making with Improvisational Puppets. In *Proceedings of the First International Conference on Autonomous Agents,* Los Angeles CA (1997) 1-7
5. Hollan, J.D., Hutchins, E.L., and Weitzman, L.M. STEAMER: An Interactive Inspectable, Simulation-Based Training System. In G. Kearsley, editor, *Artificial Intelligence and Instruction: Applictions and Methods*. Addison-Wesley (1987) 113-134
6. Jones, C. *Chuck Amuck: The Life and Times of an Animated Cartoonist*. Avon, New York NY (1989)

7. Lawler, R.W. and Lawler, G.P.   Computer Microworlds and Reading: An Analysis for their Systematic Application. In R.W. Lawler and M. Yazdani, editors, *Artificial Intelligence and Education*. Ablex (1987) 95-115
8. Lester, J.C., Converse, S.E., Kahler, S.E., Barlow, S.T., Stone, B.A., and Bhogal, R. The Persona Effect: Affective Impact of Animated Pedagogical Agents. In *Proceedings of CHI '97* (1997) 359-366
9. Malone, T.W. Toward a Theory of Intrinsically Motivating Instruction. In *Cognitive Science 4* (1981) 333-369
10. Mayer, R.E. *Educational Psychology: A Cognitive Approach*. Harper Collins, New York NY, 1987.
11. Payne, S. J., and Green, T.R. Task-action Grammars— A Model of the Mental Representation of Task Languages. In *Human-Computer Interaction 2* (1986) 99-133
12. Piaget, J. *The Construction of Reality in the Child*. Basic Books, New York NY (1954)
13. Rickel, J. and Johnson L. Intelligent Tutoring in Virtual Reality: A Preliminary Report. *In Proceedings of the Eight World Conference on AI in Education* (1997) 294-301
14. Suchman, L. *Plans and Situated Actions: The Problem of Human Machine Communication*. Cambridge University Press, Cambridge MA (1987)
15. Thompson, P.W. Mathematical Microworlds and Intelligent Computer-Assisted Instruction. *In G. Kearsley, editor, Artificial Intelligence and Instruction: Applications and Methods*. Addison-Wesley (1987) 83-109
16. Umaschi, M. Soft Toys with Computer Hearts: Building Personal Storytelling Environments. In *CHI '97 Extended Abstracts*, ACM Press (1997) 20-21

Motivation Diagnosis in Intelligent Tutoring Systems

Angel de Vicente* and Helen Pain

Department of Artificial Intelligence, The Univerisity of Edinburgh
{angelv,helen}@dai.ed.ac.uk

Abstract. Despite being of crucial importance in Education, the issue of motivation has been only very recently explicitly addressed in Intelligent Tutoring Systems (ITS). In the few studies done, the main focus has been on motivational planning (i.e. how to plan the instruction in order to motivate the student). In this paper we argue that motivation diagnosis (i.e. how to detect the student's motivational state) is of crucial importance for creating 'motivating' ITSs, and that more research is needed in this area. After an introduction, we review some relevant research on motivation diagnosis, and then we suggest directions which further research in this area might take. Although the issues discussed here are still poorly understood, this paper attempts to encourage research in the ITS community in what we believe is one of the most important aspects of instruction.

1 Introduction

Students' motivation to learn is an important issue in Education and a basic concern in classroom practice. As Goleman puts it, "The extent to which emotional upsets can interfere with mental life is no news to teachers. Students who are anxious, angry, or depressed don't learn; people who are caught in these states do not take in information efficiently or deal with it well." [1, pp. 78].

But what do we mean by motivation? The literature about this subject is extensive, and it is outside the scope of this paper to review the many theories that have been proposed to explain motivation.[1] Here, the definition given by Williams and Burden, which fits well with the meaning of motivation intended in this paper, will suffice:

> *Motivation* may be construed as
> - a state of cognitive and emotional arousal,
> - which leads to a conscious decision to act, and
> - which gives rise to a period of sustained intellectual and/or physical effort

---

* Supported by grant PG 94 30660835 from the "Programa de Becas de Formación de Profesorado y Personal Investigador en el Extranjero", Ministerio de Educación y Cultura, SPAIN.
[1] For a good introductory book to the subject see [2].

− in order to attain a previously set goal (or goals).

[3, pp. 120], (emphasis in original)

Therefore, one of the main concerns in Education is how to induce that *state of cognitive and emotional arousal* which will make the instruction an interesting and engaging experience for the student. Thus, for instance, Lepper *et al.* report after studying the motivational techniques of expert tutors in elementary school mathematics activities that "Expert human tutors, it would appear, devote at least as much time and attention to the achievement of affective and motivational goals in tutoring, as they do to the achievement of the sorts of cognitive and informational goals that dominate and characterize traditional computer-based tutors." [4, pp. 99].

Consequently, it is surprising to find that very little research has dealt explicitly with motivational aspects of instruction in ITSs. It is true that many ITSs attempt to motivate the student by using multimedia, games, etc., but this approach seems to be based on the idea that it is possible to create instruction that is motivating *per se*. We believe, on the other hand, that ITSs would benefit from being able to adapt their instruction not only according to the student's cognitive state, but also to her motivational state.

This approach has been taken on very few occasions (e.g. [5, 6]). From these, the most comprehensive work is that of del Soldato [5], who added two new modules to the traditional ITS architecture: a motivation modeller and a motivational planner. But these attempts have focused mainly on motivational planning (i.e. how to plan the instruction in order to motivate the student), rather than on motivation diagnosis (i.e. how to detect the student's motivational state). In this paper we focus on the latter.

A first concern (and the issue around which this paper is centered) is the selection of a 'communication channel' that provides the necessary information to perform the motivation diagnosis. In the case of humans the available communication channels are many (verbal communication, the eyes, the hands, posture, body rhythms, smell, touch, etc.) [7], but not all of them are always needed, and we can communicate more or less effectively using only a number of them (for instance by telephone, letter, sign language, etc). Some advantages and disadvantages of using some of these communication channels in an ITS are given throughout the paper.

In the rest of this paper we explore some of these issues: human motivation diagnosis in section 2, some of the relevant research concerning motivation diagnosis in ITSs in section 3, and lastly we present some research suggestions in section 4.

2   Human Diagnosis of Motivation

Ironically, despite the large volume of research on human motivation, we still don't understand how we diagnose other people's motivation (or more generally, other people's emotions[2]). Picard even raises the question: "How do we detect a person's emotions? Is it via some metaphysical sixth sense?" [8, pp. 4-5].

In most cases, this ability to read other people's emotions—empathy—is taken for granted, although not everybody shows the same proficiency at it. A test for measuring this ability to empathise with others has been used by Robert Rosenthal and his students. The test—or Profile of Nonverbal Sensitivity (PONS)—consists of a series of videotapes of a young woman expressing different feelings (having the words muffled), which are shown to the viewers after blanking out one or more channels of nonverbal communication [9, cited in [1]].

What seems to be undisputed is that emotion diagnosis takes place mainly through non-verbal cues. For instance, Lepper *et al.* point out that although the analyses of the tutoring sessions were not completed, "an initial hypothesis is that our tutors' affective diagnoses depend much more heavily than their cognitive assessments on inferences drawn from the student's facial expressions, body language, intonation, and other paralinguistic cues." [4, pp. 101].

An ITS would also benefit by having this ability to empathise, but observations of human empathy makes us reflect upon the real difficulty of this ability. Goleman has argued that the ability to empathise "builds on self-awareness; the more open we are to our own emotions, the more skilled we will be in reading feelings." [1, pp. 96], and points out that alexithymics (people who lack words for their feelings[3]) lack the ability to 'read' other people's emotions. These observations raise the question of whether a computer should *have* emotions in order to be able to empathise with its user.

3   Computer Diagnosis of Motivation

One of the first suggestions of endowing computer tutors with a degree of empathy was made by Lepper and Chabay [10]. They argued that motivational components are as important as cognitive components in tutoring strategies, and that important benefits would arise from considering techniques to create computer tutors that have an ability to empathise.

More recently, Issroff and del Soldato [11] have suggested that in computer-supported collaborative learning settings, the instructional planner of a system should also include the goal of motivating the learner.

Although in both cases the main focus has been on motivational planning, Lepper and Chabay [10] also suggested some additions that should be made to a computer tutor in order to provide it with an ability to detect a student's motivational state: 1) make available to the computer tutor specific background

---

[2] In this paper motivation diagnosis is considered, for simplicity, as a particular case of emotion diagnosis.

[3] "Indeed, they seem to lack feelings altogether, although this may actually be because of their inability to *express* emotion rather than from an absence of emotion altogether." (pp. 50).

knowledge about the student (gathered from aptitude tests, motivational measurement scales or even teachers' assessments) and 2) enable the computer to ask the student directly whether she would like help or not, whether she would prefer harder or easier problems, etc.

In the following sections we review the research done on computer motivation diagnosis, classifying it according to the type of information used for the diagnosis.

3.1   Questionnaires

Questionnaires have been sometimes used for collecting information about the student's motivation to learn. Thus, Arshad [12, cited in [5]], used questionnaires applied at the beginning of the first interaction in order to model the student's confidence state[4].

Matsubara and Nagamachi [6] also used questionnaires[5] at the beginning of the interaction to diagnose several factors influencing motivation, such as: Achievement Motive, Creativity, Sensation Seeking Scale, Extroversion Intention, Work Importance and Centrality, Least Preferred Co-worker and Locus of Control.

Whitelock and Scanlon used post test questionnaires (consisting of five open ended questions) to assess a number of motivational factors, such as "curiosity, interest, tiredness, boredom and expectation plus the challenge of the task and partnership itself" [13, pp. 276].

Pre-interaction questionnaires have been criticised as being static, while the student's motivational state is likely to change during the interaction [5]. On the other hand, questionnaires can be useful means for detecting motivational traits (more enduring characteristics of students) and several tests have been devised to measure motivation. For instance, Gardner [14] devised an Attitude/Motivation Test Battery (AMTB), which consists of a series of self-report questionnaires, in order to calculate an Attitude Motivation Index (AMI), and O'Bryen [15] gives an introduction to the use and development of questionnaires to assess motivation in second language classrooms.

Therefore, we could use questionnaires for collecting information about enduring characteristics of the student that can help to adapt the instruction, although other methods should be used to gather information about more transient characteristics of the student's motivation.

3.2   Verbal Communication

The system by del Soldato [5] detected information about the motivational state of the student through three main sources: direct communication with the

---

[4] One of the many factors that influence motivation.

[5] But no precise account or reference to how the questionnaires were created or what they 'look like' is given in the paper.

student during the interaction, perseverance to complete the task and student's requests for help.

Direct communication concerns the interaction and the task at hand, but not the motivational state of the student, which is inferred from the student's expressions. For example, certain answers are considered typical of low confidence students (e.g. "no, too difficult"), which would help the computer tutor to infer that the confidence of the student is low.[6]

The motivation diagnosis knowledge is implemented as a set of production rules that help the system 'decide' how to update the motivation model of the student, which is represented as a set of three numerical variables: effort, confidence and independence. For example, one of the rules indicates that the value of the confidence variable should be increased by a large constant if the student has performed a problem correctly without help.

This approach has the advantage of being relatively simple to implement, but since most of an emotional message seems to be non-verbal, it may prove to be too restricted for diagnosing student's motivation and it may be very difficult to elicit motivation diagnosis knowledge for this type of 'communication channel'. del Soldato [5] performed a preliminary study to test the accuracy of her motivational modeller, but no conclusive results were obtained, and therefore more research is needed.

3.3   Self-report

Another approach to motivation diagnosis is to have direct communication with the student about her motivational state.

This approach was taken by del Soldato [5] for the design of the system MORE, but we learn that, unfortunately, the features needed to read the self-report of the student's motivational state were not operational in the first version of the system, and hence we do not have an evaluation of how effective these features can be.

It is not clear whether or how the student's motivational state will be affected by having to report about her own motivation. But, if it is not affected significantly, this could be one of the easiest ways to diagnose it. As Briggs *et al.* put it, "confidence judgments are extremely simple to elicit, since users can give subjective ratings more easily than they can offer explanations." [16]

Different theories and models identify several factors that affect motivation. The ARCS Model by Keller [17], for instance, defines four components that influence the motivation to learn: attention, relevance, confidence and satisfaction. An interface could be easily implemented with mechanisms that would allow the student to report her subjective reading of these factors. For example, each of these factors could be represented by a slider, which could be manipulated by the student.

---

[6] The system lacks a natural language interface. Instead, the student selects her answer from a set of standard expressions.

3.4   Expert System

Hioe and Campbell [18] were concerned with performance problems in the work-place, and they devised a prototype expert system to help the employee's manager or supervisor to find which problems were affecting the employee's performance, with special emphasis on motivational problems. By reviewing different theories of human motivation, and based on the expert's diagnostic processes[7], they classified potential motivation problems into four groups: a) performance standards and goals; b) positive and negative outcomes; c) human relation issues; d) work itself. Then, they created a set of questions for specific motivational problems in these four groups, and developed an expert system that could ascertain which of these motivational conditions was causing the poor performance.

Although their work is not focused on computer tutors, we can imagine a similar approach being used in an ITS. This approach would not be as dynamic as other approaches (e.g. self-report), but neither as static as questionnaires. For instance, if at some point during the interaction a performance problem is found, the expert system could be used to directly ask the student in order to find the causes of the problem.

3.5   Sentic Modulation

Sentic modulation refers to "the physical means by which an emotional state is typically expressed" [19, pp. 25], and although still in its infancy, there has been some research addressing the issue of how a computer system could use this information to detect human emotions.

This approach has not been used, to our knowledge, in computer instruction systems, but Picard [8] reports the interest in the MIT Media Lab of building a piano-teaching computer system that could detect student's expressive timing.

In the group lead by her, the Affective Computing group, the research on detection of emotions is based primarily on the detection of patterns in physiological states. Thus, one of the areas of their research is to design sensors that will help to detect the user's emotional state. A Prototype Sensing System was developed, which includes four sensors: Galvanic Skin Response (GSR) Sensor, Blood Volume Pulse (BVP) sensor, Respiration sensor and Electromyogram (EMG) sensor.

Elias Vyzas has used this system in experiments of emotion recognition, obtaining in the best cases a 83% accuracy discriminating the physiological signals from an actress expressing different emotions [19, described in pp. 185-188].

Some work has also been done in recognising emotions from facial expressions in video, and from vocal intonation. Essa and Pentland [20, cited in [19]] developed a facial recogniser that showed an accuracy of 98% in recognising (although not in real time) six deliberately made facial expressions for a group of eight people. Roy and Pentland [21, cited in [19]] studied the possibility for a computer of discriminating between approving or disapproving sentences, obtaining

---

[7] The expert being the second author.

similar classification accuracy to humans, 65% to 88% for speaker-dependent, text-independent classification.

These methods could be used to detect the motivational state of a student in an ITS, but the approach seems much harder than some of the methods discussed in previous sections. On the other hand, we have seen that most of an emotional message is conveyed through non-verbal communication, and therefore, the use of a sentic modulation approach may prove to be the most efficient way to diagnose motivation.

In addition to the problem of efficiency of motivation diagnosis, we should also consider the difficulty of applying these methods to current ITSs, and in the case of physiological data, the possibly negative reaction of students to the use of body sensors. It could happen that despite being a very efficient way of detecting human emotions, its use could be limited to a certain type of application, as a consequence of users' reaction.

4   Research Areas Worth Pursuing

In such a new and complex area as motivation diagnosis, the list of possible research directions is extensive. Therefore, in this section we will simply present a few of the main issues that should be further explored.

Exploring Other Communication Channels. The research reviewed in this paper makes use of many different 'communication channels', but there are many other possibilities that could be studied. For example, a computer could determine the user's pupils size, which changes with different emotional states [22, cited in [7]], or could record mouse movements and typing speed and errors, or even could analyse the posture of all or some part of the body.

Eliciting Motivation Diagnosis Knowledge. In most cases, independently of the 'communication channel' that we use, the main problem is to know which pattern corresponds to which motivational state. Knowledge about motivation diagnosis may be elicited based on theories of motivation, observations of human teachers or even 'common sense', but we must devise experiments to test the validity of this knowledge.

Previously we mentioned one of the production rules used by del Soldato [5] to model student's confidence: '*increment by a large constant the confidence value if the student has succeeded solving a problem without help*'. This rule seems reasonable based on observations of human teachers, but the information available to humans is far more than the information available to the computer system, and we should study whether this knowledge is sufficient to detect the student's confidence level, or whether other factors are also influencing the decision.

Thus, we could devise experiments where humans should try to diagnose a student's motivational state by inspecting an instruction interaction where most of the 'communication channels' are blanked out (similar to the experiments mentioned in section 2 by Rosenthal *et al.*), maintaining only those channels available to the computer system (for instance, in the case of the production rule mentioned, information about the failure or success in performing the problem and information about help requests). With this type of experiments, we could start comparing the accuracy of different formalisations of motivation diagnosis knowledge.

Investigating Self-report Approaches. As we have seen, an approach to motivation diagnosis based on student's self-report would probably be the easiest to implement, but there are also many issues that should be studied. In section 3.3 we have mentioned, as an example, the use of sliders to represent each of the important factors that affect motivation. We should further investigate the effect on the user of using this approach: Does the student's motivational state change by having to inform about it? Does the student updates the sliders regularly, or only when certain 'extreme' events happen? Does she find the need to update the sliders regularly intrusive? We should also consider different ways of self-reporting motivational states: for example, we could develop an interface where several 'emoticons' are displayed, representing different states (e.g.: bored, anxious, happy,...), from which the user could select according to her own motivational state.

Developing Models of Motivation. Another interesting research direction that should be explored is the development of predictive models of motivation and their use as aids for diagnosis. Picard [19] describes some models of affective behaviour, but these have been mainly used for emotion synthesis.

The addition of these type of models could prove vital for the development of truly motivating computer instruction. Most probably, human tutors do not only react to motivational states, but make use of models of motivation to *predict* the motivational effect of possible actions, and thus to select a line of action that brings about the best possible outcome.

Exploring Individualised Motivation Diagnosis and Models of Motivation. We should consider the possibility of creating *individualised* methods of motivation diagnosis and models of motivation. del Soldato [5] considered, for simplicity, that the behaviour pattern of every student in a certain motivational state is basically the same. Similarly, we could implement general models of motivation to predict motivation outcomes for all students. But a good human tutor surely knows that each student has her own characteristics, and that different students can react differently to the same tutor actions.

As we approach the goal of creating computers systems that can detect our motivational states and even create a model of our motivational behaviour, we also face several dilemmas: Who could have access to this information? Where should we place the division between public and private emotional data? What would the reaction of the users be? It could be argued that given the state of research in this area, these questions are probably not very important at present. But the answer to these questions could give us important hints of whether or up to what point this type of research is worth pursuing.

For example, in an informal survey among 10 students in our Department we found—perhaps not surprisingly—that the use of physiological data was considered the most intrusive approach, and the one that they would least willingly use. On the other hand, the monitoring of keyboard and mouse actions was considered the least intrusive, and the approach that they would prefer to use. Although a formal study is needed, this seems to indicate that intrusiveness of the system would be an important factor when deciding whether to use it or not, and therefore it should be considered when investigating different approaches to motivation diagnosis.

5   Conclusion

In this paper we have focused on the issue of motivation diagnosis, which we believe to be of crucial importance for the development of truly effective ITSs.

We have reviewed different approaches taken for computer motivation diagnosis (or more generally emotion detection), finding that none of these approaches seem to offer a definitive solution. Therefore, we have suggested several areas of research that should be further explored.

While the efficient detection of a student's motivational state by an ITS seems to be a distant and difficult goal, we believe that research in this area can bring great benefits for computer instruction, and we hope that the issues presented in this paper are studied by the ITS community in order to make computer instruction more 'human'.

Acknowledgements

We thank Anders Bouwer, Jon Ander Elorriaga, Chi-Chiang Shei and anonymous reviewers for useful comments and suggestions on previous versions of this paper.

References

1. Goleman, D. *Emotional intelligence: Why it can matter more than IQ.* Boomsbury, London, 1996. First published by Bantam Books, New York, 1995.
2. Weiner, B. *Human motivation: metaphors, theories, and research.* Sage Publications Inc., 1992.
3. Williams, M. and Burden, R. L. *Psychology for language teachers: A social constructivist approach.* Cambridge University Press, Cambridge, UK, 1997.
4. Lepper, M., Woolverton, M., Mumme, D., and Gurtner, J. Motivational techniques of expert human tutors: lessons for the design of computer-based tutors. In S.P. Lajoie and S.J. Derry, editors, *Computers as cognitive tools.* Lawrence Erlbaum, 1993.

5. del Soldato, T. Motivation in tutoring systems. Tech. Rep. CSRP 303, School of Cognitive and Computing Sciences, The University of Sussex, UK, 1994.
6. Matsubara, Y. and Nagamachi, M. Motivation system and human model for intelligent tutoring. In Claude Frasson, Gilles Gauthier, and Alan Lesgold, editors, *Proceedings of the Third International Conference in Intelligent Tutoring Systems*, pages 139–147. Springer-Verlag, 1996.
7. Davis, F. *La comunicación no verbal*, volume 616 of *El Libro de Bolsillo*. Alianza Editorial, Madrid, Spain, 1976. Translated by Lita Mourglier from: "Inside Intuition - What we Knew About Non-Verbal Communication"; McGraw-Hill Book Company, New York.
8. Picard, R. W. Affective computing. Technical Report 321, M.I.T. Media Laboratory Perceptual Computing Section, Cambridge, Massachussetts, November 1995. Report available on-line on November 19, 1997 at http://vismod.www.media.mit.edu/cgi-bin/tr_pagemaker.
9. Rosenthal, R. *et. al.* The PONS test: Measuring sensitivity to nonverbal cues. In P. McReynolds, editor, *Advances in Psychological Assessment*. Jossey-Bass, San Francisco, 1977.
10. Lepper, M. R. and Chabay, R. W. Socializing the intelligent tutor: Bringing empathy to computer tutors. In Heinz Mandl and Alan Lesgold, editors, *Learning Issues for Intelligent Tutoring Systems*, chapter 10, pages 242–257. Springer-Verlag, 1988.
11. Issroff, K. and del Soldato, T. Incorporating motivation into computer-supported collaborative learning. In Brna et al. [23], pages 284–290.
12. Arshad, F. *The Design of Knowledge-based Advisors for Learning*. PhD thesis, School of Education, University of Leeds, UK, 1990.
13. Whitelock, D. and Scanlon, E. Motivation, media and motion: Reviewing a computer supported collaborative learning experience. In Brna et al. [23], pages 276–283.
14. Gardner, R. C. *Social psychology and second language learning: the role of attitudes and motivation*. London: Edward Arnold, 1985.
15. O'Bryen, P. Using questionnaires to assess motivation in second language classrooms. *University of Hawaii Working Papers in ESL*, 14(2), 1996.
16. Briggs, P., Burford, B., and Dracup, C. Self confidence as an issue for usermodeling. In *Proceedings of the Fifth International Conference on User Modeling*, Kailua-Kona, Hawaii, 1996. User Modeling, Inc.
17. Keller, J. M. Strategies for stimulating the motivation to learn. *Performance and Instruction Journal*, 26:1–7, 1987.
18. Hioe, W. and Campbell, D. J. An expert system for the diagnosis of motivation-related job performance problems: Initial efforts. DICS publication no. TRA3/88, Department of Information Systems and Computer Science, National University of Singapore, 1988.
19. Picard, R. W. *Affective Computing*. The MIT Press, Cambridge, Massachusetts, 1997.
20. Essa, I. and Pentland, A. Coding, analysis, interpretation and recognition of facial expressions. *IEEE Transactions on Pattern Analysis and Machine Intelligence*, 19(7):757–763, July 1997.
21. Roy, D. and Pentland, A. Automatic spoken affect analysis and classification. In *Proceedings of the Second International Conference on Automatic Face and Gesture Recognition*, pages 363–367, Killington, VT, Oct 1996.
22. Eckhard H., H. Attitude and pupil size. *Scientific American*, 212:46–54, 1965.
23. Brna, P., Paiva, A., and Self, J., editors *Proceedings of the European Conference on Artificial Intelligence in Education*, 1996.

Some Reasons Why Learning Science is Hard: Can Computer Based Law Encoding Diagrams Make It Easier?

Peter C-H. Cheng

ESRC Centre for Research in Development, Instruction and Training,
Department of Psychology, University of Nottingham, Nottingham, NG7 2RD, U.K.
peter.cheng@nottingham.ac.uk

Abstract. *Law EncodingDiagrams*, LEDs, may be an effective approach to promotingconceptual learning in science. This paper considers why by decomposing the problem of what makes science hard to learn into five generaldifficulties. How LEDs may address each of these difficulties areconsidered in the context of a novel class of LEDs for electricity, AVOW diagrams. Further, thedesign requirements of ITSs that exploit LEDs can be analysed in terms ofthe difficulties, as illustrated by the description of the positivefeatures and limitations of a computer based learning environment that has been built to exploit AVOWdiagrams for learning about electricity.

1 Introduction

There has been some success in the development of Intelligent Tutoring Systems (ITSs) for learning in domains that are mainly procedural in nature, such as programming and trouble shooting complex devices (e.g., [1][15]). However, the challenge for ITS research is now to develop systems that effectively support learning in largely conceptual domains, as exemplified by the physical sciences[1]. A possible explanation of this state of affairs is the lack of an adequate characterization of the nature of conceptual knowledge and hence the lack of a well defined target for designing systems. Any such characterization will certainly involve complex webs of meanings and multiple interconnected representations. Thus, it is essential to investigate the nature of representations that may be employed in ITSs.

The work discussed here considers conceptual knowledge from the particular perspective of a programme of research that is investigating special classes of representations that have potential for science learning, including use in ITSs. The representations are Law Encoding Diagrams, LEDs [3,4] which have interesting cognitive properties that seem to make them effective. This work includes the study of the role of LEDs in the history of science [3,7] and the development and evaluation of discovery learning environments based on LEDs [4,5]. By detailed study of problem solving with LEDs in different scientific domains, and the design of systems to support learning with LEDs, this research is attempting to broaden our

---

[1] Although the focus here is on the conceptual aspects of science, theprocedural side of science, the "scientific method", isalso important and perhaps as hard to learn.

understanding of the role of different representations for reasoning and instruction. Such knowledge will be important for developing ITSs that promote conceptual learning. This paper considers how LEDs may be effective for learning.

There is no simple single answer to what, in general, makes an effective representation for learning science. So the approach taken here is to decompose the problem by identifying various difficulties, or reasons why science is hard, and for each considering whether given representations are effect for learning that aspect of science. Here, five difficulties are first considered (sect. 2). To illustrate the difficulties electricity has been chosen as the example domain for the paper. Ample evidence of the troubles that students have in this domain are provided by a wealth of studies on students misconceptions and problem solving processes (e.g., [9] is the proceedings of a conference on this topic). A system of LEDs for electricity is introduced, AVOW diagrams, and how it addresses each of the difficulties is discussed (sect. 3). It appears to be effective for each of the difficulties, so an ITS that exploits this class of LEDs is likely to promote conceptual learning. Further, the difficulties place particular requirements on the design of such an ITS. These are considered by examining to what extent an existing prototype AVOW diagram learning environment addresses each of the difficulties (sect. 4). Empirical evaluations of AVOW diagrams and LEDs are mentioned in the conclusion (sect. 5).

2 Some Reasons Why Science Is Hard to Learn

The five interrelated explanations of why science is hard to learn, presented in this section, are not supposed to be exhaustive. Rather, they are selected aspects identified in the literature on scientific thinking and learning, which are especially relevant here.

Difficulty 1: Constraint-Based Interaction Processes. A major hurdle in learning science is the necessary conceptual change from viewing phenomena as forms of MATTER to conceptualizing them as types of PROCESSES [8]. A particularly important type of PROCESS for most sciences are *constraint-based interactions*, which are governed by a known or knowable set of constraints. For electricity these constraints include, for example, Kirchoff's laws which define conservation relations for current and voltage within a circuit. Students provided with a precursor tutorial about *constraint-based interactions*, before they study a text on electricity, may develop a more PROCESS oriented conceptualization of the domain and show greater gains in problem solving [18].

Difficulty 2: Bridging the Conceptual Gulf. Scientific domains exhibit a gulf between concrete descriptions of phenomena and abstract general laws, which must be conceptually spanned by learners [19]. For example, in electricity, concrete descriptions include the specific topological structure of a network and measured values of electrical properties, such as current, voltage and resistance. At the abstract conceptual level, there are laws for particular components such as Ohm's law and the power law. And for relations among components there are Kirchoff's laws and formulas for calculating total resistance of loads in series and parallel. Learning how electrical properties for different circuit topologies are governed by the general laws of electricity is a hard task for students. One successful approach to bridging the conceptual gulf is the use of computer based *intermediate causal representations* [19].

Difficulty 3: Phenomenal Diversity. Scientific phenomena may have a great many different manifestations, even though they are governed by the same laws or sets of constraints. A good conceptual understanding of a domain requires knowledge of: the different forms of manifestations; how each is derived from, or is a consequence of, the laws; and, how the manifestations are interrelated[16]. Such an understanding can give shape to the theoretical space that is articulated by the laws of the domain. Electricity has such complex manifestations. There are many different types of components or devices, such as conductors, insulators, switches, that each have their own particular properties. At the network level, different configurations of components serve alternative functions or have different behaviours, for instance open circuits, short circuits, parallel and series loads.

Difficulty 4: Formal Representations. A major hurdle to learning science is the formal nature of the representations that are conventionally used to express and manipulate sets of constraint-based interactions. Symbolic mathematical systems, such as algebra and differential calculus, have been used with great success to state laws and reason about their consequences. However, learning mathematics in the first place is a major difficulty on the way to a deeper understanding of science. There are different pedagogical responses to this. One is to try to reduce the mathematical content by attempting to provide a qualitative understanding (e.g., [12]). However, gaining deeper insights into the nature of the laws may be compromised, because verbal expressions cannot adequately model complex interactions nor adequately convey interesting underlying symmetries and invariants. An alternative is to embrace the mathematics and support instruction in it, perhaps by using ITSs. The approach advocated here is to use LEDs, which are as valid as the symbolic mathematics, but that have more accessible cognitive properties. LEDs were used in history of science to make original discoveries, which were only later translated into symbolic mathematical form[3,7].

Difficulty 5: Complex Interactions. In some scientific domains it is possible to treat the different levels of a phenomenon as relatively independent (or *nearly decomposable* [16]), which can greatly simplify the study of the phenomenon [2]. However, some phenomena cannot be neatly dissected and others that can exhibit complex interactions among multiple variables or components on one level. Such scientific domains with multiple dimensions will be harder to understand and learn [11]. Electrical circuits are decomposed and chunked by experts into functional units [10], such as amplifiers and rectifiers, whose internal workings may be treated as relatively independent of the internal workings of other units. However, the operation of functional units must be learned and the internal operations tend to be complex. Thus, in learning science managing the level of complexity of the interactions with which students have to cope is an important aspect of the design of instruction (independent of promoting a PROCESS based conceptualization).

These are five interrelated explanations of why science is hard to learn. How may LEDs address these difficulties in the context of learning about electricity?

Table 1. AVOW box features representing electrical properties of resistors

Property (units)	Symbol	AVOW box representation	Example: Fig. 1.
Voltage (Volts)	V	height	V = 3
Current (Amps)	I	width	I = 2
Resistance (Ohms)	r	gradient of the diagonal	r = V/I = 3/2
Power (Watts)	W	area	W = V × I = 6

3 LEDs for Electricity— AVOW Diagrams

Law Encoding Diagrams are representational systems that use diagrammatic constraints to encode the laws of a domain in the internal structure of a diagram, such that
each drawing represents a single instance of the phenomenon or one case of the laws
[3,4]. *AVOW diagrams* are LEDs for electrical circuits. AVOW (Amps, Volts, Ohms
and Watts) stands for the units of the four basic
electrical properties of components, loads or
resistors. Each resistor in a circuit is represented in
an AVOW diagram by a rectangle, or *AVOW box*,
Figure 1. Table 1 shows how AVOW boxes
represent electrical properties. An AVOW box
encodes both (i) Ohm's law and the (ii)power law:
(i) $V = I \times r$, as height = width × gradient;(ii) $P = V$
$\times I$, as area = height × width.

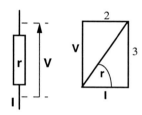

Fig.1.
A resistor and an AVOW box

Like other systems of LEDs [3,4], AVOW
boxes maybe composed to model interactions of
basic phenomena, namely configurations of
components in networks. Figures 2 and 3 show how composite AVOW diagrams
model resistors in parallel or series, by placing AVOW boxes side by side or by
stacking them, respectively. The overall height, width, area and gradient of the diagonal give the voltage, current, power and resistance of the networks. The
compositional constraints encode Kirchoff's Laws, which model the conservation of
current and voltage within networks. A well formed composite AVOW diagram

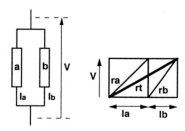

Fig.2. Parallel resistors

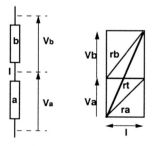

Fig. 3. Resistors in series

must be a rectangle that is completely filled with AVOW boxes, with no overlaps or gaps. Complex networks with parallel and series sub-networks nested within each other can be modelled by recursively applying the composition rules.

The potential of AVOW diagrams for learning about electricity will now be examined by considering how they address each of the five difficulties of learning science.

(1) Constraint-Based Interaction Processes. AVOW diagrams are compatible with the ontology that views phenomena as constraint-based interaction processes, because it is a constraint based representational system. LEDs use geometric, topological or spatial rules to encode the laws of the domain as constraints among the elements of the diagrams. The encoding of Ohm's law and the power law in diagrammatic form treats the relations among the properties as abstract formal relations.

As with mathematical characterizations, AVOW diagrams do not ground concepts on notions of causality or temporal order. But, it is possible to impose a causal explanation on AVOW diagrams, which in some pedagogical circumstances may be useful. For example, one can reason that increasing voltage (height) "causes" an increased current flow (width) proportional to the resistance (gradient) of the load, as depicted in Figure 4.

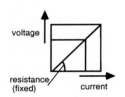

Fig. 4. AGrowing AVOW box

(2) Bridging the Conceptual Gulf. LEDs bridge the conceptual gulf between concrete descriptions of phenomena and the abstract laws by providing an integrated visualization of the magnitudes of domain properties with diagrammatic constraints that encode the abstract laws governing the domain. At the concrete level, the size of the AVOW diagrams in Figures 2and 3 may be taken to give values of the properties using appropriate scales (e.g., 1 mm=1 V or 1 A). At the abstract level the form of each AVOW box encodes Ohm's law and the power law, as described above, but further Figures 2 and 3 also encode the relations that determine the overall resistance of parallel and series pairs of resistors. For example, students often find it initially surprising that the resistance of a pair of parallel resistors is less than the smallest of the pair, but why this is so is made clear in Figure 2. For the constant voltage (height), adding another AVOW box (resistor) means the overall width (current) is greater, hence the overall gradient (resistance) must be lower. The gradient of the diagonal for the pair of boxes side by side must be less than the gradient of either box by itself.

(3) Phenomenal Diversity. By examining different configurations of AVOW boxes alone and in combination, the diversity of manifestations of electrical phenomena can be explored. Different cases and the relations among them can be investigated by visually examining the similarities and differences of the AVOW diagrams representing them. For example, consider the conceptual relations among conductors, insulators, switches, short circuits and open circuits. Conductors and insulators are extreme idealized cases of resistors with zero or infinite resistance, respectively. These extreme cases are represented by AVOW boxes that are simply horizontal or vertical line segments, because the aspect ratio must be zero or infinite for these values of resistance. These cases are not just oddities but may provide useful common conceptualizations of other things. A switch may be viewed as a special AVOW box that flips between a vertical an horizontal line segment. Similarly, common circuit problems can be explained. Figure 5 shows a circuit with two equal resistors, r1 and r2, in series and the AVOW diagram for its typical operation is shown in Figure 6a. Figures 6b and 6c are the AVOW diagrams for the problem of an open circuit (cut wire) at *a* and the problem of a short circuit (unwanted connection) between *a* and *b*, respectively. (For clarity the short and cut are represented by thin/squat rectangles rather than line segments.) On the one hand, the problems are conceptually similar, because they both require the insertion of an extreme AVOW box in the diagram for the cut or the short. On the other hand, the problems are clearly distinguishable as different diagrammatic configurations, which are direct consequences of the particular shapes of the supplementary AVOW boxes for the cut and the short.

(4) Formal Representations. One clear lesson from cognitive science and AI is that the different knowledge representations can fundamentally influence the ease of reasoning and problem solving (e.g., [13]). Diagrammatic representations have properties, due to their spatial indexing of information, that can make them more computationally efficient than informationally equivalent sentential or propositional representations, particularly with regard to search and recognition processes [14].Diagrams often obviate the need for extensive symbolic matching of labels or variables that is necessary with mathematical representations. Further, by changing representations, quite different 'regularity spotters' and operators (productions) can be used, thus reducing the number of inferences step to be taken [7].

   LEDs and AVOW diagrams benefit from being diagrams in this way but they are still suitable as the fundamental representational systems for learning science. The specification of diagrammatic constraints allows the laws of the domain to be encoded and manipulated as rigorously as the equivalent symbolic mathematical forms, whilst providing a clear visualization of the behaviour of circuits.

(5) Complex Interactions. LEDs appear to be effective for understanding complex interactions, because different cases appear as quite distinct configurations of AVOW boxes. For example, a comparison of Figure 6a with Figures 6b and6c, may be a compelling way to explain and to remember the behaviour of open and short circuits. Will students be able to quickly learn such configurations as "conceptual" chunks, which they can use as functional units in more complex problems? Supporting knowledge about functional units at a conceptual level may be an important addition

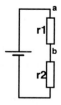

(a) Normal (b)Open circuit   (c) Short circuit

Fig. 5. SeriesNetwork   **Fig. 6.** AVOW diagrams for Fig. 5

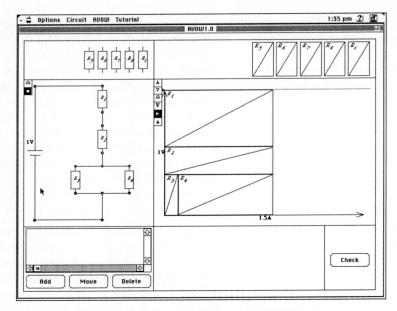

Fig. 7. A screen snap shot of AVOW-Tutor

to the perceptual chunks about function units at a domain level, which are recognized in circuit diagrams by experts [10].

Other, indirect, benefits for dealing with complex interactions follow from the points made above. LEDs represent magnitudes of properties whilst simultaneously encoding the laws of the domain, which makes it easy to switch attention from the local details to global constraints and back again. The computational savings of diagrammatic representations frees cognitive resources so that learners may be better able to deal with the demands of the multiple variables in complex interactions.

4 AVOW-Tutor —A LED Learning Environment

Designing an ITS is a complex task with many different competing requirements to be satisfied. The introduction of novel representations, such as LEDs, further complicates matters. Fortunately, the decompositional approach adopted here may be extended to help in the design of ITSs to exploit novel representations. The requirements of such an ITS may be considered with respect to each of the difficulties of learning science, identified above (sect. 2), in a similar fashion to the initial assessment of the potential of the representation (sect. 3). This section considers the design requirements imposed by the difficulties on a computer based environment for learning about electricity with AVOW diagrams.

The system, *AVOW-tutor*, already exists as a prototype and Figure7 shows a screen snap shot of the system. The user constructs circuit diagrams on the "circuit board" on the left. AVOW diagrams are interactively constructed by the user on the right, by dragging boxes down from the store and then re-sizing and positioning them. AVOW-tutor has built in test routines to provide feedback about the correctness of the diagrams (*Check* button, Fig. 7). The tests determine the correctness of an AVOW diagram, whether it is well formed, and its consistency with the circuit diagram. The system is described more fully in [6]. Here, the extent to which AVOW-tutor addresses four of the difficulties is discussed, and where it is lacking possible extensions to the system are considered.

(1) Constraint-Based Interaction Processes. This fundamental conceptualization of electricity is deliberately reflected in the different ways in which AVOW diagrams may be interactively manipulated in AVOW-tutor. At the level of individual AVOW boxes the system maintains them as rectangles through all manipulations. Further, users can to place additional constraints on the form of particular AVOW boxes. For example, by fixing the gradient of an AVOW box, as in Figure 4, the aspect ratio of the box cannot be changed during manipulations of the box, so the relations between V, I and P, for constant r, can be examined. At the compositional level, AVOW boxes may be moved around independently of each other on screen, but the built in tests determine whether the configuration of an AVOW diagram correctly matches the topology of a given circuit. In such ways the constraint-based interaction nature of electricity is already supported by AVOW-tutor.

(2) Phenomenal Diversity and (5) Complex Interactions. AVOW-tutor currently has areas on screen for a single circuit diagram and a single AVOW diagram, which is adequate for practising the construction of an AVOW diagram from a given circuit diagram, or vice versa. However, it would seem better to provide spaces for at least two circuits and two AVOW diagrams so that comparisons between different cases can be easily made. This could facilitate learning about phenomenal diversity and complex interactions. For example, to better understand the complex interaction ofa short occurring in a circuit, it would be worthwhile showing the normal and fault conditions side by side, as in Figures6a and 6c. Similarly, examining the differences and similarities between related phenomena, such as Figures 6b and 6c, would be easier with multiple AVOW diagrams on screen. Thus, the system needs to be extended to help learners form and differentiate conceptual chunks.

(3) Formal Representations. AVOW diagrams may be simpler than other formal representations, but they have a computational overhead associated with the generation and manipulation of diagrams. By making AVOW boxes interactive objects on screen, AVOW-tutor reduces the work required to reproduce large parts of AVOW diagrams. Changes can be made iteratively without extensive re-drawing.

  More importantly, the nature of the representation has implications for the design of the form of users interaction with AVOW diagrams, and of the dynamic properties of the on screen objects. For example, the AVOW-tutor goes someway towards preventing the construction of ill-formed AVOW diagrams, by stopping AVOW boxes from overlapping, and by giving feedback when a diagram is incomplete.

Such, design considerations may help to emphasise conceptually important constraints over merely contingent constraints.

(5) Complex Interactions. A different way to support the learning of complex interactions, rather than to have multiple AVOW diagrams onscreen simultaneously, as considered above, is to link the representations so that changes to either the circuit diagram or AVOW diagram will be automatically be reflected in other. Thus, the learner would be able to quickly see, for instance, the effect on an AVOW diagram of making a change to a circuit. Although AVOW-tutor can check when the represent-ations are consistent, the user is required to generate the correct AVOW(or circuit) diagram from the circuit (or AVOW) diagram in the first place. This is requires a substantial effort that will be a major distraction to learners, drawing their attention away from the details most relevant to understanding the interactions. Thus, linking the representations will be desirable in a full ITS version of AVOW-tutor.

5 Conclusions

The five difficulties of learning science provides a basis upon which the relative benefits of different representational systems for learning science can be examined. On going work is attempting to evaluate more formally the relative merits of AVOW diagrams, and LEDs in general, versus conventional representations, using the five difficulties. Further, consideration is also being given to additional difficulties and whether there is some privilege of occurrence among them.

Law Encoding Diagrams may be effective for learning science, given their poten-tial for addressing the five difficulties. In particular, AVOW diagrams may be suit-able for learning about electricity and their implementation in an interactive learning environment may further enhance the benefits. Evaluation of a discovery learning environment with LEDs for another domain has demonstrated that they can improve some forms of learning, with some subjects adopting novel problem solving strategies using LEDs [4,5]. In a pen and paper based study of learning with AVOW diagrams, which has just been completed, novice subjects were able to solve difficult problems with AVOW diagrams that they were notable to solve using conventional algebraic approaches. For example, they appear to have learned conceptual chunks based around particular configurations of AVOW boxes (like those in Figures 2, 3 and 6), and then used them for solving problems involving complex interactions. These studies give some support to the claimed benefits of LEDs for addressing the five difficulties.

Acknowledgements

This work was funded by the U.K. Economic and Social Research Council. Thanks must go to members of the ESRC Centre for Research in Development, Instruction and Training, with particular gratitude to David Wood.

References

1. Anderson, J. R., Corbett, A., T., Koedinger, K., R., Pelletier, R.: Cognitive Tutors: Lessons Learned. The Journal Of The Learning Sciences, 4(2) (1995) 167-207
2. Bechtel, W., Richardson, R. C.: Discovering complexity. Princeton University Press, Princeton, NJ (1991)
3. Cheng, P. C.-H.: Scientific Discovery with Law Encoding Diagrams. Creativity Research Journal 9(2&3) (1996) 145-162
4. Cheng, P. C.-H.: Law Encoding Diagrams for Instructional Systems. Journal of Artificial Intelligence in Education 7(1) (1996) 33-74
5. Cheng, P. C.-H.: Learning Qualitative Relations in Physics with Law Encoding Diagrams. In: Cottrell G. (ed.): Proceedings of the 18th Annual Conference of the Cognitive Science Society. Lawrence Erlbaum, Hillsdale, NJ (1996)512-517
6. Cheng, P. C.-H.: Interactive Law Encoding Diagrams for Learning and Instruction. Learning and Instruction(in press)
7. Cheng, P. C.-H., & Simon, H. A.: Scientific Discovery and Creative Reasoning with Diagrams. In: Smith, S., Ward, T., Finke, R. (eds.): The Creative Cognition Approach. MIT Press, Cambridge, MA. (1995) 205-228
8. Chi, M. T. H., Slotta, J. D., de Leeuw, N.: From things to processes: A Theory of Conceptual Change for Learning Science Concepts. Learning and Instruction. 4 (1994) 27-43
9. Duit, R., Jung, W., & von Rhšneck, C.(eds.): Aspects of Understanding Electricity. Institute for the Pedagogy of Natural Science, University of Kiel (1984)
10. Egan, D. E., Schwartz, B. J.: Chunking in Recall of Symbolic Drawings. Memory and Cognition 7(2) (1979) 149-158
11. Halford, G.: Children's Understanding. Lawrence Erlbaum, Hillsdale, NJ (1993)
12. Hewitt, P.: Conceptual Physics. 3rd ed. Harper Collins, New York, NY(1992)
13. Kotovsky, K., Hayes, J. R., Simon, H.A.: Why are Some Problems Hard? Cognitive Psychology 17 (1985) 248-294
14. Larkin, J. H., Simon, H. A.: Why a Diagram is (Sometimes) Worth Ten Thousand Words. Cognitive Science 11 (1987) 65-99
15. Lesgold, A., Lajoie, S., Bunzo, M.,Eggan, G.: Sherlock: A Coached Practice Environment for an Electronics Troubleshooting Job. In: Larkin, J., Carboy, R.(eds.): Computer Assisted Instruction and Intelligent Tutoring Systems. Lawrence Erlbaum Associates, Hillsdale, NJ (1992) 201-238
16. Simon, H.A.: Sciences of the Artificial. 2nd ed. MIT Press, Cambridge, MA (1981)
17. Reif, F.: Interpretation of Scientific or Mathematical Concepts: Cognitive Issues and Instructional Implications. Cognitive Science 11 (1987) 395-416
18. Slotta, J. D., Chi, M. T. H.: Understanding Constraint-Based Processes: A Precursor to Conceptual Change in Physics. In: Cottrell, G. W. (ed.): Proceedings of the 18th Annual Conference of the Cognitive Science Society. Lawrence Erlbaum, Hillsdale, NJ(1996) 306-311
19. White, B.: ThinkerTools: Causal Models, Conceptual Change, and Science Education. Cognition and Instruction 10(1) (1993) 1-100

Curriculum Evaluation : A Case Study

Hugo Dufort, Esma Aïmeur, Claude Frasson, Michel Lalonde

Université de Montréal
Département d'informatique et de recherche opérationnelle
2920, chemin de la Tour, Montréal, Québec, Canada H3C 3J7
{dufort, aimeur, frasson, lalonde}@iro.umontreal.ca

Abstract. In the field of Intelligent Tutoring Systems (ITS) the organisation of the knowledge to be taught (curriculum) plays an important role. Educational theories have been used to organise the information and tools have been developed to support it. These tools are very useful but not sufficient to edit a large curriculum. We need rules to help preventing incoherences, and a guideline for determining such rules. In this paper, we report on two experiments. The first one seeks of determining some rules which we shall use to improve an existing curriculum. The second experiment uses these rules during the construction of a new curriculum in order to prevent initial mistakes.

1. Introduction

Surprisingly, it is difficult to find in the ITS (*Intelligent Tutoring Systems*) literature in-depth discussions about the success or failure of ITS. It is even more difficult to find about the reasons (or the criterions) that motivate their outcomes [8],[5]. Although some studies have been on the use of ITS in a class [1] or in laboratories [7], we remark, that the motto in the literature seems to be: develop, *and later* evaluate.

Nevertheless, as we can see in most software engineering books, it has been proved for a long time that the cost for correcting an error committed while developing software increases linearly in time [15]. Keeping that in view, it would pay (or at least it would be logical) to implement software quality control techniques in the development cycle of ITS. This problem has been raised before; in the knowledge transfer process, it is possible to use automated evaluation techniques to make sure that the computer scientist does not divert from what the pedagogue stated [10]. But before going any further, we need to ask ourselves: what are we searching for, exactly? Is it possible to define what we mean by "quality in ITS"?

In this article, while focusing on the curriculum aspect of an ITS, we define three axes upon which a curriculum can be evaluated. We then pinpoint particular properties and restrictions of our sample curriculum that, when defined in a formal way, are useful to its evaluation. Using the results of the evaluation, we propose a construction methodology that permits a better quality control and we validate it by building a new curriculum from scratch.

2. A Generic Framework for Curriculum Quality Evaluation

In our search for a generic framework for curriculum quality evaluation, we faced a difficult question: are there some aspects that are present, and important, in any curriculum model? There are almost as many curriculum models as there are ITS, and each one uses a different instructional theory [11] for the knowledge representation. We chose to deal with this issue by using an indirect approach: instead of imposing strict guidelines, we defined the quality of a curriculum as: the conformity to the developer's original intentions. Even with this broad definition, though, we still need to classify these intentions.

In linguistics, and in natural language treatment [14], it is common to see a text analysed upon three axes: syntactic, semantic and pragmatic; in our opinion, it is possible to use them when analysing a curriculum. We classify the developer's initial intentions on three axes (figure 1a), which are: teaching goals, the respect of a pedagogical model and the data structure recognised by the ITS. Quality is measured in terms of conformity to each one of these axes.

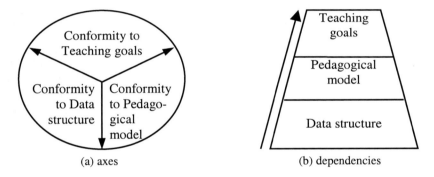

(a) axes   (b) dependencies

Figure 1. *Three aspects of curriculum quality*

The three axes (or aspects) are defined as follows:
- **Data structure**: this is the *syntaxic* aspect of a curriculum, which concerns strictly the internal and external representations of the data. Failing to conform to the data structure definition (in terms of data definitions, for instance) can affect coupling with other modules of the ITS. The initial definition will have an important influence on the implantation of the pedagogical model.
- **Pedagogical model**: this is the *semantic* aspect of a curriculum. Constraints on data elements, and on their relations are defined at this level, according to a model such as Bloom's taxonomy of objectives [2] and Gagné's learning levels [3].
- **Teaching goals**: this is the *pragmatic* aspect of a curriculum. This aspect concerns mainly the contents of the curriculum, hence the material to be taught. We leave the evaluation of teaching goals to researchers in the knowledge acquisition domain [4].

Obviously, errors in the data structure will affect the implementation of the pedagogical model, and similarly errors in the implementation of the pedagogical model will have an influence on the organisation of the material to be teached. The three axes can be seen as three levels of a hierarchy, too (figure 1b). The curriculum we have developed had the following three axes of intentions:

- Data structure: the model CREAM-O [13] (see section 3).
- Pedagogical model: Bloom's taxonomy of objectives (see section 4).
- Teaching goals: an introduction to the MS Excel spreadsheet (see section 5).

3. Curriculum Model

The curriculum in an ITS is a structured representation of the material to be taught. Today, the curriculum is often seen as a dynamical structure, that should adapt itself to student needs, subject matter and pedagogical goals [9]. The CREAM model, structures this material into three networks: the capabilities network, the objectives network and the didactic resources network.

For each of the networks, the curriculum editor leaves choice of the pedagogical model free to the developer. This flexible tool proposes Bloom's taxonomy as the default choice, but other taxonomies can be added. In this article, we pay particular attention to the objectives network. These can belong to each of Bloom's six cognitive categories. More specifically, an objective describes a set of behaviours that a learner must be able to demonstrate after a learning session [13].

The CREAM model proposes several categories of links between objectives: compulsory prerequisite, desirable prerequisite, pretext (weak relation) and constituting. In order to facilitate the analysis, we decided to simplify the theory and keep a general prerequisite relation (O_1 *is-prerequisite-to* O_2, if it must be completed before hoping to complete O_2) and a constituting relation (O_1 *is-composed-of* $O_2,O_3...$ if they are it's sub-objectives), giving the latter a higher importance.

CREAM does not propose a method for the construction nor any restrictions on the structure of the objective network. Such freedom is given to the developer in order to make the model flexible. The experiment presented in section 5 is an exploration of the effects of this freedom on the development of a curriculum and the consequences on the quality of the curriculum thus obtained.

4. Bloom's Taxonomy of Objectives

Bloom [2] sought to construct a taxonomy of the cognitive domain. He had multiple pedagogical goals: identify behaviours that enhance teaching, help pedagogues to determine objectives, analyse situations in which cognitive categories are used. He separates the cognitive domain into six broad categories organised in a hierarchy (acquisition, comprehension, application, analysis, synthesis, evaluation). The objectives belonging to a category are based on and can incorporate the behaviours of the previous categories. We will show later in this article that this detail has a great impact when one constructs a network of objectives.

Bloom's theory also describes for each category of objectives a list of sub-categories that permit an even more precise classification. Even though this part of the theory is defined for the curriculum model used, we have omitted it during the analysis. In this article we will content ourselves with examining the base categories.

5.   Evaluation of a Curriculum

In this section, we present a curriculum based on the CREAM model which has been developed between February and May 1997. Systematic methods are then presented in order to evaluate the quality of the objectives network and to correct the detected errors. A fragment of the curriculum thus obtained is also presented.

5.1.   Development Framework

In order to discover which were the most likely errors during the development of the curriculum we have worked with two high-school teachers to construct a course for the teaching of the Microsoft Excel spreadsheet. We have chosen Excel because it is a well-known tool and is often used by university students and it starts to be taught at high-school level. For four months the teacher used the curriculum editor to construct a capability network, an objective network and a pedagogical network that makes relation between capability and objective. We have used the objective network for our analysis since it was the most complete at the time of this study.

The curriculum produced by the teacher was not complete at the end of the given time period; it covered only certain aspects of the material. Some objectives were cut from the curriculum since they had not been yet linked to the other objectives (about 11% of the total objective network). This rate was higher in the other two networks and this impeded the analysis. We have regrouped the objectives into six important aspects (base tools, graphics, edition tools, format/attribute and database tools) for reasons that we will clarify in section 5.2. Except for the *Edition tools* aspect, the completion level was judged acceptable.

Figure 2 shows a fragment of the curriculum before the first step of the corrections. This fragment contains eight objectives, some of the application category and others of the acquisition category. We noticed that there are no is-composed-of relations in this fragment. In its original form the curriculum contained mostly prerequisite links.

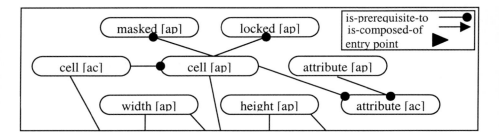

Figure 2. *Fragment of the initial curriculum*

This fragment contains numerous errors that are not easy to identify at a first glance. It is easy to get confused by the high number of nodes and links, so the only way to manage to find errors is to partially rebuild it. In this case, it is possible to make as many errors as the first time, but not necessarily at the same place; this could cause even more incoherence. So, if we want to see things more clearly, we need to use *new tools or new rules*. In the following sections, we will show some principles which permit the systematic detection of errors, the evaluation of the quality of the work and therefore, the validation of this curriculum.

5.2. Entry Points

The structure of the objective network seems to suggest that teaching any material must be done in a hierarchical manner, since some objectives are at the peak of the composition relationships. What are the characteristics of a final objective? Intuitively we can describe a final objective as an objective which:

- Is not a component of another objective (since in this case the objective which is its superior will be seen later in the learning session and therefore closer to the peak of the multi-graph)
- Is not a prerequisite to another objective (since in this case it would be assimilated before the objective for which it is a prerequisite)

If we examine a curriculum from the data structure point of view, it appears to be an oriented multi-graph. In this case, the objectives are points where one can begin an exploration. We have therefore called them "entry points". In order to analyse this characteristic in a more formal manner we use first order logic to define the following rule:

$$\forall x : (\text{entryPoint}(x) \Leftrightarrow (\neg\exists y : (\text{is-prerequisite-to}(x,y) \lor \text{is-composed-of}(y,x)))) \qquad (1)$$

The identification of the entry points in the initial curriculum has allowed us to notice that the lack of formal development methods has been directly translated into a lack of coherence in the structure. We must ask ourselves of each entry point if it is really a final objective. For example, in Figure 2, the objectives *masked* and *locked* are identified by rule (1) as entry points but they should not be so. On the contrary, the objective *attribute [ac]* should probably be a entry point but a prerequisite link stops it from being so. Of course this process is somewhat subjective but it is a guide that makes the developers ask themselves questions. The developers must constantly check if the structure being constructed corresponds to what they are trying to express.

The objectives which have been retained as entry points in the curriculum base are: *Base tools, Graphics, Edition tools, Format/Attribute, Formula, Database tools*. Table 1 shows the extent of the changes made to the curriculum just after taking the entry points into account.

Table 1. *Changes in the first phase.*

Type of change	Quantity	Ratio of change (on 90)
Relation changed destination	2	2.2%
Relation changed type	9	10.0%
Relation was inverted	0	0.0%
Relation was added	17	18.9%
Relation was removed	2	2.2%
Total	30	33.3%

The addition of a relationship was the most frequent chance. This may be surprising at the first glance, but we have discovered that curriculum incoherence is usually caused by missing relationships. Of the 17 added relationships 14 were of the *is-composed-of* type. This is due to the fact that when the structure of the curriculum lacks coherence, it is easier to trace the prerequisite links than the composition links (this shows a lack of a global vision).

Often there existed relationships but they were not of the right type. It is not always easy to determine if a relationship is one of *composition* or of the *prerequisite* type. A difficult introspection is often needed. The introduction of entry points makes this choice easier but the difference remains quite subtle. The other changes (*changed destination* and *removed*) target more serious errors, often due to a lack of attention. For example, a prerequisite link may has been drawn in a way it short-circuits a composition link.

5.3. Semantic Restrictions

As we have seen previously, the objectives in Bloom's taxonomy are organised in six levels and the competence specific to each level can necessitate competence at previous levels. One may ask the following question: does this fact influence the structure of the curriculum? We answer affirmatively. Let us observe the two types of relationships presented in the objective network:

- **is-composed-of:** let $O_1..O_n$, be sub-objectives of O in a composition relationship. These objectives should belong to a category lower than or equal to O's since "The objectives belonging to a category are based on, and can incorporate the behaviours of the previous categories " [2]. We believe that it is not desirable that a sub-objective O_i belongs to a category higher than O's. For example the relationship *is-composed-of(cell [ap], width [ac])* is not desirable from the point of view of Bloom's taxonomy.

- **is-prerequisite-to:** here it is harder to determine the categories of the objectives in question. In general, an objective O_1 prerequisite to O_2 should be of a lower category than O_2, however, it is not possible to affirm this only on Bloom's definitions. For example, in specific cases we might find *synthesis* exercises that are necessary for the *comprehension* of another objective.

The following rules related to the semantic aspects of the curriculum were obtained:

$$\forall(x,y) : (isComposedOf(x,y) \Rightarrow category(x) \geq category(y)) \tag{2}$$

$$\forall(y,x) : (isPrerequisiteTo(y,x) \Rightarrow category(x) \geq category(y)) \tag{3}$$

It is important to keep in mind that the second restriction must *generally* be respected. Table 2 shows the modifications made in the curriculum by the application of these rules.

Table 2. *Changes in the second phase*

Type of change	Quantity	Ratio of change (on 105)
Relation changed destination	2	1.9%
Relation changed type	0	0.0%
Relation was inverted	4	3.8%
Relation was added	0	0.0%
Relation was removed	2	1.9%
Total	10	9.5%

At this point of the validation process, it is important to be cautious so that the modifications made do not invalidate those made during the first phase. We observe that despite the extent of the changes being less important here, the changes do affect near 10% of the links in the curriculum. The most frequent modification was the *inversion of a link*. In all cases the change concerned an objective of the application category which was placed *prerequisite to an objective* of the acquisition category. Most of these errors were detected during the prior step.

If we add the total number of corrections made to the curriculum during both phases we obtain 42.8%, which is much higher than what we expected (we expected an error rate of approximately 20%). Figure 3 shows the fragment of the curriculum after the two phases.

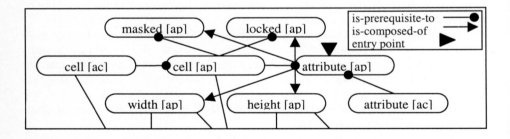

Figure 3. *Curriculum fragment after the corrections.*

In this curriculum fragment the main changes were additions: four *is-composed-of* relationships were added. These changes were justified by respecting rule (1) concerning the entry points and by the desire to complete the *attribute* definition. The two *attribute* objectives had their relationships changed in order to respect rule (3), and in order to make the *attribute [ap]* a entry point.

6. Lessons Learned

In order to understand why so many errors were found in the developed curriculum, we studied the method used by the high-school teachers. Several comments on the curriculum editor seem to suggest that a method should be proposed or even imposed on the developer: "The use of these tools tends to segment the teaching material to the point where one loses sight of the global picture" [6].

6.1. The High-School Teachers' Method

It seems that most of the errors were due to the fact that the tool allows the curriculum developers to work in an unstructured way. After having analysed the protocol used [12] we have determined that the teachers tended to use a bottom-up approach [4]. In order to build the curriculum, they enumerated the pertinent objectives, identified their types and regrouped them, traced the relationships, and repeated the process.

This method, named *content-driven*, favours the exhaustive identification of the objectives (it will cover more of the subject material). It could be useful to build a general course on a specific domain without knowing the characteristics of the learners. One of the biggest inconvenience of this approach is that some elements are defined and then discarded since they will not be connected to anything.

With this approach, there is a loss of both global vision and coherence (therefore of the global quality). The introduction of entry points addresses partially this lack. The semantic restrictions permits the detection of some errors that are less damaging but still important since they constitute 25% of the total number.

6.2. The Proposed Methodology

We have developed a methodology enabling the construction of an objective network respecting the CREAM model and Bloom's theory, while minimising the potential errors. The proposed methodology, based on a *course-driven* approach, is as follows:
1- Identify the major, most general objectives and mark them as Entry points.
2- Refine the objectives by finding their components (relations of type is-composed-of). At this step we have a set of trees, refined at the desired granularity.
3- Identify the objectives that are duplicated in different composition trees, and merge them. This has the effect of connecting some trees together.
4- Identify prerequisite relations between existing objectives (relations of type is-prerequisite-to). Special care should be taken in avoiding loops in the relations, relations contradicting Bloom's theory and, more subtly, prerequisite relations short-circuiting composition relations.
5- Add additional objectives representing particular prerequisites.

At any step of the process, the entry points should remain as such, and no further entry points should emerge. By forcing the use of a top-down approach, we keep the developer from making mistakes such as losing track of the main objectives of the course. The global organisation of the network is assured at the end of step 2. It is also easier to see the degree of refinement needed for each of the objectives, when they are in separate hierarchies. Merging subtrees and adding prerequisite links are critical operations that will be successful only if the initial hierarchy classifies clearly what's in the developer's mind.

6.3. Using the Proposed Methodology to Build a Curriculum

In order to validate the methodology described in 6.2., we built a small curriculum for teaching basic skills in racquetball. First, in order to have a starting point, we needed to identify the entry points. We decided that: *rules*, *techniques* and *match* would be the three main themes in our tutoring. The rules are technical points such as security, clothing and court specifications; the techniques are basics such as how to hold the racquet and how to move on the court; and the match objectives are related to how to play a match (serve, count points,…).

The curriculum built in this section is illustrated in Figure 4. After naming the entry points, we need to expand them. For instance, the *techniques* objective is expanded as *racquet basics* and *body location*. When each objective is refined to the desired level, it is time to merge the ones that are redundant; in this curriculum, no merging were necessary since duplicate objectives were of a different level in Bloom's hierarchy.

Prerequisite relations were then added, with the priority given to the same-name objectives which are of different levels (such as *body location/AC* and *body location/CO*). Other prerequisite relations were added until the curriculum showed enough connectivity. Finally, objectives from lower levels of Bloom's taxonomy were added as prerequisites at points where we wanted to be sure to cover all the domain.

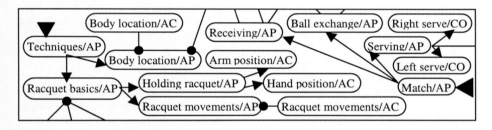

Figure 4. *Fragment of the curriculum for teaching racquetball*

7. Conclusion

The organisation of the material to be taught (the curriculum) is a key element in the building of an ITS. Since it occupies the heart of the system, any lack in curriculum quality will decrease dramatically the quality of the whole system. As we have shown, building a curriculum is an error-prone process. We believe that even if we cannot eliminate all errors because of the complexity of the structure, it is still possible to control some aspects of the process.

In this paper, we have developed a generic evaluation framework based on three axes of intention: data structure definition, pedagogical model, and teaching goals. Using a sample curriculum developed by high-school teachers, we have evaluated its conformity to the data structure definition and to the pedagogical model, leaving the teaching goals' evaluation to the teachers themselves.

Using three simple rules we developed, we tracked errors representing more than 40% of the original curriculum content (in terms of relations). This helped us in defining a methodology for curriculum development with the CREAM-O model. To test this new methodology, a sample curriculum was built and analyzed.

We hope that this work will help researchers in the ITS community in defining generic evaluation models for curriculum quality evaluation.

Acknowledgements

This work has been supported by the TeleLearning Network of Centres of Excellence.

References

1. Anderson J.R., Boyle C.F., Corbett A., Lewis M. *Cognitive modeling and intelligent tutoring*. Artificial Intelligence, 42.
2. Bloom B.J. Taxonomy of educational objectives : the classification of educational goals. New York : Longmans, Green.
3. Gagné, R. M. The conditions of Learning, 4th edn. Les éditions HRW Ltée. Montréal.
4. Gaines, B. *Knowledge Acquisition Systems*. Knowledge Engineering, vol 1, Fundamentals, pp 52-102, Edited by Hojjat Adeli, McGraw-Hill.
5. Koedinger K.R., Anderson J.R. *Effective use of intelligent software in high school math classrooms*. In Proceedings of the World Conference on Artificial Intelligence in Education, (pp. 241-248). Charlottesville, VA: Association for the Advancement of Computer in Education.
6. Lalonde M., Robert C. *Construction de cours et outils de développement*. TeleLearning 6.2.1. Internal report, Université de Montréal, DIRO.
7. Mark M.A., Greer J.E. *The VCR Tutor: evaluating instructional effectiveness*. In Proceedings of the Thirteenth Annual Conference of the Cognitive Science Society. Hillsdale, NJ: Lawrence Erlbaum Associates.
8. McArthur D., Lewis M.W., Bishay M. The role of artificial intelligence in education: current progress and future prospects. RAND, Santa Monica, CA, DRU-472-NSF.
9. McCalla G. *The search for adaptability, flexibility, and individualization: approaches to curriculum in intelligent tutoring systems*. In Adaptative learning environments: foundations and frontiers, Berlin: Springer-Verlag.
10. Millet, Gouardères. *Approche qualitative de la ré-ingénierie d'un système tuteur intelligent à partir d'une méthodologie d'évaluation*. In Proceedings of the third international conference, ITS'96, Montréal.
11. Murray T. *Special purpose ontologies and the representation of pedagogical knowledge*. In Proceedings of the International Conference for the Learning Sciences (ICLS-96), Evanston, IL, 1996. AACE: Charlottesville, VA.
12. Newell, A., Simon, H.A. Human Problem Solving. Prentice Hall, Inc., Englewood Cliffs, NJ.
13. Nkambou, R. Modélisation des connaissances de la matière dans un système tutoriel intelligent: modèles, outils et applications. Doctoral thesis. Université de Montréal, 1996.
14. Obermeier, K.K. Natural language processing technologies in artificial intelligence : the science and industry perspective. Halsted Press ed. Ellis Horwood, Chichester, England.
15. Pressman, R.S. Software Engineering: A Practitioner's Approach, 4th Edition, McGraw Hill, 1997.

A Bottom-Up Approach to Multimedia Teachware $\star,\star\star$

Jörg Caumanns

Free University of Berlin, Center for Digital Systems, 14195 Berlin, Germany
caumanns@wiwiss.fu-berlin.de

Abstract. This paper presents a bottom-up approach to multimedia teachware creation, that is completely based on self-descriptive media objects. Especially the lack of any static linkage between an application's building blocks provides the best opportunities for any kind of automatic teachware generation, that on its part offers maximum adaptability, maintainability, and extensibility.

1 Introduction

The idea of computer aided education is as old as the computer itself. During the last 50 years lots of pedagogues, psychologists, and computer scientists have tried to make use of computers for teaching and learning. Keywords as *Computer Based Training*, *Programmed Instruction*, or *Computer Assisted Instruction* show the great variety of these efforts.

The rise of powerful and inexpensive Multimedia-PCs has changed the whole picture. Concepts based on *Drill and Practice* are out of concern; web-based, adaptive, multimedia *Intelligent Tutoring Systems* are state of the art. New possibilities cause new demands, which cause new concepts. Currently favored approaches as *Situated Learning*, *Cognitive Apprenticeship*, and *Anchored Instruction* represent the rise of the new interactive, multimedia age.

But new concepts although rise new problems:

- Given that the costs of multimedia teachware applications are calculated in 100,000s of dollars and that the time to create them is counted in man years, asking for the balance of costs and benefits seems to be legal [6]. To my opinion the development of multimedia teachware is much too expensive and much too slow - much too expensive to deal with topics away from the mass interest and much too slow to react on current events.
- Runtime environment, application, and media (texts, images, video, etc.) are statically interconnected, which leads to big, monolithic software. Just inserting an additional diagram or exchanging two blocks of text may require a redesign and recompilation of the whole application.

$\star$ This research was supported by the German Research Society, Berlin-Brandenburg Graduate School in Distributed Information Systems (DFG grant no. GRK 316)
$\star\star$ This research is part of the DIALECT/DIALERN project sponsored by the German Research Network.

- Due to their monolithic nature, most applications are not well suited for any kind of adaptation to the current users special interests and preferred way of learning.
- Educational systems are stand-alone applications. There is no way to reference or even integrate pages or media from other applications.

Most of these problems can more or less directly be put down to the monolithic nature of most teachware applications. The static linkage of runtime, application, and media hinders easy maintenance, leads to nearly unchangeable applications, impedes adaptation, and makes reuse of media and design nearly impossible.

In this paper I will try to show, how reverting the teachware design process from currently preferred top-down approaches to a bottom-up design cycle can lead to a more flexible and dynamic application design, that will improve adaptability, increase reusability, and reduce costs.

2   Top-Down and Bottom-Up Teachware Design

Whenever the term "Multimedia Teachware" is used within this paper, I have educational applications in mind, that try to increase the knowledge of a delimited audience about a more or less well defined topic by using differently encoded media [3].

According to this definition, all applications designed for scholar or university further education as well as systems that provide information about certain people, events, or places are multimedia teachware.

2.1   The Building Blocks of Multimedia Teachware

Multimedia teachware in most cases consists of a hierarchy of chapters, sections, and subsections (*application structure*), which are presented to the user as a network of linked screen pages (*frame structure*). Each of these screen pages - often called *frames* - is just a set of texts, images, diagrams, audio and video files, enriched by navigational items such as "previous" and "next" buttons. Items encoding the contents of a frame are called *media objects*. Media objects can be static (e.g. text), continuous (e.g. MPEG-video), interactive (e.g. a spreadsheet), or any combination of these three properties (e.g. images containing hot zones).

The currently most widely used approach to design multimedia teachware is first to define an application structure, then to map chapters and sections to frames, and finally to fill these frames with media objects and navigational items. This top-down design cycle leads to a static linkage between application structure and frame structure, as well as between frames and media objects.

The drawbacks of this two-level static linkage become obvious, if one thinks of the impacts on extensibility and adaptability:

- Adding, removing, or modifying media objects may demand changes at the frame structure (ideally each frame should fit into a single screen page [9]).

This in turn may have impacts on the application structure. Adding, removing, or modifying chapters and sections is nearly impossible, because it
requires both a new frame structure and a new mapping of (new) media
objects to frames.
- As all linkages are static, there is no room for adaptability. Neither the
  structure of the whole application, nor the selection and sequencing of frames
  and media objects can be adapted to the current user. The only solution
  would be to create an individual application for each user.

Given the three-layered structure of multimedia teachware, designing a new
application structure and changing the selection and sequencing of media objects
in order to get adaptability and extensibility cannot be avoided. What can be
avoided is that these redesigns and modifications have to be done manually.

To reduce the amount of manual work, a dynamic linkage between the three
layers of multimedia teachware is needed. The easiest way to get such a dynamic
linkage is to keep only one layer fixed, and to automatically "calculate" the other
layers out of this base layer. If additional meta-information about the base layer
is available, even this layer can be generated automatically.

2.2   Dynamic Multimedia Teachware

One way to automatically "calculate" multimedia teachware is to revert the
design cycle from top-down to bottom-up:

Starting point of the bottom-up design cycle is an existing set of media
objects, which either have been created from scratch or have been taken from
existing applications or textbooks. According to the current user's motivation
and his/her preferred way of learning, a subset of the available media objects
is chosen. These media objects are grouped as a graph, that reflects some kind
of provides-knowledge-for relationship. Now this media object structure is converted into the application structure by combining closely related sequences of
media objects. In a last step these sequences are split up to create a set of frames.

The question left open is how to create a graph out of a given set of media
objects. There are two possible solutions: The first one is to keep some kind of
a conceptual network on all media objects. The other one is to let each media
object describes itself in a way, that enables a clever piece of software to calculate
a structure on the whole set of media objects.

The first solution is easy to implement, but based on a static structure,
which has been shown to be the cause of nearly all of the existing problems. The
second solution is not that easy to implement, but results in *dynamic multimedia
teachware*, as there is no static relationship between any of the application's
building blocks. The advantages are overwhelming:

- Adding, modifying, and exchanging media objects is as easy as possible. One
  can change the base of media objects available at will and just let the clever
  piece of software "recalculate" the application.
- Fine-grained adaptation comes for free, as the current users preferences are
  no more than a set of parameters for the application-calculating algorithm.

– The integration user-written media objects is nothing more than just extending the base of media objects available.

To make dynamic multimedia teachware came true one needs a self-description for media objects, that is powerful enough to let a clever piece of software be based on algorithms and not on magic. The first of these two requirements - a self-description for media objects - will be covered in Chap. 3, the second one - the clever piece of software - in Chap. 4.

2.3   Related Work

The idea of automatically "calculating" teachware applications is not new. Systems like DCG [15], ELM-ART [5], ITEM-IP [4], and HyperTutor [12] all dynamically generate tutoring systems from a given base of frames, media objects, questions, and other building blocks.

The main difference between these systems and the approach sketched above is, that the algorithms for "calculating" applications used by all of these systems work top-down:

The idea of top-down application-creation is to start with a set of concepts, that are interconnected by a some kind of an is-required-for relationship. Given this conceptual network, a one-to-one mapping of frames to concepts is done in order to get the frame structure of the application. These frames are than filled with media objects (if no predefined frames are used). [1]

What are the advantages of a bottom-up application generation as compared to these top-down approaches?

First, the bottom-up approach allows for a finer grained adaptation, as it is completely based on the smallest building blocks - media objects.

Secondly, it is more flexible, because any top-down generation depends on both an existing media object base (or frame base) and an predefined conceptual network, which can be seen as the applications overall structure. The static frame structure has just been replaced by a fixed mapping of a knowledge domain to a hierarchy of concepts. In contrast to this, the bottom-up approach only depends on an existing media object base and "calculates" all other layers, so that even the structure of the application can be adapted to the current user.

This directly leads to the third advantage: The conceptual network used by the top-down approach reflects the provider's model of the knowledge domain, not the users'.

The fourth advantage is a more pragmatic one: The bottom-up approach is better suited for converting existing printed texts into multimedia teachware, as it just depends on media objects, that can easily be generated from text paragraphs, diagrams, and images.

But there are also some disadvantages: The application's provider never sees any kind of structure, just a database of media objects. Nearly all the intelligence needed to create multimedia teachware is somewhere hidden within the

---

[1] Interestingly, the designers of ELM-ART used a bottom-up approach to manually build up the conceptual network from existing printed material [16].

system. This can be problematic, because the provider has no chance to force the system to use any certain application structure. He/she must trust the "clever piece of software" to be clever enough to find this structure by itself. Dynamic multimedia teachware provides the application designer with some features to influence the teachware generation algorithm, but sometimes this might not be enough. Especially for unstructured or ill structured knowledge domains, there is the danger of needing more meta-information to steer the algorithm, than to describe the application's building blocks.

3   A Content Description for Media Objects

Media objects are the building blocks of dynamic multimedia teachware as described in the previous chapter. Each media object can be described by two main properties: its form and its content. The form of a media object can be described very easily by attributes as encoding (text, image, video, etc.), size, language, and many more. What causes the real problems, is to find an appropriate content description for media objects.

One obvious solution for describing the contents of media objects might be to use one of the many existing knowledge representation mechanisms, e.g. the *predicate calculus* [10], *schemes* [8], *conceptual graphs* [14], *propositional (structural) graphs* [1, 7, 11], or *semantic networks* [13]. Although most of these representations were intentionally invented to create models of the human brain or to support logic reasoning and linguistic analysis, they recently have made their way into the domain of adaptable multimedia teachware. Especially conceptual networks are very popular for top-down generated adaptive teachware applications.

Using knowledge representation mechanisms for this kind of applications seems to be appropriate, because only one entity - the mapping of a domain to a set of concepts - has to be modeled. Using one of them for any kind of bottom-up approach is impracticable, as creating a conceptual network for each media object is a non-trivial and time consuming task. Given that an application may consist of hundreds or even thousands of media objects, any bottom-up approach will only be useful, if there exists a very easy way to describe the contents of media objects.

3.1   An Index-Based Content Description

In order to keep a media object's description as easy as possible, any semantic aspects of its content must be ignored. This is not as dramatic as it may sound, as the main need for semantics is to find a structure on media objects; and the semantics needed there for is the semantics of a media object's use, not the semantics of its contents. This could be compared to solving a puzzle: It makes things easier, if you see the picture, but if you've got enough time, you could as well solve the puzzle by just looking at the pieces' outlines.

Because of this, I propose a combination of two description mechanisms: one for describing the keywords and topics covered by a media object and one for expressing the object's preferred use (see next section).

The first description mechanism can be compared to a book's index: it lists all the keywords and topics covered, sometimes even handles structural relationships between topics, but only marginally expresses any semantics. Following this approach, a content description for media objects can completely based on indices. In contrast to a book's index, a media object's index not only lists the topics and keywords covered by the object, but even all topics and keywords the object is based on. This second group of index entries can be seen as the prerequisite knowledge of a media object.

Indices can be hierarchical; each index entry may contain subindices, which on their part may contain further subindices. Further more, index entries can be references to other index entries. Referencing index entries can be compared to "see xyz entries instead of page numbers within a book's index.

Dynamic multimedia teachware makes intensive use of subindices and references, as they can be used to "calculate some of the semantics needed to find an appropriate structure on media objects. By joining many media objects' indices, subindices and references can give an idea about the structure of a knowledge domain.

To enforce the structuring task of joined indices dynamic multimedia teachware provides a concept called *virtual indices*. An index entry is called virtual, if it is not part of any media object, but included within the joined index of all media objects available for an application. E.g. within a teachware application about statistics, references to keywords as "mean, "median, and "mode could be grouped as subindices of a virtual index entry called "measures of central tendency.

To retrieve a content description from a media object's index, all non-virtual index entries are numerically attributed according to

- the prerequisite knowledge a user must have in order to understand the media object
- the knowledge he/she has about the topic or keyword after reading the media object (taught knowledge).
- the importance of the keyword or topic within the media object (is it part of the main topic or just mentioned in parenthesis).

Applications about inherently strongly structured topics (e.g. mathematics, statistics, programming languages) can be built up just on this index based content description. But if it comes to generating applications based on constructivistic approaches that make use of case studies or video stories, the select and sequence algorithm described in the next chapter must "know" how to handle these special media objects. Even the use of examples or problems may require some further application-specific information.

3.2   Application-Specific Semantics

Dynamic multimedia teachware solves these problems by providing a mechanism called *application-specific semantics*. The idea is to give the application's provider the possibility, to specify the semantics of a media object's use whenever it makes sense according to the application's topic or to the underlying didactic concepts.

Application-specific semantics is realized through optional *application-specific attributes* on media objects. Each of an application-specific attribute's possible values is called a *layer*; a media object matching a certain attribute's layer is said to be located on that layer. E.g. if there is an application-specific attribute "purpose defined on media objects with possible values of "case study, "theory, "sample, and "problem, each media object is located one of these four layers.

For each layer of an application-specific attribute the provider can define how media objects on that layer should be used within the application. Kinds of use include the ordering (e.g. theory first, then samples, and problems last), the granularity (e.g. one sample for each topic), and the weight (e.g. less theory, more problems).

Additionally one layer of each application-specific attribute must be defined as the application's driver, which defines the overall conceptual structure. In most cases multimedia teachware will be driven by facts, but one could even imagine to generate applications based on case studies or video stories (e.g. [2]).

4   Selection and Sequencing

The heart of every bottom-up approach to multimedia teachware is a *selection and sequencing* algorithm. Its main task is to select the media objects most appropriate for the current user and to create a structure based on prerequisite-knowledge dependencies upon them.

The selection and sequence algorithm proposed in this paper works on graphs of media objects. Before the algorithm can be used, each media object has to be converted into a graph. The structure of a media object's graph is a star with the media object as its center node. The index entries of the media object are connected to the media object trough directed, weighted edges. Edges of taught keywords or topics point away from the media object, edges of keywords or topics representing prerequisite knowledge point to the media object. The weight of an edge is the set of attributes, that were assigned to the affiliated keyword or topic.

After all media objects have been converted into their corresponding graphs, all these graphs are aggregated into a set of *knowledge graphs*; one for each combination of layers of all application-specific attributes. Each knowledge graph includes all dependencies between all index entries and all media objects located within the appropriate layers. The knowledge graph containing media objects located on the intersection of all driving layers is called the *leading knowledge graph*.

It is now task of the selection and sequence algorithm to find a *learning graph* (or a set of learning graphs) inside the leading knowledge graph, that touches all topics the current user wants to learn about by just crossing media objects with all their prerequisite knowledge being part of the learning graph, too. After this has been done, the learning graph is enriched by media objects located on non-leading knowledge graphs (e.g. examples, problems, etc.).

The currently implemented select and sequence algorithm is based on a very simple local search algorithm:

1. Define a set of keywords and topics that should be taught by the application.
2. Find a minimum set of media objects that contains all of these keywords and topics as index entries within the objects' joined taught knowledge.
3. Define the set of media objects found in step 2 as the set of objects used. Define their joined taught knowledge as the knowledge provided, their joined required knowledge as the knowledge needed.
4. While the knowledge needed is not empty:
   - Find a media object within the leading knowledge graph that best fits with the current set of objects used.
   - Add this media object's taught index entries to the set of taught knowledge and take away the same index entries from the knowledge needed.
   - Join all the media object's required index entries (without the ones being members of the knowledge taught) with the knowledge needed.
5. Find media objects within the other layers that fit into the existing graph.
6. Try to improve the learning graph by adding or exchanging single media objects. Add redundant media objects from all layers according to the desired level of detail.
7. Spilt the learning graph into a set of chapters and sections by using structural information from all media objects' joined index. Add redundant media objects from all layers to make chapters and sections "look round".
8. Split each chapter into a set of frames and add hyperlinks and other navigational items.

The only problem left open is how to find the best matching media object for a learning path under construction. The current implementation uses an evaluation function based on heuristics, such as to prefer media objects with a high outer grade (many keywords taught), and to avoid index entries with a low inner grade (few explanations available). Media objects that teach keywords with a high outer grade (very often used keywords) seem always to be a good choice, while media objects teaching seldom used keywords very often produce "unwanted contents.

Further on, splitting the learning path leads to clear application structures while joining two otherwise independent learning paths into one causes problems when it comes to finding a frame structure. To take care of these rules of thumb a look-ahead mechanism is used, that tries to find splits and avoids joins by including redundant media objects.

Even with this very simple select and sequence algorithm, adaptation to the current user can be realized in many different ways; e.g. through

- the selection of the most appropriate media-mix (e.g. prefer video for text),

- the use of different didactic approaches, e.g. by including case studies or interactive tools,
- the most appropriate level of detail (e.g. by choosing redundant subentries for the most important index entries to be learnt),
- the most appropriate level of redundancy (e.g. by selecting two or more media objects providing the same taught knowledge),
- the selection and use of application-specific attributes,
- and the most appropriate sequencing (e.g. hyperlink structure vs. tree structure).

An ideal selection and sequencing algorithm should be able to find the most appropriate learning path for every user, for every set of keywords to be learned, and for every desired level of detail. Furthermore it should be very fast and highly adaptable.

The algorithm sketched above is fast enough for on-the-fly teachware generation ($O(n^2)$ with n being the number of media objects available), but does not always find the most appropriate learning path. To increase the resulting applications' quality, I'm currently "training the algorithm to make use of information retrieved by a global search on the knowledge graph. This will increases the algorithms complexity, but (hopefully) has no dramatic impacts on its speed.

5   Conclusion and Future Work

In this paper I have sketched a bottom-up design cycle for multimedia teachware. In conjunction with automatic application generation this approach provides for a much better adaptability, maintainability, and extensibility than all of the currently used, top-down oriented design processes.

Furthermore it enables a faster creation of teachware, as the single steps of the design process (media production, interface design, text authoring) can be paralleled. Even progressive applications could be imagined, starting with a small base of media objects and growing while already in use.

The question, that cannot be answered by now, is the question for the quality of the resulting applications. Despite how quality of teachware is defined, the integration of media will potentially not be as good as with "hand-made" applications. This restriction holds for all approaches based on automatic code generation - either top-down or bottom-up oriented. It has to weighed up on a per-application base, if the loss of quality can be justified by the adaptation won and the time and money saved.

Currently, a framework based on dynamic multimedia teachware is under construction at the department of economics of the Free University of Berlin. The framework will consists of some tools for easy creation and description of media objects, an implementation of the select and sequence algorithm described in Chap. 4, and an HTML-generator.

To check the framework - and the idea of an automatic, bottom-up teachware creation - we will implement a multimedia teachware application about the *European Monetary Union* (EMU). This topic is especially attractive, as it changes very fast. As with nearly all political and economic topics, easy maintainability and extensibility are must-have features for both the design process and the tools used. Further on, as people's level of knowledge about this topic is very heterogeneous, the EMU can bee seen as an ideal base for any kind of adaptation.

By now it looks as if bottom-up generation of multimedia teachware can be a real alternative to currently used top-down approaches - if it is a good one has to be proven in real life.

References

1. Anderson, J. R., Bower, G. H. (1973). *Human Associative Memory*. Washington: Winston.
2. Apostopopoulos, N., Geukes, A., Zimmermann, S. (1996). DIALECT: Digital Interactive Lectures in Higher Education. In: Carlson, P., Makedon, F. (Eds.), *Proceedings of ED-TELECOM 96 - World Conference on Educational Telecommunications*. Charlottesville: AACE
3. Baumgartner, P. (1997). Didaktische Anforderungen an (multimediale) Lernsoftware. In: Issing, L. J., Klimsa, P. (Eds.), *Information und Lernen mit Multimedia*^{2}. Weinheim: Beltz - Psychologie Verlags Union
4. Brusilovsky, P. (1992). *Intelligent tutor, environment, and manual for programming*. Educational and Training Technology International 29: 26-34.
5. Brusilovsky, P., Schwarz, E., Weber, G. (1996). ELM-ART: An intelligent tutoring system on World Wide Web. In: Frasson, C., Gauthier, G., Lesgold, A. (Eds.), *Proceedings of the Third International Conference on Intelligent Tutoring Systems, ITS-96*. Berlin: Springer.
6. Issing, L. J. (1997). Instruktionsdesign fr Multimedia. In: Issing, L. J., Klimsa, P. (Eds.), *Information und Lernen mit Multimedia*^{2}. Weinheim: Beltz.
7. Kintsch, W. (1974). *The Representation of Meaning in Memory*. Hillsdale: Erlbaum.
8. Minsky, M. (1975). A framework for representing knowledge. In: Winston, P. H. (Ed.), *The Psychology of Computer Vision*. New York: McGraw-Hill.
9. Nielsen, J. (1997). *Interface Design for Sun's WWW Site*. Palo Alto: Sun Microsystems. (http://www.sun.com/sun-on-net/uidesign/)
10. Nilsson, N. (1982). *Principles of Artificial Intelligence*. Berlin: Springer.
11. Norman, D. A., Rumelhart, D. E. (1975). *Explorations in Cognition*. San Francisco: Freeman.
12. Pérez, T., Gutiérrez, P., Lopistéguy, P. (1995). An adaptive hypermedia system. In: Greer, J. (Ed.), *Proceedings of AI-ED'95, 7th World Conference on Artificial Inteligence in Education*. Washington, DC: AACE.
13. Quillian, M. R. (1966). *Semantic Memory*. Cambridge: Bolt, Beranak and Newman.
14. Sowa, J. F. (1984). *Conceptual Structures: Information Processing in Mind and Machine*. Reading: Addison Wesley.
15. Vassileva, J. (1997). Dynamic Course Generation on the WWW. In: *Proceedings of the AI-ED'97 Workshop on Intelligent Educational Systems on the World Wide Web*. (http://zeus.gmd.de/~fink/um97/proceedings.html)
16. Weber, G., Specht, M. (1997). User Modeling and Adaptive Navigation Support in WWW-based Tutoring Systems. In: Jameson, A., Paris, C., Tasso, C., *User Modeling: Proceedings of the Sixth International Conference, UM97*. Vienna, New York: Springer.

The Authoring Assistant

Steven Ritter
Department of Psychology, Carnegie Mellon University
Pittsburgh, PA 15213, USA
sritter@andrew.cmu.edu

Abstract. In some domains, including those requiring natural language understanding, we cannot build a system that can complete the entire task. One way to deal with such cases is to encode the result of understanding the problem description along with traces of the process used to understand that description. This places the natural language understanding portion of the system in the authoring system, as opposed to the run-time system (the one used by the student). This solution, however, puts a burden on the author, who must now verify that the problem encoding reflects the desired understanding. We describe the Authoring Assistant, a component of the pSAT system [11] for authoring problems for the PAT Algebra tutor [7] which addresses these issues.

1 Introduction

Most authoring tools for intelligent tutoring systems (e.g. [8]) help users encode the task domain and pedagogical approach. The resulting tools are, essentially, software development tools that are specialized for writing educational software. The system described in [11] is a different kind of authoring tool, called the Problem Situation Authoring Tool (pSAT), which concerns itself with authoring content for an existing intelligent tutoring system. The issue of how content can be added to an intelligent tutoring system arises when problems in the domain of the system cannot be readily solved. Such cases include situations where, for computational reasons, the problem cannot be directly presented to the system in the same format as it would be presented to a student. This is typically the case, for example, with intelligent tutoring systems in which the content is composed largely or wholly of natural language text, which is the case considered in this paper. Similar situations may arise in systems which rely on complex visual or auditory processing.

In systems that are able to solve and offer assistance on all problems within the domain when presented in the same format as they would be presented to a student, content authoring is relatively straightforward. Content can be introduced to the system with the assurance that it will be understood and correctly interpreted. When this is not the case (e.g. when the system cannot be expected to correctly parse text at run-time), the author entering the text must somehow also enter a "parsed" version of the text which is computer-readable by the ITS.

This situation is problematic because the author must not only enter information in two formats (text and parsed representation) but must ensure that the two formats are consistent. If the text implies something that is not represented in the parsed representation, the system will not operate correctly. Ideally, the author would simply enter the text, and a parser would produce the representation, but our definition of the problem implies that this cannot be the case. If the parser were correct all the time, we could just put it in the run-time system and the original problem would not exist.

In this paper, we describe one solution to the authoring problem in domains which are computationally intractable. The solution takes the form of an Authoring Assistant (AA), which contains a parser specialized for understanding simple linear problem situations. The parser's goal is to produce the portion of the computer-readable representation that describes the relationship between the problem text and the procedure(s) that students are expected to use in understanding that text. By making the parser part of the authoring tool, we can avoid the requirement that the parser be correct in all instances. Instead, we consider the parser to be an assistant to the author, and the author can correct any mistakes that the parser makes, allowing the content to be verified before it is presented to a student. AA is a component of the authoring system called the Problem Situation Authoring Tool (pSAT; [11]), which is used to create content for the PAT Algebra Tutor [7]

In this paper, we discuss the problem representation used in a prototype version of the PAT Algebra Tutor and the way in which the Authoring Assistant parses the text to produce this representation. We also discuss how the authoring tool acts when the parse fails and how the author interacts with the Authoring Assistant.

2 The PAT Algebra Tutor

The PAT Algebra Tutor asks students to demonstrate their understanding of a problem situation. Problem situations are presented to the student in plain English text, and the student is given various mathematical tools with which to work through the problems. Students using the tutor learn to construct a table of values for a specific instance of the mathematical relationship, derive algebraic expressions representing the relationships and graph these relationships. For example, a simple problem might state "A worker earns $7/hour" and ask the student to construct a table showing the worker's income after 2, 5 and 20 hours. The student would also be asked to include an algebraic representation of the relationship between time and earnings in the table. As students move through the curriculum, the tools change in various ways. For example, the table tool progressing to the point where the table will operate as a spreadsheet, calculating the earnings based on the time and the algebraic expression the student enters. At various points in the curriculum, students are also asked to graph the relationship.

3 The pSAT Authoring System

The goal of the pSAT authoring system, like any authoring system concerned with entering content, is to produce a representation of the problem situation that is suitable for use by the run-time system. In an ideal situation, the problem would be completely comprehended by the runtime system, so no authoring tool would be needed. This is the case in, for example, the equation solving system described in [10]. That system provides guidance to students solving linear equations. Since the problem situation, in that case, is wholly described by an equation and since any equation can be easily parsed, there is no need for an authoring tool. The system can be presented with any linear equation, and it will immediately be able to help the student solve it.

For many domains, however, a complete solution is either impossible or impractical. This is particularly the case in domains that involve natural language understanding, such as algebra word problems. In these cases, the goal of the authoring system is to produce a problem representation that is sufficient for the run-time system to act *as if* it were understanding the natural language contained in the problem situation, even though it is doing little or no natural language understanding at run-time. Essentially, the problem representation needs to represent the result of parsing the natural language problem description along with traces of the parse itself, which are used to model the process by which the student goes from natural language input to the required activities within the tutoring system.

This approach reduces the power of the system, in that students can not simply type in a word problem and expect the system to be able to tutor them on it. The advantage of the approach is that, in cases where the authoring system cannot parse the problem text, we can ask the author to create the representation that would have resulted if the parser had been able to complete the task. That is, we allow the author to correct or override the parser's suggestions. It would be inappropriate to directly present the computer-readable representations actually used by the run-time system (since we do not want to assume that the author can understand these data structures in a computer language), so we needed to create an intermediate representation that is both comprehensible to the author and complete and accurate in its portrayal of the underlying representations. In the next section, we discuss this level of the representation.

4 Intermediate Problem Representation

Some portions of the problem representation are common to all problems. For example, all problem statements contain words which define the variables that are related within the problem. A particular problem might contain the phrases "the number of hours you work" and "your earnings," which define the independent and dependent variables to be related in the problem. The problem representation includes pointers to these phrases in the problem text so that, if students are having trouble articulating what the variables are, the system can reinforce the idea that the words used to express the variables are contained in the problem statement. Similarly, all problems contain words and pointers into problem text corresponding to appropriate units of measure and constant quantities.

Fundamentally different kinds of word problems involve fundamentally different mappings between the problem statement and the underlying representation. These mappings are, in part, a reflection of the different procedures that students must use to parse the problem text into a mental representation and to translate this mental representation into the language of algebra. As a way of explaining the fundamental differences in these two processes to our authors, we classify the relationships between the variables in the word problems. We refer to these classifications as "schemata." Problems which involve different schemata also involve somewhat different cognitive processes that students must master in order to understand them. The schemata play a similar role to Greer's [5] classification of multiplication and division problems. The basic schemata are presented below.

Standard: A standard schema is one in which the slope and intercept are given explicitly. For example, you earn $5/hour is a standard schema.

Discount /surcharge: A discount/surcharge schema is used in problems where the student might reasonably think of the algebraic representation as X +/- aX. For example, in the problem *A store is running a 20% off sale*, if the regular price is represented by X, the sale price might reasonably be represented as X-.2X.

Piecewise-slope-or-intercept: A piecewise-slope-or-intercept problem is a variant of a standard problem in which the slope or intercept (or both) is specified as the sum or difference of a number of components. For example, *Andy has saved $5545. He* *spends $125 per month for food and another $60 per month for entertainment"* is a piecewise-slope-or-intercept problem.

Percentage: A percentage problem is one in which the slope is given as a percentage instead of a decimal. For example, *34% of people in the United States are under the age of 28* is a percentage problem. These differ from standard problems in that they require students to understand the relationship between a percentage and a decimal.

Ratio: A ratio problem describes a ratio between two values (e.g. *To make 5 tons of paper requires 11 tons of wood.*). Note that this differs from a proportion, where the problem specifies some fraction of a single group of items.

Proportion: A proportion problem describes some subset of an item as a proportion (e.g. *4 out of 5 dentists recommend Trident.*). Note that this differs from a ratio, which specifies the relationship between two different things (*there are 4 dentists for every 5 doctors* would use the ratio schema).

Initial-plus-point: An initial-plus-point problem specifies an initial Y value and a new Y value after some change in X. For example, *You started with $400, and after 3 months you have $280 left* is an initial-plus-point problem.

Two-points: A two-points problem states X and Y values at two distinct points. *A candle that has been burning for 2 minutes is 8 inches long. Three minutes later it is 7 and one quarter inches long* is a two-points problem.

Initial-plus-change: An initial-plus-change problem specifies an initial Y value as well as a change in Y over some range of X. This difference between this and the initial-plus-point schema is that, here, the new Y value is given relative to the original one. For example, *A car salesperson is paid $200/month plus a bonus for each car sold. She sold four cars last month and got a bonus of $600* is a initial-plus-change problem

Distribute: A distribute problem is one in which a natural interpretation of the problem situation leads to an equation involving distribution. Usually, this results when the problem gives an initial X value and asks for an expression involving the total value of X. For example, *A builder has completed seven houses. She makes $12,000 for each house. Find her total income* is a distribution problem.

We must emphasize that these schemata do not define the complete set of skills which differ between different problems. Within each schema, there may be several sub-classes. For example, within the standard schema, we differentiate between problems in which the y-intercept is zero and those in which the intercept is non-zero. Similarly, there are differences in skills that cut across all schemata. For example, we differentiate between problems that involve negative numbers and decimals as opposed to integers. Finally, the process of developing a representation that accurately reflects the cognitive skills required to solve a problem is fundamentally empirical and iterative [3]. We fully expect this representation to continue to evolve, resulting in new schemata, the merging of different schemata and the addition or deletion of distinctions that exist both within and across schemata.

5 The Template Solution

We have presented problem schemata as representations that mediate between the underlying system representation of a particular problem and terms which the problem author will understand as relating to the problem situation. Their primary function is to explain the system's underlying representation of the problem to the author. An alternative way to use these schemata would be to consider them as the primary interfaces for inputting problems into the system. That is, their primary function would be as a way of explaining the author's mental representation of the problem to the system. In such a system, the author's first task would be to identify a problem schema, which would bring up a template which the author could use to define the problem.

We decided against this approach for three reasons. First, we wanted authors to approach the system as a way of presenting interesting problems to their students. If the problem they have in mind does not fit into one of the pre-defined schemata, that reflects a weakness with our authoring tool, not with the problem situation itself. In fact, we hope to encourage authors to include and consider problems that do not fit into the current set of schemata, since such problems represent opportunities for expanding the system. Authors can, in fact, enter problems that do not fit an existing schema into the system, although it is inevitably more work than entering problems which do fit an existing schema.

Our first argument against templates amounts to an assumption that the author's primary representation is verbal, and we would like the authoring tool to treat that representation as primary. The second reason is that, when the system can parse the author's text and recognize it as one of the existing schemas, it can save the author a substantial amount of time. In the best case, problem entry reduces to little more than typing the problem text, which would be necessary even in a template-based system. The third reason for our approach is more speculative, but it has to do with the benefits that an author can get out of working with a system constructed in this manner. We expect that authors will learn from the experience of seeing their verbal representations transformed into the intermediate problem representations, sometimes in ways that they did not expect. Empirical data from authors using the system will help us test this prediction. The next section discusses the way that the parser produces the intermediate problem representation.

6 Operation of the Authoring Assistant

6.1 Parsing Algebra Word Problems

There is a long history of efforts to write parsers for algebra (and arithmetic) word problems [2],[6],[9]. Some of this work (e.g. [2]) has focused on the computer-science perspective, in which the goal is to create a program that can produce appropriate equations representing the problem statement. Other work ([6],[9]) has focused on text understanding as a cognitive process, with the goal of understanding the conditions under which construction of appropriate mathematical understanding will succeed and when it will fail. In both lines of research, it has long been recognized that, while many problems can be understood with fairly general semantic knowledge (like the meanings of the words "increase", "times," etc.), many more require domain-specific knowledge (as in the knowledge that "a quarter" is equal to 25 cents or that when a submarine "dives", it goes down). Paige and Simon's [9] demonstration that some subjects act like Bobrow's STUDENT program [2] in constructing an algebraic representation of a word problem that has no real-world correlate is echoed in Kintsch and Greeno's [6] use of a situation model as part of the understanding of a word problem. Both point to the need for domain-specific semantics, if we wish to produce a robust and general parser for word problems.

The construction and use of semantics sufficient to understand the varied domains that we might wish to use within word problems makes this kind of solution impractical. Fortunately, the authoring assistant's goals are more limited, and it benefits from two aspects of the context in which it is used: it does not have to succeed 100% of the time in order to be useful, and the author can provide some "hints" which help the assistant do its job. In the next section, we consider the use to which the authoring assistant's parse it put, and later sections consider how the author can assist the assistant.

6.2 Parsing Output

Parsing is used for several purposes. For the parts of the problem where students are asked to reason from specific numeric instances, we ask authors to encode the questions both as text (defining the text that the student sees) and as the underlying numeric quantities. This is necessary because we need to ensure that the system's representation contains the correct numeric value (which is what the system uses for model-tracing), and this numeric value may or may not be stated directly in the text that the user sees. For example, in one problem the phrase "flat broke" might be represented by the numeric value 0. Parsing the problem text allows us to verify that the numeric quantities correspond to the meaning of the problem text. The parser also identifies places where the unit of measure used in the problem statement differs from the unit of measure used to express the specific quantity. In such cases, the student will need to convert from one unit of measure to another.

Similarly, we ask authors to state (one form of) the algebraic relationship contained in the problem separate from the text that the user reads to discern that relationship. If the parser correctly understands the text, it can verify that these two bits of information are in correspondence. In some cases, the parser identifies "special instructions," which constrain the kind of solution that the student can give. These kinds of instructions are commonly given to constrain students' solutions so that every student demonstrates ability in some area (like negative numbers) that could otherwise be avoided. For example, in a problem about a submarine diving, students might be instructed to consider depth below sea level to be a negative number.

As described above, we sometimes point students to places in the problem text where important information is contained. Parsing the text allows us to identify specific portions of the problem text which correspond to column labels, units of measure, formulas and given values. Finally, the parser automatically identifies the problem "schema", which represents the relationship between the problem text and the underlying algebraic description of the problem situation.

As an illustration of this process, consider the following (initial-plus-point) problem:

```
A college freshman started the year with $400 in spending money,
and after 3 months she has $280 left. Assume that she will
continue to spend her money at this same rate.
1. How much money will she have left after two years and one
month?
2. How much will she have if she spends at this rate for nine
months/year over four years?
```

Part of the student's task is to understand how the problem statement results in the equation $y=400-40x$. In particular, the tutor needs to be able to show a student why the amount of spending money decreases by \$40/month, and it should be able to ground its explanation with references to particular words and phrases in the problem statement. An abbreviated diagram of the underlying representation for the relationship implied by the problem is shown in Figure 1.

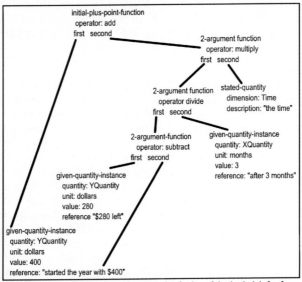

Fig. 1. Underlying representation for calculation of relationship in initial-plus-point problem

The representation captures the fact that the slope of -40 comes from subtracting the beginning y value ($400) from the ending Y value ($280) and then dividing by the change in X (3 months). The parsing process is represented in several ways. First, the topmost node identifies the schema (initial-plus-point), which is used to direct instruction to the student (when needed) and which provides semantics for interpreting lower nodes. Second, node types indicate which quantities are given and which are calculated. In this problem, for example, the intercept ($400) is given in the problem statement, but the slope (-40) must be calculated, based on 3 given quantities. Each given quantity is tagged with a "reference" which, though shown in the diagram as text, is really a pointer into the problem statement. In response to a student who is having difficulty understanding how we know that the y-intercept is $400, for example, the system could point to the phrase "started the year with $400" in the problem statement.

6.3 Domain Semantics

Although we want to accept and encourage problems from a wide variety of domains, the Authoring Assistant, for the most part, uses only general semantic knowledge. The main exception to this is that authors are asked to provide several phrases which would be appropriate for labeling the quantities in the particular problem situation. At runtime, these phrases are used to verify that the student is labeling the columns appropriately. The Authoring Assistant takes advantage of their existence to identify phrases in the problem text which refer to the appropriate quantities. This small amount of domain-specific semantic knowledge does not entirely make up for the lack of more general semantics, but it does provide substantial power.

The other major semantic knowledge base that the Authoring Assistant relies on is information about units of measure. The combination of a number and a unit of measure is tagged as a "unit phrase." The Authoring Assistant uses unit phrases to understand and verify the quantities specified in questions asking students to consider specific numeric instances and as part of the process of understanding the functional relationship included in the problem situation.

There are four kinds of unit phrases in this grammar, distinguished by the relationship between the unit used in this phrase and the standard unit used in the problem. In cases where the units are identical, no conversion need be done. In *standard* conversion phrases, the unit of measure used in the phrase differs from the standard for the problem. This might be the case when the unit phrase is "2 weeks", while the standard unit in the problem is "days." The parser has knowledge about which unit conversions factors are likely to be memorized and which calculated as chains of memorized facts. This allows the tutor to provide different instruction to a student converting from minutes to hours than to one converting from minutes to days. In the former case, the system would remind the student that there are 60 minutes in an hour. In the latter case, the system would remind the student that there are 60 minutes in an hour and 24 hours in a day and that the full conversion factor can be calculated by multiplying the two.

A *mixed* conversion involves mixed units. For example, the phrase "1 week and three days" is an example of a mixed conversion. In this case, the student must convert (at least) one of the parts to the standard unit and add the converted subparts. Finally, a *multiplier* conversion contains an implicit multiplication. For example, to understand the number of days meant by the phrase "2 days/week for a year", the student must multiply the specified number of days by the number of weeks in a year. This may involve one or two embedded *standard* conversions in some more complex cases (consider "23 days/year for a decade", when the desired unit is "months"). When the Authoring Assistant detects a unit conversion, it augments the representation to reflect the calculations that a student would have to make to perform that unit conversion, in a manner similar to that shown in Figure 1.

7 Overriding the Authoring Assistant

It is possible to use pSAT without the Authoring Assistant. The Authoring Assistant communicates with pSAT through a protocol based on the plug-in tutor architecture [12]. In cases where the Authoring Assistant either is not present or cannot parse the problem text, the user can manually enter all information that would normally be inferred by the parser. Even in cases where the assistant is operational, the user can override any values that the assistant sets. Each problem schema has a set of associated parameters. For example, in the initial-plus-point schema shown in Figure 1, there are three parameters, representing the initial and ending y values, and the change in x. The author can indicate that the Authoring Assistant's choice of problem schema is incorrect and choose a different schema. By pointing to text and filling out fields associated with the schema, the author can guide pSAT in constructing the representation shown in Figure 1. In cases where an appropriate schema does not exist, a general linear equation template can be used.

8 The Authoring Assistant's "voice"

While we are continually working to improve the heuristic parsing system, there will be, for the foreseeable future, cases where the Authoring Assistant does not correctly interpret the problem text. The system has been tested on 141 problems that were written for the PAT Algebra Tutor before pSAT existed, and the parser correctly identifies the functional relationships in the problem (and the related schema) in 67% of those problems. The parser is able to identify the numbers represented by specific situations (and any associated unit conversions) over 80% of the time. Most of these failures are cases where AA does not come up with any interpretation of the problem, but a significant fraction are cases where AA reaches an interpretation of the problem that is different than that intended. Especially problematic cases occur when AA's interpretation of the problem is only subtly different from the standard interpretation of the problem (as when it omits or adds a negative sign).

Such situations can be difficult for the author, if the author thinks of AA as an integrated part of the system, rather than a separate advisor who is usually helpful but which sometimes makes mistakes. For this reason, it is essential that the decisions make by AA appear to the author to be suggestions which can be easily changed when they conflict with the author's intention. In cases where AA identifies a different numeric quantity than that suggested by the author, the author is presented with 3 choices: use the author's value, use AA's value or use a completely different value. If the author chooses to use his or her own value (i.e., the author overrides AA), AA will remember this override and incorporate this value into the underlying representation.

Still, preliminary testing has revealed that authors resist overriding values suggested by AA. In part, this may result from the fact that messages from AA are not clearly differentiated from standard system messages. Both are presented in the same dialog format. One potential resolution to this problem would be to have AA appear as an on-screen agent [1],[4]. This might give two "voices" to the system: one used for standard system messages (which can be assumed to be correct) and another from the Authoring Assistant which, while usually helpful, might occasionally contain errors.

9 Extending the Use of Domain Semantics

One advantage of requiring authors to enter information redundantly is that the system can learn from instances where it cannot parse the problem text. Suppose an author entered a problem about spending money in which one of the specific instances asked how long it would be before the spender was "broke." If the system does not understand the word "broke," the author will be asked to highlight a phrase representing the instance. Since the author has entered the value "0" as the numeric representation for that specific instance, the system could make a reasonable inference that the word "broke" corresponds to the number 0 (at least when the unit of measure was "dollars", which would also be clear to the system). This information could then be stored and accessed the next time an author wrote a problem using the word "broke". While AA does not currently store information of this sort, this would provide a way for AA to acquire more domain semantics, without a separate tool being devoted to that purpose.

10 Conclusion

This paper describes our methodology for constructing an authoring system designed for use with an intelligent tutoring system that cannot be expected to parse natural language at runtime. In such cases, we believe it is essential to expose as much of the underlying representation to the author as possible, so that the author can verify that the student's system will behave correctly. Our experience with this system indicates that authoring assistance based on parsing natural language can be very helpful to authors, even when the parser can be expected to fail on a significant fraction of the cases. While domain semantics are needed to reach human-like comprehension levels of algebra word problems, general semantic knowledge can go a long way. It is not necessary for the authoring tool to embody a cognitive model, if it is able to output an appropriate representation for the run-time cognitive model. This can be a substantial benefit in producing intelligent tutoring systems cost-effectively.

Acknowledgments

This work was supported by the National Science Foundation and the Advanced Research Projects Agency under Cooperative Agreement CDA-940860. John Anderson helped guide this work, and Olga Medvedeva was responsible for pSAT programming.

References

1. Andre, E., Rist, T. and Muller, J.: Life-like presentation agents: A new perspective for computer-based technical documentation. In Proceedings of the AI-ED workshop on pedagogical agents, Kobe, Japan. (1997).
2. Bobrow, D. G.: Natural language input for a computer problem-solving system. In M. Minsky (Ed.): Semantic information processing. MIT Press, Cambridge, Ma. (1968).
3. Corbett, A. T., Koedinger, K. R. and Anderson, J. R.: Intelligent Tutoring Systems. In The Handbook of Human Computer Interaction. (1996).
4. Frasson, C., Mengelle, T. and Aimeur, E.: Using pedagogical agents in a multi-strategic intelligent tutoring system. In Proceedings of the AI-ED workshop on pedagogical agents, Kobe, Japan. (1997).
5. Greer, B.: Multiplication and division as models of situations. In D. A. Grouws (Ed.). Handbook on research on mathematics teaching and learning. Macmillian, New York. (1992) 276-295.
6. Kintsch, W. and Greeno, J.: Understnading and solving word arithmetic problems. Psychological Review. **92** (1985) 109-129.
7. Koedinger, K. R., Anderson, J. R.., Hadley, W. H., & Mark, M. A.: Intelligent tutoring goes to school in the big city. International Journal of Artificial Intelligence in Education. **8** (1997).
8. Murray, T.: Authoring knowledge-based tutors: Tools for content, instructional strategy, student model and interface design. The Journal of the Learning Sciences. **7** (1998).
9. Paige, J. M. and Simon, H. A.: Cognitive processes in solving algebra word problems. In B. Kleinmuntz (Ed.), Problem Solving: Research, Method and Theory. Wiley, New York.(1966).
10. Ritter, S. and Anderson, J. R.: Calculation and strategy in the equation solving tutor. In J.D. Moore & J.F. Lehman (Eds.),Proceedings of the Seventeenth Annual Conference of the Cognitive Science Society. Erlbaum, Hillsdale, NJ: (1995) 413-418.
11. Ritter, S., Anderson, J. R., Cytrynowitz, M., & Medvedeva, O.: Authoring content in the PAT algebra tutor. Journal of Interactive Media in Education (1998).
12. Ritter, S. and Koedinger, K. R.: An architecture for plug-in tutor agents. Journal of Artificial Intelligence in Education. **7** (1996) 315-347.

Explanatory Mechanisms for Intelligent Tutoring Systems

Douglas P. Metzler & Cynthia J. Martincic

Dept. of Information Science & Telecommunications
University of Pittsburgh
Pittsburgh, PA, 15260 USA
{metzler,cjmar}@sis.pitt.edu

Abstract. QUE is an exploratory environment for users of rule based intelligent systems. Its original motivation was the question of how to analyze and explain the discrepancies in rule-based intelligent tutoring systems, between "near miss" incorrect responses of a student and the system's knowledge of the "correct" line of reasoning. It is currently under development as a suite of techniques which provide explanation by supporting the exploration of a system's reasoning processes. This paper describes some of the exploratory modes, the underlying mechanisms that support them, and a number of ways in which these modes and mechanisms might be incorporated into intelligent tutoring architectures.

1 Introduction

QUE (QUerying the Expert) is a suite of techniques and interface tools currently under development that provides an interactive exploratory environment for use with rule and object based intelligent systems, and supports the determination of explanatory answers to various questions types regarding the objects, states and reasoning paths of the underlying intelligent system. The general idea is to address the complexity of the explanation problem in an approach that takes advantage of the relative simplicity of an exploratory environment architecture.

The general problem of explanation in complex systems can be viewed as a problem of mapping between the user's information need and what the system can provide to meet that information need. This mapping is complex because neither the user's information need nor the system's state is static or simple. Both are complex hierarchical structures and both change dynamically. A user's need for understanding might relate to background domain knowledge, or to understanding the dynamic reasoning processes of the system. The latter might refer to the details of local actions, or to higher level implicit strategic aspects of the procedures.

Most reasoning is non-monotonic. Shallow reasons might exist in the immediate environment but have deeper causes in the past. For instance, the explanation of why a resource is not currently available, might involve not only that it was previously used for something else, but also the *reason* for which it was used for something else. In general, states change in ways that eliminate potential actions at later points that were possible earlier. Resources are consumed, objects are combined in ways that preclude other combinations, time passes, objects move to different locations, and actions are taken that prevent alternatives.

Given the importance and complexity of the explanation problem, it is not surprising to find that the general problem has been addressed in a variety of ways. Some system architectures have provided useful explanation facilities based directly on their internal data and control structures, such as the rule traces of rule-based systems, the cases retrieved by case-based reasoning systems, or the object hierarchies of object-based systems. Since intelligent systems are based on structures that correspond closely to articulated human knowledge, these structures are relatively understandable and informative to users. In general, however such "transparent system" approaches (e.g., [1] - [2]) are not sufficient since they provide no direct access to the meta-knowledge or dynamic processes that are involved in reasoning processes.

Some have uncoupled the problem of providing explanation from the system's reasoning by providing alternative reasoning mechanisms that are separate from the underlying system's functioning. In some cases (e.g. [3]), this approach is justified by necessity since the system's reasoning mechanism is unintelligible to uninitiated users. In others, it is a means to provide additional reasoning for the sole purpose of explanation (e.g. [4]). Natural language explanation systems tend to fall into this category, typically involving the explicit data structures that support deep issues of explanation such as user modeling, dialog structure and control of dialog structure. However, although attempts have been made to analyze these issues in a general manner (e.g. [3], [5] - [7]) the complexity of this approach and its tight coupling of the explanatory data structures and the underlying knowledge structures, tends to lead to systems that are specific to one problem type, domain, or even a single application.

QUE can be understood in this framework as an attempt to extend "transparent system" ideas by providing facilities for a user to explore the dynamic aspects of explanatory mappings without attempting to build an explicit model of the meta-knowledge used by the system. We avoid the more explicit problems of user understanding by designing the system in a user driven, exploratory manner, but at the same time provide mechanisms that can be used to determine possible reasons for misconceptions.

2 The QUE System

QUE is implemented in Common LISP and functions with forward-chaining rule and object based intelligent systems written in the Harlequin KnowledgeWorks expert system shell, a general OPS-like production system which uses the CLOS object system of Common Lisp and supports developer defined LISP antecedent predicates. The ideas should be readily portable to other rule-based architectures. QUE is separate from the underlying rule-based system and thus is domain independent, but is able to take advantage of rich semantic knowledge when provided by the system developer.

QUE allows the user of a rule-based system to explore the system's reasoning processes by asking various sorts of "why not" and "what if" questions in addition to the "how" and "why" questions supported by traditional rule-based systems. These questions are critical to explaining or understanding reasoning processes in a variety of interactive situations, and to supporting user confidence in the system. These question types involve analysis of the results of potential modifications of both rules and objects, as well as a mechanism to maintain a record of the progression of state in the reasoning process itself including hypothetical branches of that process. The user can direct the system toward particular issues of interest, and can constrain the approach taken by QUE to explain the issue. In summary, QUE takes the following approach: 1) It is designed to work with a rule- and object-based production system architecture, 2) It is domain independent and can provide explanations without relying on domain specific knowledge per se, 3) It provides ways of using rich semantic knowledge if it is provided, and 4) The system consists of a set of mechanisms, currently designed to be driven by a user in an exploratory mode, but potentially detachable and usable in a variety of other architectures.

3 "Why Not" and "What If" Questions

A "why not" question is posed in the form of an object that the system has *not* created in its reasoning process. An object can represent any sort of "conclusion", e.g., a physical object that a design system might have constructed, a belief that a diagnostic system might have concluded, or a student answer to be compared to the system's conclusions. Different situations may produce the need for a "why not" query, and they call for different sorts of useful responses:

The object currently exists. Objects may be created that are not reported as part of a solution. Explaining this involves asking why the object wasn't marked as part of the solution as opposed to asking why the object doesn't exist.

The system doesn't know about objects of this type or with these properties. This can happen because the system lacks the specific rule to create such an object or because it lacks the concept knowledge that could match an appropriate general rule to create such an object. In this case, retrieving similar rules and exploring the differences between the existing rules and the desired outcome can be useful.

The object existed in the past but it was modified or deleted. QUE reveals the point of the change, and what rule caused the change. The causes of the change can then be investigated.

The object could have been created by an existing rule but the rule was never able to fire in an appropriate way because another rule or an inappropriate instantiation of the appropriate rule was preferred by conflict resolution. In this situation, the conflict set, matches and rule structures can be inspected.

The object could have been created by an existing rule but the rule was prevented from firing because of a matching problem. Here, QUE shows what prevented the rule from firing and the reasons for lack of a match, and the consequences of changes to the knowledge base can be explored.

A similar object (not fully matching the query) could have been created by an existing rule. In this situation, QUE locates rules that could create related objects.

These "why not" mechanisms are integrated in a "why not" browser that starts with an object query, employs the various matching strategies to find rules whose consequents could have potentially produced the object in question or similar ones, and displays the antecedents of those rules. The user then can investigate what was preventing those rules from producing the expected results and recursively investigate those reasons. Thus the "why not" browser facilitates a collaborative user and system directed backward search, not through the space of system actions, but through the space of reasons for which an object was not created [8].

"What if" questions address the question of how the reasoning process, and hence the conclusions reached, might have been different if the situation at some point in the reasoning process had been different. The primary focus of "what if" questions is on changes in the knowledge base, but changes in the rules can be construed as "what if" issues as well. These questions are handled by the context mechanism described below. "What if" and "why not" questions can interact, and the user is free to pursue either in the context of the other.

4 The Mechanisms of QUE

The two primary underlying mechanisms employed by QUE are a context mechanism to keep track of the past reasoning states and a set of rule relaxation mechanisms which determine how close rules come to being able to fire in given contexts and how the rule or knowledge base would have to have been different for a given action to have been taken. In addition, tools are provided to allow the user to investigate what the system knows and believes about the objects of the system at any state, to control the level of granularity of the view into the system, to modify system objects and rules, to observe the effects of their modifications, and to trace backward the reasons for the existence or the non-existence of objects.

4.1 The Context Mechanism

The context mechanism keeps track of past states ("contexts") and provides the ability to recreate past states for investigation of the objects that existed in them and the rules that were matchable in those contexts. It allows the user to create hypothetical states and reasoning paths, and is accessible through a number of graphic browsers and tools.

In nonmonotonic reasoning, as the inference engine cycles, objects are created, modified or deleted. This presents difficulties for explanation since the explanation may need to refer not only to the current state but also to the earlier ones which may have afforded possibilities that the current one no longer does. The context mechanism provides a means of determining whether objects of interest ever existed at any previous point in the expert system's reasoning path and the ability to re-establish past contexts for the user to investigate. Since past states can become the jumping off points for hypothetical lines of reasoning (triggered by "what if" questions), the context structure is a tree rather than a linear sequence of states.

To provide this functionality, the context mechanism tracks every object created during the expert system processing. All objects that have ever existed in the reasoning process are maintained in the knowledge base at all times, but are marked to indicate the contexts in which they existed. The modifications to basic object and rule definitions required to implement these mechanisms are added to standard rule and object code by a preprocessor and are transparent to a system developer.

4.2 The Relaxation Mechanisms

Relaxation processes are used in QUE at two points, matching queries to rule consequents, and relaxing rule antecedents to determine why rule instantiations are not matching into memory. Queries originate in QUE or in other potential user-driven exploratory applications of QUE in the context of "why not" questions posed by the user to determine why the system has not produced an expected result. In more structured, system directed, applications of QUE, the system might initiate a query in the attempt to understand an unexpected user input. Queries are currently limited to those that refer to a single object or class of objects and its attributes. QUE handles such queries by searching for rules that could have resulted in the object described in the query. If a rule is found that could have produced the object, the investigation turns to why that rule didn't fire. If no exact matches are found between the query and any rules, a rough-grained relaxation is used to locate inexact matches of the query to a rule consequent by relaxing numeric constraints, ignoring slot constraints or moving up the class hierarchy to which the query object belongs. Such inexact matches can be suggestive of the reason for the expectation discrepancy even if the system lacks the knowledge required for a more explicit explanation.

Relaxing Rule Constraints. The second relaxation process in QUE operates on rule antecedents to allow a user or the system to see what is preventing a rule from firing. Thus when a "why not" query returns a rule that could have produced the query, this process can show the reasons for which the rule did not fire. This is useful for identifying and debugging almost correct ("near miss") misconceptions and can be viewed as an attempt to identify the precise differences between the reasoning of the system and the user.

Conceptually, a rule antecedent consists of descriptions of objects (constraints on the properties of objects) and constraints on relations between the objects. The problem of relaxing antecedents is inherently ambiguous and combinatorial since the complex, roughly hierarchical structure of a rule can be relaxed in many different ways. If A and B are objects described by constraints a' and b' and related by relation R described by constraints r', then the ABR antecedent can be relaxed by relaxing any of a', b' or r' separately, or by relaxing them in any combination. In general, relaxing combinations is expected to find matches with less extreme relaxation of any one element. Adding to the complexity, each of a', b', and r' is, in general, a set of constraints, not an individual constraint, and so there is ambiguity and complexity within the individual constraint descriptions. Furthermore, antecedents often contain more than two objects and more than two inter-object constraints. When the set of constraints cannot be met, QUE uses processes similar to those used in machine learning, e.g., generalization, extension of references and constraint elimination [9], to modify the rules by loosening the constraints on the objects or the relations between them to find a match that is useful or to clarify why the match fails.

The issue of how to constrain the complexity of the relaxation techniques is still under investigation, but part of the solution incorporated in QUE is to allow the system designers and/or the user to control the overall structure of the relaxation process, e.g., with options on what parts of rules to relax, which to hold constant, and the ability to place limitations and priorities on the objects being relaxed, all with varying levels of granularity. While this doesn't "solve" the combinatorial complexity of the problem, it is better than leaving the user to her own (non-computational) devices. In the absence of human guidance, the system can invoke various default relaxation assumptions for guidance.

QUE begins the relaxation process with those clauses that define objects by class and slot values and are not instantiated in the current context. Once the determination has been made of which slots cannot be instantiated, the relaxation process can begin. Relaxing slot constraints depends upon the types of values that are appropriate for the slot.

Relaxation of Numeric Slots. The domain independent nature of QUE poses problems even for numeric relaxation of a single slot since the range of possible values is not explicitly known. Any choice of an increment might be too large (and jump immediately out of range) or too small (to make a difference). QUE uses the knowledge base as a guide. If there are enough objects available, QUE calculates the standard deviation of the slot values and relaxes the constraint appropriately. In the future we will add routines to notice and comply with at least simple cases of discrete values (e.g., integers) and range limits on possible values.

Relaxation of Symbolic Slots. The ability to relax a symbolic value depends on semantic knowledge. Since cross-system approaches to general semantic knowledge are prohibitively expensive [10], and susceptible to the problems of domain specific semantics in any case, we are exploring ways of taking advantage of developer supplied semantics, and ways of supporting the development of such knowledge bases by application developers.

A general approach to using developer supplied semantics is to use the topology of CLOS hierarchies. We are also developing mechanisms that would provide the application developer ways to provide information that QUE could use to control semantic relaxation in more specific ways such as: 1) the use of Rosch's [11] distinction between base level concepts, subcategories and supercategories, 2) the use of nominal ranges that describe non-numeric values, 3) the use of general ontological relationships such as "part/whole", "related concept", "causes" etc., 4) the use of priority markers to indicate the a priori importance of antecedent clauses or parts of clauses (see [12]), and 5) encoding in the knowledge base general information regarding the mutability of properties and objects.

Relaxation of Variable Constraints. Since variable binding expresses the connection constraints across various components of a rule, these constraints can be eased or broken by manipulating the variables. Tests are performed on variables in the test clauses of rules and these tests can be relaxed by relaxing constant values in the tests. The relational tests themselves can also be relaxed, but currently that is only done for basic numeric tests such as "greater than" (which can be generalized to "greater than or equal").

5 QUE AND ITS

QUE, in whole or its individual components, is potentially applicable to ITS in several ways, which correspond to different aspects of the general explanation problem. The potential applications vary on several (related) dimensions including: 1) whether the mechanisms are employed by the user/student (as in QUE) or are directed by the ITS itself, 2) how structured the ITS/learning experience is and how specifically the system directs the student to the material to be explained, and 3) how general or specific the material to be explained is.

5.1 Exploratory Learning Environments

One sense of explanation in ITS is the need for a learner to understand, or explain to herself, the knowledge which is the object of the lesson. Chi et al. [13] describe the advantage of students explicitly engaging in self-explanation activities. ITSs are characterized by explicit representations of that knowledge, typically encoded in a runnable model (i.e., a problem solving capability) or a procedural querying (e.g., question answering) capability.

The most straight forward application of QUE in ITS would be in unstructured exploratory learning environments or collaborative (intelligent assistant) learning environments. An unstructured learning environment might consist of an intelligent problem solving system, a set of examples, and a set of useful hints or questions to guide the student in understanding the functionality of the system. A collaborative learning environment might place the student in the problem solving role with the system providing partial models of the problem solving knowledge to support the student in the problem solving process. QUE capabilities would be useful in understanding what parts of a reasoning process need to be completed, the consequences of missing data or mistaken conclusions, etc.

QUE capabilities can be used in a more focused way by ITSs based on structured learning approaches. Human teaching and learning (e.g., the Socratic method) often involves a deliberate questioning of (intermediate and final) conclusions, hypotheticals, alternative possibilities, and processes involved in coming to conclusions. This is frequently done in conjunction with versions of case-based learning. Structured ITSs might utilize QUE capabilities to allow a student to explore the support for, and the various alternative possibilities surrounding known "interesting" points in the lesson. For instance, a medical ITS might ask at a particular point why a diagnosis had been narrowed in a particular way, what particular changes in the facts of the case would have led to different conclusions, and what new data would alter or narrow the current diagnosis. It might invite the student to explore the reactions of the system to various alterations to the current set of beliefs. It might even present contradictory information and ask the student to try to figure out what data is the most likely to be incorrect. All of these sorts of questions could be explored by the student using the capabilities of QUE running on an underlying intelligent model of the domain.

5.2 Generalized Working Models

A specialization of the exploratory learning environment involves domains in which part of what is being taught consists of specific working models, e.g., chemical or economic laws. Such systems sometimes utilize mathematical simulations to demonstrate the domain knowledge to the student. Mathematical simulations are powerful and robust tools when applicable, but are limited to situations that can be described by the interrelationships (shared variance, causal contributions, functional relations, etc.) between mathematical variables. Models that require a more expressive representation language, e.g., one equivalent to predicate logic, require more complex simulation techniques based on symbolic reasoning. For instance, a working model of an electronic device might require explicit predicate descriptions of the properties and connectivity of the components to support reasoning about its behavior (e.g. observed faults). The mechanisms of QUE make it possible to design demonstration models that include a range of hypothetical actions, and a detailed analysis of the consequences of incorrect actions.

5.3 Embedded Interactive Analysis

In a structured learning context, it can be useful to ask specific questions regarding the content of the lessons. In addition to providing the student with exploratory capabilities at these points (sec. 5.1), the mechanisms of QUE provide a rich palette from which the designer of an ITS can select specific interactive mechanisms to be used by the system to analyze a specific range of anticipated student responses. For instance, if the point of a question answering interaction specifically relates to a particular dimension or a particular vicinity in a semantic hierarchy, one might use specific versions of the relaxation techniques to deal with the variety of responses anticipated for that question. This can provide a way for a system to provide useful answers to narrowly defined student interactions. Rather than trying to anticipate the precise set of likely mistakes, the system might utilize relaxation techniques on the portion of the knowledge base that contains the anticipated answer to see what the relationship is between that answer and the one provided by the student.

5.4 General Analysis of Student Responses

The original motivation for QUE was an interest in providing informative responses to near miss student responses in an intelligent tutoring environment [14]. Such a near miss analysis can be far more informative and effective than simply correcting the surface mistake and/or reiterating a relevant portion of the tutor's lesson. Although it is sometimes possible to interpret student mistakes by incorporating in the ITS knowledge of the common mistakes students are likely to make in the domain, there are a number of problems with that "buggy rule" approach, including that it does not cover the general case of novel student misconceptions [15]. Neither does the very specific approach indicated in Sec. 5.3. A more general solution may be the ability to relax the expert knowledge to see how and where the student could be in error.

Employing the "why not" mechanism of QUE on the system side rather than the user/student side involves the problems of ambiguity and combinatorial complexity described above, but there are mitigating factors that make this application feasible. The most critical is that it is possible to employ such methods within the narrow confines of the knowledge base required for individual lessons. Thus only a small subset of the concept and rule base needs to be considered to interpret the discrepancy. Second, near miss mistakes may be caused by relatively simple errors such as the firing of a general rule when a more specific one should be used, or the use of a rule when a single constraint on it is incorrectly matched, and these relatively simple mistakes may be identified without a great deal of ambiguity or combinatorial complexity. Finally, QUE relaxation techniques can be employed as a back up to "buggy rule" approaches and it is always possible for a system to indicate that it does not have an informative interpretation for a student error. For instance, a language tutor might include a large number of rules that capture the common mistakes made in learning a particular language, but it might cover a wider range of possible mistakes by relaxing the feature constraints that control issues such as number and gender agreement, components of the verb structure etc. Thus, as a system driven interpreter of student errors, QUE can be seen as a way of minimizing (but not eliminating) the number of student errors about which the system has nothing interesting to say.

References

[1] Domingue, J.; *TRI: The transparent rule interpreter,* Research and Development in Expert Systems V, B. Kelly and A. L. Rector (Eds.), Cambridge Univ. Press, 126-138, 1988.

[2] Wickler, G., Chappel, H. & Lambert, S.; *An architecture for a generic explanation component,* Presented at IJCAI Workshop on Explanation and Problem Solving, 1993.

[3] Slotnick, S. A. & Moore, J. D.; *Explaining quantitative systems to uninitiated users,* Expert Systems with Applications, 8(4), 475-490, 1995.

[4] Wick, M. R., Pradyumna, D., Wineinger, T. & Conner, J.; *Reconstructive explanation: a case study in integral calculus,* Expert Systems with Applications, 8(4), 463-473, 1995.

[5] Maybury, M. T.; *Communicative acts for explanation generation,* International Journal of Man-Machine Studies, 37(2), 135-172, 1992.

[6] Cawsey, A.; Explanation and Interaction: The Computer Generation of Explanatory Dialogue, MIT Press, 1992.

[7] Suthers, D. D.; *Answering students queries: functionality and mechanisms,* Intelligent Tutoring Systems: Proceedings of the Second International Conference, C. Frasson, G. Gauthier & G. I. McCalla (Eds.), Montreal, Canada, Springer-Verlag. 191-198, 1992.

[8] Metzler, D. P., & Martincic, C. J.; *Explanation of negative and hypothetical questions in a rule-based reasoning system.* Proc. of 5th. International Symposium on Systems Research, Informatics and Cybernetics, Baden-Baden Germany, 1995.

[9] Michalski, R. S.; *A theory and methodology of inductive learning,* Artificial Intelligence, 20, 111-161, 1983.

[10] Lenat, D. & Guha, R. V.; Building Large Knowledge-Based System, Addison-Wesley, 1989.

[11] Rosch, E., Mervis, C.B., Gray, W. D., Johnson, D. M. & Boyes-Braem, P.; *Basic objects in natural categories,* Cog. Psychology, 8, 382-439, 1976.

[12] Sypniewski, B. P.; *The importance of being data,* AI Expert, 9(11), 23-31, 1994.

[13] Chi, M. T. H., de Leeuw, N. Chiu, M. H. & LaVancher, C. *Eliciting self-explanation improves understanding.* Cog. Science, 8, 439-477, 1994.

[14] Katz, S., Schmandt, L. & Metzler, D.; *A Prototype Tutoring System for Subject Cataloging.* Department of Information Science, University of Pittsburgh, Tech. Rept. IS89005, 1989

[15] Self, J. A. *Bypassing the intractable problem of student modeling.* Intelligent Tutoring Systems: At the Crossroads of Artificial Intelligence and Education. Frasson, C. and Gauthier, G. (Eds.), Norwoord, N. J.: Ablex Publishing, 110-123, 1990.

DNA - Uncorking the Bottleneck in Knowledge Elicitation and Organization

Valerie J. Shute

Air Force Research Laboratory (AFRL)
1880 Carswell Avenue
Lackland AFB, TX 78236-5508
vshute@colab.brooks.af.mil

Lisa A. Torreano

National Research Council Associate
1880 Carswell Avenue
Lackland AFB, TX 78236-5507
lisat@colab.brooks.af.mil

Ross E. Willis

Galaxy Scientific, Corp.
1880 Carswell Avenue
Lackland AFB, TX 78236-5507
rwillis@colab.brooks.af.mil

Abstract. There are two main purposes of this paper. First, we describe a novel cognitive tool that was designed to aid in knowledge elicitation and organization for instructional purposes – specifically to be used for intelligent tutoring system development. This automated approach to knowledge elicitation is embodied in a program called DNA (Decompose, Network, Assess). Our aim for this tool is to increase the efficiency of developing the expert model – often referred to as the bottleneck in developing intelligent instructional systems. The second purpose is to present a first-order summative evaluation of the tool's efficacy. Specifically, we used DNA with three statistical experts to explicate their knowledge structures related to measures of central tendency. In short, we found that DNA can be used as a standalone program to effectively elicit relevant information on which to build instruction. This was achieved in hours compared to months for conventional elicitation procedures.

1 Introduction

One of the most significant challenges we face in the prevailing "information age" is knowledge management. For information to be useful, it must be easily accessible and sufficiently organized so that it both makes sense and can potentially be conveyed to others. This challenge, however, is by no means new – especially to those persons in the teaching profession. Anyone attempting to design instruction must first develop a sound curriculum. In all cases, *what* information to include in the curriculum and *how* to ensure learners' mastery of the material must be determined, regardless of whether instructing karate beginners, nuclear physicists, mechanics, or artists.

These issues are particularly salient in computer-assisted instruction. To render such systems intelligent, and hence, more effective and efficient, three components must be included in the system: (a) an expert model, (b) a student model, and (c) an instructor model [1], [2]. The expert model represents the material to be instructed. This includes both elements of knowledge related to the domain to be instructed and their associated structure or interdependencies. In essence, the expert model is a knowledge map of what is to be taught. The student model represents the student's knowledge and progress in relation to the knowledge map or curriculum. The instructor model (also known as the "tutor") manages the course of instructional material and remediation strategy based on discrepancies between the student and expert models. Thus, the instructor model determines how to ensure learner mastery by monitoring the student model in relation to the expert model. The strength of these programs, therefore, depends on the underlying validity of the curriculum or domain expertise [3].

There are two main purposes of this paper. First, we describe a novel cognitive tool that we have designed to aid in knowledge elicitation and organization for instructional purposes – specifically to be used for intelligent tutoring system (ITS) development. This automated approach to knowledge elicitation is embodied in a program called DNA (Decompose, Network, Assess). Our aim for this tool is to increase the efficiency of developing the expert model – aptly referred to as the backbone of intelligent instructional systems [3]. We will summarize its interface and functionality, but refer the reader to more detailed information on the program [4].

The second purpose of this paper is to present a first-order summative evaluation of the tool's efficacy. We outline the results from an empirical validation of the tool that examined how efficiently and effectively DNA works in the extraction of knowledge elements related to statistics. Specifically, we used DNA with three statistical experts to explicate their knowledge structures related to measures of central tendency.

To satisfy this paper's goals and put them in perspective, we will begin with a short summary of current methods of knowledge elicitation and organization. Next, we will describe the DNA program, illustrating the niche our particular tool fills in the intelligent tutoring system arena. This will be followed by a discussion of the first-order summative evaluation results that enables us to assess the potential utility and effectiveness of DNA.

1.1   Techniques of Knowledge Elicitation and Organization

A variety of cognitive task analysis (CTA) techniques are united by the common goal of representing the underlying knowledge, skills, and goal structures of a particular domain or task performance. Typically, CTA is done in two phases: (a) initial acquisition of knowledge and skills, and (b) compilation of information into a useful database that can serve many functions (e.g., curriculum for instruction or an expert system).

How is information initially acquired? Acquisition of knowledge and skills from experts can take the form of observations, verbalizations, and interviews. The most unobtrusive procedure for obtaining data from experts involves monitoring or observing them as they perform their job or specific task. Another technique, "think aloud" protocols, involve having experts verbalize their thoughts as they perform some task, answer questions, or solve problems. Finally, interviews are a common method for eliciting expert knowledge and skills. Typically, the series of questions posed to the expert are designed around a theory of expertise or the framework in which the information will subsequently be used, e.g., in designing a cognitive model or instruction [5]. All of these approaches can vary in a number of methodological ways including whether the knowledge elicitation is structured or unstructured, and whether it is retrospective or concurrent with task performance. One drawback to these methods is that people do not always have accurate access to their cognitive processes [6]. Thus, these methods may be weak in delineating certain underlying cognitive operations or in tapping into knowledge and procedures that have been automated.

How is information optimally represented? Conceptual graphs are one popular means of representing hierarchically-structured knowledge. As the name implies, conceptual graphs are the graphical representation of concepts showing, at various grain sizes, relevant concepts (nodes) and their interrelationships (arcs or links). Another popular representation of knowledge, a means-end hierarchy, results from a production system framework using a GOMS-type analysis (GOMS= Goals, Operators, Methods and Selection rules) [7]. Each representational type produces a knowledge structure that has its own unique flavor, e.g., conceptual vs. procedural in the two examples, cited above.

Regardless of the approach for eliciting and/or structuring knowledge, current CTA procedures are usually very labor-intensive, often not standardized, potentially incomplete, and difficult to translate into instruction and assessment. For good reviews of CTA methods, see Shraagen [8] and Williams [9]. Overall, CTA remains a bottleneck in the ITS development process.

1.2   Uncorking the Bottleneck: Description of DNA

We are designing a novel cognitive tool called DNA (Decompose, Network, Assess) to help alleviate this bottleneck. Automating the bulk of the cognitive task analysis procedure can potentially expedite the CTA process without sacrificing accuracy. In addition, our goal is to create a cognitive tool that is applicable for systematic decomposition of any domain into its constituent knowledge and skill elements, whether related to task performance (e.g., troubleshooting jet engines) or not (e.g., understanding the core concepts of world religion) [4]. DNA is used to Decompose a domain, Network the knowledge into comprehensive structures, and employ other experts in a given domain to Assess the validity, completeness, and reliability of the knowledge structures. This approach is embodied within an easy-to-use program aimed at extracting and organizing knowledge and skills from experts.

1.3   Modules of DNA

Customize. The Customize module is completed by the instructional designer (ID) who provides information about the ultimate learning goal of the tutor to be developed, the prerequisite knowledge and skills of the learners, and the desired instructional emphasis or flavor (e.g., primarily procedural). This information provides the SME with the superordinate goal of the analysis and the lowest-level subordinate goal at which point the SME should stop decomposing the domain. Using the instructional designer's input, the Customize module generates a personalized letter that explains the purpose of the project and a set of floppy diskettes, which are to be mailed to prospective SMEs. The diskettes contain files for a SME to install on his or her computer that DNA needs to elicit and store knowledge structures.

Decompose. The Decompose module is a semi-structured, interactive dialog between computer and SME designed to elicit most of the explicit knowledge associated with the domain/topic of analysis. DNA utilizes the "What, How, Why" questioning procedure which has been shown in the past to successfully elicit knowledge from experts (e.g., [10]). "What" questions (e.g., "What is a definition of _____?") are designed to obtain symbolic knowledge, or definitions of terms. "How" questions (e.g., "How do you _____?" or "What is the first step you do when you _____?") are designed to elicit procedural knowledge and skills. Finally, "why" questions (e.g., "Why is _____ important?") are designed to elicit conceptual knowledge, or higher-level relationships among concepts.

All information given by experts is stored in a database as a record of curriculum elements (CEs) which are components of knowledge needed to develop expertise in the domain. By storing information in a CE record, it should become easy to translate the information into teachable units and thereby generate curricula.

Network. The Network module transforms CEs elicited during the Decompose module into graphical nodes which experts spatially arrange and link to form knowledge hierarchies, conceptual graphs, or production rules. Each node contains the name of the CE and its contents as defined during the Decompose module. Links placed between CEs can differ in terms of *strength* (i.e., weak, moderate, strong - showing the degree to which the items are related), *type* (e.g., is a, causes, fixed serial order, etc. - denoting the nature of the relationship between nodes), and *directionality* (i.e., uni-, or bi-directional - indicating which CEs are prerequisites to other CEs and the flow of causation).

The use of a graphical representation should make relationships among knowledge units salient, which can also highlight missing knowledge components. This module is similar to conceptual graph analysis except that, with DNA, experts generate the conceptual graphs instead of the instructional designers. Thus, we speculate that DNA will enable experts to recognize gaps in the knowledge and skills they provided earlier. Moreover, they have a chance to readily correct inadequacies as they can return to the Decompose module and update the CE record with new information.

After SMEs complete the Network module, data are stored on floppy diskettes and returned to the ID. The ID reviews the CE record and conceptual graphs for any glaring omissions in content. If any omissions are present, the ID can ask the expert to expand the inadequate CEs.

Assess. The final module is used to validate the CE records and conceptual graphs generated by SMEs. This is accomplished by having other experts in a domain review the conceptual graphs generated by the first group of experts. Multiple experts can also be used to edit initial conceptual graphs as a method of modifying and validating the externalized knowledge structures.

The modules are repeated until the instructional designer is satisfied with the content of the revised CE records and conceptual graphs. Efforts have been made to elicit a range of outcome types: symbolic knowledge (SK), procedural knowledge and skills (PK and PS), and conceptual knowledge (CK).

1.4   DNA Promises and Purposes

Conventional CTA methods have been described as being inefficient, limited to procedural tasks, laborious to translate into usable instruction, and difficult to use. We have attempted to address each of these limitations when we designed DNA [8].

Efficiency. Traditional CTA methods typically involve extensive interviews with experts, transcription of ensuing protocols, and organization of knowledge and skill units. This process normally requires many months of work and many person-hours to achieve. These traditional methods often employ knowledge engineers to interview and observe experts, others to transcribe sessions, and cognitive psychologists to summarize the data into a hierarchical representation. In contrast, DNA automates the bulk of the interview, transcription, and organization processes which is intended to significantly decrease both time and personnel resources required for the cognitive task analysis.

Broad applicability. A common limitation of traditional CTA methods is that most are only applicable to procedural domains. DNA's specific purpose, and thus strength, relates to ITS development and being applicable across a range of domain topics - procedural and conceptual in nature. This is achieved via its underlying hybrid representational structure of knowledge and skills elements - functionally a cross between a semantic net and production system.

Instructional design framework. Another common limitation of traditional CTA methods is that it is often difficult to translate the pages of interview transcriptions and conceptual graphs into a usable curriculum. DNA is structured such that its output is directly compatible with an existing instructional system framework (i.e., SMART; [11]) which further enables efficient tutor development. DNA's resulting database of CEs contains rich and useful information at the individual CE level (e.g., unique CE number, outcome type category, detailed description, and hierarchical information such as parents, siblings, and children). The database also includes embellishments from the SME such as: typical points of difficulty (impasses) in understanding CEs, good examples and counter-examples of CEs, and specific questions that can serve to assess understanding of CEs. All of this information is well suited for developing subsequent and principled instruction.

User-friendly. As previously mentioned, traditional CTA methods often rely on several individuals trained in knowledge elicitation techniques. However, DNA was designed to be very user-friendly, thus the program is not limited for use by individuals with CTA experience. Rather, any instructional designer who wants to develop a curriculum will be able to use this tool to elicit knowledge.

2   Preliminary DNA Evaluation

What we present here is the summary of an investigation testing the Decompose module of the DNA system. In general, the different evaluation issues relate to the system's consistency, validity, and efficiency. DNA promises a great deal in its potential to render the CTA process faster, cheaper, and better. However, before assessing its relative benefits, we need to determine a more fundamental issue: Can DNA indeed extract comprehensive knowledge from subject-matter experts that could serve as the basis for curriculum development?

2.1   Participants and Design

Three volunteer subject-matter experts participated in this preliminary study. While none are formally "statisticians," all have graduate degrees in psychology and a minimum of 10 years experience conducting statistical analyses. Further, all reported that they were quite familiar with "measures of central tendency."

Before the experts arrived, the authors completed the Customize module of DNA to produce the letter informing the experts of the curriculum goals for students to achieve. These included: (a) identify the main measures of central tendency, (b) identify the formulas for the measures of central tendency, (c) know how to calculate each measure of central tendency, and (d) understand the relationship(s) between each measure of central tendency and different underlying distributions. In addition, this letter informed the SMEs that the intended learner population would have (a) basic math skills (with algebra), (b) basic reading skills, and (c) basic computer skills (Windows 95 interface). This provided the SMEs with parameters for their decomposition of the domain. Each SME devoted several hours to decomposition via DNA, and at least one of the authors was present during each of the three interactions to answer only general questions posed by the SMEs.

We are interested in testing the degree to which our SMEs' data agree with a benchmark representation of the domain. Williams [9] conducted a similar analysis using a production system representing cutting and pasting text with a word processor. We are interested in seeing whether this technique can be used for more conceptual data as well. Therefore, because we have an existing tutor that focuses on this topic (i.e., Stat Lady; [11]), we chose the domain of "measures of central tendency". The curriculum for this module of Stat Lady was derived from a traditional cognitive task analysis involving document analysis and interviews with SMEs. The CEs that were obtained for the Stat Lady curriculum required about six months to obtain.

The degree to which knowledge elements derived from the experts using DNA map onto a curriculum already embodied in an existing tutor, will shed light on the consistency of DNA's output as well as potential effectiveness, a validity issue. That is, if the obtained outputs are close to the "idealized" domain structure of a tutor that has already been shown to improve learning, we can infer that the outputs are valid.

To assess incoming levels of expertise, the SMEs completed an on-line test of measures of central tendency used in conjunction with Stat Lady. The test assesses knowledge and skills related to all CEs contained within the Stat Lady curriculum (a total of 127 CEs). Our experts required between 1-1.5 hours to complete the test (no time limits were imposed), and scores ranged from 71.3% to 87.5%. Ideally, however, expert scores would have been in the 90% range. Following the test, each expert completed the Decompose portion of DNA.

2.2   Analysis and Results

The output from DNA comes in two forms: (a) Microsoft Access database of CE records, and (b) graphical array of the hierarchical knowledge structure. However, because the focus of this DNA evaluation was on the Decompose module, only the CE databases were analyzed for the consistency assessment.

We used the Stat Lady database of curriculum elements as the basis for comparing completeness and consistency of output among the SMEs. A few example CEs from Stat Lady include knowing: the notation for sample size (N) and summation (Σ), the steps involved in the computation of the mean when all frequencies are 1, and the location of the mean within a negatively-skewed distribution relative to the median and mode. In total, 78 CEs from this particular Stat Lady module were appropriate for the topic of analysis (i.e., measures of central tendency).

The first stage of analysis involved assessing the contents of each SME database. We created a spreadsheet that included a column listing all Stat Lady CEs, as well as three columns representing our SMEs' data. We then placed a "1" next to the Stat Lady CE to indicate that the SME did, in fact, include it in his or her decomposition and a "0" to denote its absence. Partial credit was also assigned for some CEs. For example, if there was a 3-step procedure, and an expert only reported 2 of the 3 steps, we assigned a value of .67 for that CE. And finally, there were some instances where a SME delineated a CE that was not present in the benchmark listing. Those instances were noted, but not included in the current analysis.

How well do the experts capture the benchmark curriculum? Our three SMEs matched the Stat Lady database 25%, 49% and 23% respectively. Further, each required 285, 170, and 100 minutes to complete DNA. One expert (SME-2) was clearly more in line with Stat Lady than the others, producing her array of CEs in less than 3 hours of decomposition time. The outputs produced by all three experts were subsequently combined to determine the degree of total overlap with the benchmark. Results showed that 62% of the Stat Lady CEs were delineated by at least one of our three experts. Thus, the agreement between the aggregate and benchmark data showed that we can capture 62% of the CEs present in an existing database in a reasonable amount of time (i.e., approximately 9 hours, the total of all time required by the 3 experts).

With regard to our benchmark CEs, some of them were reported by more than one expert, while others were omitted completely. The duplicated CEs included definitions of the Mean, Median, and Mode, as well as the basic steps required in determining the values of each of these measures of central tendency. Other knowledge bits specified by multiple experts related to information about distribution types and relevant notations. Benchmark elements that were omitted by all three experts included the specification of: (a) particular types of distributions (e.g., leptokurtic), (b) the location of the central tendency measures within distributions, and (c) different ways to compute measures of central tendency (e.g., finding the Median when N is odd versus even).

These data provide preliminary information about the efficacy of DNA as a knowledge elicitation tool. That is, given limited direction via one introductory letter of expectations for the decomposition of the domain and minimal guidance in use of the DNA program, experts appear to be able to use the tool to efficiently explicate their knowledge structures. Moreover, the obtained data are consistent with an existing curriculum. Thus we are gaining confidence that our tool has potential value as an aid to the bottleneck in ITS development.

3 Summary and Discussion

This paper describes an ongoing effort to develop a knowledge-elicitation tool called DNA, to be used by subject-matter experts across a variety of domains. We also describe an exploratory test of the effectiveness and efficiency of the program. Preliminary results show that DNA can produce valid and reliable data within reasonable amounts of time. This has direct implications for streamlining the ITS development process, previously defined as the bottleneck in developing automated instructional systems. In addition, given these data were obtained from individuals who are not "statisticians" suggests that DNA can be used by persons varying in levels of expertise.

There are several key features of DNA that, we believe, make this a viable alternative to current and costly knowledge-elicitation techniques. That is, it is automated, uses a hybrid representational scheme, provides an interplay between elicitation and organization of evolving knowledge structures, and is based on an effective instructional design framework (SMART; [12]).

In general, DNA is a computer program that automates the interview, transcription, and organization processes. This automation allowed us to obtain data simply by giving each expert the program along with a short letter explaining the goals of the curriculum. Thus automation obviates the need for transcribing lengthy interviews. Additionally, experts are able to explicate and organize their knowledge within the same elicitation session, translating into expected savings of time and money without sacrificing accuracy. This will be examined in future studies.

DNA's applicability is enhanced because it elicits, and then allows SMEs to graphically represent, a range of knowledge types. Specifically, the Network module can produce a conceptual graph that is a hybrid between a production-rule (or GOMS-type) structure and a semantic net. The result is that this hybrid representational scheme enables DNA to obtain both procedural- and conceptual-flavored curricula, promoting applicability across multiple topics.

Another design feature of DNA is its compatibility with an empirically validated instructional framework (i.e., SMART; [12]). First, DNA's Network module empowers the SME with tools to create a complete hierarchical structuring. The SME can create and manipulate CEs, as well as establish links between them and specify their relationships. An accurate representation of the knowledge structure directly affects the efficacy of the expert model used in an ITS, and thus learning. Specifically, SMART relies on information present in hierarchical-knowledge structures (e.g., parent/child relations) to manage instruction and remediation. Second, DNA's Decompose module's what, how, and why questions map onto the instructional framework of symbolic, procedural, and conceptual knowledge types embodied by SMART. Specifically, SMART relies on these knowledge types to provide differential instruction and remediation. For instance, procedural knowledge is instructed within a problem-solving context, while conceptual knowledge may use analogies for instruction. Therefore, DNA's capacity to identify different knowledge types facilitates SMART's management of more customized instruction.

In conclusion, the results from this preliminary evaluation are encouraging. In a relatively short amount of time and with minimal resource cost, DNA (the Decompose module) was able to elicit more than 60% of the curricular elements that are in place in an extant tutor. Our initial question for this paper concerned whether, indeed, DNA can extract comprehensive and reasonable knowledge from experts. Results suggest that the general approach implemented by DNA works to produce valid data that could potentially serve as the basis for curriculum development. Future studies will examine DNA's efficiency relative to standard knowledge elicitation techniques. Additional questions we will explore include, among others: (a) Can DNA be used across a broad range of domains? (b) Is it differentially effective in eliciting symbolic, procedural, or conceptual knowledge elements? and (c) Do differing levels of expertise result in data structures that vary in kind, rather than simply quantity? In short, future development and research will focus on identifying where we have and have not succeeded in our aim to uncork one of the main bottlenecks in ITS development.

References

1. Polson, M. C., & Richardson, J. J.: Foundations of Intelligent Tutoring Systems. Lawrence Erlbaum Associates, New Jersey (1988)
2. Shute, V. J., & Psotka, J.: Intelligent Tutoring Systems: Past, Present, and Future. In: Jonassen, D. (ed.): Handbook of Research on Educational Communications and Technology: A project of the Association for Educational Communication. Macmillan, New York (1996) 570-600
3. Anderson, J. R.: The Expert Module. In: Polson, M. C., Richardson, J. J. (eds.): Foundations of Intelligent Tutoring Systems. Lawrence Erlbaum Associates New Jersey (1988) 21-50
4. Shute, V. J., Torreano, L. A., & Willis, R. E.: Cognitive Task Analysis: Towards an Automated, Powerful Tool. In: Lajoie, S. (ed.): Computers as Cognitive Tools, Vol. 2. Lawrence Erlbaum Associates, New Jersey (in press)
5. Ryder, J. M., & Redding, R. E.: Integrating Cognitive Task Analysis Into Instructional Systems Development. Educational Technology Research and Development 41 (1993) 75-96
6. Nisbett, R. E., & Wilson, T. D.: Telling More Than We Can Know: Verbal Reports on Mental Processes. Psychological Review 8 (1977) 231-259
7. Card, S., Moran, T. P., & Newell, A.: The Psychology of Human-Computer Interaction. Lawrence Erlbaum Associates New Jersey (1983)
8. Shraagen, J. M. C., Chipman, S. E., Shute, V. J., Annett, J., Strub, M., Sheppard, C., Ruisseau, J. Y., & Graff, N.: State-of-the-Art Review of Cognitive Task Analysis Techniques. Deliverable Report of RSG.27 on Cognitive Task Analysis NATO Defense Research Group (Panel 8/RSG.27). TNO Human Factors Research Institute Group: Information Processing (1997)
9. Williams, K. E.: The Development of an Automated Cognitive Task Analysis and Modeling Process for Intelligent Tutoring System Development. Contract final report on N00014-97-J-5-1500. Manpower Personnel and Training Program, Office of Naval Research (1993)
10. Gordon, S. E., Schmierer, K. A., & Gill, R. T.: Conceptual Graph Analysis: Knowledge Acquisition For Instructional System Design. Human Factors 35 (1993) 459-481
11. Shute, V. J., Gawlick, L. A., & Lefort, N. K.: Stat Lady [Unpublished computer program]. Brooks Air Force Base, TX: Armstrong Laboratory (1996)
12. Shute, V. J.: SMART: Student modeling approach for responsive tutoring. User Modeling and User-Adapted Interaction 5 (1995) 1-44

Evaluating Subject Matter Experts' Learning and Use of an ITS Authoring Tool

Brenda M. Wenzel, Mary T. Dirnberger, Pat Y. Hsieh, Tom J. Chudanov, and
Henry M. Halff

Mei Technology Corporation, 8930 Fourwinds Dr, Suite 450, San Antonio, TX 78239,
USA
{brenda, mary, pat, tom, henry}@meitx.com

Abstract. Because ITSs offer knowledge-based instruction, ITS authoring shells can use knowledge acquisition systems to bring courseware development within the reach of subject-matter experts unskilled in instructional design and development. The Experimental Advanced Instructional Design Advisor (XAIDA), a simple ITS shell, was evaluated in a study of 17 Air Force medical-technician trainers. The study examined XAIDA's learnability, usability, and acceptability to the participants using a one-week combined training and evaluation program. All participants were able to produce courseware using XAIDA. Measures of cognitive structure indicated that their conception of XAIDA's features became more similar to that of an expert as the result of training. Performance tests, skill ratings and usability ratings indicated that XAIDA is both usable and learnable. Participant's attitudes were generally positive except at a point when training required a difficult cognitive shift. Attitudes remained focused throughout training on personal and low-level concerns, indicating the participants were not likely to be early adapters of the technology. The results have implications for the deployment of ITS shells in operational environments.

1   Introduction

This paper concerns the oft-neglected potential of Intelligent Tutoring System (ITS) development shells [2] [16] to bring Interactive Courseware (ICW) development within the reach of those unskilled in instructional design and development. In particular, the paper describes the evaluation of one ITS shell for use by Subject-Matter Experts (SMEs). The shell evaluated was the Experimental Advanced Instructional Design Advisor (XAIDA) [11], and the evaluation investigated its use by instructors, supervisors, and program directors in an Air Force organization (the 383rd Training Squadron (TRS) at Sheppard Air Force Base) responsible for training medical technicians

The work is particularly relevant the deployment of ITS authoring shells since XAIDA is a knowledge-based system that actually preempts the instructional design process. Thus, unlike users conventional authoring system, who specify *instructional procedures*, XAIDA developers use a knowledge-acquisition system to specify *subject-matter knowledge*. The evaluation described here addresses the learnability, usability, and acceptability of this approach as embodied in XAIDA.

1.1   XAIDA

XAIDA is a prototype computer system that supports the development and delivery of ICW. XAIDA was designed for use by Subject Matter Experts (SMEs) with no pre-existing skills in instructional design or computer-based training. XAIDA was developed under the sponsorship of the Air Force Research Laboratory [10] [20] [21].

XAIDA, in the version (5.1) evaluated here, addresses two aspects of maintenance training, a system's *physical characteristics* and its *theory of operation*. Each of these aspects is addressed with a separate transaction shell [14] consisting of a knowledge representation system, a knowledge acquisition system called *Develop*, and an instructional delivery system called *Deliver*. Instructional materials such as multimedia can be attached to particular parts of the knowledge structure. A brief description of each shell, with an emphasis on Develop, follows. A more complete description can be found in [11].

1.1.1   Physical Characteristics

Knowledge representation and instructional Delivery. Physical characteristics knowledge is represented as a semantic network describing a system, its parts and their locations, and other attributes of the system and its parts. Deliver provides a browser for the network and an ITS-directed system for practicing recall of the knowledge.

Knowledge acquisition. Develop is a collection of WYSIWYG and form-based editors for the semantic network and instructional materials. The main steps in authoring include entering the part structure of the system using an outline editor, selecting pictures of the system and each part and designating the locations of subparts, associating multimedia resources with each part, entering author-defined attributes of each part (e.g., their functions), and fine-tuning the behavior of the ITS.

1.1.2   Theory of Operation

Knowledge representation and instructional delivery. The theory of operation shell teaches students to reason about a system's behavior under specified conditions. The conditions and behaviors are represented as *variables*. A set of *rules* relating variables supports reasoning about their values. In addition to variables and rules, authors designate particularly salient sets of conditions called *cases*, that are used to illustrate device behavior. Deliver for theory-of-operation provides a browsers for cases and variables, an exploratory environment in which students can build their own cases, and an ITS for practice in reasoning about device behavior.

Knowledge acquisition. Like the physical characteristics shell, the theory of operation shell provides a collection of editors for entering specifying variables, rules, and cases. Authoring is a two-step process. In the first step, the author creates each variable and specifies its possible values or the rules that determine its values. In the second step, the developer creates the cases by specifying values of input variables for each.

2   XAIDA Developer Training Program

2.1   Participants

Nineteen Air Force military personnel from the 383 TRS at Sheppard AFB were scheduled to receive XAIDA training. The participants possessed subject matter expertise in the medical field. Two participants dropped out, due to conflicts in their schedules. Of those who participated, 17 percent were instructors, 53 percent served in supervisory roles, and 29 percent were training coordinators or program directors. Results of a survey administered on the first day of training indicated that participants were, for the most part, familiar with computers, Windows, and Microsoft Word, less familiar with graphic programs and unfamiliar with authoring systems.

2.2   Training Objectives

The primary training objective was to enable participants to effectively use physical characteristics Develop, but all were given the option to learn how to develop XAIDA lessons that teach theory of operation. Only four exercised this option. As the consequence, this report focuses on the physical characteristics shell.

2.3   Training Materials

Materials used in physical characteristics training included a pre-training handout on the type of lesson materials and multimedia to bring to training, example XAIDA physical characteristics lessons, and two tutorials—one for a specific example, the other more general.

The pre-training handout described the type of text, graphics, and other media needed for lesson development. Participants were encouraged to assemble these materials on a topic of interest to them. Participants used the materials to develop courseware on a topic of their choosing during training. Advantages of this approach include increased participant motivation through an increase in the relevance of training and the production of usable courseware during training.

2.4   Training Design

The training design incorporated practical findings from the training literature [3] [4] [12] [15]. Training was conducted in an open learning setting where interaction was encouraged. A minimalist training approach was employed [4]. Accordingly, we (a) left the amount of reading from manuals to the users discretion, (b) coordinated demonstrations, group discussions, and hands-on participation, (c) were prepared to deal with user errors, (d) focused on real tasks and lesson development activities, and (e) kept motivation high by allowing the participants to choose the topics for their lessons.

3   Evaluation Techniques and Results

The evaluation focused on XAIDA's learnability, usability, and acceptability. Multiple evaluation techniques, *viz.*, self-report, task check-list, open-ended responses, and cognitive assessment, were used to address these issues [12]. Each technique used in the evaluation is presented next along with its result.

3.1   Abilities Assessment

The most direct evidence that the training objective was achieved is the 17 different XAIDA physical characteristics lessons successfully developed during training:

Air Force specialty codes	Medical surgical terminology
Blood pressure diagnostic equipment	Nursing inservice
EKG machine	Nursing skills assessment
Emergency response guidebook	Patient transport
Flexible gastrointestinal endoscope	Sager traction splint
Human heart	Six part folder
IV setup	Skeletal system
Mayo tray setup	Soft tissue injuries
	Surgical attire

3.2   Skills Assessment

Ratings of self-perceived computer skills, including newly acquired skills using XAIDA, were taken across the five-day training period. Figure 1 presents participants' perceived levels of expertise using XAIDA *Develop* across the five training days. Participants rated their expertise on a 10-point scale where "1" represented a *novice* user and "10" represented an *expert* user. Statistically significant increases in perceived levels of expertise were found at the end of each subsequent training day. On average participants rated themselves 4.5 points higher on the 10-point scale after training than before training ($t(14) = 8.4$, $p < .0001$).

A measure of general computer skills, including those pertinent to using XAIDA, was administered immediately before and after training. Ratings were made on a four point scale where "1" represented *none*, "2" represented *poor*, "3" represented *good*, and "4" represented *expert*. Table 1 shows the average ratings for the various skills before and after training. Ratings of skill levels using XAIDA Develop and Deliver increase significantly ($p < .0001$) during training. The amount of incidental learning that occurred as a function of using XAIDA is apparent in the significant ($p < .05$) increases in the self-reported levels of skill involved with general computer use-- managing files and directories, typing, creating graphics, and using a database. These skills are needed to develop courseware with XAIDA.

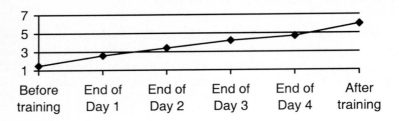

Fig. 1. Mean ratings of XAIDA develop proficiency before, during, and after training. ($N = 15$).

Table 1. Mean ratings of general computer skills before and after training

Skill	Before	After
Using XAIDA Develop	1.2	2.8
Using XAIDA Deliver	1.8	3.1
Creating Graphics	1.6	2.5
Managing Files	1.8	2.5
Managing Directories	1.8	2.5
Typing	2.8	3.1
Word Processing	2.9	3.1
Programming	1.3	1.5
Creating Video	1.3	1.4
Scanning	1.5	1.6
Using DOS	1.9	1.9
Using a Database	1.6	2.3

3.3   Cognitive Assessment of Procedural Knowledge

Drawing on techniques for assessing the growth of cognitive structures during learning [7] [12] [17] [18] and during procedural learning in particular [5] [17], we conducted a structural analysis of participants' knowledge of XAIDA commands using a technique known as Pathfinder [19]. The input to Pathfinder is pair-wise relatedness ratings between concepts in the domain being studied. Participants were asked to judge the *temporal* relatedness between 14 computer commands (e.g., select question type) used to develop physical characteristics courseware with XAIDA. Relatedness ratings were collected from participants before and after formal training with the physical characteristics shell. Relatedness ratings were also obtained from an XAIDA expert to serve as the standard to which the participants' ratings were compared.

We used two measures of cognitive structure to assess the effects of training, both based on participant-expert comparison. First, the average correlation between participant and expert ratings increased from 0.14 before training to 0.46 after training ($t_{15} = 7.1$, $p < .0001$). Second, we used Pathfinder to identify the 13 most interrelated pairs in each data set and computed the overlap between the expert's 13 most related and each participant's 13 most related. The average overlap, expressed as a proportion, was 0.20 before training and 0.32 after training; the difference was significant ($t_{15} = 4.7$, $p < .0001$).

3.4   Performance Assessment

Participants' skills and abilities using XAIDA Develop were assessed by examining their performance on a set of 13 tasks requiring particular manipulations of a specially constructed XAIDA lesson. For instance, task #3 involved the replacement of one graphic for a part with another graphic.

On average participants completed the Navigation Task in 33.8 minutes (range 17-47). The 13 tasks were collapsed into four categories: lesson content, background graphics, practice, and general navigation. The highest average error rates (38 percent) occurred when participants interacted with the content editors. The majority of content editing errors were due to confusion concerning the storage of multimedia resources and their assignment to lesson elements. Low average error rates occurred when tasks involved navigating from one section of the lesson to another (8 percent) or tuning practice exercises (7 percent).

3.5   Attitude Assessment

Acceptance and the willingness of personnel to adopt new technology is important to an organization planning to successfully integrate the technology [6]. Therefore, an exploration was made of participant attitudes toward XAIDA. For the majority of participants, their first exposure to XAIDA was on the first day of training.

Participants responded to an open-ended item asking for their impressions of XAIDA physical characteristics shell before training and at the end of each training day. Responses were coded into categories identified in earlier research to reflect users' concerns when adopting educational innovations [1] [8] [9]. The seven categories and examples of coding criteria follow:

1. *Awareness*-- have heard of it, interested in the area,
2. *Information*-- what are the requirements, what are the possible applications,
3. *Personal*-- time and energy required, how my role will change,
4. *Management*-- coordination of tasks and people, conflict between interests and responsibilities,
5. *Consequences*-- how it affects training,
6. *Integration* --coordinating efforts with others, help others with the innovation, and
7. *Refocusing*--revise the approach, modify based on use.

Concerns of those willing to adopt innovative technology tend to fall into the fourth, fifth, sixth, and seventh categories. Responses were further coded as positive, negative, or neutral concerns. Results are presented in Figures 2 and 3.

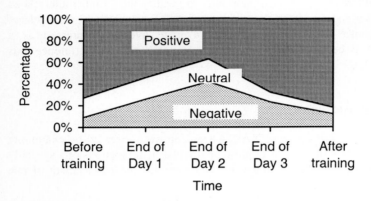

Fig. 2. Proportion of comments by valence and training day.

As indicated in Figure 2, the majority of participants expressed a positive impression of XAIDA. Before XAIDA training began, 73 percent of the statements made expressed a positive interest in XAIDA. At the end of training, 82 percent of the statements made were positive. However, at the end of the second day, when participants were working on developing courseware within their areas of expertise the proportion of positive statements decreased to around 40 percent.

Of particular interest in these data are attitudes toward XAIDA at the end of Day 2, when negative comments peaked. Participants spent Day 2 developing lessons on topics they had chosen. While developing their own lessons, participants were faced with the practical problem of thinking about their lesson topics in a manner that was acceptable to XAIDA. Problems facing these novice users were evidenced in their *Personal* concerns-- "My understanding of what I thought was fairly clear is not, ..."

Although attitudes were generally positive at the end of training, only thirty percent of the statements made at the end of training were classified in the higher level categories of *Management, Consequences, Integration,* and *Refocusing.* The other 70 percent were classified in the lower level categories of *Awareness, Information,* and *Personal.* Research suggests that staff of the 383rd TRS attending training would not be early adopters of XAIDA [1] [8]. This turned out to be the case. Only one of the 17 participants from the 383rd TRS went on to complete the courseware that was begun in training. That lesson was evaluated and found to be highly effective in a distributed training setting. [22].

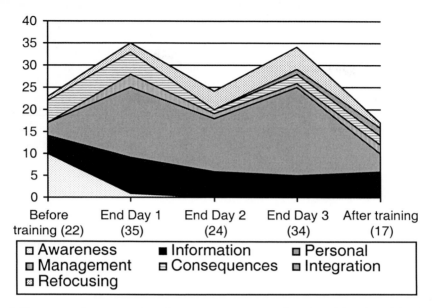

Fig. 3. Frequency of comments in each concern category as a function of time in training. Note: Comments are specific to the XAIDA physical characteristics shell.

3.6   Usability Assessment

A questionnaire, referred to as the Editor Usability Questionnaire, was developed to assess the ease of use and comprehensibility of a number of XAIDA's critical editing capabilities. The instrument also gave users an opportunity to provide comments and suggestions on each of these capabilities. The Editor Usability Questionnaire was administered at the end of formal training with the physical characteristic shell. Most of the features received high ratings, but ratings for several indicated a need for improvement. These data have provided valuable feedback to the design team.

Discussion

This study concerns the potential of ITS authoring shells to bring ICW development within the reach of SMEs otherwise unskilled in instructional design and development. We approached the issue by examining how such SMEs interact with a shell that preempts instructional design so that the author's role is that of specifying content knowledge and instructional materials.

The results indicate that the shell-based approach, in this implementation, allows SMEs to develop usable courseware within a very short period of time. Although attitudes towards the approach were, in general, positive, these concerns remained focused on low level issues so that the participants were not prepared to introduce the approach into their organization. In addition, when, during training the participants had reorganize their thinking in order to deal with the development of their own lessons, attitudes became considerably less positive.

These results suggest that the knowledge-based approach to instructional development does indeed deliver on its promise of making ICW development both easy and fast. The minimalist approach to training worked well, in general, but could benefit from specific attention to cognitive barriers encountered in mastering the knowledge-based approach. Finally, successful deployment of the approach in an organization requires that the entire organization, and its corps of early adopters, be prepared for and committed to the technology before implementation. See [23] for a description of an XAIDA deployment in which these measures were taken.

Acknowledgements

The research reported here was sponsored by the Air Force Research Laboratory under Contracts F1624-93-C-5002 and F41624-96-C-5006. The opinions expressed in this paper are those of the author and do not necessarily reflect those of the Air Force.

References

1.   Bailey, D. B., & Palsha, S. A. (1992). Qualities of stages of concern questionnaire and implications for educational innovations. *The Journal of Educational Research, 85,* 226-232.
2.   Bloom, C., Linton, F., & Bell, B. (1997). Using evaluation in the design of an intelligent tutoring system. *Journal of Interactive Learning Research, 8,* 235-276.
3.   Cannon-Bowers, J. A., Tannenbaum, S. I., Salas, E., & Converse, S. A. (1991). Toward an integration of training theory and technique. *Human Factors, 33,* 281-292.
4.   Carroll, J. M. (1984). Minimalist Training. *Datamation,* November, 125-136.
5.   Cooke, N. J. (1994). Varieties of knowledge elicitation techniques. *International Journal of Human-Computer Studies, 41,* 801-849.
6.   Geoghegan, W. H. (1994). Whatever happened to instructional technology? Paper presented at the 22nd Annual Conference of the International Business Schools Computing Association. Baltimore, Maryland.
7.   Glaser, R. (1983). Expertise and learning: How do we think about instructional processes now that we have discovered knowledge structures? In E. Klaher and K. Kotovsky (Eds.) Complex information processing: The impact of Herb Simon. Lawrence Erlbaum: Hillsdale, NJ.
8.   Hall, G. E. (1979). The concerns-based approach to facilitating change. *Educational Horizons, 4,* 202-208.
9.   Hall, G. E., George, A. A., & Rutherford, W. L. (1986). *Measuring stages of concern about the innovation: A manual for the user of SoC Questionnaire.* Austin, TX: Southwest Educational Development Laboratory.
10.   Hickey, A. E., Spector, J. M., & Muraida, D. J. (1991). *Design specifications for the advanced instructional design advisor (AIDA)* (Vols 1 & 2) (AL-TR-1991-0085). Brooks

AFB, TX: Technical Report for the Air Force Armstrong Laboratory, Human Resources Directorate.

11. Hsieh, P. Y, Halff, H. M., & Redfield, C. L. (1996). *Four easy pieces: Development systems for knowledge-based generative instruction.* (Manuscript submitted for publication).

12. Kraiger, J., Ford, K., & Salas, E. (1993). Application of cognitive, skill-based, and affective theories of learning outcomes to new methods of training evaluation. *Journal of Applied Psychology, 78,* 311-328.

13. Kraiger, J., Salas, E. & Cannon-Bowers, J. (1995). Measuring knowledge organization as a method of assessing learning during training. *Human Factors, 37,* 804-816.

14. Merrill, M. D. (1993). An integrated model for automating instructional design and delivery. In J. M. Spector, M. C. Polson, and D. J. Muraida (Eds.) *Automating Instructional Design: Concepts and Issues* (pp. 147-190). Englewood Cliffs, NJ: Educational Technology Publications.

15. Palmiter, S., & Elkerton, J. (1993). Animated Demonstrations for learning procedural computer-based tasks. *Human-Computer Interaction, 8,* 193-216.

16. Redfield, C. (November, 1997) *AAAI Fall Symposium on ITS Authoring Tools* (Technical Report FS-97-01). Cambridge, MA, AAAI.

17. Rowe, A., Cooke, N., Hall, & Halgren, (1996). Toward an on-line knowledge assessment methodology: Building on the relationship between knowing and doing. *Journal of Experimental Psychology: Applied, 2,* 31-47.

18. Royer, J. M., Cisero, C. A., & Carlo, M. S. (1993). Techniques and procedures for assessing cognitive skills. *Review of Educational Research, 63,* 201-243.

19. Schvaneveldt, R. W. (Ed.). (1990). *Pathfinder associative networks: Studies in knowledge organization.* Norwood, NJ: Ablex.

20. Spector, J. M. (1990). *Designing and developing an advanced instructional design advisor.* (AFHRL-TP-90-52). Brooks AFB: TX: Technical Paper for the Training Systems Division of the Air Force Human Resources Laboratory.

21. Spector, J. M., Polson, M. C., & Muraida, D. J., Eds. (1993). *Automating Instructional Design: Concepts and Issues.* Englewood Cliffs, NJ: Educational Technology Publications.

22. Wenzel, B. M., Dirnberger, M. T., & Ellis, R. (1997). Evaluation of the effectiveness of distributed interactive multimedia courseware for emergency medical technician training. Manuscript submitted for publication.

23. Wenzel, B. M., Keeney, C., Licklider, J., Roberts, J. D., & Reyna, H. (1997). *Evaluation of the courseware developed and delivered using the Experimental Advanced Instructional Design Advisor.* Presentation at the annual meeting of the Texas Association of College Technical Editors. Austin, Texas.

Component-Based Construction of a Science Learning Space

Kenneth R. Koedinger, Daniel D. Suthers,[1] and Kenneth D. Forbus

Human-Computer	Information and	Institute for the
Interaction Institute	Computer Sciences	Learning Sciences
Carnegie Mellon University	University of Hawaii	Northwestern University

E-mail: koedinger@cs.cmu.edu, suthers@hawaii.edu, forbus@ils.nwu.edu

Abstract. We present a vision for learning environments, called Science Learning Spaces, that are rich in engaging content and activities, provide constructive experiences in scientific process skills, and are as instructionally effective as a personal tutor. A Science Learning Space combines three independent software systems: 1) lab/field simulations in which experiments are run and data is collected, 2) modeling/construction tools in which data representations are created, analyzed and presented, and 3) tutor agents that provide just-in-time assistance in higher order skills like experimental strategy, representational tool choice, conjecturing, and argument. We believe that achieving this ambitious vision will require collaborative efforts facilitated by a component-based software architecture. We have created a feasibility demonstration that serves as an example and a call for further work toward achieving this vision. In our demonstration, we combined 1) the Active Illustrations lab simulation environment, 2) the Belvedere argumentation environment, and 3) a model-tracing Experimentation Tutor Agent. We illustrate student interaction in this Learning Space and discuss the requirements, advantages, and challenges in creating one.

The Science Learning Space Vision

Imagine an Internet filled with possibility for student discovery. A vast array of simulations are available to explore any scientific field you desire. Easy-to-use data representation and visualization tools are at your fingertips. As you work, intelligent tutor agents are watching silently in the background, available at any time to assist you as you engage in scientific inquiry practices: experimentation, analysis, discovery, argumentation. This is our vision for Science Learning Spaces. Table 1 summarizes how this vision contrasts with typical classroom experience.

Table 1. What Science Learning Spaces Have to Offer

	Typical Science Class	Science Learning Space Vision
Content	Lectures, fixed topics, fixed pace, focus on facts	Vast options, student choice and pace, focus on scientific process
Activity	Inquiry process hampered by mundane procedure & long waits	Simulations speed time, leave technique lessons for later
Tools	Paper and pencil	Data representation & argument construction
Assistance	Limited, 1 teacher for 30 students	Automated 1:1 assistance of tutor agents
Assessment	Large grain, limited assessment-instruction continuity	Tutor agents monitor student development at action level

---

1 Work performed while at Learning Research and Development Center, University of Pittsburgh

A Science Learning Space can be created by coordinating software components of three types: 1) *lab/field simulations* in which experiments are run and data is collected, 2) *modeling/construction tools* in which data representations are created, analyzed and presented, and 3) *tutor agents* that provide just-in-time assistance in higher order skills like experimental strategy, representational tool choice, conjecturing, and argument. Although the full Science Learning Space vision is currently out of reach, we have created a demonstration of its feasibility. This demonstration serves as a model for future work and a call for further community authoring toward achieving this vision.

The Need for Collaborative Component-Based Development

Research in intelligent learning environments typically involves designing and implementing an entire system from scratch. Time and resources spent on software engineering is taken away from the education and research the software is designed to support. Today the typical solution is for research labs to work within the context of an in-house software investment, evolving each new system from previous work. This makes replication and sharing more difficult and can lead to maintenance and deployment difficulties as restrictive platform requirements accumulate over time.

This situation is growing intolerable, and so recently there has been a surge of interest in architectures and frameworks for interoperable and component-based systems [Ritter & Koedinger, 1997; Roschelle & Kaput, 1995; Suthers & Jones, 1997]. This has led to a number of successful workshops on the topic (e.g., http://advlearn.lrdc.pitt.edu/its-arch/), the emergence of several standards efforts specifically targeted to advanced educational technology (e.g., www.manta.ieee.org/p1484/), and new repositories for educational object components (e.g., trp.research.apple.com). These efforts gain leverage from the rise of interactive Web technology and its associated emphasis on standards-based interoperability. Solutions for component-based systems are arriving, in the form of shared communication protocols, markup languages, and metadata formats. Although the component-based solutions developed to date are useful, they are inadequate for those building component-based *intelligent* learning environments in which the components must respond to the meaning of the content as well as its form and presentation. We see the development of techniques for sharing *semantics* across components and applications to be a critical research direction for the field.

Recently we conducted a demonstration of the feasibility of integrating three different, independently developed components. Two of the components were complete intelligent learning environments in their own right: Active Illustrations [Forbus, 1997] enable learners to experiment with simulations of scientific phenomena, and to receive explanations about the causal influences behind the results [Forbus & Falkenhainer 1990; 1995]. Belvedere [Suthers & Jones, 1997; Suthers *et al.,* 1997] provides learners with an "evidence mapping" facility for recording relationships between statements labeled as "hypotheses" and "data". A Scientific Argumentation Coach [Paolucci *et al.,* 1996] guides students to seek empirical support, consider alternate hypotheses, and avoid confirmation biases, among other things. The third component was an instance of a model-tracing Tutor Agent [Ritter & Koedinger, 1997] that contains a cognitive model of general experimentation and argumentation process skills. This "Experimentation Tutor Agent" dynamically assesses student performance and is available to provide students with just-in-time feedback and context-sensitive advice. Our Learning Space Demonstration took place in the context of meetings of ARPA's Computer Aided Education and Training Initiative program contractors. Using a MOO as a communication infrastructure, we demonstrated a scenario in which a student poses a hypothesis in the Belvedere evidence-mapping environment, uses the simulation to test that hypothesis in the Active Illustration environment and sends the results back to Belvedere for integration in the evidence map. Throughout this activity the Experimentation Tutor Agent was monitoring student performance and was available to provide assistance.

From this experience we abstracted the notion of a Science Learning Space. In our demonstration, the Space was filled with Active Illustrations as the lab/field simulation component, Belvedere as a modeling/construction tool, and the Experimentation Tutor Agent and Argumentation Coach in tutor roles. In this paper we discuss how interoperability of these components was achieved through the use of Translator components that enable communication between existing functional components with little or no modification to them. We begin by examining the constraints that developing intelligent learning environments impose on the nature and types of components and their interactions, focusing on the importance of semantic interoperability. We then describe the demonstration configuration in detail, showing how it exploits a limited form of semantic interoperability. Finally, we reflect on the requirements, advantages, and future directions in creating Science Learning Spaces.

Components for Intelligent Learning Environments

Component-based development has a number purported economic and engineering benefits. Component-based systems are more economical to build because prior components can be re-used, saving time for new research and development efforts. They are easier to maintain due to their modular design and easier to extend because the underlying frameworks that make component-based development possible in the first place also make it easier to add new components. We can also expect better quality systems as developers can focus their efforts on their specialty, whether in simulation, tool, or tutor development.

However, there is a deeper reason why we believe component-based educational software is important: It will enable us to construct, by composition, the multiple functionalities needed for a pedagogically complete learning environment. Various genres of computer-based learning environments have had their advocates. Each provides a valuable form of support for learning, but are insufficient in themselves. Yet today, the high development costs associated with building each type of environment leads to the deployment of systems with only a small subset of desirable functionality.

For example, microworlds and simulations enable students to directly experience the behavior of dynamic systems and in some cases to change that behavior, experimenting with alternate models. These environments are consistent with the notion that deeper learning takes place when learners construct their own knowledge through experience. However, simulations lack guidance: Taken alone, they provide no tools for the articulation and reflection on this knowledge and no learning agenda or intelligent assistance.

On the other hand, intelligent tutoring systems provide substantial guidance in the form of a learning agenda, modeling of expert behavior, and intelligence assistance. This form of guidance is particularly important in domains where the target knowledge is not an easy induction from interactions with the artifact or system of interest. In such domains, intelligent tutors can lead to dramatic, "one sigma", increases in student achievement [e.g., Koedinger, Anderson, Hadley, & Mark, 1997].

However, tutoring systems are themselves subject to the criticism. Emphasis on knowledge engineering usually leaves little time for careful design of performance tools to enhance pedagogical goals. Thus, there is a third need for representational tools for manipulating data, searching for patterns, or articulating and testing new knowledge. Spreadsheets, outliners, graphers, and other such tools provide representational guidance that help learners see certain patterns, express certain abstractions in concrete form, and discover new relationships. Representational tools can be designed based on cognitive analysis to address particular learning objectives [Koedinger, 1991; Reiser et al., 1991] and can function as "epistemic forms" [Collins & Ferguson, 1993] that afford desirable knowledge-building interactions. Yet representational tools provide only a subtle kind of guidance. As with simulations and microworlds, direct tutoring interventions are sometimes needed as well. Fortunately there is a double-synergy: Inspection of learners' representations and simulation actions can provide a tutor with valuable information about what kind of guidance is needed.

We believe that the ability to routinely synthesize new intelligent learning environments from off-the-shelf components that combine multiple functionalities rarely found today is sufficient justification for moving to a component-based development approach. The potential advantages of component-based systems must, of course, be weighed against their costs. Creating composable software components requires exposing enough of their internal representations, through carefully designed protocols, so that effective communication is possible. Doing this in ways that minimize communication overhead while maximizing reuse is a subtle design problem which can require substantial extra work.

A Feasibility Demonstration of a Science Learning Space

In this section we describe the Science Learning Space demonstration that we undertook. We begin with the learning activity that motivates our particular combination of tools; then we describe the underlying architecture and step through an example interaction scenario.

The Learning Activity: Scientific Inquiry

There is no point in combining components unless the learner benefits - in particular, the functionality provided by each component must contribute to the facilitation of effective learning interactions in some way. Consider scientific inquiry. Students have difficulty with the basic distinction between empirical observations and theoretical statements. They need to learn that theories are posed to explain and predict occurrences and that theories are evaluated with respect to how consistent they are with all of the relevant observed data. They need to seek relevant evidence, both confirming and disconfirming, perform observations, and conduct experiments to test hypotheses or to resolve theoretical arguments between hypotheses. Experimentation requires certain process skills, such as the strategy of varying one feature at a time. Evaluation of the results of experiments requires scientific argumentation skills. Thus, this is a learning problem that could benefit from (1) experimentation in simulation environments, aided by coaching based on a process model of effective experimentation; and (2) articulation of and reflection upon one's analysis of the relationships between hypotheses and evidence, aided by coaching based on principles of scientific argumentation.

In our demonstration scenario, we imagine a student engaging in an investigation of the climate of Venus. She starts by posing a plausible hypothesis that Venus is cold because its excessive cloud cover makes it so. Next, she uses the multiple tools and intelligent assistance of the Science Learning Space to record, test, revise and argue for this hypothesis.

The Implementation Architecture
We describe the abstract implementation architecture (see Figure 1) behind our demonstration as one illustration of how several technologies enable the construction of component-based systems. Our collaboration began with a Learning Space demonstration involving an Experimentation Tutor Agent and Active Illustration [Forbus, 1997] communicating through a Lambda-MOO derivative using the "MOO Communications Protocol". Forbus had already made use of the MOO for communication between the Active Illustration simulation engine and a simulation user interface (bottom right of Figure 1). A MOO was chosen as the infrastructure because its notion of persistent objects and multi-user design made it easy for participants in experiments (both human and software) to be in a shared environment despite being on different machines, often in different parts of the country. The open, ASCII-based MOO Communications Protocol made it easy to add a Tutor Agent to monitor student performance as the basis for providing context-sensitive assistance. Koedinger used the plug-in tutor agent architecture [Ritter & Koedinger, 1997] which employs a simple Translator component (small box upper right of Figure 1) to manage the communication between tools and tutor agents. The Translator watched for messages between the Simulation Interface and the Active Illustration server, extracted messages indicating relevant student actions, and translated these student actions into the "selection-action-input" form appropriate for semantic processing by the Tutor Agent's model-tracing engine.

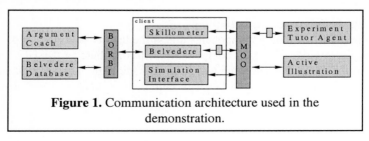

Figure 1. Communication architecture used in the demonstration.

Subsequently, the Belvedere system and Argumentation Coach were added (left side of Figure 1). Belvedere itself provides a communication architecture, described in Suthers & Jones [1997] and abstracted as "BORBI" in Figure 1. Integration of the Belvedere subsystem into the MOO required the addition of one translator component (the other small box in the figure): no modification to Belvedere itself was required. The translator watched the MOO for Hypothesis and Simulation Run objects sent by the Simulation Interface. When seen, these were converted to Belvedere Hypothesis and Data objects and placed in the user's "in-box" for consideration.

Learning Scenario

Returning to our student who is thinking about planetary climate, we illustrate a learning interaction scenario supported by our multi-application Learning Space. In the opening situation (Figure 2), the student has recorded in Belvedere's evidence-mapping facility the hypothesis that Venus is cold because it is cloudy. On the left are the Active Illustration simulation interface and the Tutor Agent's Skillometer showing initial estimates of the student's level of skill on several subskills. Next, Belvedere's Argumentation Coach suggests that the student find some evidence for this hypothesis (Figure 3). Since the student can't go to Venus to experiment, she decides to use an Active Illustration simulation of the Earth's atmosphere as an analog instead.

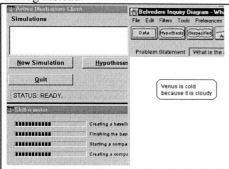

Figure 2. Opening situation: An initial hypothesis.

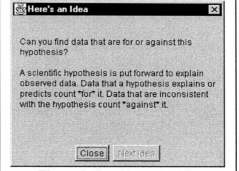

Figure 3. Coaching scientific argumentation

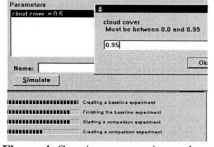

Figure 4. Creating an experimental run of the simulation.

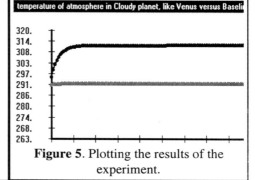

Figure 5. Plotting the results of the experiment.

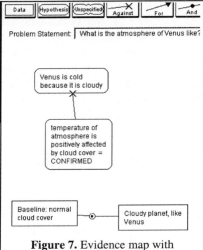

Figure 6. Making a new hypothesis in Active Illustration.

Figure 7. Evidence map with experimental results.

In the Active Illustration interface, the student runs a baseline simulation using normal cloud cover parameters for Earth. The Tutor Agent observes these events in the MOO and updates estimates of baseline experimentation skills (lower portion of Figure 4). Then the student constructs a comparison simulation by increasing the Earth's cloud cover to 95%, much more like Venus (Figure 4). If the student had attempted to change more than one parameter of the simulation, the Experimentation Tutor Agent would recognize this action as an instance of the change-more-than-one-variable bug (see Table 2), and would have generated a feedback message to prompt the student toward designing a more discriminating experiment. Having created baseline and comparison experiments, the student uses Active Illustration's plotting facility to show the results (Figure 5). To her surprise, Earth gets *hotter* when cloud cover increases. The student realizes that a new hypothesis is required. Using Active Illustration's hypothesis recording facility, the student creates the hypothesis that the temperature of the atmosphere is affected positively by cloud cover and marks it as confirmed (Figure 6).

The student then decides to send this hypothesis along with the results of the two experiments back to the Belvedere application. She does this by selecting these objects and clicking a "send to other tools" button. The objects are sent out on the MOO, where they are observed by the Belvedere-MOO Translator. It filters messages and translates hypothesis and data objects into Belvedere's representations and places them in Belvedere's "in-box". The in-box is a place where new information is kept until the student is ready to integrate it into the evidence map. The student selects information objects from the in-box and places them in her evidence map. At this point she uses Belvedere to construct the argument shown in Figure 7. The two experiments are connected with an "and" link and then connected to the hypothesis that temperature increases with cloud cover using an evidential "for" link. Finally, this experimentally derived hypothesis is used to argue against the original idea that Venus is cold because it is cloudy by making an evidential "against" link.

The Experimentation Tutor Agent is able to understand the semantics of the experiment and hypothesis objects because it observed the history of the creation of these objects in the Simulation. As a consequence, this agent can provide the student with advice on the semantics of the argument. If, for instance, the student were to try to use only the comparison experiment as evidence for the hypothesis, the agent can remediate this argumentation bug (see Table 2): "Just because the temperature was high with high cloud cover is not enough to argue for your hypothesis; you must also cite the contrasting baseline experiment where the temperature was lower with normal cloud cover."

Table 2. Domain-Independent Productions for Experiments and Argument

```
Change-more-than-one-variable-bug (Pre-conception)
IF  the  goal  is  to  discover  a  hypothesis  and  you  have  a  first
experiment
THEN change some variable values to create a second experiment

Change-one-variable
IF the goal is to discover a hypothesis
   and you have a baseline experiment
THEN change one variable value to create a comparison experiment

One-trial-generalization-bug (Pre-conception)
IF the goal is argue for hypothesis "The greater the <cloud cover>
   the higher the <atmospheric temperature>"
   and you did an experiment where <cloud cover> was high
   and the resulting <atmospheric temperature> was high
THEN argue the hypothesis is true by citing this experiment

Argue-from-controlled-comparison
IF the goal is argue for hypothesis "The greater the <cloud cover>
   the higher the <atmospheric temperature>"
   and you did two experiments, a baseline and comparison
   and in one <cloud cover> was low and <temp> was low
   and in the other <cloud cover> was higher and <temp> was higher
THEN argue the hypothesis is true by citing these two experiments
```

Semantic Interoperability for Constructive Learning Interactions

Since all three systems made reference to the same set of objects (e.g., experiments, data, hypotheses), it was critical that a shared semantics was achieved. Below we discuss some alternate solutions and their roles.

Shared Ontologies

One possible approach to achieving semantic interoperability is to have a common ontology of educational objects that each system accesses. Significant portions of our communications were in effect a process of negotiating an informal shared ontology. The process may have been more efficient and involved fewer misunderstandings if a standard ontology or even reference vocabulary were available and known to all.

However, while shared ontologies may be worthy goals in the long term, they require a high level of community consensus and standardization that is still well out of reach (if not in defining the standards, certainly in having them take hold). Furthermore, there is good reason to believe that multiple alternative representations of the same objects or concepts are not only inevitable, but useful. Different representations afford different kinds of processing. For example, the representation of an experiment in the simulation stores numerous simulation-related details whereas the Tutor Agent's representation of an experiment is at a more abstract level appropriate for reasoning with, rather than about, experiments.

Translators to Preserve Advantages of Alternative Representations

The use of Translator components allow developers of component systems to make their own representational decisions. Once these decisions have been made, developers can get together to identify the shared semantics and specify translators to implement them. It is not necessary to work out ahead of time the precise meaning and structure of all symbol structures in a shared ontology. The Translator components were critical to the relative ease in which we composed the three systems. Our composition task would not have been as easy, however, if Active Illustrations and Belvedere had not built from the start in an open client-server architecture. These tools were "recordable" and "scriptable" by the Tutor Agent [Ritter & Koedinger, 1997] and by each other. Unfortunately, too few office applications or educational objects are currently built in this open architecture.

Granularity and Persistence of Identity
The Active Illustrations simulation and Simulation Interface used the MOO to communicate in terms of the multiple parameter settings that define a simulation run or experimental trial, however, we wanted experimental trials to appear in Belvedere as single nodes in the evidence map. We needed a way to coordinate this difference in granularity while preserving the essential semantic identity of object representations as they are moved from tool to tool. This design problem ultimately led us to better understand how the software need for persistence of identity can sometimes be solved by addressing the learner's same need.

We initially considered solving this problem by using the Belvedere-MOO Translator to aggregate individual parameter setting and simulation events into "data" objects that record the results of a particular trial. These data objects would then appear automatically in Belvedere's in-box. However, focusing on the needs of the learner, we elected to follow a different approach for three major reasons. (1) Not all simulation runs will be informative enough to use. We wanted to avoid cluttering the in-box with many not so useful objects. (2) We wanted to encourage the learner to reflect on which runs were worth recording, by requiring that the learner make the decision of which to record. (3) The learner needs to make the connection between her experiences in the simulation environment and the representational objects that she manipulates in Belvedere. Hence the aggregated objects representing simulation runs should be created while still in the simulation environment and given visual identities recognizable to the learner, preferably by learner herself.

The Simulation Interface already enabled the user to provide textual labels for simulation runs and we took advantage of that. We modified the Simulation Interface to provide a facility for broadcasting labeled simulation summary objects to the MOO (and hence to the Belvedere in-box) thereby enabling the learner to select relevant results without leaving the simulation context. This example reveals one limitation of a pure "plug and play" approach to component based systems: Communication protocols cannot anticipate all future needs.

Conclusions

We described a case study of component-based construction of a *Science Learning Space*, consisting of a simulation tool (Active Illustrations), a modeling tool (Belvedere), and tutoring agents (the Experimentation Tutor Agent and Argumentation Coach). We discussed several approaches to reducing the effort required to "hook up" diverse components and demonstrated the value of sharing semantics between applications. Information objects created with particular semantic identities in Active Illustrations retained their identity in their treatment in Belvedere and its Argumentation Coach. Furthermore, the Experimentation Tutor Agent treated these objects as having the same semantics in both situations.

The Science Learning Space vision is to combine the pedagogical benefits of simulations, modeling tools, and intelligent assistance to support students in cycles of inquiry -- questioning, hypothesizing, modeling, reflecting and revising -- to both acquire new scientific content and to improve reasoning and learning skills. A major obstacle at this point is that too few developers are creating open components that are recordable and scriptable by other applications. Although *media* interoperability is widely available between "office" tools in current software environments, our vision is of a *semantic* interoperability between knowledge-based software for learning. In this vision, learner-constructed objects will maintain their meaning (though not necessarily the same underlying representation) when moved from one tool to another. They will remain meaningful not only to the human user, but also to the software agents that interact with each tool. Consistent treatment of the learner's constructions in different contexts by different software agents reinforces the deep semantics that we want learners to extract and generalize from specific experiences. At the same time, the contextual semantics of these objects accumulate as they are used. In a Science Learning Space, students experience the concept of experimental trial, for instance, by first *thinking about it*, designing discriminating trials in the simulation, and then *thinking with it*, using these trials to construct an argument. Tutor agents support students in properly encoding these learning experiences and in engaging in effective scientific reasoning processes. We hope our initial efforts to integrate components in a Science Learning Space point the way to future, more complete efforts.

Acknowledgments

The DARPA CAETI program funded the Active Illustrations, Belvedere, and Tutor Agents projects. Thanks to Kirstie Bellman for providing inspiration for this collaboration, to Danny Bobrow and Mark Shirley for providing the MOO infrastructure, and to programming staff Ray Pelletier, Dan Jones, Leo Ureel, and Tamar Gutman.

References

Anderson, J. R., Corbett, A. T., Koedinger, K. R., & Pelletier, R. (1995). Cognitive tutors: Lessons learned. *The Journal of the Learning Sciences*, 4 (2) 167-207.

Anderson, J. R. & Pelletier, R. (1991). A development system for model-tracing tutors. In *Proceedings of the International Conference of the Learning Sciences*, 1-8. Evanston, IL.

Collins, A. & Ferguson, W. (1993). Epistemic Forms and Epistemic Games: Structures and Strategies to Guide Inquiry. *Educational Psychologist*, 28(1), 25-42.

Forbus, K. (1997). Using qualitative physics to create articulate educational software. *IEEE Expert*, 12(3).

Forbus, K. & Falkenhainer, B. (1990.) Self-explanatory simulations: An integration of qualitative and quantitative knowledge, Proceedings of AAAI-90.

Forbus, K. & Falkenhainer, B. (1995.) Scaling up Self-Explanatory Simulators: Polynomial-time Compilation. Proceedings of IJCAI-95, Montreal, Canada.

Koedinger, K.R. (1991). On the design of novel notations and actions to facilitate thinking and learning. In *Proceedings of the International Conference on the Learning Sciences*, (pp. 266-273). Charlottesville, VA: AACE.

Koedinger, K. R., Anderson, J.R., Hadley, W.H., & Mark, M. A. (1997). Intelligent tutoring goes to school in the big city. *International Journal of Artificial Intelligence in Education*, 8, 30-43.

Paolucci, M., Suthers, D., & Weiner, A. (1996). Automated advice-giving strategies for scientific inquiry. *Intelligent Tutoring Systems, 3rd International Conference*, Montreal, June 12-14, 1996.

Reiser, B. J., Beekelaar, R., Tyle, A., & Merrill, D. C. (1991). GIL: Scaffolding learning to program with reasoning-congruent representations. In *Proceedings of the International Conference on the Learning Sciences*, (pp. 382-388). Charlottesville, VA: AACE.

Ritter, S. & Koedinger, K. R. (1997). An architecture for plug-in tutoring agents. In *Journal of Artificial Intelligence in Education*, 7 (3/4), 315-347. Charlottesville, VA: Association for the Advancement of Computing in Education.

Roschelle, J. & Kaput, J. (1995). Educational software architecture and systemic impact: The promise of component software. Presented at *AERA Annual Meeting*, San Francisco, April 19, 1995.

Suthers, D. & Jones, D. (1997). An architecture for intelligent collaborative educational systems. *AI-Ed 97, the 8th World Conf. on Artificial Intelligence in Education*, Kobe Japan, August 20-22, 1997.

Suthers, D., Toth, E., and Weiner, A. (1997). An Integrated Approach to Implementing Collaborative Inquiry in the Classroom. Computer Supported Collaborative Learning (CSCL'97), Toronto, December, 1997.

'Do It Yourself' Student Models for Collaborative Student Modelling and Peer Interaction

Susan Bull

School of Languages, University of Brighton, Falmer, East Sussex, BN1 9PH, UK.
s.bull@brighton.ac.uk

Abstract: An approach to student modelling is presented where learners build their own student models. A more accurate model may thereby be obtained, and learners may reflect on their beliefs while constructing their model. The diyM system is illustrated in four environments: two collaborative student modelling systems, and two learner modelling systems with peer interaction as their focus.

1 Introduction

Interest is growing in student models which involve the student in their construction and repair, as illustrated by the recent development of systems using this approach. One thing these systems have in common is the aim of achieving greater accuracy in the student model by taking account of student contributions. Other reasons for the involvement of learners in the modelling process are varied. MFD (Beck et al, 1997) seeks to afford the learner some feeling of control over the interaction. Mr Collins (Bull & Pain, 1995) uses a process of negotiating the student model to promote learner reflection. ADI (Specht et al, 1997) allows the openness of the model to become an additional method of accessing target educational material. The student mod-els in the latter two systems are inspectable by the learner, thus may "help, or chal-lenge, the student to be aware of what the system thinks she believes" (Self, 1988).

This paper presents DIY ('do it yourself') modelling in the form of diyM, to offer a method for learners to construct their own inspectable student models as a supplement to system-created inspectable models. An example of the diyM environment is presented, and possible uses of diyM in different collaborative student modelling and peer interaction settings are introduced. The focus is accuracy of the student model to improve the educational potential of learning environments; and promoting learner reflection through the self-evaluation which takes place when constructing the model.

2 The diyM Environment

DiyM is applicable to different learning environments. The illustration below is object pronouns in European Portuguese–implemented to supplement collaborative student modelling in Mr Collins (Bull & Pain, 1995). The environment has menus for student initiated interaction, with the options *build model; run model; clause types*.

2.1 The 'Build Model' Menu Option

Build Model displays a task to construct the student model (which then remains accessible). Fig. 1 shows the first method of model construction: for each rule of pronoun placement the learner selects the option they believe correct. The choices are: *pre-verbal; post-verbal; infix*, except for 'aux & pp', which has the options: *before aux; between aux & pp; after pp*. Students also state whether they are *sure* or *unsure*. In this example a student is in the process of constructing their model: they have stated their beliefs for five rules. The student believes the pronoun to be pre-verbal in negative clauses and open questions, but is more confident about negatives. They think the pronoun is post-verbal in affirmative main clauses and adverbial phrases, being sure in the latter case. The fourth rule was not attempted. They think the pronoun is probably an infix with infinitives, but are unsure. Selections will continue for each rule.

I think			
the pronoun is [pre-verbal ▼] in NEGATIVE CLAUSES.		I am	[sure ▼]
the pronoun is [pre-verbal ▼] in OPEN QUESTIONS.		I am	[unsure ▼]
the pronoun is [post-verbal ▼] in POSITIVE MAIN CLAUSES.		I am	[unsure ▼]
the pronoun is [▼] in POSITIVE IMPERATIVES.		I am	[▼]
the pronoun is [infix ▼] with INFINITIVES.		I am	[unsure ▼]
the pronoun is [post-verbal ▼] in SOME ADVERBIAL PHRASES.		I am	[sure ▼]
the pronoun is [▼] in RELATIVE CLAUSES.		I am	[▼]
the pronoun is [▼] in SUBORDINATE CLAUSES.		I am	[▼]
the pronoun is [▼] with AUX & PP.		I am	[▼]
the pronoun is [▼] in YES/NO QUESTIONS.		I am	[▼]
the pronoun is [▼] in the FUTURE TENSE.		I am	[▼]
the pronoun is [▼] in the CONDITIONAL TENSE.		I am	[▼]

Fig. 1: Constructing the student model (method 1)

In Fig. 1 the learner's selections for the first three rules are correct. For imperatives the learner has made no selection, indicating they are less confident than if they had selected an option and the confidence 'unsure'. In the last two attempts the learner is wrong both times. The selection of 'unsure' with infinitives shows that the difficulty with this rule may be less problematic to resolve than with adverbial phrases, where the learner holds a misconception they strongly believe.

In this manner students construct their own simple student models. DiyM stores a series of facts from which it can infer information, and from which it can present alternative viewing modes as requested. The facts are recorded as follows:

`clause_type(Clause,Position,Confidence,[Method])`. So, the first clause type in the current example is: `clause_type(1,pre_verbal,sure,[1])`. At this stage the goal is not necessarily to get answers right, but to create an accurate model of learner beliefs. The knowledge that accuracy may lead to more effective system help should provide motivation. The task is also an exercise in self-evaluation and promoting learner reflection. The ways a system will use information from a DIY student model will depend on the aims, domain and educational philosophy of the system.

Methods 2 and 3 of building the student model are similar to method 1 (the default), but the information is submitted in a different form (illustrated for rule 1):

Method 1: I think the pronoun is   pre-verbal / post-verbal   in negative clauses.

Method 2: I think the following sentence is correct: Não os compra / Não compra-os.

Method 3: I think the rule for pronoun placement in negative clauses is:

s --> neg, obj-pronoun, v. / s --> neg, v, obj-pronoun.

With method 2 the learner selects the sentence they believe is correct. *Não os compra* ('he does not buy them') is right–i.e. the pronoun (os) is before the verb (comprar). Method 3 offers the grammar. All methods use the same representations in the underlying (system's) student model. Students may, if they wish, repeat the task of constructing their student model using more than one method. In such cases conflicts may occur, for example, as given above for clause type 1 the representation might be: `clause_type(1,pre_verbal,sure,[1])`. A student may also submit information by another method, producing: `clause_type(1,post_verbal,sure,[2])`. This produces a conflict: with the different methods the learner states explicitly that they believe both P ('The pronoun is pre-verbal in negative clauses'), and ¬P:

	learner choice: belief:	representation:
system's model: ----		
clause_type(1,pre_v)		P
student model (1): pre-verbal		
clause_type(1,pre_v,sure,[1])	P	
student model (2): Não compra-os clause_type(1,post_v,sure,[2])		Q (¬P)

Fig. 2: Representing conflicts in the student model

The way in which this situation is dealt with is as follows:

1. On submitting a second (or third) set of beliefs, the learner is asked which method should be considered most reliable. In the above example they select from:

   o Method 1 (statement of pronoun position) o Method 2 (example sentence) o Both 1 & 2

   The resulting representation is: priority(Methods), where *Methods* is a list of the methods which should be given priority.

2. DiyM uses the representations from the method with highest priority, if only one is listed. If more than one method is assigned priority, for each clause type where there is *no* conflict of beliefs the representations are combined–e.g. if the following were provided for clause 3: clause_type(3,post_verbal,sure,[1])

clause_type(3,post_verbal,unsure,[2])

   the representation used is: clause_type(3,post_verbal,unsure,[1,2]).

   The value *unsure* is recorded because its weighting is greater than that for *sure*. This can be amended afterwards by the student if they wish.

3. Where there is a conflict of beliefs, all are represented. DiyM regards the representation(s) assigned the confidence *sure* as likely to be more reliable. There may be more than one of these: each is given equal weighting. On viewing their model, all representations for each rule are displayed to the student, so they remain aware of conflict. Depending on the system using diyM, the student's attention may be drawn to the conflict at the time, and they may be expected to resolve it.

In summary: in constructing their student model, learners provide their views directly to the system, thereby experiencing some degree of reflection. DiyM allows the model to be built in a number of different ways, to suit the preferred representation.

2.2 The 'Run Model' Menu Option

Run Model has two sub-menus: *System's Model; Student Model.* Selecting *System's Model* instructs the system to run its domain model, and present the results. The information is displayed three ways: grammar rules; example sentences; statements of the rule for the position of the pronoun as illustrated in the grammar and examples. Reference to clause types for each rule is also available–i.e. *1 negative clause; 2 open question*, etc. Students may view all information types, or just those they wish. Information is displayed on the right of the screen, on a blue background to emphasise to the viewer that these are the system's 'beliefs' about the domain (Fig. 3).

student's rules				system's rules			
THE POSITION OF THE PRONOUN IS:				THE POSITION OF THE PRONOUN IS:			
1	pre-verbal	7		1	pre-verbal	7	pre-verbal
1	*post-verbal	8		2	pre-verbal	8	pre-verbal
2	pre-verbal	9		3	post-verbal	9	betw aux & pp
3	post-verbal	10		4	post-verbal	10	post-verbal
4			11	5	post-verbal	11	infix
5	*infix		12	6	pre-verbal	12	infix
6	*post-verbal						

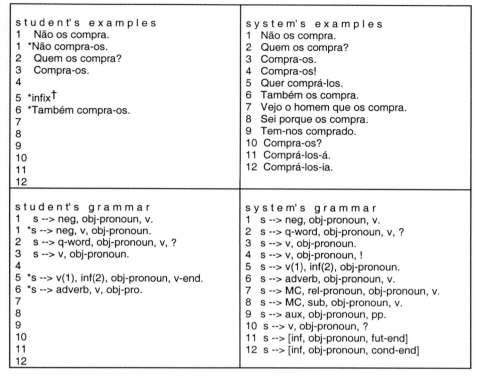

student's examples	system's examples
1 Não os compra.	1 Não os compra.
1 *Não compra-os.	2 Quem os compra?
2 Quem os compra?	3 Compra-os.
3 Compra-os.	4 Compra-os!
4	5 Quer comprá-los.
5 *infix†	6 Também os compra.
6 *Também compra-os.	7 Vejo o homem que os compra.
7	8 Sei porque os compra.
8	9 Tem-nos comprado.
9	10 Compra-os?
10	11 Comprá-los-á.
11	12 Comprá-los-ia.
12	
student's grammar	system's grammar
1 s --> neg, obj-pronoun, v.	1 s --> neg, obj-pronoun, v.
1 *s --> neg, v, obj-pronoun.	2 s --> q-word, obj-pronoun, v, ?
2 s --> q-word, obj-pronoun, v, ?	3 s --> v, obj-pronoun.
3 s --> v, obj-pronoun.	4 s --> v, obj-pronoun, !
4	5 s --> v(1), inf(2), obj-pronoun.
5 *s --> v(1), inf(2), obj-pronoun, v-end.	6 s --> adverb, obj-pronoun, v.
6 *s --> adverb, v, obj-pro.	7 s --> MC, rel-pronoun, obj-pronoun, v.
7	8 s --> MC, sub, obj-pronoun, v.
8	9 s --> aux, obj-pronoun, pp.
9	10 s --> v, obj-pronoun, ?
10	11 s --> [inf, obj-pronoun, fut-end]
11	12 s --> [inf, obj-pronoun, cond-end]
12	

Fig. 3:   The learner's student model and the system's domain model

Selecting *Student Model* leads to the system running the student model built by the learner. Information is displayed in the same three ways, illustrated in Fig. 3 for the first six rules (as completed in Fig. 1). These representations are on the left of the screen, on a yellow background to show that these are the student's beliefs. As stated above, conflicts within the model are displayed. If both *System's Model* and *Student Model* are selected, the models can be directly compared.

2.3 The 'Clause Type' Menu Option

The student model can also be displayed by clause type, coded according to correctness (compared to domain model), and sureness of the learner. Combinations of correctness and sureness are awarded a 5-point grading to determine how to present each rule (Table 1). For example, if a student's entry in their student model reflects 'correct knowledge', and the learner is sure of their view, the score awarded by the system for the clause type is 5. The window with the representations for that rule uses the pen colour green (illustrated in Fig. 4 by bold text). All backgrounds are yellow.
- *green* (bold) indicates the student knows the rule, and knows they know the rule.
- *black* (plain text) shows the learner knows the rule, but is unsure of the knowledge.
- *red* (italic) is 'danger'. The student does not know the rule but recognises a problem.
- *strong red* (italic/underline) shows a learner does not know a rule, but thinks they do.
- if no text is entered the learner does not know a rule and knows they do not know it.

---

† Pronouns are infixes in future and conditional, between infinitive stem and verb ending. In other tenses an infix cannot be used this way. An example therefore cannot be given.

Table 1: Determining presentation according to correctness and sureness

COMBINATION	SCORE	PEN COLOUR	EXAMPLE
correct + sure	5	Green	bold text
correct + unsure	4	Black	plain text
no selection	3		
incorrect + unsure	2	Red	italic
incorrect + sure	1	strong red	italic + underlined

negative clauses	imperatives
s --> neg, obj-pronoun, v. **Não os compra.** **pre-verbal** *s --> neg, v, obj-pronoun.* *Não compra-os.* *post-verbal*	
open questions	infinitives
s --> q-word, obj-pronoun, v, ? Quem os compra? Pre-verbal	*s --> v (1),inf(2),obj-pro,v-end.* *infix* *infix*
main clauses	some adverbials
s --> v, obj-pronoun. Compra-os. Post-verbal	*s --> adverb, v, obj-pronoun.* *Também compra-os.* *post-verbal*

Fig. 4: The student model presented according to clause type

Varying presentation helps learners notice problems. Conflicts in the model are clear.

2.4 Methods of Building the Student Model: Early Reactions

A small-scale early study was undertaken to determine whether potential users would use the different approaches to building their student models with diyM.

Subjects: The subjects were 3 lecturers; 6 postgraduate students; 4 undergraduate language students; 6 undergratuate students of other subjects; 5 'others'–a total of 24.

Method: Subjects were shown paper versions of the 3 methods to construct the student model. They completed a questionnaire stating how often they would use each.

Results: There was no difference in choice of methods across groups, except for 'other', which had only one instance of method 3 (as first choice). The groups are therefore not distinguished in the analysis below.

Table 2: Combinations of method chosen by experimental subjects

none	1 only	2 only	3 only	1 & 2	1 & 3	2 & 3	1, 2 & 3
1	0	3	1	6	4	1	8

Table 3: Frequency of choice of method

	1st choice	2nd choice	3rd choice	Never chosen	total choices
method 1	6	5	3	5	14
method 2	11	6	1	5	18
method 3	3	9	2	9	14

Table 2 shows most potential users would use a combination of more than one method to describe their beliefs. Only 4 subjects stated they would use one method only. 11 of the 24 subjects would use a combination of two methods, and 8 would use all three. 1 student would not use any. The most common combination was method 2 as first choice, and 1 as a second option (4 subjects). The second most common combinations, with 3 subjects each, were: 2 only, and 1 followed by 3.

Table 3 shows that most users would opt for method 2 as their first choice, and a total of 18 subjects would use this method at some time. The other methods would also be used–each by 14 users. The questionnaire options were as follows:

	always	mostly	sometimes	occasionally	never
Method 1	☐	☐	☐	☐	☐
Method 2	☐	☐	☐	☐	☐
Method 3	☐	☐	☐	☐	☐

14 subjects stated there was a method they would *always* use. For 4 subjects–method 1; for 8 subjects–method 2; and for 4 subjects–method 3. Amongst these were the 4 who would use one method only. 6 would use two, and 4 would use all. 2 of these subjects wanted to be able to use two methods simultaneously in all cases: 1 subject methods 1 & 2; and 1 subject methods 2 & 3 as a combined first option.

Of the remaining 10 who would not always use the same method(s), there were varying, but not significantly different spreads of two or three methods across *mostly, sometimes* and *occasionally*, except for the 1 subject who chose *never* for each.

Discussion: This study, although small, indicates that inclusion of different methods of constructing diyM in this context is important: a large majority of users would use more than one method; and there was a wide range of order of preference and frequency of choice for each method, irrespective of user group.

Limitations to this study include the following. Subjects were not asked whether they would like further methods of constructing their model–it might be necessary to allow more choices. Although subjects were able to identify the methods they would use in model construction, it has not yet been shown that they will do so in practice. It is also not known whether users would continue to maintain their student model longer term. Finally, results from this study are not necessarily transferable to other contexts in which diyM may be used, as it applies to different types of learning environment (see section 3). More studies need to be undertaken. It is suggested that these issues be considered further to determine the extent to which it is practical to promote learner reflection and achieve a more accurate student model with DIY modelling.

3 Uses of diyM

DiyM aims to address a specific problem: how to enable students to provide information to student models explicitly. The two main aims are to facilitate construction of a more accurate model by taking account of what a learner says they believe; and to enhance learner reflection through the need to state their beliefs, as self-evaluation is important in learning (e.g. Klenowski, 1995). DiyM may be used alone, or combined with a learning environment sharing at least one of diyM's aims. Implementations were designed for collaborative student models and systems encouraging peer interaction. The further use to which a DIY model will be put depends on its context of use.

3.1 DiyM by Itself

Explicit access to the contents of a student model has been argued to be useful in increasing learner awareness and reflection (Bull & Pain, 1995; Crawford & Kay, 1991; Morales et al, 1998; Paiva et al, 1995; Self, 1988). DiyM is inspectable. Its construction encourages students themselves to make explicit their views, to help them reflect on their knowledge. Moreover, it practices their skills of self-evaluation. DiyM also allows comparison of learners' own beliefs, to the rules or concepts of the domain.

3.2 DiyM and Student/System Collaborative Student Modelling

Student/system *collaborative student modelling* is a special case of inspectable student models: in addition to viewing their model, learners can *negotiate* the contents with the system (Bull & Pain, 1995). This differs from co-operative learner modelling (Beck et al, 1997) which more likely aims for accuracy in the model. While collaborative modelling will usually have this as a goal, it also strives to promote reflection.

The domain of pronoun placement above is identical to part of that in Mr Collins (*coll*aboratively maintained, *in*spectable student model). Mr Collins has 2 exercise types: 1 placing a (given) pronoun in a (given) sentence; 2 translating an English sentence into Portuguese. The system infers its student model (Sys-SM) from a learner's input, and constructs the student's student model (Stu-SM) from learner statements of confidence. The inspectable model is viewed as in Fig. 5. A breakdown is available.

	YOUR CONFIDENCE
SYSTEM CONFIDENCE	
Negative clauses: • almost sure	• very sure

Fig. 5: The inspectable student model of Mr Collins

Learner access to their model (Stu-SM & Sys-SM) provides a focus for negotiation in cases of conflict, by menu-based discussion (Bull & Pain, 1995). This is designed to enhance learner awareness of beliefs and approaches to learning, while building a more reliable model. The addition of diyM to Mr Collins provides a means to indicate to both system and learner the presence of inconsistencies within Stu-SM, as well as those between Stu-SM and Sys-SM which are identified by Mr Collins–i.e. in addition to awareness of differences between their own beliefs and those of the system about their beliefs, students are presented with problems *in their own model*.

3.3 DiyM and Student/Teacher Collaborative Student Modelling

See Yourself Write (Bull, 1997a) is a different kind of collaborative student model: it does not use student/system discussion of the model, but rather, has an inspectable learner model to facilitate interaction between student and *teacher*. A (human) tutor gives feedback on a student's foreign language writing, which is supplemented by student responses. Qualitative and quantitative feedback is given in a number of categories. An inspectable student model is automatically created from this feedback, with additional system generalisations based on the teacher's quantitative comments. The aims of *See Yourself Write* are to provide feedback to learners in a form they will take notice of, also providing a method to help them reflect on their feedback, since many learners do little with feedback on writing (Cohen & Cavalcanti, 1990). At the same time, teachers are not restricted in the kind of feedback they give. Fig. 6 shows a learner's initial view when inspecting the student model built from teacher feedback. The quantitative evaluations from the tutor for each category are displayed for each assignment completed to date. By clicking any of the cells, the learner may view qualitative feedback for that category and assignment. A summary column contains system-inferred comments to give an overview of performance in each category across all assignments so far. These are also accessed by clicking on the cell (see Bull, 1997a).

In addition to viewing structured feedback, learner reflection is achieved by system prompts about the student's approach to the task, based on the contents of the student model; by teacher requests for clarifications; by encouraging learners to state whether they agree with feedback, and allowing them to argue if they feel this is justified. This latter facility is designed as much to provoke self-explanation as to offer a route for student views to reach the tutor. The aim of a more accurate student model has a different purpose in *See Yourself Write*: the accuracy is more important for the *teacher*, as student contributions will help them to understand the student's problems and misconceptions. This is crucial with a domain such as writing where system reaction to a student's text can only occur if some kind of constraints are placed on input.

See Yourself Write	assignment1	assignment2	assignment3	summary
content	SUPERFICIAL	SUPERFICIAL	GOOD	OKAY
struct / arg	INCONSISTENT	INCONSISTENT	INCONSISTENT	INCONSISTENT
grammar	GOOD	OKAY	OKAY	OKAY
spelling	WEAK	GOOD	WEAK	OKAY
punctuation	OKAY	GOOD	GOOD	GOOD
style / vocab	GOOD	GOOD	GOOD	GOOD

Fig. 6: The inspectable student model of *See Yourself Write*

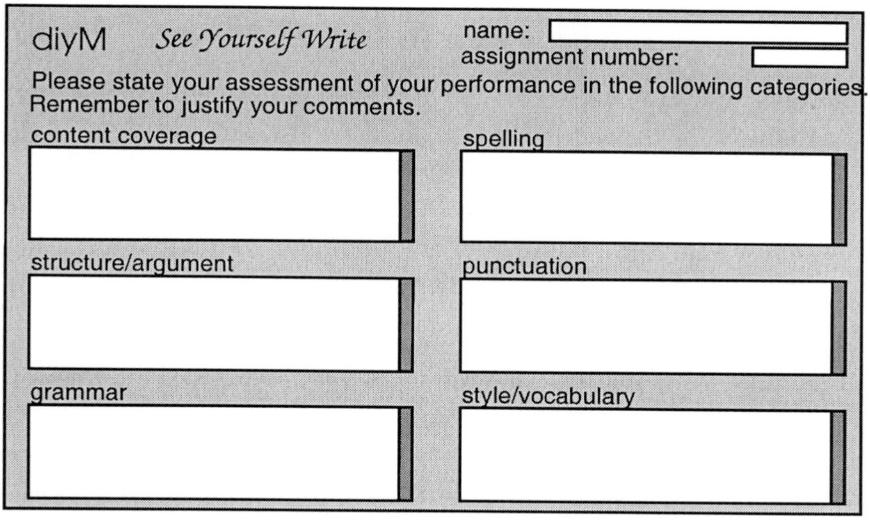

Fig. 7: DiyM for *See Yourself Write*

DiyM with *See Yourself Write* offers another way to help learners reflect–*at the time of writing*. Fig. 7 shows diyM for *See Yourself Write*. It is necessarily simpler than diyM for Mr Collins, designed primarily to get learners thinking about their writing from different perspectives. They are reminded of some of the criteria of assessment, and may experience some of the benefits decribed by Mowl and Pain (1995) for self-assessment in undergraduate essays–they may: think about how they are writing; better understand assessment; improve their future writing. As with Mr Collins, feedback can be viewed with the learner's own assessment when teacher and system comments are available.

3.4 DiyM and Peer Interaction

PeerSM (Bull & Brna, 1997) and S/UM (Bull, 1997b) are based on *See Yourself Write*, but involve *peer* feedback. The aim is similar in terms of promoting reflection with an inspectable model to prompt interaction about feedback. However, peerSM and S/UM also encourage reflection for educational benefit in the *givers* of feedback.

In peerSM the inspectable model is created from self-assessment, peer feedback and system inference from self- and peer evaluation of a linguistics exercise (Fig. 8). The inspectable model of S/UM is built from feedback on writing from peers (Fig. 9).

In peerSM one peer is involved. S/UM mediates interaction of multiple peers–the model of an individual is usually open to all (unless permission has not been given). The two systems are designed for participants to be both feedback givers and receivers.

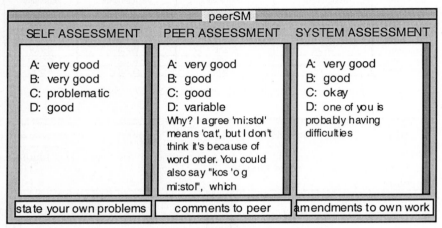

Fig. 8: The inspectable student model of peerSM

Categories:	content	structure	argument	style	other
Summary:		**OKAY**	**WEAK**		
Feedback 2:		GOOD	WEAK		

I find the structure of your paper a little hard. Instead of introducing related work as a starting point in the introduction, you have weaved it in throughout the paper.

Feedback 1:   WEAK

Although you support your argument well, there are counter-arguments you have not given. (e.g. you could explain why other studies produced different results).

Fig. 9: The inspectable student model of S/UM

System Evaluation
    Category: Content
Overall the content of your document appears OKAY.
The most recent feedback was GOOD, but no explanations or justifications were provided by the author of this feedback.
Earlier feedback suggests that the content of your document was WEAK.
Your improvement may be because you have considered these comments.
Your own assessment of the content of your document is OKAY.

Fig. 10: System comments based on S/UM and diyM

DiyM for S/UM is similar to diyM for *See Yourself Write*. However, students may also give quantitative evaluations which feed into S/UM's inspectable student model, so that it may take the learner's own beliefs about their performance into account when making generalisations. Fig. 10 shows a system generalisation from peer feedback in S/UM and self-assessment through diyM. This is constructed using hierarchically structured templates. Although information is from system generalisations, it may be inaccurate as it is based on as-sessments of non-experts. Hence use of 'appears'; 'may'. The aim, as stated above, is to encourage learner reflection in *all participants*. Thus accuracy is not as important here as in a collaborative student model, though *interaction* to produce accurate contents to *promote reflec-tion* still applies.

The peerSM exercise is one word answers input textually into edit boxes which can be evaluated by the system, and longer textual responses which cannot be evaluated computationally. DIY modelling in this context provides an alternative way of completing the exercise, using an interface similar to Fig. 1. As with diyM for Mr Collins this may result in conflicts in the model. This is handled in a similar manner: conflicts within the learner's own model (Stu-SM) are salient when viewed. Implementation of diyM for peerSM is not yet complete: although the diyM component can be viewed (in an additional field), the system does not take account of the information. Therefore the issue of learner reflection is served, but the question of increased accuracy in this version of diyM has not yet been addressed.

4 Summary

This paper has presented DIY student modelling to enable students to contribute information directly to their student models, to improve the accuracy of the models and to support reflection on learning. The approach was illustrated with four learning environments. Further work is required, to examine the extent to which students will embrace the approach in practice, in the different contexts of use.

References

Beck J, Stern M & Woolf BP (1997). Cooperative Student Models, B du Boulay & R Mizoguchi (eds) *Artificial Intelligence in Education*, IOS Press, Amsterdam, 127-134.

Bull S (1997a). See Yourself Write: A Simple Student Model to Make Students Think, A Jameson, C Paris & C Tasso (eds) *User Modeling Proceedings of Sixth International Conference*, Springer Wien New York, 315-326.

Bull S (1997b). A Multiple Student and User Modelling System for Peer Interaction, R Schäfer & M Bauer (eds) *ABIS-97 Adaptivität und Benutzermodellierung in interaktiven Softwaresystemen*, Universität des Saarlandes, 61-71.

Bull S & Brna P (1997). What does Susan know that Paul doesn't? (and vice versa): Contributing to Each Other's Student Model, B du Boulay & R Mizoguchi (eds) *Artificial Intelligence in Education*, IOS Press, Amsterdam, 568-570.

Bull S & Pain H (1995). 'Did I say what I think I said, and do you agree with me?': Inspecting and Questioning the Student Model, *Proceedings of World Conference on Artificial Intelligence and Education*, Washington DC, 501-508.

Cohen AD (1987). Student Processing of Feedback on their Compositions, A Wenden & J Rubin (eds) *Learner Strategies in Language Learning*, Prentice-Hall, London, 57-69.

Cohen A & Cavalcanti M (1990). Feedback on Compositions teacher & student verbal reports, B.Kroll (ed) *Second Language Writing,* Cambridge University Press, 155-177.

Crawford K & Kay J (1991). *Metacognitive Processes and Learning with Intelligent Educational Systems*, Report 91/3/3.1, Systems Group, University of Sydney.

Klenowski V (1995). Student Self-Evaluation Processes in Student-Centred Teaching and Learning Contexts of Australia and England, *Assessment in Education* 2(2), 145-163.

Morales R, Ramscar M & Pain H (1998). Modelling the Learner's Awareness and Reflection in a Collaborative Learner Modelling Setting, presented at *Workshop on Current Trends and Applications of AI in Education*, Mexico City.

Mowl G & Pain R (1995). Using Self and Peer Assessment to Improve Students' Essay Writing, *Innovations in Education and Training International* 32(4), 324-335.

Paiva A, Self J & Hartley R (1995). Externalising Learner Models, *Proceedings of World Conference on Artificial Intelligence and Education*, Washington DC, 509-516.

Specht M, Weber G & Schöch V (1997). ADI ein adaptiver Informations- und Lehragent im WWW, R Schäfer & M Bauer (eds) *ABIS-97 Adaptivität und Benutzermodellierung in interaktiven Softwaresystemen*, Universität des Saarlandes, 53-60.

Self JA (1988). Bypassing the Intractable Problem of Student Modelling, *ITS-88*, 18-24.

Promoting Effective Peer Interaction in an Intelligent Collaborative Learning System[1]

Amy Soller, Bradley Goodman, Frank Linton, and Robert Gaimari

The MITRE Corporation
202 Burlington Road, Bedford, MA, 01730-1420
soller@mitre.org

Abstract. Placing students in a group and assigning them a task does not guarantee that the students will engage in effective collaborative learning behavior. The collaborative learning model described in this paper identifies the specific characteristics exhibited by effective collaborative learning teams, and based on these characteristics, suggests strategies for promoting effective peer interaction. The model is designed to help an intelligent collaborative learning system recognize and target group interaction problem areas. Once targeted, the system can take actions to help students collaborate more effectively with their peers, maximizing individual student and group learning.

1   Introduction

Research has shown that classroom learning improves significantly when students participate in learning activities with small groups of peers [2]. Students learning in small groups encourage each other to ask questions, explain and justify their opinions, articulate their reasoning, and elaborate and reflect upon their knowledge, thereby motivating and improving learning. These benefits, however, are only achieved by active and well-functioning learning teams. Placing students in a group and assigning them a task does not guarantee that the students will engage in effective collaborative learning behavior. While some peer groups seem to interact naturally, others struggle to maintain a balance of participation, leadership, understanding, and encouragement. Traditional lecture-oriented classrooms do not teach students the social skills they need to interact effectively in a team, and few students involved in team projects or exposed to integrated working environments learn these skills well [11].

The collaborative learning model (CL Model) described in this paper identifies the characteristics exhibited by effective collaborative learning teams, and based on these characteristics, suggests strategies for promoting more effective student interaction. The model is designed to help an intelligent collaborative learning system recognize and target group interaction problem areas. Once targeted, the system can take actions to help students collaborate more effectively with their peers, maximizing individual student and group learning.

---
[1] This work was supported by the MITRE Sponsored Research Program.

The next section describes the characteristics exhibited by effective collaborative learning teams, and section 3 proposes strategies for helping groups achieve these characteristics. Section 4 describes our ongoing efforts to implement the strategies in an intelligent collaborative learning system, and section 5 summarizes the CL Model.

2 Characteristics of Effective Collaborative Learning Teams

This section describes the characteristics exhibited by effective collaborative learning teams based on a review of research in educational psychology and computer-supported collaborative learning [2] [10] [11] [13] [18], and empirical data from a study conducted by the authors of this paper [16]. The study was conducted during a five day course in which students learned and used Object Modeling Technique to collaboratively design software systems. The students were videotaped as they worked in groups of four or five. The videotape transcriptions were coded with a speech act based coding scheme, and studied using summary and sequential analysis techniques.

The characteristics studied and seen to be exhibited during effective collaborative learning interaction fall into five categories: participation, social grounding, collaborative learning conversation skills, performance analysis and group processing, and promotive interaction. The following five subsections describe these categories and their corresponding characteristics.

2.1 Participation

A team's learning potential is maximized when all the students actively participate in the group's discussions. Building involvement in group discussions increases the amount of information available to the group, enhancing group decision making and improving the students' quality of thought during the learning process [10]. Encouraging active participation also increases the likelihood that all group members will learn the subject matter, and decreases the likelihood that only a few students will understand the material, leaving the others behind.

2.2 Social Grounding

Teams with social grounding skills establish and maintain a shared understanding of meanings. The students take turns questioning, clarifying and rewording their peers' comments to ensure their own understanding of the team's interpretation of the problem and the proposed solutions. "In periods of successful collaborative activity, students' conversational turns build upon each other and the content contributes to the joint problem solving activity [17]."

Analysis of the data collected from our study [16] revealed that students in effective collaborative learning teams naturally take turns speaking by playing characteristic roles [5] such as such as questioner, facilitator, and motivator.

2.3 Collaborative Learning Conversation Skills

An individual's learning achievement in a team can often be determined by the quality of his communication in the group discussions [10]. Skill in learning collaboratively means knowing when and how to question, inform, and motivate one's teammates, knowing how to mediate and facilitate conversation, and knowing how to deal with conflicting opinions.

The Collaborative Learning Skills Network (shown in part by Figure 1) illustrates the conversation skills which are key to collaborative learning and problem solving, based on our study [16]. This network is a modified version of McManus and Aiken's Collaborative Skills Network [13], which breaks down each *cooperative* learning skill type (Communication, Trust, Leadership, and Creative Conflict) into its corresponding subskills (e.g. Acknowledgment, Negotiation), and attributes (e.g. Appreciation, Asking for information). Each attribute is assigned a sentence opener which conveys the appropriate dialogue intention.

The goal of collaborative learning is for *all* the students to help each other learn *all* the material together, whereas in cooperative learning each student individually performs his or her assigned learning task, independently contributing to the group's

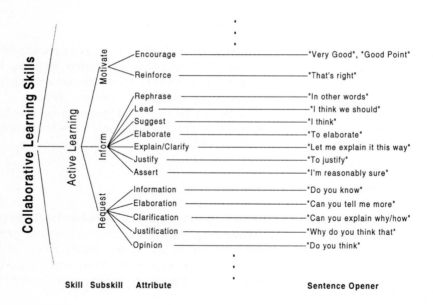

Fig. 1. The Active Learning Skills section of the Collaborative Learning Skill Network (adapted from McManus and Aiken's Collaborative Skill Network, [13])

final solution [8]. Effective collaborative learning interaction differs from cooperative learning interaction in that students learning collaboratively utilize fewer *Trust* and *Leadership* skills, and more *Active Learning* skills such as Justify, Elaborate, Encourage, and Explain [16]. The Collaborative Learning Skills Network reflects this difference.

2.4 Performance Analysis and Group Processing

Group processing exists when groups discuss their progress, and decide what behaviors to continue or change [11]. Group processing can be facilitated by giving students the opportunity to individually and collectively assess their performance. During this self evaluation, each student learns individually how to collaborate more effectively with his teammates, and the group as a whole reflects on its performance.

2.5 Promotive Interaction

A group achieves *promotive interdependence* when the students in the group perceive that their goals are positively correlated such that an individual can only attain his goal if his team members also attain their goals [7]. In collaborative learning, these goals correspond to each student's need to understand his team members' ideas, questions, explanations, and problem solutions.

Students who are influenced by promotive interdependence engage in *promotive interaction*; they verbally promote each other's understanding through support, help, and encouragement [11]. If a student does not understand the answer to a question or solution to a problem, his teammates make special accommodations to address his misunderstanding before the group moves on. Ensuring that each student receives the help he needs from his peers is key to promoting effective collaborative interaction.

3 Strategies for Promoting Effective Peer Interaction

This section suggests implementation strategies for helping students attain the collaborative learning skills required to excel in each of the five CL Model categories.

3.1 Encouraging Participation

An intelligent collaborative learning system (ICLS) can encourage participation by initiating and facilitating round-robin brainstorming sessions [10] at appropriate times during learning activities. Consider the following scenario. An ICLS presents an exercise to a group of students. After reading the problem description to himself or herself, each group member individually formulates procedures for going about solving the problem. A student who is confident that he has the "right" procedure may naturally speak up and suggest his ideas, whereas the student who is unsure (but may actually have the best proposal) may remain quiet. During this phase of learning, it is key that all students bring their suggestions and ideas into the group discussion, especially since quiet students of lower ability have particular difficulty learning the material [18]. The ICLS initiates and facilitates a round-robin brainstorming session a few minutes after the students have read the problem description. Each student in the group is required to openly state his rationale for solving the problem while the other students listen. Round-robin brainstorming sessions establish an environment in which each student in turn has the opportunity to express himself openly without his teammates interrupting or evaluating his opinion. An ICLS can help ensure active participation by engaging students in these sessions at appropriate times.

Personal Learning Assistants (PaLs), personified by animated computer agents, can be designed to "partner" with a student, building his confidence level and encouraging him to participate. Providing a private channel of communication [12] between a student and his personal learning assistant allows the student to openly discuss his ideas with his PaL without worrying about his peers' criticisms. A student's PaL could help him develop his ideas before he proposes them to the other students. The personal learning assistant may also ask the student questions in order to obtain a more accurate representation of his knowledge for input to the student model. A more accurate student model allows coaching to better meet student needs.

3.2 Maintaining Social Grounding

An ICLS can model the turn-taking behavior that is characteristic of teams with social grounding skills (section 2.2), by assigning the students roles [5] such as questioner, clarifier, mediator, informer, and facilitator (among others), and rotating these roles around the group for each consecutive dialogue segment. The beginning of a new dialogue segment is identified by the start of a new context, often initiated by sentence openers such as, "OK, let's move on", or "Now, what about this" [16].

One or more critical roles, such as questioner or motivator, may be missing in a group if there are too few students to fill all the necessary roles. A missing role can be played by a simulated peer, or *learning companion* [6] [9]. The learning companion can be dynamically adapted to best fit the needs of the group, playing the role of critic during one dialogue segment, and facilitator during the next.

Identifying and characterizing the natural role switches that take place between dialogue segments will aid in further developing advanced strategies for maintaining social grounding through role playing.

3.3 Supporting Collaborative Learning Conversation Skills Practice

Students solving open-ended problems, in which an absolute answer or solution may not exist, must explain their viewpoints to their peers, and justify their opinions. Assigning students open-ended activities encourages them to practice these essential active learning conversation skills. A learning companion in an ICLS can also encourage students to elaborate upon and justify their reasoning by playing the role of devil's advocate [10].

Providing students with collaborative learning skill usage statistics (e.g. 10% Inform, 50% Request, 40% Argue) raises their awareness about the types of contributions they are making to the group conversation. This capability, however, requires either the ICLS to understand and code the students' dialogue, or the students to tell the system from which skill categories their utterances belong. Section 4 describes an alternate method of obtaining collaborative learning skill information.

3.4 Evaluating Student Performance and Promoting Group Processing

An ICLS can promote group processing by evaluating students' individual and group performance, and providing them with feedback. Students should receive individual evaluations in private, along with suggestions for improving their individual performance. The team should receive a group evaluation in public, along with suggestions for improving group performance. The purpose of providing a group evaluation is to inspire the students to openly discuss their effectiveness while they are learning and determine how to improve their performance. This introspective discussion may also be provoked by allowing the students to collaboratively view and make comments on their student and group models [4].

3.5 Supporting Promotive Interaction

Webb [18] outlines five criteria for ensuring that students provide effective help to their peers in a collaborative environment. These criteria are (1) help is timely, (2) help is relevant to the student's need, (3) the correct amount of elaboration or detail is given, (4) the help is understood by the student, and (5) the student has an opportunity to apply the help in solving the problem (and uses it!). The following paragraphs suggest strategies to address each criteria.

When a student requests help, the ICLS can encourage his teammates to respond in a timely manner. Assigning a mentor to each student provides them with a personal support system. Student mentors feel responsible to ensure their mentee's understanding, and mentees know where to get help when they need it.

In response to their questions, students must be provided with relevant explanations containing an adequate level of elaboration. Their peers, however, may not know how to compose high-quality, elaborated explanations, and may need special training in using examples, analogies, and multiple representations in their explanations [1]. To increase the frequency and quality of explanations, and ICLS could strategically assign students roles such as "Questioner" and "Explainer" to help them practice and improve these skills.

Webb's fourth and fifth criteria can be met by an ICLS by observing and analyzing a student's actions in conjunction with his communicative actions to determine whether or not a student understood and applied the help received.

4   Applying the CL Model to an ICLS

This section describes our ongoing research in the development of an intelligent collaborative learning system based on the CL Model. Ideally, an ICLS would be able to understand and interpret the group conversation, and could actively support the group during their learning activities by applying the strategies described in section 3. In working toward the realization of this vision, we have focused our efforts on implementing group support strategies; later these strategies may draw upon natural language understanding functionality.

Fig. 2. Sentence opener based communication interface

To enable student communication over a computer network, a chat style interface (Figure 2), based on the Collaborative Learning Skill Network, was developed [15] (see also [13] [14]). Students begin their statement with a sentence opener by selecting one of eight subskill categories: Request, Inform, Motivate, Argue, Mediate, Task, Maintenance, or Acknowledge. The sentence openers represent characteristic sentence starters from the subskill categories to which they belong. Students view the group conversation as it progresses in the large window displaying the students' names and utterances. This sentence opener interface structures the group's conversation, making the students actively aware of the dialogue focus and discourse intent.

Each time a student makes a contribution to the group conversation, the communication interface records the date, time, student's name, and subskill applied in the student action log (Figure 3). By dynamically performing summary analysis on a group's logged interaction data, an ICLS can determine to what extent each student is participating, and from which subskill categories he is contributing. This type of data may allow the system to determine a student's role within the group and what skills he needs to practice. For example, although John has been following the group conversation closely and interacting often, his summary CLC skill statistics show that 90% of his contributions are from the category Acknowledge.

The information in the student action log combined with knowledge of the student actions taken on a shared workspace provides insight into the students' competence in the subject matter. For example, consider the sequence of actions shown in Figure 3. Brad asks Amy a question and Amy responds. Brad asks Amy a second question and Amy responds again. Brad acknowledges Amy's response and then creates a link on the shared workspace, showing the relationship between his proposed hypothesis and some new evidence he has discovered. Finally, Amy praises Brad for taking a correct action. From this interaction sequence, the ICLS could deduce that Amy helped Brad learn and apply the rule relating his hypothesis and the new evidence. This information could be used, for example, to enrich Amy and Brad's student models, enabling the ICLS to provide more effective coaching to them

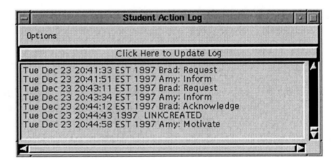

Fig. 3. Example log generated from student communication and actions on a shared workspace

The components of an ICLS, based on the CL Model, are responsible for using the information obtained from the communication interface and shared tools to determine when and how to apply the strategies described in section 3. For example, the instructional planning component may be responsible for not only selecting appropriate exercises to present to the students, but also selecting roles to assign to students. Table 1 summarizes the strategies that address each of the five CL Model categories, and shows how the ICLS components can implement these strategies.

In the next stage of this research, a second study will be conducted in which students from the first study will be asked to collaboratively solve problems similar to those they solved before, however this time they will be required to communicate

Table 1. The CL Model support strategies that could be executed by each ICLS component

		ICLS Component			
CL Model Facet	CL Skill Coach	Instructional Planner	Student/ Group Model	Learning Companion	Personal Learning Assistant
Participation	Facilitate round-robin brainstorming sessions	Initiate round-robin brainstorming sessions			Encourage participation
Social Grounding		Assign roles to students, and rotate roles around group		Fill in missing roles in group	Ensure students are playing their assigned roles
Collaborative Learning Conversation Skills	Provide feedback on CL skill usage	Assign tasks that require students to practice CL skills	Store student/ group CL skill usage statistics	Play devil's advocate to encourage active learning	
Performance Analysis & Group Processing	Provide feedback on group/ individual performance		Allow students to inspect and comment on their student/ group models		
Promotive Interaction	Ensure adequate elaboration is provided in explanations	Assign mentors or helpers to students	Update student/group models when students receive help		Alert students to their peers' requests for help

using the sentence opener interface. The students will jointly design their software system using a shared workspace. This study will test the usability of the communication interface, and reveal any refinements needed to the collaborative learning skill network. The ICLS components shown in Table 1 will then be developed and tested to evaluate the CL Model.

5   Conclusion

Learning effective collaboration skills is essential to successfully learning course material with peers [3]. These skills are often not inherent, however they can be learned through practice and support during structured group learning activities.

The CL Model described in this paper provides ICLS developers with a framework and set of recommendations for helping groups acquire effective collaborative learning skills. The model describes the characteristics exhibited by effective learning teams, namely participation, social grounding, performance analysis and group processing, application of collaborative learning conversation skills, and promotive interaction.

References

1. Blumenfeld, P., Marx, R., Soloway, E., & Krajcik, J. (1996). Learning with peers: From small group cooperation to collaborative communities. Educational Researcher, 25(8),37-40.
2. Brown, A. & Palincsar, A. (1989). Guided, cooperative learning and individual knowledge acquisition. In L. Resnick (Ed.), Knowledge, learning and instruction (pp. 307-336), Lawrence Erlbaum Associates.
3. Bruffee, K. (1993). Collaborative learning. Baltimore, MD: The Johns Hopkins University Press.
4. Bull, S. & Broady, E. (1997). Spontaneous peer tutoring from sharing student models. Proceedings of the 8th World Conference on Artificial Intelligence in Education (AI-ED 97), Kobe, Japan, 143-150.
5. Burton, M., Brna, P., & Treasure-Jones, T. (1997). Splitting the collaborative atom. Proceedings of the 8th World Conference on Artificial Intelligence in Education (AI-ED 97), Kobe, Japan, 135-142.
6. Chan, T.W. & Baskin, A. (1988). Studying with the prince: The computer as a learning companion. Proceedings of the ITS '88 Conference, Montreal, Canada, 194-200.
7. Deutsch, M. (1962). Cooperation and trust: Some theoretical notes. In M. Jones (Ed.) Nebraska Symposium on Motivation (pp. 275-320). Lincoln: University of Nebraska Press.
8. Dillenbourg, P., Baker, M., Blaye, A., & O'Malley, C. (1995). The evolution of research on collaborative learning. In H. Spada and P. Reinmann (Eds.), Learning in Humans and Machines, Elsevier Science.
9. Goodman, B., Soller, A., Linton, F., & Gaimari, R. (1997). Encouraging student reflection and articulation using a learning companion. Proceedings of the 8th World Conference on Artificial Intelligence in Education (AI-ED 97), Kobe, Japan, 151-158.
10. Jarboe, S. (1996). Procedures for enhancing group decision making. In B. Hirokawa and M. Poole (Eds.), Communication and Group Decision Making (pp. 345-383). Thousand Oaks, CA: Sage Publications.
11. Johnson, D., Johnson, R., & Holubec, E. (1990). Circles of learning: Cooperation in the classroom (3rd ed.). Edina, MN: Interaction Book Company.
12. Koschmann, T., Kelson, A., Feltovich, P., & Barrows, H. (1996). Computer-supported problem-based learning. In T. Koschmann (Ed.), CSCL: Theory and Practice of an Emerging Paradigm (pp. 83-124). Mahwah, NJ: Lawrence Erlbaum Associates.
13. McManus, M, & Aiken, R. (1995). Monitoring computer-based problem solving. Journal of Artificial Intelligence in Education, 6(4), 307-336.
14. Robertson, J. (1997). BetterBlether: An educational communication tool. Unpublished undergraduate honours dissertation, Departments of Computer Science and Artificial Intelligence, University of Edinburgh.
15. Soller, A. (1997). Toward an intelligent CSCL communication interface. Proceedings of AI-ED 97 Workshop IV, Kobe, Japan, 94-95.
16. Soller, A., Linton, F., Goodman, B., & Gaimari, R. (1996). [Videotaped study: 3 groups of 4-5 students each solving software system design problems using Object Modeling Technique during a one week course at The MITRE Institute]. Unpublished raw data.
17. Teasley, S. & Roschelle, J. (1993). Constructing a joint problem space. In S. Lajoie & S. Derry (Eds.), Computers as cognitive tools (pp. 229-257). Hillsdale, NJ: Lawrence Erlbaum.
18. Webb, N. (1992). Testing a theoretical model of student interaction and learning in small groups. In R. Hertz-Lazarowitz and N. Miller (Eds.), Interaction in Cooperative Groups: The Theoretical Anatomy of Group Learning (pp. 102-119). New York: Cambridge University Press.

Acknowledgments

Special thanks to the students in the OMT class we studied, and to the instructor for being exceptionally cooperative. Thanks also to Brant Cheikes and Mark Burton for their support.

Using Induction to Generate Feedback in Simulation Based Discovery Learning Environments

Koen Veermans[1] & Wouter R. Van Joolingen[2]

[1] Faculty of Educational Science and Technology University of Twente, PO Box 217
7500 AE Enschede, The Netherlands
veermans@edte.utwente.nl
[2] Faculty of Educational Science and Technology University of Twente, PO Box 217
7500 AE Enschede, The Netherlands
joolingen@edte.utwente.nl

Abstract. This paper describes a method for learner modelling for use within simulation-based learning environments. The goal of the learner modelling system is to provide the learner with advice on discovery learning. The system analyzes the evidence that a learner has generated for a specific hypothesis, assesses whether the learner needs support on the discovery process, and the nature of that support. The kind of advice described in this paper is general in the sense that it does not rely on specific domain knowledge, and specific in the sense that it is directly related to the learner's interaction with the system. The learner modelling mechanism is part of the SimQuest authoring system for simulation-based discovery learning environments

Key words: Intelligent Tutoring Systems, Simulation-Based Learning, Scientific Discovery

Introduction

Historically discovery learning has never attracted much attention from the field of Intelligent Tutoring Systems (ITS) because of the high degree of freedom for learners in discovery learning environments.

Influenced by problems with the traditional approach towards ITS, like the difficulty of handling uncertainty, and new directions in the field of education, the view on ITS has changed [3]. This move, away from systems with detailed learner and expert models that aim at remediating 'incorrect' knowledge, created opportunities to extend the scope of ITS to less directive approaches towards learning, like discovery learning.

Good examples of systems that do combine these two fields are *Belvedere* [14], and *Smithtown* [17]. *Belvedere* is a system that gives advice to learners engaged in scientific inquiry in textual format. *Smithtown* offers a free discovery environment combined with all kinds of support for the discovery process in the domain of economics. However, a system like *Smithtown* requires a large effort of knowledge engineering in order to generate dedicated discovery support.

The objective of simulation based discovery learning is to engage the learner actively in the learning process. In a discovery environment learners have to set their own learning goals. At the same time, the learner has to find the methods that help to achieve these goals. These activities would result in deeper rooting of the knowledge, enhanced transfer [1], the acquisition of regulatory skills [13], and would yield better motivation.

Learning with simulation based discovery environments has not always resulted in better learning results; see [7] for a full report. One of the reasons is that the processes involved in discovery learning appear to be difficult. De Jong & Njoo [8] describe discovery learning as comprising *transformative processes* that include analysis, hypothesis generation, testing and evaluation, and the *regulative processes* planning, verifying, and monitoring. A number of studies have indicated problems with one or more of these processes. Klahr & Dunbar [11] found that learners failed to draw the right conclusions from disconfirming evidence for a hypothesis. In the same experiment they also found a reversed effect: learners rejecting a hypothesis without evidence supporting the rejection. A number of other researchers [15, 17, 18] found that learners varied too many variables over experiments making the interpretation of the outcomes virtually impossible.

This paper describes an attempt to apply techniques used in ITS to provide learners with support on some of the problems they encounter in discovery learning.

Learner Modelling in Discovery Environments

Discovery learning environments and learner modelling are not natural companions. The traditional ITS systems containing learner models usually cannot be designated as discovery environments in the sense that they do not offer the amount of learner freedom necessary for genuine discovery learning. Although the degree of learner control varies, the stereotypical ITS has traditionally been system controlled. Conversely, known simulation based discovery environments do not offer learner modelling in the sense of creating a cognitive model of the learner's knowledge. There are two reasons for the latter observation:

- the amount of learner freedom offered by discovery environments is so large that a full learner model is beyond the scope of practical application: the number of parameters is simply too large.
- often learner modelling is seen as incompatible with discovery learning, and the related concept of constructivism, for which 'measuring' the learners' knowledge conflicts with the idea that learner builds their own representation of the external world. For a discussion on this point the reader could refer to [4].

These arguments explain why traditional ITS techniques such as learner modelling and instructional planning have not been used very often for discovery learning.

The role we see for learner modelling in discovery learning is to generate support for the learner in the *process* of discovery, by inferring the inductive and deductive steps the learner takes in the discovery. The claim is not that the system can maintain a full cognitive model of the discovery skills and steps taken by the learner, but to infer just enough from the learner's behaviour to direct the learner's search through experiment and hypothesis space. Following Self [16] we use a pragmatic approach in which we attempt to:

- design interactions such that the information needed by the system is provided by the learner
- link the content of the system's model of the learner to specific instructional actions
- assume a modest role for the system

The ideas behind discovery learning call for a different attitude towards tutoring than traditional ITS. If the ITS is to give up control in favour of the learner this implies that the tutoring should not be imperative, instead, the ITS should opt for a role of advising the student. The implication for the learner model is, since the ITS is advising, that the validity of the learner model is less important. Discovery learning is concerned with open domains where there are no explicit criteria for success. Therefore, instruction cannot be aiming primarily at remediating misconceptions, but rather should aim at a critical attitude. The aim is therefore not to establish a complete model of the learner's knowledge, but to assist learners in their discovery processes enabling the learner to acquire the domain knowledge. The advice should address certain parts of the task that are difficult for learners, but the student should feel free to discard the advice. In addition, since support for the learner aims at a generic mechanism for generating advice, the mechanisms for generating it should also not depend on specific domain characteristics.

Based on these constraints we have adapted techniques used in ITS to create a mechanism that can generate useful advice to learners active in discovery learning.

Using Induction to Support Discovery Learning

In this section we describe a mechanism to generate a learner model from learners' behaviour in a discovery learning environment. The mechanism is created for and integrated in the SimQuest authoring system for simulation-based discovery [5, 6]. SimQuest is an authoring system for creating simulations embedded in instructional support. Currently, SimQuest supports the following types of instructional support:

- *Model progression:* dividing the domain in manageable portions, for instance going from simple to complex models.
- *Assignments:* providing the learner with subgoals, for instance promting to investigate a certain relation in the domain. SimQuest offers six types of assignments
- *Explanation:*. Providing extra domain information, in the form of text, graphics, sounds, video or hypertext.
- *Monitoring:* allowing the learner to keep track of the experiments performed within the domain.

The learner modelling mechanism operates as a self standing module within the applications created by SimQuest, and strengthens the relation between one type of assignments, Fig. 1, and the learner's experimentation. In the present paper we outline the principles of how this system functions and present an example of how the system operates in a real situation. We will show that by restricting the analysis to assessing the correctness of the hypotheses put forward by the learner we are able to collect valuable information that can be utilized to give advice concerning the experiment space search without relying on extensive domain knowledge.

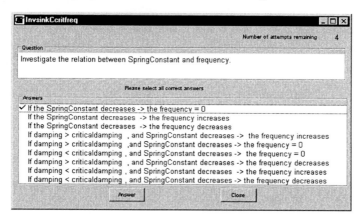

Fig. 1. *An assignment in the SimQuest environment. The first alternative is in focus.*

A Mechanism for Generating Learner Models from Discovery Behaviour.

The mechanism we use in our system for generating a learner model, which serves as a base for generating tailored advice on discovery learning, is based on the principles of induction and deduction. An induction process tries to infer a hypothesis from a given set of data, while a deduction process tries to predict experimental outcomes from a given hypothesis. In the mechanism we invert both processes: instead of reasoning forward from given data to a candidate hypothesis, or from a given hypothesis to predicted data, we reason back from a candidate hypothesis to supportive data or from experimental outcomes to a given hypothesis. In this way we assess the steps the learner takes and use this as a basis for generating tailored advice.

As a starting point, we always take a set of experiments performed by the learner, described as a set of values assigned to input and output variables. A second input for the learner model is the hypothesis[1] the learner is investigating. The source is an as-

---

[1] In the current version the hypothesis is a statement about the relation that is offered to the learner as an answer alternative in an assignment like the one in Fig. 1. Although it might be argued that these are not hypotheses in the true sense we will refer to them as hypotheses in the rest of the paper.

signment in the environment. In the assignment (see Fig. 1) the learner has to investigate the relation between the variables *spring constant* and *frequency*. The hypothesis the learner is working on is: *If the spring constant increases then the frequency = 0*.
In order to assess if an hypothesis can predict a given set of data, a stepwise process is applied to the set of data:

- First, a set of *informative experiments about the relation* is filtered from the complete set of performed experiments. An experiment (or pair of experiments) is considered to be informative when the input variables which have been manipulated take part in the relation. If this set is empty, the process stops here.
- Then, a set of *informative experiments about the hypothesis* is filtered. This process uses the form of the hypothesis to divide the set of hypotheses resulting from the previous filter into sets which each can generate a prediction using the hypothesis. For instance, for a hypothesis with the form: "If a doubles, b is divided by two", experiments will be selected where a is doubled, quadrupled etc. where all other input variables are kept constant.
- For each of the informative sets for the hypothesis, *predictions* are generated for the output variables. This can be done using the hypothesis. For instance, if the hypothesis is a quantitative relation, such as $y = 2x$. Then the output variable y can be computed directly from the input variable x. If the hypothesis is qualitative, such as: "When x increases, y increases", it can be inferred from the (x,y) pairs: $(1,5)$, $(2,?)$ that the value on the question mark must be greater than 5. The more information available, the more accurate the prediction can be.
- The predictions generated are compared to the values actually found in the experiments. On mismatches, advice can be generated.

The analysis of experiments as described here yields two kinds of information. First, the availability of sets of experiments about a certain hypothesis contains information about what a learner *could* have inferred about a certain relation in the domain Second, the information collected can be used as a source to assess the learner's discovery behaviour as such. In this sense the information collected forms a learner model of both the discovery behaviour of the learner and the domain knowledge collected using the discovery environment. In both cases, this information can be used to generate advice, directed at improving the efficiency and effectiveness of the discovery process, without disrupting the self-directed nature of this process.

Using the Learner Model to Generate Advice

The assessment of the support for a hypothesis reveals whether the experiments contain information about the relation and/or the hypothesis, and, if so, whether the hypothesis is confirmed or disconfirmed. The contents of this assessment will be discussed along two lines: (1) that the assessment is valuable and (2) how this information can be used to generate advice.

Why is this information valuable?
The information on the experiments related to a relation or hypothesis can be used to draw a distinction between 'good' and 'bad' experimenters. If there is no information about the relation this is either caused by floundering behaviour, i.e. varying too many variables at the same time, by not changing the dependent variable, or by a combination of the two. When the hypothesis is semi-quantitative the same distinction can be made as well, and additionally it can be determined whether the experiments performed match the condition(s) in the hypothesis. If not, this indicates that the learner is not able to generate experiments that match the condition of the hypothesis.

The evidence being confirming or disconfirming for the hypothesis can be matched with the conclusion of the learner. A discrepancy between the learner's belief and the generated evidence indicates that the learner has not interpreted the evidence correctly.

How can this information be used to generate advice?
In the advice the relation between the experiments and the hypothesis or the conclusions can be questioned, followed by a suggestion on how to improve this aspect in the future. Being able to distinguish 'good' and 'bad' experimenters gives an opportunity to present 'bad' experimenters with information that concerns their experimenting behaviour. This advice is presented in the from of questioning the relation between the experiments and the hypothesis and a suggestion on how to conduct experiments that contain information on the hypothesis. When the experiments contained no information about the hypothesis the content of this suggestion depends on the kind of experiments that the learner has done. If the learner has changed more than one variable at a time, it is questioned whether this kind of experiments can serve as a basis to draw conclusions, and at the same time it will be suggested that it might be a better idea to change just one variable at a time in order to be able to keep track of the changes for the independent variable. For not manipulating the dependent, the value of experiment outcomes will be questioned and it is suggested to focus on the dependent variable.

A discrepancy between the learner's belief and the evidence that is generated for a specific hypothesis can be translated into advice as well. If the learners refuse to reject the hypothesis confronted with disconfirming evidence, they might either oversee this information or misinterpret the evidence. In either case the attention is drawn to the evidence that should have led to the rejection of the hypothesis. This can be done by presenting the predicted outcomes and the observed outcomes for the experiment(s) under this hypothesis. In case of rejection, when no evidence disconfirming the hypothesis was generated, the learner will be asked to reconsider his rejection.

It is important to note that no assumptions are made on the correctness of a confirmed hypothesis. No knowledge of correct and incorrect hypotheses is involved and any hypothesis can, in principle, be disconfirmed by future evidence, because strictly speaking, evidence within the induction paradigm can never be conclusive [12]. If this were to be the case this could be brought to the attention of the learner. For now the conclusion is that, based on the current evidence, the hypothesis can not be rejected.

Example

The mechanism as described above has been implemented within the SimQuest system [5]. In the current section we will illustrate how this mechanism works within a learning environment created with SimQuest. The domain is that of oscillatory motion. The simulation consists of a mass, a spring and a damping force. The student is asked to find out the relations between the mass, spring constant, and the frequency of the oscillation in the situation where there is no friction (damping =0), and in the situation where friction is present, represented by a damping force. The learner can change the input variables mass, force constant and damping. There are two output variables: the frequency of the oscillation and critical damping indicating the point beyond which the system will no longer oscillate. For this simulation let us assume that a learner performs the set of experiments presented in table 1 and states a hypothesis; and see what kind of information we can extract from this based on the analysis.

Table 1. Set of experiments used in the first example

experiment	mass	spring constant	damping	critical damping	frequency
1	1.00	1.00	10.00	2.00	0.00
2	8.00	3.00	10.00	9.80	0.00
3	3.00	5.00	10.00	7.75	0.00
4	1.00	4.00	10.00	4.00	0.00
5	1.00	2.00	10.00	2.83	0.00
6	8.00	8.00	10.00	16.00	0.78
7	8.00	4.00	10.00	11.31	0.33
8	8.00	12.00	10.00	19.60	1.05
9	8.00	6.00	10.00	13.86	0.60

The hypothesis the learner will start to investigate is:
If the spring constant increases then the frequency = 0
    In case a learner only conducted the first three experiments in table 1, the result of the analysis is that the set of experiments that are informative about the relation is empty because there are no two experiments for which the spring constant is changed and the mass is not changed at the same time. At this moment we can stop our analysis knowing that the learner had no support for the hypothesis because the experiments were not relevant for the relation that was under investigation.
    If the learner was to proceed with the next two experiments and again claimed this hypothesis to be correct, the system would re-evaluate the evidence starting with selecting the experiments that are informative about the relation. This time, the experi-

ments 1, 4 and 5 form a set that is informative about the relation. As the hypothesis is qualitative the same set is informative about the hypothesis. From experiment 1 we can generate predictions for experiments 4 and 5 and conclude, that for this set of experiments, the hypothesis holds. If later on the student conducts experiment 6 and 7 there are two sets of experiments that are informative about the relation/hypothesis. In this case both experiment 1, 4, and 5 and experiment 2, 6 and 7 are informative. The first set supported the hypothesis as we have seen, the latter, however, predicts a frequency of zero for the experiments 6 and 7, whereas the observed frequencies are not equal to 0. This means that the hypothesis can no longer explain the observations and has to be rejected. Fig. 2 shows the kind of feedback that the learner receives in this situation.

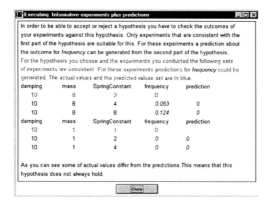

Fig. 2. Feedback after the experiments 1-7

Table 2. Set of experiments used in the second example

Experiment	mass	spring constant	damping	critical damping	frequency
1	3.00	3.00	0.00	6.00	1.00
2	3.00	5.00	0.00	7.75	1.29
3	6.00	4.00	0.00	9.80	0.82
4	2.00	3.00	0.00	4.90	1.22
5	2.00	12.00	0.00	9.80	2.45
6	3.00	4.00	0.00	6.93	1.15

A second example is the investigation of the semi-quantitative hypothesis stating:
If the mass doubles then the frequency will become twice as large.

After the first four experiments from table 2 the learner concludes that the hypothesis is correct. This conclusion is false. The information the analysis offers is as follows: there is a set of experiments for which the mass doubles (1 and 3) but for these two experiments the spring constant is not left constant; this means that the values for the frequencies cannot be interpreted to confirm or disconfirm the hypothesis. If the learner had performed the complete set of experiments in table 2, the conclusion would still have been false but now, because there is evidence, viz., experiments 6 and 3, which yielded a different result than would have been predicted by the hypothesis. In the first situation the learner receives feedback pointing out that the experiments are not suitable for testing this hypothesis and how to conduct experiments to test this hypothesis. In the second situation, the system confronts the learner with the conflict between the prediction generated by the hypothesis and the actual outcome of the experiment in a similar way as shown in Fig.2.

Discussion

In this paper we have outlined a mechanism for learner modelling of experimentation behaviour in discovery environments. The resulting system is capable of analyzing the experiments learners perform and, based on the information generated, draws conclusions about the developing domain knowledge of the learner and the quality of the learner's discovery behaviour. We have also demonstrated how the model generated is capable of generating support directed at improving the learner's learning activities in a discovery environment.

The system is a learner modelling system in the sense that it builds a model of the behaviour of the learner. To a lesser extent the system models the *knowledge* of the learner, only to what extent the learners have investigated the hypotheses they have stated is monitored. There are two main features of the system which are worth mentioning:

- *The mechanism is domain independent*

Nowhere in the mechanism is there a reference made to the actual model of the domain. All the system needs is a formalized description of the hypothesis the learner is investigating. This can be retrieved from the context offered by the learning environment, or by an input device like a hypothesis scratchpad [10]. This means that the system can be used in any domain for which a more or less formal description of knowledge is possible. This applies to most domains for which simulation models can be constructed.

- *The system can support searching the experiment space*

By generating hints, indicating where information is needed, pointing at the interpretation of experiments, the system supports the search for experiments relevant for testing hypotheses. The system does not support the learner's search in hypothesis space.

References

1. Bruner, J. S. (1961).The act of discovery. *Harvard Educational Review, 31*, 21-32.

2. Glaser, R., Schauble, L., Raghavan, K., & Zeitz, C. (1992). Scientific reasoning across different domains. In E. de Corte, M. Linn, H. Mandl & L. Verschaffel (Eds.), *Computer-based learning environments and problem solving* (pp. 345-373). Berlin, Germany: Springer-Verlag.

3. Holt, P., Dubs, S., Jones, M & Greer (1994). The State of Student Modelling. In J.E. Greer, & G. I. McCalla (Eds.), *Student Modelling: The key to Individualized Knowledge-Based Instruction* (NATO ASI series F: Computer and Systems Series, Vol 125) (pp. 3-35). Berlin, Germany: Springer-Verlag.

4. Jonassen, D.H. (1991). Objectivism versus constructivism: Do we need a new phi- losophical paradigm? *Educational technology research & development, 39*, 5-14.

5. Jong, T. de, Joolingen, W. R. van, Swaak, J., Veermans K., Limbach R., King S. & Gureghian D. (in press). Combining human and machine expertise for self-directed learning in simulation-based discovery environments. *Journal of Computer Assisted Learning.*

6. Jong, T. de, Joolingen, W. R. van, & King, S. (1997). The authoring environment Sim-Quest and the need for author support. In T. de Jong (Ed.) *Supporting authors in the design of simulation based learning environments.* Servive project, deliverable D 8.1. Enschede: University of Twente.

7. Jong, T. de & Joolingen, W. R. van, (in press). Discovery learning with computer simulations of conceptual domains. *Review of Educational Research.*

8. Jong, T. de & Njoo, M. (1992). Learning and instruction with computer simulations: learning processes involved. In E. de Corte, M. Linn, H. Mandl, & L. Verschaffel (Eds.), *Computer-based learning environments and problem solving.* Berlin: Springer-Verlag.

9. Joolingen, W.R. van, & Jong, T. de (1993). Exploring a domain through a computer simulation: traversing variable and relation space with the help of a hypothesis scratchpad. In D. Towne, T. de Jong & H. Spada (Eds.), *Simulation-based experiential learning* (pp. 191-206). Berlin, Germany: Springer-Verlag.

10. Joolingen, W.R. van, & Jong, T. de (1997). An extended dual search space model of learning with computer simulations. *Instructional Science, 25*, 307-346.

11. Klahr, D., & Dunbar, K. (1988). Dual space search during scientific reasoning. *Cognitive Science, 12*, 1-48.

12. Klayman, J. & Ha, Y-W. (1987). Hypothesis testing in rule discovery: strategy, structure, and content. *Journal of Experimental Psychology: Learning, Memory, and Cognition, 15 (4)*, 596-604.

13. Marchionni, G. (1988) Hypermedia and learning: Freedom and Chaos. *Educational Technology, 28* (11), 8-12.

14. Paolucci, M., Suthers, D. & Weiner, A. (1996) Automated advice giving strategies for Scientific inquiry In C. Frasson & G. Gauthier & A. Lesgold (Eds.). *Proceedings of the 3nd International Conference on Intelligent Tutoring Systems,* (pp. 372-381). Lecture Notes in Computer Science, Vol. 1086, Berlin: Springer Verlag.

15. Reimann, P. (1991). Detecting functional relations in a computerized discovery environment. *Learning and instruction, 1*, 45-65.

16. Self J. A. (1990) Bypassing the intractable problem of student modeling. In C. Frasson & G. Gauthier (Eds.). *Intelligent Tutoring Systems: At the Crossroadsof Articicial Intelligence and Education* (pp. 107-123). Norwood, NJ: Ablex.

17. Shute, V.J., & Glaser, R. (1990). A large-scale evaluation of an intelligent discovery world: Smithtown. *Interactive Learning Environments, 1*, 51-77.

18. Tsirgi, J. E. (1980) Sensible reasoning: A hypothesis about hypotheses. *Child development, 51*: 1-10.

An Interactive Graphical Tool for Efficient Cooperative Task Acquisition Based on Monaco-T Model

Serge Guepfu Tadié[1], Jean-Yves Rossignol[1], Claude Frasson[1], Bernard Lefebvre[2]

1: Université de Montréal , Département d'Informatique et de Recherche Opérationnelle, Case postale 6128, succursale Centre-Ville, Montréal (Québec), H3C 3J7 Canada. Email: (tadie, rossigno, frasson)@iro.umontreal.ca

2: Université du Québec à Montréal, Département d'Informatique, Case postale 8888, succursale Centre-Ville, Montréal (Québec), H3C 3P8, Canada. Email: lefebvre.bernard@uqam.ca

Abstract. In the past, Knowledge Acquisition represented a barrier for developing intelligent systems, and particularly intelligent tutoring systems. In a recent work we proposed a model (Monaco-T) for structuring and representing cooperative tasks. These tasks can be used directly in a cooperative learning environment, or in a simulation environment able to show how the cooperative task is effectively realized. To help experts representing knowledge with this model, we have built an editor able to produce tasks in Monaco-T format. The editor has graphic capabilities for editing rules, trees and layers, that are the basic elements of Monaco-T. Our editor also provides tools to directly link cooperative tasks to an external system able to react to direct manipulation. It represents an environment for component oriented programming.

Keys words: Knowledge elicitation, Collaborative learning, Cognitive task analysis Authoring tools.

Introduction

The construction of a knowledge base is known as an iterative process involving multiple refinements performed by a human, the *knowledge engineer*, who acts as an intermediary between the expert and the system [8].

However, the knowledge engineer creates as many problems as he solves [9]. Recent research aims to allow the expert to directly perform this task using computer [2] bypassing the knowledge engineer.

In the TeleLearning project[1], we have created Monaco-T [14], a model for teaching and simulating cooperative tasks which can be used by the knowledge engineer to extract his knowledge. However, as Monaco-T is simply a model we have decided to build a computer-based acquisition tool to facilitate this task. Monaco-T is a model

---

[1] This project is supported by the Telelearning Network Center of Excellence

for handling procedural knowledge including rules and layers. More precisely, the tasks are decomposed using trees and, consequently, we need interactive graphical tools to facilitate the acquisition and presentation of rules, together with facilities for representing multiple layers of knowledge.

Monaco-T can modeling cooperative task of manipulating system, for this purpose, tools for acquisition have to give us the way to link the task to the manipulated system. This characteristic allows our editor to be an environment for making component oriented programming. Tree

In this paper, we present first an overview of Monaco-T, a three-levels knowledge model we have developed for representing cooperative tasks. Each level contains rules that we detail. Then we present the main characteristics of the editing tools for manipulating the task and how the edited task can be linked to a real system. Finally, we show how to construct the set of rules at the dynamic and scenario levels.

An overview of Monaco-T: A Model to Represent Cooperative Tasks

In reviewing the ITS literature we obtain some answers to following questions: how knowledge is organized [10], what kind of strategy the tutor has to 1], how can we model learning strategies to reuse them [7], how can we analyze student reasoning [5], how to integrate cooperative learning and other aspects of social learning [13], [4]? However, all these goals assume that we have one student who faces the system and tries to learn an individual task or knowledge. In reality, many tasks are performed cooperatively. An example can be the task that consists on taking care of a patient in an intensive care unit. This task involves at least three actors: the doctor, the nurse and a laboratory technician.

Conceptually, what is a *cooperative task*? According to [11], [6], [15] [13], a task is called cooperative if it needs two or more actors to be performed. To teach this kind of task, a learning system has to provide an environment, which takes into account many working-places and tools to support cooperative work. In this environment, the learning system has to coach every learner as if he was working in a classic ITS on an individual task.

Because a cooperative task needs coordination between several expertise, a *model* of a cooperative task used in a learning system should help people to know how to coordinate their actions and how to execute them. The efficiency of the model should be improved by tools able to build a simulation of each role of the cooperative task. Monaco-T, which is a task-oriented model, focuses on the problems of explaining different reasoning failures and simulations of the cooperative task. It is also a model for representing tasks of manipulating systems such as piloting an airplane.

Monaco-T is organized in three levels (Figure 1): the *static, the dynamic* and *the scenario* levels. The first one represents the *tree structure* of a cooperative task and all the information describing this structure. The second one represents the *rules*, which define the general behaviour of the entire cooperative task. The third one guides the execution of the task by following some particular *strategies*.

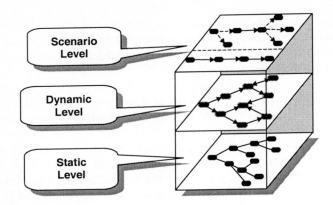

Figure 1 The three-levels subdivision of a cooperative task.

2.1 The Static Layer

The static representation gives us a way to analyze the whole task and split it into sub-tasks. The link between a task and its sub-tasks is a composition link. This decomposition is similar to the GOMS (Goals, Operators, Methods and Selection Rules) decomposition [3]. The differences between these two models are the following :

In Monaco-T a task is not an abstract goal, but represents a concrete action. When this task has some sub-tasks, its action consists in the composition of the results of his sub-tasks.

We take into account a cooperative execution of a task by allowing each task (action) to be executed by an agent.

The static representation of a task is a tree, whose root is the task, the nodes are the sub-tasks, and the leaves elementary ones.

Formally, the static level is defined as a space of ten dimensions. In this space, there are many relations between each dimension. At the end of the construction the static level implements some functions, which are useful in an environment for teaching or for simulation.

In a cooperative task based on Monaco-T, we have a set of working roles, a set of sub-tasks, a set of manipulated systems (system manipulated by the task. They are called Monaco-T component), a set of actions (representing the protocol of manipulated systems), a set of execution stage of sub-task (Activation, Realization, Termination), a set of characteristic variables (used to represent the state of the cooperative task. We define four kinds of characteristic variables *State*, *Status*, *NumberOfRealization*, *Results*), a set of possible values for characteristics variables, a set of operators of comparison, a set of activities of functional dependencies (each afd defines the fact that a characteristic variable pass from o value to another), a set of homogeneous groups of sub-tasks (gives us the way to designate some groups of sub-tasks by a unique name).

To structure the static layer of Monaco-T, we have to combine the different dimension found in our model. These combinations allows us to link action of external system to sub-task, to construct the tree of sub-task, to distribute afd among stage of execution of sub-task, to distribute sub-task to the team of role agent, etc.

Because Monaco-T has several layers, each layer has to communicate with the others. This communication is held by a set of functions built inside different layers of the model. The static layer implements several functions. These functions enable the static layer to transmit to others layer information about sub-tasks such as child, descendent, parent, working role, afds and so on.

2.2 The Dynamic Layer

The dynamic level defines the behavior of the task when a team of agents achieves it. While the GOMS model uses selection rules to determine the behavior of a task, Monaco-T builds its dynamic on the basis of the static task tree by creating in each node, three rule bases : the activation, the realization and the termination rule bases. These rules behave like pre-conditions, invariant and post-conditions rules in the domain of program proofs. They can be used by a computerized tutor to determine at what time a task has to be activated, executed and terminated. They also have to synchronize the partner's actions in the cooperative task.

Formally, the dynamic level is defined following three axis:
- the description of the semantic of each characteristic variable,
- the evolution of the cooperative task due to the activity of the team of agents (behavior of sub-task activities) and
- the rules or conditions, which define when each stage of execution of each sub-task that can be realized.

Based on these axis, we built some functions, which handled communication with every Monaco-T environment

In Monaco-T we used four types of characteristic variables: *State* (determine the stage of a sub-task), *Status* (determine the active path in the tree of sub-task), *NumberOfRealisation* (contain the number of time a sub-task has been executed) and *Results* (contain the result of the action involve in a sub-task. For example if we have a sub-task "Blood test", we can have a result variable called "quantity of blood"). Each sub-task in Monaco-T includes one *State* variable, one *Status* variable, one *NumberOfRealisation* variable and a set of *Result* variables.

The evolution of the cooperative task when a team of agents are working is maintained by assigning afds to the different stages of execution in each sub-task. This define the behavior of each of the three sub-task stages of execution. Because the role of afd is to update characteristic variables of cooperative task, when an agent decides to execute a stage of execution in one of its sub-task, the whole task is updated through the afds included in that stage.

The rules in our model have this form: if `Condition` then `Action`. The action in the rules represents the different stages of execution of the sub-task in the cooperative task. We affect a condition in the description of a stage of execution of a sub-task. We can then read it like this: To activate a stage of execution, we need that the condition in it has to be evaluated as true.

The conditions are built like a disjunction of conjunctions of terms. A term is a comparison between a characteristic variable and a possible value, using the value scope and the operator scope of the characteristic variable. A term can also be defined like a comparison between two characteristics variables using the operator scope of the first one. The unique constraint is that the value scope of the two characteristic variables has to be compatible.

There are many kinds of functions in this level. Functions to know the different rules in each sub-task, Functions to evaluate conditions of a rule, function to known which sub-task can be executed (activated, realized, terminated), function for advice. We are going to focus only on the functions for the construction of advice. These functions answer two kinds of question:

- Why a sub-task can't be executed?
- Who has to do what for allowing a sub-task to be executed?

Like we saw in [13]], these questions can be answered depending on some stages of reasoning. In Monaco-T we define five stages of reasoning: reactive, simple cooperative, extended cooperative, simple social, extended social. This function uses a kind of inference engine, which exploit an AND/OR tree.

2.3 The Scenario Layer

This level gives us the way to define different strategy to resolve the cooperative task. We have two kind of strategies: cooperative strategy and individual strategy.

The cooperative strategy or cooperative scenario is used to make a static demonstration to a team of agent who has to realized the cooperative task. His structure is a fixed planning of stage of execution of sub-tasks, where each stage of execution of sub-tasks has a moment of intervention.

The individual strategy or scenario is used to give or to control a precise behavior when an agent (human or simulated) has to execute a role in a cooperative task. Because agent behavior depend of the behavior of his partner, we have to define individual strategies like rules. It means that when some conditions are present, the agent can use a particular behavior.

At this moment, we have defined three kinds of rules: rules of ordering, rules of sub-tasks deactivation, and rules of terms deactivation.

Implementing Monaco_T Editing Tools

The manipulation of a task based on Monaco_T can be cumbersome. Indeed, as the number of sub-tasks increases, the possibility for the expert to keep track of the whole task decreases dramatically. The construction of the different rules of the dynamic and the scenario level need to be interactive. The expert need not know how to structure the rule base. He must be allowed to concentrate on the task construction. Also, Monaco_T does not define the domain of the different fields included in the sub-task nodes. The knowledge acquisition tool must implement data types to limit the range of the sub-task fields to be used in the construction of the rules.

In order to overcome these problems, a graphical interface has been developed so as to ease the work of the expert. As seen in figure 2, this interface allows for the expert to develop the sub-task tree graphically.

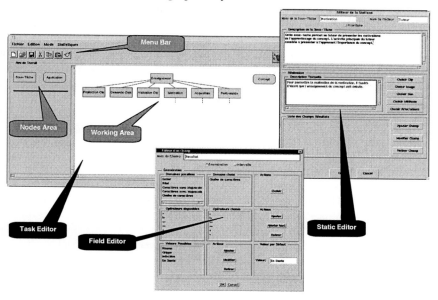

Figure 2   The graphical interface of the sub-task tree editor.

3.1 Manipulating the sub-task tree of a cooperative task

The task editor is divided in three zones. First, the working area is where the sub-task tree is constructed. This zone allows the construction of multiple sub-task trees in parallel for future assembly. It also allows for the interchanging of the nodes amongst brother nodes and displacement of sub-trees using cut and paste functions. Second, the nodes area is where the blank nodes are kept to be selected by the expert assembly in the working area. For now, only two types of node have been added, the sub-task nodes, and the application nodes. Future implementations will feature more advanced types of nodes such as typed sub-task nodes.

This task editor has a number of features that eases the work of the expert. First, the editor allows for a graphical construction of the static level. This is a great enhancement over textual editors that oblige the expert to keep a mental representation of the task. Second, it allows the expert to focus its work on a restrained part of the sub-task tree. This is done by closing or opening sub-tasks. As seen in figure 3, a closed sub-task, when it has children sub-tasks, draws a dotted line instead of its sub-tree. This way, when a whole part of the sub-task tree is completed, it can be temporarily closed.

Third, it implements all the standard editing functions such as copy, cut and paste in all the different editors of the application. Finally, at all times, the expert can press the F1 key to get a contextual help on hoe to use all the different editor functions.

During the construction of this tool, the emphasis has been put on eliminating the possibility for the expert to add syntactically incorrect data to the model and on getting a very high level of interactivity. To this end, data types have been added so as to enable the interactive construction of sub-task fields and rules. The elaboration of such data types allows for the construction of editors that are almost exclusively mouse driven, thus very interactive, disabling the possibility of incorrect rule construction.

3.2 Linking the task to a real system

When the task manipulate a system, our application give us the way to link different systems to a cooperative task by distributing actions (protocol) of the system among sub-tasks. The task will then be able to use the external system as means of interaction with the user. The possibility of linkage with external systems makes the application a component driven programming environment. This is done simply by adding an application node in the working area and specifying, by double clicking on it (figure 3), the concrete application it represents. Obviously, the available applications must respect certain constraints such as having specific methods that can be called from the task server, being written in Java, being available on the disk, etc.

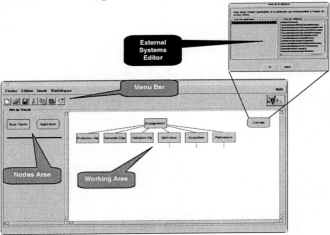

Figure 3 Interface for linking Monaco_T external components with the task

3.3 Constructing the sets of rules which define the dynamic level

The construction of the rule base representing the dynamic level of the task can be very difficult depending on the number of nodes in the sub-task tree. Indeed, even a small cooperative task can require a large set of rules to accurately correspond to the constraints imposed on a real cooperative task. Interactivity is a major factor here as the system must, not only ease the work of the expert, but also eradicate syntax errors from the rule base.

To this end, the construction of the set of rules defining the dynamic level is done mostly by use of the mouse. Indeed, every term composing the conditions (pre-condition, condition for execution, post-condition) is done by mouse, easing the task of the expert. A condition is constructed in three steps: the construction of the terms, their assembly in conjunctions and the assembly of conjunctions into a disjunction A term is constructed in three steps. First the left operand is chosen by selecting one field of any sub-task node. This sub-task node is selected in the graphical interface by mouse. Second, the operator is selected according to the ones available with the field of the left operand. Finally, the right operand is either a possible value of the left operand or another field, as in the left operand.

3.4 Constructing the different set of rules of the scenario level

The size of this set of rules is bound to be large. Hence, the number of data to be entered by the expert is large enough as to discourage any motivated worker. Some form of short cuts have to contribute in eliminating as much steps as possible by, again focusing on interactivity.

The scenario level is constructed with three sets: the set of sub-tasks orderings, the set of sub-tasks deactivation and the set of rules deactivation. In every element of the sets, applicability conditions (contexts) have to be constructed. As stated earlier, standard editing functions can be used to copy and paste different parts of the contexts, for reuse in the construction of others. Those contexts are built the same way the dynamic conditions are and are used by the task to determine if an element of the scenario is applicable given its state (of the task). The first set is the definition of the orderings of the sub-tasks. For every element of the set, once the applicability condition has been built, an ordering is generated by the system that can be altered by the expert. The default ordering is one that gives a pre-order traversal of the sub-task tree. The second set is the definition of the sub-tasks deactivations. The expert can, for specific contexts described by the applicability conditions, deactivate sub-tasks in the sub-task tree. This is done by simply selecting in the list of all the sub-tasks the ones to be deactivated. Finally comes the definition of the deactivation of rules in the dynamic set of rules. Again, given a context, the expert can select, with the mouse, the sub-task nodes and their disjunctions, conjunctions or terms to be deactivated. In every case, sub-task ordering, sub-task deactivation and rules deactivation, a number of contexts can be defined.

3.5 Improving the validity of the sets of rules

Since Monaco_T allows for the construction of conditions based on any node of the sub-task tree, it can become difficult to keep track of the interactions amongst the set of rules. In fact, as the rule base grows, it becomes impossible to predict the behavior of such a rule base in a real environment.

The construction of the scenario level poses the same challenges as in the construction of the dynamic one, only in a larger scale. Indeed, instead of a simple set of conditions found in the dynamic level, the scenario level is based on three different sets of rules, interacting with each other and with the dynamic rule through the applicability conditions. At this point, it become essential to have a validation tool.

In order to improve the validity of the sets of rules, and to be able to exploit the tasks and external systems built, an architecture has been developed. In this architecture, agents, representing the different task roles, can connect to the task server using Internet.

These agents can be human or simulated ones. The validation of the dynamic and the scenario set of rules is done mostly by connecting human agents to the server. Needless to say that those persons need to be experts of the task. This task allows the expert(s) to see if any constraint is missing or if there are too many.

After apply the scenario rules, by using functions defined in the dynamic level like those which help us to respond to question like why a sub-task can't be executed?, who has to do what for allowing a sub-task to be executed?, the expert who supervise the simulation can easily verify if the dynamic and scenario rules are consistent and valid.

Conclusion

The Monaco-T acquisition tools we have built matches all the characteristics required by the Monaco-T model. Despite the fact that Monaco-T model manipulate several kind of knowledge such as rules, tree, layer, object, component, the tools of acquisition we build are efficient.

This tools is divided in three modules, where each module corresponding at each layer of Monaco-T structure. The module of the acquisition of the static contains tools for: Decomposing a cooperative task in sub-tasks and link them to construct a tree of sub-tasks. Creating set of element, which define the dimension of the static. Constructing the different relation in the static by defining which element is in relation with which. Open a Monaco-T component and link his available action to the sub-tasks of cooperative task. This last characteristic allows Monaco-T tools for acquisition to be an environment of component oriented programming.

The module of the acquisition of the dynamic level contains tools for interactively construction of rules. Using the ATN, which define the behavior of each characteristic variable of Monaco-T model, the rules are well controlled in this tools.

The module of the acquisition of the scenario level is based on the tools of the dynamic level because both are structured in Monaco-T with rules techniques.

This tools also has the capability to improve the rules defined in dynamic and the scenario level. This improvement is realized by enabling the cooperative task to be executed by a team of artificial agent and let the expert watch the result and change some rules if the behavior of the cooperative task is not like he had imagined.

This editor work very well and was presented at the Second Telelearning conference [12] as a demonstration.

Bibliography

[1] Aimeur, E. et Frasson, C. (1996). Analyzing a New Learning Strategy According to Different Knowledge Levels *In Computers Educ volume 27 Numbers 2, pp 115-127.*

[2] Boose, J.H.. (1989). A survey of knowledge acquisition techniques and tools. *Knowledge Acquisition,* March, 1 (1), 3-37

[3] Card, S., Moran, T. & Newell, A. (1983). The Psychology of Human-Computer Interaction, Hillsdale, NJ : Erlbaum.

[4] Chan T.W. et Baskin A.B.(1990). Learning companion systems. *InIntelligent Tutoring Systems : At the Crossroad of Artificial Intelligence and education (Edited by Frasson C. And Gauthier G.) Chap. 1. Ablex, N.J.*

[5] Djamen J.Y. (1995). Une architecture de STI pour l'analyse du raisonnement d'un apprenant. Thèse de Ph.D., DIRO, Université de Montréal, Montréal, CANADA, Juin 1995.

[6] Ellis, C., Gibbs, S.J., et Rein, G.L. (1991). Groupware: Some issues and experiences. *CACM,* 34(1), pp. 38-58.

[7] Frasson C., Mengelle T., Aimeur E., Gouarderes G, (1996). An Actor-Based Architecture for Intelligent Tutoring Systems, In *The Proceeding of Thirth international Conference of Intelligent Tutoring Systems*, June, Montreal, Canada.

[8] Brian R Gaines & Mildred L G Shaw. (1992). Eliciting Knowledge and Transferring it Effectively to a Knowledge-Based System *In IEEE Transactions on Knowledge and Data Engineering* September 1992

[9] Brian R Gaines. (1988). An Overviwe of Knowledge-Acquisition and Transfer *In Knowledge Acquisition for Knowledge-Based Systems, Gaines,B.R & Boose, J.H., Eds, Knowledge-Based Systems, Vol.1, New York: Academic Press, 3-22*

[10] Nkambou, R., Gauthier, G., (1996) Un modèle de représentation de connaissances dans les STI. In Proceeding of 3th International Conference on Intelligent Tutoring System ITS96. Springer-Verlag.

[11] Schmidt, K. et Bannon, L. (1992). Taking CSCW Seriously. *In Computer Supported Cooperative Work Journal, 1,1,* pp. 7-40.

[12] Tadie, G.S., Rossignol, J-Y, Frasson, C. et Lefebvre, B. (1997). Collaborative Learning System in Industry. In *Demonstration at the Second Annual Conference on the TeleLearning NCE*, November 4-6, 1997, Toronto, Canada.

[13] Tadié, G.S., (1996) Coopération et Système Tutoriel Intelligent. Rapport de l'examen prédoctoral oral. Département d'Informatique et de Recherche Opérationnelle. Université de Montréal.

[14] Tadie, S., Lefebvre, B. et Frasson, C. (1996). Monaco-T âche: un modèle à nature coopérative pour la modélisation de tâche dans un STI. In *The Proceeding of Thirth international Conference of Intelligent Tutoring Systems*, June, Montreal, Canada.

[15] Terveen, L.G.(1995). Overview of human-computer collaboration. *In Knowledge-Based Systems volume 8 Numbers 2-3.*

Acknowledgments

This work is supported by the Tele Learning Network Center of Excellence of CANADA.

Learning in the Workplace: Initial Requirements of a Lessons Learned Centred Corporate Memory

Leila Alem

CMIS
Locked Bag 17, North Ryde, NSW 2113,
Australia
leila.alem@cmis.csiro.au

Abstract. Many organisations have recognised that the construction, communication and sharing of their corporate knowledge and know how is key to improving business effectiveness. This has lead to the design of a number of corporate memories. Such systems have so far failed to demonstrate how they can contribute to the effectiveness or learning of the organisation. This paper investigates the requirements of a corporate memory designed for promoting individual and collective learning within an organisation. Individual and collective learning are promoted by assisting the articulating and sharing of lessons learned. A set of initial functional requirements of a corporate memory centred around the lessons learned processing (L2Corp) is presented. Some consequences of such requirements are then presented in terms of knowledge modelling, authoring and associated architecture of L2Corp. This paper is a follow up to preliminary investigations in this area [Alem 97].

1. Introduction

Few organisations have recognised that a great portion of their everyday activities generates information that, when recognised for its potential usefulness, can be captured, stored in a corporate memory for future use and made available to decisions makers when needed. Such organisations have began to implement such corporate memories usually using either Lotus Notes or Intranet technology. This has lead to systems such as ACTION [Gasser et al 93], AIMS [Damiani et al 93], CARNOT [Huns et al 93], CKV [Barthes 93]. The main drive of such efforts has been to maximise knowledge development, storage and distribution. But as stated by Stein in [Stein & Zwass 95], the basic knowledge processes proposed in the literature on knowledge management (construction, embodiment, dissemination and use) do not provide the right level of abstraction for specifying the requirement that a corporate memory should satisfy, because they are not directly related to either the business model/task, neither to the goals of the organisations. The ultimate goal of organisations is not to maximise knowledge development, storage, distribution per se, but to improve the competitive power by continuously adapting the organisation to the external environment (market, social political climate, customer preferences etc.). In this paper we take the view that the requirements of a corporate memory implementation should be formulated in terms of these adaptations (= learning). This is aligned with the view that the main source of competitive advantage of an organisation is its knowledge assets and its learning capacity [Argyris 78].

Our aim is to specify the requirement of a corporate memory in term of forms of organisational learning that the corporate memory may want to support. This paper proposes a set of requirements of a corporate memory centred around the lessons learned processing as a means for promoting individual and collective learning within an organisation. Section two presents the type of learning taking place in an organisation, section three elaborates on the lessons learned processes, section four presents the initial functional requirements of the lessons learned centred corporate memory(L2Corp), section five presents L2Corp lessons learned models and conceptual framework, then comes the conclusion.

2. Organisational learning

Gertjan van Heijst in [Gertjan van Heijst 97] defines the relation between corporate memories and learning in organisations. He argues that a corporate memory should support three types of learning in organisations: Individual learning, learning through direct communication, and learning using a knowledge repository. His model of organisational learning involves two forms of learning: top-down learning and bottom-up learning. Top-down learning occurs at the management level when a particular knowledge area is recognised as promising and deliberate action is undertaken to acquire that knowledge. Bottom-up learning occurs when a worker (either on the management level or on the work floor) learns something which might be useful and this lesson learned is then distributed through the organisation. With the term "lessons learned", Gerrtjan van Heijst refers to any positive or negative experience or insight that can be used to improve the performance of the organisation in the future. It includes problems, worst practices, recommendations, most often repeated mistake, etc.

In this paper our focus is on the bottom-up learning which is centred around the lessons learned concept. In our view lessons learned processes are key in supporting individual learning (ie when an individual creates a new piece of knowledge) as well as collaborative learning (ie when individual experiences are shared among co-workers leading to collective learning). Sharing lessons learned is the sharing of individual experiences among co-worker , which may lead to one individual applying the lesson learned of another. This can potentially improve efficiency by helping in preventing the two classical problems: 1) reinventing the wheel, ie repeating activities/work which has already been performed in the past, and 2) repeating failure : failures tend not to be well-recorded and are therefore the type of activity/work most likely to be repeated. The agent accessing the lesson learned formulated by a peer may also engage in sharing of the experience and perception of the experience with peers which then promotes collective learning and increases collective and individual level of awareness. Articulating and sharing lessons learned can stimulate a number of type of learning that may occur in the workplace, such as learning by reflection, case based learning, learning through communication as defined by [Gertjan van Heijst 97].

As stated Peter Senge [Senge 90], in the Fifth Discipline "Learning in organisations means the continuous testing of experience, and the transformation of that experience into knowledge accessible to the whole organisation and relevant to its core purpose".

This has lead to the design of a number of experiences/lessons learned based corporate memories. Next section presents some limitations of such efforts.

3. Limitations of existing experienced based corporate memories

A number of corporate memories have been designed based on collecting, storing and retrieving lessons learned. such as: SELL a system which has been developed by the Nasa to capture lessons learned in flight system design development, integration , test and evaluation, CALL : a system which collects and distribute lessons learned in combat missions of the US army , and other systems developed using REX methodology such as REX-SPX, CAUSE, ELODIE, DIESEL, etc. [Malvache and Prieur 93].

- all of such systems are adopting a documentation approach to capturing experiences using data base techniques (relational objects, SGML document, hyper document for modelling, and indexing and retrieval for delivery). Their focus has been on organisational documents, technical notes, design document etc.. all of which capture in writing some form of implicit or explicit knowledge. Such knowledge when delivered is difficult to put into action.
- none of such systems (as far as we know) relates explicitly to the goals of the organisations such systems have been designed for. They , therefore, can not demonstrate how they can contribute to the effectiveness and learning of the organisation.
- the level of adaptation of such systems is low, the user model is often limited to key words.

These considerations lead to the following research problems:

- What are the means for representing individual experiences in a way that articulates the approach taken, the faced problems and what the individual had learned from the experience. This a *knowledge modelling and representation problem.*
- What functional help should be provided (by the system) to assist the user in making the best use of existing experiences. The purpose here is not to generate ready made solutions but more to guide and support thinking and understanding in ill structured activities by generating value added knowledge based on existing experiences. This problem can be described as the problem of *designing appropriate computer mediated effective learning tool.* This is aligned with Argyris and Schon view that the primary leverage of any organisational learning

effort lies not in policies, budgets or organisational charts, but in the way its members think and interact [Argyris 78].

- What type of learner/worker model can be built based on individual experiences so that learning can be evaluated and the functional help made adaptive. The is a *learner modelling problem.*

The next section presents the initial functional requirements of a lessons learned centred corporate memory (L2Corp), based on such considerations.

4. L2Corp initial functional requirements

The aim of L2Corp design is to both support the articulation and sharing of lessons as well as enabling the evaluation of L2Corp in term of learning.

The L2Corp should satisfy the following requirements:

1. it should provide assistance for articulating lessons learned
2. it should index lessons learned by the task and the characteristics of the lesson learnt
3. it should provide the contact of the agent who entered the lesson learnt, ie L2Corp should provide access to peer helper. This is aligned with the PHelpS Personal Assistant system idea proposed by McCalla and Greer in [McCalla and al 97], the difference being that L2Corp will not only provide the contact of the peer helper but also the lessons learned as described by the peers.
4. the collection and distribution of lessons learned should be passive in order not to intrude to the worker. An example of this type of system is the Nasa Space Engineering Lessons Learned (SELL) system.
5. there should be mechanisms for amending, aggregating and deleting lessons learned in a dynamic way
6. there should be mechanisms for relating lessons learned with tasks and goals of the organisations.
7. there should be means for generating learners models based on analysis of the content and history of user's lessons learned.

Requirements (6) and (7) will allow an evaluation of the L2Corp in terms of both its contribution to the effectiveness of the organisation, and in term of learning. This will constitute the main difference between existing lessons learned based corporate memory (such as a SELL, DoeE and CALL) and L2Corp.

Following such requirements, L2Corp requires

- An explicit representation of the organisational business processes,
- A representation of individual experiences and their link to business processes,
- A computer mediated tool to support the authoring of experiences in a way that promotes reflection and assessment of individual experience,
- A computer mediated learning tool to assist users interpreting individual experiences.

The next section presents some answers to the knowledge modelling problem and the computer mediated authoring learning tool problem underlying L2Corp's functional requirements.

5. L2Corp lessons learned model

In L2Corp, the lesson-learned class is described as:
1. author of the lesson learned and his/her contact,
2. the business process related to,
3. a general description: actors, date and place,
4. the initial situation,
5. the action taken and its objective
6. the resulting situation,
7. type of the lesson.

A lesson learned could be of three types: it could be a positive lesson (LL+), a negative lesson (LL-) or it could be a neutral lesson (LLo). A positive lesson learned is one in which the objective of the action is met or partially met. A negative lesson learned is one in which the objective of the action has not been met leading to a resulting situation that is worst than the initial situation. A neutral lesson learned (LLo) is one in which the resulting situation can not be assessed as being better or worst than the initial one.

This lesson learned model adds value to existing experience based systems, by assisting the worker in reflecting on their own experience in order to gain insight and understanding from experience through reflection, assessment of own experience in light of both successes and failures. The main conceptual differences are:

- An explicit representation of the assessment of the worker's owns experiences in term of the impact of their action, the outcomes reached.
- An explicit representation of the workers reflection on what are the elements of the situation that have contributed to a success or a failure of the actions taken, ie what had helped (enabling factors) and/or what were the barriers.
- an explicit link to organisational business processes

These conceptual differences enable the articulation of the worker's know-how used in their experience. This approach implies that the ability of workers is not only reflected by what they know, but also by how they learn.

In L2Corp, authoring lessons learned need to be done in a way that assists workers in articulating the knowledge related to their experience in a way that promotes learning.

5.1 Authoring lesson learned

When authoring a lesson the user needs first to provide the general context of the lesson, this is done by selecting a task or a number of tasks from an existing list of tasks. Such a list of tasks includes all possible tasks related to the activity for which the corporate memory is designed for. L2Corp needs therefore a representation of such activity. It should be task based, each task containing a description of :
1. situation patterns ie the typical type of situations one can encounter,
2. general ways of handling the task,
3. key factors related to the task.

The situation patterns as well as the key factors will assist the user in describing the specific situation in which the lesson has been learned.

The end user then needs to specify/evaluate the situation at hand, this is done by scoring the factors related to the task. The scoring of these factors will force discrimination and will help focusing the interaction with the system. The objective of the action undertaken by the agent needs to be expressed in terms of increasing or decreasing the scores of one or more key factor(s).

The objective of the action as well as the description of the situation are expressed in terms of key factors some of which will directly relate to the key success factor of the organisation. The representation of the activity in terms of task, situation patterns and factors and the representation of the lessons learned in terms of task and factors enables the bridging between lessons learned and the goals of the organisation as expressed in requirement (6).

For example if the activity for which L2Corp is developed is the development of commercial projects with clients, L2Corp's activity will be composed of a number of tasks including: establishing the client interest, producing a proposal for discussion, determining the commercial contract, managing the project etc. Each of such task will be associated with a number of key factors. Scoring factors allows the description of the situation.

Here factors related to establishing the client interest could include:
1. Re-working (RW : score 1 to 3, 1 being first time and 3 being more than twice)
2. Alignment with business strategy (ABS : score from 1 to 5)
3. Match of interest (MI : score from 1 to 5, 1 being poor match)
   A situation, in this example, can be described as: RW=1, ABS=3 and MI=1

The factor Re-Working is a key success factor for the organisation, it is also used as a factor for describing a number of situations.

So, lets' say that, in the previous example, when establishing the client interest with client X the organisation of a workshop in order to look for a better match of interest had worked and the presence of XYZ had helped. This piece of knowledge is represented as :

LL33
task = establishing the client interest
Client X, Actors = JohnF from end-user group and PierreB from management
Sit-initial : RW=1, ABS=3, MI=1
Action : organise a workshop with client
Objective: increase the match of interest
Sit-final : RW =1, ABS =3, MI =2
Peer-Contact :Leila (3151)

5.2 Retrieving lessons learned

In this case workers are trying to identify which part of the corporate experience is most relevant to their needs. They need to first describe the situation they are in. This could be done by determining
1. the task,
2. the client,
3. an initial scoring of the key factor = initial situation.
   Based on this information, L2Corp should then be able to
1. Retrieve all LL+, LL- and LLo which have similar initial situations. and tasks
2. Select the most relevant lessons learned
3. Present them in terms of what worked (LL+) in which context, what didn't work (LL-) and (LLo) in which context, each LL with related actions undertaken, objectives pursued and peer contact.

6. Future work

This paper presents initial functional requirements and concepts of L2Corp, a lessons learned centred corporate memory in a way that promotes learning from experience. L2Corp design supports the formulation of lessons learned as well as the sharing of such. Lessons learned are described using the notion of key factors which relates to the key success factors of the organisation. We have presented in this paper some consequences in terms of knowledge modelling, authoring and the associated architecture L2Corp's functional requirements imply. Examples have been given in the area of dealing with commercial customers. Evaluation of this approach beyond the scope of the feasibility study reported in this paper requires the definition of methods for associating (1) the lesson learned creation process within the corporate memory with (2) the evaluation of individual learning based on individual experiences. Such methods/metrics will allows us to evaluate the business benefits we can expect to gain from the use of corporate memory for organisational learning based upon the development and evaluation of prototypes.

References:

Alem L.1997, "Knowledge Management and organisational memory : preliminary investigations", June 1997, CMIS internal document.

Argyris C. and Schon C. 1978, " Organizational Learning : a theory of action Perspectives. Reading Massashusett, Addison Wesley.

Barthes J.P. 1993, The "Corporate knowledge Vaults" project. In ISMICK Management of Industrial and Corporate Knowledge, October 1993.

Damiani M., Randi P., Bertino E and Spampinato L. 1993, The AIMS projects: An information server architecture integrating data, knowledge abd multimedia information. In Entreprise Integration modelling-proceedings of the first International conference, 1993.

Gasser L., Hulthage I., Leverich B., Lieb J.and Majchrzak A. 1993, "Organisations as complex, dynamic design problems. In proceedinga of the sith Portuguese on AI, October 1993.

Gertjan van Heijst, Rob van der Spek, Eelco Kruizinga, 1997, " Organizing Corporate Memory" Proceedings of the 10th Banff Knowledge Acquisition for knowledge based systems workshop. Banff, Alberta, Canada. Nov 9-14, 1996.

Huber G.P. 1996, " Organisational learning : a guide for executives in technology-critical organisations :Int J. Technology Management, Special Publication on Unlearning and Learning for technological inovation, Vol. 11. Nos. 7/8, 1996.

Huhns M., Jacobs N., Ksiezyk T., Shen WM., Sing M.P., and Cannata P.E 1993. "Enterprise information modelling and model integration in CARNOT. In Enterprise Integration Modelling. Proceedings of the first International Conference, 1993.

McCalla G., Greer J., Kumar V., Meagher P., Collins J., Tkatch R., Parkinson B. 97 " A Peer Help System for workplace training", Proceeding of Artificial in Education 97. B. du Boulay and R. Mizoguchi (Eds). IOS Press 1997.

Malvache P and Prieur P, «Mastering corporate experience with the REX method», Proceedings of ISMICK-93, Management of Industrial and Corporate Knowledge, Compiegne, France, October 1993, pp. 33-41

Senge P., "Fith Discipline : Theory and Practice of the learning Organisation", Douleday, new York 1990.

Simon G. 1996, "Knowledge Acquisition and modelling for corporate memory : lesson learnt from experience". Proceedings of the 10th Banff Knowledge Acquisition for knowledge based systems workshop. Banff, Alberta, Canada. Nov 9-14, 1996.

Stein, Zwass 1997, " Actualizing organizational memory with information technology", Information Systems Research, 6(2): 85-117.

An ITS for Dutch Punctuation

Anders Bouwer

Faculty of Mathematics and Computer Science
Vrije Universiteit Amsterdam
The Netherlands[*]
andersb@dai.ed.ac.uk

Abstract. This paper describes a prototype Intelligent Teaching System aimed at improving Dutch university students' use of punctuation in writing and editing texts. Not only grammatical aspects of punctuation are considered, but also the effect of using different punctuation marks with respect to the rhetorical structure of the text. The system offers a student texts in which he should check the punctuation, and if necessary, make corrections. The system then analyses the student's answer and the differences with respect to possible correct solutions, and gives specific feedback based on these analyses. Formative evaluation of the prototype suggests that it has some advantages over using textbooks, because it allows students to understand the way punctuation actually works, rather than merely teaching prescriptive rules.

1   Introduction: Teaching Punctuation

This paper describes a prototype Intelligent Teaching System for improving students' understanding of punctuation. The system is based on the educational material of an existing course on writing skills for Dutch university students in linguistics [1, 2]. In this course the focus is not on giving prescriptive rules for writing the best text possible in one go, but rather on making clear the effects different choices of linguistic elements can have on the resulting text, and how changing some of these elements can improve, damage, or simply just change the text. This *functional* approach has the advantage that students become aware of the different possibilities they have in writing and reformulating texts.

Following [1], only a subset of punctuation marks is taken into account: the comma, the colon, the semicolon and the full stop. These four are among the most frequently used, especially in formal texts. Writers often have to choose between these four, whereas other punctuation marks, like parentheses, dashes, single quotes, quotation marks, exclamation marks and question marks are mostly reserved for a special occasion, which simply triggers that specific (pair of) mark(s). These special occasions can be adequately learned using ordinary textbooks, but the many possible ways of using the four punctuation marks mentioned can only be acquired by reading and writing both correctly and imperfectly punctuated texts, and receiving feedback about them.

---

[*] At the Department of Artificial Intelligence, University of Edinburgh, 80 South Bridge, Edinburgh EH1 1HN, Scotland, UK until October 1998.

1.1   Different Approaches to Punctuation

In the nineteenth century, punctuation was considered to mirror the syntactical structure of a sentence. There are indeed grammatical constraints on the use of punctuation marks, but they don't tell the whole story. Consider, for example, two sentences with a colon between them, where the second sentence is an explanation of something in the first. Changing the colon into a full stop won't affect the syntactical structure of either of the sentences; it will however change the meaning of the fragment, or even cause it to become meaningless. Another classic view is that punctuation is a reflection of the way we pronounce a text, with pauses and intonation. However, different kinds of pauses do not clearly match with different punctuation marks; moreover, speech normally encompasses many more pauses than there are punctuation marks in the corresponding written text. More recently, a third view has developed, called the functional approach. Here, the main focus is on the effect of using a specific punctuation mark with respect to the interpretation of the surrounding text, in terms of structure and meaning. For (American) English punctuation (including intra-word, inter-word and higher-level), this approach is perhaps best described in [3]. Dutch punctuation is slightly less constrained, however; therefore, the functional approach as adopted in [1] and the corresponding course module is used in this study.

1.2   Common Punctuation Errors

A small survey (done manually by the author, based on initial error marking by teachers) of first drafts of papers written by first-year university students revealed that some students have a strong habit of chaining multiple clauses and fragments by the use of commas, where either stronger punctuation is required, or no punctuation at all.[1] Sometimes they use a semicolon where a colon would actually be better. Overall, students don't use semicolons or colons very often, thereby missing some opportunities to improve their texts, as interviews with teachers suggested.

1.3   Types of Exercise

Looking at different books on punctuation [5, 6] and writing skills [1, 2], several types of exercises are found. The most popular one, which is adopted in this system, is the *check-and-correct* exercise: the student has to check a piece of text for punctuation errors (which may or may not be there), and correct them if necessary. The difficulty level of such exercises is hard to formalize, but crude factors are the length of the text and the sentences within it, and the number of errors; all these factors affect the complexity of the search space.

Another kind of exercise consists of punctuating texts where all punctuation marks have been removed, aided (or not) by indicating positions of punctuation marks. This kind of *completion* exercise seems more unnatural, however, because

---

[1] This is very similar to results from a French punctuation study [4].

texts without any punctuation are rarely found, whereas the *check-and-correct* exercise is encountered regularly by writers, proof readers and editors. A third type of exercise found is to reflect and describe the use of punctuation in a piece of text. And of course, writing texts and receiving feedback on them by punctuation experts is yet another way of acquiring punctuation skills. However, automating these last two ways requires natural language processing capabilities beyond the level presently available.

2   The System: Domain Knowledge

As explained earlier, the punctuation of a text should structure the text in such a way that it matches both the grammatical and rhetorical structure. Therefore, the system has knowledge about the effects of the different punctuation marks, knowledge about the rhetorical and grammatical structure of the texts, and knowledge about constraints on the use of different punctuation marks.

2.1   Hierarchy of Punctuation Marks

Of the four punctuation marks mentioned, the comma delivers the least separation. This can lead to errors when a stronger boundary is needed. The semicolon is used to separate segments on a higher level than the comma. Clauses connected by semicolons together form a functional unit within the context. Often such a segment consists of a pair of clauses, with one of the following relations holding between them: restatement, justification, elaboration, or contrast. An exception is the use of semicolons in a list or enumeration, where they can be used to separate any number of elements. A colon can be used to announce an explanation, a quote, or an enumeration. Both a semicolon and a colon are in principle preceded by a main clause which could stand on its own as a full sentence, except in the case where semicolons are used in an enumeration. Because the semicolon and colon are similar in strength, caution is necessary when they are combined in one sentence. The full stop, at the top of the hierarchy, ends a sentence, without giving further information about the relation which might hold between the sentences around it. This is why a text containing only full stops and no other punctuation marks often seems to lack structure.

2.2   Encoding Texts

The texts used in the exercises are about 2 to 8 lines long, and are decomposed into basic elements, separated by punctuation marks. Each element is assigned a grammatical status: *clause, subordinate clause,* or *fragment,* a catch-all category. In addition, relations which hold between two segments (segments can be basic elements, or combinations of them, resulting in hierarchical structures of segments) are stored explicitly. Some of these relations are similar to Rhetorical Structure Theory relations [7] like *elaboration, contrast* and *joint;* others are of a more syntactic nature, *e.g.,* subordinality of clauses with respect to other ones. Moreover, most relations above the sentence level are ignored, while more attention is paid to the structure below the clause level.

Finally, all correct punctuation combinations are stored for each text, as well as the one which is shown initially, with or without errors. While in the study described here all annotation tasks were done by hand, current Natural Language Processing techniques could help automating the parsing into elements and the grammatical analysis [8], [9]. Recently, automatic extraction of rhetorical structure has also been investigated [10].

2.3   Combination Rules of Punctuation

At the heart of the system are the rules for combining two (or more, in the case of an enumeration) segments of text together into one more complex segment. These rules are used when a text is parsed to extract its punctuation structure, which guides the generation of feedback. An example of such a rule is abstractly depicted in figure 1.

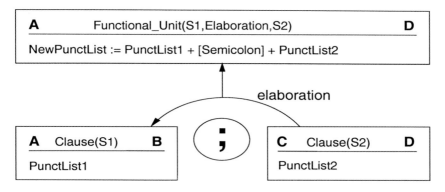

Fig. 1. A rule for combining two clauses with a semicolon in between, marking an elaboration relation

This rule states that segment A–D can be seen as one functional unit with structure [S1, elaboration, S2], if the interval A-D can be split in two segments A-B and C-D, for which the following holds: C-D is an elaboration with respect to A-B; segment A-B is a clause with internal structure S1; segment C-D is a clause with internal structure S2; neither A-B nor C-D contain semicolons. PunctList1 and PunctList2 keep track of which punctuation marks are contained within a segment; these lists are combined together with the new semicolon into NewPunctList. Other rules take care of other combinations like two contrasting clauses with a comma or semicolon in between, or enumerations, which can have multiple fragments separated by commas (or by semicolons, in case commas are not strong enough to separate the elements of the enumeration). The system currently comprises about 40 rules in total, accounting for different combinations of segments and the punctuation marks *comma, colon, semicolon* and *full stop.*

3   The Prototype: An Example Session

The prototype, implemented in SWI-Prolog[2], comprises a number of modules; using the exercise definitions and parsing rules, different modules take care of exercise presentation, problem highlighting, difference analysis/explanation, and structure analysis/explanation. To give an idea of the system's capabilities, a session trace is displayed, together with some comments about the underlying mechanisms. The text and the feedback of the system are translated into semi-English for the purpose of this paper.[3] In this example, all punctuation issues in Dutch seem preserved in the English version. All feedback texts consist of pre-stored templates with dynamically generated segment numbers and relation types. The input from the student is prompted by `Punctuation >>>`, followed by his alternative solution.

3.1   Presentation of Exercises: The Interface

After a short introduction to the goal of the system, its user interface and an example, the system presents an exercise in the following manner:

```
Please check the use of punctuation marks in the following fragment:

  Maybe it is exactly this criticism which makes people want to grab for
  these books, as a way of supplementing the regular approach. Whatever's
  the case; these books can boast a huge popularity, they go over the
  counter by thousands.

Consider whether you would like to alter the way this text is punctuated.
Maybe this would also involve capitals being changed into lowercase or
vice versa, but you don't have to worry about that. The division into
segments is as follows:

1. Maybe it is exactly this criticism which makes people want to grab for
   these books
2. as a way of supplementing the regular approach
3. whatever's the case
4. these books can boast a huge popularity
5. they go over the counter by thousands

To give your proposal for a new punctuation, you have to enter the
numbers of segments, followed by the punctuation mark of your choice.
For example, the way the text is punctuated right now can be displayed
as 1,2.3;4,5.
```

---

[2] Copyright (c) 1993-1995 University of Amsterdam. All rights reserved.

[3] The Dutch version of the text, with the same punctuation errors, is: *Misschien is het juist deze kritiek die mensen naar deze boeken doet grijpen, bij wijze van aanvulling op de reguliere aanpak. Hoe dan ook; deze boeken kunnen bogen op een grote populariteit, ze gaan bij duizenden over de toonbank.*

Do you have any idea on how to improve the punctuation of this text? If
yes, please enter your proposal in the way described above. If you think
the punctuation is fine as it is, type 'ok'. If you don't know, just type
RETURN.

Punctuation >>> 1,2:3,4.5.

3.2   Analysis of Differences

Now that the student has given an alternative punctuation, the system first tries
to find out what the changes are with respect to the original version as shown
in the exercise, and the optimal version(s) of the text[4] . This leads to a global
evaluation of the student's answer based on the number of *corrected errors* (the
semicolon between 3 and 4 has been replaced correctly by a comma); *neglected
errors* (none in the example); *changed errors* (the comma between 4 and 5 was
changed to a full stop instead of a semicolon, which would have been the best
choice); and *introduced errors* (the full stop between 2 and 3, which was already
correct, was changed to a colon). Simple rules involving calculations on these
four variables determine what kind of feedback will be given as introductory
remarks. In the example, the number of *corrected errors(1)* + *changed errors(1)*
> *the number of introduced errors(1)*, therefore the following will be given as
feedback:

Well, that's better than it was, but there's still room for improvement.

  You have localised some problems correctly, but you haven't handled
  them in the best possible way: ...

You have also introduced some new problems: ...

The detailed treatment of each problem is done by a module called *difference
explanation*.

3.3   Difference Explanation

This module has rules about why the chosen punctuation mark is not the best
one possible, compared to an ideal solution. In the example, the student correctly
changed the semicolon to a comma, but chose to replace the comma between 4
and 5 by a full stop, where a semicolon would have been even better. Therefore,
the system replies:

The full stop between segment 4 and 5 creates too big a separation.
Segment 3-4 forms a functional unit together with segment 5. Therefore,
a semicolon is the better choice here.

---

[4] The optimal punctuation for this text is considered 1,2.3,4;5.

Unfortunately, the student also chose to replace the full stop between 2 and 3 (which was already correct) by a colon, thereby introducing a new problem. In this case, the system says:

```
The colon between 2 and 3 would suggest that an explanation or
enumeration follows. What seems to be case here is just a new step in
the reasoning process. Therefore, a full stop is the better choice here.
```

3.4   Structure Explanation

After the student has been shown all problems, a correct solution will be given as a final version of the text. Before moving on to a next exercise, however, the student can ask the system to generate an explanation of the structure of the text, based on the parsing rules together with the encoded features of the text:

```
This punctuation segments the text into two full sentences, each ending
with a full stop. The first sentence comprises segments 1-2; the second
comprises segments 3-5.

Within the first sentence
  - segment 2 is an adjunct to segment 1; both segments are bound
    together by a comma.

Within the second sentence
  - segment 3 is a relative clause preceding its head, segment 4; both
    segments are bound together by a comma.
  - segment 5 is an elaboration of segment 3-4; this relation is marked
    by a semicolon.
```

First, the system describes how the text is segmented into full sentences; then each sentence is treated in turn, by describing the internal structure in a bottom-up fashion. This way, the student can see how the small elements are combined to form larger ones, and how the punctuation marks are related to this hierarchical structure.

4   Evaluation

The prototype was tested informally by both teachers and students separately, while the experimenter was present to answer questions and to observe the subjects' and system's behaviour. After the test session, which lasted for about 15 minutes for students and 30 minutes for the teachers, findings were discussed within each group.

4.1   Teachers

Two teachers from the writing skills course evaluated the behaviour of the system from both a linguistic and didactic viewpoint. They were given a short description of how the system worked and asked to evaluate the system's feedback.

They were instructed to work through each of the six exercises several times, giving different answers each time. This allowed them to see how the system would respond to students giving different answers. Positive comments from the teachers about the system were:

1. The feedback really applies to the student's answer. This is a real advantage over systems which can only give the right answer and leave the comparison completely to the student.
2. The explicit use of text segments while interacting with the system (by referring to their numbers), facilitates understanding the structure.[5]
3. The introductory remarks, structuring the feedback into three different kinds of errors (introduced, changed, and unchanged) were regarded as useful in interpreting the information.

Negative comments they gave were:

4. The fact that the system displays much text creates problems; it is impossible to see both the text and feedback at the same time when the fragment is more than a few lines long.
5. The system does not have much to say about combinations of punctuation marks, *e.g.*, it is usually a bad idea to include both a semicolon and a colon within the same sentence, as this might induce multiple possible readings.
6. The feedback texts are not always convincing. When the system says a particular relation is present in the text, it doesn't tell why it thinks this is the case. The system should perhaps be able to justify its claims by pointing to specific lexical elements in the text suggesting a particular reading.
7. According to one teacher, the system acts too pedantically. If a student disagrees with the system about the feedback it gives, there is no way of expressing this disagreement. Allowing interactive argument is difficult, but the system could simply send these cases to a human teacher.

4.2   Students

Five artificial intelligence students participated in the formative evaluation session. Following explanation of how the system worked, they were asked to try some of the exercises and to evaluate the system in terms of what they thought they had learned, and what they liked or disliked in the system's behaviour. The students agreed with the teachers on points 1-4. In addition:

8. Most subjects liked using the system, and some commented that it made them think more clearly about their own use of punctuation marks, especially colons and semicolons.

---

[5] In some exercises, however, the teachers preferred to divide some segments into smaller ones, to add some punctuation marks where there were none in the original text. They also wanted to be able to leave out punctuation marks, which is not possible in the current version.

9. Some subjects didn't like the fact that the system corrected their errors by giving the right answer immediately afterwards; they would prefer the system to give them a second chance.

10. Some subjects said that after a while, they did not really look at the original texts anymore; they just looked at the segments, and tried to think of the best way of adding punctuation marks from scratch. This essentially changes the nature of the task from a *check-and-correct* to a *completion* exercise, as described in section 1.3.

11. Some subjects felt a desire to insert conjunctions, or alter the text in other ways. This is not possible in the current prototype.

5   Further Work

Besides the mere addition of many more exercises with some more linguistic knowledge to fully cover them, and more rigorous evaluation of the actual learning effects, future work might include the following:

— Changing the interface to a graphical one, where students may click in the text to make changes. In this way, a distinction can be made between the skill of locating errors, and the skill of correcting them.
— Modelling students' behaviour over time, focussing on recurring error patterns, to allow more general comments like *'You don't seem to use the semicolon at all; maybe you should try one sometime'*.
— Looking more into the *process* of placing punctuation marks. For example, in a *completion* exercise, teachers will often break up the text into sentences first by placing full stops, before choosing the smaller punctuation marks in between; students tend to work more from left to right.
— A more holistic treatment of structural differences in punctuation. Although the prototype is capable of explaining the structure of correct solutions, it treats differences for each position separately.
— Have the system transform texts (annotated as in section 2.3) into exercises automatically, by picking text fragments to suit its current teaching goal in terms of complexity, structure, and use of specific punctuation marks.
— Combine the work outlined here with NLP techniques for segmenting texts and parsing grammatical and rhetorical structure (and some help of the writer), to allow for better treatment of punctuation in grammar checkers.

6   Conclusion

This paper shows that a functional approach to punctuation can be implemented in an Intelligent Teaching System for students learning how to write and edit texts. The current prototype is able to give intelligent feedback on students' answers to exercises which involve checking and correcting the punctuation of texts. This is done using not only the kind of prescriptive syntactic rules found in handbooks, but also the rhetorical relations present in a text.

Formative evaluation of the prototype has led to positive remarks from both students and teachers about the way it showed how punctuation actually works, but also resulted in many ideas for improving the system. Besides changing the textual interface to a graphical one, this includes adding student modelling techniques for adapting the curriculum to a particular problem a student is having, which may be related to the strategies the student is using while performing the task. Also discussed are possibilities for the automatic generation of exercises, and improvements to grammar checkers.

Acknowledgements

This work was part of a MSc project at the Vrije Universiteit Amsterdam (see [11], in Dutch, for more details), supervised by Rineke Verbrugge (AI) and Gisela Redeker (Linguistics), with help from Margreet Onrust (Linguistics) in the evaluation of the prototype. I would also like to thank Shari Trewin, Angel de Vicente, Helen Pain and Geraint Wiggins of the AI Department of the University of Edinburgh, as well as three anonymous reviewers, for commenting on earlier drafts of this paper.

References

1. Onrust, M., Verhagen, A., and Doeve, R. *Formuleren.* Bohn Stafleu Van Loghum, Houten/Zaventem (1993a)
2. Onrust, M., Verhagen, A., and Doeve, R. *Docentenhandleiding bij Formuleren.* Bohn Stafleu Van Loghum, Houten/Zaventem (1993b)
3. Nunberg, G. *The Linguistics of Punctuation.* CSLI Lecture Notes, No. 18. Stanford (1990)
4. Simard, M. Considerations on parsing a poorly punctuated text in french. In Bernard Jones, editor, *ACL/Sigparse International Meeting on Punctuation in Computational Linguistics*, pages 67–72. HCRC Publications (1996)
5. Horst, P. J. van der. *Leestekenwijzer.* SDU Uitgeverij, 's-Gravenhage (1990)
6. Vervoorn, A. J. *Prisma Leestekens en hoofdletters. Over een goede interpunctie.* Het Spectrum, Utrecht (1991)
7. Mann, W. C. and Thompson, S. A. Rhetorical structure theory: Toward a functional theory of text organization. *TEXT*, 3(8), pages 243–281 (1988)
8. Shuan, P. L. and Ann, C. T. H. A divide-and-conquer strategy for parsing. In Bernard Jones, editor, *ACL/Sigparse International Meeting on Punctuation in Computational Linguistics*, pages 57–66. HCRC Publications (1996)
9. Briscoe, T. The syntax and semantics of punctuation and its use in interpretation. In Bernard Jones, editor, *ACL/Sigparse International Meeting on Punctuation in Computational Linguistics*, pages 1–7. HCRC Publications (1996)
10. Marcu, D. *The rhetorical parsing, summarization, and generation of natural language texts.* PhD thesis, University of Toronto (1997)
11. Bouwer, A. Intellipunctie: een intelligent onderwijs-systeem voor interpunctie. Master's thesis, Faculty of Mathematics and Computer Science, Vrije Universiteit Amsterdam (1996)

Cognitive Task Analysis in Service of Intelligent Tutoring System Design: A Case Study in Statistics

Marsha C. Lovett

Center for Innovation in Learning, Carnegie Mellon University
Pittsburgh, PA 15213, USA
lovett@cmu.edu

Abstract. Cognitive task analysis involves identifying the components of a task that are required for adequate performance. It is thus an important step in ITS design because it circumscribes the curriculum to be taught and provides a decomposition of that curriculum into the knowledge and subskills students must learn. This paper describes several different kinds of cognitive task analysis and organizes them according to a taxonomy of theoretical/empirical ∞ prescriptive/descriptive approaches. Examples are drawn from the analysis of a particular statistical reasoning task. The discussion centers on how different approaches to task analysis provide different perspectives on the decomposition of a complex skill and compares these approaches to more traditional methods.

Introduction

One of the first steps of intelligent tutoring systems (ITS) design involves performing a cognitive task analysis of the curriculum to be taught. There are a variety of approaches to cognitive task analysis. This paper argues for a new taxonomy of those approaches.   Theoretical   approaches   tend   to   emphasize   the   informational requirements of the task: what information is included in a problem description? how is this information represented? how must it be transformed to produce a solution? Empirical approaches, on the other hand, emphasize the processes people are engaged in as they perform the task. Another distinction is between prescriptive approaches that analyze a task in terms of how it *should* be performed and descriptive approaches that analyze a task in terms of how it *is* performed. One can combine these various features to get a variety of cognitive task analysis styles. As a structure for this paper, take the two distinctions (theoretical vs. empirical and prescriptive vs. descriptive) as orthogonal dimensions and cross them to create four distinct combinations. This paper will demonstrate how all four cognitive task analysis styles can be useful in service of ITS design.

The task domain to be analyzed is a topic in statistics called exploratory data analysis (EDA). EDA involves using statistical tools to describe, summarize, and draw conclusions about data. It is a good example for demonstrating cognitive task analysis for several reasons. First, EDA is a complex problem-solving skill that requires the solver to bring several different types of knowledge to bear on real-world problems (e.g., domain-specific and domain-general knowledge, higher-level reasoning and low-level perceptual processing, and both declarative and procedural knowledge). Thus, providing a cognitive analysis of this task will shed some light on the structure of what is sometimes considered to be more of an art than a science. Second, the need for EDA arises frequently across a wide variety of disciplines and in everyday life [2]. As such, it is commonly viewed as an important target of instruction [11]. Third, teaching EDA is a challenge [4, 17]. Many students at the undergraduate level, even after a statistics course, lack the necessary skills for selecting appropriate data-analytic tools [17], interpreting statistical graphs [13], and drawing conclusions from data [7]. Thus, identifying the key components of this complex skill could help improve instructional design and hence student learning.

The outline of this paper is as follows. The next section describes related work to set this research in context. The subsequent section presents a taxonomy of four types of cognitive task analysis and exemplifies how each applies to the domain of EDA. The final section discusses how these different task analyses contribute different perspectives to ITS design and relates them to more traditional methods.

2 Related Work

Although there has been a good deal of computer-assisted instruction in the domain of statistics, very little of this research specifically addresses the domain of EDA. There are two standard ways that computers are used in statistics instruction. The first is as a computational tool. Many introductory statistics classes include off-the-shelf statistical software packages to help students in analyzing real data sets, but these packages do not have an instructional component. The second standard way that computers are used in statistics instruction is as a simulation tool. These simulation programs are used as vehicles for students to view certain statistical phenomena in a discovery-world context. Examples include ExplorStat [9] and StatVisuals [10]. Although these simulations have an instructional component, they generally focus on isolated statistical concepts (e.g., standard deviation, confidence interval) and so do not deal with the larger skill of EDA.

The most notable exception to this rule is StatLady, an ITS for teaching probability and statistics [14]. This system has been shown to lead to substantial learning gains both in terms of pre- to post-test measures and when compared with other (non-StatLady) instructional conditions [15, 16]. The descriptive statistics module of StatLady is most closely related to EDA, so it will be discussed here. The StatLady Descriptive Statistics Modules covers a range of skills from sorting data to generating informative data displays. The Descriptive Statistics-1 component of StatLady was based on a task analysis that identified approximately 80 different curriculum elements. These elements are arranged into groups of elements that are closely related to each other and that tend to be taught in a unit. These curriculum elements also are categorized as representing three types of knowledge: procedural, symbolic, and conceptual. This short description shows that analyzing a task in the domain of statistics can lead to a highly complex, but also highly structured, set of task components.

2.1   The Context for the Examples

Because the different kinds of cognitive task analysis will be exemplified in the context of EDA, it is important to have a more specific idea of what is involved in this complex task. We take an EDA problem to include (1) a set of data, (2) some description of those data (e.g., what the different variables contain, how the data are represented) and (3) a question that requires one to draw conclusions from the data. For example, take the following problem statement:

> A weather modification experiment was conducted in south Florida to investigate whether "seeding" clouds with silver nitrate would increase the amount of rainfall. Clouds were randomly assigned to the treatment group (to be seeded) or to the control group (not to be seeded), and data were collected on the total rain volume falling from each cloud. A variable named *group* contains data on whether each cloud was seeded or not (1 = seeded, 2 = not seeded), and a variable named *rain* contains data on each cloud's rain volume. Does cloud seeding increase rainfall?

In this problem, (1) there are data available, (2) the data are described as coming in the form of two variables, *group* and *rain*, and (3) the question being posed is "Given these data, does cloud seeding appear to increase rainfall?" These three features compose the initial state of this problem. The goal state or "solution" to such a problem includes the following: (1) interpretation of appropriate statistical analyses performed on the data (e.g., interpretation of a graphical display of the distribution of rain volume for each of the two groups) and (2) discussion of how those results address the question that was posed (e.g., was the seeded group's rain volume larger, on average, than the not-seeded group's rain volume). Getting from the initial state to the goal state requires many steps—some mental steps (e.g., transforming the problem statement into a plan for action) and some physical steps (e.g., working with a statistical software package to produce the displays). In general, a cognitive task analysis is aimed at identifying the separate task components necessary to progress through all the necessary steps and reach a solution.

3   Different Types of CTA

Figure 1 presents the 2∞2 table of analysis styles to be explored in the following sections.

	Theoretical	Empirical
Prescriptive	Information-theoretic analysis of how the task should be performed	Analysis of how experts produce high-quality solutions
Descriptive	Complexity analysis to predict how people actually do the task (e.g., typical errors)	Analysis of how novices actually do the task (e.g., their misconceptions)

Fig. 1. Two-by-two table of dimensions along which cognitive task analyses can vary.

3.1 Theoretical/Prescriptive

One approach to deriving a theoretical/prescriptive cognitive task analysis is to consider the information present in the initial state and in the goal state and then to specify how this information must be transformed to progress from one state to the other. In the case of EDA, the initial state includes a data set, a description of the data, and a question. The problem solver must somehow take this information and produce interpretations of analyses performed on the data and conclusions regarding the original question (see Figure 2, top row). Given this, it is logically implied that an intermediate step in the task must involve producing an analysis (i.e., the analysis to be interpreted, see Figure 2 middle row). To progress with a theoretical analysis then, one continues to ask, for each intermediate step generated, what is required to go from the preceding state to that intermediate state or from that intermediate state to the next state.

In the EDA example of Figure 2, we can apply this technique to the middle row and ask how a solver would get from the initial state to a state that has an appropriate analysis of the data. In EDA there are many different kinds of analyses that are appropriate in different situations. One must choose an analysis based on the type of variables involved in the problem (e.g., are they categorical or quantitative). Therefore, we must add a preceding intermediate state specifying the proper identification of variables (Figure 3, bottom row). Repeating this process to identify intermediate states between each pair of adjacent states leads to the cognitive task analysis in Figure 3. This task analysis could be refined further still, but we stop at this level for current presentation purposes.

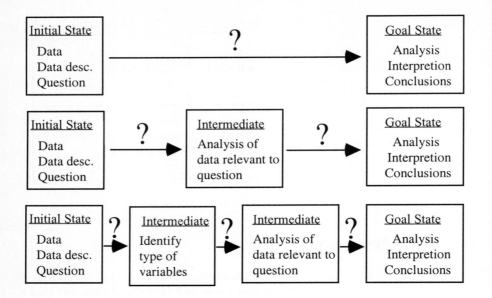

Fig. 2. Progressive revinement of a theoretical/prescriptive cognitive task analysis.

Note that this style of cognitive task analysis is similar to means-ends analysis [12] in that one repeatedly evaluates the difference between two problem states and establishes an intermediary to link them, eventually creating a complete solution path from initial state to goal state. Thus, the resultant analysis emphasizes the goal structure of the task more than the methods for achieving those goals. Thus, this technique is most appropriate for domains where planning is very important to good problem solving. This is true of EDA, especially in complex problems, where several planning steps must be taken before any analysis is initiated. Also, any situation where the ITS design involved an emphasis on goals or planning would be well informed by this style of task analysis. For a detailed enumeration of the procedures involved in performing a task, however, this approach should probably be combined with one or more of the other approaches described below.

3.2   Theoretical/Descriptive

The difference between a theoretical/*prescriptive* and a theoretical/*descriptive* task analysis involves a consideration of how people will actually perform the task, not just how they should perform the task correctly. This can involve an analysis of where errors are likely to occur or what parts of the task will be difficult to learn. One can apply cognitive psychological theories to make these predictions. For example, tasks that involve high working-memory demands are predicted to produce more errors [3].

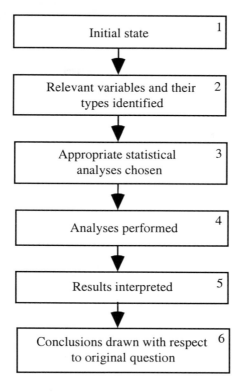

Fig. 3. Resulting cognitive task analysis.

One can apply this type of task analysis at more detailed level as well. Previous research suggests that steps that are not overt (e.g., "mental" planning steps) will be more difficult for students to learn than steps that have coresponding observable actions [8]. This suggests that the first three steps depicted in Figure 3 will be difficult to learn because students will tend not to see these steps modeled often and will tend not to be corrected when they make mistakes on these steps. It may spotlight particular areas where special attention should be directed during ITS design. This approach to task analysis is especially useful when data on student performance and errors are not already available.

3.3 Empirical/Prescriptive

The next type of cognitive task analysis involves an empirical/prescriptive approach. Here, experts can be asked to solve a series of problems *while* they are providing concurrent talk-aloud protocols [6]. Such protocols provide step-by-step information about what features of the problem the experts are attending to, what intermediate results they are producing, and what goals they are posting during the solution of a problem. The experts are ideally those who will produce high-quality (i.e., accurate and complete) solutions. This could range from a professional in the target domain to a "good" student, where "good" is defined in terms of some performance criterion.

1	So, it looks like what the problem is asking for is a comparison between breeder A and Breeder B puppies and specifically it says that Breeder A wants to compare the heights of the Great Dane puppies.
2	So actually the information on weight and litter is not necessarily going to be useful. ...
2	So, we've got 2 variables heights , well actually 1 var which is height.
2	And that would be the response variable and the explanatory variable is breeder.
3	So, one of the first things I'd like to do is do a boxplot to compare the heights for breeder A vs Breeder B. ...
4	<S selects boxplot in statistics package; display appears>
5	Ok there we go. Ok so now what do I see? Well, I'm looking at boxplots of heights of these Great Danes. Um. for the two breeders.
5	Immediately what I see is that the central part of the distribution for breeder A's puppies seems to be shifted lower than, relative to the central part of the distribution for breeder B's puppies.
5	And being specific, the third quartile for the distribution of heights of breeder A is actually even lower than the median for breeder B, the distribution of puppies from breeder B.
5!	So that means that 75% of the pups were shorter than the median height pup for breeder B, that's for group A.
5	There's, I would say the IQR in the two groups is about the same.
5	The overall range is bigger in breeder A. Breeder A also has a low end outlier,
5!	a little dwarf Great Dane.

Fig. 4. Expert protocol excerpt

Figure 4 presents some excerpts from a statistics instructor solving an EDA problem that asked whether puppies bred by two different breeders tend to differ in height. To the left of each line in the protocol is a number indicating the step number (from the task analysis in Figure 3) that the expert's verbalization appears to represent. One can see by a quick scan of the column of numbers in Figure 4 that this problem solver is following the theoretical/prescriptive task analysis quite closely. He makes one statement corresponding to step 1 from Figure 3, then three statements corresponding to step 2, etc. This analysis can be useful to confirm a previously generated theoretical/prescriptive task analysis.

Also noted in Figure 4 are two cases where the expert makes some particularly insightful comments during interpretation of his analyses. These lines are noted with a bold exclamation mark (!). In the first, the expert makes a specific inference about the proportion of data in one group that would be lower than the median for the other group. This step demonstrates not only that he can "read off" the values on a graphical display, but that he can use these values flexibly and appropriately. The final step shown in Figure 4 shows not only that this expert is willing to make a pun (not yet part of the EDA curriculum!) but that he takes into account the context of the problem in making his interpretations. This is important for the final step of drawing conclusions even though it was not present in the earlier theoretical/prescriptive analysis. Thus, seeing such features of expert performance can suggest revisions and additions to a theoretical/prescriptive analysis that might not have included them. In particular, it may revise the ITS design to emphasize the use of contextual information in interpreting statistical displays.

This theoretical/descriptive analysis style is also useful on its own. For example, it may be the preferred approach when the ITS designer does not have a lot of domain knowledge and hence would have difficulty in applying a theoretical/prescriptive analysis based on first principles. In addition, the theoretical/descriptive analysis focuses more on procedures required for good performance because it focuses on the expert's problem-solving processes. Therefore a domain that involves learning a lot of procedural knowledge would be well analyzed under this approach.

3.4 Empirical/Descriptive

Finally, empirical/descriptive cognitive task analysis can be performed by collecting talk-aloud protocols from students who are currently learning the target domain or from people who may perform the target task but have not received formal training. Since EDA is covered in many introductory statistics classes and yet students often exit these classes with misconceptions and incorrect strategies, we collected data from students whose problem-solving protocols might reveal such areas of difficulty.

Because the technique for collecting the data was similar to that in the empirical/prescriptive analysis above, we will just summarize the results of this analysis. Several areas of weakness were revealed as students often did incomplete or incorrect exploratory data analyses. By studying their talk-aloud protocols, the following difficulties were identified:

- Skipping of steps 2 and 3 (from Figure 3) such that students began carrying out statistical analyses without having considered the variable and analysis types
- Selecting incorrect statistical analyses (step 3) or just guessing at analyses
- Incompletely interpreting the statistical analyses generated (e.g., forgetting to describe the spread of a distribution and only describing its mean value)
- Failing to address the results of the statistical analyses to the question (step 7)

The first two of these areas of difficulty are consistent with the predictions of the theoretical/descriptive analysis, i.e., that planning steps would be difficult for students to learn because they are not overtly taken. The other areas of weakness help to highlight problem areas that may be representative of student misconceptions. For example, previous research has shown that students learning statistics often fail to understand the importance of variability. This could be related to some students failing to mention the spread of distributions in their interpretations of graphical displays.

4 Discussion

Each of the cognitive task analysis styles described above provided important results about EDA to inform the design of ITS for this domain. Here we summarize some of the strengths and weaknesses of these approaches, highlighting that different styles may be more effective for different domains or at different stages of ITS design. Theoretical/ prescriptive analysis helps identify the goals that must be achieved for high-quality performance of a task.   This can lead to the specification of the knowledge components an ITS needs to cover. It is especially useful in providing an abstract picture of the goal structure of a task; this may be helpful in the early phases of ITS design. However, it does not emphasize the methods for achieving task goals, so heavily procedural domains may require further task analysis of another style. The theoretical/descriptive approach similarly derives its results from theory-based predictions but deals more with how actual performance may depart from the prescriptive model. This is useful in highlighting areas where special attention to student errors and difficulties in learning is warranted. When data on typical student difficulties and misconceptions are not available, this approach can be very useful. The empirical approaches differ from the theoretical in that they are based on studies of people performing the target task.   This provides a "reality check" on the theoretical analysis at the cost of additional data collection and coding time. Empirical/prescriptive cognitive task anlaysis focuses on studying people who will produce high-quality solutions, whereas empirical/descriptive cognitive task analysis focuses on "typical" performance. These analysis styles are also useful on their own (not just as validation methods) because they (a) emphasize the processes involved in problems solving and (b) offer the potential for very fine-grained analyses. Thus, empirical analyses are appropriate for domains requiring a good deal of procedural knowledge of for later stages of ITS design where detailed refinements of the task analysis are helpful.

It is also important to note the relationship between these analysis methods and those described in other work. Durkin, for example, contrasts interview and case-study methods of task analysis [5]. Interview methods are quite different from those covered in this paper; they primarily rely on people's introspections about the knowledge required for good performance in a domain. Case study methods, on the other hand, relate to the empirical approaches described here. In particular, observational case studies performed with experts correspond to the empirical/prescriptive approach, and observational case studies performed with end users or novices correspond to the empirical/descriptive approach. Retrospective case studies, which involve someone's retrospective report on a previously solved problem, are in some sense intermediate between interview and observational case study in that they require some amount of actual problem solving (the empirical side) and some introspection (a recollection of why/how particular solution steps were taken). Like those described in this paper, these traditional methods are best suited to different situations. The general rule, however, is that *some* type of task analysis (or possibly several types) will aid ITS design because the better we understand the problem, the better we can solve it.

References

1. Anderson, J. R., Corbett, A. T., Koedinger, K. R., & Pelletier, R. (1995). Cognitive tutors: Lessons learned. *The Journal of the Learning Sciences, 4*(2), 167-207.
2. Becker, B. J. (1996). A look at the literature (and other resources) on teaching statistics. *Journal of Educational and Behavioral Statistics, 21*(1), 71-90.
3. Byrne, M., & Bovair, S. (1997). A working memory model of a common procedural error. *Cognitive Science, 21,* 31-61.
4. Cohen, S., Smith, G., Chechile, R. A., Burns, G. & Tsai, F. (1996). Identifying impediments to learning probability and statistics from an assessment of instructional software. *Journal of Educational and Behavioral Statistics, 21,* 35-54.
5. Durkin, J. (1994). Knowledge acquisition. In J. Durkin (Ed.) Expert systems: Design and development. (pp. 518-599). New York: Macmillan.
6. Ericcson, K. A., & Simon, H. A. (1993). *Protocol Analysis* (Rev.). Cambridge, MA: MIT.
7. Garfield, J. & delMas, R. (1991). Students' conceptions of probability. In *Proceedings of the Third International Conference on Teaching Statistics*, D. Vere-Jones (Ed.), Volume 1. pp. 340-349. Voorburg, The Netherlands: International Statistical Institute.
8. Koedinger, K. R., & Anderson, J. R. (1993). Reifying implicit planning in geometry: Guidelines for model-based intelligent tutoring system design. In Lajoie, S., & Derry, S. (Eds.) *Computers as Cognitive Tools.* Hillsdale, NJ: Erlbaum.
9. Lang, J., Coyne, G., & Wackerly, D. (1993). ExplorStat. Computer Program.
10. Loomis, J., & Boynton, G. (1992). Stat Visuals. Univ. of Calif. Computer program.
11. National Council of Teachers of Mathematics (1989). *Curriculum and Evaluation Standards for School Mathematics.* Reston, VA.
12. Newell, A., & Simon, H. A. (1972). *Human Problem Solving.* NJ: Prentice Hall.
13. Pittenger, D. J. (1995). Teaching students about graphs.*Teach. of Psych.* 22(2), 125-128.
14. Shute, V. J., & Gluck, K. A. (1994). Stat Lady Descriptive Statistics Tutor: Data Organization and Plotting Module. Brooks AFB, TX: Armstrong Laboratory.
15. Shute, V. J. (1995). SMART: Student Modeling Approach for Responsive Tutoring. *User Modeling and User-Adapted Interaction, 5,* 1-44.
16. Shute, V.J., Gawlick-Grendell, L. A., Young, R.K., and Burnham, C.A. (1995). An Experiential System for Learning Probability: Stat Lady Description and Evaluation. *Instructional Science (4),* 1-22.
17. Ware, M. E., & Chastain, J. D. (1991). Developing selection skills in introductory statistics. *Teaching of Psychology, 18*(4), 219-222.

Diagrammatic Reasoning for Geometry ITS to Teach Auxiliary Line Construction Problems

Noboru Matsuda *and* Toshio Okamoto

Graduate School of Information Systems,
University of Electro-Communications

Abstract. A new model of problem solver for geometric theorems with construction of auxiliary lines is discussed. The problem solver infers based on schematic knowledge with diagrammatic information (diagrammatic schema, DS for short). The inference algorithm invokes forward and backward chaining. The diagrammatic schema as well as the inference algorithm was designed through a series of observations of human problem solving. This paper also describes that DS is beneficial for instructions, especially for teaching students how to draw auxiliary lines.

1 Introduction

The main issue of this study is on a development of geometry ITS to teach how to solve problems that require the construction of auxiliary lines. Many geometry ITSs / CAIs have been developed so far (for example, [1, 3, 4, 10, 17]). Geometry Tutor[1] is one of the earliest geometry ITS based on the formal geometry rules as knowledge to solve problems as well as to teach students. CABRI CAI[17] is one of the most recent learning environment with GUI in which students can construct arbitrary geometric figures and modify them.

However, no geometry ITS with a capability to teach students how to construct auxiliary lines has been introduced in the past, while there have been several studies done on automatic construction of auxiliary lines in the field of AI[5, 7, 15, 16, 18]. All of them are based on a procedural knowledge of construction in terms of goals and constraints. When students receive explanations generated by such systems, they might understand how the solution was reached using the auxiliary lines given for that particular situation, but could they be able to construct similar lines in different situation? The answer might be NO without understanding the reasoning process of the system for the construction of the auxiliary lines.

We have noticed, through several experiments, that students strongly rely on diagrammatic information when they solve geometric problems. Indeed, many preceding researches have mentioned the importance of diagrammatic information[9, 8, 12–14, 19].

In this paper, we propose a theorem prover with knowledge to interpret diagrammatic information, which is further capable of automatic construction of the auxiliary lines. We then discuss an effectiveness of diagrammatic information for tutoring systems.

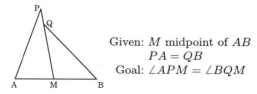

Given: M midpoint of AB
$$PA = QB$$
Goal: $\angle APM = \angle BQM$

Fig. 1. An example of a proof problem.

2   Problem Solving Based on Diagram

We have conducted an experiment on geometric theorem proving to observe students' thinking and solving process. In this section, we describe an outline of the experiment, and then list several observed characteristics upon which the further discussions are based.

There were twenty one junior high school students participated in the examination. One third of the subjects were asked to solve problems alone, while the rest of them solved in pairs. Each of the subject or the pair of subjects solved 2 to 4 problems selected from 6 different problems. Fig. 1 shows an example of a problem used for the examination.

The students were instructed to solve problems out loud. All utterances given by a subject during problem solving were recorded as a verbal protocol. Analysis of the data revealed the following distinctive behavior.

(C1) They like to refer to the elements in figures visually (e.g., *"this angle,"* *"that segment, "* or simply say *"it"*), instead of using symbolic labels (e.g., *"angle A-B-C,"* *"side X-Y,"* etc).

(C2) A particular configuration of the figure reminds students strategies for solving problems, or facts related with the given figure (for example, theorems, definitions, etc).

(C3) They often construct auxiliary lines that complements the present figure so that the modified configuration matches against a particular configuration in their memory toward solving the problem.

(C4) When they can not think of any suitable operation to accomplish the proof, they take a deductive inference strategy like *"writing the facts in the figure which are directly drawn from the current problem situation."*

(C5) They sometimes invoke a hypothesis verification. If they think of a statement that seems to be beneficial to the proof but is later found not to be valid in that particular situation, then they dismiss the statement with a proper reason.

Each characteristic listed above is supported by the facts observed in the verbal protocols. Here are detailed explanation of the characteristic with some sample protocols from 7 subjects solving the problem shown in Fig. 1.

In regards to constructing auxiliary lines, a strong evidence to support the characteristic C3 mentioned above is apparent in Table 1. This table shows clas-

Intention of construction	Example of Auxiliary Lines[†]	Frequency
Parallel Line	$BX \parallel PM$, $MX \parallel AP$, $MX \parallel BQ$, etc.	7
Extension of a segment	X on the extension of BQ, X on PM	3
Congruent segment	$BX = BM$ where X is on an extension of PM, etc.	2
Transferring of a triangle	Move $\triangle QBM$ as MB overlaps MA and Q overlaps X on an extension of PM	4
Bisector	AX of $\angle A$	1
Construct a familiar figure	PB as $\triangle QPB$, etc.	5

[†]Note: X is a newly added point by construction

Table 1. Example of auxiliary lines for the problem in Fig. 1.

sifications of the analyzed result from observing students construct 22 auxiliary lines in 18 different patterns for solving the problem in Fig. 1.

C4 indicates that students often invoke a forward inference chaining that is not necessarily towards the goal. Indeed, several researchers have mentioned the importance of forward inference not only in geometry[9, 15], but also in many other domains like decision making in intensive care medicine[11] and designing in biology[2], etc. During our experiment of the problem in Fig. 1, 31 out of 46 (67.4%) statements made by students on geometric theorems were verified as the act of invoking the forward inference.

Hypothesis verification (C5) is one of the distinctive feature of human problem solving. During the experiment, 3 out of 7 subjects invoked this strategy. For example, a subject mentioned that "$\angle PAM$ *is not equal to* $\angle QBM$, *because if they are the same measure then* $\triangle PAM$ *should be congruent with* $\triangle QBM$ *which is contradictory to the difference between a length of PM and QM.*" Another example of the hypothesis rejection is appeared in a statement like "$\triangle PAM$ *and* $\triangle QMB$ *are not congruent, because they have the segments of the different length.*" Since hypothesis verification works as a powerful heuristics for a computerized problem solver, we will discuss this issue in detail at 3.3.

All of the subjects were referring to geometric elements in the visual way (C1), and it is obvious from above protocols that they invoke diagrammatic information to solve geometric theorems (C2).

Though many other characteristics were observed in the experiment, we have focused on the above five listed and designed a new model of theorem prover for geometry based on the diagrammatic information.

3   Diagrammatic Reasoning

This section describes the knowledge structure and the reasoning algorithm for geometry theorem prover. The knowledge represents diagrammatic information as well as mathematical information (for example, theorems, relationships among

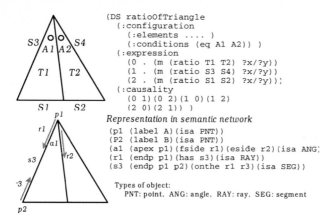

```
(DS ratioOfTriangle
   (:configuration
      (:elements .... )
      (:conditions (eq A1 A2)) )
   (:expression
      (0 . (m (ratio T1 T2) ?x/?y))
      (1 . (m (ratio S3 S4) ?x/?y))
      (2 . (m (ratio S1 S2) ?x/?y)))
   (:causality
      (0 1)(0 2)(1 0)(1 2)
      (2 0)(2 1)) )
```

Representation in semantic network

```
(p1 (label A)(isa PNT))
(P2 (label B)(isa PNT))
(a1 (apex p1)(fside r1)(eside r2)(isa ANG)
(r1 (endp p1)(has s3)(isa RAY))
(s3 (endp p1 p2)(onthe r1 r3)(isa SEG))
```

Types of object:
    PNT: point, ANG: angle, RAY: ray, SEG: segment

Fig. 2. Example of diagrammatic schema and semantic network.

Table 2. The semantics of links.

Link	Meaning	Link	Meaning
endp	Terminal point of a segment	apex	Vertex of an angle
fside	Segment from which an angle begins	eside	Segment at which an angle ends
onthe	Ray which a segment overlap	has	Segments lying on a ray
label	Label of a geometric object	isa	Type of an object

some objects, etc) for particular figures which are often accessed to solve problems. We call this knowledge *diagrammatic schema* (DS for short), since they represent a knowledge of problem solving based on diagrammatic information.

3.1 Architecture of Diagrammatic Schema

DS consists of two parts as symbolic declarations; (i) *structural declaration* (hereafter, refer to it as a *S-part* of DS) that represents a configuration of a particular figure, and (ii) *operational declaration* (*O-part*) that suggests the mathematical relations held in the figure. Fig. 2 shows an example of diagrammatic schema and semantic network.

S-part is written in semantic network basically equivalent to the one developed in PERDIX[6]. Each node in the network corresponds with a geometric element of the figure (that is, segment, angle, point, etc). The links among the networks specify relationships between nodes, for example, a point *is an apex* of an angle, a segment *is a side* of an angle or a triangle, 'X' *is a label* of a point, etc. The semantics of the links is shown in Table 2. An example of the network is shown in Fig. 2 with association list in LISP.

S-part also describes the constraints called *permanent constraints*. They are permanent because they must be satisfied to activate the corresponding schema;

the problem solver never tries to generate subgoals when these constraints are not satisfied in a given problem figure.

O-part describes the mathematical relationships between geometric objects in S-part as well as the causality among the relationships. It therefore consists of two subparts;

Expression part : A set of mathematical expressions about the relationships between geometric objects, that is, measurement, equality, parallelism, orthogonality, etc. The expressions are written with the nodes in S-part.

Causality part : A set of causal relationship exists in the expression part. The relationships are described a pair of premises and a consequence.

The mathematical expressions in the expression part refer to the geometric objects by an ID of the node in semantic network instead of a label of the object. This feature, corresponds with the first characteristic (C1) listed in the previous section, prevents a problem on the combination of the label which makes a search space to be huge.

For example, given there are two nodes a1 and a2 which are angles, and they are labeled $\angle ABC$ and $\angle DEF$ respectively. If the two angles are equal, then they are expressed in the relational expression as equal(a1,a2) instead of using the labels as in equal($\angle ABC, \angle DEF$). In the latter form, angle a1 is also represented as $\angle CBA$ while a2 has another representation as $\angle FED$, so that a number of equivalent expressions representing equal(a1,a2) is four. If there is a point on the segment AB, then a number of the combination for the label doubles.

3.2   Reasoning Algorithm with DS

Before explaining a reasoning algorithm with DS, some definitions on the state of DS are needed.

Given a problem P with a figure N_P represented by semantic network, a goal G to solve, and a set of premises.

DS_i is a diagrammatic schema with suffix i as a discriminater. Refer to the semantic network in S-part of DS_i as N_{DS_i}. $\overline{N_{DS_i}}$ consists of the same links and nodes as N_{DS_i} except all node IDs are substituted with unique variable. N'_{DS_i} is a subset of N_{DS_i}.

DS_i is *active* if $\overline{N_{DS_i}}$ is unifiable with a subset of N_P, and all the permanent constraints in S-part are satisfied. An active schema DS_j should be *applicable* if any of the causal expressions of DS_j is satisfied in the current state of N_P. An active schema DS_k should be *effective* if some expression in O-part of DS_k is unifiable with G. Any DS which is not active is *invalid*.

A diagrammatic schema DS_i is *potentially active* if N'_{DS_i} is unifiable with a subset of N_P. In this situation, a difference between N_{DS_i} and N'_{DS_i} corresponds with the geometric figures which are short of N_P. It means that if the lacking part existed in the problem figure, then the schema DS_i is to be active.

The inference steps to solve a geometric problem with diagrammatic schemata is shown below;

S1: (Termination Test) If there exists a relationship that corresponds with G in N_P, then the problem P is solved.

S2: Examine a state of every DS against the current problem situation. The state of DS is one of four; active, applicable, effective, or invalid.

S3: For each applicable DS, apply it to N_P. Application of the DS causes new relational expressions described in O-part to be added into N_P. This step corresponds to the fourth characteristic (C4) listed in the previous section. Take termination test.

S4: For each effective DS, re-examine the causality and then apply it if the schema is applicable, otherwise spawn unsatisfied causal expressions as disjunctive subgoals for G.

S5: For each generated subgoal, examine it for validity and reject the one if it is invalid. Otherwise, try to solve the valid subgoal.

At step S5, the inference procedure spawns subgoals that are well related to the problem situation at that moment. In this way, the subgoal'ing with DS based inference prevents a node, where human does not feel it is worth considering from being a subgoal. On the other hand, ordinal production systems invoke a strategy as "subgoal'ing unknown conditions in any case" to activate a rule that may have an effect to solve a goal. So, many irrational subgoals are evaluated, resulting in a combinatory explosion on the search.

3.3 Goal Rejection

The fifth characteristic — C5: rejection of invalid subgoals — of human problem solving mentioned earlier is one of the most significant heuristics that enhance the performance of computer problem solver as well, because it causes serious reduction in a search space.

An early example of goal rejection in geometry was implemented by Gelernter[5]. He has addressed to this issue by rejecting the subgoals that are not valid in the diagram by comparing the subgoals represented in strings with the diagram. A subgoal is invalid if those strings do not appear in the diagram.

Obviously, Gelernter's rejection heuristics are not powerful as compared with human behavior, because sometimes people mention about a conflict between a subgoal and the problem situation. For example, to solve a problem shown in Fig. 3 which is one of the problems used for the experiment, a subject expected that $\triangle ECF$ is an isosceles triangle as he knew a measure of EC is 1 so that a measure of FC might be also 1. But he noticed that it is not true, because the hypothetical subgoaling of "$\triangle ECF$ is an isosceles triangle" deduces $EC = CF$ as a consequence which is contradictory to the fact that "a ratio of EC to CF is 3:4."

We have designed a conflict based goal rejection heuristics for a computerized problem solver (see step S5 in the previous section). Before trying to solve a subgoal, the problem solver infers its logical consequences by applying all applicable DSs as well as a set of *ad hoc* inference rules. The inference rules are designed to deal with non diagrammatic deductions; for example, "*If A equals to X, B equals to Y, and A equals to B, then X equals to Y.*"

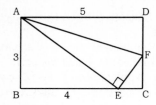

Problem: Give a rectangle $ABCD$ where $AB = 3cm$, $BE = 4cm$, and $AD = 5cm$. The bisector of $\angle EAD$ intersects with DC at a point F. What is a measure of CF?

Fig. 3. Example of conflict based goal rejection

3.4   Focus Control

The inference step with DS fairly depends on a pattern matching with S-part against a problem figure. Since a number of different DS, however, might be fired (that is, to be active, applicable, or effective) at each situation, we have introduced heuristics to control the firing of DS.

This control mechanism is suggested by an observation of the ways human pays attention to the elements within a problem figure. Hereafter, we refer to a part of the figure to which an attention is paid as the *focus*.

The focus limits an extent of problem figure against which S-part is matched. In our system, the focus is continuously changed according to the progression of an inference as follows.

- At the beginning of a problem solving, the focus is on the given premises and the goal.
- Given, a schema DS_i is fired under the focus F_i at a time t_i. A focus for the next inference step (F_{i+1}) is taken one by one in the following way until some DS is fired;

  F_{i+1}^e: The newly added expressions by DS_i
  F_{i+1}^s: F_{i+1}^e + A part of N_P corresponding with N_{DS_i}
  F_{i+1}^x: F_{i+1}^e + F_i
  F_{i+1}^o: Entire elements of a problem figure

A focus gradually shifts from a narrow scope to a broad one. Since F_{i+1}^o covers the entire part of a problem figure, this heuristics do not prevent the problem solver from finding a solution.

4   Auxiliary Line Construction

Some geometric problems require construction of auxiliary lines into a given problem figure in order to achieve a solution. We refer to this type of problems as AL-problems. The inference system with DSs can solve a set of AL-problems. The key idea is to use a lacking part of the figure specified by a potentially active DS.

If an inference system gets stuck while carrying out the inference steps from S1 to S5, then the system invokes a following operation to construct an auxiliary line(s).

AL1: Select a potentially effective DS that is, it has a relational expression matched against a goal to solve. Let the DS be referred to as DS_{G_b}. If no DS_{G_b} is found, then this operation is failed.

AL2: Select a potentially applicable DS (say, DS_{G_f}) that has the same lacking part as DS_{G_b} at that moment.

AL3: If DS_{G_f} is found then add the lacking parts of S-part into the problem figure, otherwise get back to AL1 to select another DS_{G_b}.

An auxiliary line is constructed when two DSs suggest the same hidden geometric elements that might both contribute to a solution. The S-part of DS_{G_f} covers a figure to which the inference system (a human may also) pays attention as a forward step, and O-part of DS_{G_b} suggests a geometric theorem on the figure which will achieve the goal.

5   Application of Diagrammatic Reasoning for ITS

Using DS, an ITS can provide students following two types of instruction; diagrammatic explanations on the proof, and guided discovery of the auxiliary lines.

5.1   Diagrammatic Explanations on Proof

The explanations on proof in terms of diagrammatic objectives are easy to understand and memorize for students. During the experiment mentioned in section 2, the observer occasionally gave subjects suggestions to pay attention to some elements by just pointing the figure without any explanations. Many of these hints were proved to be quite helpful by the way students were reminded of some related theorem, thereby completing the proof while concentrating on the suggested area or elements.

The proposed ITS can generate such kind of hints by highlighting all elements that correspond to S-part of applicable or active DS at a given situation, and just say "*consider these figures.*"

5.2   Guided Discovery of Auxiliary Lines

As mentioned above, the problem solver constructs auxiliary lines, for a goal G, by two different DSs; DS_{G_b} and DS_{G_f}. Using these schemata, the tutoring system can give students two different kinds of advise.

DS_{G_b} suggests that if a lacking part of the problem figure is supplemented by the auxiliary line(s), then the goal is proven by the theorem related to DS_{G_b}. So, the tutoring system can expect students to notice a plausible auxiliary line by just giving some advice about the theorem related to DS_{G_b}.

On the other hand, DS_{G_f} suggests some hidden geometric relation in the figure that might remind the theorem related to DS_{G_b}. The tutoring system can use this hidden information to make students be aware of a lacking part of the figure, which in turn will result in constructing an auxiliary line(s).

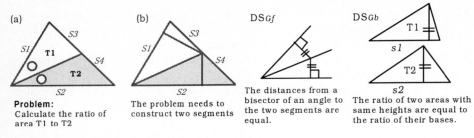

Fig. 4. Example of a AL-problem.   **Fig. 5.** DS for construction in Fig. 4 (b)

For example, suppose that a problem shown in Fig. 4 (a) is given to a student. This problem requires two segments as auxiliary lines as shown in Fig. 4 (b) to be constructed for achieving a solution. The construction of these lines is supported by two DSs, DS_{G_f} and DS_{G_b} shown in Fig. 5.

With DS_{G_b}, the tutoring system can provide an advice like; *"The ratio of two areas of two triangles which have the same heights is equal to the ratio of their bases."* When a student receives this advice, he or she might think of two lines representing the height of T1 and T2 respectively, because the goal is to prove the ratio between T1 and T2.

With a schema DS_{G_f} that is potentially applicable for this situation, the system can provide an advice like; *"The distances from a bisector of an angle to two segments are equal."* A student when provided this advice, may think of two lines even without an insight into the usefulness of the lines. Afterwards, an opportunity for his or her awareness of the theorem corresponding to DS_{G_b} might greatly increase, due to the lines (which are one of the key factor for reminding the theorem) he or she can now visualize.

6   Conclusion

In this paper we discussed a construction of a geometry theorem prover based on diagrammatic information, and its application for a geometry ITS. We implemented a knowledge of theorem proving as a set of diagrammatic schemata which describes what is drawn from a particular configuration of a figure.

Diagrammatic schema enables the theorem prover to construct auxiliary lines inferentially. The inference procedure invokes backward inference from a given goal as well as forward inference towards a goal from the constraints (i.e., known facts). When one potentially active DS of a forward inference step and another DS of a backward step both suggest a common missing element(s), then all appropriate hidden lines (auxiliary lines) are added to the problem figure.

Geometry ITS with diagrammatic schema has a capability of teaching students how to construct auxiliary lines. The tutor can give students advises using diagrammatic information towards a solution, as well as guide students to find necessary auxiliary lines by themselves.

References

1. J. R. Anderson, C. F. Boyle, and G. Yost. The geometry tutor. In *Proceedings of the 9th IJCAI*, pages 1–7, 1985.
2. L. M. Baker and K. Dunbar. Constraints on the experimental design process in real-world science. In *Proc. of Cognitive Science Society*, pages 154–159. Lawrence Erlbaum Associates, 1996.
3. P. Bernat and J. Morinet-Lambert. A new way for visual reasoning in geometry education. In *Proc. of ITS96*, pages 448–456. Springer Verlag, 1996. Lecture Notes in Computer Science No.1086.
4. C. Desmoulins. On relationship between semantics and explanation in an ITS for teaching geometry. In *Proc. of Artificial Intelligence in Education*, pages 129–136, 1993.
5. H. Gelernter. Realization of a geometry-theorem proving machine. In E. A. Feigenbaum and J. Feldman, editors, *Computers and Thought*, pages 134–152. McGraw-Hill Book Company, 1963.
6. J. G. Greeno. *A Study of Problem Solving*, volume 1 of *R. Glaser (Ed.), Advances in Instructional Psychology*. Erlbaum, Hillsdale, N.J, 1978.
7. J. G. Greeno and M. E. Magone. Theory of constructions and set in problem solving. *Memory & Cognition*, 7(6):445–461, 1979.
8. K. R. Koedinger. Emergent properties and structural constraints: Advantages of diagrammatic representations for reasoning. In *Working Notes of AAAI Stanford Spring Symposium on Diagrammatic Reasoning*, pages 151–156, 1992.
9. K. R. Koedinger and J. R. Anderson. Abstract planning and perceptual chunks: Elements of experties in geometry. *Cognitive Science*, 14:511–550, 1990.
10. K. R. Koedinger and J. R. Anderson. Reifying implicit planning in geometry: Guidelines for model-based intelligent tutoring system design. In S. Lajoie and S. Derry, editors, *Computers as Cognitive Tools*. Erlbaum, 1993.
11. A. W. Kushniruk, V. L. Patel, and D. M. Fleiszer. Complex dicision making in providing surgical intensive care. In *Proc. of Cognitive Science Society*, pages 287–292. Lawrence Erlbaum Associates, 1995.
12. J. H. Larkin and H. A. Simon. Why a diagram is (sometimes) worth ten thousand words. *Cognitive Science*, 11:65–99, 1987.
13. T. McDougal and K. Hammond. A recognition model of geometry theorem-proving. In *Proc. of Cognitive Science Society*, pages 106–111. Lawrence Erlbaum Associates, 1992.
14. N. H. Narayanan and B. Chandrasekaran. Reasoning visually about spatial interactions. In *Proc. of IJCAI*, pages 360–365, 1991.
15. A. J. Nevins. Plane geometry theorem proving using forward chaining. *Artificial Intelligence*, 6:1–23, 1975.
16. M. Suwa and H. Motoda. Acquisition of associative knowledge by the frustration-based learning method in an auxiliary-line problem. *Knowledge Aquisition*, 1:113–137, 1989.
17. University Joseph Fourier of Grenoble and the CNRS. *CABRI Geometry*. http://www-cabri.imag.fr/index-e.html.
18. R. Wong. Construction heuristics for geometry and a vector algebra representation of geometry. Technical report, Project MAC, MIT, 1972.
19. J. Zhang. The nature of external representation in problem solving. *Cognitive Science*, 21(2):179–217, 1996.

Providing Feedback To Equation Entries In An Intelligent Tutoring System For Physics

Abigail S. Gertner

Learning Research and Development Center
University of Pittsburgh
Pittsburgh, PA 15260
gertner+@pitt.edu

Abstract. Andes, an intelligent tutoring system for Newtonian physics, provides an environment for students to solve quantitative physics problems. Andes provides immediate correct/incorrect feedback to each student entry during problem solving. When a student enters an equation, Andes must (1) determine quickly whether that equation is correct, and (2) provide helpful feedback indicating what is wrong with the student's entry. To address the former, we match student equations against a pregenerated list of correct equations. To address the latter, we use the pregenerated equations to infer what equation the student may have been trying to enter, and generate hints based on the discrepancies. This paper describes the representation of equations and the procedures Andes uses to perform these tasks.

1   Introduction

Providing meaningful feedback that can help a student correct her mistakes is an essential ability for any Intelligent Tutoring System. This is especially true for Andes, an ITS for Newtonian physics, since it will be used by students in an unsupervised setting. If a student makes an error while solving a problem with Andes, the feedback it gives must allow her to recognize and correct the error as quickly as possible and continue solving the problem.

The issue addressed in this paper is how to provide effective feedback allowing students to correct their errors in *equations* while solving quantitative physics problems. This problem arose as a result of feedback from a formative evaluation of Andes that was carried out in the Fall of 1997, in which Andes was used for approximately three weeks by students in the introductory physics course at the US Naval Academy.

Since Andes is a system for teaching college physics, and students are expected to be familiar with basic algebra when they take this course, Andes *does not* attempt to tutor students on their algebraic derivations. Instead, each equation entered by the student is evaluated independently as to whether it is a correct part of the solution or not, and immediate feedback is given after each entry. To guarantee a fast response time, all equations that may be derived for each problem are pre-generated and stored in a hash table, which can then be checked very quickly at run time.

After using Andes, however, one of the main complaints from students was that they often entered "correct" equations that Andes would mark incorrect. Examination of the records saved by Andes showed that there were three primary reasons for this:

- The equations were actually not correct, but the system was not very good at explaining what was wrong with them. If the student eventually got the right answer, they assumed that all of their intermediate equations were also correct.
- The equations were correct for some interpretation of the variables used, but not the interpretation that Andes had been given.
- The equations were correct, but they did not follow from the abstract solution produced by Andes' problem solver, which is used to generate the equation hash table.

The third point will be partially addressed in the future by adding more alternative solutions to Andes' problem representations. Andes will then give a different kind of feedback if an entry is correct but not part of the most efficient solution. Unfortunately, it is not always possible to pre-enumerate every such equation that a student might derive, and so there will continue to be some correct, but not useful, equations that the system will mark as incorrect.

The first and second points have been addressed by changes to the equation feedback procedures that are described in this paper. Deciding what feedback to give in response to an incorrect equation is complicated because there may be different reasons for the student's error requiring different kinds of response. An error in an equation may be algebraic, such as multiplying two numbers incorrectly or getting a sign wrong. The error may be semantic, such as using the wrong variable to refer to the intended quantity. Alternatively, the error could reflect a more fundamental misconception in the student's understanding of the problem or the domain, which may result in errors in converting abstract physics laws into equations, or even in using the wrong physics laws to generate equations.

To decide how to respond to erroneous equations, Andes uses a two step procedure. First, it searches the pre-generated equation hash table to find the closest match to the student's entry (Section 5.1). Then it compares the two equations and displays a hint describing the most salient discrepancy (Section 5.3). If a reasonable match cannot be found for the student's equation, Andes will give a hint aimed at guiding the student back to the correct solution path.

2   The Andes Tutoring System

The Andes interface is shown in Figure 1. On the upper left, the text of a problem is given, along with a picture illustrating the situation described in the problem. Below the problem text is an area for entering diagrams. Every object

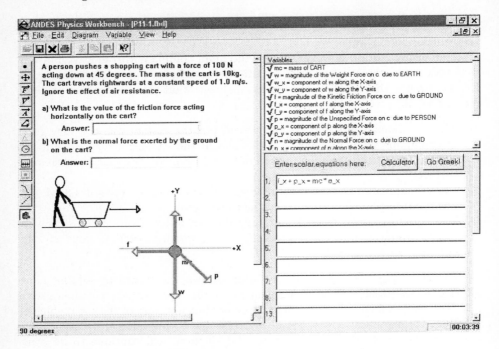

Fig. 1. The Andes problem solving interface.

that is drawn in the diagram area is given a label by the student, and that label is subsequently available for the student to use as a variable in equations. Variables may also be defined using a "variable definition" dialog box.

On the upper right is the list of variables the student has defined so far, and below that is the equation entry pane. Students enter one equation per line in plain (unformatted) text. For example the equation, $v_f^2 = v_i^2 + 2 * a * s$, would be entered as, `vf^2 = vi^2 + 2*a*s`. There is a flexible parser for equations so that, for example, $2 * a * s$ may also be entered as `2as`, `2(as)`, etc. The student is notified immediately if there is a syntactic error in an equation entry.

While Andes is concerned with encouraging students to plan their solutions by doing a qualitative analysis and deciding what laws of physics to apply, it does not attempt to teach any particular heuristics for traversing the search space of the problem. Despite early reports to the contrary, later studies have found no expert-novice difference in the order in which solvers produce equations [6], nor have we be able to find any good reasons for preferring one order over another. Thus, Andes does not put any constraints on what order equations may be entered. Furthermore, since students are assumed to be familiar with the basic rules of algebra, Andes does not require that every step be explicitly entered in the process of deriving the answer. Rather, the equation pane is intended to serve as a flexible problem solving aid – allowing students to enter as much or as little of their work as they need (of course, the instructor may require students to show their work in the homework they hand in).

Every entry the student makes in Andes, whether it is a diagram object or an equation, receives immediate feedback by turning the entry green if it is correct or red if it is incorrect. Once an entry turns red, the student may ask for a followup explanation, by selecting the question "What's wrong with that?" from a menu. When this happens in the case of an equation entry, Andes decides how to respond based on what it determines to be the most likely equation the student was trying to enter.

The student's equation is compared with the most likely match, and a hint is generated suggesting how the student might correct the entry. For example, suppose that in the problem shown in Figure 1, the student enters the incorrect equation, $P_x = m * a_x$. The hint that Andes gives in response to this equation is "Maybe you should include a term for F_x in this equation." Here, Andes has determined that the student was trying to enter the equation for Newton's second law applied to the shopping cart, which should be entered as $P_x + F_x = m * a_x$, but has left out a term for the friction force on the cart.

3   Related Work

Two areas of work in the ITS literature are relevant to the problem of responding to students' incorrect equations. The first deals with identifying the misconceptions underlying students' errors. The second, more closely related work, deals with finding the most likely intended equation as part of a physics solution.

Finding the algebraic error to which to attribute a student's incorrect equation has typically been done in ITS's using a pre-coded collection of bugs or mal-rules, and searching for the sequence of rules and mal-rules that could have led to the derivation of the student's entry [7]. However, this approach is computationally very expensive, and in the context of a physics tutoring system it seems unnecessary to find specific bugs in the student's algebraic derivations.

An algorithm for computing a match between a student's equation and potentially correct target equations is described by Gürer [3]. This algorithm assigns weights to different components of an equation, such as function type, variable, etc., and then recursively calculates a weighted match for each segment of the equations. Gürer's algorithm relies heavily on the specific representation she used for equations and also on the surface structure of the two equations being comparable. In contrast, the algorithm we use for matching equations makes use of a canonical form for equations, and so is not dependent on their surface form. In addition, rather than pre-enumerating all possible equations, Gürer's method requires additional manipulation of equations at run time (simplification and substitution of known values), which will increase the time needed to find a match.

4   Representation of problems

Andes' representation of physics problems is designed to support a *model tracing* approach to tutoring [8]. Andes uses a rule-based problem solver to generate a compact graphical model of the reasoning needed to solve each problem. This model, called the *solution graph* includes all acceptable solutions to the problem in terms of qualitative propositions and applicable physics laws, as well as the abstract plans for how to generate those solutions. The solution graph also marks each piece of information with the domain rule(s) that generated that information.

Unfortunately, including every correct equation the student might enter for a problem would result in a prohibitively large and complex solution graph. A typical physics problem can have between 10 and 30 primitive equations, all of which are necessary to derive the final solution. Whenever two equations share a variable, a new equation can be written with one equation substituted into the other. Thus, instead of having N primitive equations to work with, the student really has approximately $2^N - 1$ equations. Furthermore, each of these equations can potentially be expressed in a number of different surface forms.

Since Andes is intended to teach physics and not algebra, the problem solver stops short at representing these algebraic derivations in the solution graph. Instead, the solution graph contains (possibly more than one) sets of primitive equations that are sufficient to derive the solution. To avoid the computationally expensive task of deciding at run time whether a student's equation can be derived from the primitive equations, we pre-generate the set of all equations that can be derived from the primitive equations by algebraic substitution.[1] The *equation hash table* is used to store these equations. The hash table is keyed on the list of variables in each equation, so that new equation entries can be looked up quickly for immediate feedback.

Each entry in the equation hash table contains a derived equation, along with the sets of primitive equations from the solution graph from which that equation was derived. When a student's equation is matched with an equation from the hash table, that equation is added to Andes' student model [1], linked to the corresponding primitive equations. In this way, Andes can model the relevant physics knowledge that the student has, or has not, brought to bear in generating her equations.

4.1   Canonical form

An additional consideration in producing the equation hash table is the fact that each correct equation may appear in several mathematically equivalent surface forms. For example, the equation $T + W = m * a$ is equivalent to $(T + W)/a = m$ or $T = (m * a) - W$ etc. Rather than generating every possible surface form of

---

[1] Within reason – we do not include tautological equations (e.g. $x = x$) or equations that do not make sense from the point of view of the physics (eg. combining components along different coordinate axes).

every equation, each equation is converted into a *canonical form* before it is saved in the hash table. The method of canonicalizing equations is the same that was used in OLAE [4], a precursor of Andes. The equation is rearranged to produce a polynomial that is equal to zero by moving all terms to one side, and then that polynomial is converted into a vector in which the first element is a variable and the coefficient of the nth power of that variable is in position $n + 2$ of the vector. If there is no nth power for the variable, the $n + 2$th coefficient is 0.

Using this representation, the canonical form of the polynomial $x^2 + 2$ would be the vector [x 2 0 1]. The first position specifies the main variable of the polynomial. The remaining numbers indicate that the coefficient of x^0 is 2, the coefficient of x^1 is 0 (i.e. there is no term for x^1), and the coefficient of x^2 is 1.

If there is more than one variable in the polynomial, for example $x^2 + xy + 2$, the variables are sorted in alphabetical order and put in the vector in relation to each other: [x 2 [y 0 1] 1]. In this vector, the coefficient of x^0 is 2, the coefficient of x^1 is the polynomial y^1, and the coefficient of x^2 is 1.

When the student enters an equation, Andes converts the equation into canonical form, and looks it up in the hash table to see whether the entry is equivalent to the equation stored in the hash table with the same variables (numbers must be equal to within two significant digits).

5   Deciding how to respond

When the student asks "What's wrong with that?" in reference to an incorrect equation, Andes decides how to respond by searching for the closest match between the student's equation and one of the correct equations in the equation hash table. If a good enough match is found (above a pre-determined threshold), Andes compares the two equations and generates a hint pointing to what might be wrong with the student's equation.

If no good match is found, however, the student may be trying to enter an equation that is not part of the solution, indicating a possible misconception on the procedural level, regarding how to solve the problem. In that case, Andes' procedural help module [2] generates a hint regarding what problem solving goal the student might want to pursue instead of entering the erroneous equation. The hint might point to a different equation, or to part of the qualitative analysis of the problem that has not yet been done.

5.1   Finding the most likely match

To find the closest match to a student's equation, Andes calculates a match score between the canonical form of the student's equation and the hash table equations. The match between two canonical equation vectors, V_1 and V_2, is calculated as a score between 0 and 100 by comparing individual elements of each vector based on the following rules:

1. If the two elements are both variables, then the match score is determined according to a function that calculates the similarity between two variables: (e.g. If one variable represents a vector magnitude, and the other variable represents the X-component of that vector, then the match factor is .70).
2. If the two elements are both numbers, then the match score is 100 if the numbers are equal, 80 if $e_1 = -e_2$, 70 if $e_1 = 1/e_2$, $e_1 = \cos(e_2)$, or $e_1 = \sin(e_2)$, otherwise it is 30.
3. If the two elements are not both numbers or both variables, the score is zero.
4. The match score for each pair of elements is multiplied by a factor based on the relative positions of the elements in the equation vector. The further apart the elements are, the lower the score.

The normalized total match score between two equation vectors, V_1 and V_2, is computed as:

$$\frac{\sum_{i,j}^{m,n} M(e_1^i, e_2^j)}{avg(m,n)}$$

where $M(e_1^i, e_2^j)$ is the match score between corresponding elements of V_1 and V_2, and $avg(n,m)$ is the average length of the two vectors. Consequently, the shorter an equation, the more each individual element contributes to the score.

During canonicalization, all numerical expressions in an equation are evaluated. For example, the equation $W = 9.8 * 5$ would be canonicalized to $W = 49$. If the student enters $W = 9.8 * 3$ where $W = 49$ is correct, it will be matched with $W = 49$ as the most likely target, but the information about which part of the student's entry was wrong will be lost. To avoid this loss of information, an additional pre-processing step substitutes variables into the student's equation wherever it finds a number that is equal to the value of a quantity that Andes knows. In the above example, if $g = 9.8$, $m = 5$ and $W = g * m$, then the student's entry, $W = 9.8 * 3$, would be transformed into $W = g * 3$ which would match $W = g * 5$ rather than $W = 49$. This allows a more helpful explanation to be found during the equation comparison stage.

Finally, the equation from the equation hash table that has the highest normalized match with the student's entry is taken to be the most likely intended target equation. Andes then goes on to generate feedback based on the discrepancies between the target equation and the student's entry.

5.2   Finding the threshold

To determine the threshold to use for accepting a match between the student and target equations, we looked at the equations entered into Andes by students in the formative evaluation described earlier. We chose 42 representative log files that were collected from that study. Each log file records all of the actions done by the student during a session with Andes. In these log files, a total of 624 equations were entered. After removing identical entries, in which a student entered the same equation string in the same problem session, 526 unique equations remained.

Since the log files were generated by the previous version of Andes, each file was processed to generate the match scores for the new equation matching algorithm. Out of the 526 equations that were entered, 170 of them were correct, 158 of them contained variables that had not yet been defined by the student and thus could not be interpreted by Andes, 47 contained a variable representing a quantity that was not part of Andes' solution, and 32 contained syntactic errors and could not be parsed. Based on the distribution of match scores for the remaining 119 equations, together with an examination of the actual equations that were matched with various scores, we chose to use a threshold of 67 as the point below which Andes will not accept a match. Andes failed to find a match above 67 for only 17 of the 119 equations, leaving 102 matches to compare in the following stage.

5.3 Comparing two equations

Given a student's equation and a correct target equation, Andes next compares them and attempts to find the most significant discrepancy to report to the student. In this stage, it is necessary to preserve the surface form of the student's entry so that the result will be in a form that she will understand. For example, before comparing the student equation $\frac{F}{v} = m$ with the target equation $F = m * a$, Andes first transforms the target equation to the form, $\frac{F}{a} = m$.

Next, both equations are separated into terms, and the two corresponding terms with the lowest match (calculated using a similar method as the equation match score), are compared. The function that compares two terms looks for a number of possible discrepancies, resulting in the sample output shown in Table 5.3.[2]

The output is generated from templates with the form given in Table 5.3. The slots in the templates (indicated by square brackets) are filled with the appropriate variables, values, or descriptions from the student and target equations. For example, if the student has entered an equation containing the variable S which stands for the magnitude of a vector, and Andes determines that she should really have used the vertical component of the vector, the output would be "Do you want to use S_y rather than S?" or "Do you want to use the vertical component of S rather than S?" depending on whether or not the student has defined the variable S_y.

5.4 Following up feedback

Evidence from studies of human tutors suggests one of the main reasons that human tutors are effective is that they are able to let students do most of the work in correcting errors and overcoming impasses, while providing just enough guidance to keep them on a productive solution path [5]. For this reason, the hint templates listed in the previous section are designed to point to the incorrect

---

[2] The numbers in the last column show how many instances of that discrepancy were found in the 102 equations that were compared in the evaluation.

Type of discrepancy	Output	# seen
The terms are identical except for a +/- sign.	"Make sure you are using the correct signs in this equation."	35
Dividing instead of multiplying (or multiplying instead of dividing)	"Maybe you should multiply [a] by [m] instead of dividing them."	0
Missing a factor	"Maybe you should multiply [V_1] by something."	5
Extra factor	"Are you sure you want to multiply [V_1] by [2]?"	5
Wrong factor	"Maybe you should multiply [t] by [V_1] here rather than by [V_2]."	7
Wrong function	"Are you sure you want to take the [sin] of [60]?"	0
The terms are two different numbers	"Did you mean to use [34.5] here?"	17
The terms have nothing in common	"Do you want to use [S_y] rather than [S]?"	14
The student term is blank	"Maybe you should include a term for [W] here."	3
The target term is blank	"Are you sure you want to include a term for [W] here?"	9
One term contains factors that are in different terms in the other equation	"Do you really want to multiply [$T1$] by [$T2$]?"	7

Table 1. Hints generated in response to equation errors.

part of the equation without giving the correct answer away. If the student still cannot correct her error after seeing one of these hints, in most cases she can ask for additional explanation and get a more specific hint by clicking a button labeled "Explain more." For example, the followup explanation for the hint, "Maybe you should multiply V_1 by something." might be, "Try multiplying V_1 by 2." The student can keep clicking the "Explain more" button until she has seen the most specific hint available. In most cases, Andes will finally tell the student what equation to write. However, it will not give away an equation if it states the value of a single quantity. So it might say, "Enter the equation: $T + W = m * a$," but it will not say "Enter the equation $a = 2.35$."

6   Conclusion

An informal inspection of the hints produced by Andes in response to the 119 incorrect equations saved in the log files analyzed indicates that the algorithm is quite good at determining the students' intended meaning, and at pointing out the errors in their equations.

One potential enhancement to the types of feedback presented here might be to connect the equation feedback to Andes' conceptual help module [8], so that the student could get a more extensive tutorial on the physics concepts underlying an incorrect equation when the student model indicates a probable lack of understanding of those concepts. For example, students seem to have a lot of trouble understanding the relationship between vector magnitudes (which are always positive values) and the scalar values of their components (which may be negative). They therefore have a lot of sign errors in their equations. A more detailed explanation of the relationship between the direction of a vector and the signs of its components when these errors occur might be very helpful in preventing them in the future.

During the Spring semester of 1998, Andes will again be used by students at the Naval Academy, and we will analyze their log files to see how helpful the explanations produced are at helping the students to correct erroneous entries. These log files will then be used as input to evaluate further enhancements to the system, such as the Conceptual help feature described above.

7   Acknowledgements

This research is supported by ARPA's Computer Aided Education and Training Initiative under grant N660001-95-C-8367, by ONR's Cognitive Science Division under grant N00014-96-1-0260, and by AFOSR's Artificial Intelligence Division under grant F49620-96-1-0180. I would like to thank Kurt VanLehn and the Andes group for their comments and suggestions.

References

[1] Cristina Conati, Abigail S. Gertner, Kurt VanLehn, and Marek J. Druzdzel. On-line student modeling for coached problem solving using Bayesian networks. In *Proceedings of UM-97, Sixth International Conference on User Modeling*, pages 231–242, Sardinia, Italy, June 1997. Springer.

[2] Abigail S. Gertner, Cristina Conati, and Kurt VanLehn. Procedural help in Andes: Generating hints using a Bayesian network student model. In *Proceedings of the 15th National Conference on Artificial Intelligence*, Madison, WI, 1998. to appear.

[3] Denise Gürer. *A Bi-Level Physics Student Diagnostic Utilizing Cognitive Models for an Intelligent Tutoring System*. PhD thesis, Lehigh University, 1993.

[4] Joel Martin and Kurt VanLehn. Student assessment using Bayesian nets. *International Journal of Human-Computer Studies*, 42:575–591, 1995.

[5] Douglas C. Merril, Brian J. Reiser, Michael Ranney, and J. Gregory Trafton. Effective tutoring techniques: A comparison of human tutors and intelligent tutoring systems. *The Journal of the Learning Sciences*, 3(2):277–305, 1992.

[6] A. G. Priest and R. O. Lindsay. New light on novice-expert differences in physics problem solving. *British Journal of Psychology*, 83:389–405, 1992.

[7] Derek H. Sleeman. Inferring student models for intelligent computer-aided instruction. In R.S. Michalski, J.G. Carbonnel, and T.M. Mitchell, editors, *Machine Learning: An Artificial Intelligence Approach*, pages 483–510. Tioga Publishing Company, Palo Alto, CA, 1983.

[8] K. VanLehn. Conceptual and meta learning during coached problem solving. In C. Frasson, G. Gauthier, and A. Lesgold, editors, *Proceedings of the 3rd International Conference on Intelligent Tutoring Systems ITS '96*, pages 29–47. Springer, 1996.

Using Automatic Methods for Structuring Conceptual Knowledge in Intelligent Learning Environments

Baltasar Fernandez-Manjon, Juan Cigarran, Antonio Navarro,
Alfredo Fernandez-Valmayor

Escuela Superior de Informática, Universidad Complutense de Madrid
Avda. Complutense s/n, 28040, Madrid, Spain
bfmanjon@dia.ucm.es

Abstract. Re-using pre-existing electronic information has become a new perspective able to reduce the development costs of intelligent learning environments (ILE). This approach has to face the problem of organizing and structuring this pre-existing information in a way that ease users' understanding and assimilation. The automation of the Formal Concept Analysis (FCA) theory is proposed as a way to structure conceptually the reused information and as a suitable method to implement different interaction techniques. Therefore, the FCA can be a relevant and competitive method for the production of ILEs, and specifically in the construction of intelligent assistants.

1 Introduction

Because it is so expensive to develop intelligent learning environments (ILE), such as ITS or intelligent assistants, methods and techniques that simplify its production are needed. Presently, the construction of a new ILE typically starts from scratch; developers are forced to design their own system architecture, implement all system components, acquire and encode all relevant content knowledge (domain and instructional knowledge), and develop knowledge representation strategies and reasoning mechanisms [1, 2]. The above reasons make the construction of ILEs non cost-effective.

Due to the advent of Internet and the massive dissemination of bibliographic collections, software libraries and multimedia repositories, the amount of electronic information available has rapidly grown. In many educational contexts re-using all this knowledge to provide part of the tutorial content would avoid constructing ILEs from scratch and it will reduce their final production costs. Reusing this knowledge leads us to solve the problem of how to make useful for users this information that was originally created without educational purposes. To obtain this educational aim we propose to structure and to organize this pre-existing information in a way that ease users' understanding and assimilation. With this goal we propose to integrate different organizations of the domain information (based on different techniques) within one ILE. This will allow multiple kinds of interactions with users [3].

In ILEs the representation of knowledge is crucial to its performance. Normally, ILEs are built around some kind of conceptual network (or knowledge base) representing experts' view of the domain, with nodes corresponding to domain concepts and with links reflecting several kinds of relationships between concepts. This network determines the content, processing and organization of all the system information. The gathering of experts' knowledge identifies the domain key concepts; their attributes and their interrelations is an essential and difficult phase in the software design process [4]. This is usually done in a manual way which complicates its maintenance, checking and application in complex domains. We consider that in many real scenarios the main objective is to face the problem of extracting, organizing and structuring the domain information in order to build low cost, pragmatic and "easy to access" conceptual networks.

In this paper we propose the automation of the Formal Concept Analysis (FCA) theory as a relevant technology to simplify the development of ILEs. We think that FCA can provide the basis for educational tools that use a conceptual network as a learning tool. The FCA application allows the construction of conceptual networks whose concepts are (semi) automatically extracted from the objects and attributes of the domain. The idea behind our approach is that FCA can be used by ILE developers to model the language that experts use when they describe their domain expertise. Applying FCA, the organization of the information and the concept hierarchy obtained depends only on the domain objects considered and on the description provided regarding those objects. We choose the Unix operating system as a complex and well known domain to exemplify our approach. We integrated FCA as a complementary technique in the construction of intelligent assistants for Unix, and presently we are extending FCA use as a standalone technique [5, 6].

The rest of the paper is organized in the following way: First, we present what is necessary to turn the pre-existing information into an effective educational medium; Then we introduce the basics of the formal concept analysis theory and how this theory can be used to support the design and production of educational software; Finally, we briefly discuss the benefits and drawbacks of our approach.

2   Information Re-use, Organization and Interaction in Educational Systems

As previously stated, we understand the construction of ILEs (and more specifically of intelligent assistants) not only as a process of software development, but also as a process of organizing, accessing and structuring pre-existing electronic information to obtain an useful and effective educational system. The *information re-use* approach proposed, discussed herein (partially) solves the problem of how to extract, organize and structure the domain knowledge embedded in a set of documents whose final objective is to be presented to the user in a comprehensible way. Also, the application should allow different and "easy to use" interaction methods (e.g. information retrieval or browsing) to simplify accessing, understanding and the relation of the information presented.

Usually the help systems or assistants are accessed by the user in a free learning way (not in a driven learning way) to retrieve some items of interest, to obtain complementary information or to explore the related contents of the domain [4]. In this situation it is appropriate to organize the domain information into some kind of structure that could be explored by the user in a simple and "browsable" way [7].

The idea is to merge information retrieval and browsing methods in order to provide the user with a flexible way to interact with the domain knowledge without knowing precisely how it is organized or what the needed information is. The main difference between browsing methods and the more classical accessing methods, based in information retrieval techniques, is that browsing allows a "free" examination of the indexed information without any preliminary knowledge of the domain. On the contrary most of the information retrieval methods make necessary a previous knowledge of the domain in order to access the information required (e.g. to construct queries able to specify the user's needs) [8]. Also, when applying information retrieval techniques users can not directly explore the structure of the domain knowledge and, as a consequence, the learning component of the system is reduced due to it not being possible to view similar or related concepts at first sight.

The domain knowledge in such a navigational educational system should be arranged in a conceptual network (or hierarchy) permitting the user to easily move around and examine concepts. Within this network similar domain concepts should be clustered allowing direct accessing to other related concepts. The construction of such networks is usually done manually by human experts that select and index the main concepts of the domain. Concepts obtained and arranged following this approach may be perceived to be similar in many senses and the corresponding mapping to a specific conceptual network may often turn out to be quite arbitrary, depending on the subjective judgment of the expert. Moreover, systems created using this manual approach are expensive, and very difficult to check and to maintain. Besides these conceptualization difficulties, the attempts to provide efficient network navigation and interaction in real domains are hindered by visualization problems. To fully exploit the conceptual network created and not to overcharge the user with extra information the browser interface should allow to make a partial exploration of the hierarchy.

Our approach to the construction of educational software reusing pre-existing electronic information is supported by the use of FCA theory. FCA suits the needs of the organizing-navigational paradigm presented above in that it can be understood as a technique able to extract and organize the domain knowledge embedded in a document collection within a structure suitable for browsing. As FCA is an automatic method, the development and the maintenance costs of systems based on this approach are competitive.

3   Basics of Formal Concept Analysis Theory: Concepts, Contexts and Hierarchies

FCA provides a complete set of mathematical tools to analyze and to obtain conceptual hierarchies [9]. Here we introduce in an informal way the main notions of FCA without using the mathematical formulation of the theory found in [9, 10]. FCA provides a conceptual tool for the analysis of data, which is relatively new and has already successfully been applied not only in technical domains, but also in more descriptive disciplines (e.g. biology or psychology) [11, 12]. Though, up to our knowledge, its use in the field of educational technology has been very limited.

The central idea is the *formal concept* which is a mathematical abstraction consisting of two parts, the extension and the intension. The extension covers all the objects belonging to a concept while the intension comprises all the attributes valid for all those objects. When the objects and attributes of a domain are fixed we call this a formal context. For a better understanding of the idea of formal concept we propose the following example. Table 1 shows a context where some Unix commands are described by some keywords or descriptors (obtained from the command documentation). In this case the objects are a subset of Unix commands, the attributes are a subset of keywords used to describe the commands and the crosses in the table hold a "has a" relationship between a Unix command and a specific descriptor. An empty cell in Table 1 indicates that the corresponding descriptor does not describe or does not apply to the corresponding command.

Table 1. Formal context produced by seven Unix commands and their descriptions

	file	printer	directory	job	copy	change	send	display	remove
rm	X		X						X
cd			X			X			
cp	X		X		X				
ls	X		X					X	
lpq		X		X				X	
lpr		X		X			X		
lprm		X		X					X

Usually common understanding of a concept lies in the collecting of individuals into a group with certain common properties. Keeping this idea in mind we will consider the attributes corresponding to the object "lpr" and ask for those commands (within the context) which share attributes with the object "lpr". We can see that no object shares all the attributes belonging to "lpr" but the objects "lpq" and "lprm" share the attributes "printer" and "job" with it. Hence we get the set A consisting of {"lpr", "lprm", "lpq"}. This set of objects is closely connected to the set B consisting of the attributes {"printer", "job"}. It is possible to conclude that the set A is the set of all objects having all the attributes of B, and B is the set of all attributes which are valid for all the objects in A. In FCA each of these pairs (A, B) is called a formal concept.

Concepts of a given context are naturally ordered by the generalization-specialization relation (subconcept-superconcept) producing a hierarchy for the given context (this hierarchy is a complete lattice and it is not limited to be a simple tree). The top will consist of the more general concepts that have a smaller intension and larger extension than any of the more specialized concepts below. If we look again at our example we can see that the concept A1 = ({"lpr"}, {"printer", "job", "send"}) is a subconcept of the concept A2 = ({"lpr", "lpq", "lprm"}, {"printer", "job"}).

Particular kinds of formal concepts are those concepts generated by only one attribute or object belonging to the context. These concepts are called attribute and object concepts respectively; they are useful because an object concept represents the smallest concept with this specific object in its extension while an attribute concept represent the largest concept with this specific attribute in its intension. In our example, the concept ({"lpr"}, {"printer", "job", "send"}) is an object concept and it can be considered the most specific concept with the object "lpr" in its extension. On the other hand, the concept ({"rm", "lprm"}, {"remove"}) is the attribute concept corresponding to the attribute "remove". This attribute concept is the most general concept with the attribute "remove" in its intension.

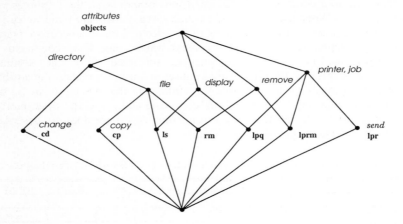

Fig. 1. Hasse diagram of the hierarchy of concepts obtained from the context presented in Table 1.

Moreover, hierarchies of formal concepts can be represented graphically by line (or Hasse) diagrams. These diagrams are composed of nodes representing formal concepts and links representing the subconcept-superconcept relationships. Object concepts are named with the object that produces the concept; attribute concepts are labeled with the attribute that generates the concept. A diagram contains all the context information [11]; an object has an attribute if and only if there is an upwards leading path from its object concept to this attribute concept. Fig. 1 shows the diagram of the Unix example (notice that this hierarchy is not limited to be a simple tree). That means that most of the FCA applications can be supported by graphical representations that simplify the presentation of information and the interaction with users.

4   FCA as a Learning Tool: Information Retrieval, Browsing and Application Design

There are several learning alternatives that can be implemented to exploit the organization of the information around the domain formal concepts provided by the FCA. We analyze three different uses: information retrieval, browsing and application design.

The domain structuring provided by FCA can be used to support an easy and effective retrieval of information. For instance, in the Unix example, the problem of a user looking for information about a specific command can be expressed in FCA terms as a process of helping users obtain the smallest concept that has this command in its extension (i.e. the object concept).

As FCA gives us all the formal concepts of the domain and their organization within the conceptual hierarchy it is possible to implement different retrieval interactions with the two following characteristics: a) the user does not need a previous knowledge of the domain because it is not necessary to know the keywords or structure used to index the information; and b) the searching process is driven in a quick and incremental way. In order to construct the "queries" that define the search path to the object concept requested two kind of interfaces may be implemented: a table based interface and a hierarchy diagram based interface. Table based interfaces show a set of selectable descriptors that the user can incrementally choose in order to describe his needs (see Fig. 2) [13]; in another separate column the interface presents the set keywords selected by the user and; in a third column, the interface shows the items selected by the system as possible objects to be retrieved. This way of presenting hierarchical information has several advantages: the user always obtains at least one object in his searching process avoiding the overspecification of the query; the user gets a rapid and effective feedback regarding the information search; the user can easily control the number of objects obtained by selecting or unselecting keywords.

We have applied this information retrieval tabular interface in Aran, an intelligent assistant for the Unix domain, that integrates FCA with other techniques (e.g. user modeling, manual knowledge base) to provide help facilities [3,5,6]. Now we are extending FCA applicability as a standalone technique with a new cross-platform implementation (Aran was developed in Lisp and the new applications are being developed in C language and Metacard with allows its execution in several platforms). An example of the new interface is presented in Fig. 2. In this example the user needs to find information about the commands used to change the working directory in Unix. In initiating the user choice, the system will present as selectable descriptors all the descriptors available in the conceptual network allowing the user to select the keyword "directory". Then the system will show as possible items to retrieve the objects "rm", "ls", "cp" and "cd" updating the list of selectable descriptors to those keywords related with the attribute "directory" (i.e. "copy", "remove", "file", "change", "display"). The next interaction will refine the searching path by adding the descriptor "change" to the incremental query. This last selection drives the search to the object concept {("cd"), ("directory", "change")} that will be used to retrieve the information related with the command "cd".

On the other hand, a second approach to the construction of information retrieval interfaces based on FCA is to present the hierarchy of concepts in a graphical way. This approach would arrange the formal concepts around a graphical diagram where users could access directly to the indexed information. In this case, if the domain were complex, problems could arise making the visualization of the complete set of concepts difficult. Solutions to this problem should avoid presenting the whole diagram by solely focusing the view in the sub-hierarchies related with the user's interests [14] or merging the tabular representation with a graphical representation of sub-hierarchies. The above approach to graphical concept hierarchy representation is closely related to a domain browsing approach.

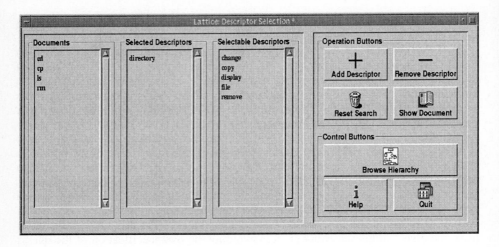

Fig. 2. Incremental query construction where the user specifies the keyword "directory". The commands and the descriptors compatible with the partial query specification are also shown (Screenshot obtained in a SUN WorkStation with Unix).

Domain browsing is an approach to the exploration of indexed domains that allows the user to interact with the domain without knowing precisely the contents of the domain or the way it is organized. Relations between concepts obtained using FCA define structures suitable for browsing. Conceptual networks appeal to the browser's intuitive notions of distance, closeness and dimensions clustering similar concepts within the concept diagrams. Browsing methods not only can be used in a domain exploration way, they can be also exploited as powerful learning tools. This allows users to solve their direct information needs (short term learning process) and finally acquire a global view of the domain where browsing is applied (long term learning process). Because the way browsing is going to be done and how it is going to present the domain concepts and their relations clearly determine the domain users' learning process.

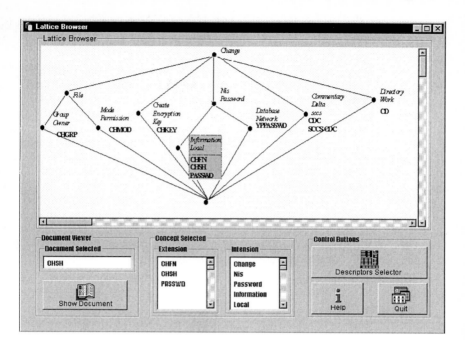

Fig. 3. Hierarchy browsing corresponding to the user's selection of the keyword "change". (Screenshot obtained in a compatible personal computer with Windows 95).

We will explain a typical browsing session within a conceptual network implemented using FCA and we will try to observe how the learning process is going to be done. Coming back to a (simplified) Unix example, suppose that the user explores the domain in order to obtain information related with the commands used to change his password. He will browse to the node "change" unfolding the part of the domain corresponding to the subdiagram shown in Fig. 3. This subdiagram only contains as object concepts those related with changing actions such as "cd" or "passwd". The selection of a specific descriptor reduces the number of navigational concepts within the diagram to those concepts that are specialization of the attribute concept "change". The application of a browsing technique over the concept hierarchy allows the system not to show other management commands that are related with typical user actions, but that are not described by the keyword "change". As a consequence, the user's attention will concentrate only in the information that he wants to know about and, at the same time, he will acquire a global notion of all the commands that can be used to change things in Unix by inspecting related electronic information. The following user's interactions will refine the learning objectives browsing down in the diagram in an incremental way until the browsing process obtains an object concept.

Finally, FCA can be used as a previous step in the design of ILE and educational applications in general. The automatically extracted formal concepts can be later refined by the domain experts in order to manually construct the definitive conceptual network or to check an already existing knowledge base. The number and the quality of the concepts obtained by FCA varies because it depends on the objects and the description of these objects (that is the formal context). However, we have the warranty that all the information is indexed.

Also it is necessary to notice that FCA permits a more labored analysis of the data and even can be used to create different views of the same domain as described in [9, 11, 12, 14]. One possibility is that the analysis of the domain can be done taking into account the relationships between the attributes, that is, including expert' information, and not only considering those attributes as simple and independent characteristics. For example, we could include in the analysis of the domain the experts' perception that the attributes "display" and "list" are specific instances of a more general action that is "inform". This will produce an automatic organization of the information while taking into account the background information provided by the domain experts. Another possibility is to play with the attributes and how many different attributes are used to describe one object. Usually, this process will modify the number of concepts obtained and the depth of the conceptual network. Therefore, FCA allows the construction of different views of the domain depending only on the selected objects and on the vocabulary used to describe those objects.

5   Discussion

In this paper we have introduced FCA as a relevant and competitive method to develop ILEs reusing pre-existing electronic information. Systems that implement this technique have low development costs and are easy to maintain. This is possible due to FCA feature able to process the electronic information automatically.

Compared with other approaches used to construct ILEs the conceptual networks created using FCA may improve the effectiveness of hierarchy navigation for interactive searches and the general learning process of a specific domain. The main reason is that concept relations generated by FCA provide a conceptual structure that can support different methods to manage and to present information without changing the domain structure created. Therefore, we propose FCA as an information extracting and structuring method that can be used standalone or as a complementary technique for the production of ILEs, for example, to provide an alternative way to access to the information or a different view of the domain.

Nevertheless, this approach also has some limitations. Even if the tabular information retrieval scales up well, the graphical browsing approach is more difficult to implement for complex domains because it is difficult to implement a simple interface. The FCA conceptual networks usually have no relevant or nonsense concepts that should be discarded by a domain expert. FCA should be understood as a first step method able to create a first organization of the domain that considerably reduces the efforts and costs of developing the structure of a domain from scratch.

Presently, we are using FCA as a tool to unfold the domain data supporting the construction of better user interfaces. We are applying this approach not only in the Unix domain but also in a different application for teaching text comprehension in a second language. The next step of the project is to evaluate the interfaces produced using this technique with real users.

Acknowledgments

The EU project Galatea (TM-LD-1995-1-FR89) and the Spanish Committee of Science and Technology (TIC96-2486-CE) have supported this work.

References

1. Architectures and Methods for Cost-Effective and Reusable ITS: An Electronic Community, 1998. [WWW document, URL:http:// advlearn.lrdc.pitt.edu/its-arch/]
2. Sokolnicki, T. "Towards knowledge-based tutors: a survey and appraisal of Intelligent Tutoring Systems". *The Knoledge Engineering Review*, 6(2), 59-95, 1991.
3. Buenaga, M., Fernandez-Manjon, B., Fernandez-Valmayor, A. "Information Overload At The Information Age". Adults in Innovative Learning Situations, Elsevier Science B.V., Amsterdam, pp. 17-30, 1995.
4. Winkels R. Explorations in Intelligent Tutoring and Help IOS Press, Amsterdam, 1992.
5. Fernandez-Manjon, B., Fernandez-Valmayor, A., Fernández Chamizo, C. Pragmatic User Model Implementation in an Intelligent Help System. *British Journal of Educational Technology*, 29(2), 113-123, 1998.
6. Fernandez-Manjon, B., Fernandez-Valmayor, A. Building Educational Tools based on Formal Concept Analysis. D. Dicheva, I. Stanchev (Eds.) HCI-ET, Proceedings of the IFIP WG3.3 Working Conference, Sozopol, Bulgaria, May 27-28, pp 39-48, 1997.
7. Wasson B and Akselsen S. An Overview of On-line Assistance: from On-line Documentation to Intelligent Help and Training. The Knowledge Engineering Review 7 (4) 289-322, 1992.
8. Salton, G. Automatic Text Processing: The Transformation, Analysis And Retrieval Of Information By Computer, Edit. Addison Wesley, 1989.
9. Wille, R. Concept Lattices and Conceptual Knowledge Systems. Computers and Mathematics with Applications, 23(6-9), 493-515, 1992.
10. Davey, B. and Priestley, H. (1990) Introduction to Lattices and Order. Cambridge, UK: Cambridge University Press
11. Wolff, K. E. A First Course in Formal Concept Analysis - How to Understand Line Diagrams. Faulbaum, F. (ed.) SoftStat'93, Advances in Statistical Software 4, Gustav Fischer Verlag, 429-438, 1994.
12. Godin, R., Mineau, G. W., Missaoui, R. and Mili, H. Méthodes de Classification Conceptuelle Basées sur les Treillis de Galois et Applications. Revue d'Intelligence Artificielle, 9(2), 105-137, 1995.
13. Lindig, C. Concept-Based Component Retrieval, Proceedings of. IJCAI-95, Workshop on Formal Approaches to the Reuse of Plans, Proofs, and Programs, Montreal, 1995.
14. Carpineto, C., Romano, G. Automatic Construction of Navigable Concept Networks Characterizing Text Databases. M. Gori, G. Soda (Eds.) Topics in Artificial Intelligence, Lectures Notes in Artificial Intelligence 992, Springer-Verlag, Berlin, pp. 67-78, 1995.

Two-Phase Updating of Student Models Based on Dynamic Belief Networks

Jim Reye

Queensland University of Technology
Brisbane, Australia
j.reye@qut.edu.au

Abstract. When a belief network is used to represent a student model, we must have a theoretically-sound way to update this model. In ordinary belief networks, it is assumed that the properties of the external world, modelled by the network, do not change as we go about gathering evidence related to those properties. I present a general approach as to how student model updates should be made, based on the concept of a dynamic belief network, and then show this work relates to previous research in this area.

1   Introduction

When a belief network is used to represent a student model (e.g. [1], [2]), we must have a theoretically-sound way to update this model. Such updates are based on information from two sources: (i) the student, via their inputs to the system (e.g. requests for help, answers to questions, and attempts at exercises); and (ii) the system, via its outputs (e.g. descriptions and explanations given). In this paper, I present a general approach as to how such updates should be made, and show this work relates to previous research in this area.

In ordinary belief networks, it is assumed that the properties of the external world, modelled by the network, do not change as we go about gathering evidence related to those properties. That is, even though the system gathers information from the external world that causes it to modify its measures of belief about items in that world, those items remain either true or false. This is useful, for example, in medical diagnosis, where the cause of a disease is assumed not to change during a (single) medical examination.

But, such an approach is clearly inadequate for student modelling in a tutoring system, where we must be able to reason about:

(a)   the dynamic evolution of the student's knowledge, over a period of time, as we gain new information about the student; and

(b)   the likely effects of future tutorial actions (relative to what is currently known about the student), so that the action with maximum likely benefit to the student can be chosen.

Dynamic belief networks [3] allow for reasoning about change over time. This is achieved by having a sequence of nodes that represent the state of the external item over a period of time, rather than having just a single temporally-invariant node. For real-world continuous processes, the sequence of nodes may represent the external state as it changes over a sequence of time-slices. For tutoring, it is often more useful to represent changes in the student model over a sequence of interactions, rather than time-slices (as illustrated by the example in the following section).

2   Two-phase updating of the student model

In general, an interaction with a student must cause the system to revise its beliefs about the student's state of knowledge. On first consideration, it might appear that this updating of beliefs should be modelled as a single process, representing the transition from prior beliefs to posterior beliefs.

However, in the general case, an interaction with a student may provide clues about two distinct (but related) pieces of information: (i) how likely it is that the student knew a topic *before* the interaction; and (ii) how likely it is that the student knows a topic *after* the interaction, i.e. what change (if any) is caused by the interaction.

Consequently, I advocate a *two-phase approach to updating the student model*, at each interaction:

(a)   phase 1: the incorporation of evidence (if any) from the interaction, about the student's *state of knowledge as it was prior to the interaction*; and

(b)   phase 2: the expected changes (if any) in the student's *state of knowledge as a result of the interaction*.

Many ITS architectures have clearly distinguishable Analysis (input-processing) and Response (output-generating) components. The two-phase approach maps naturally onto these architectures: phase 1 covers updates made by the Analysis component; and phase 2 covers updates made when executing tutorial actions chosen by the Response component.

But, this two-phase approach is applicable to *any* architecture that uses probability theory for student/user modelling. This is the case even if probability theory is just used to model uncertainty about isolated nodes (rather than structuring these into a belief network).

In any system, phase 1 is clearly important for gathering information at the *first* interaction on a given topic, i.e. topics for which there has not been any previous interaction with the particular student. But phase 1 is especially important for gathering information at *each* interaction, because the model must allow for the possibility that the student's knowledge will change independently of interactions with the system, i.e. the student may forget, may study independently, etc. It is necessary that the system be able to handle the fact that substantial periods of time (hours, days, weeks) may elapse from one interaction to the next, depending on how the student wishes to make use of the system.

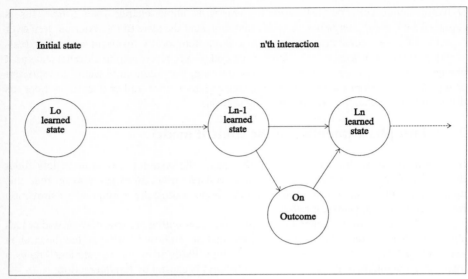

Figure 1. Two-phase updating

Figure 1 is an overall illustration of a dynamic belief network representing this two-phase approach. As this figure shows, following the n'th interaction, the probability that the student is *now* in the *learned state*, L_n (i.e. student-knows (*topic*)), depends both on whether the student was already in the learned state, L_{n-1} , and on the outcome, O_n, of the interaction. (The figure also shows that there must be some initial assumption about how likely it is that the student is in the learned state, prior to any interactions with the system, L_0, so that the updating process has somewhere to begin.)

In the sections that follow, I derive the mathematical formulae that follow from the two-phase approach. I then illustrate my claim for its generality, by showing that the student modelling approaches of Corbett and Anderson [4] and Shute [5] are actually special cases of this approach, even though these two papers appear totally unrelated to each other!

3 Phase 1: incorporation of evidence about the student's knowledge

With regard to Figure 1, let:

(a) O_n be an element in a *set of possible outcomes* of a given tutorial interaction involving a given domain topic, i.e. the set of allowed student responses for that interaction, e.g. (a) correct or incorrect; (b) no-help, level-1-help, level-2-help, etc;

(b) $p(L_{n-1})$ represent the system's belief that the student *already knows the given domain topic*, prior to the n'th interaction (where $n = 1, 2, ...$);

(c) $p(O_n \mid L_{n-1})$ represent the system's belief that *outcome O_n will occur when the student already knows* the domain topic;

(d) $p(O_n | \neg L_{n-1})$ represent the system's belief that *outcome O_n will occur when the student does not know the domain topic*;

where (c) and (d) are the two conditional probabilities needed to fully define the single link between the "L_{n-1} learned state" node and the "O_n Outcome" node, shown in Figure 1.

Given values for each of these, the system must be able to revise its belief in $p(L_{n-1})$ when outcome O_n occurs. This is done by using the well-known Bayes's rule:

$$p(L_{n-1} | O_n) = \frac{p(O_n | L_{n-1})p(L_{n-1})}{p(O_n | L_{n-1})p(L_{n-1}) + p(O_n | \neg L_{n-1})p(\neg L_{n-1})} \tag{1}$$

Let $K(O_n)$ be the likelihood ratio:

$$\gamma(O_n) = \frac{p(O_n | L_{n-1})}{p(O_n | \neg L_{n-1})} \tag{2}$$

Then, equation (1) can be simplified to:

$$p(L_{n-1} | O_n) = \frac{\gamma(O_n)p(L_{n-1})}{1 + [\gamma(O_n) - 1]p(L_{n-1})} \tag{3}$$

4   Phase 2: expected changes in the student's knowledge due to tutoring

In phase 2, we model the expected changes in the student's knowledge as a result of the interaction. Doing this requires a formula for $p(L_n | O_n)$, so that we know what probability to assign to $p(L_n)$ for each possible outcome, O_n, in the set of possible outcomes.

To fully define the double link from the "L_{n-1} learned state" node and the "O_n Outcome" node to the "L_n learned state" node shown in Figure 1, requires two conditional probabilities for each possible outcome:

(a) $p(L_n | L_{n-1}, O_n)$

This function represents the probability that the student will remain in the learned state as a result of the outcome, i.e. it is the *rate of remembering* (or "not forgetting"). As we do not expect an ITS's interactions to cause the student to forget something they already know, this probability will have the value 1 in most implementations. However, for completeness, I leave it as a function here.

(b) $p(L_n \mid \neg L_{n-1}, O_n)$

This function represents the probability that the student will make the *transition from the unlearned state to the learned state* as the result of the outcome, i.e. it is the rate of learning.

From this, the revised belief after the interaction is simply given by:

$$p(L_n \mid O_n) = p(L_n \mid L_{n-1}, O_n) \, p(L_{n-1} \mid O_n)$$
$$+ \, p(L_n \mid \neg L_{n-1}, O_n) \, p(\neg L_{n-1} \mid O_n) \tag{4}$$

For notational simplicity, let:

(a) $\Psi(O_n) = p(L_n \mid L_{n-1}, O_n)$; and
(b) $\Sigma(O_n) = p(L_n \mid \neg L_{n-1}, O_n)$.

Then equation (4) can be simplified to:

$$p(L_n \mid O_n) = \lambda(O_n) + [\rho(O_n) - \lambda(O_n)] \, p(L_{n-1} \mid O_n) \tag{5}$$

The equations for each phase, (3) and (5), can be used separately in an implementation. But, it is also useful to combine them together, so that one can conveniently describe the effects of an entire interaction. This combination is given in the following section.

5   Combining the two phases

Combining (5) with equation (3) gives:

$$p(L_n - O_n) = \lambda(O_n) + \frac{[\rho(O_n) - \lambda(O_n)] \, \gamma(O_n) \, p(L_{n-1})}{1 + [\gamma(O_n) - 1] \, p(L_{n-1})} \tag{6}$$

which can be rewritten as:

$$p(L_n \mid O_n) = \frac{\lambda(O_n) + [\rho(O_n)\gamma(O_n) - \lambda(O_n)] \, p(L_{n-1})}{1 + [\gamma(O_n) - 1] \, p(L_{n-1})} \tag{7}$$

When $p(L_{n-1}) = 1$, equation (7) gives:

$$p(L_n \mid O_n) = \rho(O_n) \tag{8}$$

I.e. $\Psi(O_n) = p(L_n \mid O_n)$ when $p(L_{n-1}) = 1$, illustrating the earlier description of $\Psi(O_n)$ as the "rate of remembering".

When $p(L_{n-1}) = 0$, equation (7) gives:

$$p(L_n \mid O_n) = \lambda(O_n) \tag{9}$$

I.e. $\Sigma(O_n) = p(L_n \mid O_n)$ when $p(L_{n-1}) = 0$, illustrating the earlier description of $\Sigma(O_n)$ as the "rate of learning".

   Figure 2 illustrates equation (7) for some particular values of K, Ψ and Σ. For each tuple of such values, there is a direct visual interpretation of these three parameters: the height of each end-point directly portrays the values of parameters Ψ and Σ (in accord with equations (8) and (9)); and the curvature depends directly on the value of K, i.e. concave when $K > 0$, convex when $K < 0$, and straight when $K = 0$.

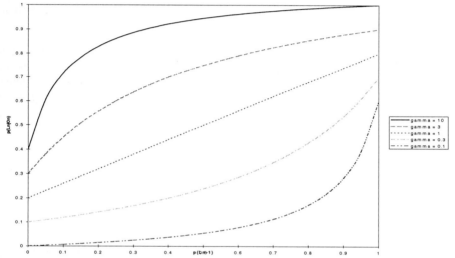

Figure 2. Example curves for equation (7)

6   A dynamic belief network for probabilistic modelling in the ACT Programming Languages Tutor

The ACT Programming Languages Tutor [4] uses a two-state psychological learning model, which is updated each time that the student has an opportunity to show their knowledge of a production rule in the (ideal) student model. In an appendix to their paper, the authors briefly state equations for calculating the probability that a production rule is in the learned state following a correct (C_n) or erroneous (E_n) student response, at the nth opportunity.

   In this section, I illustrate the applicability of my approach of using dynamic belief networks by showing how Corbett and Anderson's equations can be derived as a special case of my earlier equations. In their paper, Corbett and Anderson did not describe how they derived these equations. Even though they did not make any explicit use of the concept of dynamic belief networks, their learning model is clearly based on the mathematics of probability theory. So, it is not too surprising that there should be a direct relationship between their work and mine. Here, I show that my work is a generalisation of their model, by adding constraints to my model until I obtain their equations. (This is an extension of the research reported in [2].)

The authors make the following simplifying assumptions:

(a)   the set of outcomes has only two values: C_n (i.e. correct) and E_n (i.e. error).

(b) $p\ (L_n \mid L_{n-1}, O_n) = \Psi\ (O_n) = 1$, i.e. no forgetting.

(c) $p\ (L_n \mid \neg L_{n-1}, O_n) = \Sigma\ (O_n)$ is a constant, i.e. the probability that the student will make the transition from the unlearned to the learned state is *independent of the outcome*. The authors use the symbol $p(T)$ for this constant.

(d)   there are no conditional probabilities linking different rules, i.e. no prerequisite constraints.

Assumption (c) means that there is no direct dependency between the L_n node and the O_n node shown previously in Figure 1. By dropping this arrow, it should be clear that this is the simplest possible (structurally) dynamic belief network for student modelling (and simplicity may be a virtue rather than a vice). Under the above assumptions, equation (5) becomes:

$$p(\ L_n \mid O_n\ ) = p(T) + [1 - p(T)]\ p(\ L_{n-1} \mid O_n\ )$$

I.e.

$$p(\ L_n \mid O_n\ ) = p(\ L_{n-1} \mid O_n\ ) + p(T)(1 - p(\ L_{n-1} \mid O_n\ ))$$

When O_n is replaced by each of the two possible outcomes, C_n and E_n, we obtain:

$$p(\ L_n \mid C_n\ ) = p(\ L_{n-1} \mid C_n\ ) + p(T)(1 - p(\ L_{n-1} \mid C_n\ ))$$

$$p(\ L_n \mid E_n\ ) = p(\ L_{n-1} \mid E_n\ ) + p(T)(1 - p(\ L_{n-1} \mid E_n\ ))$$

which are the two equations that Corbett and Anderson number as [1] and [2], in their paper. Under these same assumptions, equation (2) becomes:

$$\gamma(\ C_n\ ) = \frac{p(\ C_n \mid L_{n-1}\ )}{p(\ C_n \mid \neg L_{n-1}\ )}$$

when O_n has the value C_n. Substituting this into equation (3), a version of Bayes's theorem, gives:

$$p(L_{n-1} \mid C_n) = \frac{p(C_n \mid L_{n-1})p(L_{n-1})}{p(C_n \mid L_{n-1})p(L_{n-1}) + p(\neg L_{n-1})p(C_n \mid \neg L_{n-1})}$$

which is the same as the equation marked [3] in Corbett and Anderson's paper, except for: (i) some rearrangement of terms; and (ii) they use the symbol "U_{n-1}" (for "unlearned") where I use "$\neg L_{n-1}$". For brevity, I omit the analogous derivation of their equation [4] for $p\ (L_{n-1} \mid E_n)$.

As a result of their assumptions, Corbett and Andersen's model has only four parameters associated with each rule. I list these parameters below, and, for clarity of reference, use the same notation utilised by the authors:

$p(L_0)$ the probability that a rule is in the *learned* state prior to the first opportunity to apply the rule (e.g. from reading text);

$p(C|U)$ the probability that a student will guess correctly if the applicable rule is in the *unlearned* state (same as my $p (O_n=C_n|\neg L_{n-1})$);

$p(E|L)$ the probability that a student will slip and make an error when the applicable rule is in the *learned* state (same as my $p (O_n=E_n|L_{n-1})$);

$p(T)$ the probability that a rule will make the transition from the *unlearned* state to the *learned* state following an opportunity to apply the rule (same as my $\Sigma (O_n)$).

In the most general case, the values of these parameters may be set empirically and may vary from rule to rule. Corbett and Anderson [4] describe a study in which these parameters were held constant across 21 rules, with $p(L_0) = 0.5$, $p(C|U) = 0.2$, $p(E|L) = 0.2$ and $p(T) = 0.4$. In my notation, these values are equivalent to $K (C_n) = 4$, $K (E_n) = 0.25$ and $\Sigma (C_n) = \Sigma (E_n) = 0.4$.

7   Another example of a dynamic belief network: SMART

While developing SMART, Shute [5] created a number of functions for updating her student model, as illustrated in Figure 3. The mappings in these functions were developed mainly by hand, based on the opinions of domain experts. Shute's empirical validation of her system, which is based on this approach, makes this student modelling approach worthy of further study.

As is clear from Figure 3, Shute's model is a probabilistic one, thus raising the interesting question as to how it relates to my own work. Like Corbett and Anderson, Shute does not make any use of the concept of dynamic belief networks. However, in this section, I show that such networks are a good way to provide a theoretical foundation for her work, by showing how Shute's graphs can be represented using my equations.

When solving each problem posed by Shute's SMART system, the student is allowed to choose from four levels of help (or "hints"), where level-0 covers the case where the student required no help at all. Unlike Corbett and Andersen, Shute does not make the assumption that the probability of learning is independent of the outcome. This is obvious from the fact that there are four separate curves in Figure 3.

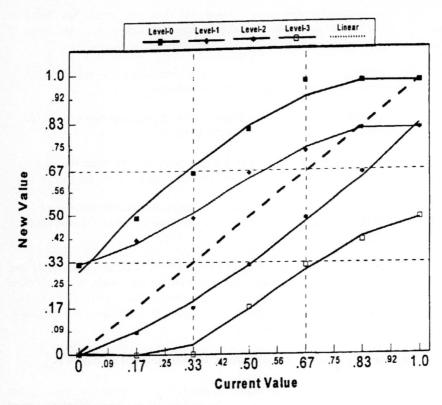

Figure 3. SMART's updating function

Figure 4 shows the curves obtained when plotting equation (7) with the following values for K, Σ and Ψ:

Outcome	K	Σ	Ψ
Level-0 help	2.35	0.33	1
Level-1 help	2.12	0.33	0.83
Level-2 help	0.66	0	0.83
Level-3 help	0.52	0	0.5

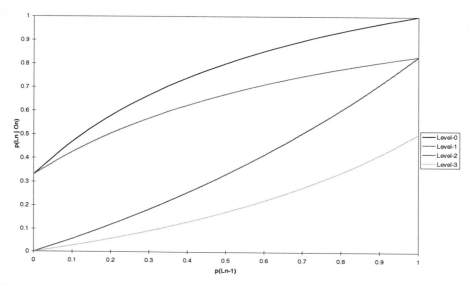

Figure 4. Curves from equation (7) for chosen values of K, Σ and Ψ

By inspecting this figure, it is clear that equation (7) provides a good theoretical basis for Shute's graphs.

8   Conclusion

This paper gives a general theory of how a student model should be updated, based on the concept of a dynamic belief network. This work shows that the student modelling approaches of Corbett and Anderson [4] and Shute [5] are actually special cases of this general approach, even though this is far from obvious at first glance.

References

1. Villano, M. (1992) Probabilistic student models: Bayesian belief networks and knowledge space theory. In Frasson, C., Gauthier, C. and McCalla, G.I. (eds.) *Intelligent Tutoring Systems (Proceeding of the Second International Conference, ITS'92, Montreal, Canada)*, 491-498. Berlin: Springer-Verlag.
2. Reye, J. (1996) A belief net backbone for student modelling. In Frasson, C., Gauthier, C. and Lesgold, A. (eds.) *Intelligent Tutoring Systems (Proceeding of the Third International Conference, ITS'96, Montreal, Canada)*, 596-604. Berlin: Springer-Verlag.
3. Dean, T., and Kanazawa, K. (1989) A model for reasoning about persistence and causation. *Computational Intelligence* 5, 142-150.
4. Corbett, A., and Anderson, J. (1992) Student modeling and mastery learning in a computer-based programming tutor. In Frasson, C., Gauthier, C. and McCalla, G.I. (eds.) *Intelligent Tutoring Systems (Proceeding of the Second International Conference, ITS'92, Montreal, Canada)*, 413-420. Berlin: Springer-Verlag.
5. Shute, V. (1995) SMART evaluation: cognitive diagnosis, mastery learning & remediation. In Greer, J. (ed.) *Artificial Intelligence in Education, 1995*, 123-130. Charlottesville, VA: Association for the Advancement of Computing in Education.

Teaching and Learning with Intelligent Agents: Actors

Thierry MENGELLE, Charles DE LÉAN, Claude FRASSON

Université de Montréal - Département d'informatique et de recherche opérationnelle
2920 Chemin de la Tour - Montréal (Québec) - H3T 1J4 - Canada
E-mail :{mengelle, delean, frasson}@iro.umontreal.ca

Abstract. Various research projects suggest to use intelligent agents inside Intelligent Tutoring Systems (ITS). We have designed a new kind of agent (actor) to model the pedagogical expertise of ITS. Actors aim to help a student to learn using powerful cooperative pedagogical strategies. Such systems involve complex expertise that evolves continuously. To improve the knowledge acquisition process and to foster revision of expertise, we give the actors some learning abilities. The paper first describes how to use pedagogical actors to implement ITS. This involves three main points: the actor paradigm, the communication protocol with the domain-related material, and the representation of this material. The second part of the paper focuses on the learning abilities of actors. We discuss different learning approaches and illustrate one of them with an example involving two simple actors.

1. Introduction

From the very beginning, artificial intelligence was a key element of ITS research. Most tutoring systems were built around expert systems. The drawbacks of classical expert systems (knowledge acquisition, revision of expertise,...) were even more crucial for ITS, due to their multiple expertise (domain, pedagogy, interface, ...). For a few years now, another field of artificial intelligence has influenced ITS research: agents and multi-agent systems. Most conferences now propose workshops on pedagogical agents. Many reasons promote the emergence of this new field...

From a software-engineering point of view, agents have advantages of modularity and flexibility. Several works on artificial intelligence study knowledge acquisition and learning abilities for agents: instructable agents [9], Disciple agents [14], etc. Agents are also efficient assistants for groupware or Internet search.

Regarding the ITS field, we find various applications of agents: structuring the expertise of an ITS [4] [12], coaching [10], animated characters [2] [6], etc.

Our research on pedagogical actors [7], a new kind of agents, deals with all these aspects. In this paper, we will however focus on two points only: modeling of pedagogical expertise and actors' learning abilities. The first part will describe the basic characteristics of actors and the protocol they use to communicate with the elements of the domain. The second part will deal with learning.

2. Managing domain-related materials with pedagogical actors

2.1. Cooperative pedagogical strategies

We are mainly interested in cooperative strategies such as *learning with a companion* [3] or *learning by disturbing* [1]. In our ITS, the learner interacts with domain-related materials, that are named resources (exercises, simulations, problems, ...) under the supervision of a society of pedagogical actors. The works of [12] and the design of the MATHEMA system [4] stem from the same approach. Before describing the structure of resources and the protocol that the actors use to dialog with these domain-related elements, next paragraph will present this new agent paradigm.

2.2. Actor paradigm

Actors, which have been defined as a *reactive, instructable, adaptive* and *cognitive* agents [7], exhibit two main properties. They react to the activity of others and are able to learn. The first property stems from the combination of three approaches: reactive agents, deliberative agents and interacting agents [13]. To ensure these three kinds of reactions, we defined a modular architecture [7], which is summarized in the bottom-right part of figure 2. Reactivity results from a direct association between perception and action modules (the detection of a typical situation can directly trigger an action task). The third module (control module) supports deliberation and the abilities for social behavior. This module involves several control tasks that are in charge of planning, decisions and invoking services of other actors. Regarding the last point, we propose two general protocols for communication/cooperation among agents: direct request of a specific service of a given actor (see the arrow between 'pedagogical actor 1' and 'dialog actor' on figure 2) and broadcasting of a request to the whole society using the blackboard structure (see the broadcast of a message by the 'dialog actor'). The second property (learning) is ensured via a cognitive module and will be described in the second part of the paper.

The influence of personality on agents' activity and on emotional state forms another advanced feature of actors. To deal with this point we are presently interested in the virtual theater project [5], the animated characters [2] [10], the work on affectivity [6]. Detailing this aspect is however outside the scope of the paper.

We defined an interpreted language allowing to build actors. An actor is defined as a set of typical situations that trigger some tasks. Figure 1 presents some of the language features. This example describes a task that the *Companion* actor triggers when the learner asks for help (the human learner is faced to two computerized agents: a teacher and a companion). First, an exchange of structures via the blackboard allows the actor to dialog with the resource (this is a simplified version of the real structure which consists of only two fields: one contains a hint, the other contains the complete answer in text form). Then, the *Companion* calls the task *shouldGiveAnswer* (primitive `calltask`) in order to decide whether to give the complete response or a simple hint. Because some of the tasks can take a few seconds to execute, we want to allow executing them while waiting for the learner. The new task will be executed concurrently and the calling task will get an id of the task. With that id, the calling task may check if the task is over (with the primitive `existreply`), or simply wait after the result with the `getreply` primitive. A task may request a service of another actor through the `req` primitive whose grammar is very similar as the one of `calltask`. If the requested actor accepts to give the service (it can refuse), it will start a task and give its result. Here, the *Companion* requests the *Teacher* to give a hint (*GiveHint*) when the learner refuses its help.

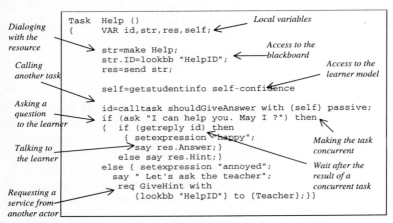

Fig. 1. The actor language: example of a task definition

2.3. The dialog protocol between actors and resources

The protocol the actors use to communicate with resources (figure 2) involves four kinds of messages. A pedagogical actor first loads a given resource. The resource answers with some static information (for instance its type (e.g. MCQ)). Then, after each interaction with the learner, the resource informs actors about what presumably happened (diagnosis of student action) and about all the possible reactions. The diagnosis describes the global situation (it's a good answer, a partial answer...) and specifies a partial learner model which is supposed to explain this situation. We defined a very simple structure for this model: the status of each knowledge involved in the pedagogical activity (basic status are: *mastered*, *not mastered* or identification of a *frequent mistake*). The possible reactions describe what the resource is able to do at this point (for instance it may: reformulate the question, give a correct hint about <a-knowledge-id>, try to mislead the learned with a frequent error about <a-knowledge-id>, display the correct answer, etc). Then, the actors use their own pedagogical expertise to choose one of the possible reactions and then inform the resource (`ApplyDecision`).

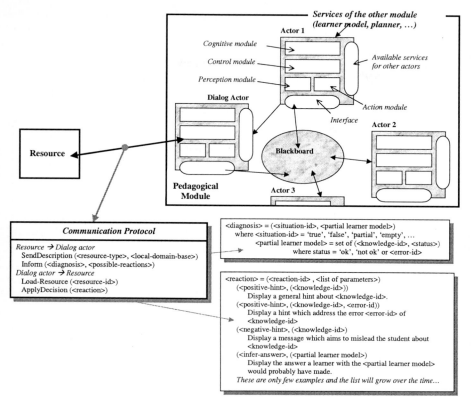

Fig. 2. Managing the dialog between a resource and a society of pedagogical actors

2.4. Building resources

The main principle which underlines the previous protocol is that the resource is in charge of the diagnosis of student knowledge and informs the actors about what they can do next. So, clearly, the global quality of the ITS also depends on the expertise of the resources. One can build powerful domain-specific resources. We took this approach to model exercises for an ITS in the field of radiology [11] [7]. These resources were time-consuming to implement because of the complex and domain-related algorithms they need for diagnosis. It appears however that most of the elements of a domain don't require such specific diagnosis. So we are also interested in building generic resources. Here, we take the example of a classical tool for knowledge assessment: Multiple Choice Questions (MCQ). This well-known tool for student's evaluation allows a very straightforward diagnosis, and hence fits our problematic of quickly building efficient resources.

Figure 3 presents a simplified version of the structure we use to implement MCQ manageable by actors. Each MCQ consists of four main parts:

- an *identification part* with an identifier and a list of the pieces of knowledge that are useful to answer the question (*Capital* and *Communism* paradigms),
- a *subject part* which specifies the text of the question and, eventually, some other texts to display more information on question and answers,
- an *answer processing* part for the diagnosis of the student's knowledge,
- and a *set of hints* related to the various knowledge elements that are involved in this question (wrong hints allows the troublemaker to mislead the learner).

Question-ID		<xxxx>	
Related knowledge		<capital-id>, <communism-id>	
Question		Choose the towns that are or have been capital of communist countries: 1. Rome 2.Moscow 3. Stalingrad 4.Bucarest	
Refinement of the question		Null	
Refinement of the answers		1	Rome is a town located in Italy. It is well…
		3	Stalingrad is now named…
Answer	Knowledge ok		Knowledge not ok
1---	<capital-id>		<communism-id>
-2--	<capital-id>, <communism-id>		
(…)			
Hints	T/F	Text	
<capital-id>	true	Generally speaking, capitals are important cities.	
<communism-id>	true	Most of communist countries were in East Europe.	
<communism-id>	false	The proportion of communist countries is the same in each continent.	

Fig. 3. A generic structure to implement MCQ manageable by actors

We took a very simple approach to process answers. The designer links each possible answer with a set of mastered knowledge and with a set of not-mastered knowledge. For instance, the fact that the student chooses *Rome* as a capital of a communist country may reflect a good master of the *Capital* paradigm and some problem about *Communism*. Considering this structure, when the student chooses an answer, the resource can establish a diagnosis in a very straightforward fashion. Let us assume the learner answers '1'. The resource sends the actors its diagnosis (the student masters <capital-id> and has problems on <communism-id>) and the possible reactions it can ensure (detailing answers 1 or 3, positive hints on <capital-id> and <communism-id>, wrong hint on <communism-id>). Actors choose one of these possible reactions and inform the resource of their choice. So, if some of the elements of the structure are not specified, the resource will offer fewer potentialities but the whole system will still work.

An editor helps the teacher to build pedagogical efficient MCQ using this simple structure. Regardless of the definition of resources, the other point on which we want to make the designer's work easier concerns the definition of new pedagogical strategies. Because the pedagogical expertise is often complex, we promote an incremental development and have decided to supply actors with learning abilities.

3. Learning in pedagogical actors

3.1. Basic learning features of actors

Improving the expertise of an actor requires two distinct tasks: diagnosis of a problem then revision of the actor expertise in order to solve it. The diagnosis stage checks that the behavior of the actor respects its goals. Each actor considers two distinct global goals: its individual goal (e.g. the aim of the *Troublemaker* [1] is to mislead the learner) and the collective goal of the society (the goal of the whole *learning by disturbing* strategy is to help the student to learn and to improve his self-confidence). In most cases, these goals can be divided in several subgoals. The aim of the diagnosis stage is hence to check every subgoal and to notify the possible problems. Once a subgoal failure is detected, the revision stage aims to modify the expertise of the actor in order to improve its future behavior.

Each of these two tasks (diagnosis and revision) can be ensured whether by the human expert, by the actor or by cooperation between these two partners. In the instructable agent approach [9], the actor is in charge of diagnosis and dialogs with the human to improve its expertise. We also promote another kind of instructability where the human can interrupt the actor in order to provide it with some new knowledge. This process of dynamic instruction is described in [11]. Besides instructability, we also study situations where actors can do diagnosis and reparation, using some learning algorithm. We design an environment which offers all these forms of learning. The choice of a given learning approach will depend on various parameters such as: the availability of the human expert, or the expected performance... Another key factor will influence the kind of learning: will the reparation occur during the actor's activity (like in classical instructable systems) or after it (during a specifically dedicated learning stage)? To summarize, a learning approach is characterized by the entity (actor, human, or both entities) that will be in charge of each stage (diagnosis and revision) and by the time where the revision will take place (during or after the activity).

To allow actors to ensure diagnosis, we have to specify some functions that allow them to assess their goals (individual and collective goals). One of the main sources of knowledge these functions may use is the learner model, which generally reflects the influence of the actors' activity on the student. When dealing with reparation, we aim to supply actors with different kinds of learning algorithms. The next paragraph illustrates the use of a classification learning algorithm in order to improve the expertise of two simple actors.

3.2. A first experiment

This learning process we used in this example is quite simple. A human expert, that will be next named programmer, runs actors on several problems. Then a learning algorithm will try to find what are the differences between the actors' traces in cases of failure or success. The programmer will interpret this result in order to improve the actors' expertise (adding of modifying rules). The process will re-start until results become satisfactory. To summarize this situation: actors are in charge of the diagnosis and the reparation will be ensured in a distinct stage using a cooperation between the actor and the human programmer.

To reduce complexity, we illustrate this process with an example which is outside of the ITS field (see figure 4).

> Two actors are trying to build words. The alphabet consists of 4 letters: red square, red circle, blue square and blue circle. The *tracer* chooses the form while the *painter* decides the color. They are not allowed to communicate and look only at the current state of the word to make their decision. We define four basic rules:
> - A red letter must follow a square
> - A blue letter must follow two consecutive red letters
> - A circle must follow a blue letter
> - A square must follow two consecutive circles.
>
> The *tracer* knows only about rules 1 and 2, while the *painter* knows rules 3 and 4. It is therefore possible for our actors to come to a dead end. For instance, if the two last letters are red and the last one is a square, the *painter* can't paint. The tracer has likewise problems. The actors aim to reach 20-letter words.

Fig. 4. A simple example: Rules of the game.

We are here mainly interested in the learning phase. The learning algorithm we use is a class regression tree. We feed it with a bank of examples. It returns a classification tree which will allow human experts to infer some new rules in order to improve the actors' performance (see figure 5). Each example describes a previous sequence of interactions between the two actors in order to build a word and the result of this activity (assessment of the actors' goals, here: to build 20-letters words respecting the basic rules). The basic description we have about actors' activities is the trace of the activation of the various tasks. But, this trace first requires some processing before learning. We need to give some hints to focus learning. Here, the programmer may have the intuition that the number of blue circles is a key factor for success. Hence, it may be useful to examine the various traces of actors' activities and count the number of occurrences of the tasks *Paint-Blue* and *Draw-Circle*. The indicators a programmer may want to focus on are quite independent from this example; they may concern for example the number of occurrences of a task, the number of occurrences of a task after another one, the presence of a specific pattern inside the trace... The approach we adopt to solve this problem is to supply the human expert with a set of heuristics that have been already used on other examples to extract pertinent indicators. We promote a two-step process (see figure 5). Because a trace of tasks' activation can be complex, the first step allows filtering it. We give the programmer various tools that allow him to hide some actors, some tasks or to consider only certain period of time. In the above example, the view we defined considers only two tasks for each one of the two actors. The second step concerns the extraction of pertinent indicators from this filtered trace. Figure 5 presents some of the heuristics we defined; roughly, they compute the number of times a task occurred. In this example, we consider 48 indicators, for instance: number of times the task *Draw-Circle* follows the *Paint-Blue* task (i.e. circle following a blue letter).

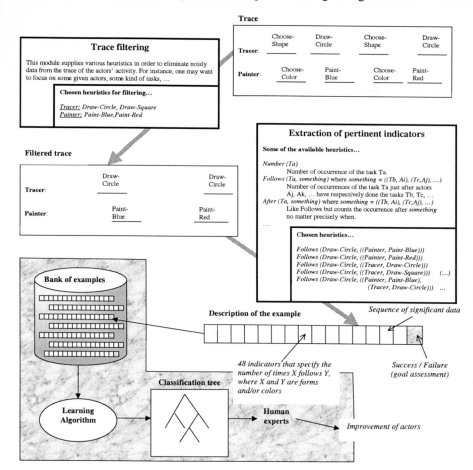

Fig. 5. Learning from sequences of traces of actors' interactions

At the beginning the choice is at random and about half of the traces are failures. Applying the learning algorithm tells us that the most discriminating factor (i.e. head of the original tree on figure 6) between failure and success is choosing a blue square after a red circle (this must happen at least 5 times to succeed). We consider that only one of the two actors can learn at each time; so, we make the *Painter* learn a new rule: "after a red circle, choose the color blue if possible" (this heuristic is added to the Painter expertise by the programmer). With this new rule, we run the actors another 2000 times and we notice that results significantly decrease (a success each 8 attempts). The programmer interprets the new tree (tree 1) and adds a new heuristic in the tracer: "after a blue circle, choose a square if possible". This time, performance is improved and actors build 2 good words each 3 tries. Tree 2 leads to generalize the previous heuristic of the *Tracer*: "after a circle, choose a square if possible". The performance remains however unchanged. A new application of the learning algorithm (tree 3) doesn't tell us any new information.

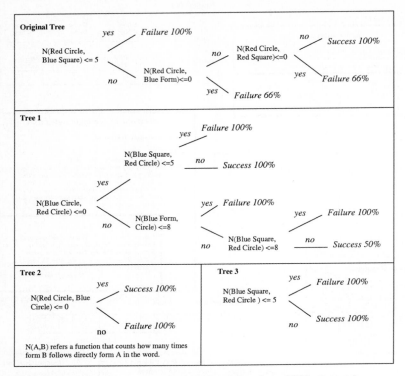

Fig. 6. Classification trees that result from learning (after about 2000 attempts)

This basic example told us that a thing as simple as the trace of actors' activity can provide a programmer interesting features in order to improve the expertise of a society of actors (here, the ratio of success grows from 1/2 to 2/3). In the begining of the paper, we addressed the problem of the complexity of ITS expertise; we think that tools such as this learning algorithm can be usefull in order to help human designers to improve the expertise of a society of pedagogical actors.

Conclusion

The actor paradigm allows intelligent tutoring systems to foster learning using various powerful cooperative strategies such as *learning by disturbing*. After having described the basic features of actors, we detailed the communication protocol that actors use to dialog with the resources. Actors can manage complex, domain-related and powerful resources. In this paper, we have however promoted the use of generic and quickly implemented resources such as MCQ. Then, we have discussed another interesting feature of actors: learning. Several approaches have been presented. The example that we have described shows that learning from the trace of actors' activities can help a designer to improve the expertise of an ITS. Our work on learning is still ongoing. We are also presently dealing with personality and affectivity issues for actors.

Acknowledgements

This research has been supported by the MICST (Ministère de l'Industrie, Commerce, Science et Technologie du Gouvernement du Québec) under the Synergie program. We also thank the CRSNG for his financial support.

References

1. Aïmeur, E. and Frasson, C.: Analyzing a new learning strategy according to different knowledge levels. Computers in education, Vol 27, No. 2, (1996) 115-127.
2. André, E., Müller, J., Rist, T.: Life-Like Presentation Agents: A New Perspective for Computer-Based Technical Documentation. Proceedings of the workshop on Pedagogical Agents, AI-ED 97, Kobe, Japan (1997) 1-8.
3. Chan T. W. and Baskin A. B.: Learning companion systems. In Intelligent Tutoring Systems : At the crossroads of Artificial Intelligence and Education (Edited by Frasson C. and Gauthier G.), Chap 1. Ablex, N.J. (1990)
4. Costa, E.B., Perkusich, A.: A Multi-Agent Interactive Learning Environment Model. Proceedings of the workshop on Pedagogical Agents, AI-ED 97, Kobe, Japan (1997) 9-16.
5. Doyle, P., Hayes-Roth, B.: Computer-aided exploration of virtual environments. Working Notes of AAAI-96 WorkShop on AllALife, AAAI Press, Menlo Park, CA, (1996).
6. Elliott, C.: Affective Reasoner Personality Models for Automated Tutoring Systems. Proceedings of the workshop on Pedagogical Agents, AI-ED 97, Kobe, Japan (1997) 33-39.
7. Frasson, C., Mengelle, T., Aïmeur, E., Gouardères, G.: An Actor-based Architecture for Intelligent Tutoring Systems, ITS'96 Conference, LNCS, No 1086, Springer Verlag, Montréal (1996) 57-65.
8. Frasson, C., Mengelle, T., Aïmeur, E.: Using Pedagogical Agents in a Multi-Strategic Intelligent Tutoring System. Proceedings of the workshop on Pedagogical Agents, AI-ED 97, Kobe, Japan (1997) 40-47.
9. Huffman, S.B.: Instructable Autonomous Agents. PhD Thesis, University of Michigan, Dept of Electrical Engineering and Computer Science, (1994)
10. Lester, J.C., Callaway, C. B., Stone, B. A., Towns, S. G.: Mixed Initiative Problem Solving with Animated Pedagogical Agents. Proceedings of the workshop on Pedagogical Agents, AI-ED 97, Kobe, Japan (1997) 56-62.
11. Mengelle, T., Leibu, D., Frasson, C., Aïmeur,E.: Processus d'instruction d'acteurs pédagogiques, Colloque Cinquièmes journées EIAO de Cachan, Hermés, France (1997) 251-262.
12. Morin, JF., Lelouche, R. Tutoring Knowledge Modelling as Pedagogical Agents in an ITS. Proceedings of the workshop on Pedagogical Agents, AI-ED 97, Kobe, Japan (1997) 63-70.
13. Müller, P.J.: The Design of Intelligent Agents, A Layered Approach, LNAI, No. 1177, Springer-Verlag: Heidelberg, Germany (1996)
14. Tecuci,G., Hieb M.R.: Teaching intelligent Agents: the Disciple Approach. International Journal of Human-Computer Interaction (1996).

Self-Organized Goal-Oriented Tutoring in Adaptive Hypermedia Environments

Elmar Schwarz

Department of Computer Science,
University of Karlsruhe
ukgo@rz.uni-karlsruhe.de

Abstract. Goal-oriented tutoring in adaptive hypermedia has been proved to be a powerful technique in educational environments. By providing guided sequencing, link annotation, sorting and hiding of links, adaptive systems support the student individually in navigating through complex hyperspaces. Those basic techniques adapt the interface according to the student's current state of knowledge and the current educational goal. State of the art systems often implement these adaptation techniques, but remain static with respect to the educational goal the system adapts to. Our approach supports the user in defining his or her own learning goal by requesting help from an automated guard, which sets the new learning goal according to the current teaching operation, for which the guard was called. This allows the system to provide the student with adaptation specific to his or her current self-defined goal.

1   Introduction

Goal-oriented adaptive hypermedia is a new promising technique to provide students with navigation support in complex intelligent learning environments. The basic idea yields in teaching a student according to a goal, some knowledge or skills the user should or wants to acquire. According to this basis the problem of goal-adapted navigation support results in two basic questions: First, what is the current goal of the student that makes him or her using the intelligent tutoring system; and second, what is the most optimal next teaching operation to complete this goal by acquiring the desired pieces of knowledge. In recent years, many approaches have been taken and several techniques were developed (cf. [2]) and implemented in several contexts to answer these questions (cf. [10; 12; 13; 15; 16]).

Surprisingly, most systems mainly address the second question, whilst the first one remains unanswered in almost any context. Often the underlying assumption, that the student is supposed to acquire any piece of knowledge a system can provide, allows system designers and instructors to leave this question unanswered. With the growing complexity of educational systems and the increasing size of an educational domain this approach becomes more and more inappropriate. A large domain as a current learning goal does not allow to focus on one particular subgoal, which the student might be interested in. For this reason the current mental goal of the student can not be covered by the system's support, which usually results in frustrating the student by missing preciseness of navigation support or even misleading information. Providing the student by precise and appropriate support means providing him or her with an opportunity for affecting the system's behavior by setting his or her own individual goals to which the system should adapt. For an efficient and user friendly implementation of this kind of self-directed teaching, we suggest *adaptive guarding*. Once this guard is called by the student for a certain teaching operation, our system recognizes the pieces of knowledge, the student is lacking to successfully proceed on that current teaching operation, as the student's current learning goal. The system will change its behavior by adapting to that new goal until it is sufficiently learned by the student. Doing so, the student can take advantage of the adaptation of the system to his or her specific self-defined learning goal or ask for another teaching operation which supports exactly the current self-defined goal the most.

2   Goal-Oriented Adaptive Educational Hypermedia

To allow a better understanding of the answer to the first of these two basic questions, we want to give a short introduction to goal-oriented adaptive tutoring in general. We will state some paradigms of user modeling and goal-oriented adaptive hypermedia, which are used in recent implementations (cf. [10; 15]) and show how our approach relates to recent research (cf. [12; 16]).

2.1   User Modeling and Indexing

User modeling represents the backbone of any adaptive intelligent tutoring system. The user model of an intelligent tutoring system tries to cover the student's mental state at any particular point in time. Different systems reflect different aspects of these states. Most systems mainly point out the student's knowledge about the particular domain that is taught. Other systems also try to summarize student's preferences, goals, procedural knowledge (cf. [1]) or episodic experience (cf. [17]). In our context mainly the current goal and the supposed state of knowledge have to be considered. As a simple technical implementation of modeling student's state of knowledge overlay models are a commonly used technique. Although the overlay technique is not essential for the presented approach which could also be extended to other representations of students knowledge (cf. [1; 17]) its simplicity led us to choose this technology. [3] gives an example, how to built a bridge between several heterogeneous representation and how to make them suitable for our context.

The overlay technique associates any concept, elementary pieces of knowledge, with a certain score which reflects the student's supposed knowledge about it. A simple model may only implement the two grades "seen" and "unseen". More sophisticated models distinguish more states (cf. [15]) or even use probabilistic ones. Some open architectures combine some of those scores to improve the reliability of the estimation (cf. [3; 18]).

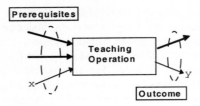

Fig. 1. A teaching operation, indexed by concepts of the domain model as outcome and prerequisites of the teaching operation. Prerequisite x and outcome y are not yet marked as being known.

Based upon those scores the system can predict, which knowledge a user might have and which he is still lacking. To collect information about the student's state of knowledge, student's actions can be tracked and by applying certain rules estimations about his or her knowledge can be made. A simple and direct way to do this is called *indexing* which attaches any possible teaching operation, like text, multimedia, examples, tests, or problems, with a set of concepts from the domain model (see figure 1). Those concepts may have different roles as indices, like being the outcome or the prerequisite of such an operation. Using the outcome concepts of a teaching operation, the system can estimate how much knowledge a user has already gained by tracking the student's actions, e.g. by marking the outcome concepts of a successfully taken teaching operation as being more familiar to the student.

2.2   Adaptation Techniques

One of the more promising techniques in adaptive navigation support is *adaptive link annotation*. This technique tries to support the user in navigating through hyperspaces by attaching an annotation to each link. Based upon the user model, reflecting the goal and the current knowledge state of the user, the system can make conclusions whether or not a page is suitable for the user. Following these conclusions, the user is either suggested to take a link or advised to avoid it for the moment by annotating the link in different ways (cf. [9]). If there is any prerequisite that is not yet sufficiently learned by the student, a teaching operation will not be suggested. For the case, that an outcome concept is part of the current learning goal and the knowledge about it is missing in the user model, the page will be suggested.

Another important goal-oriented technology is *adaptive sequencing* (cf. [7; 14; 18]). The underlying algorithms try to select an item, which is ready to be learned and further supports the current learning goal the most. For the selection of the next item often heuristics algorithms are employed. Popular strategies are the focus of attention mechanism, which tries to select items having prerequisites that have been recently learned (cf. [7]). Other systems select the next suggested teaching operation from the current context (cf. [18]). In ELM-ART II (cf. [18]) a simple implementation of adaptive link annotation can be found a simple as well as a basic sequencing mechanism, which selects the next suggested item from the current context.

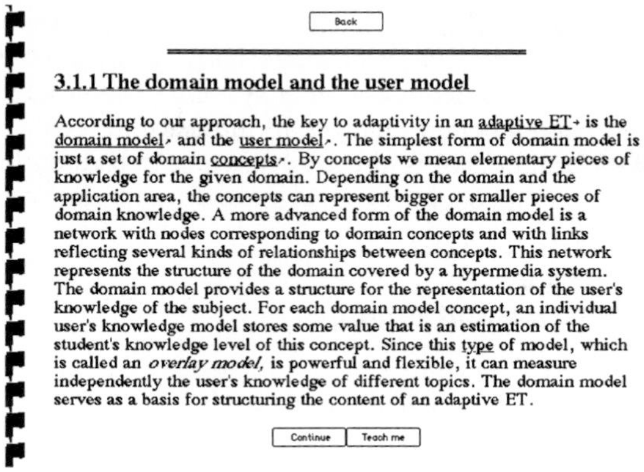

Back

3.1.1 The domain model and the user model

According to our approach, the key to adaptivity in an adaptive ET is the domain model and the user model. The simplest form of domain model is just a set of domain concepts. By concepts we mean elementary pieces of knowledge for the given domain. Depending on the domain and the application area, the concepts can represent bigger or smaller pieces of domain knowledge. A more advanced form of the domain model is a network with nodes corresponding to domain concepts and with links reflecting several kinds of relationships between concepts. This network represents the structure of the domain covered by a hypermedia system. The domain model provides a structure for the representation of the user's knowledge of the subject. For each domain model concept, an individual user's knowledge model stores some value that is an estimation of the student's knowledge level of this concept. Since this type of model, which is called an *overlay model*, is powerful and flexible, it can measure independently the user's knowledge of different topics. The domain model serves as a basis for structuring the content of an adaptive ET.

Continue | Teach me

Fig. 2. At the bottom of the figure, which show a part of a textbook window, you can see the 'Teach me' button, which involves the sequencing mechanism build-in InterBook.

Some other systems do further provide feedback about the supposed state of the current page. This can either be performed by showing a summarized state of the current teaching operation or by explicitly listing and annotating the indexed concepts, which cause this state. Both techniques are described in more detail in [4]. [11] implements a similar technique, showing a list of unlearned concepts, when the student is accessing a page that is not yet ready to be learned.

2.3 Origins of the Current Learning Goal

We have seen a couple of efficient navigation support techniques supporting the user in finding the next relevant teaching operation - up to a certain level - autonomously. Those techniques are often implemented in a way, that systems and models pay a lot of attention in modeling the user's current state of knowledge. But the current mental goal of an user acting in the hyperspace is either not explicitly represented at all or statically set by the system designer or instructor. In the introduction we have already discussed the inappropriateness of static goals in complex learning environments. For those reasons the need of a technique that tries to adapt the goal of the user itself becomes evident.

The simplest approach for setting the current learning goal is also the most commonly used: The student is supposed to acquire any piece of knowledge that is provided in the courseware. Systems like ELM-ART (cf. [18]) assume any unlearned concepts as being part of the goal. The students are simply supposed to walk through all the course. There is hardly any support just to learn a small subset of the knowledge presented in the tutorial. The sequencing mechanism does not take into account any preferences of the student, looking in general for the next suggested teaching operation. A small progress is made by allowing the instructor to set a certain learning goal (cf. [7]). In this case, at least the instructor of the course is able to take into account certain requirements of individual students in advance. But the current learning goal remains fixed throughout the course and it is not able to adapt temporarily to specific interests of the student. Another small step is taken by [16].

The presented system can compile a course according to a certain set of goals taken from the domain. This allows one to generate individualized courseware and represents a significant progress compared to other systems. The system is still not capable to take into account contemporary changes in the learning goal. Further, it demands for the fact, that the learning goal is already known before compiling the course. Free exploration of the underlying course is made more difficult due to this situation.

3   Towards Self-Defined Goals

3.1   Motivation: Why to Use Self-defined Goals?

For a better understanding of our implementation of user-adapted learning goals, we want have a short look at typical students behavior and its abstraction in the terms of user modeling, indexing and adaptive hypermedia: The student starts out from a certain point of knowledge accessing a hypermedia learning system. From any point in the hyperspace a student wants to find the next teaching operation of his or her interest, which can be reached by buttons or hyperlinks. Usually a student will follow some given structure, like the structure of the underlying educational material or some focus-of-attention based sequencing support. Many of the techniques discussed in the previous section apply to this kind of support. As long as the goal of the student and the goal that was explicitly or implicitly set by the instructor remain equivalent, the student will feel comfortable with this kind of *forward support*. In certain cases the instructor or the student him- or herself might overestimate the his or her current skills, requiring some *backward support*. In simple cases some techniques like prerequisite-based help and visualization of missing prerequisites can be sufficient. For the case, that the student has stepped so far ahead, that he is not even able to understand the items that might be listed by those features, these techniques will fail. The student would likely call these mechanisms recursively until he or she has found a suitable piece of information. While doing so, he would loose his current goal of understanding the page from which he or she has requested help.

The user demands for a more complex backward support (s. figure 3), that will enable him or her to collect the missing pieces of knowledge by a set of teaching operations, but will not let him or her loose the original focus. To do this, we make use of the basic principle of goal-adapted tutoring: we change the learning goal. By setting the current goal basically to the list of outstanding prerequisites, any navigation support provided by the system will now help the user to understand this self-defined goal and help the student to find his or her individual, but still optimal, way to the understanding of the item whose prerequisites defined the new goal.

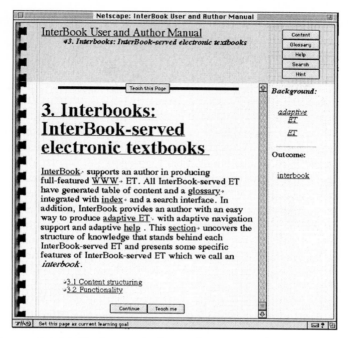

Fig. 3. A not suggested InterBook page. At the top the system indicates, that the page is not suggested for the student, who can set the new learning goal by selecting underlying button "'Teach this page".

Since some concepts in the prerequisites might be introduced only on "not suggested" pages, the goal might have to be extended recursively by prerequisites of supportive teaching operations. This algorithm is described in more detail in the next section. The essence of the presented technology enables the user to focus the intelligent support of a tutoring system onto any action, which might help the student to understand a chosen teaching operation associated with a certain learning goal.

3.2   Self-Organized Goal-Adapted Tutoring in InterBook

In figure 3 we can see the basic idea of self-organized goal-adapted tutoring in our system: When the student accesses a not suggested page, the system will bring up a visual cue that indicates, that this page is not ready to be learned. Additionally, the student will be provided with a button that enables him or her to set the current page as his or her new learning goal (see figure 3). Doing so, the system's behavior will change. Any kind of adaptation will now be performed according to this new goal. Annotation, sorting and sequencing algorithms will be adapted to this set of concept, that was defines the new learning goal. From now on the system will support the student in learning his or her individually set learning goal. When the current learning goal is sufficiently learned, the current goal will be popped and the next sequencing request will bring the user back to the page from which he has called for help. Instead of learning what a course instructor wants him or her to learn, the student can receive individualized support for his or her specifically defined learning goal.

4   Implementing Self-Defined Goals

4.1   Sequencing in InterBook

InterBook (cf. [6]) employs a complex modular sequencing mechanism, that can be adapted to support different teaching issues by tuning weights that influence the systems behavior. Like most sequencing mechanisms InterBook searches the pool of available teaching operations. Each of them is assigned by a certain score, which is depending from user's current goal and learning experience. The item with the highest sequencing score is chosen as the next teaching operation. InterBook combines well-known strategies for computing these sequencing scores, like focus-of-attention and picking next suggested item. Many similar scores reflecting the supportiveness, the educational state, the current focus-of-attention, the student's familiarity with a teaching operation and more educational aspects of the teaching operations are integrated into a single score by a weighted sum. The integration of these scores can be adapted by tuning the weights of the scoring sum. Usually an instructor is supposed to choose one major strategy, whilst the others rather perform fine-grained discrimination between different items. This enables the student to understand this major strategy, what make the system more predictive and lowers frustration for the students.

Items are further distinguished by certain punishments. For instance, teaching operations that are more close to the current item in the curriculum are favored by punishing more distant teaching operations. As well, teaching operations that occur later in the curriculum may be punished in general, like items from the glossary or items from different sections. All those punishing scores try to avoid certain misbehavior of the system, like jumping between book or sections. These punishments might be understood as determining a learning path with the least expensive misbehavior. Like scores for different strategies these punishment scores are computed in a weighted sum, whose parameters are adaptable as well. Finally, the fraction of strategy and punishment scores results in the final score on a teaching operation as given in equation 1:

$$score(TO) = \frac{\sum_{strategy} weight_{strategy} \cdot score_{strategy}(TO)}{1 + \sum_{punish} weight_{punish} \cdot score_{punish}(TO)} \qquad (1)$$

It is evident, that once the learning goal changes, being set by the student, all those scores will change for the teaching operations, since the score for the educational state will assume different value. InterBook can further distinguish between goals defined by the student and those ones, which were implicitly set by the system or the instructor. This enables the system to choose stronger support for self-defined goals.

4.2   Computing Minimal Closure

The major problem when establishing a new learning goal based on the prerequisites of an item, is the computation of all teaching operations and concepts that are required to teach these prerequisites. Since there might be no suggested teaching operations available for certain prerequisites, the mechanism has to be applied recursively. Based upon considerations in [8] a hyperspace of indexed teaching operations can be seen as graph, whose nodes are represented by the teaching operations and edges by the domain concepts. The abstraction becomes more complex, since some concept may be introduced and required by different teaching operations. Those concepts are considered as the virtual nodes in the graph. A first reasonable approach based on figure 4 could perform the computation of the minimal closure of teaching operations and concepts might by using efficient algorithms for computing minimal closures in general graphs. In principal, these algorithms apply, but they neglect two important facts. On the one hand, they do not take into account the dynamic changes of the students knowledge, while the student is taking particular teaching operations. Since these operations may influence the supportiveness, the educational state, the degree of familiarity and other scores, they can seriously affect the selection of the next most optimal teaching operation. On the other hand, those mechanisms do not sufficiently take into account the heuristic character of the available data on student's knowledge.

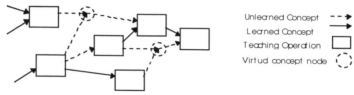

Fig. 4. Network of teaching operations and concepts. The given problem consists of finding the minimal set of teaching operations and concepts to provide the student with the knowledge required for this item.

For these reasons we tried to carry out a more heuristical approach, that can perform this calculation with linear worst case effort, when either all concepts or all teaching operations are required for teaching the requested page. The estimation of an upper bound assumes, that all teaching operations are indexed by a limited number of concepts and all concepts are outcome of a limited number of teaching operations. These assumptions are obviously reasonable.

Our heuristic algorithm (cf. fig. 5) starts out with the set of unlearned prerequisite concepts (preU) of the current teaching operation (TO). As the next step the next most relevant teaching operation will be selected by the sequencing mechanism amongst all supportive TOs; i.e. among all TOs teaching at least one concept from preU. To ensure that only those items are selected, that support the new goal most, we increase weights for the supportiveness and familiarity scores, whilst weights for scores representing the current educational state are lowered, since items to be selected might be not suggested yet. For the same reason the sequencing score is computed with preU as the current learning goal.

Having selected the most optimal item, the `closure` is extended by the list of unknown prerequisites of the selected item and the outcome concepts are removed from the current goal, which is used as the current goal in the sequencing mechanism. If this goal is empty, items for all missing prerequisites have been selected and the algorithm stops, returning the minimal closure. For the case, that the instructor has encoded the domain incompletely, i.e. no teaching operation introduces a prerequisite of another TO, we have implemented a security exit to the loop that checks, whether no new supportive items for the remaining goal could be found. In this case the remaining goal is removed from the closure before returning the result.

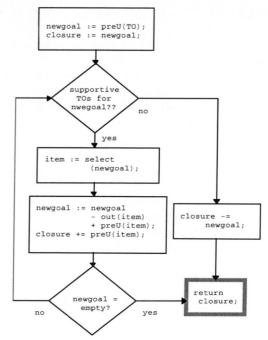

Fig. 5. Heuristic algorithm for the calculation of the minimal closure.

5   Conclusion

We have seen, how current adaptation methodologies are logically derived and implemented. We could present a new technology called *adaptive guarding*, which hopefully will extend the benefits of those technologies. This technique combines latest approaches in goal-oriented adaptive educational hypermedia yielding in higher flexibility of the system. We showed how this technique can be employed to take into account individual goals of particular students for adaptive intelligent student support at any point in time during their learning process. Goal-oriented adaptation of learning material was extended by mechanisms that provide students with an opportunity to influence system's behavior in order to provide an simplified opportunity to the user to navigate autonomously through a complex amount of learning material. This was achieved by making the current goal represented in an tutoring system adaptive to the requirements of individual students.

References

1. Anderson, J. R., Corbett, A. T., Koedinger, K. R., and Pelletier, R. (1995) 'Cognitive tutors: Lessons learned'. *The Journal of the Learning Sciences* **4** (2), 167-207.
2. Brusilovsky, P. (1996) 'Methods and techniques of adaptive hypermedia'. *User Modeling and User-Adapted Interaction* **6** (2-3), 87-129.
3. Brusilovsky, P., Ritter, S., and Schwarz, E. (1997) 'Distributed Intelligent Tutoring in the Web'. *Proceedings of AI-ED'97: 8th World Conference on Artificial Intelligence in Education*, Kobe, Japan, pp. 482-489.
4. Brusilovsky, P. and Schwarz, E. (1997) 'Concept-based navigation in educational hypermedia and its implementation on the WWW'. *Proceedings of ED-MEDIA*, Calgary.
5. Brusilovsky, P., Schwarz, E., and Weber, G. (1996) 'ELM-ART: An intelligent tutoring system on World Wide Web'. Berlin: Springer Verlag, 261-269.
6. Brusilovsky, P., Schwarz, E., and Weber, G. (1996) 'A tool for developing adaptive electronic textbooks on WWW'. *Proceedings of WebNet'96, World Conference of the Web Society*, San Francisco, CA, pp. 64-69.
7. Brusilovsky, P. L. (1992) 'A framework for intelligent knowledge sequencing and task sequencing'. Berlin: Springer-Verlag, 499-506.
8. Capell, P. and Dannenberg, R. B. (1993) 'Instructional design and intelligent tutoring: Theory and the precision of design'. *Journal of Artificial Intelligence in Education* **4** (1), 95-121.
9. de La Passardiere, B. and Dufresne, A. (1992) 'Adaptive navigational tools for educational hypermedia'. Berlin: Springer-Verlag, 555-567.
10. Eklund, J. and Sawers, J. (1996) 'Customising Web-based course delivery in WEST® with navigation support'. *Proceedings of WebNet'96, World Conference of the Web Society*, San Francisco, CA, pp. 534-535.
11. Lai, M.-C., Chen, B.-H., and Yuan, S.-M. (1995) 'Toward a new educational environment'. *Proceedings of 4th International World Wide Web Conference.*
12. Lai, M.-C., Lien, H.-M., and Yuan, S.-M. (1995) 'Navigation control in educational hypermedia'. *Proceedings of ED-MEDIA'95 - World conference on educational multimedia and hypermedia*, Charlottesville, pp. 773.
13. Lin, F., Danielson, R., and Herrgott, S. (1996) 'Adaptive interaction through WWW'. *Proceedings of ED-MEDIA'96 - World conference on educational multimedia and hypermedia*, Charlottesville.
14. McArthur, D., Stasz, C., Hotta, J., Peter, O., and Burdorf, C. (1988) 'Skill-oriented task sequencing in an intelligent tutor for basic algebra'. *Instructional Science* **17** (4), 281-307.
15. Schwarz, E., Brusilovsky, P., and Weber, G. (1996) 'World-wide intelligent textbooks'. *Proceedings of ED-TELECOM'96 - World Conference on Educational Telecommunications*, Boston, MA, pp. 302-307.
16. Vassileva, J. (1997) 'Dynamic Course Generation on the WWW'. *Proceedings of AI-ED'97: 8th World Conference on Artificial Intelligence*, Kobe, Japan, pp. 498-505.
17. Weber, G. (1992) 'ELM-PE: A knowledge-based programming environment'. *Proceedings of the Fifth Workshop of the ``Psychology of programming interest group" (PPIG5)*, Paris, pp. 159-168.
18. Weber, G. and Specht, M. (1997) 'User Modelling and Adaptive Navigatio Support in WWW-based Tutoring Systems'. *Proceedings of UM97: The Sixth International Conference on User Modeling*, Chia Laguna, Sardinia, Italy.

Ecolab: Exploring the Construction of a Learning Assistant

Rosemary Luckin

School of Cognitive and Computing Sciences
University of Sussex
Falmer
Brighton
BN1 9QH
phone: +44 (0)1273 678647 (direct) or 678195
fax: +44 (0)1273 671320
email: rosel@cogs.susx.ac.uk

Abstract. The Ecolab is an interactive learning environment constructed with the aim of providing a tool to investigate how software can offer help and support to an individual learner. The design framework is informed by Vygotsky's Zone of Proximal Development (ZPD) and previous work on face to face tutorial assistance. Three Ecolab versions implement different variations and combinations of design features with the purpose of providing a means of evaluating what constitutes effective assistance. The evaluation of the system illustrates that the differing qualities and quantities of collaborative assistance offered by the three system variations influenced both the child user's learning gain and the nature of her interactions with the system. It also highlights the impact which each user's ability and learning style has upon their experiences with an interactive learning environment.

1 Introduction

The Ecolab software described in this paper consists of a trilogy of system variations designed around the common theme of providing collaborative assistance in an interactive learning environment with which children aged 10 and 11 years can investigate food chains and webs. The theory of instruction which underpins the design framework is inspired by the Zone of Proximal Development (ZPD) concept [7] [8]. This theory has been interpreted and formulated into a software design framework (for a full description of this framework and its implementation within the Ecolab see [4]). Each system variation implements different aspects of this underpinning framework to provide collaborative support and to adopt the role of a more able learning partner. The purpose of the three variations is to allow evaluation of the design framework. The ZPD provides a theoretical fabric within which an investigation into the nature of collaborative support and assistance can be constructed. The problems addressed by this paper are the specification of what it means for one party to assist another in the process of learning and the implementation of this specification within educational software design. The aim is to demonstrate the possibilities offered by software design which integrates a collaborative or partnership role for the computer with an effective instructional theory.

2 The Nature of Collaborative Assistance

One way to investigate how the computer can play the role of a learning partner is to consider how face to face assistance is offered to learners. Wood [9] coined the term "scaffolding" to describe tutorial assistance. Effective scaffolding is presented as something more than the provision of hints and graded help. It represents one way of pinning down the nature of the assistance that teachers can provide for children as they learn, it is not however a straightforward process. Before scaffolds can be constructed, or even planned, a careful analysis of the domain, indicating potential links to the child's existing, intuitive knowledge is essential [1]. In order to explicate a framework within which a more able partner assists a less able one, attention needs to be paid to more than help interventions [5].

The notion of *scaffolding* has been used in the development of educational software in various ways [10] and [2] for example).   Model-It [2] and McBagal [3] are examples of computer based scaffolding which side-step some of the problems associated with the limited ability of computers to create social interactions, by concentrating upon the authenticity and grounding of the problem domain, the structuring of its presentation or the use of the computer to support human collaboration.   In contrast, the EXPLAIN [10] developed as an implementation of the contingent strategy, concentrates on the provision of different qualities of help intervention. Ecolab combines a structured environment of variable complexity and multiple viewpoints with the provision of specific instances of help.

3 The Zone of Collaboration

The specification of assistance is complex; the scaffolding process introduced by Wood et al [9] has its roots within Vygotskian theory and provides an illustration of a successful interpretation. The Ecolab design framework reconsiders this theoretical foundation and investigates what more can be gained from the Zone of Proximal Development concept. Two additional constructs: the Zone of Available Assistance (ZAA) and the Zone of Proximal Adjustment (ZPA) are used in an attempt to clarify the interpretation of the ZPD which is being used within the Ecolab.   The ZAA describes the variety of qualities and quantities of assistance which need to be available to enable the more able partner (whether human or computer) to offer appropriate assistance to the target user group. The assistance which is selected and actually offered to the child needs to be matched to that particular child's ZPD. This is where the Zone of Proximal Adjustment [6] comes into play. The ZPA represents a selection from the ZAA appropriate for the given educational situation. Clearly, if the

ZAA is impoverished then this will limit the possibilities for the ZPA. Moreover, even if the ZAA is versatile, an inappropriate selection of ZPA can be made. So the aim for the software designer becomes that of maximising the ZAA and providing a means of targeting the ZPA so that it as close as possible to the child's ZPD. The framework developed here and used in the implementation of the Ecolab, is concerned with the implementation of a system which can interact with respect to the ZPD of a single user. It is not suggested that this is the only way of viewing the ZPD concept's application to software design, merely that it is *one* way to use the concept.

4 The Ecolab Software

The Ecolab software consists of 3 variations: VIS (the Vygotskian Instructional System), WIS (the Woodsian Inspired System) and NIS (No Instructional-intervention System). Each variation implements different variations and combinations of the features in the design framework with the purpose of providing a means of evaluating what constitutes effective assistance. The learning environment provided by the Ecolab can be presented to the user in various formats and complexities. This versatility is part of the ZAA of the system and provides a means of adjusting the system to the individual user.

4.1 Interacting with the Ecolab

The metaphor underlying the presentation of the Ecolab to the child is that of an Ecology Laboratory. The Ecolab is an environment into which the child can place different organisms and then explore the relationships which exist between them. The overall motivation which is presented to her is that she should explore which sort of organisms can live together and form a food web. In addition to providing the child with the facilities to build, activate and observe a simulated ecological community, the Ecolab also provides the child with small activities of different types. The activities are designed to structure the child's interactions with the system. They provide a goal towards which the child's actions can be directed and vary in the complexity of the relationships which the child is required to investigate. There are, for example, investigative activities which challenge the child to examine the relationships which exist between the organisms she has selected. She might be asked to see how many links she can add to a food web diagram for example.

The Ecolab operates in two modes: *build* and *run* and is controlled by the child's mouse driven commands. *Build* mode allows the child to construct her mini world of plants and animals by adding those of her choice. When switched to *run* mode she can activate these organisms. If the action specified is possible it will occur and the changes can be observed. If the action is not possible the child will be guided (in accordance with the system variation in use) towards a possible alteration so that the effects of the selected action can be observed.

4.2 The Zone of Available Assistance (ZAA)

The ZAA has already been described as the variety of qualities and quantities of assistance which need to be available to enable the more able partner (whether human or computer) to offer appropriate assistance to the target user group. Within the Ecolab the features which comprise the system's ZAA fall into six categories:

- Variations to the phase of complexity of the Ecolab environment.
- Variations to the terminology used to describe the Ecolab environment.
- Alternative Views of the Ecolab environment.
- *Help* of varying levels of control and specificity
- Variations to the difficulty of the activities: *Activity differentiation*
- Variations in the content of the activities

Variations to the phase of complexity of the Ecolab environment.
When a learner interacts with the Ecolab she does not need to deal with the full complexity of possible food web inter-relationships at once. The learning environment provided by the Ecolab can operate in 4 phases of complexity. This means that not all the possible methods of activating the Ecolab are available all the time. In phase one, which is the simplest, the relationships which can be formed by the Ecolab objects are only those between a food and a feeder: the *eat* or *eaten by* relationship. The second phase of complexity allows the formation of food chains and interactions between more than two organisms. The third and fourth phases allow the formation of food webs and interactions between all the different members of the web. The system can switch between these four phases from the less to the more complex, or in reverse from the more to the less complex. The activities available to direct the child's actions are consistent with the phase of complexity at which the Ecolab is currently operating.

Variations to the terminology used to describe the Ecolab environment.
Like the complexity of the relationships, the terminology used to identify the organisms can be varied. It can increase or decrease in its generality. For example, whilst initially the child may be working out what happens to the energy level of a *thrush* when it eats a *snail*, as she moves through the activities this may become an *omnivore* eating a *herbivore* or a *secondary consumer* eating a *primary consumer*. Within the levels of generality available, the terminology in use can be varied to be less or more abstract.

Alternative Views
The Ecolab environment built by the child can be viewed in different ways, each of which emphasises a particular aspect of the relationships which currently exist within the Ecolab. *World* view shows a picture of the organisms which are currently members of the Ecolab environment.   *Web* view provides a diagrammatic representation of the organisms and the links which exist between them in a manner similar to the food web diagrams used in text books. *Energy* view illustrates each of

the live organisms in terms of their current level of energy. *History* view is a textual description of what has happened in the Ecolab world to date. *Log* view shows the Ecolab logs which summarise all that has happened and the current state of the world.

Within each of these views most of the screen objects will provide the child with information when clicked on with the mouse. For example, clicking on an organism in world view will yield the organism's name, what it eats and what eats it. Figure 1 illustrates *Energy* Ecolab views.

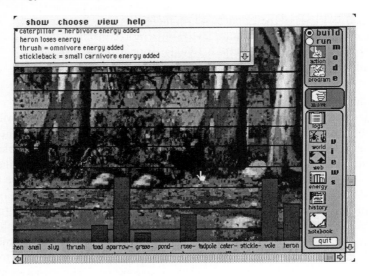

Fig. 1. Ecolab Energy View

Help of varying levels of control and specificity

The Ecolab can offer graded help specific to the particular situation. There is a 5 level set of help templates which vary with regard to the quality of the help which they provide. The higher the level of help the greater the control taken by the system. At level 5 the system completes the activity for the child. There is no notion of failure in the Ecolab, only variations in the levels of support offered to ensure success. If the level of help offered to the child is insufficient, then the level can be increased until the system completes the particular activity for the child.

Variations to the difficulty of the activities: *Activity differentiation*

In addition to offering the child specific help to ensure the activity is completed, the difficulty level of the activity itself can be adjusted. This is referred to as *Activity differentiation* and comes in three levels: 0 to 2. Level 0 involves the child in the most difficult activities, Level 2 the simplest. At this latter level the possibility of confusion is reduced through partial completion of the activity, for example.

Variations in the content of the activities

The activities which the child completes as she interacts with the Ecolab vary in the complexity of the relationships they encompass in line with the phases of the learning environment.

4.3 The Zone of Proximal Adjustment (ZPA)

Each of the three variations of the Ecolab aims to act as a different type of instructional partner for the child. This difference results from the way each variation uses the assistance which is available in the Ecolab in the construction of its ZPA and the manner in which the child's capability is represented in the system's learner model. These variations are summarised in Table 1 The learner model of VIS is the most sophisticated of the three, it is a Bayesian Belief Network (BBN) of values representing the system's beliefs about child's ZPD. These values are calculated from the amount of collaborative support she has used to date. WIS maintains a record of the help which the child has used to permit the contingent calculation of the next help level. A record of the curriculum areas presented is also maintained to allow the system to make suggestions about what the user might try next. NIS simply maintains a record of curriculum areas presented to help child keep track.

	VIS	WIS	NIS
Levels of Help Available	5	5	2
Decision about Level of Help made by	system	system and child	child
Levels of Activity Differentiation Available	3	3	3
Decision about type of Activity and Differentiation level made by	system	child - system makes suggestions	child
Extent of Learner Model	BBN	Record of help used and curriculum areas presented.	Record of Curriculum areas presented.
Abstractness of Terminology selected by	system	child	child
Curriculum Area and phase of Ecolab World Differentiation selected by	system	child - system makes suggestions	child

Table 1. Collboration in the Ecolab

5 Evaluating the Ecolab

In order to test the hypothesis that the nature of the collaborative learning support offered by the system variation used would influence both the resultant learning gain and the nature of the system: child interactions an evaluation study of the Ecolab software was conducted. A group of 30 children were divided into three matched groups each of which used a different Ecolab system variation. Prior to using the software each child completed a written and a verbal pre-test. Each child used the Ecolab software as an individual for a total of 60 minutes over two sessions, these interactions were logged. After the system intervention subjects were given a written and verbal post-test, identical to the pre-test. The results of the pre and post-test were used to assess the efficacy of the three variations of the Ecolab software. The records of the interactions between each child and the system were examined to investigate what sorts of interactions had resulted in the greater learning gains and which system variations had supported and encouraged various types of interaction and collaboration. To be an effective learning partner the system needs to be able to adjust to learners of differing abilities. The children's school assessments were therefore used to allocate each child to one of three ability grouping: High, Average and Low.

5.1 Results - Learning Gain

Improvement in performance between pre and post test was investigated using an [2 by 3 by 3] ANOVA on the pre-test and post-test data. The design being 2 (T1:pre-test -T2:post-test) by 3 (VIS, WIS, NIS) by 3 (High Ability, Average Ability, Low Ability). The overall effect of the interaction between Time and the System variation was significant ($F(2,17) = 3.79$ p <.05). This indicates that the system variation which the child used was relevant to her subsequent learning gain. A post hoc analysis indicated that the significant difference (p < .05) was between VIS and both WIS and NIS. The interaction between Time, System variation and Ability group was also significant ($F(2,17) = 5.63$ p <.01). The means (and standard deviations) which relate to these interactions are contained in Table 2.

Table 2. Summary of Mean Learning Gains

Mean improvement between pre and post-test. Score % (S.D.)	VIS	WIS	NIS
Totals across ability groups.	16.67	10.92	7.29
	(6.72)	(10.54)	(6.42)
High Ability group	20	23.33	1.66
	(6.38)	(6.00)	(2.35)
Average Ability group	13.88	3.75	5.42
	(6.73)	(6.14)	(2.84)
Low Ability group	14.16	6.66	16.66
	(8.24)	(0)	(2.35)

The significant interaction between the system variation used and the learning gains made by the children supports the selection of constituents which make up the ZAA and ZPA of VIS. It also supports the efficacy of the allocation of control for the composition of the ZPA in VIS to the system. However, whilst VIS resulted in the most consistent learning gains across all abilities it was not the optimal system with children of all abilities. The mean improvements amongst WIS users who were in the high ability group was greater than those for VIS and NIS. Likewise the mean learning gains for low ability NIS users were higher than those for WIS and VIS. Consistency of performance is a useful attribute for any piece of software, but pinpointing the elements of WIS and NIS which led to their superior performance with particular ability groups is informative for future adaptation of the design framework. This is where the analysis of the records of interaction proved useful.

No. of users	System Var.	Ability group	Interaction Profile	Collaboration Profile	Average Improvement from pre- to post-test %	Average no. of actions done
3	VIS	high	BE	LD	15.9	131
2	WIS	high	BE	NLD	27.2	109
2	NIS	high	BC	NLND	1.7	145
1	WIS	high	BE	LD	17	95
1	NIS	high	QC	NLND	9	78
2	VIS	ave	BE	LD	19.9	103
1	WIS	ave	BC	LD	3.8	164
2	VIS	ave	QE	LD	12.4	52
1	NIS	ave	BC	NLND	.1	119
3	WIS	ave	BE	LD	4.1	105
1	NIS	ave	QC	LND	8.1	61
1	NIS	ave	QC	NLD	7.3	54
2	VIS	low	QE	LD	13.1	68
1	WIS	low	QE	NLD	7.1	77
1	NIS	low	QC	NLND	19.2	41
1	WIS	low	QC	NLD	5.4	66
1	NIS	low	BC	LND	14.9	90
mean					11.5	85

Table 3. Individual user summary. 26 children completed all stages of the evaluation.

Key to Table 2: BE = Busy - Exploring; BC = Busy - Consolidating; QC = Quiet - Consolidating; QE = Quiet - Exploring; LD = Lots and Deep; LND = Lots and Shallow; NLD = Little and Deep; NLND = Little and Shallow

5.2 Results - Profiles

Interaction Profiles

There were two characteristics which could clearly be seen as either present, or largely absent within the children's interactions. These were used to allocate children to Interaction Profiles and were: *Busyness,* which was considered to be a characteristic of interactions in which the children completed an average or above average number of actions of any type, and *Exploration* which was considered to be a characteristic of an interaction if the child had been involved in some sort of action which allowed her to experience more than one phase of learning environment complexity or abstraction. Table 3 summarises information about each child including their membership of Interaction and Collaboration Profile groups.

Collaboration Profiles

Two characteristics were found to be the most useful for differentiating collaborative style within the interactions: *Amount of support*: An above average amount of either activity differentiation or instances of help was the criteria necessary for a child to be considered as using 'Lots' of collaborative support. *Depth of support*: Help or differentiation above the average level for the class resulted in a child being considered as using 'Deep' or higher level support.

A Pearson Chi-squared statistical test indicated that there was a significant association between System variation membership and Collaboration Profile membership ($X^2 = 28.52$, df = 6, p < .0001), and between System variation membership and Interaction Profile membership ($X^2 = 25.79$, df = 10, p < .01).

6 Discussion

These results suggest that simply providing children with the means for extension through challenging activities is not enough to ensure that these challenging activities are undertaken. The consistency within the high and average ability groups for above average learning gain achievement to be linked to the "Exploring" profile characteristic is not reflected in the low ability group. Children appeared to need to be explicitly directed towards activities which were beyond their ability. The success of WIS indicates however that a suggestion about what and how to proceed is often sufficient.

The manner in which each variation of the system collaborates with the child is a design feature of that variation. This is reflected in the significant association between system variation and Collaborative Profile membership. However, it is possible, in principle, for a user of any of the variations to interact in line with any of the Collaboration Profiles described. In reality only VIS and WIS children used a large amount *and* a high level of help. The only system which allocated both help and differentiation to users was VIS, so the fact that VIS children all used a high quantity and quality of help is unsurprising. It would however have been possible, for example, for a WIS user to engage in the same nature of collaborative interaction as a VIS user. The truth is however, that they did not do this in all cases. WIS users often used a high level of assistance, but in smaller quantities. An even more noticeable difference can be seen between the WIS and NIS users. In terms of collaborative support all WIS users belong to profiles where the support used was of a high level. In contrast all NIS users are in profile groups in which the level of support is low. What is perhaps surprising is that these two groups of users, who could all choose the amount and level of support they wanted, did not opt for the same quantity and quality of support. The choice of help available to NIS users was admittedly more limited, being of only two levels, however none of the NIS users ever chose to use the higher level of help offered. As with extension, children's effective use of assistance appears to benefit from the provision of some guidance.

The Ecolab offers one way of exploring the use of the ZPD as the basis for a software Design Framework. The concepts of a Zone of Available Assistance (ZAA) and a Zone of Proximal Adjustment (ZPA) clarify the interpretation of the ZPD used within the Ecolab and explain the role of the more able learning partner. The evaluation has demonstrated that the design framework is effective and that different styles of interaction and collaboration can be supported within an interactive learning environment.

References

1. Bliss, J., Askew, M. & Macrae, S. (1996). Effective teaching and learning: scaffolding revisited. Oxford Review of Education, 22(1), 37-61.
2. Guzdial, M., Kolodner., J., Hmelo, C., Narayanan, H., Carlson, D., Rappin, N., Hubscher, R., Turns, J., and Newstetter, W. (1996). Computer support for learning through complex problem solving. Communications of the ACM, 39(4), 43-45.
3. Jackson, S. L.,. Stratford, S. J., Krajcik, J. and Solloway, E. (1994). Making dynamic modeling accessible to precollege students. Interactive Learning Environments, 4(3), 233-257.
4. Luckin, R. (1997) 'Ecolab': Explorations in the zone of proximal adjustment. CSRP No. 496. School of Cognitive and Computing Sciences, University of Sussex, Brighton.
5. Mercer, N. (1995). The guided construction of knowledge: talk amongst teachers and learners Clevedon: Multilingual Matters Ltd.
6. Murphey, T. (1996). Proactive adjustment to the zone of proximal development (conference presentation). In the abstracts of the IInd Conference for Socio-Cultural Research 1896-1996. Geneva, September 11-15 1996.
7. Vygotsky, L. S. (1978). Mind in society: the development of higher psychological processes (M. Cole, V. John-Steiner, S. Scribner, E. Souberman, Trans.). Cambridge, MA: Harvard University Press.
8. Vygotsky, L. S. (1986). Thought and language. Cambridge, MA:MIT Press.
9. Wood, D. J., Bruner, J. S. & Ross, G. (1976). The role of tutoring in problem solving. Journal of Child Psychology and Psychiatry, 17(2), 89-100.
10. Wood, D., Shadbolt, N., Reichgelt, H., Wood, H. & Paskiewitz, T. (1992). EXPLAIN: Experiments in planning and instruction. Society for the Study of Artificial Intelligence and Simulation of Behaviour Quarterly Newsletter, 81, 13-16.

Information Types and Cognitive Principles in Program Comprehension: Towards Adaptable Support for Novice Visual Programmers

Judith Good[1] and Paul Brna[2]

[1] University of Edinburgh, Human Communication Research Centre,
Edinburgh EH8 9LW, Scotland UK,
judithg@cogsci.ed.ac.uk,
WWW home page: http://www.hcrc.ed.ac.uk/~judithg
[2] University of Leeds, Computer Based Learning Unit,
Leeds LS2 9JT, England UK
paul@cbl.leeds.ac.uk

Abstract. The authors describe work on the GRiP (Graphical Representations in Programming) Project[1], which aims to build a support environment for novices learning to program using a visual programming language (VPL). The design of the environment is based on a series of experiments which investigate issues of visual programming language paradigm, and the ways in which novices extract information from a representation in order to make sense of a program. This paper focuses particularly on the multivariate nature of program comprehension, the difficulties associated with attempting to teach skills of this kind, and suggests a solution in the form of a modular support system.

1 Program Comprehension: Current Theories

Program comprehension is considered to be an important part of the process of programming [1]. It comes into play whether one is reviewing one's own work in order to extend it, attempting to comprehend a program written by someone else, or trying to understand a program for a particular task (debugging, maintenance, communicating some aspect of the program to another person, etc.). It therefore makes sense to consider the notion that novice programmers should be taught how to comprehend a program [2].

However, teaching program comprehension may be problematic for various reasons. Firstly, there is no unique model of the program comprehension process. For example, a number of theories conceive of program comprehension in terms of top-down processing [3], while others argue for a bottom-up process occurring in two stages [1]. Von Mayrhauser and Vans provide an "integrated meta-model" which seeks to include both top-down and bottom-up elements [4]. They argue that trying to understand large programs requires the use of a

---

[1] Funded by EPSRC grants GR/L36987 and GR/L37045 and carried out in collaboration with Jon Oberlander and Richard Cox.

variety of approaches, a view shared by Tilley and Smith, who state that "the combination approach opportunistically exploits top-down and bottom-up cues as they become available" [5, p.3].

Secondly, program comprehension can't be seen as a unique, invariant activity comprising the same cognitive processes in all situations. Although in some cases, the comprehension of an entire program may be required, in others, "partial" comprehension occurs at different levels of granularity, for different purposes and involving greater or lesser sections of the program. In the latter case, comprehension is grounded in a context and usually associated with a task (e.g. von Mayrhauser's adaptive, perfective, corrective, reuse and code leverage maintenance tasks [4]). In other words, comprehension covers a range of activities which require different types of information and are task dependent.

Given that there is increasing agreement about the opportunistic nature of comprehension, there is also decreasing certainty about the ability to delineate expert strategies in some simple manner. Tilley, in his forecast of future developments in the area of program understanding, argues that "by investigating comprehension strategies that better reflect the actual understanding approaches used by expert software engineers, identifying when specific comprehension approaches are best used will become clearer" [5, p.3].

There currently is not much prospect of a single model of comprehension, and it seems unreasonable to assume that there could ever be one given the range of activities it would need to cover. However, there is strong agreement that program comprehension involves various types of information which must be extracted from the program text in order for comprehension to take place.

2   (How) Can Program Comprehension be Taught?

Trying to teach a unique way of comprehending programs is not currently a very promising prospect. In attempting to alleviate novice difficulties with program comprehension, various methods have been suggested, which break down crudely into a) changing the notation, in other words, modifying the language or even designing a new one, b) providing support tools for use as and when they are required, and c) augmenting the existing system by teaching.

We argue that each solution is not without its own problems, particularly in the first case. Any change in the notation highlights some information at the expense of other information, therefore, one would expect that there will be gains in comprehension for some aspects of the program, but consequent losses for other types of information[2].

In the last case, that of teaching, it has already been argued that there is no one normative model of learning to comprehend a program. Instead, there is

---

[2] Proponents of VPLs have often uncritically accepted the idea that the change in notation as a result of moving from a textual to a visual language would alleviate a range of novice difficulties (see [18] for examples). However, despite the claims made for VPLs, very little is known about the relative benefits of their use: studies investigating these issues have shown mixed results.

an ill structured set of activities relating to information finding and information integration. Therefore, we propose to follow the middle road of a support environment for novice visual programmers: tools will be provided that highlight information types (e.g. control flow, data flow) and provide ways of representing progress in comprehension activities. We feel that the graphical nature of VPLs make them particularly suited to allowing information to be selectively highlighted in a way which would be difficult in a conventional, textual notation. These tools will provide a useful scaffold for the comprehension activities inherent in programming and be designed in such a way that they can be individually removed in order to achieve a 'fading' effect.

The rest of the paper is organised as follows: we first describe the theoretical and empirical bases for the support system. This includes a discussion of the types of information that are relevant to program comprehension (embodied in Pennington's information types [1]), and a brief description of the experiments conducted. This work is reported more fully in [15, 16]: here we provide an overview of the experiments as they relate to the analysis of program comprehension errors. We then describe an analysis of the results in terms of their implications for the design of the learning system. This is followed by a description of a set of adaptive support tools allowing novice visual programmers to develop their own strategies for program comprehension, with examples of each feature. Finally, we conclude with a general discussion of possible extensions to the system based on further empirical work and consider prospects for an ITS.

3   A Flexible Support Tool for Novice Comprehension

The learning environment being developed is based on both theoretical and empirical work: Pennington's classification of information types [1] provides the basis for structuring the support, while experiments focusing on programming language paradigm and the way in which novices extract information from a representation in order to make sense of a program allowed us to uncover: 1) student errors and misunderstandings, 2) undesirable features of the languages in their unsupported state, and 3) difficulties in representation navigation.

3.1   Information Types

Information types have been defined as distinct categories of information which are present in a program, and which must be detected in order to arrive at an understanding of the program [1].

Pennington identified five types of information, as follows:

Function: information about the overall goal of the program, essentially, "What is the purpose of the program? What does the program do?"

Control-flow: information about sequences of events occurring in the program, e.g. "What happens after X occurs? What has occurred just before X?"

Data: essentially concerned with the transformations which data objects undergo during execution, including data dependencies and data structure information, e.g. "Does variable X contribute to the final value of Y?"

Operations: information about specific actions which take place in the code, such as "Does a variable become instantiated with a particular value?"

State: time-slice descriptions of the state of objects and events in the program, e.g. "When the program is in state X, is event Y taking place?"

Pennington sought to map these information types onto van Dijk and Kintsch's theory of text comprehension [8] in order to describe comprehension as a two-stage progression from a procedural low-level account of the program to a more abstract, functionally based account. However, it is not necessary to subscribe to this particular model of program comprehension in order to make use of the concept of information types. Instead, information types can be viewed as entities which are extracted from the program and composed according to the task at hand. The process by which this occurs (e.g. the order or the types of information involved) will tend to be prescribed by the particular theory adopted.

3.2   Experimental Work on Program Comprehension

Design of the learning environment began with experiments using two unsupported, micro visual programming languages: one based on a data flow paradigm (as defined in [11]) and the other on a control flow paradigm (involving minor variations on standard flowchart techniques). Using a methodology similar to [1, 2], participants were required to study short recursive programs (equivalent to 10-15 line programs in a conventional textual language), represented in either the control flow or the data flow language. An example of a program in the data flow language is shown in figure 1[3]. Participants then answered multiple-choice questions about the program. Each question was designed to elicit various "information types" (as described in section 3.1), in other words, it required participants to scan the representation in order to identify and reason with a particular type of information present in the program.

In keeping with the methodology used in [1, 2], subjects were asked to write a summary of the program they had just seen. The request was open-ended, which led to great variety in the form and content of the summaries produced. These summaries were analysed, among other ways, in terms of reporting errors subjects made about the function of the program and the way in which it worked [16].

In the experiment described in [15], retrospective verbal protocols were taken by showing participants a screen recording of their mouse movements during the experiment and asking them to explain their actions to the experimenter [4]. The protocols obtained provided insight into navigational errors and misunderstandings.

---

[3] Although only the data flow language is shown here, the support features proposed could be adapted equally well to both languages.

[4] This article also addresses the methodological issues surrounding the use of retrospective verbal protocols.

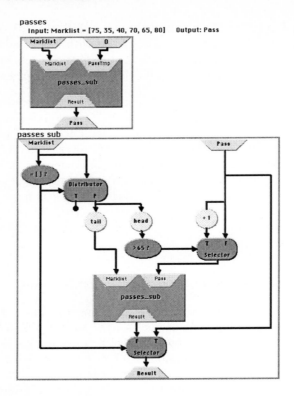

Fig. 1. A Simple Recursive Program in the Data Flow Visual Programming Language

In analysing the results, it should be noted that the two types of error elicitation each favour a particular category of error over the other: the retrospective verbal protocol analysis highlights the navigational errors related to finding one's way around the diagram, while the program summary analysis highlights informational errors related to the program's function and behaviour.

3.3 Results of the Analyses

The results of the analyses described above suggested a series of changes which can be roughly divided into permanent and non-permanent changes (with the latter being further divided into changes which are either generic or task dependent).

Permanent changes imply "pathological" features of the representation for which it is difficult to see a benefit in any comprehension situation. This categorisation is based on Green's cognitive dimensions [12], which comprise a small vocabulary of terms, and capture those features of a notation which are cognitively relevant. In so doing, they provide a broad-brush analysis of both textual and graphical programming notations and environments [6]. These changes are not covered here as they relate to changes to the notation itself rather than support features built around the notation.

Non-permanent, non-task variant changes to the representation involve adding support which can be used as needed, and which does not vary on a task by task basis. These changes tend to revolve around the properties of external representations, navigation issues and management of memory resources.

Non-permanent, task-dependent changes to the representation are based upon the match-mismatch conjecture and the concept of information types. According to the match-mismatch conjecture, "the structure of a notation affects the ease with which information can be extracted both from the printed page and from recall" [7, p.47]. Therefore, if a language (or notation) highlights a given type of information, then a task requiring that information should be easier to perform than one requiring another type. Likewise, the same task performed using a representation in which the required information is present, but needs to be inferred, will also be more difficult. The implication for program understanding is that various types of information contained in the program will be relevant in particular contexts, and so could usefully be made salient in those situations.

Support features in the proposed learning environment fall into either the second or third category: changes which can be made to the representation on an as-needed basis: either at any stage of the program comprehension process or in relation to a specific task. These features are described below.

3.4   System Design

The support features of the proposed system are divided into generic features and task based features. The generic features correspond to non-permanent, non-task specific changes to the representation. They are designed to provide support for navigation through the representation and to allow the student to off-load onto the representation some of the information which must normally be kept in memory while trying to comprehend the workings of the program.

In contrast, task based features are designed to highlight a particular information type. The aim, by making the information more salient, is to help alleviate the errors and misunderstandings which students encounter as they attempt to extract information from the representation.

All of the available features are presented in the form of a panel of buttons: clicking on a button toggles its feature either on or off. When the feature is on, clicking on the relevant part of the representation will apply the particular feature, as described below.

Generic Navigation Support Features The following tools provide general support for navigation in the following forms:
Jump Support
- *Error:* actions occurring at the node immediately preceding or following a "jump" in the diagram are ignored ("jumps" are defined as moves to a different part of the diagram which cannot be followed via an arc, e.g. the

calling of a subprocedure). This is a very frequent error: students often do not take into account anything which occurred prior to the jump and/or don't return to the point of the jump in order to continue execution.
— *Support Feature:* allows a process to be marked as unfinished before jumping.

Path Tracing
— *Error:* difficulty in keeping track of the paths which have already been examined, i.e. essentially a memory management error.
— *Support Feature:* with this feature on, tracing the path with the mouse button down would cause it to change colour up to the point at which the user releases the mouse button. This is particularly important in the case of a data flow diagram, where each data object is represented by its own arc: it is often useful to trace one object to a particular point, and then break off to trace another data object up to the same point in order to capture some of the sequential nature of the program.

Annotations
— *Error:* difficulty in remembering what has been gleaned from the program, e.g. intermediate results of execution, comments about the function of a part of the program, particularities of data input, etc.
— *Support Feature:* allows students to annotate parts of the diagram with comments of any sort.

Task Based Support Features Some of the errors which occurred in the experiments concerned misunderstandings which can be linked a particular information type: task based features are based on information types. Particular difficulties observed and proposed support are described below (with corresponding information type shown in parentheses). Note that as the motivation for these features is empirically based, features described relate only to the actual errors which students encountered (e.g. state errors are not represented). However, other features could easily be added.

Understanding Function (FUNCTION)
— *Error:* attributing an incorrect function to an action or to the entire program (e.g. "it adds the numbers to the output list" when the program produces a single number).
— *Support Feature:* places a black box over the program, showing only inputs to the program and the corresponding outputs.
   Note that highlighting function proves to be problematic. As function is a high level abstraction of what the program does, it is built from the component parts of the representation: one cannot point to a part of the program which denotes its function. A true functional description would provide abstractions of the input and corresponding output rather than actual input and output. However, from a pedagogical point of view, this is akin to "giving the game away": no further inferences need be made. We felt it was preferable in this instance to provide concrete input and output

so as to require the student to infer the abstract relationship which holds between them. Note also that the "intelligence" of this feature can vary depending on whether the input/output pairs are canned, or students are allowed to provide their own input.

Control Structure (CONTROL FLOW)

- *Error:* difficulty in understanding recursion, particularly the termination of a recursive call (this error is specific to our ongoing study of recursion, but would apply equally to misunderstandings about other types of control structure: loops, case structure, etc).
- *Support Feature:* recursion would be "unfolded" into its various calls in order to make the recursive process more explicit [18]. The cyclic graph, in which recursion is represented as a node having the same name as the entire graph, would be "unravelled" in such a way that each call became a separate, but interconnected, graph. This could also be done with other control structures *e.g.* loops of various kinds.

Evaluation (CONTROL FLOW)

- *Error:* students are at a point in the diagram and skip to another, incorrect, point, based on an incorrect evaluation of a choice point.
- *Support Feature:* allows students to selectively display one output branch of a test box at a time, based on the hypothesised outcome.

Data Object (DATA FLOW)

- *Error:* a misunderstanding about the identity of the data being acted upon.
- *Support Feature:* for a given action node, students can click on one (or all) of the inputs to the node. This will highlight the data path back to the point at which the data object was introduced and explicitly named.

Data Dependency (DATA FLOW)

- *Error:* a misunderstanding about the interrelatedness of data objects (e.g. how a change in one object will affect another).
- *Support Feature:* students can click on two data flows, which will show the dependency relationship which exists between them, if any.

Data Flow (DATA FLOW)

- *Error:* a misunderstanding about the origin of a data object, or how it arrived at a particular node in the diagram, or where it will go after a reaching particular point in the program.
- *Support Feature:* students will be able to click on a data object, which will highlight to show its path through the program.

Understanding Operations (OPERATIONS)

- *Error:* an erroneous description of an operation, or a description of a non-existent one ("operations" are contained in nodes through which data flows).
- *Support Feature:* provides a list of the nodes present in the program. Clicking on the name of a node in the list would cause that node to be highlighted.

4   Conclusions and Prospects for an ITS

Program comprehension is an activity which, while important, is difficult to pin down: various strategies are appropriate depending on the situation and will vary across individuals, and according to expertise. From this perspective, program comprehension cannot be taught directly. However, we hope that by focusing on an awareness of the types of information which are important for comprehension, rather than on rigid strategies for comprehension, students will go on to build up flexible, personalised strategies which they find useful.

We are designing a system which aims to provide support for this activity. The approach we have taken is to develop an adaptable system rather than a traditional ITS, i.e. there are no rules for selecting the most appropriate viewpoint, there is no 'curriculum' and there is no student model. Our aim is that this system will be able to offer the opportunities for growth, motivation and diversity that Soloway argues are essential for learner centred design [9].

Given such a flexible system, it would be possible to add intelligence to the environment by following a learner centred methodology as developed by Brna and Cox. This approach requires that we first build a learning environment, empirically test it and analyse the results, and only then add judiciously selected ITS functionalities [10]. Therefore, we will examine individual differences (cognitive style, prior experience, etc.) against use of tools with a view to determining effective patterns of tool use. Given additional results indicating which aspects of comprehension are still problematic, we plan to provide limited intelligent support. For example, we can expect that there will be occasions when the user will benefit from advice to switch focus from one type of information to another, say, from control flow to data flow: we hope to be able to advise students on the appropriateness of such a move at any given time, and provide them with tools to perform the move with ease.

From a practical perspective, such an approach may offer an initial step towards solving the difficult problem of transfer. By developing features which could be integrated directly into a language, the novice would not be required to first learn to use a specially designed teaching environment, then negotiate the transfer to the full-scale target language (often with very different syntactic features), which may involve 'unlearning' some constructs and relearning others.

To conclude, it is our hope that by not constraining students to a rigid program comprehension strategy, flexible approaches will be fostered which are applicable to a variety of languages (although this hypothesis will need testing). On a wider level, rather than creating additional programming environments, one could envisage the integration of support of this type within a full-scale language. These features would provide a form of scaffolding as the novice learns to program, and be switched off as the novice gains in competency.

References

1. Pennington, N.: Comprehension Strategies in Programming. In: Olson, G.M., Sheppard, S., Soloway, E. (eds.): Empirical Studies of Programmers: Second Workshop. Ablex Publishing Corporation, New Jersey (1987a) 100–113
2. Corritore, C.L., Wiedenbeck, S.: What Do Novices Learn During Program Comprehension? International Journal of Human-Computer Interaction, **3** 2 (1991) 199–222
3. Soloway, E., Adelson, B., Ehrlich, B.: Knowledge and Processes in the Comprehension of Computer Programs. In: Chi, M.T.H., Glaser, R., Farr, M.J. (eds.): The Nature of Expertise. Lawrence Erlbaum Associates, Hillsdale (1988) 129–152
4. von Mayrhauser, A., Vans, A.M.: Program Understanding — A Survey. Technical Report, Colorado State University. (1994)
5. Tilley, S.R., Smith, D.B.: Coming Attractions in Program Understanding. Technical Report CMU/SEI-96-TR-019, Carnegie Mellon University. (1996).
6. Green, T.R.G., Petre, M.: Usability Analysis of Visual Programming Environments: A Cognitive Dimensions Framework. Journal of Visual Languages and Computing **7** (1996) 131–174
7. Gilmore, D.J., Green, T.R.G.: Comprehension and Recall of Miniature Programs. *International Journal of Man-Machine Studies* **21** (1984) 31–48
8. van Dijk, T.A., Kintsch, W.: Strategies of Discourse Comprehension. Academic Press, New York. (1983)
9. Soloway, E., Jackson, S.L., Klein, J., Quintana, C., Reed, J., Spitulnik, J., Stratford, S.J., Studer, S., Jul, S., Eng, J., Scala, N.: Learning Theory in Practice: Case Studies of Learner-Centered Design. In: Bilger, R., Guest, S., Tauber, M.J. (eds.): CHI '96 Proceedings: Conference on Human Factors in Computing Systems: Common Ground. ACM. (1996).
10. Brna, P., Cox, R. Adding 'Intelligence' to a Learning Environment: A Case of Learner-Centred Design? Journal of Computer Assisted Learning. Accepted for publication in November/December 1998.
11. Davis, A.L., Keller, R.M.: Data Flow Program Graphs. IEEE Computer 1 (1982) 526–541
12. Green, T.R.G.: Cognitive Dimensions of Notations. In: Sutcliffe, A., Macaulay, L. (eds.):People and Computers V. Cambridge University Press, Cambridge (1989)
13. Sweller, J., Chandler, P., Tierney, P., Cooper, M.: Cognitive Load as a Factor in the Structuring of Technical Material. Journal of Experimental Psychology General **119** (1990) 176–192
14. Cooper, G.: Cognitive Load Theory as an Aid for Instructional Design. Australian Journal of Educational Technology **6** 2 (1990) 108–113
15. Good, J.: The 'Right' Tool for the Task: An Investigation of External Representations, Program Abstractions and Task Requirements. In: Gray, W.D., Boehm-Davis, D.A. (eds.): Empirical Studies of Programmers: Sixth Workshop. Ablex Publishing Corporation, New Jersey (1996) 77–98
16. Good, J.: Visual Programming Languages, Programming Paradigms and Program Comprehension. Technical Report, Human Communication Research Centre, The University of Edinburgh. (In Preparation).
17. Pennington, N.: Stimulus Structures and Mental Representations in Expert Comprehension of Computer Programs. Cognitive Psychology **19** (1987b) 295–341
18. Good, J., Brna, P.: Scaffolding for Recursion: Can Visual Languages Help? In: IEE Colloquium on Thinking with Diagrams. IEE. (1996) 7/1–7/3

A Domain Theory Extension of a Student Modeling System for Pascal Programming

Rhodora L. Reyes

Software Technology Department, College of Computer Studies, De La Salle University, Manila, Philippines
ccsrlr@dlsu.edu.ph

Abstract. Student models play an important part in intelligent tutoring systems. Its primary objective is to understand the student behavior, especially erroneous behavior. However, it is difficult to determine all possible errors that a student commit while solving problems for a particular domain. Thus, there is a need to extend the domain theory of the Student Modeling System (SMS). This paper discusses the design of the extension algorithm using Pascal programming as its domain.

1. Introduction

An *Intelligent Tutoring System* (ITS) is a computer-based tutor that qualitatively models the cognitive process of its learners in order to effectively diagnose and correct their errors and misconceptions [12]. Although many architectures have been proposed for Intelligent Tutoring Systems, a few components seem to be present in all. These are the student model, tutor model, domain model and the interface. The *student model,* which is one of the major components of an ITS, assesses a student's performance by determining what the student knows, his or her misconceptions and the causes of these misconceptions. Thus, the primary function of the student model is to interpret the learner's behavior.

Clancey, in his tutorial survey of ITSs, presented *Turtle, Meno* and *Proust* which are some of the existing tutors concerned with teaching computer programming [5]. Other student simulation programs are *Marcel* and *Grapes* [14]. Despite the success of these existing programming tutors, there still is a need for domain extension. These tutors all rely on a static library of misconceptions. If the errors committed by the student are not in the library, these tutoring systems will no longer be able to determine the misconceptions underlying their errant behavior.

Student modeling systems form models of the student's ability based on the observed behavior of the student, which in the case of this paper, is usually in the form of student solutions (i.e., programs) to a given programming problem. It is impossible to determine all students' programming errors and preprogram these in the student model. This paper focuses on the design of an extension algorithm for a domain theory for Pascal programming. This helps determine the cause (or causes) of the student's error even if it is not preprogrammed in the student model.

2.   The Domain Theory Structure[1]

A major prerequisite in developing a student model is to identify the errors students commit and the origin of these errors. Anderson [1] stated that it is important to identify the errors student make, to understand the origin of these errors, and code the inferred buggy productions one by one into the system .

An analysis of the non-syntactic errors found in programs written by novice Pascal programmers' errors was performed. Six programming problems were given to the students. These are functions, for-do, while-do, repeat-until, if-then and arrays[11]. A domain theory subnetwork was created for each of these problems. The set of programming plans and codes, both correct and incorrect, taken from the analysis form the initial domain theory.

2.1 Levels, Frames and Slots

In this design, the domain theory is represented as a *network*. Each state in the network is represented using *frame-based structure* and each frame has *slots*.

The domain network structure has four levels: the *root level,* the *plan level,* the *subplan level* and the *instance level* (Fig.1 shows an example). The root level has only one frame which represents the *start state*. All frames in all four levels have a *name slot* which contains the name (or description) of the frame. In addition to the *name slot*, the start state has a *plan slot* for the alternative plans that the domain theory has for solving a given programming problem. The connections from the start state to the *plan frames* are *disjunctive*.

At the *plan level,* each state (called as *plan frame*) is used to represent programming plans. *Plans* are stereotypic methods for implementing the problem requirements that appear in the problem descriptions. Each of these frames has *constant slot* and *variable slot* for the constants and variables used in the plan, respectively.   The variables placed in the *variable slot* are also called *pattern variables*, that is, variables used in the student program will be used to substitute these pattern variables. The plan frame also have a slot for the set of subplans in implementing the plan called the *subplan slot*. Since all these plans are necessary to carry out a plan, the links from the plan frames to the *subplan frames* are *conjunctive*. These subplans must also be checked in the order they were placed in the *subplan slot.*

---

[1] The end-product programs and video/verbal protocols that were collected from the Computer Science freshmen provided the basis for an initial formulation of the domain theory [11].

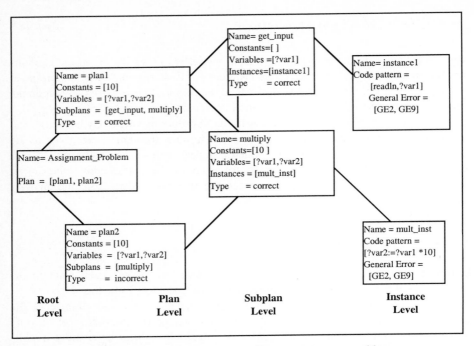

Fig. 1. A sample domain theory structure for an assignment statement problem.

The *subplan frames* also have *constant* and *variable slots*. The constant and variable slots have the same definition as those defined in the plan frame. Only, these slots identify the constants and variables used in the subplan. The *instance slot* identifies alternative code implementation of the subplan. This indicates that the subplan is implemented similarly (i.e., have the same meaning) but appears differently in code. Fig. 2 shows an example of a subplan that adds two numbers with two *instances*. Both implementations have the same meaning but appears differently in code. At the subplan level, *subplan frames* may have the same value for the *name slot* but different values in other slots. In this situation, the intention of the subplans is the same but is implemented differently. Fig. 2 shows an example of subplans with the same name, one is correct and the other is not.

In addition, both the *subplan* and *plan frames* have a type slot for determining if it is the correct or incorrect implementation of the plan/subplan. This will serve as a guide in determining the errors in the student programs.

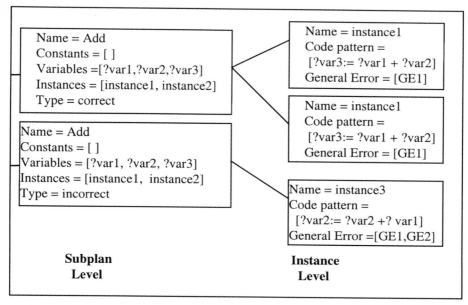

Fig. 2. An example of subplans with the same name and a subplan with two instances.

The last level is the *instance level*. The states in this level are called *instance frames*. The three slots in this frame are the name slot, *general error slot* and the *code pattern slot*. The most important slot is the *code pattern slot* which describes the form the Pascal code has in implementing the subplan. The *general error slot* indicates the general error or type of statement categories to which the code belongs.

A subplan frame can have a link to one or more plan frames but an instance frame can only have a single link to a subplan frame (i.e., subplan frames can not have the same value for their instance slots).

3.   The Domain Theory Extension

The impossibility of pre-enumerating all student's errors and represent these in the domain theory creates the need for extending the domain theory. This section discusses the design of an algorithm that uses both induction and deduction to infer missing operators from the initial formulation of the domain theory.

3.1 The Extension Algorithm

Learning occurs at the plan, subplan and instance level. Learning at the instance level implies that the programming plans and subplans used by the student are present in the domain theory but are written differently in code. Learning at the subplan level, on the other hand, implies that the programming plan is present in the domain theory but the subplans are implemented differently and are logically different. In this case, there is also learning at the instance level. Learning at the plan level indicates that the student's programming plan is not present in the domain theory.   Table 1 states the summary of the extension algorithm [10].

Table 1. Summary of the extension algorithm.

---

1. Given the domain theory, traverse the network forward from the start state (at the root level) towards the goal state (i.e., student program) by :
    a.   Finding a match between the instances (i.e., values of the code pattern slot) of the plans and the statements in the student program
    b.   Applying *valid statement transformations* (if a match has not been found) and matching the newly transformed code pattern to the statement in the student program
    c.   Repeating steps (a) and (b) until all plans have been traversed and the goal was not found. Declare an impasse.
2. Apply deductive inference to the impasses and continue the traversal towards the goal state. This may involve creating a new rule at the subplan level and at the instance level.
3. Apply inductive inference to completely connect the gap between the   network and the goal state. This involves creating a new rule at the plan level and/or at the subplan and instance level.

3.2 Deduction

Deductive inference [2],[3],[4] in this algorithm can be classified into three categories: *valid sentence transformation, valid program transformation*   and *perturbation*.

Valid Sentence Transformation

The first step in the algorithm requires that the forward traversal of the network towards the goal state. During the matching of the plan instances to the student's program statements, *valid sentence transformations* are applied to the *instance frame* if the expected Pascal code differ from the statement in the student program. Valid sentence transformations are legal Pascal transformation rules.   They are applied in the first instance that the student code does not match with the database code.

The following are the valid sentence transformation:

1. If the statement contains a Pascal expression then alter the expression using the commutative, associative and distributive law. A Pascal expression may be an arithmetic or Boolean expression. For example:

    `a := b + c` can be transformed to   `a : = c + b`

2. If the statement is a Pascal input/output statement then interchange the position of the variables.

Valid Program Transformation

The purpose of the *valid program transformation* is to generate all possible sequences of the statements without altering the programming plan. Table 2 shows the summary of the rules for valid program transformation.

Table 2. Summary of Valid Program Transformation Rules

1. Generate the read/write sets. A read set is the set of variables that are read, and a write set is the set of variables that are written to. For example, in the statement `a := b + c`, the read set is {b, c} and the write set is {a}. This determines the dependencies among the statements.
2. A *dependency graph* is created based on the dependencies of the statements. An edge from node S_i to S_j means that statement S_j is dependent on S_i.

For example, given a program (with line numbers) in the following sequence:

```
1 begin                RS(1) = {a, b};   WS(1) = {a, b}

2 readln(a);           RS(2) = {};       WS(2) = {a}

3 readln (b);          RS(3) = {};       WS(3) = {b}

4 a:= a + b;           RS(4) = {a, b};   WS(4) = {a}

5 end.                 RS(5) = {a, b};   WS(5) = {a, b}
```

The dependency graph is shown in Fig. 3.

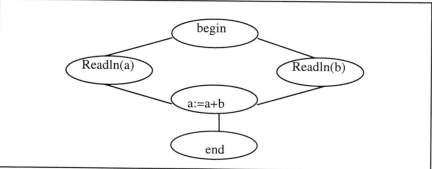

Fig. 3. Dependency graph for the sample program.

One valid transformation is:

```
1 begin                   since,
3 readln(b);                 read set(2)∩ write set (3) = {null}
2 readln(a);                 write set(2) ∩ write set(3) = {null}
4 a := a + b;                write set(2) ∩ read set (3) = {null}
5 end
```

The read and write sets of the instances in the database were first generated, followed by the level of each statement with respect to its depth in the program (i.e., if it belongs to a block).

Perturbation

Perturbation [13] is applied only after the first two classifications of deductive inference fail to reach the goal. In perturbation, each instance frame of the plans is matched to its corresponding statement in the student program. If an impasse occurs, perturbations are implemented to the instance frame.

The design was to generate all possible combinations. However, it is only up to the point where the expressions did not match. For example, if the expression did not match at an operator, it will be perturbed by modifying only that operator, thus generating all possible combinations of expressions where different operators are involved at that particular point/node. If it did not match on an operand, it will be perturbed to produce a list of the same expression but with different operands at the point where the statement did not match. If a match is not found after the perturbation, the original statement will be used for succeeding perturbations. Approaches to perturbation are as follows:

1. Modify operators
The mathematical and logical operators are modified. All possible permutations of operators are applied. The rules for modification are as follows:
   a.   If the operator is a mathematical operator (i.e., +, -, *, /, div, mod) or a logical operator (i.e., >,<,=, >=, <=, <>), choose a new mathematical/ logical operator (e.g., the new operator is different from the original operator).
   b.   If the operator is a logical connective (i.e., and, or), choose a new operator different from the original operator. If the operator is "not", remove the operator

2. Delete sub-expressions
This type of perturbation removes a mathematical operator and an operand (e.g., constants or variables) to the expression. For example, given the statement x:=y/12/100, one valid perturbation is x:=y/12 .

3. Exchange operands
Another type of perturbation is to swap operands. Operands may be in the form of variables or constants. For example, a:=b/c+10 can be perturbed to a:=c/b+10 or a:=b/10+c; .

4. Alter variables
When assigning values to the *pattern variables* in the domain theory, one policy is that only variables in the student program are allowed to be substituted to the pattern

variables. Two ways of altering the variables are to allow constants to be bound to the free variable and to allow substitution of variables in the student program to the bound variables in the domain theory. The bound variable is converted to a pattern variable so that a different variable can be substituted to it. If the goal is reached after this alteration then this implies that the student used a variable different from what is expected in the domain theory.

5. Alter Constants

Constants used in the expression are changed to other constant values. The constant values that are used as substitution are taken from the list of constants used in the plan.

6. Delete input/output arguments

Some of the arguments in the input/output statements are deleted as part of the perturbation. For example, `readln(a); readln(b)` can be perturbed to `readln(a); or readln (b);`.

7. Modify Construct

Statements that have almost the same purpose are used as basis for modifying the construct. An example of modification is to change the *if-then statement* to *while-do statement* and vice versa. If-then and while-do statement have almost the same objective, that is, to check first its condition before executing the statement after it. Their only difference is that if-then executes the statement after it once, whereas while-do statement executes the statement after it several times (depending on the happening of an event).[2] Other statements that may be interchanged are *writeln* and *readln*.

If the perturbations applied result to the attainment of a match in the program statement in the goal then the perturbation is learned as a rule at the subplan level and the program code is learned as a rule at the instance level.

3.3 Induction

If after applying deductive inference the goal is still not reached then inductive inference [2],[3],[4] is applied. This means that the student program (or goal) have a different programming plan. The following states how a plan is learned:

1. Inductive inferencing uses *backward chaining*. From the goal, each statement is matched to the instance frames.
    a. If the statement matches the instance frame, then the subplan is determined. It is possible that the subplans used by the student are in the domain theory but they are used differently.
    b. Otherwise, apply perturbations to the code pattern slot . If the perturbed statement matches the student's statement, determine its subplan. Learn this as a new subplan (with the same subplan name).
    c. Otherwise, learn an entirely new subplan. This involves inductive inference of a new subplan.

---

[2] This perturbation is based on the analysis of novice Pascal programmers' errors [11].

2.   The subplan that has been determined at (1) will be included in the list of subplans of the new plan while the variables and constants used will be included in the list of constants and variables for the plan.

In learning a new value for the code pattern in the instance slot, the variables in the student program statement must be converted to pattern variables. This pattern variables to be used is determined by specifying which pattern variables were the program variables substituted to.

4. Conclusion

A structure of the domain theory for Pascal programming was presented   as a collection of domain subnetworks for each problem type. This design organizes the domain theory such that the programming knowledge of the student is represented from the plans to the implementation of the plans.

In the domain theory extension, it was shown that the initial domain theory can be extended given any type of programming solution to the problem. Both deductive and inductive inferencing were used to extend the domain theory. Extensions that can not be learned through perturbations are learned through induction.

The extension algorithm presented in this paper does not automatically learn perturbations nor induce new statements because programming statements can be written in several ways (if they are independent statements) and each statement may have different forms (although it is logically the same). The extension algorithm checks first if a match can be found through valid sentence transformation or valid program transformation before applying perturbations or induction.

A prototype was built to verify the extension of the domain theory. This is just a subset of the student model, which is a major component of the system. A truth and consistency maintenance system was also included in the prototype. This is used for updating the domain theory database and for faster matching of plans. Also, the student model is responsible for determining the errors and misconceptions of the student. Based on the domain theory and the newly learned plan, subplan or instance, the system will be able to determine the errors and misconceptions of the student. Thus, this prototype can be extended such that it will be able to determine the errors and misconceptions.

Based from the design of the domain theory for Pascal programming and the algorithm that extends it, three major results were found. First, approaches to program analysis can be based upon the concept of programming plans. This concept was also used by Cutler, Draper, Johnson and Soloway [6] and according to the authors, empirical evidences show that the notion of programming plans facilitate the processing and storage of information by providing background knowledge or context. Another result is that most subplans can be learned as perturbations of the subplans in the initial domain theory. The domain theory extension algorithm does not heavily depend on the initial formulation of the domain theory. If the initial domain theory was well constructed, most of the extensions are learned through perturbations. Otherwise, the domain theory will still be extended, that is, through the use of induction. In both cases, the domain theory is extended.

References

1. Anderson, J., Boyle, C.F., Corbett, A. and Lewis, M.: Cognitive Modeling and Intelligent Tutoring. *Artificial Intelligent.* Elsevier Science Publishers, B.V., North Holland, (1990) 7-40
2. Carbonell, J., Michalski, R., Mitchell, T.: Machine Learning : An Artificial Intelligent Approach, Volume I. Tioga Pub. Co., Palo, Alto, California.(1983)
3. Carbonell, J., Michalski, R., Mitchell, T.: Machine Learning : An Artificial Intelligent Approach, Volume II. Tioga Pub. Co., Palo, Alto, California. (1983)
4. Carbonell, J., Michalski, R., Mitchell, T.: Machine Learning : An Artificial Intelligent Approach, Volume III. Tioga Pub. Co., Palo, Alto, California. (1983)
5. Clancey, W. : Intelligent Tutoring System: A Tutorial Survey. Technical Report No. KSL-86-58. Stanford Knowledge Systems Laboratory, Palo, Alto, California. (1986)
6. Cutler, B., Draper, S., Johnson, W.L. and Soloway, E.: Bug Catalogue I. Cognition and Programming Project. Department of Computer Science, Yale University, New Haven, Connecticut (1983)
7. Freiman, S., Johnson, L., Lipman, M., Littman, D., Pope, E., Sack,W., Soloway, E. and Spohrer, J.: Bug Catalogue: II, III, IV. Research Report. Department of Computer Science. Cognition and Programming Project, Yale University, New Haven, Connecticut.(1985)
8. Kearsley, G.: Intelligent Computer-Aided Instruction. Park Row Software (1987)154-159
9. McCalla, G.: Knowledge Representation Issues in Automated Tutoring. Research Report 87-1. ARIES Laboratory, Computational Science Department, University of Saskatchewan, Canada.(1987)
10. Reyes, R. L.: The Design and Extension of a Domain Theory for Pascal . A Masteral Thesis. Graduate Program of the College of Computer Studies, De La Salle University, Manila. (1995)
11. Reyes, R.L.: Understanding Novice Pascal Programmers' Errors. URCO Project No: 28 RP, De La Salle University, Manila.(1995)
12. Sison, R.: Intelligent Tutoring Systems: Objectives, Components and Design Issues. Computer Issues, 28(3), De La Salle University, Manila. (1989) 1-30
13. Sleeman, D., Hirsh, H., Ellery, I. and Kim, I.: Extending Domain Theories: Two Case Studies in Student Modeling, Machine Learning. Kluwer Academic Publishers, Netherlands (1990). 11-37
14. Spohrer, J. and Soloway E.: Simulating Student Programmers. Proceedings of the 11th International Joint Conference in Artificial Intelligence. San Mateo, California. (1989) 543-549

The Foundations and Architecture of Autotutor

Peter Wiemer-Hastings[1,2], Arthur C. Graesser[1,2], Derek Harter[2], and the
Tutoring Research Group[*,1,2,3]

[1] Department of Psychology
[2] Department of Mathematical Sciences
[3] College of Education
The University of Memphis
Memphis TN 38152-6400
{pwmrhstn, a-graesser, dharter}@memphis.edu

Abstract. The Tutoring Research Group at the University of Memphis
is developing an intelligent tutoring system which takes advantages of
recent technological advances in the areas of semantic processing of natural language, world knowledge representation, multimedia interfaces, and
fuzzy descriptions. The tutoring interaction is based on in-depth studies
of human tutors, both skilled and unskilled. Latent semantic analysis
will be used to semantically process and provide a representation for the
student's contributions. Fuzzy production rules select appropriate topics
and tutor dialogue moves from a rich curriculum script. The production
rules will implement a variety of different tutoring styles, from a basic
untrained tutor to one which uses sophisticated pedagogical strategies.
The tutor will be evaluated on the naturalness of its interaction, with
Turing-style tests, by comparing different tutoring styles, and by judging
learning outcomes.

1 Introduction

At the University of Memphis, our team of researchers from Psychology, Computer Science, and Education has begun development of an intelligent tutoring system that is fundamentally different from previous ITS's. We are taking advantage
of recent technological developments as well as advances in our understanding
of human tutoring protocols in order to make a tutor (called Autotutor) that
can interactively communicate with a student in natural language, and produce
a wide range of appropriate responses. This paper describes the motivation and
foundations of this project, the basic architecture that is being developed and
types of behaviors that it will support, the methods we will use for evaluating
the system, and the future directions for research and development.

* The Tutoring Research Group includes Stan Franklin, Max Garzon, Barry Gholson,
Doug Hacker, Xiangen Hu, Roger Kreuz, Bill Marks, Natalie Person, Fergus Nolan, Ash-
raf Anwar, Myles Bogner, Derek Harter, Lee McCauley, Zhaohua Zhang, Jim Hoeffner,
Bianca Klettke, Kristen Link, Brent Olde, Victoria Pomeroy, Katja Wiemer-Hastings,
Holly Yetman, Scotty Craig, Patrick Chipman, Melissa Ring, Charles Webster and the
authors. This project is supported by grant number SBR9720314 from the National
Science Foundation's Learning and Intelligent Systems Unit.

2   Motivation

Researchers have long been attempting to develop a computer tutor that can interact naturally with students to help them understand a particular subject domain. Unfortunately, however, language and discourse have constituted a serious barrier in these efforts. Language and discourse facilities have been either nonexistent or extremely limited in the most impressive and successful intelligent tutoring systems available, such as Anderson's tutors for geometry, algebra, and computer languages [1], Van Lehn's tutor for basic mathematics [26], and Lesgold's tutor for diagnosing and repairing electronic equipment [17]. There have been some attempts to augment ITS's with language and dialog facilities [13]. But such attempts have been limited by three major obstacles: (1) the inherent difficulty of getting a computer to "comprehend" the language of users, including utterances that are not well-formed syntactically and semantically, (2) the difficulty of getting computers to effectively use a large body of open-ended, fragmentary, and unstructured world knowledge, and (3) the lack of research on human tutorial dialogue.

Advances in research during the last five years make it much more feasible to develop a computer tutor which tackles the above three barriers. Our Autotutor system will "comprehend" text that the learner types into the keyboard (i.e., the initial version of our tutor will not support spoken input from the student). It will generate discourse contributions in the form of printed text, synthesized speech, graphic displays, animation, and simulated facial movements and expressions [18, 21]. The primary technological contribution of this research, however, lies in formulating helpful discourse contributions based on an analysis of human – human tutoring sessions.

3   Advances Facilitating ITS Development

As mentioned above, three major barriers (natural language, world knowledge, and tutorial dialog) have prevented ITS researchers from implementing tutorial dialog facilities in natural language. Recent advances have provided approximate solutions to minimizing these barriers, so an ITS with a natural language and dialog facility is much more feasible. In sections 3.1 and 3.2, we will address the two most important advances: world knowledge representation and tutorial dialogue. Space limitations force us to only briefly mention the following technical advances which will have also have a significant affect on Autotutor's chances for success:

Natural language processing The DARPA Message Understanding initiative [7], has pushed researchers away from toy problems to dealing with real-world texts, which use a wide variety of words and include complex and often ill-formed grammatical constructions.

Multimedia The ability to fluidly present not just text, but also synthesized speech, graphic displays, simulated facial movements, and animation has moved from the state-of-the-art to the commonplace.

Synthesized speech Pitch, pause, duration, amplitude, and intonation contours are among the variety of intonation cues that signal back channel feedback, affect, and emphasis [12]. Synthesized speech will allow us to provide this type of feedback to the students.

Talking heads Several researchers have recently developed relatively realistic animated talking heads that have facial features synchronized with speech [21]. This allows us to provide facial gesture feedback as well.

Fuzzy descriptions of figures and diagrams For each picture or graph that is be presented as a teaching aid, Autotutor uses a fuzzy description to specify the set of components in the picture, properties of components, spatial relationship between components, motion depicted by arrows, and so on [25].

3.1   World Knowledge representation

The fact that world knowledge is inextricably bound to natural language comprehension is widely acknowledged in psycholinguistics, cognitive science and discourse processing [9, 15, for example], but researchers in computational linguistics have not had a satisfactory approach to handling the deep abyss of world knowledge. The traditional approach to representing world knowledge in artificial intelligence has been structured representations, such as semantic networks, conceptual graphs, and rules [10]. World knowledge is frequently open-ended, imprecise, vague, and incomplete, so simple computational procedures cannot handle the role of world knowledge in understanding language and in tutoring.

Latent Semantic Analysis (LSA) provides the critical backbone for representing world knowledge in Autotutor. LSA has recently been proposed as a statistical representation of a large body of world knowledge [8, 16, for example]. LSA capitalizes on the fact that particular words appear in particular texts; the occurrence of words in texts reflects the constraints that exist in world knowledge. A statistical method called *singular value decomposition* reduces a very high-dimensional co-occurrence matrix to K dimensions (typically, 100 to 300 dimensions). Each word, sentence, or text is represented as a weighted vector on the K dimensions. The "match" (i.e., similarity in meaning, conceptual relatedness) between two words, sentences, or texts is computed as the cosine between the two vectors, with values ranging from -1 to 1. The match between two language strings can be high even though there are few if any words in common between the two strings. LSA goes well beyond simple string matches because the meaning of a language string is determined in large part by the company (other words) that each word keeps.

The empirical success of LSA has been promising and sometimes remarkable. Landauer and Dumais [16] created an LSA space from a large subset of Grolier's Academic American Encyclopedia, and then gave it the Test of English as a Foreign Language (TOEFL) from ETS. The LSA model answered 64.4% of the questions correctly, which is essentially equivalent to the 64.5% performance for college students from non-English speaking countries. Foltz et al., [8] and Kintsch [15] report other successful applications of LSA to different tasks.

LSA plays a central role in Autotutor. The *truth* of a student's contribution is evaluated by computing the maximum cosine match between a student's contribution and the entire corpus of related texts. The *relevance* of a student's contribution is evaluated by computing its match with expected answers to a question, or expected solutions to a problem. Prior to LSA, there was no empirically defensible computation of the truth and relevance of expressions with respect to a large knowledge base that is open-ended, fragmentary, imprecise, and vague. We believe that LSA will allow us to bootstrap the ITS enterprise to accommodate natural language and dialog for the first time. Autotutor provides a research platform to allow us to test this claim.

3.2 Tutorial Dialog

Researchers in education and ITS development have identified a number of ideal tutoring strategies, such as: the Socratic method [6], modeling-scaffolding-fading [24], reciprocal training [20], anchored learning [3], and others. Researchers who have examined these tutoring strategies have frequently pointed out that tutors need extensive training on the use of these sophisticated ideal tutoring strategies. Not surprisingly, therefore, these strategies do not spontaneously emerge in the repertoire of strategies of unskilled tutors — the tutors that predominate in actual school systems [11]. Previous ITS developers have abandoned attempts to incorporate most of these ideal tutoring strategies in the tutoring systems because of the barriers of natural language and world knowledge. We will implement some of these ideal tutoring strategies in Autotutor, to the extent that they are technically feasible.

Aside from these ideal tutoring strategies, recent projects have dissected the strategies used by skilled and unskilled human tutors. In some of these studies, the tutors have been highly skilled and knowledgeable about the topic [14, for example]. Our previous work on tutorial dialog [22, for example], funded by the Office of Naval Research, has examined untrained tutors with moderate domain knowledge because these tutors are most representative of tutors in actual school systems. Even though most tutors in school systems are untrained, they are surprisingly very effective compared to teachers in normal classroom environments. One-on-one human tutoring has shown effect sizes of .4 to 2.3 standard deviation units compared to classroom teaching and other suitable controls [2]. Our detailed conversational analyses of normal tutors unveiled the characteristics of the dialog that apparently are responsible for the robust learning gains [11].

One conceivable advantage of tutoring in general is an enhanced "meeting of the minds" between student and tutor. That is, the tutor infers the idiosyncratic knowledge, bugs, and misconceptions of the student – and the student's knowledge drifts toward the tutor's knowledge base. Designers of some ITS's have implemented "student modeling," to attempt to infer the student's knowledge states [1]. Discourse theories have frequently emphasized the importance of establishing shared meanings for successful communication [5]. There is a radically different perspective on the matter of common ground and student modeling, however. Researchers have cast doubt on the possibility, the need, and the pedagogical utility of detailed student modeling [19]. Our detailed analysis of actual tutoring sessions revealed that there is a very slow convergence towards shared meanings during tutoring [11]. The gap in knowledge between the tutor and student is so wide that the two parties in the conversation frequently misunderstand each other and give each other incorrect feedback. For example, tutors normally give positive responses ("Yeah", "Uh-huh") to student contributions that are vague, incoherent or error ridden; students who are lost usually say yes or nod their heads when asked "Do you understand?" [22]. The fact that the tutor manages conversation when there is a breakdown in common ground and feedback mechanisms makes tutoring a fascinating phenomenon to study from the standpoint of theories of communication and discourse processing.

The large gulf that frequently exists between the knowledge of tutors and students gives us reason to believe that it is feasible to develop a computer tutor that parallels human tutors. A key feature of effective tutoring lies in assisting students in actively constructing subjective explanations and elaborations of the material [4]. The tutor's dialog moves in a collaborative exchange might provide effective scaffolding for a student to build such self-explanations – without the computer fully knowing what the student knows.

Autotutor will simulate dialog moves in tutorial dialog of different classes of tutors. One class is unskilled tutors, the sort of tutors that exist in real school systems. Another class will be untrained tutors who acquire more experience in tutoring; the computer tutor will augment its knowledge base by storing answers that students give to questions and solutions to problems (segregating good and bad contributions). More sophisticated classes of tutors will implement various ideal tutoring strategies (such as a Socratic tutor, modeling-scaffolding-fading, and strategic hinting).

4   Autotutor Architecture

A schematic view of the architecture of Autotutor is shown in figure 1. This section describes the major processing components and knowledge bases of the system, and its overall behavior.

4.1   Topic selection

At every stage in the tutoring session, a set of production rules controls selection of a subtopic that is appropriate to the student's needs and the teacher's goals. The subtopics come from a set of instructional materials called the curriculum script, developed by experts in education and in the subject domain.

4.2   Curriculum script

The material in a curriculum script covers one topic, for example, the internet in a computer literacy class. For each topic, there is an information delivery item to

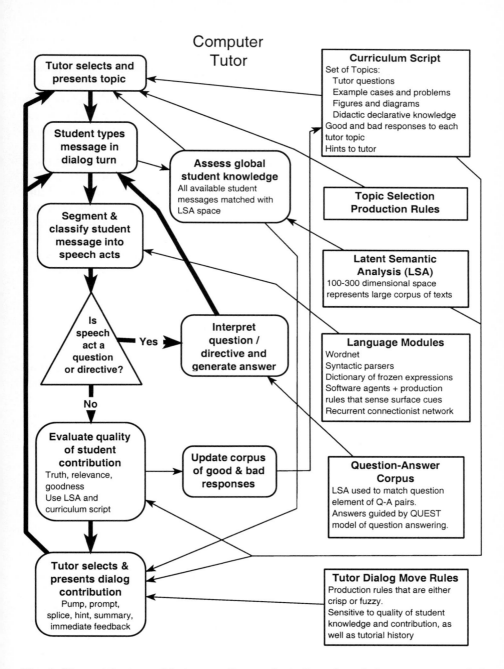

Fig. 1. The architecture of Autotutor. Rectangles indicate knowledge sources, rounded rectangles are processes, the triangle is a choice point, and the very heavy arrows indicate the general flow of control.

set up the common ground between the student and Autututor and a seed question to "get the ball rolling." The remainder of the curriculum script consists of a set of subtopics. There are four types of subtopics: (1) simple question/answer, (2) question/answer with didactic content, (3) problem solution, and (4) picture question/answer.

Each subtopic is ranked on sophistication (high, medium, low) and on chronological order (early, middle, late). Some topics may have specific ordering constraints, for example that subtopic A must be covered *before* subtopic B. Associated with each subtopic is: an ideal complete and correct answer; a set of additional good answers (which grows with experience), ranked good, better, best; a set of bad answers (which grows with experience); a set of hints, ranked for low, medium, and high-quality student contributions (i.e. a low-ranked hint provides more basic information than a high-ranked hint); a set of question that the student would be likely to ask, with appropriate answers; and a good succinct summary.

The set of curriculum scripts provides a rich set of responses from which Autotutor can choose, based on the evaluation of the student's contribution (described below) and on the dialogue selection rules (described in section 4.4).

4.3   Evaluating the quality of student contributions

Human tutors are sensitive to the overall quality of student contributions during the collaborative process of answering a question or solving a problem. This component evaluates the quality of the students' speech acts that are classified as Contributions, but not Questions and Directives. As mentioned above, latent semantic analysis will be used in these assessments of the contributions' truth, relevance, and quality.

4.4   Tutor dialogue moves

Our analysis of untrained tutors uncovered a set of dialogue moves that are triggered under specific conditions during the collaborative evolution of an answer to a question or a solution to a problem [11]. Some of these moves are specified below:

Pumping: The tutor pumps the student for more information during the early stages of answering a particular question (or solving a problem).

Prompting: Tutors supply the student with a discourse context and prompt them to fill in a missing word, phrase, or sentence.

Immediate feedback: Tutors are normally polite conversation partners, so they are reluctant to give negative feedback after student contributions that have poor quality [23]. Instead, they give positive, neutral, or indirect feedback.

Splicing: A tutor jumps in and splices correct information as soon as the student produces a contribution that is obviously error-ridden.

Hinting: When the student is having problems answering a question or solving a problem, the tutor gives hints by presenting a fact, asking a leading question, or reframing the problem.

Summarizing: Unskilled tutors normally give a summary that recaps an answer to a question or solution to a problem.

Autotutor will implement these dialogue moves to the extent possible using the dialogue move production rules described below.

4.5   Dialogue move production rules

Autotutor includes another set of fuzzy production rules that specify which dialogue response the tutor will make after a student turn. These are conditionalized on the content of the curriculum script, the dialogue history, and the quality of the student's contribution during the last turn, the cumulative quality of the student's knowledge, and the cumulative quality of the student-tutor exchange. For example, the following simple production rule is associated with immediate positive feedback for student contribution C:

```
IF [scriptComponent = Question(j)
    AND max(similarity(C, good-answer(j)) > Threshold]
THEN [produceFeedback: "That's right."]
```

The style and expertise of the tutor is defined in part by the production rules that capture these dialogue rules and the values of the threshold parameters. The production rules will be different for the unskilled tutor with minimal experience and a tutor with much experience (i.e., a large accumulated list of good answers and bad answers) which uses frontier learning. An important goal of this project is to simulate the contributions of different classes of tutors which vary in experience and in the use of particular pedagogical strategies.

5   Evaluating Autotutor

The primary objective of the evaluation is to assess the pedagogical quality and conversational aptness of the simulated tutor contributions. A tutor contribution should have pedagogical value, be relevant to the conversational context, and be informative. While a stable prototype version of Autotutor is still being developed, informal assessments of the system will prevail. When the computer tutor approaches the arena of supplying reasonable contributions, we will make more systematic evaluations of the tutor's contributions. The following types of evaluations are planned:

Initial evaluations: College students will interact with the computerized tutor and supply a sample of tutorial dialogs. The students will enter information by keyboard and the tutor will display information on computer screen and through simulated speech during these interactions. The content of the tutor's contributions in these transcripts will be analyzed by experts in discourse analysis, experts in education, and graduate research assistants.

Turing tests: College students will read transcripts in which half of the contributions are generated by Autotutor, and half by human experts. Then they will make a decision as to whether a human or computer generated each contribution. We will perform a standard signal detection analysis that segregates a true discrimination between human and computer from response biases in making these judgments; we will collect hit rates, false alarm rates, d scores, and Ag discrimination scores.[1]

Comparison of tutors: As discussed earlier, we will compare different classes of tutors that embrace different ideal tutoring strategies. These models will be the same except for the production rules that select topics and dialogue moves. Trained judges will assess the tutor's contributions with respect to conversational smoothness and pedagogical value, as discussed above.

Learning outcomes: Although the primary objective of this research does not address how well students learn with these computerized tutors, we do plan on conducting preliminary evaluations during the third year of the project. College students in a Computer Literacy course will be randomly assigned to use one of the different classes of tutors described above, or to a reading control. The students' learning of the domain material will be tested with a variety of measures of understanding.

6   Conclusion

We are in the first year of development of the system. As of mid-April 1998, we have a running prototype which includes latent semantic analysis, the talking head, the curriculum script, and the topic and subtopic selection rules. Later versions of the system will include in-depth natural language processing and a mechanism for automatically inferring from a picture a set of fuzzy descriptions of the relationships between the objects in the picture. As mentioned above, the focus of our efforts will now shift to evaluating the technical components of the system, evaluating the naturalness of its interactions, and developing the additional, more challenging components.

References

1. J. R. Anderson, A. T. Corbett, K. R. Koedinger, and R. Pelletier. Cognitive tutors: Lessons learned. *The Journal of the Learning Sciences*, 4:167–207, 1995.
2. B. S. Bloom. The 2 sigma problem: The search for methods of group instruction as effective as one-to-one tutoring. *Educational Researcher*, 13:4–16, 1984.
3. J. D. Bransford, S. R. Goldman, and N. J. Vye. Making a difference in people's ability to think: Reflections on a decade of work and some hopes for the future. In R. J. Sternberg and L. Okagaki, editors, *Influences on children*, pages 147–180. Erlbaum, Hillsdale, NJ, 1991.

---

[1] An alternative method of performing a Turing test would be to have a human expert provide contributions on-line during the tutorial sessions at random points in the dialogue; the computer would supply contributions at the remaining points.

4. M. T. H. Chi, N. de Leeuw, M. Chiu, and C. LaVancher. Eliciting self-explanations improves understanding. *Cognitive Science*, 18:439–477, 1994.
5. H. H. Clark and E. F. Schaefer. Contributing to discourse. *Cognitive Science*, 13:259–294, 1989.
6. A. Collins. Teaching reasoning skills. In S. Chipman, J. Segal, and R. Glaser, editors, *Thinking and learning skills*, pages 579–586. Erlbaum, Hillsdale, NJ, 1985.
7. DARPA. *Proceedings of the Sixth Message Understanding Conference (MUC-6)*. Morgan Kaufman Publishers, San Francisco, 1995.
8. P. Foltz. Latent semantic analysis for text-based research. *Behavior Research Methods, Instruments, and Computers*, 28:197–202, 1996.
9. M. A. Gernsbacher, editor. *Handbook of Psycholinguistics*. Academic Press, San Diego, CA, 1994.
10. A. Graesser and L. Clark. *Structures and procedures of implicit knowledge*. Ablex, Norwood, NJ, 1985.
11. A. C. Graesser, N. K. Person, and J. P. Magliano. Collaborative dialogue patterns in naturalistic one-to-one tutoring. *Applied Cognitive Psychology*, 9:359–387, 1995.
12. J. Hirschberg and G. Ward. The interpretation of the high-rise question contour in english. *Journal of Pragmatics*, 24:407–412, 1995.
13. V. Holland, J. Kaplan, and M. Sams. *Intelligent language tutors*. Erlbaum, Mahwah, NJ, 1995.
14. G. D. Hume, J. Michael, A. Rovick, and M. W. Evens. Hinting as a tactic in one-on-one tutoring. *The Journal of the Learning Sciences*, 5:23–47, 1996.
15. W. Kintsch. *Comprehension: A paradigm for cognition*. Cambridge University Press, Cambridge, MA, inpress.
16. T. Landauer and S. Dumais. A solution to Plato's problem: The latent semantic analysis theory of acquisition, induction, and representation of knowledge. *Psychological Review*, 104:211–240, 1997.
17. A. Lesgold, S. Lajoie, M. Bunzo, and G. Eggan. Sherlock: A coached practice environment for an electronics troubleshooting job. In J. H. Larkin and R. W. Chabay, editors, *Computer-assisted instruction and intelligent tutoring systems*, pages 201–238. Erlbaum, Hillsdale, NJ, 1992.
18. D. Massaro and M. Cohen. Perceiving talking faces. *Psychological Science*, 4:104–109, 1995.
19. D. Newman. Is a student model necessary? Apprenticeship as a model for ITS. In D. Bierman, J. Breuker, and J. Sandberg, editors, *Artificial intelligence and education*. IOS, Amsterdam, 1989.
20. A. S. Palinscar and A. Brown. Reciprocal teaching of comprehension-fostering and comprehension-monitoring activities. *Cognition and Instruction*, 1:117–175, 1984.
21. C. Pelachaud, N. Badler, and M. Steedman. Generating facial expressions for speech. *Cognitive Science*, 20:1–46, 1996.
22. N. K. Person, A. C. Graesser, J. P. Magliano, and R. J. Kreuz. Inferring what the student knows in one-to-one tutoring: The role of student questions and answers. *Learning and Individual Differences*, 6:205–229, 1994.
23. N. K. Person, R. J. Kreuz, R. Zwaan, and A. C. Graesser. Pragmatics and pedagogy: Conversational rules and politeness strategies may inhibit effective tutoring. *Cognition and Instruction*, 13:161–188, 1995.
24. B. Rogoff. *Apprenticeship in thinking*. Oxford University Press, New York, 1990.
25. B. Tversky and K. Hemenway. Categories of environmental scenes. *Cognitive Psychology*, 15:121–149, 1983.
26. K. Van Lehn. *Mind bugs: The origins of procedural misconceptions*. MIT Press, Cambridge, MA, 1990.

Verbal Coaching During a Real-Time Task

Bruce Roberts, Nicholas J. Pioch, and William Ferguson

BBN Technologies,
A division of BBN Corporation,
A unit of GTE Internetworking,
10 Moulton Street,
Cambridge, MA 02138
{broberts, npioch, wferguson}@bbn.com

Abstract. TRANSoM is a collaborative effort among university and industry researchers aimed at producing an intelligent tutoring system for training pilots of remotely operated vehicles (ROVs). ROVs are unmanned, tethered, underwater vehicles used in a range of applications such as inspection, search and salvage, and mine countermeasures. Pilots have to learn to maneuver the ROV, keeping track of its tether and its surroundings, using little more than a video camera and sonar. To minimize workload while a trainee is practicing, the primary mode of feedback during a mission is verbal. The design of this verbal coaching was modeled closely on techniques observed in human instructors. We report on several of the issues faced in implementing this coaching paradigm that make it effective yet unintrusive.

1 Introduction

The TRANSoM (Training for Remote Sensing and Manipulation) project is a combined industry and university effort applying the technologies of intelligent tutoring systems and virtual environments to the task of training pilots of remotely operated underwater vehicles (ROVs). ROVs are used widely for scientific exploration, construction, inspection, search and salvage, survey, and other activities in both military and commercial settings. They are controlled by an operator on board ship, which communicates with the ROV via a tether. The pilot controls thrusters on the ROV with a joystick and receives information from the ROV by means of a video camera and sonar mounted on it. Navigation aids, which track the ROV with respect to a global reference frame, are sometimes available.

Piloting an ROV is a challenging task despite the aid of video, sonar and guidance systems. As one pilot described it, "You can get so disoriented." In the underwater environment visual capabilities are limited by the natural turbidity of the water and backscatter from the lights needed to illuminate the scene. Unseen currents and the drag of the tether have significant influence on the dynamics of the ROV. Nevertheless, ROV operators must maintain a mental model of the vehicle, its tether, and its physical surroundings based on often incomplete and confusing data.

We are addressing these piloting skills in our training system: first by trying to understand how good pilots construct and maintain their world model, and second by devising a set of apprenticeship learning activities which foster this type of reasoning in novice pilots. As part of this effort, we have built a tutor to develop the maneuvering skills that form the foundation of good piloting. These predominately sensorimotor skills present an instructional challenge to the ITS, not the least of which is the inherently high workload associated with the task itself. We have been exploring the use of verbal feedback as the chief modality for real-time critique. This paper describes our experience integrating verbal coaching within an ITS for ROV maneuvering skills.

2 Practice Environment

Several component maneuvering tasks have been identified. They differ in the control strategies and information sources a pilot uses during their execution. We assembled these tasks as phases of a single "mission" to serve as the context for practicing maneuvering skills (Figure 1). Taken together, these phases exercise all of the basic maneuvering skills identified by our expert pilots.

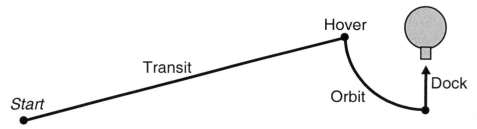

Fig. 1. Phases of the Maneuvering Task (Plan View)

We have created a virtual environment (VE) that incorporates the salient dynamical, visual, and aural features of the ROV's underwater environment (e.g., obstacles, strength and direction of current, visibility, particulate flow, and lighting) and makes these features easily reconfigurable by the ITS. The ITS guides a student's progress through a curriculum of increasingly challenging situations. The VE allows us to augment the world with additional features chosen for their instructional value and to populate the world with agents responsible for critiquing, guiding, and reviewing the student's progress. The role these agents play in instruction is borrowed from research on the value of coached practice and apprenticeship learning and the successful application of this approach in intelligent tutoring systems [1] [2].

The general coaching framework is to demonstrate the mission, allow the student to practice the mission, and then review the student's performance.

• The *demonstration* features an expert flying the mission accompanied by a talkthrough of the important aspects of the mission. It is an opportunity to present to the student explicit strategies for control (e.g., dealing with currents) and information assessment (e.g., how to use the displays).

• During *practice* the student can solicit help in the form of reminders about maneuvering goals and how to achieve them. Various "bird's eye" views of the ROV and its path are available to reorient the pilot. Unsolicited coaching is triggered by monitors that assess the student's progress and deviations from expert performance, such as drifting too far from the prescribed path. This feedback is delivered verbally in order to minimize the workload impact on the student, whose visual attention is already divided among several displays.

• During the *review* phase of instruction, the student can replay portions of the mission, see a summary of measures compared with expert performance, see a view of the actual path and an expert's path, and re-fly segments of the mission where errors occurred.

The practice environment includes several visual and aural features that act as instructional scaffolding and invite the student's own interpretation of what went wrong and how to improve his or her performance. In general they provide extra information to improve awareness of a) the vehicle in its environment, b) the consequences of pilot actions, c) the effects of external forces, and d) information available in the typical ROV displays. For more details on the implementation of the VE and its visual and aural cues, see [3].

3   Verbal Coaching

Task analysis led us to investigate ways of incorporating verbal coaching in addition to visual coaching aids as part of the maneuvering task training. The fact that a pilot's hands and eyes are fully occupied with flying the ROV makes it problematic to introduce additional visual features and practically impossible to present the student with something he or she would have to read. On the other hand, the speech modality is relatively underutilized in normal ROV operations, where speech is used to coordinate with other crew members, such as the sonar operator or tether handler. Although the demonstration and review phases of the session permit extended textual interactions, the student is not *doing* the task at that point in the instruction. We feel that timely feedback and suggestions during the mission itself are an extremely important form of coaching. This presented a unique opportunity to build on the relatively few precedents that exist in applying ITS technology to a real-time task [4] [5].

Several challenges arose in the course of creating verbal coaching for the maneuvering task.

• Simplistic schemes that trigger commentary based on exceeding a performance threshold rapidly become intrusive and distracting. To be acceptable to a student, the tutor must offer a dialogue, not a collection of repetitive or disconnected utterances.

• We wanted to structure dialogues in the tutor to reflect those often used by instructors that we had observed. One common technique was to give the student just enough information to allow him or her to make a correction without giving too much away. For example, "Check your depth" allows the student to diagnose the problem and correct it, while "Apply upward thrust" allows the student to correct the deviation without realizing what was wrong or how the situation arose.

• Multiple deviations can occur simultaneously or in rapid succession. Coaching responses must be coordinated to avoid a cacophony of suggestions and feedback.

• Behavior that is questionable at one moment may be entirely appropriate in other circumstances. An obvious example is the difference in the primary maneuvering goals during hover (stay motionless) and transit (make steady progress toward the destination). The mix of the coaches must vary as the task progresses.

The verbal coaching implementation must allow for the authoring and tuning of tutor behavior in light of these considerations. We have developed a theoretical framework and implementation that monitors violations and the student's response to corrective feedback over time. Follow-up feedback to uncorrected problems becomes increasingly specific, and multiple simultaneous violations are managed by establishing priorities among the violations so that feedback triggered by multiple problems is not interleaved. The framework defines a collection of coaching agents focused on particular performance features, imposes a common dialogue structure on the feedback generated by these agents, and incorporates a multi-threaded control structure to coordinate the activity of the agents.

4 Sensors and Coaches

Sensors provide a mechanism for monitoring student performance during a practice session. They act as instrumentation on the simulation to provide information needed by the coaches. They are also the basis for curriculum decisions that control progress through a sequence of scenarios and the source for the student assessment provided during the review stage of a trial. Sensors track properties of the mission scenario as it unfolds and detect conditions that trigger coaching responses to situations as they arise. Sensors have direct access to control movements and other control panel inputs, the status of the ROV (x, y, z, heading, and velocity), simulated time, collisions, and inputs from the student in the form of button presses or simple speech commands. The output of sensors can be recorded for later analysis, monitored with respect to a threshold, and have other properties derived from it.

The following sensors are currently used by the tutor:
• *Path Sensor*—horizontal deviation from a prescribed path.
• *Depth Sensor*—vertical deviation from a prescribed path.
• *Bearing Sensor*—angular deviation between ROV heading and bearing to target.
• *Hover Sensor*—distance to a prescribed hover point in 3-D space.
• *Progress Sensor*—rate of motion with respect to a prescribed path.
• *Control (Smoothness) Sensor*—variance of the commanded thrust.
• *Collision Sensor*—collisions with the sea floor or other objects.

Similarly, a coach uses one or more sensors to monitor a particular aspect of the student's maneuvering. The coach's interaction with the student follows a "correction" template, which captures a common type of interaction observed between human tutors and their students [6].

A coach is defined as a linear sequence of actions. It first alerts the student to the type of the error ("What's your heading?"). If, after a time, the error goes uncorrected, the coach tells the student the specific nature of the error ("Your heading is drifting to the right."). If, after another interval, the error continues unabated, the coach finally tells the student exactly how to remedy the error ("Twist left 5 degrees."). All the while, the coach is checking to see if the student corrects the problem. If this occurs, the coach first acknowledges the student's response and then restarts itself after a refractory period.

Coaches are tied into the phase structure of the mission; each phase has its own possible student deviations and so has its own set of coaches to help the student correct them. The control structure manages transitions between the phases by shutting down one set of coaches and activating another. The tutor author specifies how phase transitions are to be detected and which coaches should be active for each phase.

Although our primary emphasis has been on how to provide unsolicited coaching for a student in trouble, we also allow the student to ask for help directly. Currently, the student can ask these four general questions:

- *Where am I?*—Show a God's eye view of the scene.
- *What should I be doing?*—Describe the current goal.
- *How do I do it?*—Describe what actions to take and what information is needed to achieve the current goal.
- *Tell me more?*—Elaborate the most recent coaching message.

5   Defining a Coaching Agent

To provide versatility in defining verbal coaching dialogues, a multi-threaded control mechanism was implemented along with a set of process primitives to allow parallel execution and non-local returns from within executing process threads. Using these primitives allowed coaching agents to be defined separately while at the same time establishing interdependencies to be maintained during their execution. In addition, coaching agents can be nested; that is, agents can spawn sub-agents and still retain control of the overall flow of the coaching activity.

Defining a coach consists of writing a sequence of actions or condition-action pairs that execute in sequence. Two special types of primitive actions mediate the simultaneous execution of multiple coaches. The primitive action `race`, borrowed from the ACTOR language [7], spawns multiple threads of execution and terminates when any one of its spawned threads terminates:

```
race <coach1> <coach2> ...
```

The following family of primitive actions pause execution of their thread until a condition is satisfied:

```
wait <duration>
wait-for <condition>
wait-until <duration> <condition>
```

The action `wait` simply pauses for the specified `<duration>`; the action `wait-for` pauses until the specified `<condition>` becomes true; the action

`wait-until` pauses until the specified `<condition>` remains true for the `<du-`
`ration>`.

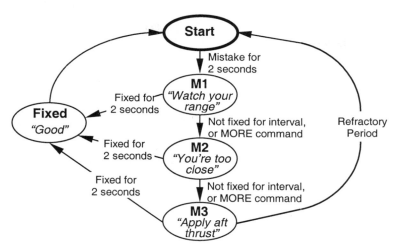

Fig. 2. Finite State Machine representation of the "Maintain Range" coach, which is active
during the orbit phase.

A typical coach definition is shown in Figure 2 as a Finite State Machine. This
coach is used to monitor the range of the ROV to the target during the orbit phase.
When activated (**Start**) it will "wait-until" a triggering condition holds, in this case,
the range sensor going above the sensor threshold for a minimum time. Once triggered, it outputs the first level coaching message (**M1**), and then enters a "race" to
detect either a corrective action, an interval during which the triggering condition
remains unrectified, or a button press asking for more information. In the first case
the coach acknowledges the correction (**Fixed**) and resumes monitoring (**Start**). In
the latter two cases, it outputs the next coaching message (**M2**); and similarly the third
level coaching message (**M3**). After the final message, the coach enters a refractory
period before it resumes monitoring.

The same parallel control structure has proved to be valuable for managing multiple simultaneous coaches during the practice stage of a trial. For example, a portion
of the definition for the orbit phase is shown in Figure 3. It instantiates three coaches,
assigning each a priority, an interval to pause between coaching levels, and an associated sensor. The coaches remain active until the phase terminates; i.e., the orbit is
completed or the student quits. A coach in any state will be interrupted when a higher
priority coach is triggered. In this case, the lower priority coach enters a dormant
state until the interrupting coach completes. Then, after a global refractory period, all
coaches are reset to their initial state (**Start**).

```
(race
  (run-coaches
    (maintain-target-view-coach high    10
      (orbit-bearing-sensor))
    (maintain-range-coach         medium 12
      (orbit-range-sensor))
    (maintain-depth-coach         low     8
      (orbit-depth-sensor)))
  (wait-for (orbit-complete? (orbit-bearing-sensor)))
  (wait-for (quit-button-pressed)))
```

Fig. 3. Typical phase definition

These examples illustrate several temporal parameters that have been found helpful for adjusting the behavior of the verbal coaching to make it more effective and acceptable by students. Collectively they control the intrusiveness and sense of urgency associated with the coaching. The parameters include:

• *Interval between successive levels of coaching within a single coach.* The coach's correction template defines a progression of utterances containing increasingly specific advice to the student. A parameter determines the amount of time the coach waits for a corrective response after each utterance. For the maneuvering task, coaches allow the student about 10 seconds to respond before offering the next piece of advice.

• *Interval between successive activations of a single coach.* To avoid appearing to harp, each coach enters a refractory period after it has finished. For the maneuvering task, a coach cannot be triggered again for about 7 seconds.

• *Interval between successive utterances regardless of their source.* To avoid too many interruptions in general, a global refractory period was added that inhibits *any* coaching for 5 seconds after a coach has finished, regardless of its source.

Other parameters are defined for each coach which convey its apparent seriousness or importance to the student:

• *Priority.* A scalar parameter assigned to each coach determines whether one coach can interrupt another. Once a coach has been triggered, it "keeps the floor" until it terminates; i.e., it becomes the sole discourse focus. Coaches with lower priorities cannot break into the sequence of coaching defined for the active coach. However, if a condition appears that triggers a higher priority coach, it effectively grabs the focus by terminating the active coach. For example, keeping the target in view when orbiting is more important than maintaining the proper distance and depth.

• *Leniency.* In theory, the condition under which a coach is triggered can be an arbitrarily complex function of the student's performance. In practice, simpler functions tend to be preferred since they are more easily computed and more easily understood by the student. Typically a sensor associated with each coach continuously monitors the simulation and computes derived values that are compared against predefined bounds. To this is added a "grace period," the amount of time a sensor value must be out of bounds before triggering the coach. For example, during orbiting the "Maintain Range" coach is triggered when the student drifts 2 meters closer or farther from the target for more than 2 seconds.

The values for these parameters have been derived empirically, starting from a priori estimates and refined through user feedback, evaluation by expert pilots, and our ongoing experience with the tutor. User validation and software verification continue to be critical activities in developing an effective and acceptable verbal coaching capability.

Currently, all parameter values are fixed for the duration of a session. This does not preclude incorporating adaptive changes as our theory of how to manage these details of verbal coaching matures. The tutor might adjust the priority and the leniency of a coach based on the level of mastery of the student; e.g., to lower the priority of well learned skills (thus shifting the training focus to weaker skills), or to lower the leniency (thus "raising the bar" and urging the student toward higher standards of performance). For novices, the tutor might turn some coaches off altogether in order to focus on a few key skills at a time.

6 Lessons Learned

Our experience with the verbal coaching scheme has led to the following additional qualitative suggestions for integrating verbal coaching in a tutor:

• *Discourse cues*. Two situations arise during the corrective verbal coaching that benefit from special verbal cues:

a) *Acknowledgement*. Whenever the student corrects the problem, the coach utters an acknowledgement of the form "Good. You have..." This signals the end of the interaction with that activation of the coach.

b) *Interruption*. Whenever a higher priority coach interrupts an active coach, it precedes its first-level advice (stating the problem) with the phrase, "New problem." This signals the end of the interaction with the interrupted coach and the introduction of another.

• *Short utterances*. Brief coaching messages are less intrusive than lengthy ones. The correction template in Figure 2 provides an example of how to decompose coaching feedback into smaller statements. The student's ability to ask for elaboration or clarification (using the *Tell Me More* command) provides some control of when and how much information is delivered.

• *Recorded speech*. Despite advances in speech generation and text-to-speech technology, our subjects prefer the natural quality of pre-recorded speech. We continue to use recorded speech fragments wherever possible.

• *Simultaneous visual cues*. When a coach is triggered, the visual cues associated with being able to recognize and correct the problem are highlighted during the coach's initial utterance. For example, on hearing "What's your heading?" the student simultaneously sees the compass and target bearing indicators illuminate. This is meant to suggest that by paying increased attention to these information sources the student will be better able to detect and correct deviations.

• *Corrections*. In response to suggestions from our expert advisors, we added an additional layer of monitoring to each of the coaches in order to detect two prevalent types of novice reaction to errors: over-correction ("Too far!") and reverse-correction

("Wrong way!"). There is a cost to this second layer of coaching, however. Adding conditions to the set of situations being monitored by a coach requires careful tuning in order to balance the timeliness of a coach's response against its confidence in interpreting the subject's actions. For example, waiting to see if the pilot will over-correct requires delaying the response to *any* correction, including a good one.

7 Future Work

The verbal coaching machinery we have developed can be extended to include additional features of natural instructional dialogues. The correction template can be enhanced to include other parts of the discourse context:

• *Pedagogical context.* It is useful instructionally to connect feedback to prior examples of the same class of error, in order to emphasize recurring errors or situations; e.g., "You're too low *again*." [8] [9]

• *Control context.* The shift in focus required when one coach interrupts another could be made less abrupt by explicitly acknowledging the status of the other currently active coaches: e.g., "Forget your depth, you're about to collide with that mine!"

New classes of templates can also be defined. For example, a control template actively talks the student through a maneuver; e.g., "Get ready to stop...OK, ease back on the stick now...not too much...good."

We have concentrated on the micro-structure of natural coaching utterances, but need to devote similar resources to the macro-structure. A cross-session mechanism for dynamically tailoring the selection of a suite of coaches and priority assignments according to the student's abilities or preferences needs to be developed and tested. For example, since we already suggest a training focus for each trial based on prior performance, we could limit the coaching interactions to skills associated with that single focus. Furthermore, a mechanism for the student to verbally acknowledge awareness of a coached problem would prevent subsequent redundant messages and provide a greater sense of dialogue with the coach.

We have shown how a general verbal coaching paradigm has contributed to the instructional effectiveness and reconfigurability of an ITS in a real-time task. The style and format of the coaching was driven largely by observations of expert pilots and instructors. Preliminary transfer experiments on the overall effectiveness of the maneuvering tutor are reported in [10]. Further study is planned to refine the coaching parameters and policies. TRANSoM's coaching template framework could be adapted for use in training systems in other real-time maneuvering tasks, such as piloting unmanned aerial vehicles, submarine navigation, or flight simulators. Implementation of coaching interactions for situation awareness tasks such as searching for underwater objects while avoiding tether entanglements is underway. We plan to use a variety of verbal probes to solicit information about the quality of the student's mental model of his or her surroundings.

8 Acknowledgements

The authors wish to acknowledge the contributions of the entire TRANSoM team: Dick Pew, Yvette Tenney and Jason Vantomme (BBN); Stewart Harris, Barbara Fletcher, and Jason Fritz (Imetrix); Nat Durlach, David Zeltzer, Johnny Yoon, Jonathan Pfautz and David Manowitz (MIT); Bruce Perrin, Barbara Barnett, Jim Curtin, and Katja Helbing (Boeing); Sandy Katz and Jenny Hwang (LRDC). This work was sponsored under the Office of Naval Research contract N00014-95-C-0181. Terry Allard and Harold Hawkins at ONR deserve special thanks for their continuing support.

References

1. Collins, A., Brown, J.S., Newman, S.E.: Cognitive Apprenticeship: Teaching the Craft of Reading, Writing and Mathematics. In: Resnick, L.B. (ed.): Cognition and Instruction: Issues and Agendas. Lawrence Erlbaum Associates, Hillsdale, NJ (1987).
2. Lesgold, A., LaJoie, S., Bunzo, M., Eggan, G.: SHERLOCK: A Coached Practice Environment for an Electronics Troubleshooting Job. University of Pittsburgh Learning Research and Development Center, Pittsburgh, PA (1988).
3. Pioch, N.J., Roberts, B., Zeltzer, D.: A Virtual Environment for Learning to Pilot Remotely Operated Vehicles. Proceedings of the International Conference on Virtual Systems and Multimedia 1997. IEEE Computer Society Press, Los Alamitos, CA (1997).
4. Ritter, F., Feurzeig, W.: Teaching Real-Time Tactical Thinking. In: Psotka, J., Massey, L.D., Mutter, S.A. (eds.): Intelligent Tutoring Systems: Lessons Learned. Lawrence Erlbaum Associates, Hillsdale, NJ (1988).
5. Eliot, C., Woolf, B.P.: Reasoning about the User within a Simulation-based Real-time Training System. Proceedings of the Fourth International Conference on User Modeling. The MITRE Corporation, Bedford, MA (1994).
6. Freedman, R.: Using Tutoring Patterns to Generate More Cohesive Text in an Intelligent Tutoring System. Proceedings of the Second International Conference on the Learning Sciences. Evanston, IL (1996).
7. Agha, G.: Actors: A Model of Concurrent Computation in Distributed Systems. MIT Press, Cambridge, MA (1986).
8. Moore, J.D.: Indexing and Exploiting a Discourse History to Generate Context-Sensitive Explanations. Proceedings of the DARPA Human Language Technology Workshop. Morgan Kaufmann Publishers, Princeton, NJ (1993).
9. Rosenblum, J., Moore, J.: Participating in Instructional Dialogues: Finding and Exploiting Relevant Prior Explanations. Proceedings of World Conference on Artificial Intelligence and Education. Edinburgh, Scotland (1993).
10. Fletcher, B.: TRANSoM ROV Pilot Training: Test Results. Underwater Intervention '98 Conference Proceedings, Marine Technology Society, Washington, D.C. (1998).

Successful Use of an Expert System to Teach Diagnostic Reasoning for Antibody Identification

Philip J. Smith, Jodi Heinz Obradovich, Stephanie A. Guerlain, Sally Rudmann, Patricia Strohm, Jack W. Smith, John Svirbely, Larry Sachs

Cognitive Systems Engineering Laboratory, The Ohio State University
210 Baker Systems, 1971 Neil Avenue, Columbus OH 43210-1271
Phil+@osu.edu

Abstract. A previously reported study indicated that, when used by an instructor as a tool to assist with tutoring in a class laboratory setting, use of the Transfusion Medicine Tutor (TMT) resulted in improvements in antibody identification performance of 87-93% (p<.001). Based on input from teachers requesting that TMT be designed for use without the presence of an instructor, a new study on the use of TMT without instructor assistance found that performance improved by 64-66% (p<.001). Finally, based on the results of these two studies, TMT was mailed to 7 sites for beta-testing. In exchange for a free copy of the kit, the instructors (and their students) were asked to fill out questionnaires. Results of these questionnaires are summarized.

1 Introduction

This research project, involving the design, development, and empirical evaluation of a computer-based tutoring system, was highly interdisciplinary in scope, requiring consideration of aspects of artificial intelligence (specifically, expert systems), education, psychology, and human factors engineering, as well as the domain of study (i.e., allo-antibody identification).

More specifically, the focus of this project has not been on the invention of new features for an underlying expert system, although two especially interesting forms of expertise have been noted in the development of the system:

1. The use of initial data to form an abstract model of the solution in order to decompose the task into simpler subproblems ("It looks like I have a two antibody problem with one antibody accounting for these reactions and a second accounting for the others");

2. The use of self-directed models of potential errors ("In a situation like this, it's likely I erroneously ruled out a weakly reacting antibody") to direct attention when an impasse has been reached [1].

Thus, from the perspective of advancing the design of the expert systems underlying tutoring systems, the project is primarily an application that helps to demonstrate that a rule-based system can provide an efficient means of encoding domain expertise, and can do so with sufficient completeness to cope with the varieties of interactions encountered when used in actual instructional settings.

What the project does focus on is the integration of interface design concepts (providing an interface that not only is unobtrusive in collecting data about the student's thought processes, but that in fact makes performance by the user easier because of the embedded perceptual and memory aids) with instructional design strategies, such as the use of part-task training and scaffolding, and the presentation of instructional messages that generalize based on the specific error made by a student in order to teach him/her how to deal with the broader class of relevant knowledge.   In short, the major research question has been: What is required to successfully integrate expert systems technology into an effective instructional and interface environment that teachers and students want to use, and that results in significant learning?

Below, the domain of study is briefly described in terms of its abstract characteristics. Then TMT is described and the underlying design principles are listed. Finally, the results of empirical studies of its use are presented.

2 Antibody Identification as a Testbed

Antibody identification is a laboratory task where medical technologists must run a series of tests to determine the antibodies in a patient's blood. It has the classical characteristics of an abduction task, including masking and problems with noisy data.

2.1 The Antibody Identification Procedure

In going from raw data to a diagnostic conclusion, blood bankers must call upon a large body of factual knowledge, apply strategies that have either been taught or derived from past experience, and make hypotheses and predictions to help them through the problem-solving process [1].

2.2 Expert Strategies

Studies by Smith et al. [1] have shown that, like experts studied in other medical domains, expert blood bankers try to sort out which antibodies are causing the reactions by recognizing typical reaction patterns and making early hypotheses upon which to base further analyses. In order to minimize the chance for an incomplete or incorrect diagnosis and to protect against human error and the fallibility of the heuristic methods, the expert blood banker also tries to collect independent, converging evidence to both confirm the presence of hypothesized antibodies and to rule out all others. Thus, there is a high level of skill involved in knowing how to combine various problem-solving strategies such that the overall protocol is likely to succeed.

3 The Design of TMT

Based on studies of the expert strategies and erroneous/inefficient strategies found to be used in this domain, as well as studies of current teaching methods, TMT was designed as a coaching system [2-11]. TMT uses a rule-based system to monitor the student's actions for evidence of errors and provides feedback if errors are detected. To help ensure use of this strategy, TMT monitors for both errors of commission and errors of omission. The types of knowledge encoded into the system include detecting:

1) Errors of commission (due to slips or mistakes):
   - Errors in ruling out antibodies.
2) Errors of omission (due to slips or mistakes):
   - Failure to rule out an antibody for which there was evidence to do so.
   - Failure to rule out all clinically significant antibodies besides the antibodies included in the answer set.
   - Failure to confirm that the patient did not have an auto-immune disorder (i.e., antibodies directed against the antigens present on their own red blood cells).
   - Failure to confirm that the patient was capable of forming the antibodies in the answer set (i.e., that the patient's blood was negative for the corresponding antigens, a requirement for forming antibodies in the first place if the possibility of an auto-immune disorder has been ruled out).
3) Errors due to masking:
   - Failure to detect and consider potentially masked antibodies.
4) Errors due to noisy data:
   - Failure to detect situations where the quality of the data was questionable.
5) Data unlikely given answer (low probability of data given hypothesis):
   - Failure to account for all reactions.
   - Inconsistency between the answers given and the types of reactions usually exhibited by those antibodies (e.g., that a warm temperature antibody was accounting for reactions in cold temperatures)
6) Unlikely answers according to prior probabilities (regardless of the available evidence)
   - Antibody combinations that are extremely unlikely due to the way the human immune system works.

3.1 Design Strategy

As reported in a previous paper [12], based on the literature, several design principles were used to guide the design of TMT:

Principle 1. If the goal is to offer students an opportunity to actively apply relevant knowledge and develop important problem-solving skills, provide a problem-solving environment that allows them to integrate this declarative knowledge into the procedural knowledge that they need to develop.

Principle 2.   Use expert systems technology to efficiently provide students with immediate, context sensitive feedback or critiques as they perform the problem-solving tasks.

Principle 3.   Design a user interface that allows the expert system to unobtrusively collect data on the student's reasoning during the problem-solving tasks, thus allowing the computer to give immediate, context-sensitive feedback.

Principle 4.   Design the system to support rather than replace the teacher.

Principle 5.   If appropriate, decompose a complex task into subtasks, and teach the subtasks first.

Principle 6.   Use a mixture of proactive and reactive teaching methods to teach and reinforce the student's knowledge.

Details on the application of these principles to the design of TMT can be found in [12].

4 Previously Reported Findings: TMT with Instructor Assistance

In a previous paper [12], an empirical evaluation of TMT was reported in which it was used in a classroom lab setting *with an instructor present* to supplement the tutoring provided by the computer. That study is reviewed here, before presenting new work.   In that study, thirty students in the medical technology program at a major U. S. university were tested on TMT. These students were college juniors and had completed the didactic portion of their immunohematology coursework and an associated student lab, but had not yet begun their clinical rotation. The study was conducted at a university where the staff had not been involved in the development of the system.

Since a major goal of this instructional system is to teach antibody identification, a major test is whether the students learn effectively from it. This previous study collected data on two groups of students using the Transfusion Medicine Tutor. The Treatment Group received a version of TMT with all of the intelligent functions turned on, use of a Checklist, the Reference Manual, and *access to instructor assistance*; while the Control Group used a version of the system with the immediate intelligent feedback turned off and with no other support except for the end-of-case summaries.

A within-subjects analysis (using McNemar's chi square test) of the students' performance in the Treatment Group showed a significant ($p < 0.001$) improvement in performance (an improvement of 87%) from the pre-test case to a matched post-test case (Post-test Case 1). Students in the Control Group showed a 20% reduction in errors that was not significant from the pre-test to post-test Case 1 ($p > 0.05$).

Between-subject analysis using Fisher's Exact Test results showed that there was no significant difference in the misidentification rates on the Pre-test case for the Control and Treatment Groups ($p = 0.50$). However, analysis showed a significant difference in performance on each of the post-test cases between the two groups ($p < 0.005$). On Post-test Case 1, subjects in the Treatment Group had a misidentification rate of 13% (2 out of 15 incorrectly identified the antibodies present) while subjects in the Control Group had a misidentification rate of 73% (11 out of 15 students incorrectly identified the antibodies present) ($p=0.0013$).   On Post-test Case 2, students in the Treatment Group had a 7% misidentification rate (1 out of 15 students incorrectly identified the antibodies present), while students in the Control Group had a 73% misidentification rate (11 out of 15 students incorrectly identified the antibodies present) (p=0.0002). Thus, something about the Treatment Group (the use of intelligent tutoring, the checklist, the reference manual and/or instructor assistance) produced a sizable and statistically significant improvement in performance. (Additional details are available in [12]).

5 New Findings: TMT without Instructor Assistance

In this new study, a within subjects design was used to study the effectiveness of TMT as a stand alone tutoring system.

5.1 Subjects

Thirty-six students in Medical Technology Programs at three major U. S. universities were tested on TMT. These students were college juniors and had completed the didactic portion of their immunohematology coursework and an associated student lab. Thus, they were similar to the students in the previous study, except that they were attending different schools. The staff at these universities had not been involved in the development of the system.

5.2 Experimental Design

The students completed five lessons; each of the first four lessons consisted of subtasks involved in solving a complete case. Lessons 1 - 4 each had four to six subtasks to solve. The fifth lesson, Complete Cases, consisted of solving complete patient cases, and included the use of all the subtasks covered in the first four lessons, along with more global strategies for gathering converging evidence to test hypotheses. All of the participants saw the lessons and test cases in the same order, with the exception of the pre-test case and the post-test case, which were randomized with respect to their order of use for each student. The students were allowed to work at their own pace and the entire study took no more than 4 1/2 hours to complete, with most students finishing in approximately 4 hours.

Interface training. In order for the participants to interact as efficiently as possible with the computer, they were introduced to the interface by viewing a 10 minute video while they sat at a computer with TMT running. The video ran through the interface functions available with TMT, instructing them to perform specific actions using TMT. The video did not review any problem-solving strategies. It simply reviewed use of the interface.

Pre-Test. Following the interface training the participants were asked to solve a case, a "pre-test," that did not contain any intelligent tutoring. This case was used to provide a benchmark, allowing the researcher to determine a student's overall level of understanding of the task of antibody identification prior to any training using TMT. The purpose of this pre-test case was explained to the students, and they were encouraged to do their best work.

Lessons. Following the pretest case, the students completed five lessons. Each of the first four lessons consisted of subtasks involved in solving a complete case. The fifth lesson allowed the students to work on complete cases. While completing these lessons, the students had access to the following resources:

Checklist. In addition to the immediate, context-sensitive tutoring provided by the computer, the students in the Treatment Group were given a paper checklist that made explicit the high-level goal structure that guided the expert system's error detection and tutoring.

Reference Manual. The students also received a manual consisting of a concise set of the underlying rules used by TMT when tutoring students. The Reference Manual was meant to be used by the students when they needed a more in-depth explanation of the rules and procedures than was provided by the Checklist.

Post-Test Case. Following Lesson 5 (Complete Cases), a "post-test" case was given to all students in order to assess each student's overall level of competence on the material just taught. This case was one of two cases matched in characteristics. This post-test case was randomly selected for each subject from one of the two "matched" cases, the other of which was used as the pre-test case. These two cases were matched in that the original testing panel seems to indicate that only one antibody is present, but in actuality, two different antibodies are together accounting for the reactions. For the post-test case, the intelligence was turned off.

Debriefing. A questionnaire was administered to each student to gather additional demographic data (including the student's age, gender, and previous computer experience), to assess the students' subjective reactions to TMT and its various functions, and to elicit suggestions for improvement in its design and use. For brevity, however, those results are not reported here.

Data Collection.   The computer system logged all of the student's actions, including final answers. In order to better understand the problem-solving strategies and the errors made by the student (and the possible misconceptions underlying those errors), computer logs for each student were analyzed and coded for certain key behaviors.

5.3 Results

A between-subjects analysis was done on the results for each of the three universities to determine whether there were any significant differences among the three groups which would prevent us from combining the results of the data from the three schools. No significant differences were detected, so the data sets were merged for later analysis. Using McNemar's Chi Square test for a within-subjects analysis, a significant reduction in errors (from 80% wrong on the pre-test to 13.9% on the post-test) was found from the Pre-Test Case to the matched Post-Test Case ($p < 0.001$) for these students.

Thus, as measured in this manner, the use of TMT (along with the associated checklist and reference manual) was quite effective even without instructor assistance.

Classes of Errors.   In order to better understand the impact of the Treatment condition on learning for the students in Study 2, the computer logs were used to identify error frequencies for four classes of errors (1. Ruling out correct answer due to ruling out incorrectly; 2. Failure to rule out when appropriate; 3. Failure to collect converging evidence; 4. Failure to check for consistency of data with answer). A within-subjects analysis (using McNemar's chi square test) of the students' end-of-case errors showed a significant (p < 0.001) reduction in errors on Errors 2, 3 and 4 from the pre-test case to the matched post-test case. Thus, the tutoring provided to students in this study appeared to be effective in significantly reducing some of the errors that the computer detected immediately after the student marked a final answer for a case.

6 Beta-Testing

Following completion of the two studies described above, copies of the TMT "kit" (software, video, checklist, user's manual and reference manual) were sent to seven medical technology programs around the country. (Several of these programs were hospital-based and teach only 2-3 students at a time.) A cover letter was included that described the purpose of TMT, and that asked the instructor if he/she would consider using the system on a trial basis. The instructor was told that in exchange for a free copy of the kit, we would appreciate it if he/she would return questionnaires for the instructor and the students after its use.

6.1 Objectives

The goal of this study was to determine whether TMT could and would be used in a setting where the designers were not present to assist or motivate the instructor, and to solicit subjective evaluations of its use in such a setting.

6.2 Procedure

A kit containing the software, video, checklist, user's manual and reference manual was sent to each of seven medical technology programs. These materials were the same as those described in the study above, except that the video was redone so that it not only introduced the interface, but that it did so by running through a complete, correct analysis of a full patient case. Thus, the video provided an introduction to the problem-solving strategies taught by TMT.

The cover letter indicated that TMT could be used in a classroom setting or for stand alone instruction. It also indicated that studies had found use of TMT in both settings to result in significant learning, but that the most effective use appeared to be in a classroom lab setting with the instructor present.

If they chose to use TMT, the instructors and students were asked to fill out short questionnaires following its use.

6.3 Results

Results from all seven programs are summarized below.

Instructors. On an ordinal scale with levels of Strongly Disagree, Disagree, Neutral, Agree and Strongly Agree, responses by the 7 instructors to a subset of the rating questions asked are summarized below.

This tutorial provided a useful teaching strategy: 2 Agree; 5 Strongly Agree

The software was easy to use: 1 Disagree; 2 Agree; 4 Strongly Agree

I would like to incorporate this tutorial into my classroom: 4 Agree; 3 Strongly
  Agree.

Responses to open-ended questions indicated that 6 of the 7 instructors chose to use TMT to provide stand alone instruction, without the instructor present. The 7th used in it a classroom lab setting. Comments about its use included (the range of positive and negative comments are listed):

"It's appropriate for their level of knowledge"

"A good review of information"

"Makes the student think logically"

"I liked that it thoroughly covered antigen/antibody identification"

"This is a great program for the student who is not strong"

"It doesn't have the ability to resume where you left off"

"I am very pleased with TMT and look forward to using it in the future."

Students. Responses by the 23 students to a subset of the rating questions asked are summarized below.

The program was easy to use: 3 Disagree; 3 Neutral; 9 Agree; 8 Strongly Agree

I learned a great deal from the program: 2 Disagree; 2 Neutral; 14 Agree; 5
  Strongly Agree

I would recommend this program to other students: 1 Disagree; 3 Neutral; 10
  Agree; 9 Strongly Agree

A representative set of comments to open-ended questions includes:

"[I liked that it] led you step by step through identification procedures"

"It introduced many small details about the procedure and helped
    you remember them"

"[I didn't like] having to correlate the video with the tutorial"

"The case studies were very helpful for practicing for exams for the
    class and the boards"

"I was confused at first on how to run the program, which buttons
    to push"

"[I didn't like] a separate manual from the computer program"

"It was thorough and was a great help in my understanding of
    blood bank"

"It was easy to click on rule outs for the panels"

"Good review and useful scenarios"

"Comments were too negative when errors were made. Positive
    reinforcement would be nice"

As with the instructors, note that most of these comments focus on and are very positive regarding the content and the instructional strategy with the exception of one ("Comments were too negative when errors were made"). The remaining comments deal with interface design.

7 Conclusion

The results of these studies suggest that a principled and multi-disciplinary approach to design can lead to the successful development of an effective computer-based tutoring system. Broadly speaking, our conclusions are the following:

1. Expert systems technology offers an efficient and successful approach for helping to teach problem-solving skills like antibody identification.

2. The successful use of this technology is critically dependent on:

   a. The design of an interface that unobtrusively obtains data on the student's thought processes, so that context-sensitive feedback can be provided. (Of particular significance in this regard is the provision of memory and perceptual aids that, in the process of helping the user to more easily accomplish his/her task, also serve to encourage the user to provide the computer with a rich set of data about the user's intermediate thought processes);

   b. Selection of effective teaching strategies in which to embed the use of the technology (a problem-based curriculum; part-task instruction; proactive as well as reactive teaching);

   c. Careful design of the target material (identification of effective problem-solving strategies and structuring of knowledge) to be taught.

More specifically, the studies indicate that, even without the presence of an instructor to supplement the tutoring provided by TMT, use of the system resulted in significant learning. Given this is an often cited benefit from the use of such technology (and one that instructors in this domain specifically noted as highly desirable), such empirical support for the stand-alone use of such an educational tool is important.

References

1.   Smith. P.J., Smith, J.W., Svirbely, J.R., Galdes, D.K., Fraser, J., Rudmann, S., Miller, T.E., Balzina, J., and Kennedy, M. (1991). Coping with the complexities of multiple-solution problems: A case study. *International Journal of Man-Machine Studies*, 35, 429-453.

2.   Albanese, M. and Mitchell, S. (1993). Problem-based learning: A review of literature on its outcomes and implementation issues. Academic Medicine, 68, 52-81.

3.   Anderson, J.R. (1984). Cognitive psychology and intelligent tutoring. Proceedings of the Cognitive Science Society Conference. Boulder, Colorado, Lawrence Erlbaum Associates, Inc., 37-43.4.

4.   Brown, J.S. & Burton, R.R. (1978). Reactive learning environments for teaching electronic troubleshooting. In Rouse, W.B. (Ed.), Advances in man-machine systems research. Greenwich, Connecticut: JAI Press

5.   Burton, R.R. (1982). Diagnosing bugs in a simple procedural skill. In D. Sleeman and J.S. Brown (Eds.), Intelligent tutoring systems. London: Academic Press, Inc., 157-184.

6.   Collins, A., Brown, J.S., & Newman, S.E. (1989). Cognitive apprenticeship:

Teaching the crafts of reading, writing and mathematics. In L. B. Resnick (Ed.), Knowing, learning, and instruction. Hillsdale, N.J.:   Lawrence Erlbaum

7.   Corbett, A.T. & Anderson, J.R. (1992). LISP intelligent tutoring system: Research in skill acquisition. In J.H. Larkin, R.W. Chabay, & C. Sheftic (Eds.), Computer-assisted instruction and intelligent tutoring systems: Shared goals and complementary approaches. Hillsdale, N.J.: Lawrence Erlbaum Associates, Inc., 73-109.

8.   Dempsey, J.V. and Sales, G.C. (Eds.) (1993). Interactive instruction and feedback. Englewood Cliffs, NJ: Educational Technology Publications.

9.   Gabrys, G., Weiner, A., & Lesgold, A. (1993). Learning by problem solving in a coached apprenticeship system In M. Rabinowitz (Ed.), Cognitive science foundations of instruction. Hillsdale, NJ: Lawrence Erlbaum Associates

10.   Lajoie, S.P., & Lesgold, A.M. (1989). Apprenticeship training in the workplace: Computer-coached practice environment as a new form of apprenticeship. Machine- Mediated Learning, 3, 7-28.

11.   VanLehn, K. (1996). Conceptual and Meta Learning during coached problem solving. In Frasson, Gauthier and Lesgold (eds.), Proceedings of the Third International Conference on Intelligent Tutoring Systems, 29-47.

12.   Obradovich, J., Smith, P.J. (1996). The Transfusion Medicine Tutor: Using expert systems technology to teach domain-specific problem-solving skills. In Frasson, Gauthier and Lesgold (eds.), Proceedings of the Third International Conference on Intelligent Tutoring Systems, 521-530.

Combatting Shallow Learning in a
Tutor for Geometry Problem Solving

Vincent Aleven, Kenneth R. Koedinger, H. Colleen Sinclair, and Jaclyn Snyder[*]

HCI Institute
School of Computer Science
Carnegie Mellon University

[*]Langley High School / Pittsburgh Public Schools
E-mail: aleven@cs.cmu.edu, koedinger@cs.cmu.edu, colleens+@andrew.cmu.edu,
jsnyder@pps.pgh.pa.us

Abstract. The PACT Geometry tutor has been designed, with guidance from mathematics educators, to be an integrated part of a complete, new-standards-oriented course for high-school geometry. We conducted a formative evaluation of the third "geometric properties" lesson and saw significant student learning gains. We also found that students were better able to provide numerical answers to problems than to articulate the reasons that are presumably involved in finding these answers. This suggests that students may provide answers using superficial (and possibly unreliable) visual associations rather than reason logically from definitions and conjectures. To combat this type of shallow learning, we are developing a new version of the tutor's third lesson, aimed at getting students to reason more deliberately with definitions and theorems as they work on geometry problems. In the new version, students are required to state a reason for their answers, which they can select from a Glossary of geometry definitions and theorems. We will conduct an experiment to test whether providing tutoring on reasoning will transfer to better performance on answer giving.

Introduction

A problem for many forms of instruction is that students may learn in a shallow way [Burton and Brown, 1982; Miller, *et al.*, submitted], acquiring knowledge that is sufficient to score reasonably well on some test items, but that does not transfer to novel situations. One manifestation of shallow learning is that students construct superficial domain heuristics that may allow them to solve some problems quite well, even though that "knowledge" is ultimately not correct. For instance, in the context of geometry, most students will learn how to find the measures of unknown quantities in diagrams. However, they may rely on the fact that certain quantities look equal rather than reason from geometric definitions and theorems. Such superficial perceptual strategies, enriched with some correct geometric knowledge, can be very serviceable and lead to correct solutions on many naturally-occurring problems. However, they fall short on more complex problems or when students are asked to discuss reasons for their answers.

Superficial strategies occur in many domains. In physics problems solving, consider a problem where students are asked to draw an acceleration vector for an elevator coming to a halt while going down. They often draw a downward arrow, assuming, incorrectly, that the acceleration has the same direction as the velocity. Also, when asked to categorize physics problems, novices tend to do so on the basis of surface level features, while experts use the deeper physics principles involved [Chi, *et al.*, 1981].

We can interpret the shallow learning problem within the ACT-R theory of cognition and learning [Anderson, 1993], as follows: In the ACT framework, learning a procedural skill means acquiring a set of production rules. Production rules are induced by analogy to prior experiences or examples. Superficial knowledge may result when students pay attention to the wrong features in those experiences or examples, features that may be readily available and interpreted, but that do not connect to deeper reasons. However, not much is known about what types of instruction are more likely or less likely to foster shallow learning.

Evaluations of cognitive tutors indicate that they can be significantly more effective than classroom instruction [Anderson, et al., 1995; Koedinger, et al., 1998]. In spite of this success, cognitive tutors (and other computer-based learning environments) may not be immune from the shallow learning problem. It is important to determine to what degree students come away with shallow knowledge, when they work with cognitive tutors. This may help to find out how these tutors can be designed to minimize shallow learning and be even more effective.

We study these issues in the context of the PACT Geometry Tutor, a cognitive tutor developed by our research group used in four schools in the Pittsburgh area. In a formative evaluation study, we found that the instructional approach of which the tutor is part, leads to significant learning gains. We also found evidence of a form of shallow learning: Students cannot always give a reason for their answers to geometry problems, even if the answer itself is correct. Such a reason would be, for example, a definition or theorem applied in calculating certain quantities in a diagram. We have redesigned the tutor in an attempt to remedy this kind of shallow learning. Currently, we are pilot-testing the new tutor.

In this paper, we give a brief overview of the PACT Geometry tutor. We present results from our formative evaluation study that motivated the redesign of the tutor. We describe how we have modified the tutor, and finally discuss why the changes may lead to a more effective tutor, in geometry and potentially also in other domains.

The PACT Geometry Tutor

The PACT Geometry Tutor was developed at the PACT Center at Carnegie Mellon University, as an adjunct to classroom instruction, in tandem with the PACT geometry curriculum, which covers high school geometry from a problem-solving perspective, consistent with the standards for mathematics instruction developed by the National Council of Teachers of Mathematics [NCTM, 1989]. The PACT Geometry Tutor is different from the earlier Geometry Proof Tutor [Anderson, 1993] and the ANGLE tutor [Koedinger and Anderson, 1993], reflecting changes in the geometry curriculum de-emphasizing the teaching of proof skills. As shown in Figure 1, the PACT Geometry tutor curriculum consists of four lessons (a fifth lesson on circle properties will be added soon), each divided into a number of sections. The topics in each section are introduced during classroom instruction. Students then use the tutor to work through problems, proceeding at their own pace. Usually, students spend 40% of classroom time solving problems on the computer.

The PACT Geometry Tutor provides intelligent assistance as students work on geometry problems, aimed at making sure that students successfully complete problems and that students are assigned problems that are appropriate to their skill level. In each problem, students are presented with a geometry diagram and are asked to calculate the measures of some of the quantities in the diagram, as is illustrated in Figure 2, which shows the tutor interface. The problem statement and diagram are presented in separate windows on the top left and top right, respectively. The tutor has a store of 56 problems for lesson 3.

Lesson 1. Area
1. Area of parallelograms
2. Area of triangle
3. Area of trapezoid
4. Area of circle
5. Area

Lesson 2. Pythagorean Theorem
1. Square & square root
2. Pythagorean Theorem
3. 45-45-90 right triangle
4. 30-60-90 right triangle
5. Pythagorean & area Problem

Lesson 3. Angles
1. Angles
   Linear pair angles
   Vertical angles
   Complementary angles
   Supplementary angles
   Angle addition
   Angle Subtraction

   Triple angles sum
   Linear pair formula
   Vertical angles formula
   Complementary angles formula
   Supplementary angles formula
2. Angle associated with triangles
   Triangle sum
   Isosceles triangle, base angle
   Isosceles triangle, vertex angle
   Exterior angle of triangle
   Interior angle of triangle
   Equilateral triangle
3. Parallel lines
   Corresponding angles
   Alternate exterior angles
   Alternate interior angles
   Supplementary interior angles

Lesson 4. Similar triangles
1. Similar triangles

Fig. 1. PACT Geometry tutor curriculum, organized by lessons, sections, and skills.

Students enter answers in the Table Tool, a spreadsheet-like device shown on the left, second window from the top. The table cells correspond to the key quantities in the problem, such as the givens, the target quantities, or intermediate steps. As students enter values into the table, they receive immediate feedback indicating whether their answer is correct or not. When students are stuck, they can ask for hints, which the tutor presents in a separate Messages window (see Figure 2, left, third window from the top). The hints become more specific as students repeat their request for help. Students can move on to the next problem only when they have entered correct values for all quantities in the table.

The Diagram Tool presents an abstract version of the problem diagram (Figure 2, bottom right) with cells for students to record the measures of angles, as one often does when solving geometry problems on paper. This makes it easier for students to relate the quantities in the problem to the entities in the diagram and to keep track of information. For problems that involve difficult arithmetic operations, students can use the Equation Solver (not shown, see [Ritter and Anderson, 1995]), a tool which helps students to solve equations step-by-step.

Finally, the PACT Geometry Tutor provides a skillometer, which displays the tutor's assessment of the student, for the skills targeted in the current section (see Figure 2, bottom left). The skillometer helps students keep track of their progress. The skills for which a student has reached mastery level are marked with a "✓". When students have reached mastery levels for all skills, they graduate from the current section of the curriculum.

The PACT Geometry Tutor is a cognitive tutor, an approach based on the ACT theory which has proven to be effective for building computer tutors for problem-solving skills [Anderson, 1993; Anderson, *et al,* 1995]. The PACT Geometry tutor is based on a production rule model of geometry problem solving, organized by lessons and sections as shown in Figure 1. The model, which contains 77 geometry rules and 198 rules dealing with equation-solving, is used for *model-tracing* and *knowledge tracing*. The purpose of model-tracing is to monitor a student's solutions and to provide feedback and hints. When the student enters a value into the Table Tool, the tutor uses the model output as a standard to evaluate the student's answer. To provide hints, the tutor applies its production rule model to the current state of problem-solving and displays the hint messages associated with the applicable rule that has highest priority.

The purpose of knowledge-tracing is to compile detailed measures of an individual student's competence (i.e., a student model), based on that student's performance over a series of problems. The student model is an overlay on the production rule set. For the critical production rules, the tutor uses a Bayesian algorithm to estimate the probability that the student knows the skill [Corbett and Anderson, 1995]. The estimate for a given rule is updated each time the rule is applicable, taking into account whether the student's action is correct or not, or whether the student asks for help. The tutor uses this information to select appropriate remedial problems for each student and to decide when a student is ready to advance to the next section of the curriculum. The information in the student model is displayed on the screen in the skillometer. The system is implemented using the plug-in Tutor Agent architecture [Ritter and Koedinger, 1997] and the Tutor Development Kit [Anderson and Pelletier, 1991].

Formative evaluation of the angle properties lesson

In the spring of '97, we collected data to evaluate how effective the combination of classroom instruction and practice with the PACT Geometry tutor is, primarily to identify areas where the instruction or tutor can be improved. Also, we wanted to assess how well students are able to explain answers to geometry problems. The study focused on lesson 3 of the PACT geometry

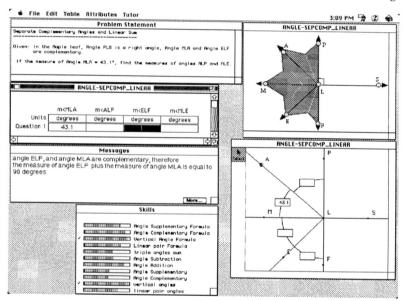

Fig. 2. The PACT Geometry Tutor provides tools and intelligent assistance

curriculum, which deals with geometric properties relating primarily to the measures of angles (see Figure 1). A total of 71 students in two schools participated. All students received classroom instruction on the topics of lesson 3 and used the tutor to work through problems related to this lesson. The students took a pre-test before working with the tutor and a post-test afterwards. The classroom instruction took place in part before the pre-test, in part in between pre-test and post-test.

Each test involved four multi-step geometry problems in which students were asked to calculate certain measures in a diagram and were asked also to state reasons for their answers, in terms of geometry theorems and definitions. Students were given a sheet listing relevant definitions and theorems and were told that they could use the sheet freely. We used two different test forms, each of which was given (randomly) to about half the students, during pre-test and post-test, to counterbalance for test form difficulty. An example question is shown in Figure 3, together with correct and incorrect reasons that students gave for correct numeric answers (e.g., correct angle measures), when they took the post-test.

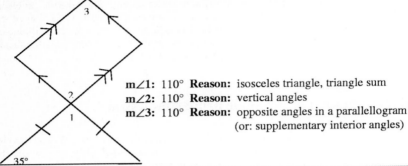

m∠1: 110° **Reason:** isosceles triangle, triangle sum
m∠2: 110° **Reason:** vertical angles
m∠3: 110° **Reason:** opposite angles in a parallellogram
(or: supplementary interior angles)

	Correct	**Incorrect**
∠ 1	• triangle sum, isosceles triangle • third # to the sum of triangle • you subtract 180 - 35 - 35 and get 110	• only angle besides congruent angles; opposite congruent sides • linear pair • alt. Interior angles are congruent
∠ 2	• vertical pair of angles	• because it 2 is a linear pair with 1 • it is opposite ∠1 • corresponding angles are congruent
∠ 3	• Opposite Angles of a Parallelogram are equal • Interior angles on same side of transversal are supplementary • all the lines are parallel so there will be 2 pairs of equal angles	• parallel lines --> Alt. Int. angles are congruent • ANG 2 & 3 are CONG cause of parallel sides • same as m∠2

Fig. 3. Sample test question with correct answers and reasons (top) plus a sample of reasons given by students for correct answers on the post-test

The criterion for grading the reasons was whether students were able to justify their answers in terms of geometry definitions and theorems, possibly stated in their own words. For example, to calculate the measure of angle 1, one needs to apply the isosceles triangle theorem and the triangle sum rule, as shown in Figure 3, first correct reason for angle 1. Since the grading was lenient, listing only one of the two rules was deemed correct, as can be seen in the second correct reason for angle 1. Even a procedural description which did not mention any geometry rules was deemed (borderline) correct, as in the third correct reason for angle 1. We see also that some of the incorrect reasons were more incorrect than others. Some are very close to being correct (e.g., the first incorrect answer for angle 1), some are plain wrong (e.g., the first incorrect reason for angle 2 mentions the wrong theorem), some are in between.

As shown in Figure 4, students' test scores improved from pre-test to post-test. Numeric answer-finding increased from an average of 0.74 on the pre-test to 0.86 on the post-test, reason-giving improved from 0.43 on the pre-test to 0.60 on the post-test. A two-factor ANOVA with test-time (pre v. post) and action type (numeric answer vs. reason) as subjects factors, revealed significant main effects of both test-time ($F(1, 70) = 39.1$, $p < .0001$) and action type ($F(1,70) = 191.4$, $p < .0001$). This indicates that students improved significantly from pre-test to post-test and were significantly better at giving answers than at giving reasons. The two factors did not interact ($F(1, 70) = 3.3$, $p = .075$), indicating that there was as much improvement on reason-giving as they did on numeric answer finding.

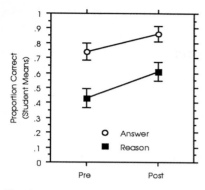

Fig. 4. Students' scores for answers and reasons (proportion correct) at pre-test and post-test

These results indicate that a combination of classroom instruction and practice with the PACT Geometry tutor, based on the PACT curriculum, is effective. The high pre-test scores may reflect the fact that the bulk of the classroom instruction took place before the pre-test. Much of the improvement in students' test scores may be due to students' working with the tutor. Students' ability to state reasons for their answers improved, in spite of the fact that the instruction did not focus on teaching them to do so. This may be due to transfer from answer-giving, the tutor's hints (which often mention the reason), or from the classroom instruction between pre-test and post-test.

Students may use shallow knowledge

The results from the formative evaluation show that students are better at finding numerical answers than at articulating the reasons that are presumably involved in finding these answers. We hypothesize that this is due to the use of shallow knowledge.

At best, students may have a fairly robust visual encoding of the knowledge involved, associating diagram configurations with inferences that can be drawn from them, but may not know the name of the definition or theorem involved. (Geometry experts organize their knowledge in this way, but they also know the name of the rules involved or at least, are able to identify corresponding rules on a reference sheet [Koedinger and Anderson, 1990].) At worst, students may draw on superficial knowledge that enables them to get the answer right in some

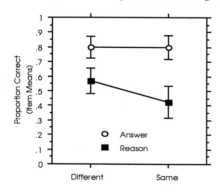

Fig. 5. Students' answer and reason scores on test items where a quantity sought is different from the quantities from which it is derived (Different) vs. scores on items where a quantity sought is equal to a quantity from which it is derived (Same)

circumstances but that may be overly general or inappropriately contextualized. This knowledge may take the form of "guessing heuristics" such as: If two angles look the same in the diagram, their measures are the same. Or even: An unknown measure is the same as that of another angle in the diagram. Or: The measure of an angle may be equal to 180• minus a measure of another angle. Such guessing heuristics can be quite helpful. For example, by looking at the diagram shown in Figure 3, one could guess correctly that the measures of angles 1, 2, and 3 are equal. Thus, once one has the measure of angle 1, one can find the measures of angles 2 and 3. But one also needs more robust knowledge to solve this problem. It seems difficult if not impossible to find the measure of angle 1 solely using guessing heuristics, without using (something like) the triangle sum rule.

We found evidence that students use guessing heuristics by comparing their scores on two classes of test items, namely (1) items where a quantity sought is equal to a quantity from which it is derived (in one step) and (2) test items where the quantity sought is different from the quantities in the problem from which it is derived. We found that the difference between students' answer scores and reason scores is greater on "same measure" items than it is on "different measure" items (see Figure 5). This suggests that students are, in part, relying on a heuristic that says: If angles look equal, their measures are equal.

Finally, we found evidence of the use of guessing heuristics in the logs of students' work with the tutor. For example, consider the problem shown in Figure 6. In an attempt to find the measure of ∠ELF (which is 50•), one student entered values of 90, 40, and 130 (on successive, unsuccessful attempts), evidence of the use of guessing heuristics. For example, she may have entered 40 because a given quantity in the problem is equal to 40•. She then turned to ∠ALP (leaving open the answer for ∠ELF) and found that its measure is 50•. She proceeded to enter 50 for both m∠ELF (correct) and for m∠MLE (incorrect), illustrating further use of the same heuristic. If she had entered 50 only for m∠ELF but not for m∠MLE, it would have been harder to argue that she was guessing. However, the quick entry of 50 for both quantities indicates a lack of deliberate processing characteristic of shallow learning.

This example is not unusual. It should be noted from our classroom experience (the fourth author is currently a teacher and the second author has taught high school geometry previously) that such guessing behavior is not unique to our computer tutor, but is also commonly observed in classroom dialogues.

Hypothesis: Teaching to give reasons is beneficial

We hypothesize that students acquire more reliable knowledge when they are trained consciously to interpret rules (definitions, theorems, etc. written in English) and apply them in a logical manner to find answers. By doing so, students may learn to rely less on implicit, recognition-based inferencing that results from the shallow perceptual coding of geometric knowledge. Encouraging students to reason logically from definitions and theorems may result not only in better performance on reason-giving, but may transfer to better performance on quantitative answers. First, this kind of instruction may help students to induce the correct geometry knowledge and therefore lessen the need to form shallow rules such as the ones illustrated above. The verbal encoding of the rules focuses students on the right features when inducing rules from practice examples. Consistent with this line of reasoning, studies in both a statistics and a logic domain [Holland, et al., 1986] showed that students learn better from instruction using both examples and rules than either one alone. Our interpretation is that example instruction facilitates the same kind of implicit, perceptual level learning that our students are engaged in while practicing answer finding, while rule instruction facilitates the kind of explicit, verbal learning we expect to support in glossary search and reason giving.

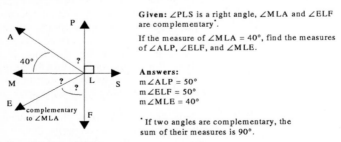

Given: ∠PLS is a right angle, ∠MLA and ∠ELF are complementary*.

If the measure of ∠MLA = 40°, find the measures of ∠ALP, ∠ELF, and ∠MLE.

Answers:
m∠ALP = 50°
m∠ELF = 50°
m∠MLE = 40°

* If two angles are complementary, the sum of their measures is 90°.

Fig. 6. Sample tutor problem

A second argument for the transfer of deliberate rule use to answer finding is based on memory research. In explaining experimental results showing that concrete words are remembered better than abstract words, Paivio (1971) posed a "dual code" theory. Concrete words are stored in memory both perceptually and verbally and these redundant codes make retrieval of them more likely than equally frequent abstract words which are stored in memory only in a verbal code. In our case, providing more practice in deliberate rule use should complement student's natural inclination toward perceptual encoding of geometric properties and encourage students toward a second verbal encoding that can enhance the probability of reliable recall. In both these arguments, we are not suggesting stamping out the use of perceptual encodings and heuristics in geometric reasoning, but rather bolstering them with complementary verbal-logical encodings.

Extensions to the tutor

We have modified and extended the PACT Geometry tutor, so as to get students to reason more deliberately with definitions and theorems. In the extended version of the tutor, students are required to provide reasons for their answers, usually the name of a definition or theorem. Students enter the answers and reasons in a new "answer sheet", shown on the left in Figure 7. To complete a problem, students must give correct answers and reasons for all items. Students can look up relevant definitions and theorems in a Glossary, shown on the right in Figure 7. The Glossary contains entries for all geometry rules that students may need in order to solve the problems. Students can cite the Glossary rules as reasons for their answers, as illustrated in Figure 7. They can click on Glossary items to see a statement in English of the definition or theorem, illustrated with an example and a diagram. Students can browse the Glossary as they see fit. Our intention is that students will consult the Glossary when they do not know how to proceed with a problem, interpret the English rules, aided by the examples, and judge which rule can be applied.

The tutor's hint messages have been changed to encourage students to use the Glossary and to help narrow the search for applicable rules in the Glossary, as is illustrated in Figure 7. When a student asks for help, the tutor initially suggests a quantity to work on and points to items in the diagram that are relevant (i.e., the tutor points to the next subgoal and to the premises to use to infer the goal quantity). If the student repeats the request for help, the tutor suggests that the student look at a certain category of rules in the Glossary (e.g., rules dealing with parallel lines). At the next level of help, the tutor highlights in the Glossary the rules that are within that category. If the student asks for even more help, the tutor states which definition or theorem to use. Finally, the tutor points out how the rule can be applied to the current problem. The tutor's production rule model has been extended to accommodate these changes. In all other respects, the tutor is the same as the previous version.

Thus, the new tutor provides opportunities to work with English descriptions of the rules and to some extent forces students to do so. We have begun pilot-testing the new tutor. Initial reactions of two geometry teachers and a student were favorable. The student remarked that he liked the tutor better than the original version, "because you have the reasons."

Discussion and conclusion

Shallow learning is a problem for many forms of instruction and current computer-based tutors may not be an exception. Students who have worked with the PACT Geometry tutor do well on problem-solving tests, but are not always able to state reasons for their answers. We hypothesize that we can reduce this kind of shallow learning by having students work more deliberately with (textual statements of) definitions and theorems as they solve geometry problems with the tutor. Towards this end, we have added a Glossary of definitions and theorems to the tutor and have modified the tutor so that students are required to state which definition or theorem was used to arrive at answers. By providing a textual representation of the geometry definitions and theorems, we aim to focus students on the right features to use in constructing the geometry production rules, as is required according to ACT theory of cognition and learning. There is also an argument that having both a visual and a textual encoding of an item may make that item easier to recall.

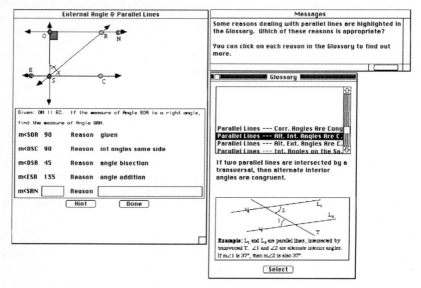

Fig. 7. Extensions to the tutor, to get students more deliberately to reason with definitions and theorems

We will carry out a controlled experiment to evaluate how effective the new tutor is, as compared to the old version of the tutor. We hypothesize that training students to reason more deliberately in this way results not only in greater ability to state reasons for quantitative answers, but also that there will be transfer to better scores on quantitative questions, especially on more difficult problems. We have designed two types of challenge problems to better discriminate the use of shallow versus deep reasoning to find numerical answers. *Misleading problems* have deceptive diagrams in which superficial perceptual strategies will yield the wrong answers. *Possibly unsolvable problems* ask students to compute unknown quantities when there is sufficient information, but to answer "not enough information" when there is not. The pre- and post-test in our evaluation will contain problems of these types, in order to test our hypothesis.

The approach to combatting shallow learning presented in this paper is not specific to geometry instruction, but could also be applied to other cognitive skills. In teaching Lisp programming, for example, it may help to have students articulate what a Lisp operator does in order to get them better to work with unfamiliar Lisp objects such as lists of lists.

If our hypothesis turns out to be true, the work will be significant in the following ways: From a practical point of view, creating instruction, computer-based or otherwise, that leads to deeper learning is an important goal. From a theoretical perspective, if it can be shown that one can effectively combat the learning of shallow knowledge by providing for both implicit perceptual and explicit textual modes of learning, that is a significant result for cognitive science generally.

Acknowledgments
Ray Pelletier and Chang-Hsin Chang contributed to the development of the PACT Geometry tutor. The PACT Geometry curriculum was developed by Jackie Snyder. The research is sponsored by the Buhl Foundation, the Grable Foundation, the Howard Heinz Endowment, the Richard King Mellon Foundation, and the Pittsburgh Foundation. We gratefully acknowledge their contributions.

References
Anderson, J. R., 1993. *Rules of the Mind*. Hillsdale, NJ: Addison-Wesley.

Anderson, J. R., A. T. Corbett, K. R. Koedinger, and R. Pelletier, 1995. Cognitive tutors: Lessons learned. *The Journal of the Learning Sciences*, 4, 167-207.

Anderson, J. R., and R. Pelletier, 1991. A development system for model-tracing tutors. In *Proceedings of the International Conference of the Learning Sciences*, 1-8. Evanston, IL.

Burton, R. R., and J. S. Brown, 1982. An Investigation of Computer Coaching for Informal Learning Activities. In D. H. Sleeman and J. S. Brown (eds.), *Intelligent Tutoring Systems*, 79-98. New York: Academic Press.

Chi, M. T. H., P. J. Feltovich, and R. Glaser, 1981. Categorization and representation of physics problems by experts and novices. *Cognitive Science*, 5, 121-152.

Corbett, A. T., and J. R. Anderson, 1995. Knowledge tracing: Modeling the acquisition of procedural knowledge. *User Modeling and User-Adapted Interaction*, 4: 253-278.

Holland, J. H., K. J. Holyoak, R. E. Nisbett, and P. R. Thagard, 1986. *Induction: Processes of Inference, Learning, and Discovery*. Cambridge, MA: The MIT Press.

Koedinger, K. R., and J. R. Anderson, 1990. Abstract planning and perceptual chunks: Elements of expertise in geometry. *Cognitive Science*, 14, 511-550.

Koedinger, K. R., and J. R. Anderson, 1993. Reifying implicit planning in geometry. In S. Lajoie and S. Derry (eds.), *Computers as Cognitive Tools*, 15-45. Hillsdale, NJ: Erlbaum.

Miller, C. S., J. F. Lehman, and K. R. Koedinger, 1997. Goals and learning in microworlds. Submitted to Cognitive Science.

NCTM, 1989. *Curriculum and Evaluation Standards for School Mathematics*. National Council of Teachers of Mathematics. Reston, VA: The Council.

Paivio, A., 1971. *Imagery and verbal processes*. New York: Holt, Rinehart, and Winston.

Ritter, S., and K. R. Koedinger, 1997. An architecture for plug-in tutoring agents. *Journal of Artificial Intelligence in Education*, 7 (3/4), 315-347. Charlottesville, VA: AACE.

Ritter, S., and J. R. Anderson, 1995. Calculation and strategy in the equation solving tutor. In Proceedings of the Seventeenth Annual Conference of the Cognitive Science Society, 413-418. Hillsdale, NJ: Erlbaum.

A Formative Evaluation of the PACT Algebra II Tutor: Support for Simple Hierarchical Reasoning

Albert T. Corbett, Holly J. Trask, K. Christine Scarpinatto, and William S. Hadley

Human Computer Interaction Institute
Carnegie Mellon University, Pittsburgh PA 15213, USA

Abstract. This paper reports a formative analysis of a principal interface tool in the PACT Algebra II Tutor (PAT2). PAT2 employs modern computational tools to support student reasoning about real-world problem situations. This paper examines a curriculum section on general linear form equations and evaluates the effectiveness of a worksheet tool in reifying the hierarchical structure of the problem situations. Performance analyses suggest that the worksheet effectively supports students in mapping from natural language situations to hierarchical symbolic structures, and that this accounts for the preponderance of observed learning gains. Analyses also suggest that students incur a performance cost in using the worksheet and that the worksheet might be deployed more efficiently in problem solving.

1 Introduction

This paper reports a formative analysis of an early curriculum section in the new PACT Algebra II Tutor (PAT2). PAT2 is cognitive problem solving tutor [5] currently undergoing development at Carnegie Mellon University and piloting in four Pittsburgh area schools. This evaluation focuses on an interface design principle that guides PAT2 development. As recommended in the National Council of Teachers of Mathematics [7] curriculum standards, PAT2 employs modern computational tools to support students in analyzing real-world problem situations. In this paper we examine whether a worksheet representation effectively supports students' reasoning about simple hierarchical problem situations.

2 The PACT Algebra II Tutor

The PACT Algebra II Tutor builds on a successful collaboration between the Pittsburgh Urban Mathematics Project in the Pittsburgh School District and the Pittsburgh Advanced Cognitive Tutor (PACT) Center at Carnegie Mellon University. This collaboration previously yielded the PUMP Algebra I Tutor [6], which is now in use in approximately 40 middle and high schools and two colleges in the United States and Europe. Currently the PACT Center is developing cognitive tutors for Geometry as well as Algebra II. The tutors reflect the National Council of Teachers of Mathematics [8] curriculum standards, and tutor development is guided by three major goals: (1) to support students in applying academic mathematics in real-world problem situations, (2) to encourage students to reason among multiple representations, including tables, graphs, symbolic representations, and natural language and (3) to employ modern computational tools.

Fig. 1 displays the PAT2 tutor screen near the conclusion of a vertical motion quadratics problem. The problem statement window in the upper left corner presents a problem situation and seven questions. Students answer the questions by filling in the worksheet in the lower left corner. Students (1) identify relevant quantities in the problem and label the columns accordingly; (2) enter appropriate units in the first row of the worksheet; (3) enter a symbolic formula for each quantity in the second row; and (4) answer the questions in the successive table rows. Students graph the function with the graphing tool in the lower right corner. The quadratic formula tool in the upper right is available for use in answering questions, and is one example of a suite of symbol manipulation tools in PAT2. Tutor feedback is available in the tutor window at the lower left. The tutor provides immediate feedback on each problem solving action in the worksheet, graphing and symbol manipulation tools. Students can also ask for advice at each step in problem solving. Three levels of help are available: (1) advice on a goal to achieve, (2) an abstract description of how to achieve the goal, and (3) problem-specific advice on how to achieve the goal.

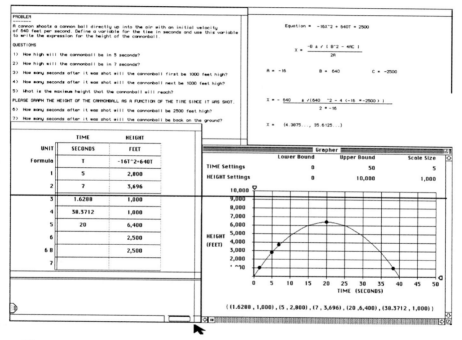

Fig. 1. The PACT Algebra II Tutor interface near the end of a vertical motion problem.

3 A Formative Evaluation of the Worksheet: Applying Algebra in Problem Solving

Students face two fundamental challenges in applying algebra to problem situations. The first task is to identify the interdependent quantities in the situation, analyze the relationship among the quantities and map that relationship onto a formal structure. The second task is to manipulate the structure in answering questions. This paper focuses on problems that can be represented by the general form of linear equations:

$$c = ax + by .$$

(1)

Fig. 2 displays a problem situation that can readily be represented in this form. This problem situation can equivalently be represented as an operator hierarchy, as depicted in Fig. 3. In both the linear equation and hierarchical representation in this figure, the variable x represents the number of Optimas to be sold, the product $250x$ represents the income from Optima sales, the variable y represents the number of Futuras to be sold and the product $500y$ represents the Futura sales income. The sum $250x + 500y$ represents total income and is set to the constant $750,000$ in this situation. Questions can be formed in this problem situation by instantiating one variable or product node in the hierarchy with a given value and asking students to compute the value of another variable node or product node. Students can answer the questions by traversing the operator hierarchy and successively applying the operators (in moving up through the hierarchy) or the operator inverses (in moving down through the hierarchy). More specifically, students may be asked to reason from one product (e.g., ax) to the other (by), as in question 1, from one product (e.g., by) to the other variable (x), as question 3, and so on. Logically, students need to traverse 0, 1 or 2 subgoals in deriving these answers.

PROBLEM SITUATION

We own a company that makes and sells two different models of televisions. We need to decide how many Optimas and how many Futuras to make. The Optima sells for $250 and the Futura sells for $500. Our goal is to reach $750,000 in total income.

QUESTIONS

(1) If the company makes $300,000 from selling Optimas, how much income do we need from selling Futuras.

(2) If the company sells 500 Futuras, how much income do we need from selling Optimas?

(3) If the company makes $600,000 from Futuras, how many Optimas do we need to sell?

(4) If the company sells no Futuras, how many Optimas do we need to sell?

(5) If the company sells 1000 Optimas, how many Futuras do we need to sell?

Fig. 2. A General linear form problem situation and questions.

In completing the tutor problems, students fill in a worksheet as shown in Fig. 4. Students identify the five quantities represented by the two variable nodes, two product nodes and the sum node in the hierarchical representation, and label the five columns in the table with the quantity names. Students also type the unit of measurement for each quantity and type in a formula for each quantity, as shown in the figure. Finally, students answer each question by filling in cells in the corresponding rows of the worksheet. For each question in this curriculum section, students are required only to type the given value and the answer in the appropriate cells (shown in bold). Students may fill in the any other cells they choose and are free to fill in cell values in any temporal order.

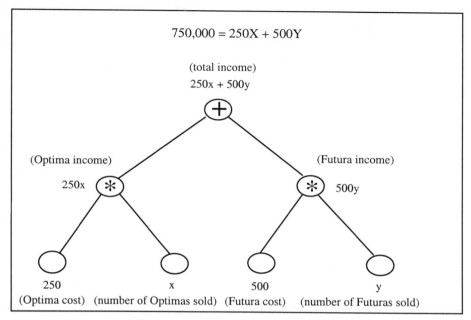

$$750{,}000 = 250X + 500Y$$

(total income)
$250x + 500y$

(Optima income)   (Futura income)

$250x$ $500y$

250   x   500   y
(Optima cost) (number of Optimas sold) (Futura cost) (number of Futuras sold)

Fig. 3. Symbolic and hierarchical representation of the problem situation in Fig. 2.

Note that the spatial layout of the worksheet in Fig. 4 does not preserve the hierarchical relationships among the quantities that are graphically depicted in Fig. 3. Instead, the hierarchical structure is represented symbolically, via the expressions in the formula row, and dynamically, via the underlying cognitive model, as described in the next section.

3.1 The Cognitive Model.

PAT2 reflects the ACT-R theory of skill knowledge [1]. It assumes that cognitive skills can be modeled as a set of independent production rules and that each step in performance is governed by one of these if-then rules. PAT2 is constructed around a set of such problem solving rules, called the *ideal student model*. The cognitive model enables the tutor to trace the student's solution path through a complex problem solving space, providing feedback on problem solving actions and, if requested, advice on steps that achieve problem solving goals. This *model tracing* process has been shown to speed learning by as much as a factor of three and increase achievement levels, compared to students solving problems on their own [2].

The PAT2 worksheet ideal model is tied to the hierarchical structure of the problem situation. In solving each question, the model begins by identifying the given quantity. If the quantity has not yet been labeled, it finds an open column, labels the column and enters the unit, then enters the given value in the appropriate row. It then follows the hierarchical solution path through the question. For example, in question 4, the cognitive model recognizes it needs to compute the product ax , then chains forward to the sum (constant) term, chains forward to the *by* product and then finally chains forward to find the variable quantity *y*.

Students are *not* required to follow these canonical solution paths. They are only required to fill in the given and answer quantity for each question and they can fill in the cells in any order. However, if help is requested, the student is guided to the canonical path. If the student selects a cell and asks for help, the tutor evaluates whether the student is ready to fill that cell, and if so, offers help. If not, the tutor guides the student to the next appropriate step in the solution path.

	Number of Optimas	Number of Futuras	Optima Income	Futura Income	Total Income
Units	tvs	tvs	$	$	$
Formulas	x	y	250x	500y	250x + 500y
1	1200	900	**300,000**	**450,000**	750,000
2	2000	**500**	**500,000**	250,000	750,000
3	**600**	1200	150,000	**600,000**	750,000
4	**3000**	**0**	750,000	0	750,000
5	**1000**	**1000**	250,000	500,000	750,000

Fig. 4. Worksheet solution to questions in Fig. 2. Students are required to type the given value and answer for each question, shown in bold. Other values are optional.

4 The Study

While the worksheet is a flat two-dimensional representation, the formula row and help facility are intended to reinforce the hierarchical structure of these problem situations. This study provides an initial formative evaluation of the worksheet's effectiveness in supporting students' problem solving. The study goals are to examine the worksheet's overall impact on learning and to understand the learning process more fully by examining tutor performance in some detail. In this capacity the study contains no comparison conditions, but should provide guidance in enhancing tutor effectiveness.

In addition to completing tutor problems, students in the study completed a paper-and-pencil pretest and posttest in this study to assess the tutor's effectiveness. These paper-and-pencil tests provide a problem situation and questions similar to the tutor problems, but the tests provide no explicit support in analyzing the problem situation. Students are not asked to write a formula and no worksheet is provided to reify the problem situation.

4.1. Students
Twenty-two students in one PACT Algebra II class in a Pittsburgh high school participated in this study. Math SAT scores in this school average around 400 and about 15% of the students go on to college. The class was approximately 40% African-American.

4.2 Design
The general linear form was introduced largely through small-group classroom activities. Upon completion of these classroom activities, students completed a paper-and-pencil test (a pretest with respect to the tutor). Students then worked through the

section of PAT2 general linear form problems at their own rate.   Each student completed a paper-and-pencil posttest after his or her last general linear form tutor problem, before moving to the next tutor section.

Test Design. The pretest and posttest each contained a single problem situation with five questions analogous to the tutor questions. Students were only required to write down the answer to each question. No worksheet was provided, and no explicit algebraic representation of the situation was provided by, or for, the students. The tutor's worksheet tool is intended to support students' analysis of quantity relations by requiring the students to explicitly post the interdependent quantities and to characterize their relationships symbolically. The goal of the study is to examine if these analytical activities support learning in the tutor and transfer to the test environment. Four versions of the paper-and-pencil tests were generated. Each version was completed by 25% of the students in pretesting and a different 25% in posttesting.

4.3 Results

Students completed an average of 5 general linear form problems in this lesson and a maximum of 8.   The number of problems each student completed was largely determined by class attendance.

Test Performance. Table 1 displays the paper-and-pencil pretest and posttest results. As can be seen, students scored 44% correct on the pretest following their small-group problem solving activities.   Scores climbed to 72% correct on the posttest, following individual problem solving with PAT2. This achievement gain represents a 64% increase in performance and is significant ($t = 3.08$, $p < .01$).

Tutor Performance. As students work with PAT2, their growing knowledge of the component productions in the underlying cognitive model is monitored in a process we call *knowledge tracing*. As the student practices, the tutor maintains an estimate for each production of $p(L)$, the probability that the production is in the learned state. At each opportunity to apply a rule in problem solving, the estimate of $p(L)$ for the rule is updated with a Bayesian computational procedure. This procedure employs two learning parameters and performance parameters, and has been shown to accurately model student performance in cognitive tutor problem solving and to accurately predict posttest performance [3,4]. We generated best-fitting parameter estimates for students' worksheet performance in this study to quantify learning rates. The first column in Table 2 displays the probability that students have learned the component productions prior to the first attempt to use them in tutor problem solving. As can been seen, these probabilities are relatively high, ranging from 0.34 to 0.98. In large part, these probabilities reflect the success of the whole-group and small-group problem solving activities that preceded individual problem solving with the tutor. The second column reflects learning rate in the tutor - the probability that the students will learn a rule at each opportunity to apply it. Again, these learning probabilities are quite high, replicating earlier findings that cognitive tutors are effective learning environments [2].

Table 1. Pretest and posttest accuracy (probability correct) for five problem types.

Question Type	Pretest Accuracy	Posttest Accuracy
ax -> by	.39	.78
by -> x	.44	.56
y -> ax	.33	.72
y -> x	.39	.72
y=0 -> x	.67	.83
Average	.44	.72

Test Performance vs. Tutor Performance. Note that average pretest accuracy in Table 1, 0.44, is lower than the $p(L_0)$ estimates in Table 2 that students know the component productions before beginning tutor work. Average pretest accuracy is expected to be appreciably lower than the $p(L_0)$ estimates for two reasons. First, the model assumes a probability that students will slip and make mistakes even when they know necessary rules. Second, and more importantly, correct performance on each paper-and-pencil question depends on the correct firing of multiple productions.

Table 2. Best fitting learning probabilities for students' problem solving performance.

Production Rule	$p(L_0)$	$p(T)$
Worksheet Headers		
Quantity Labels	0.34	0.46
Units	0.73	0.67
Formulas	0.69	0.60
Question Cells		
Given Values	0.98	1.0
Answers	0.80	0.5
Optional Values	0.93	0.33

$p(L_0)$ = probability the student has learned a rule prior to its first application
$p(T)$ = probability of learning a rule at each opportunity to apply it

We can compare test performance and tutor performance more directly. On the surface the test and tutor questions are comparable. Under the assumption that production rules are independent, the probability of answering a <u>pretest</u> question correctly should equal the <u>product</u> of the probabilities that the student fires each of the component question-answering productions correctly in the <u>first</u> tutor problem. Consider question 4 in Fig. 2. The probability of answering such a pretest question correctly should be similar to the probability, in the first tutor problem, that students enter the given value correctly, times the probabilities of entering each intervening subgoal value correctly, times the probability of entering the answer correctly.

Similarly, accuracy levels in answering posttest questions should be similar to the product of the probabilities of firing productions correctly in the final tutor problem.

Table 3 presents mean paper-and-pencil test accuracies and predicted accuracies derived from students' tutor performance. There are two interesting patterns in this table. The most important is that actual learning gains (posttest minus pretest scores) exceed predicted gains. Actual test accuracy rises 63%, while gains are predicted to rise only 18%. As described below, this offers indirect evidence that the worksheet effectively supports students in learning to map the problems onto hierarchical quantity structures. The second interesting pattern is that actual pretest performance falls short of predictions, while posttest performance exceeds predictions. A further examination of this pattern supports our interpretation of learning gains, but also reveals an interface cost of employing the worksheet.

Table 3. Performance accuracy (probability correct) in the first test and final test and predicted accuracy based on students' performance on their first and last tutor problems.

	Pretest	Posttest
Paper-and-Pencil Test	0.44	0.72
Predicted Scores	0.51	0.60

Learning Gains. Recall that in problem solving, students must perform two tasks: (1) mapping the real-world situation onto a representation of quantity relationships, and (2) manipulating this representation to answer questions. In completing the tutor worksheet, students receive the guidance needed to complete a correct mapping, by filling in the column labels and formula rows, *before* they begin answering questions. In answering questions, students need only perform the second task of manipulating this conceptual structure. Thus, the tutor-derived test predictions and the predicted gain reflect only this second subtask. To successfully answer the pretest and posttest questions, however, students must perform both the mapping and manipulation subtasks on their own. We contend that actual learning gains exceed predicted gains because students are successfully learning to perform the situation mapping, in addition to manipulating the resulting representation. The fact that predicted gains are more than three times larger than predicted gains suggests that the initial mapping is the more challenging of the two subtasks.

Actual vs. Predicted Performance Levels. An inspection of student answers in completing worksheet questions reveals that they are making two types of performance errors that do not happen in the paper-and-pencil tests. First, they make typing errors (e.g., typing 30,000 or 3,000,000 when the correct answer is 300,000). Second, they sometimes type a correct answer in the wrong worksheet cell. It is difficult to quantify this performance slip rate, since any given error could conceivably be a calculation error. But, it seems clear that correcting for pure performance errors would increase paper-and-pencil accuracy predictions by 10-15% and attenuate the predicted gains from pre-test to post-test.

This has several implications. First, it tends to increase the difference between actual and predicted pretest performance and to shrink the difference between actual and predicted posttest performance. This tends to support the argument that much of what students are learning is the mapping from the real world to the hierarchical structure that is mediated more by the worksheet column headers than question answering in the tutor. Second, students are encountering a performance cost associated with the learning effectiveness of the worksheet. Third, the attenuation in predicted gains further suggests that a large component of student learning gains derives from filling in column headers rather than answering questions. Perhaps we can increase learning rate in the tutor by reducing the number of questions per problem.

Problem Completion Order. A final analysis reinforces the claim that students are learning the hierarchical structure of the general linear form problems. In this analysis we examined the *order* in which students completed the worksheet cells in answering tutor questions. The underlying cognitive model demonstrates two types of regularity when filling in the question cells. First, it completes each question before moving on to the next question. Second, it follows a canonical solution path through the hierarchical structure in completing each question. This path begins with the given in the question, proceeds through any subgoal quantities on the solution path, in the appropriate order, follows with the answer value, and concludes with any extra, irrelevant values. (For example, when both the given and answer are products, both variable values are irrelevant). Students are free to enter table values in any order, but if they are learning to map the problems onto hierarchical structures, we would expect to see a growing regularity in their solution orders.

To examine this hypothesis, we examined the order in which students filled in the worksheet question cells in their first tutor problem and in their final tutor problem. We computed two measures, (1) the probability that students complete each question before moving to another, and (2) the probability that students follow the canonical solution path within each question. The results are displayed in Table 4. As can be seen, the probability that students complete each question before jumping to another rises slightly from 0.62 on the first problem to 0.79 on the last. This increase is marginally significant, $t = 2.06$, $p = .05$. More importantly, the probability that students follow the canonical solution path through the questions increases considerably, from 0.46 in the first tutor problem to 0.76 on the final tutor problem. This increase is significant, $t = 2.81$, $p < .05$ and provides compelling evidence that students are learning the hierarchical mathematical relations in each problem situation.

5 Conclusion

This formative evaluation of the PACT Algebra II Tutor is quite encouraging. Pretest-to-posttest achievement gains and best-fitting parameter estimates both demonstrate that PAT2 is an effective learning environment. Analyses suggest that entering column headers (labels and formulas) can effectively support students' mapping from problem situations to hierarchical representations of quantity relations. This understanding successfully transfers to the test environment and accounts for the preponderance of learning gains. This conclusion, in turn, suggests that we might increase learning rate in the tutor by reducing the number of questions per problem.

Table 4. The probability that students follow canonical solution order in answering questions in the first and last tutor problem.

	Tutor Problem	
	First Problem	Final Problem
Probability of completing each question before proceeding to the next	0.62	0.79
Probability of following the canonical solution path through each question	0.46	0.76

Acknowledgment

This study was supported by the Office of Naval Research grant N00014-95-1-0847.

References

1. Anderson, J.R.: Rules of the mind. Lawrence Erlbaum, Hillsdale, NJ (1993)

2. Anderson, J.R., Corbett, A.T., Koedinger K.R., Pelletier, R.: Cognitive tutors: Lessons learned. Journal of the Learning Sciences, (1995), 4, 167-207

3. Corbett, A.T., Anderson, J.R.,: Knowledge tracing: Modeling the acquisition of procedural knowledge. User modeling and user-adapted interaction, (1995), 4, 253-278

4. Corbett, A.T., Bhatnagar, A.: Student modeling in the ACT Programming Tutor: Adjusting a procedural learning model with declarative knowledge Proceedings of the Sixth International Conference on User Modeling. Springer-Verlag Wein, New York (1997)

5. Corbett, A.T., Koedinger, K.R., Anderson, J.R.: Intelligent tutoring systems. In M.G. Helander, T.K. Landauer and P. Prabhu (Eds.) Handbook of human computer interaction, 2nd edition. Elsevier Science, Amsterdam (1997)

6. Koedinger, K.R., Anderson, J.R., Hadley, W.H., Mark, M.A.: Intelligent tutoring goes to school in the big city. Artificial Intelligence and Education, 1995: The Proceedings of AI-ED 95. AACE, Charlottesville, VA (1995)

7. National Council of Teachers of Mathematics: Curriculum and Evaluation Standards for School Mathematics. The Council, Reston, VA (1989)

Evaluation Of Data Aging: A Technique For Discounting Old Data During Student Modeling

Geoffrey I. Webb and Mark Kuzmycz

School of Computing and Mathematics
Deakin University, Geelong, Vic, 3217, Australia.

Abstract. Student modeling systems must operate in an environment in which a student's mastery of a subject matter is likely to change as a lesson progresses. A student model is formed from evaluation of evidence about the student's mastery of the domain. However, given that such mastery will change, older evidence is likely to be less valuable than recent evidence. Data aging addresses this issue by discounting the value of older evidence. This paper provides experimental evaluation of the effects of data aging. While it is demonstrated that data aging can result in statistically significant increases in both the number and accuracy of predictions that a modeling system makes, it is also demonstrated that the reverse can be true. Further, the effects experienced are of only small magnitude. It is argued that these results demonstrate some potential for data aging as a general strategy, but do not warrant employing data aging in its current form.

1 Introduction

A student modeling system seeks to develop a model of the student from observations of the student's past performance. A fundamental difficulty confronting such a system is that while it seeks to construct a model of the student's current state, the evidence upon which the model is constructed is based upon observations of performance arising from previous states. Education aims to transform the student, from whatever initial state in which the student begins the educational interaction, to a state of mastery of the instructional subject matter. Thus, unless a student starts in a state of mastery, in which case educational interactions are not necessary, successful educational interactions will change student states. In consequence, in a successful educational environment, one should not expect the evidence on which a model is based to reflect the current state of the student. But, such evidence is the primary information available to a system on which to base a model.

Most student modeling systems have ignored this problem, or have circumvented it by avoiding the use of historical data, basing a model on only a single recent action (for example, [1, 5, 6]).

One approach to solving this problem is to use a truth maintenance system [3, 2], or an alternative approach [7] to sequentially refine and modify a model so that it is always consistent with the most recent observed behavior. However, such an strategy has difficulty dealing with noisy data. In particular, when should an observed action that deviates from an existing model be treated as an isolated exception to the student's normal behavior, and when should such an action be treated as the first realization of a new approach to a domain?

Feature Based Modeling has sought to tackle the problem using an alternative mechanism called *data aging*. Data aging discounts older evidence, placing greater weight on recent evidence. This is motivated by the assumption that the more time that has elapsed between an observation and the formation of a model, the greater the probability that the evidence is no longer relevant.

The original formulation of this mechanism [10] assigned each observation an initial weight of 1. The weight of each observation was then discounted by a set proportion each time another relevant observation was incorporated into the model. The induction system took account of weights when developing a model.

While the system incorporating this mechanism demonstrated high accuracy in the challenging task of predicting elementary subtraction results, no evaluation of the contribution of data aging as opposed to other aspects of the mechanism was undertaken. This paper rectifies this situation by evaluating the effect of differing levels of data aging upon system performance.

2   Feature Based Modeling

Feature Based Modeling constructs a black-box model of an agent. It seeks to capture the relationships that hold between the inputs and outputs of the agent, but not the mechanisms that underlie those relationships.

Feature Based Modeling employs a simple form of attribute-value machine learning. The context of an action is described by a set of attribute values called *context features*. Each action is described by a set of attribute values called *action features*.

A model takes the form of a set of *associations*. Each association can be thought of as a production rule associating a set of context features to a single action feature.

A model consists of all associations that satisfy the following conditions:

1. $\#(C- > a) \geq min\_evidence$;
2. $\frac{\#(C->a)}{\#(C->a)+\#(C->\neg a)} \geq min\_accuracy$; and
3. there is no association between a specialization of C and a sibling (alternative feature from the same attribute) of a.

where

- $\#(C- > a)$ is the number of observed cases in which all features in C and feature a have been present;
- $\#(C- > \neg a)$ is the number of observed cases in which all features in C and a sibling of a have been present; and
- $min\_evidence$ and $min\_accuracy$ are implementation dependent parameters.

Associations are allowed that are contradicted by some of the evidence in order to accommodate noise, inconsistent behavior, and changes in behavior.

Most implementations of FBM have used *min_evidence* set to 3 and *min_accuracy* set to 0.8. Although *min_accuracy* of 0.8 ostensibly allows for an association to be accepted when almost 20% of the evidence contradicts it, clause 3 limits the probability of this occurring by suppressing an association if there is a regularity detected in the contrary evidence.

A set of associations can be used to make predictions. To predict an agent's actions in a particular context it is necessary only to extract the set of associations that have all their context features satisfied by the given context. The set of action features for these associations can then be used to make predictions. The action features might fully specify a precise action, or may simply indicate constraints on possible actions, depending both upon the types of action features that are employed and the number of associations that match the current context.

The interested reader is referred to [10] for a more detailed description of Feature Based Modeling and its application.

3   Between and Within Test Data Aging

Feature Based Modeling was initially developed in the context of an intelligent tutoring system [8]. In this context, the evidence from a student was presented to the system in the order in which it was generated by the student (each student response was observed immediately). Further, each task followed immediately one after the other. In such a setting it seemed sensible to discount data at a single set rate after each interaction with the student.

However, this design decision may be less appropriate in other domains. Recent research has considered the application of Feature Based Modeling to the development of models of subtraction performance in a non-tutoring environment [10]. Students are administered a sequence of tests, each comprising 40 three column subtraction problems. Tests are administered at one week intervals. After each test, individual student models are created from the test results for the student to date. Each such model is used to predict the student's answers to the questions on the next test. It is not possible for the computer to determine the order in which questions are answered during a test. However, the original data aging mechanism caused the results for the first question processed by the computer to be discounted 117 times (each column is treated as a separate task, so three discountings occur for each subsequent three column problem that is examined). In contrast, the data for the last column of the last problem will not be discounted at all. This does not appear to be appropriate as:

- a student may tackle the problems in a different order to that in which the system processes them; and
- the changes in the student's state over the interval between tests is likely to be greater than that between tasks within a single test, but greater discounting occurs during a test than between tests.

To address these issues it would appear appropriate to perform discounting between tests rather than discounting within tests.

In more abstract terms, a break in the link between individual tasks and the data aging schedule is advocated. Rather than discounting the data after each task, it should be possible to specify a data aging schedule that reflects the probable impact on the relevance of data within the model of different intervals between observations. One can imagine a schedule that is sensitive to whether specific forms of educational interaction have occurred (lectures, practical work, etc.) and the interval of time between observations.

4   Evaluation

Previous evaluation of Feature Based Modeling has each time employed a set discounting rate [4, 10]. This has not permitted the evaluation of any of:

- the relative performance of different discounting rates; or
- whether discounting is in itself beneficial.

To evaluate these factors Feature Based Modeling was applied to a large modeling task using discounting rates of 0%, 5%, 10%, 20%, 30%, 40%, and 50%.

The task to which each of these alternatives was applied was the task used by [10] and [9]. This involves a body of results of three column subtraction tests administered to eight to nine year old Australian primary school students.

This data was collected as follows:

1. 73 nine to ten year old primary school students were divided into two treatments: Random and Error Repeat. This was achieved by sorting the students at each of the three participating schools into alphabetical order and then assigning them to alternating treatments in order.
2. An initial set of 40 three column subtraction problems were randomly generated as follows:

$$minuend = (random() \text{ modulo } 900) + 100$$

$$subtrahend = random() \text{ modulo } (minuend + 1)$$

where *minuend* and *subtrahend* are the two values in a subtraction problem such that the *subtrahend* is subtracted from the *minuend*, and *random()* is a pseudo random number generator that generates 32 bit unsigned integer values. This resulted in random three digit subtraction problems such the minuend contained three digits and the correct result was positive.
3. The initial test was presented to all subjects.
4. The following was repeated three times
   (a) a new set of 40 three column subtraction problems were generated for each subject as follows:

    i. for each subject in the Error Repeat treatment, all problems from the last test sheet for which the subject made an error were copied to the new problem set and then new random problems were generated, as per step 2, to make a total of 40 problems,

    ii. for each subject in the Random treatment, 40 random problems were generated, as per step 2.

  (b) the tests were administered to the subjects.

5. A single final set of 40 three column subtraction problems was generated as per step 2 and administered to all subjects.

Successive tests were all administered at weekly intervals. (As variations over time were not relevant, [10] used only the first two of this series of tests.) Normal tuition proceeded between tests. Thus, students' approaches to the domain could be expected to alter between sessions.

The two treatments were created for research purposes that do not relate to the current study. For this reason, the groups were not distinguished for analysis in the current study. Our past experience suggests that there is unlikely to be any substantial difference in the performance of the systems on the two groups.

The following evaluation is performed by forming a model from a sequence of tests, 1, ... n, which is then applied to predict the subject's precise answers in test $n + 1$. This process is repeated for n set to each of $2, 3$ and 4. The same modeling and prediction techniques were employed as in [10] except that the data aging procedures were systematically manipulated.

Data aging was implemented by reducing the accumulated score for each of $\#(C- > a)$ and $\#(C- > \neg a)$ for every a and C by the set aging rate after the prediction phase of each test round. Hence, with an aging rate of 30%, if for some a and C $\#(C- > a)$ was 1 on every test, for prediction on round 5 the cumulative value of $\#(C- > a)$ would be 2.533. The round 4 item would contribute 1.0, as it would not yet be aged. The round 3 item would contribute 0.7, as it would have been aged once. The round 2 and 1 items would contribute 0.49 and 0.343 as they would be aged twice and three times, respectively.

The following are lists of the context and action features employed to model subtraction skills in this study. For more detail, the interested reader is directed to [10].

Context Features: Minuend > Subtrahend; Minuend < Subtrahend; Minuend = Subtrahend; Minuend > Subtrahend in the column to the right; Minuend < Subtrahend in the column to the right; Minuend = Subtrahend in the column to the right; Minuend > Subtrahend two columns to the right; Minuend < Subtrahend two columns to the right; Minuend = Subtrahend two columns to the right; Minuend is zero; Minuend is not zero; Minuend is zero in the column to the left; Minuend is not zero in the column to the left; Minuend is zero in the column to the right; Minuend is not zero in the column to the right; Minuend is one in the column to the left; Minuend is not one in the column to the left; Subtrahend is zero; Subtrahend is not zero; Subtrahend is nine; Subtrahend is not nine; Subtrahend is nine in the column to the right; Subtrahend is not nine in the column to the right; Subtrahend is blank; Subtrahend is not blank; This column is right-most; This column is left-most; This column is neither left nor right-most.

Action Features: Result = Minuend − Subtrahend; Result = Minuend − Subtrahend − 1; Result = Minuend − Subtrahend + 10; Result = Minuend − Subtrahend + 9; Result = Minuend − Subtrahend + 8; Result = Minuend; Result = Subtrahend; Result = zero; Result = Minuend − Subtrahend − 2; Result = Subtrahend − Minuend; Result is correct; Result is incorrect.

Each prediction relates to a single column of a subtraction problem. The prediction is considered correct if the precise digit for the column is predicted. For some columns no predictions will be made. This can arise because: no associations apply to the column; multiple associations apply that make differing predictions; or the associations that do apply do not fully specify a single digit.

5   Results

The treatments were evaluated on six metrics:

Cover: the percentage of columns for which a prediction was made;
Accuracy: the percentage of predictions that were correct;
Student error cover: the percentage of those columns for which a student made an error, for which a prediction was made;
Student error accuracy: the percentage of the student error cover for which the predictions were correct;
Error predictions: the number of predictions that a student would make an error; and
Error prediction accuracy: the percentage of error predictions that were correct.

Figures 1 to 6 summarize the round by round performance on these metrics. Each of these figures plots the relevant outcome for each condition. Each of the data aging levels are labeled by the percentage level.

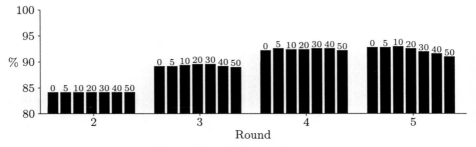

Fig. 1. Round by round cover

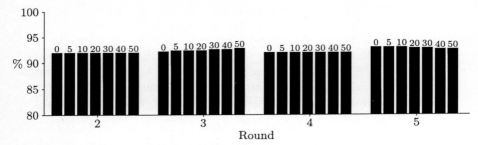

Fig. 2. Round by round accuracy

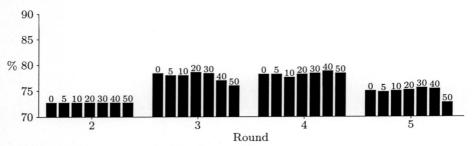

Fig. 3. Round by round student error cover

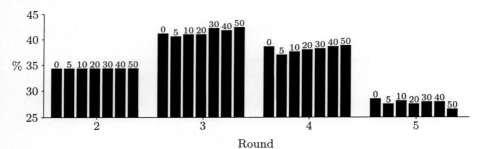

Fig. 4. Round by round student error accuracy

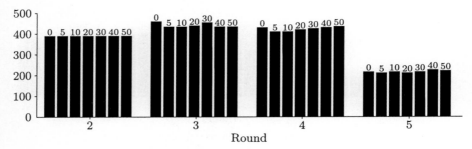

Fig. 5. Round by round error predictions

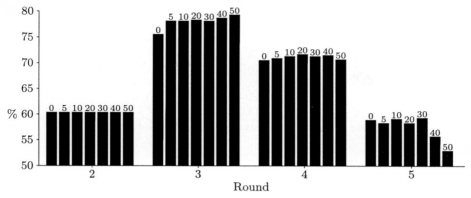

Fig. 6. Round by round error prediction accuracy

All treatments are equivalent for the first set of predictions (round 2), as aging of data only occurs immediately before the round 2 data is incorporated into the model and thus has no effect at the time when predictions are made with respect to round 2.

It can be seen that moderate levels of data aging lead to small increases in both the numbers (Figure 1) and accuracy (Figure 2) of predictions for rounds 3 and 4. However, 20% and higher aging values lead to small decreases in both numbers and accuracy of predictions on the last round. There is no clearly discernible pattern to how aging affects the number of errors for which a prediction is made (Figure 3), the accuracy of those predictions (Figure 4) or the number of predictions that the student would make an error (Figure 5). However, data aging does appear to improve the accuracy of error predictions (Figure 6) for rounds 3 and 4, although differing levels of aging lead to greatly differing outcomes on round 5.

Visual inspection of these results figures suggests that data aging at 30% leads to reasonable overall performance. A statistical comparison of the performance of this level of data aging against no data aging was performed. For each round, the relative performance of no data aging and 30% data aging was compared on a subject by subject basis. On each of the six criteria examined in the figures, the number of subjects for which each treatment outperformed the other was determined. A binomial sign test was used to evaluate whether there was a statistically significant difference in the performance of the two treatments on the criterion. The results of this evaluation are presented in Table 1. (The columns labeled 0% provide counts of the number of times no data aging outperformed 30% data aging, and those labeled 30% provide counts of the number of times 30% data aging outperformed no data aging.)

Table 1 shows that 30% data aging is leading to increases in cover and accuracy significantly more often than not for round 3 but that such an advantage is not apparent for round 4 and the reverse is true for round 5.

Criterion	Round 3			Round 4			Round 5		
	0%	30%	p	0%	30%	p	0%	30%	p
Cover	39	78	<0.001	57	52	0.351	60	29	0.001
Accuracy	36	64	0.003	43	50	0.267	47	30	0.034
Student error cover	79	70	0.364	78	75	0.209	75	72	0.271
Student error accuracy	15	18	0.364	16	22	0.209	14	10	0.271
Error predictions	20	15	0.250	20	17	0.371	17	10	0.124
Error prediction accuracy	13	12	0.500	9	15	0.154	13	9	0.262

Table 1. Sign tests comparing 0% and 30% data aging

With respect to student error cover and student error accuracy, there is no significant advantage to either treatment in any of the rounds.

With respect to the predictions that the student would make an error, neither treatment demonstrated a significant advantage with respect to either the number or accuracy of such predictions.

6   Discussion

The significant increases in both cover and accuracy on round 3 demonstrates that data aging can provide a significant benefit. The significant losses incurred on round 5 demonstrate that such benefits are far from guaranteed, however.

There is reason to believe that round 5 might be atypical in some respects. It should be recalled that all subjects were given the same randomly generated test on this round. All treatments experience a significant drop in average performance on all metrics for this round. This suggests that the single test presented to the students was not typical.

There are two possible explanations of why the significant improvements on round three are reflected in the overall number of predictions and accuracy of the system but not in respect to predicting just errors. It might indicate that discounting some of the student's errors enables the system to more successfully model those aspect of the domain that a student has mastered. On the other hand, it could be that the numbers of errors are so low that the power of the statistics employed is not great enough to uncover such an advantage even though it exists.

7   Conclusions and Further Research

A formal evaluation of data aging has led to inconclusive results. 30% data aging demonstrates a small but statistically significant improvement in the number and accuracy of predictions on the third of a series of five tests, but leads to small but statistically significant decreases in performance on the fifth test. While there is some reason to doubt the typicality of the fifth test, it is clear that data aging in its current form is not providing large improvements in system performance.

The small but significant improvements in performance that are demonstrated in the third round suggest that there is some merit in the general strategy. To this end it might be valuable to explore alternative approaches to data aging. One possibility that might be worth exploring is differential aging rates. One possibility is that errors should be discounted more rapidly than correct performance, given the evidence that students only repeat an error on approximately one third of occasions [10]. Another possibility is that data that has been aged once should subsequently be aged at a lower rate, on the assumption that there is less difference between the relevance of evidence that is two or three weeks old than between that of evidence that is one or two weeks old.

In summary, data aging in its current form does not appear to warrant use. Experimental evaluation suggests, however, that there may be merit in further refinement of the technique.

References

1. Beller, S., Hoppe, H. U.: Deductive error reconstruction and classification in a logic programming framework. In *Proceedings of AIEd'93 The World Conference on Artificial Intelligence in Education* (1993) pp. 433–440. Edinburgh.
2. Giangrandi, P., Tasso, C.: Temporal reasoning in student modelling. In du Boulay, B., Mizoguchi, R. (Eds.), *Proceedings of AI-Ed 97 World Conference on Artificial Intelligence in Education* (1997) pp. 514–521 Kobe, Japan. IOS Press.
3. Ikeda, M., Kono, Y., Mizoguchi, R.: Nonmonotonic model inference: A formalization of student modeling. In *Proceedings of the Thirteenth International Joint Conference on Artificial Intelligence: IJCAI'93* (1993) pp. 467–473 Chambery, France. Morgan Kaufmann.
4. Kuzmycz, M., Webb, G. I.: Evaluation of Feature Based Modelling in subtraction. In Frasson, C., Gauthier, G., McCalla, G. I. (Eds.), *Intelligent Tutoring Systems* (1992) pp. 269–276 Berlin. Springer-Verlag.
5. Langley, P., Ohlsson, S.: Automated cognitive modeling. In *Proceedings of the Second National Conference on Artificial Intelligence* (1984) pp. 193–197.
6. Sleeman, D. H.: Inferring student models for intelligent computer-aided instruction. In Michalski, R. S., Carbonell, J. G., Mitchell, T. M.(Eds.), *Machine Learning: An Artificial Intelligence Approach* (1984) pp. 483–510. Springer-Verlag, Berlin.
7. VanLehn, K.: Learning one procedure per lesson. *Artificial Intelligence* **31** (1987) 1–40.
8. Webb, G. I.: Inside the Unification Tutor: The architecture of an intelligent educational system. In Godfrey, B. (Ed.), *Proceedings of the Eighth Annual Conference of the Australian Society for Computers in Learning in Tertiary Education* (1991) pp. 675–684 Launceston. ASCILITE.
9. Webb, G. I., Chiu, B. C., Kuzmycz, M.: Comparative evaluation of alternative induction engines for Feature Based Modelling. *International Journal of Artificial Intelligence in Education* **8** (1997).
10. Webb, G. I., Kuzmycz, M.: Feature Based Modelling: A methodology for producing coherent, consistent, dynamically changing models of agents' competencies. *User Modeling and User Assisted Interaction* **5** (1996) 117–150.

Student Modelling by Case Based Reasoning

Mohammad E. Shiri A.   Esma Aïmeur   Claude Frasson

Université de Montréal, Département d'informatique et de recherche opérationnelle
2920 Chemin de la Tour, Montréal, H3C 3J7, Québec, Canada
E-mail: {shiri,aimeur,frasson } @iro.umontreal.ca

Abstract. The student model is the key to providing adequate assistance in teaching and adaptive instruction by Intelligent Tutoring Systems (ITS). Student modelling has been recognized as a complex and difficult but important task by researchers. We propose a new approach to student modelling based on Case-Based Reasoning (CBR), which is simple and does not require computationally expensive inference algorithms. This paper presents the application of this approach in developing an ITS, which analyzes the student's problem solving ability in order to obtain the knowledge component of the student model. We apply the formalism of Graph with Classified Concepts and Relations (GCR), an extended model of conceptual graph previously defined by us, to represent the problems, the cases, and the knowledge component of the student model in such systems.

Keywords: student modelling, knowledge component of the student model, case based reasoning, knowledge representation, graph with classified concepts and relations, problem solving, intelligent tutoring systems.

1   Introduction

A student model can be described as the information that an Intelligent Tutoring System (ITS) keeps about the knowledge of a student. It is used to drive instructional decisions in order to make an ITS adaptable to individual learners. There are many techniques for generating student models in the literature [6], however most of these techniques are computationally complex and expensive, for example numerical techniques [7]. There are three major paradigms of such numerical techniques: Bayesian Networks [13] [10], the Dempster-Shafer theory of evidence [3], and the fuzzy student modelling approach [5]). Other techniques, although computationally cheap (e.g., the model tracing approach [1] [2]) can only record what a student knows and not the student's behaviour and characteristics.

We propose a new technique based on the idea of Case-Based Reasoning (CBR). In this technique, we submit a problem to a student and allow him to find a solution by adapting existing solutions of similar problems (called cases) stored in a database. We compare this solution with the solution generated by the system using the same case. Our modelling technique is simple and does not require a computationally expensive inference algorithm. Furthermore, we believe that our approach can be applied to obtain various types of information related to the the knowledge of the learner, such as the knowledge level (in term of Gagné scale [4]), the capabilities (analogy and adaptation), and the solution known by the learner. We call this type of information the *knowledge component*.

This paper focuses on this component and shows how a CBR approach can be used to obtain this information through problem solving situations. The paper is organized as follows. First, our previous work on using CBR in ITS is briefly reviewed. Secondly, the content of a student model is described. Thirdly, the process of student modelling using CBR techniques is presented. Fourthly, this process is illustrated with an example. Finally, our approach is compared with other approaches and its implication in future research is discussed.

2   Using CBR in ITS

Case-Based Reasoning [8] [9] consists in using the previous cases or experiences to suggest a mean of solving a new problem, to critique a new solution, to explain or interpret a new situation, or to focus attention on some part of a situation or a problem. Case-Based Reasoning is often used in teaching, planning, design or argumentation. Recently, there has been a focus on Case-Based intelligent tutoring systems [11]. In such systems a set of solved problems (cases) is presented to the student who is expected to learn through these cases to solve a new problem. However, to our knowledge, no work has been done on specific issues of student modelling using CBR. In this paper we focus on the problem of how to integrate the CBR's techniques in order to construct the knowledge component of the student model.

2.1   Representing the required knowledge base

Case-Based Reasoning is based on a theory of how expertise is represented and how new knowledge is assimilated. In this section we briefly review our previous work about the representation of cases and problems for an ITS. We begin by briefly reviewing the definition of a Graph with Classified Concepts and Relations, and then by showing how the problems and cases are modelled by this formalism.

Definition: A Graph with Classified Concepts and Relations (GCR) is a particular case of conceptual graph [12], where each concept and relation consists of two parts, the type part and the referent part.

Modelling the problems: A problem consists of *Indexed information* (or *ID*, since it will be used for indexing the problems), a *statement* (or description of the problem), and the *solutions*. It should be emphasized that in the representation of a problem only two types of relations will be used: relations of *STatement type (ST)* and relations of *SIMilarity type (SIM))* (see Figure 1). This will be sufficient because, as we will show in section(3.3), the problems solutions will automatically be obtained from the solutions of similar cases and will be stored in the system dynamically.

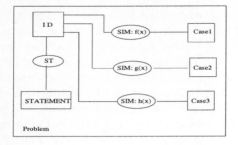

Fig. 1. Representation of a problem

An Example:

- *ID* : Problem1;
- *Statement* : Determine the function y, such that $y = \int \frac{(\ln x)^2}{x} dx$.
- *Similar to* : Case1   [* *Similarity function* : $T = \ln x$, (so $dT = \frac{1}{x} dx$)];
- *Similar to* : Case2   [* *Similarity function* : $(U, dV) = ((\ln x)^2, \frac{1}{x} dx)$];

Modelling the cases: A case is a solved problem. Likewise, it consists of *Indexed information* (or *ID*), a *statement* (or description of the case), and the *solutions*. As we already did in previous work, we use the GCR to represent the cases. In such a representation, two types of relations are used: (1) relations of *STatement type (ST)*, which link the statement to the ID; and (2) relations of *SOLution type (SOL)*, which link a solution to the ID. For a given case we can have two types of solutions: *inductive* or *deductive*. Figure 2 reflects the representation of a case.

An example:

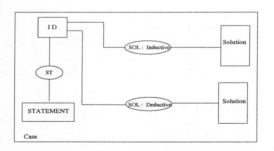

Fig. 2. Representation of a case

- *ID* : Case1;
- *Statement* : Determine the function y, such that $y = \int T^n dT$.
- *SOL* : Deductive   [* *Solution* : $y = \frac{1}{n+1} T^{n+1} + C.$]

3   Student modelling

3.1   Elements of the student model

A student model represents knowledge about a student, which is used by the ITS to provide adaptive instruction to the student. The information which must be contained in a student model depends on the instructional tasks to be supported and on the characteristics of the subject matter to be taught. Some identified contents are: level of knowledge, goals and plans, capabilities, attitudes, and knowledge or beliefs. In this paper, we are particularly interested in the knowledge level, the capabilities (analogy and adaptation), and the solutions known by the learner, all of which constitutes the *knowledge component* of the student model.

3.2   Case-Based student modelling as a subsystem

In an attempt to explain and understand the student modelling task we represent the Case-Based Student Modelling (CBSM) as a subsystem of the global (ITS) system. Three types of information which can be identified as input flows to this subsystem are: *"problem"*, *"case selected by the student"*, and the *"student's solution"*. The information which can be identified as output flows are: *"knowledge component"* of the student model and the *"solution generated to the problem"*. The CBSM subsystem contains a number of components; as shown in Figure 3, the main components are the following: *"Verificator"*, *"Solutions Generator"*, and *"Analyzer"*. We now describe the role of these components and the related flows of information in more detail.

3.3   Student modelling process

Figure 3 shows a scheme for constructing the knowledge component of a student model. The process of construction involves several steps:

- *Selection of a problem.* First, the ITS selects a problem to propose to the student. The selection of the problem is based on: "elements of the student model" and "the concepts of interest to be taught".
- *Selection of cases by the student.* When the student is faced with a new problem, he searches into the cases base for a relevant case that best matches the problem. In order to enable the student to do this, the ITS should be equipped with a tool which can return the list of cases for the student to inspect.
- *Adaptation of the case (by the student).* Once the case has been selected by the student, he creates a solution to the current problem by adapting the solution of the selected case. Adaptation can take several forms [8]: something new might be inserted into the case solution, something might be deleted from it, some item might be substituted for another, or some part of the case solution might be transformed.

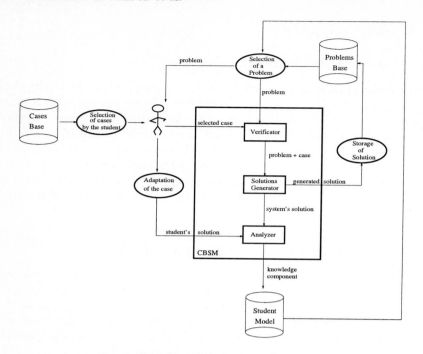

Fig. 3. The process of student modelling

Two different ways of adaptation can be identified: (1) *Accessible solution mode.* In this method the cases solutions are accessible by the student. He adapts the solution of the selected case, which he thinks is similar to the given problem, to obtain a solution for the problem. This method is useful when the ITS deals with a novice. (2) *Unaccessible solution mode.* In this method the cases solutions are not accessible. Therefore, the student must remember the steps of the solution of the selected case, which he thinks is similar to the given problem, to suggest a mean of solving the new problem.

- *Solutions generation.* Before attempting to analyze the student's solution, the CBSM should generate all the possible solutions to the problem by using the same case selected by the student. We remind that the solutions generated by the system will compared with the student's solution. In short, the process of generating can be summarized in the following steps: (1) *Verify the similarity between the problem and the case selected by the student.* The case selected by the student may not really be similar to the problem. In this condition, the *Verificator* can verify the student's selection by using the information existing in each problem. (2) *Adapting the solutions of the case.* In order to obtain the solutions for the problem the *Solutions Generator* adapts the solution(s) of the case selected by the student if it is applicable, i.e., if the case selected by the student is truly similar to the problem.

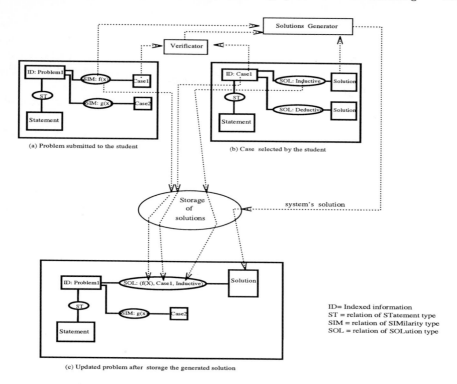

Fig. 4. Generation and storage of problems solutions.

– *Storage of solutions.* Once the solutions of a problem are generated by the CBSM, they are stored in the system for future reference. The generated solutions can be included in the representation of the problem by modifying (see Figure 4) the structure of this representation. This can be done by: (1) eliminating the relation between the problem and the case selected by the student (from the representation of the problem); (2) and then linking the generated solutions to the problem. In general, in order to identify the linked solutions, a relation of *SOLution type (SOL)* must be used; the referent of this relation becomes a triplet *(f(x), Case-i, RM)* where *Case-i* is the case selected by the student, *f(x)* is the function of similarity between the problem and the case, and *RM* is the Reasoning Mode of the solutions (for example: inductive, deductive etc.). Figure 4 illustrates how these elements *(f(x), Case-i, RM)* have been selected for a given problem.

Remark: The problems base changes dynamically each time solutions are generated by the CBSM system. Therefore, each time the system faces the task solutions generation for a problem it first checks the problems base. If the solutions of this problem relative to the case selected by the student has already been stored in the problems base, then it does not need to implement the last two tasks. It is only sufficient to verify the similarities between the problem and the case selected by the student. The implementation of this task is necessary to make sure that the student has selected a suitable case for his reasoning. As a result, the system needs to generate and store the solutions to each problem relative to each similar case only once.

- *Analyzing the student's solution.* The analysis of the student's answer leads to what we call the knowledge component of a student model. This process is activated by the answer provided by the student to the problem. Then, the *Analyzer* compares the student's solution with those generated by the *Solution Generator*, which can be considered as an expert's solutions. The information issued from this analysis can be: (1) the *level of student's knowledge* in terms of the Gagné scale; assuming that it is at level 6 before problem solving, we will increase it to level 7 when the problem is successfully solved, and reduce it to level 5 when the problem remains unsolved; (2) the *student's capabilities* of analogy and adaptation for the cases he used to solve the problems; (3) and the *solutions known* by the student for these problems.
- *Achieving the knowledge component of the student model.* Finally, the ITS uses the results of the *Analyzer*'s activities to update the student model. We apply the GCR to model the knowledge component of the student model. This component contains: (1) all the problems solved by the student. We have to note that each problem is attached to a solution which is identified by the student for this problem. The solution is linked to the problem by a relation of *SOLution type(SOL)*; the referent of this relation is a triplet *(f(x), Case-i, RM)* where *Case-i* is the case selected by student, *f(x)* is the function of similarity between the problem and this case, and *RM* is the reasoning mode of the solution (see Figure 4); (2) all the problems submitted and unsolved by the student. It will be useful to add these problems to the knowledge component, because they indicate the student's points of difficulty.

4   An example

In order to understand the steps of the process mentioned above we give an example.

- Let us assume that the system has selected the following problem to present to the student.
  - Problem submitted to the student :
    * *ID* : Problem1;
    * *Statement* : Determine the function y, such that $y = \int \frac{(\ln x)^2}{x} dx$.
    * *Similar to* : Case1   [* *Similarity function* : $T = \ln x$, (so $dT = \frac{1}{x} dx$)];
    * *Similar to* : Case2   [* *Similarity function* : $(U, dV) = ((\ln x)^2, \frac{1}{x} dx)$];
- In order to enable the student to solve new problems, the previously solved cases should be stored in the system. For instance, in our current example the following cases are stored.
  - Some existing cases in the cases base :
    1. Case1 :
       * *ID* : Case1;
       * *Statement* : Determine the function y, such that $y = \int T^n dT$.
       * *SOL* : Deductive   [* *Solution* : $y = \frac{1}{n+1} T^{n+1} + C.$]

2. Case2 :
   * ID : Case2;
   * Statement : Determine the function y, such that $y = \int U dV$.
   * SOL : Deductive   [* Solution : $y = UV - \int V dU + C$.]
- The student is now searching for resemblance between the submitted problem and one that he has been previously solved.
  • The case selected by the student : Case1
- The process of problem solving by the student.
  • The student's solution using Case1 :

$y = \int \frac{(\ln x)^2}{x} dx = \int T^2 dT + C$

$y = \frac{1}{3}T^3 + C$

$y = \frac{1}{3}(\ln x)^3 + C.$

- The process of problem solving by the system.
  • Verify the similarity between the problem1 and the case1 : OK
  • The function of adaptation : $T = \ln x$
  • A solution of the problem generated by the system using Case1 :

$y = \int \frac{(\ln x)^2}{x} dx = \int T^2 dT + C$

$y = \frac{1}{3}T^3 + C$

$y = \frac{1}{3}(\ln x)^3 + C.$

- For the purpose of future reference, the generated solution should be stored in the system.
  • The state of the problem1 after the storage of the generated solution :
    * ID : Problem1;
    * Statement : Determine the function y, such that $y = \int \frac{(\ln x)^2}{x} dx.$
    * SOL(relation of solution type) : ($T = \ln x$, Case1, Deductive)
      · Solution :

$y = \int \frac{(\ln x)^2}{x} dx = \int T^2 dT + C$

$y = \frac{1}{3}T^3 + C$

$y = \frac{1}{3}(\ln x)^3 + C.$

   * Similar to : Case2   [* Similarity function : $U = (\ln x)^2$, $dV = \frac{1}{x} dx$];

- Now, the analyzer compares the student's solution with the solutions generated by the system.
- Updating the student model.
  • The information added to the student model
    * ID : Problem1;
    * Statement : Determine the function y such that $y = \int \frac{(\ln x)^2}{x} dx.$
    * SOL(relation of solution type) : ($T = \ln x$, Case1, Deductive)
      · Solution :

$y = \int \frac{(\ln x)^2}{x} dx = \int T^2 dT + C$

$y = \frac{1}{3}T^3 + C$

$y = \frac{1}{3}(\ln x)^3 + C.$

As a result, the updated student model contains the student's solution for this problem and indicates: (1) that the student has the capability (of analogy and adaptation) to solve the problems similar to case1; (2) the student's level of knowledge goes form level 6 to level 7 in term of the Gagné scale.

5   Conclusions and Future Work

We propose a new approach to student modelling based on Case-Based Reasoning. Our technique differs from some types of student modelling and shares several features with other modelling approaches. In fact unlike the Bayesian student modelling and fuzzy student modelling approaches, there is no need for sophisticated and computationally expensive inference mechanisms. Furthermore, this approach can be used to construct different components of the student model. This paper proposed the application of our approach in constructing the knowledge component of the student model.

In the near future, we plan to improve this approach in order to be able to construct the other components of the student model, such as the student characteristics model. For the moment, we have implemented a prototype system called P-SARA[1]. This prototype is a first step toward an ITS that integrates CBR to model the student's modes of inferences. We hope to improve our current prototype in order to enable it to achieve a complete student model.

Acknowledgments: This research has been supported by the TLNCE (Telelearning Network Centers of Excellence in Canada), to which we give thanks. The first author also wishes to thank the Ministry of Culture & Higher Education of Iran for its scholarship during his studies.

References

1. Anderson, J.R., Boyle, C. F., Corbett, A.T., and Lewis, M. W. Cognitive modeling and intelligent tutoring. *Artificial Intelligence, 42*, pages 7–49, 1990.
2. Anderson, J.R., Corbett, A.T., Koedinger,K., and Pelletier, R. Cognitive tutors: Lessons learned. *The Journal of the Learning Sciences vol. 4, no. 2*, pages 167–207, 1995.
3. Bauer, M. A dempster-shafer approach to modeling agent references for plan recognition. *User Modelling and User-Adapted Interaction, 5*, pages 317–348, 1996.
4. Gagné, R. M. *The condition of learning and the theory of instruction.* CBS College Publishing, Fourth ed., 1985.
5. Hawkes, L. W., Derry, S. J., and Rundensteiner, E. A. Individualized tutoring using an intelligent fuzzy temporal relational database. *International Journal of Man-Machine Studies, 33*, pages 409–429, 1990.
6. Holt, P., Dubs, S., Jones, M., and Greer, J. The state of student modelling. In *Greer, J.E. and McCalla, G.I.(Eds): Student Modelling: The Key to Individualized Knowledge-Based Instruction*, pages 3–35, NATO-ASI Series F, Springer-Verlag, 1994.
7. Jameson, A. Numerical uncertainty management in user and student modeling: An overview of systems and issues. *User Modelling and User-Adapted Interaction, 5*, pages 193–251, 1996.
8. Kolodner, J. *Case-Based Reasoning.* Morgan Kaufmann Publisher Inc., San Mateo CA, 1993.
9. Leake, D.B. *Case-Based Reasoning: Experiences, Lessons and Future Directions.* AAAI Press, Menlo Park, California, 1996.
10. Petrushin, V. A. and Sinista, K. M. Using probabilistic reasoning techniques for learner modelling. *World Conference on AI in Education, Edinburgh, Scotland*, pages 418–425, 1993.

---

[1] Petit Système d'Analyse des Raisonnements de l'Apprenant.

11. Schank, R. and Edelson, D. A role for AI in education: using technology to reshape education. *Journal of Artificial Intelligence in Education, 1(2)*, pages 3–20, 1990.
12. Sowa, J.F. *Principles of Semantic Network: Exploration in the Representation of Knowledge*. Morgan Kaufmann Publisher Inc., San Mateo CA, 1991.
13. Villano, M. Probabilistic students models: bayesian belief networks and knowledge space theory. In *Second International Conference on Intelligent Tutoring System*, pages 491–498, Montréal, Canada, 1992.

Tutoring Prolog Novices Based on Programming Techniques

Jun Hong

School of Information and Software Engineering
University of Ulster at Jordanstown
Newtownabbey, Co. Antrim BT37 0QB, United Kingdom
j.hong@ulst.ac.uk

Abstract. We present a techniques-based approach to the tutoring of Prolog programming. The concept of a programming technique is used to characterise and classify programs. We define a set of technique grammar rules for each class of programs, which can be used for program classification, technique and program recognition, and program construction. We use both technique and program frames to represent technique-related and program-related knowledge that provides the basis of error diagnosis and explanation generation for tutoring. Our approach to error diagnosis and explanation generation, however, does not rely on the representation of buggy versions of the program.

1 Introduction

Because Prolog has a simple syntax and few program constructs, it is fairly easy to start Prolog programming. Even though the language knowledge itself does not give the novice any serious problems, studies show that they often have many difficulties with Prolog programming due to the lack of Prolog programming knowledge [9], [10]. This type of metaknowledge in contrast to the language knowledge is therefore essential in Prolog programming.

Many efforts have been made to identify this type of knowledge, and help the Prolog programmer to learn and use it. Brna et al [2] described the concept of a Prolog programming technique. They showed that a knowledge of programming techniques can be useful in both program construction and program debugging. Gegg-Harrison [3] described the notion of basic Prolog construct schemata and showed how they could be used to represent the basic constructs of a structured Prolog for recursive list processing. The basic constructs of Prolog can be viewed as Prolog programming techniques.

All these efforts [2], [3] have been mainly focused on facilitating program construction rather than program debugging and tutoring. Looi [7] described an algorithms-based approach to the debugging of the student Prolog program, that detects errors in the program and proposes the corrections. Looi's work however has some limitations: The algorithms are randomly picked up without characterisation; All the possible implementations of an algorithm have to be represented; It relies on the representation of buggy versions of programs for error explanation; It can only give code-related tutoring commentaries to the student.

In this paper, we present a techniques-based approach to the tutoring of Prolog programming, that can overcome the limitations in Looi's algorithms-based approach. The concept of a programming technique is used to characterise and classify programs. We define a set of technique grammar rules for each class of programs. These grammar rules can be used for program classification, technique and program recognition, and program construction. The technique-related knowledge is represented for each class of programs in a technique frame. The coding-related knowledge is represented for each program in a program frame. These two types of knowledge provide the basis of error diagnosis and explanation generation for tutoring. Our approach to error diagnosis and explanation generation however does not rely on the representation of buggy versions of the program.

We present a system for tutoring Prolog programming to the student. It poses programming exercises to the student and asks him to do the exercises in the form of Prolog programs. It analyses the student's programs and the techniques used in the programs, and gives comments, suggestions or corrections when appropriate. If the student is not able to program on his own and has failed to use a programming technique in his program, he is given directive guidance and provided with program templates in which the relevant programming techniques have been embedded.

2   Representation of Prolog Programming Techniques

A Prolog programming technique is a common pattern of code used by the Prolog programmer in a fairly systematic way [2]. Prolog programs can, therefore, be characterised and classified into different categories, with each category of programs corresponding to a particular programming technique.

2.1   Schema Representation of Prolog Programming Techniques

Gegg-Harrson [3] provided a Prolog schema language for defining the basic Prolog construct schemata that represent the common syntactic features shared by the corresponding sets of programs. This schema language is an extension of Prolog supporting first-order schema variables, second-order predicate variables, optional, arbitrary, and permutable arguments and goals. For example, in the following schema, any number of arguments can replace schema variables &1, ..., &7 while the terms pre_pred<<&3>>,H,<<&4>>) and post_pred(<<&6>>,H, <<&7>>) may be instantiated to either the null string or a single invocation of the goal.

```
schema_A([],<<&1>>).
schema_A([H|T],<<&2>>)  :-  <pre_pred(<<&3>>,H,<<&4>>),>
                            schema_A(T,<<&5>>)
                            <,post_pred(<<&6>>,H,<<&7>>)>.
```

Since a basic Prolog construct schema represents a programming technique that is the generalisation of a set of programs, it might be useful for presenting the general idea of the technique to the student. It might also be useful for being presented to the student in the form of templates for instantiation and modification. A basic Prolog construct schema is however less useful for recognising a program since it does not provide much grammatical information and relies on pattern matching to match the schema to the student program.

2.2 Grammatical Representation of Prolog Programming Techniques

We define a Prolog technique grammar to represent Prolog programming techniques. The Prolog technique grammar is a type of context sensitive grammar and an extension of Prolog grammar that defines the general form of Prolog clauses. We use a set of technique grammar rules to define the set of programs that correspond to a Prolog programming technique.

Gegg-Harrison [3] defined a set of Prolog construct schemata to represent the corresponding Prolog programming techniques. We need to define a set of Prolog technique grammar rules for each set of programs that can be made to instantiate a basic Prolog construct schemata. Let's look at schema_A described in Section 2.1. The programming technique used in this schema is to process a list until it is empty by splitting it into the head and the tail, making a recursive call with the tail. We can define a set of Prolog technique grammar rules as shown in Fig. 1 to represent this technique that can be used to generate and parse all programs in which this technique has been used.

```
<technique_A program> ::= <base case>{Pred}<recursive case>{Pred}
<base case>{Pred} ::= <pred>{Pred}([],<optional args>)
<optional args> ::= <arg>|<arg>,<optional args>
<recursive case>{Pred} ::= <rule head>{Pred,H,T} :-
                                      <rule body>{Pred,H,T}
<rule head>{Pred,H,T} ::= <pred>{Pred}(<list split>{H,T},
                                      <optional args>)
<list split>{H,T} ::= [<list head>{H}|<list tail>{T}]
<rule body>{Pred,H,T} ::= ......
......
```

Fig. 1. A set of technique grammar rules for a Prolog programming technique

In the above set of grammar rules, those strings enclosed in a pair of brackets {} such as Pred, H and T are context variables. Using this set of grammar rules, the following naive reverse program can be parsed as shown in Fig. 2.

```
reverse([],[]).
reverse([X|Y],L) :- reverse(Y,M),append(M,[X],L).
```

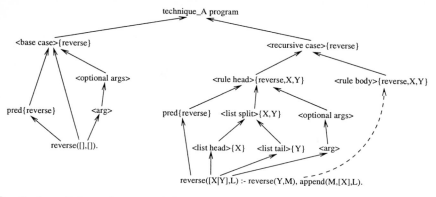

Fig. 2. A partial parsing tree of the naive reverse program using a set of technique grammar rules.

2.3   Prolog Programming Technique Hierarchies

We can create a Prolog programming technique hierarchy that contains all programming techniques and programs for simple recursive list processing. Gegg-Harrison [3] described two major viewpoints, termination and execution, to differentiate Prolog programs along two primary dimensions. Since the two viewpoints both group together Prolog programs on the basis of their common patterns of code, they are consistent with the way in which Prolog programming techniques group together Prolog programs. They can, therefore, group together Prolog programming techniques as well. We use the termination viewpoint to create a Prolog programming technique hierarchy as shown in Fig. 3.

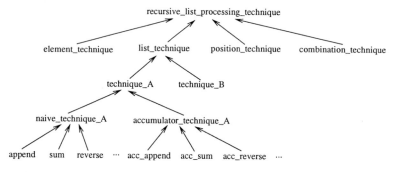

Fig. 3. A partial Prolog programming technique hierarchy based on a viewpoint

3   Representation of Semantic Knowledge and Programming Exercises

Apart from syntactical knowledge such as technique grammar rules and the standard codes, we also need to represent the semantic knowledge including technique-related and program-related knowledge, and the programming exercises.

3.1 Representation of Technique-Related and Program-Related Knowledge

The semantic knowledge associated with each of the nodes on the programming technique hierarchy is represented by either a technique frame or a program frame. There are also clause frames that represent the semantic knowledge associated with individual clauses within a program. The Fig. 4 shows the representation of technique, program and clause frames.

```
Frame type: technique
Name: naive_technique_A
Description: To process a list until it is empty by splitting it
            into the head and the tail, ...
Programs: reserve, sum, length, ...

Frame type: program
Name: reverse
Program type: recursive
Invocation: Code: reverse(List,Revlist).
            Description: Check or get the reverse of a list.
                        If List and Revlist ...
Base cases: reverse_clause_1
Recursive cases: reverse_clause_2

Frame type: base case
Name: reverse_clause_1
Head: Code: reverse([],[]).
      Description: Reversing an empty list gets ...

Frame type: recursive case
Name: reverse_clause_2
Head: Code: reverse([H|T],L).
      Description: Reversing a non-empty list consisting of a
                  head, H, and a tail, T, gets a list, L.
Body: Recursive call: Code: reverse(T,L1)
                      Statement: The tail, T, is reversed to
                                 get a list, L1.
      Post predicate: Code: append(L1,[H],L)
                      Statement: The list, L, is obtained from
                                 appending the list, L1, ...
```

Fig. 4. Representation of technique, program and clause frames

3.2 Representation of Programming Exercises

There are a set of exercise frames to represent the programming exercises given to the student. An exercise frame is shown in Fig. 5.

```
Frame type: exercise
Name: list_reversal
Description: Write a program which reverses the elements of a list
            into another list.
Likely techniques: naive_technique_A, accumulator_technique_A
```

Fig. 5. Representation of an exercise frame

4   Program Tutoring Based on Technique and Program Recognition, Error Diagnosis and Explanation Generation

First of all, the system poses a programming exercise to the student by accessing the exercise frame and asks him to write a program for doing the given task in the exercise. The system then runs a tutoring process at both the technique and coding levels.

4.1   Recognition and Tutoring of Programming Techniques

When the exercise is given to the student, he is not told about the programming techniques to be used for the exercise. The student then answers the exercise question in the form of a Prolog program that consists of a number of clauses. The program is parsed and a path of programming techniques from the most general one at the top of the programming technique hierarchy to the most specific one just above the program itself may be recognised. When this path of programming technique is a complete one, the student has no problems with the techniques. So the tutoring is shifted to the program itself.

In some cases, only those more general programming techniques can be recognised because the student has not been able to use those more specific programming techniques in his program which therefore does not give sufficient information for the recognition of these more specific programming techniques. The system will then start with the most specific technique among the ones recognised so far. It will tutor the student on the more specific techniques so the student can further complete the program.

In the following transcript, the student program can not be recognised to fit into one of the most specific programming techniques because the student has not been able to implement a specific programming technique properly. The system therefore tries to tutor the student on the relevant programming techniques that can be used to further complete the program.

System: Write a program which reverses the elements of a list into another list.
Student: Help.
System: You can use a technique that recursively processes all elements in the list.

```
reverse(<arguments>).
reverse(<arguments>) :- <pre-predicates>,
                        reverse(<arguments>),
                        <post-predicates>.
```

Student: More help.
System: You can use a technique that processes a list until it is empty by splitting it into the head and the tail, making a recursive call with the tail.

```
reverse([],<optional arguments>).
reverse([H|T], <optional arguments>) :-
                            <pre predicates>,
                            reverse(T, <optional arguments>),
                            <post predicates>.
```

Student: More help.
System: You can further complete your program using either a naive technique or an accumulator technique.
Student: I want to use the naive technique.
System: The naive technique allows you to process a list until it is empty by splitting it into the head and the tail, making a recursive call with the tail and putting the result from the recursive call and the processed head together as required.

```
reverse([],<argument>).
reverse([H|T],<argument>) :- reverse(T, <argument>),
                            <post predicate>.
```

Student:

```
reverse([], Reversed).
reverse([H|T], Reversed) :- reverse(T, ReversedT),
                            append(H, ReversedT, Reversed).
```

System: You seem to have known the correct programming technique for doing this exercise. You will be given more tutoring on your program itself next.

4.2   Error Diagnosis and Explanation Generation

When the student has no problems with the programming technique used, the tutoring is shifted to the program itself at the coding level. The program frame that contains the implementation of the exercise using that particular technique is accessed. The programming codes are parsed using the set of technique grammar rules associated with the most specific programming technique. The parsing of the student program is then compared with the parsing of the standard program given in the program frame. Several types of errors can be recognised. These include missing clauses, extra clauses, missing subgoals, extra subgoals, wrong ordering of clauses, wrong ordering of subgoals, term type errors, missing arguments, extra arguments, wrong ordering of arguments, and inconsistent uses of arguments.

In the following transcript, a student program has been recognised to fit into one of the most specific programming techniques. The program implementation of the technique for doing the given exercise is retrieved and parsed. The parsing of the student program and the one of the standard program are compared. Two errors are found in the base case and the recursive case respectively. These errors are explained to the student who is then asked to correct the program.

System: Write a program which reverses the elements of a list into another list.
Student:

```
reverse([],List).
reverse([H|T],L) :- reverse(T,L1), append(H,L1,L).
```

System: You seem to have used a programming technique that processes a list until it is empty by splitting it into the head and the tail, making a recursive call with the tail and putting the result from the recursive call and the processed head together as required.
Student: Yes. That's right.
System: Great! You have picked up an appropriate programming technique for this exercise. The base case in your program is, however, not quite right. It is supposed to say that reversing an empty list gets the empty list itself. The second argument of your base case, List, is a variable but it is supposed to be an empty list. Now can you correct your base case?
Student:

```
reverse([],[]).
```

System: Yes, correct. Your base case says that reversing an empty list gets the empty list itself.
System: The recursive call in the body of your recursive case is correct but the post goal isn't. The first argument in the post goal should be a list rather than a variable because the post goal is supposed to say that the list, L, is obtained from appending the list, [H], and the list, L1. Now can you correct your recursive case?
Student:

```
reverse([H|T],L) :- reverse(T,L1), append([H],L1,L).
```

System: That's correct. Your recursive case says that reversing a non-empty list consisting of a head, H and a tail, T gets a list, L if the tail, T is reversed to get a list, L1, and the list, L is obtained from appending the list, L1 and the list, [H].

5   Related Work

The way our system tutors the student on Prolog programming at the coding level is similar to Looi's APROPOS2 [7]. However there are a number of fundamental differences between the two systems. The tutoring of APROPOS2 is only restricted to the coding level. It can not tutor the student on the use of appropriate programming techniques. Our system tutors the student at both the programming technique level and the coding level.

The program recognition in APROPOS2 relies on the code matching of the student program and a reference program. Any discrepancies between the two programs are treated as errors. The student program is then made to match one of the buggy versions of the reference program and the pre-generated commentaries associated with the buggy version are given to the student telling him which parts of the program are wrong and how to correct them. The program recognition in our system is based on the comparison of the parsing trees of the student program and the standard program respectively. The parsing trees are generated using the technique grammar rules and they carry grammatical information explicitly. So the system is able to automatically generate the explanation on the syntactic errors in the student program and suggest the corrections to the errors based on the standard program. Our system is therefore not dependent on the representation of the buggy versions of the standard program.

Gegg-Harrison [3] emphasised the importance of using structured programming constructs in Prolog programming [2]. A basic Prolog construct schema is the structural representation of the corresponding group of programs. This kind of schema representation is useful for program construction because the student can be provided with the relevant program templates to complete. The schema representation is, however, not quite suitable for program debugging because it does not contain detailed grammatical information. Gegg-Harrison's system can not detect any errors in the student program and give the explanation on the errors to the student.

Soloway and his colleagues [4], [5], [8] introduced the notion of programming plans for the detection and explanation of the semantic errors produced by novice Pascal programmers. The plan-based approach may suit the analysis of structured programs written in a procedural programming language. Its suitability for declarative programs written in Prolog is an issue to be addressed.

The Lisp Tutor [1] contains a set of ideal rules to represent the programming knowledge to be acquired by the student, a large set of buggy rules to represent misconceptions and the corrections to them. The Lisp Tutor, however, only has specific problem-solving rules which do not explicitly represent conceptual structures of the programming language [6].

6   Conclusions

In this paper, we have discussed how to use programming techniques to group together Prolog programs. We have described how to use a set of technique grammar rules to represent a programming technique, and how to organise these programming techniques in a hierarchical structure called the programming technique hierarchy.

We presented a new approach to the tutoring of Prolog programming to the novice. Different types of frames are used to represent technique-related, program-related and clause-related programming knowledge respectively. There are also a set of exercise frames that represent all exercises given to the student. These different types of frames provide a knowledge source to our tutoring system that can give directive guidance on the programming techniques to be used, recognise the specific technique used, detect different types of errors in the student program, generate tutorial explanation on the errors to the student, and suggest corrections to the errors.

We have implemented the system in LPA Prolog. We have tested the system using a variety of correct and buggy Prolog programs. It can recognise all the correct and buggy programs that fit into the programming techniques the system has at moment. More programming techniques need to be defined before we can carry out a larger scale of quantitative evaluation.

Further developments could be done in a few areas: How to automatically extract a new programming technique shared by a set of programs and represent it in a set of technique grammar rules? Is the representation of a technique sufficient for recognising any program supposed to in the class and rejecting any program not supposed to be in the class? How to deal with the variations of the standard program?

References

1. Anderson, J.R. and Reiser, B.J. (1985) The Lisp Tutor. BYTE, April, 159-175.
2. Brna, P., Bundy, A., Dodd, T., Eisenstadt, M., Looi, C.K., Pain, H., Robertson, D., Smith, B. and van Someren, M. (1991) Prolog programming techniques. Instructional Science 20: 111-133.
3. Gegg-Harrison, T.S. (1991) Learning Prolog in a schema-based environment. Instructional Science 20: 173-192.
4. Johnson, W.L. and Soloway, E. (1985) PROUST: knowledge-based program understanding. IEEE Transactions of Software Engineering, SE-11(3): 267-275.
5. Spohrer, J.C., Soloway, E. and Pope, E. (1985) A goal-plan analysis of buggy Pascal programs. Human-Computer Interaction 1:163-207.
6. VanLehn, K. (1996) Conceptual and Meta Learning During Coached Problem Solving. Intelligent Tutoring Systems. Proceedings of the Third International Conference, ITS'96, Montreal, Canada, 29-47.
7. Looi, C.K. (1991) Automatic debugging of Prolog programs in a Prolog tutoring system. Instructional Science 20: 215-263.
8. Soloway, E.M. (1985) From problems to programs via plans: the content and structure of knowledge for introductory LISP programming. Journal of Educational Computing Research: 1, 157-172.
9. Taylor, J. and du Boulay, B. (1987) Studying novice programmers: why they may find learning Prolog hard. Computers, cognition and development: issues for psychology and education, J.C. Rutkowska and C. Crook (Eds.), New York: John Wiley and Sons.
10. van Someren, M.W. (1990) Whats wrong? Understanding beginners problems with Prolog. Instructional Science 19: 257-282.

Experiences in Implementing Constraint-Based Modeling in SQL-Tutor

Antonija Mitrović

Computer Science Department, University of Canterbury
Christchurch, New Zealand
tanja@cosc.canterbury.ac.nz
http://www.cosc.canterbury.ac.nz/~tanja

Abstract. The problem with most student modeling approaches is their insistence on complete and cognitively valid models of student's knowledge. Ohlsson [10] proposes Constraint-Based Modeling (CBM) as a way to overcome intractability of student modeling, by generating models that are precise enough to guide instruction, and are computationally tractable at the same time. The paper presents our experiences in building SQL-Tutor, an ITS built upon CBM. CBM is extremely computationally efficient. State constraints, which form the basis of CBM, are very expressive; we have encountered no situations where constraints were unable to diagnose student answers. The time needed to acquire, implement and test a constraint is less than times reported for the acquisition of production rules. The initial evaluation of SQL-Tutor proved the validity of design and appropriateness of CBM.

1 Introduction

Student modeling (SM) is crucial for Intelligent Teaching Systems (ITS) to be able to adapt to the needs and knowledge of individual students. However, the process of generating student models is intractable in nature [7] [10] [12]. Search spaces involved are huge and the modeling environment gets very limited student input with a lot of noise, caused by the loss of concentration or tiredness, dynamic and non–monotonic nature of human learning, ambiguities and indeterminacy in student's answers.

Although the complexity of student modeling is well-known, many existing SM approaches insist on cognitive validity and completeness of generated models. We have strong objections towards such approaches. If the goal is to model student's knowledge completely and precisely, student modeling is bound to be intractable. However, a student model can be useful even if it is not complete and accurate [10] [12]. Even simple and constrained modeling is sufficient for instruction purposes, and this claim is supported by findings that human teachers also use very loose models of their learners, and yet are highly effective in what they do [7] [12]. Anderson [2] also argues against such modeling, saying that it is not very useful for students to be told about the sources of their misconceptions, and that students benefit much more by being given an informative error message.

Fortunately, recently there has been a new wave of SM approaches that do not insist on completeness and cognitive validity, but rather on models precise enough to guide instruction and computationally tractable at the same time. One of such approaches is Ohlsson's Constraint-Based Modeling (CBM) [10]. This paper presents our experiences in implementing CBM in SQL-TUTOR, an ITS for SQL programming. Section 2 introduces CBM. We turn to SQL-TUTOR in section 3, which discusses the domain, system's architecture and components. The implementation of CBM within SQL-TUTOR is the topic of section 4, followed by discussion and conclusions.

2 Learning from Errors and Constraint-Based Modeling

Ohlsson [11] presents a theory of learning from errors, which views errors as the results of applying overly general knowledge. Ohlsson explains the process of learning from errors as consisting of two parts: error recognition and error correction. A student needs declarative knowledge in order to detect an error; only then, the error can be corrected by specializing faulty knowledge so that it is applicable only in situations in which it is appropriate.

CBM is built upon learning from errors. The approach identifies errors, which is extremely important for students lacking declarative knowledge, and therefore unable to detect errors themselves. The basic assumption of CBM is that diagnostic information is not hidden in the sequence of student's actions, but in the situation (or the problem state) that the student arrived at. This assumption is supported by the fact that there can be no correct solution of a problem that traverses a problem state which violates the fundamental ideas or concepts of the domain. The student model does not represent student's actions, but the effects of his/her actions instead.

Because the space of false knowledge is vast, Ohlsson suggests the use of an abstraction mechanism which he realizes in the form of state constraints. A state constraint is an ordered pair (C_r, C_s), where C_r is the relevance condition and C_s is the satisfaction condition. Each constraint specifies one property of the domain which is shared by all correct paths. C_r is used to identify a set of problem states for which the constraint is relevant, while C_s identifies a subset of these states in which the constraint is satisfied. In other words, if C_r is satisfied in a problem state, in order for that problem state to be a correct one, it must also satisfy C_s. An example of a constraint in the arithmetic domain is [10]:

If the problem is $n_1/d_1 + n_2/d_2$, the student's solution is n/d and $n = n_1 + n_2$, then it had better be the case that $d_1 = d_2 = d$.

The relevance condition focuses on a class of problems in which two fractions are to be added and the numerator of the result equals to the sum of the numerators of operands. In all such problems, the solution can only be correct if the denominators of the starting fractions are identical.

CBM represents domain knowledge as a set of state constraints, which define equivalence classes of problem states. An equivalence class triggers the same instructional action; hence all states in an equivalence class are pedagogically equivalent. A violated constraint signals an error, which translates to incomplete/incorrect knowledge.

The most important feature of CBM is its computational simplicity. Instead of using complex reasoning as required by other SM approaches, CBM reduces student modeling to pattern matching. Conditions are combinations of patterns, and can therefore be represented in compiled forms, such as RETE networks [5], which are very fast and for which off-the-shelf software is available. In the first step all relevance patterns are matched against the problem state. In the second step, the satisfaction components of constraints that matched the problem state in the first step (i.e., relevant constraints) are matched. If a satisfaction pattern matches the state, then the constraint is satisfied, and the ITS is not to take any action. In the opposite case, the constraint is violated. The student model consists of all violated constraints.

CBM does not require extensive studies of students bugs required by enumerative modeling, as in [1]. Furthermore, Ohlsson's approach is not sensitive to the *radical strategy variability phenomenon*, by being able to completely ignore procedures used by students to solve problem and thus allowing for student's inconsistency in choosing problem-solving strategies. CBM is neutral with respect to the pedagogy, since different pedagogical actions (immediate or delayed ones) may be generated on the basis of the model.

Another advantage of CBM is that it allows for a simpler architecture of ITSs, since there is no need for a runnable expert module. CBM-based ITSs are able to generate instructional actions even without being able to solve problems on their own, by focusing on violated constraints. Of course, CBM does not prevent an ITS from having a domain module; on the contrary, the existence of a domain module can be very beneficial to the student, as it can provide the answer to questions such as "What do I do next?".

So far, there have been no ITSs based on CBM. Ohlsson claims that CBM may prove to be superior to other approaches, because of the advantages discussed. However, there are some potential disadvantages that need to be checked for. It is not clear whether constraints provide the right type of abstraction for representing knowledge in various domains. It may also be true that constraints provide too loose a net so that some of the student inconsistencies may not be identified by the tutor. One of the goals of this research is to test CBM in reality. The following section presents the design and implementation issues of SQL-TUTOR, an ITS based on CBM.

3   SQL-TUTOR

SQL is the dominant database language today, used both for interactive and programmed access to databases. SQL is a simple and highly structured language; yet, students have lots of difficulties learning it. Students have to learn about new environments (DBMS interfaces), learn the syntax and semantics of SQL, strategies for developing queries and also how to test and repair queries.

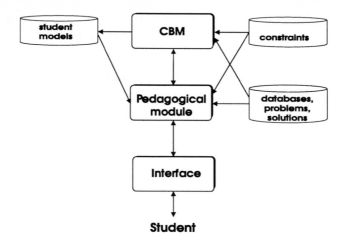

Fig. 1. The architecture of SQL-TUTOR

We discussed typical misconceptions and the inadequacy of DBMSs as learning environments elsewhere [8] [9].

SQL-TUTOR is aimed at upper-level undergraduate students. The system is implemented in CLOS [6] on SUN workstations and PC compatibles. The system is designed as a practice environment; we suppose that students have previously been exposed to the concepts of database management in lectures. Only the SELECT statement of SQL is covered currently, but the same approach could be used with other SQL statements. This focus on the SELECT statement does not lessen the importance of SQL-TUTOR, since queries do cause most misconceptions for students. Moreover, many of the concepts covered by SELECT are directly relevant to other SQL statements and other relational database languages in general.

The architecture of SQL-TUTOR is illustrated in figure 1. Domain knowledge is represented in the form of constraints. The system contains definitions of several databases, which are also implemented on the RDBMS used in the labs (currently Ingres). New databases can easily be added to SQL-TUTOR, by supplying the same SQL files used to create the database in the RDBMS.

SQL-TUTOR also contains a set of problems for each specified database and the ideal solutions to them. The solutions are necessary because SQL-TUTOR has no domain module and is not capable of solving problems. The system evaluates students solutions by comparing them to the correct ones.

The basic components of the system are the interface, pedagogical module and the CBM student modeler. The pedagogical module (PM) observes every student's action performed in the interface, and reacts to it appropriately. At the beginning of the interaction, a problem must be selected for the student to work on. When the student enters the solution for the current problem, PM sends it to the student modeler, which propagates the solution through the relevance network first, and then through the satisfaction network for those constraints that were found relevant. All the violated constraints are identified and the student model is updated accordingly. PM then generates an appropriate feedback message. The level of feedback determines how much information is provided to the student. Currently, there are five levels of feedback in SQL-TUTOR, arranged in the increasing order of information content: positive or negative feedback, error flag, hint, partial solution and complete solution. At the lowest level (positive/negative feedback), the student is only told whether the solution is correct or not and, in the latter case, how many errors there are (i.e. how many constraints were violated). An error flag message informs the student about the clause in which the error[1] occurred. A hint-type message gives more information about the cause of error. Partial solution feedback displays the correct content of the clause in question, while the complete solution simply displays the correct solution of the current problem. When the current problem is solved, or the student requires a new problem to work on, the pedagogical module selects an appropriate problem on the basis of student model.

The interface of SQL-TUTOR (figure 2) supports problem-solving in several ways. It reduces the memory load by displaying the database schema and problem text, providing the basic structure of the query and also by providing explanations about the elements of SQL. The main window of SQL-TUTOR is divided into three areas which are always visible to the student. The upper part of the window displays the text of the problem being solved and the student can always remind him/herself easily of the elements requested in the query. The middle part contains the clauses of the SQL SELECT statement, thus visualizing the goal structure. Students need not remember the exact keywords used and the relative order of clauses. The lowest part displays the schema of the currently chosen database. The schema name is given first, followed by the descriptions of tables. Each table is shown by its name and schema enclosed in a box. The name(s) of the attribute(s) forming the primary key is underlined and given in blue. The foreign key attributes are given in red.

Schema visualization is highly important; all database users are painfully aware of the constant need to remember table and attribute names and the corresponding semantics as well. SQL-TUTOR users can ask for the description of databases, tables, attributes or any element of SQL, such as functions, expressions, predicates, operators and others. The motivation here is to remove from the student some of the cognitive load required for checking the low-level syntax and to enable the student to focus on higher-level query definition problems.

4   Student Modeling in SQL-TUTOR

Student modeling approach adopted in SQL is CBM. There are several reasons in favour of such a SM approach in the context of SQL. Firstly, database queries are given in a natural language; however, the current state-of-the-art in Natural

---

[1] In case that there are several errors in various clauses, the pedagogical module will select one of them to start with.

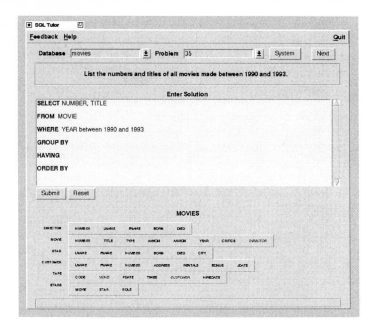

Fig. 2. The interface of SQL-TUTOR

Language Processing (NLP) is still far from being able of handling various problems present in such queries, such as references and synonyms. There is a possibility to circumscribe the NLP problem: the text of the problem may be represented not in its natural-language form, but in a form which could be the product of NLP, as done in [3]. However, it is hard not to build parts of the solution into such a representation. Furthermore, even if we overlook the NLP problem, the knowledge required to write SQL queries is very fuzzy. Therefore, it would be very difficult, if not entirely impossible, to develop a problem solver in this area. On the other hand, CBM does not require a problem solver; it is very efficient computationally, since it reduces the modeling process to pattern matching. The main complexity of the approach comes from the need to represent domain knowledge in the form of constraints.

The process of identifying constraints is the knowledge acquisition process, with all problems associated with it. SQL-TUTOR models students by looking at the student's solution and by comparing the student's solution to the ideal one. Because of this decision, constraints are divided into two groups: one dealing with the syntax of SQL and the other dealing with the semantics of queries, by focusing on the differences between the student's and the expert's solutions. The constraint base of SQL-TUTOR currently consists of 392 constraints, which are acquired by analyzing the domain knowledge [4] and on the basis of a comparative analysis of correct and incorrect solutions.

Each constraint in SQL-TUTOR has a unique number, two conditions (relevance and satisfaction), a list of problems to which the constraint applies, an error message that is displayed to the student as a hint when the constraint is violated and also the name the clause of the SELECT statement that is the focus of the constraint. Relevance and satisfaction conditions can be any logical formulas, consisting of any number of tests. Some of the tests match parts of the student's solution to prespecified patterns or the ideal solution, while others may be ordinary Lisp functions.

The constraints differ significantly. An example of a very simple constraint is given below. The relevance condition of this constraint is 't, which is always satisfied; therefore, this constraint is relevant to all student's solutions. The satisfaction condition specifies that the FROM clause cannot be empty.

```
(p 3
"FROM is a mandatory clause - specify the tables to retrieve data from."
t
(not (null (slot-value ss 'from)))
"FROM")
```

However, constraints can be much more complex. Constraint 22, given below, checks whether the student used the BETWEEN predicate correctly. Its relevance condition makes sure that the WHERE clause is specified firstly, and then finds all conditions in WHERE which are based on BETWEEN. Next, the satisfaction part of the constraint checks that each such condition is specified on a valid attribute, checks for the use of NOT within the condition, checks whether the *AND* keyword separates the lower and upper value of the interval and finally checks that the constants used are of the appropriate type. Constraints comparing student and ideal solutions may be even more complex [8].

```
(p 22
"If the BETWEEN operator is used in a search condition, there must be
two constants of the same type as the attribute used in the condition
separated by the AND keyword."
(and (not (null (where ss)))
     (member "BETWEEN" (where ss) :test 'equalp)
     (bind-all '?a (names (where ss)) bindings)
     (match '(?*d1 ?a ??n "BETWEEN" ?*d2) (where ss) bindings))
(and (attribute-in-from ss '?a)
     (member '?n '(nil "NOT") :test 'equalp)
     (match '(?v1 "AND" ?v2 ?*d3) '?d2 bindings)
     (equal (find-type '?a) (find-type '?v1))
     (equal (find-type '?a) (find-type '?v2)))
"WHERE")
```

As said earlier, CBM reduces student modeling to pattern matching, a simple, but potentially time-consuming operation, especially in situations when the number of patterns is large. SQL-TUTOR uses a modification of the RETE network [5] to speed up the process. There are two networks that are generated on the basis of constraints: the relevance network contains the relevance conditions, and the other network contains the satisfaction parts of constraints. The student's solution is first propagated through the relevance network, and is propagated next through the satisfaction network, but only for those constraints that are relevant.

The student model is a structure consisting of general student characteristics (name, level of expertise, history etc.) and the model of student's knowledge. The latter is represented in the form of statistics of how the student used various constraints. For each constraint the student model contains the total number of times the constraint has been used, the number of times it was relevant, and the number of times it was used correctly. These three indicators are used by PM for selecting new problems and are updated by the student modeler [8].

5 Discussion and Future Work

Ohlsson [10] proposes Constraint-Based Modeling as a way to overcome intractability of student modeling. Instead of generating exact models of student's knowledge, Ohlsson suggests we focus on student errors, i.e. the violations of basic principles of a domain. These basic principles are realized in CBM in the form of state constraints, which are, in essence, patterns. State constraints can be matched to student answers in order to identify student errors, and therefore SM is reduced from inducing an exact model to simple pattern matching.

This paper presented SQL-TUTOR, an ITS for SQL programming based on CBM. SQL-TUTOR supports three kinds of learning: conceptual, problem solving and meta-learning. A student can learn about concepts and elements of SQL by asking for explanations. SQL-TUTOR is a problem-solving environment which supports the acquisition of domain knowledge in a declarative form (i.e. constraints) and strengthening of this knowledge in practice. The system assists students in problem solving and arguments against incorrect actions. Finally, SQL-TUTOR encourages meta-learning by supporting self-explanation on the basis of error messages and correct solutions. All these kinds of learning are supported by the pedagogical module, which generates appropriate instructional actions on the basis of the student model, formed by CBM.

The strength of CBM lies in a well-formed constraint base. Constraints are modular, they are not related to each other in any way and are therefore easy to implement and test. The language for representing constraints we chose is general and expressive enough to allow us to check very subtle features in student solutions and to compare them to correct solutions.

One of the possible disadvantages of CBM Ohlsson reported was the appropriateness of constraints as an abstraction mechanism for representing knowledge in various domains. We had no problems representing the syntax and semantics of SQL in the form of constraints, and believe that CBM would be suitable for all types of domains where solutions have an internal structure. Ohlsson has originally suggested CBM as suitable for checking the correctness of each problem-solving step; we have used it for checking the final answer only, because of the nature of the domain, and it proved to be very effective.

Another possible difficulty reported in [10] is that it might turn out that the acquisition of constraints is no easier than acquisition of expert rules or bug libraries. It is well known that knowledge acquisition is a very slow, time-consuming and labour-intensive process. Anderson [3] reports 10 or more hours necessary for a production rule to be induced. The time spent on identification, implementation and testing of SQL-TUTOR's constraints averages at 1.1 hours per production, which is significantly shorter than those above. This may be the consequence of the same person serving as the domain expert and knowledge engineer (and the system developer, at that matter), but may also illustrate the appropriateness of constraints as a formalism for representing domain knowledge. It is important to note that the relatively high number of constraints was dictated by the design decisions made. Namely, constraints are modular and each focuses on only one aspect of the solution. Even though the same aspect may appear in various clauses (i.e. various parts of the solution) and therefore may be covered by a single constraint, we have chosen instead to have as many different constraints as there are options. The speed of evaluating queries is not compromised by such a decision, as pattern matching is fast. On the other hand, this allows us to attach a very specific hint message to each constraint, thus greatly simplifying the process of finding appropriate feedback.

The last doubt about CBM was the chance that constraints provide too loose a net so that some of student inconsistencies may not be identified by the tutor. This problem appears in all knowledge-based systems with incomplete knowledge bases. The current prototype of SQL-TUTOR contains 392 constraints identified from reference material and by examining incorrect student solutions. The constraint base is not perfect yet, it needs further testing and it is very likely that the number of constraint will grow, as we encounter new situations.

An initial study of SQL-Tutor was performed in early April 1998. The purpose of the study was twofold: to test the completeness and correctness of the constraint base and to evaluate the interface and interactions. There were 20 students involved in the study, concurrently enrolled in a database course, who had already learnt about SQL in the lectures (roughly 6 sessions), and had 4 weeks of practical labs. The study involved students using SQL-Tutor in a 2-hour laboratory session. All students' actions were logged, and the students filled a questionnaire at the end of the session. The collected data have not been analyzed completely yet, and the results would be available from http://www.cosc.canterbury.ac.nz/~tanja/sql-tut.html. The study identified a number of problems, mainly coming from incompleteness and bugs in the constraint base, and also some minor drawbacks in the interface, which provide the basis for completing the system. The observers reported that students were very enthusiastic about using SQL-TUTOR and were eager to explore various possibilities. Generally, students liked the system, especially the self-paced nature of learning, and the usefulness and variety of feedback messages. They enjoyed the interface and different kinds of learning available in the system.

Our experiences with CBM have been very good. Constraints have provided a means for dealing with all kinds of learning situations encountered so far. Student models generated by CBM enable SQL-TUTOR to select problems and generate feedback to students. We are confident that the next version of the constraint base would provide perfect diagnosis of students' solutions and enough details for generating effective pedagogical actions.

Acknowledgements

This work was supported by the University of Canterbury research grants 6242 and 2313728. We thank Kendrick Elsey and Andrew King for implementing the interfaces.

References

1. Anderson, J.R., Jeffries, R.: Novice LISP Errors: Undetected Losses of Information from Working Memory. Human–Computer Interaction **22** (1985) 403–423
2. Anderson, J.R.: Rules of the Mind. Lawrence Erlbaum Associates, Hillsdale, NJ (1993)
3. Anderson, J.R, Corbett, A.T., Koedinger, K.R., Pelletier, R.: Cognitive Tutors: Lessons Learned. The Journal of the Learning Sciences **4**(2) (1995) 167–207
4. Elmasri, R., Navathe, S.B.: Fundamentals of database systems. 2nd edn. Benjamin/Cummings, Redwood (1994)
5. Forgy, C.L.: Rete: a Fast Algorithm for the Many Pattern/Many Object Pattern Match Problem. Artificial Intelligence **19**, (1982) 17–37
6. Franz Inc. Allegro Common Lisp (1996)
7. Holt, P., Dubs, S., Jones, M., Greer, J.E.: The State of Student Modelling. In: Greer, J.E., McCalla, G.I. (eds.): Student Modeling: the Key to Individualized Knowledge–based Instruction. NATO ASI Series, Vol. 125. Springer–Verlag, Berlin Heidelberg New York (1994) 3–35
8. Mitrović, A. SQL-Tutor: a Preliminary Report. Technical Report TR-COSC 08/97, Computer Science Department, University of Canterbury (1997)
9. Mitrović, A. Learning SQL with a Cimputerized Tutor. Proc. 29th SIGCSE Tech. Symp. (1998) 307–311
10. Ohlsson, S.: Constraint–based Student Modeling. In: Greer, J.E., McCalla, G.I. (eds.): Student Modeling: the Key to Individualized Knowledge–based Instruction. NATO ASI Series, Vol. 125. Springer–Verlag, Berlin Heidelberg New York (1994) 167–189
11. Ohlsson, S.: Learning from Performance Errors. Psychological Review **103**(2) (1996) 241–262.
12. Self, J.A.: Bypassing the Intractable Problem of Student Modeling. In: Frasson, C., Gauthier, G. (eds.): Intelligent Tutoring Systems: at the Crossroads of Artificial Intelligence and Education. Ablex, Norwood (1990) 107–123

A Practical Approach to Bayesian Student Modeling

William R. Murray

Teknowledge Corporation
Embarcadero Road
Palo Alto, CA 94303
wmurray@teknowledge.com

Abstract. Bayesian modeling techniques provide a rigorous formal approach to student modeling in contrast to earlier ad hoc or certainty-factor based approaches. Unfortunately, the application of Bayesian modeling techniques is limited due to computational complexity, conditional independence requirements of the model, and difficulties with knowledge acquisition. The approach presented here infers a student model from performance data using a Bayesian belief network. The belief network models the relationship between knowledge and performance for either test items or task actions. The measure of how well a student knows a skill is represented as a probability distribution over skill levels. Questions or expected actions are classified according to the same categories by the expected difficulty of answering them correctly or selecting the correct action. With this model only a small number of parameters are required: an expected probability distribution for the skill categories, and the expected conditional probabilities for slips and lucky guesses. By limiting the complexity of the user model in this way, and to a single level of propagation, updating can be performed in time linear to the number of test items and typically only about a half a dozen model parameters are required. Test items can be added or taken away without changing these parameters, provided only that their skill level is specified. We contrast this approach with other uses of Bayesian models in intelligent tutoring systems for diagnostic plan recognition or assessment. Other assessment approaches typically require 100's of conditional probabilities or an explicit authoring of the structure of the belief network; this approach requires neither.

Introduction

This paper describes a simple approach to using Bayesian modeling and belief networks to provide student modeling for intelligent tutoring systems. Early approaches to student modeling relied on certainty factors (e.g., GUIDON [Clancey 87]), or ad hoc approaches. The more recent use of Bayesian models provides a more rigorous foundation, but at a higher cost in knowledge acquisition[1] and in the time to

---

[1] In some cases hundreds of conditional probabilities are required [Collins, Greer, and Huang 96].

update the student model. For example, in some cases the updating can take as long as 40 seconds.[2]

The Bayesian modeling approach presented here restricts the complexity of the student model knowledge representation and the belief network used to model it. In return, updating is linear in the number of input items (e.g., test items or student questions), knowledge acquisition requires the specification of only a small number of parameters, and the input items can be treated in a modular way: they can be added or dropped with no changes to the algorithm or parameters.

Difficulties in using Bayesian modeling

Some difficulties in applying Bayesian modeling as an approach to student modeling are:

- *Computational complexity*—in general inference in belief networks is NP-hard. [Russell and Norvig 95]
- *Knowledge acquisition*—the model requires prior probabilities and conditional probabilities. For a large network and without conditional independence assumptions, an astronomical number of probabilities must be specified.
- *Conditional independence assumptions*—alternatively, conditional independence assumptions can be used to reduce the number of probabilities required.

How this approach works

The approach described here, used in the Desktop Associate knowledge-based performance support system [Murray 97], trades off complexity of knowledge representation and depth of modeling for a linear-time algorithm for belief updating and a small set of model parameters.

Skills and performance data are represented by trees

The model interprets a *single* skill with any number of performance data. It can be applied multiply to separate skills, but it does not model the relationships between the skills, such as prerequisite, general-specific, or part-of links. The performance data can be actions that can be taken to solve some problem, questions to be answered, or any other data that can be classified as either being correct or not.

Consider an example from the Desktop Associate. The skills in that system are knowledge of desktop application tools and features, such as the use of styles,

---

[2] The ANDES physics tutors [VanLehn 97] uses a stochastic simulation approach to evaluating the belief networks. In that tutor the student model is used only for task selection so a slow updating time is acceptable.

templates, macros, and embedded objects in Word documents or Excel documents[3]. The performance data are multiple choice questions. For a skill such as "knowledge of Word formatting" there could be any number of questions covering styles, tabs, indenting, fonts, columns, etc.

The range of user skill is represented by levels. For example, these could be beginner, intermediate, and advanced levels. In the Desktop Associate there are five levels, ranging from novice level (no exposure to the concept or skill), through beginning level (can apply the skill in some stereotypical ways but with limited understanding), intermediate level (has a basic understanding and ability to apply the skill but with only a limited understanding of the interactions with other skills), advanced level (increased understanding of interactions), to expert level (innovative applications and a deep mental model of the skill and its interactions with other skills). The student modeling approach presented here does not assume these 5 levels, only that there is some discrete number of levels placed in a total order.

If we assume the skill has 5 levels as in this example, then to apply Bayesian modeling we need the prior probabilities of each level along with conditional probabilities for each question[4]. For example, for question i we would need to supply the following conditional probabilities:

	Nov	Beg	Int	Adv	Exp
P(correct)	P(cor|Nov)	P(cor|Beg)	P(cor|Int)	P(cor|Adv)	P(cor|Exp)
P(incorrect)	P(inc|Nov)	P(inc|Beg)	P(inc|Int)	P(inc|Adv)	P(inc|Exp)

Since the bottom row is 1 minus the top row, we really only need 5 probabilities for each question. For 8 questions 40 probabilities are needed. In general, if we have n skill levels and q questions for each we need nq probabilities plus the n prior probabilities of the skill levels if we are to calculate a probability distribution of skill levels given all the question scores. That is just to model the *one* skill that the questions pertain to. For k different skills, using the same skill levels for each, we would need knq probabilities. As we can see even for a simple model the number of probabilities is large. Assuming 10 skills, 5 skill levels, and 8 questions per skill we need 400 conditional probabilities. Even this simple single-level-of-propagation model seems impractical at first.

Note that this model also assumes that the performance on each question is independent of every other question. If this were not the case then even more complex joint probabilities would be required.

---

[3] Word and Excel refer to the trademarked products Microsoft™ Word 97 and Microsoft™ Excel 97.

[4] Rather than use the more abstract term "performance item" we will use "question" to refer to a question (true-false, multiple-choice, short-answer, matching, etc.) that can be scored as either correct or not, along with any action taken to solve a task that can be scored as either correct or not.

Conditional probabilities are determined by difficulty level

The key to the simplified approach used in this student model is to group the questions into categories of similar difficulty and then to tie the conditional probabilities of answering each set of questions correctly to the possible skill levels. By partitioning the questions into difficulty categories, each question in the same category has the same probability parameters as the other members. Now we need only provide knc probabilities where c is the number of categories rather than knq probabilities where q is the number of questions per skill. Typically the number of categories is much smaller than the number of questions for a skill when there are multiple questions in each category. For example, the questions for a single skill could be partitioned into four categories of difficulty with each category having ten or more questions.

Next we can tie the question categories to the skill levels. For example, if we have 5 skill levels (e.g., novice, beginning, intermediate, advanced, and expert) we can have 4 corresponding question categories (e.g., beginning-level questions, intermediate-level questions, advanced-level questions, and expert-level questions). The reason we have $n+1$ skill levels when we have n question categories is that we need one extra skill level for users whose skill is below the questions in any of the n question categories. In the Desktop Associate, the novice skill level corresponds to users who typically cannot even answer beginner-level questions. This partitioning of question categories to match the skill levels is shown in Figure 1.

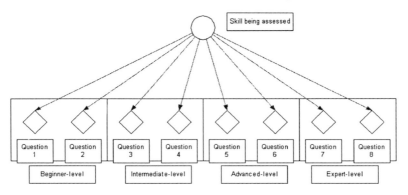

Fig. 1. Partitioning questions into categories reduces the number of model parameters

The final reduction in probabilities results from the transitive nature of these skill categories: if a user has reached a certain skill level then that user should be able to answer all questions at that skill level *and all easier questions*. Similarly we expect them to miss all questions at any higher skill level. But in the real world users can make mistakes and sometimes miss questions they should know, or be lucky and guess the right answer or perform the right action even though they do not have the knowledge that supports that choice. Without these slips and guesses the conditional probabilities would be either 1 or 0, depending on the user's skill level. For example, an expert level user would have probability 1 of answering any question at the expert, advanced, intermediate, or beginning level. Conversely, an intermediate-level user would have probability 0 of answering an advanced or expert question. But to account for noise in the data the expert's probability should be less than 1 by the probability of a slip, and the intermediate-level user's probability should be greater than 0 by the probability of a lucky guess.

Call the probability of a slip s and the probability of a lucky guess g. s and g will both be numbers close to 0. For example, s is modeled as 0.1 in the Desktop Associate. If our performance data consists of multiple choice questions then we may be able to provide a better estimate for g as $1/m$ where m is the number of choices in each question. For example, in the Desktop Associate there are typically 5 questions so g is 0.20.

Using these parameters the conditional probabilities for correct and incorrect answers to questions of increasing difficulty, from beginning level questions to intermediate level questions, is shown below:

		Nov	Beg	Int	Adv	Exp
Beginning	P(correct)	G	1-s	1-s	1-s	1-s
	P(incorrect)	1-g	s	s	s	s
Intermediate	P(correct)	g	g	1-s	1-s	1-s
	P(incorrect)	1-g	1-g	s	s	s
Advanced	P(correct)	g	g	g	1-s	1-s
	P(incorrect)	1-g	1-g	1-g	s	s
Expert	P(correct)	g	g	g	g	1-s
	P(incorrect)	1-g	1-g	1-g	1-g	s

The probability that a beginning level question will be answered correctly is shown in the first two rows, or to make the example more concrete, using s = 0.1 and g = 0.2.

		Nov	Beg	Int	Adv	Exp
Beginning	P(correct)	0.2	0.9	0.9	0.9	0.9
	P(incorrect)	0.8	0.1	0.1	0.1	0.1

The top row (Novice, Beginner, etc.) is the *actual* skill level of the student. The Bayesian analysis provides a probability distribution for the different possible skill levels. We interpret this table to mean that a user who is actually a novice has a 0.2 chance of answering a beginner-level question correctly and 0.8 chance of answering it incorrectly. We typically expect them to *not* answer it correctly but the 0.2 probability is the probability that they guess it correctly. On the other hand we would expect a user whose true skill level is beginner to answer a beginner-level question correctly. But allowing for a slip, that probability is modeled as 0.9 and the chance that they will answer it incorrectly is modeled as 0.1. Any user whose skill level is intermediate, advanced, or expert should also certainly be able to handle a beginning level question, unless they also make a slip. So their probability of a correct answer is also modeled as 0.9 and their probability of an incorrect answer is again 0.1.

The key point is that we have reduced the total number of probabilities required to just the prior probabilities for the skill levels and two other probabilities:

1. s—the probability that a user will slip up on a question that they should know the answer to,
2. g—the probability that a user will correctly guess the right answer when they do not really have the knowledge to answer it.

In this example only seven parameters are required: the five prior probabilities for the skill levels plus the two conditional probabilities of a slip (s) and a lucky guess (g).

Updating takes place in linear time

Now we derive the equation for determining the probability distribution of the skill levels given performance data. We start with the general Bayesian model and apply the simplifying assumptions. The Bayesian model for a single discrete probability variable X conditionally dependent on n different pieces of evidence is given by:

$$p(X = x_j | \vec{e}) = \alpha \, p(X = x_j) \, p(\vec{e} | X = x_j)$$

where the evidence vector e has n elements and represents the evidence gathered and where α is normalization constant. X will be a vector of skill levels so variable x_j represents a particular skill level (e.g., intermediate in the example above). Similarly, e will be a vector of evidence data (e.g., three questions of beginner level difficulty were answered correctly but one was missed, and one expert level question was answered correctly and two were missed). If we assume that each piece of evidence in e is independent of the others than this equation becomes

$$p(X = x_j | \vec{e}) = \alpha p(X = x_j) \prod_{i=1}^{i=n} p(e_i | X = x_j)$$

The next step is to note that each of these conditional probabilities is either s, $(1\text{-}s)$, g, or $(1\text{-}g)$. Then we can count the number of questions correct and incorrect in each category and use them to compute the answer as shown below:

$$p(X{=}x_j|\vec{e}) = \alpha \, p(X{=}x_j) \left((1-s)^{\sum\limits_{i=1}^{i=j} e_i} \right) \left(s^{\sum\limits_{i=1}^{i=j_-} e_i} \right) \left(g^{\sum\limits_{i=j+1}^{i=n} e_i} \right) \left((1-g)^{\sum\limits_{i=j+1}^{i=n_-} e_i} \right)$$

All that is required to compute this formula is that we add up correct and incorrect answers in the various question categories and plug in these values along with the values for s, g, and the prior probabilities for each X=x_j (e.g., p(Novice), p(Beginner), etc.). If the actual skill level of the student is level x_j (e.g., Intermediate), then the four exponents above correspond to the number of correct and incorrect answers in the various categories. These exponents, from left to right, are the questions:

1. Answered correctly (as expected)
2. Answered incorrectly (slips)
3. Answered correctly, by chance (lucky guesses)
4. Answered incorrectly, as expected (too hard)

The normalization constant α is easily computed by adding all the unnormalized values for each skill category and then dividing into 1. It is the inverse of the probability that the evidence vector occurs in *any* of the skill categories, i.e., the a priori probability of the evidence vector itself. Formally,

$$\alpha = \frac{1}{\sum_{j=1}^{j=n} p'(X = x_j \mid \vec{e})} = \frac{1}{p(\vec{e})}$$

where p' is computed using the formula above without the normalization constant α.

Trade-offs with this approach

Now we consider the pros and cons of this approach compared to Bayesian analysis without these simplifications.

Advantages

First we consider advantages.

Modularity: questions can be added, dropped, or moved between categories

The overhead in adding new performance items (e.g., multiple-choice questions) is simple: they need only be placed in the proper question category. So one can easily add new questions to one category such as the beginner level, with no changes to the underlying algorithm. No new conditional probabilities must be ascertained from a subject matter expert.

Similarly, particular questions can be dropped, or different numbers of questions in each category can be asked.

The model allows for both slips and lucky guesses

Unlike purely abductive approaches based on logic and searching for misconceptions, this approach is uncertainty based and explicitly allows for both slips and guesses in student performance.

Linear-time updating

Although updating belief networks is in general NP-hard, taking time exponential in the number of belief nodes, the algorithm presented is linear in the number of data items. It avoids the NP-hard problems by only dealing with one level of propagation, from data to the skill.

Simplified knowledge acquisition: only a small number of parameters
Typically only about a half dozen parameters are required: the probabilities for a slip and a lucky guess, plus the a priori probabilities of each skill level.

Disadvantages

We have gained these advantages by trading off some complexities.

Propagation of values from one skill to another
First, only one skill can be modeled at a time. For more complex student models where we would like to model composite skills some means of propagating values upward in the network is required. If Bayesian belief network updating algorithms are used this can take time that is exponential in the number of nodes.

In the Desktop Associate application this is not a problem as it only needs to model sets of skills for each application. Given a profile of the user's competence in, say, Word styles, formatting, templates, macros, and formatting knowledge, then the Desktop Associate can select appropriate tasks for that user. It does not need to determine an overall rating for the user's knowledge of Word itself as it would have no use for it. Instead, each different kind of task (e.g., doing a newsletter, preparing a budget, etc.) requires a different profile of skills.

Only binary-valued evidence data can be used
Second, only binary-valued evidence that is either correct or incorrect is modeled with this approach. For example, time is not taken into account: we could not penalize answers that are correct but which took a long time to be answered and score those lower in some way than a correct answer given immediately.

Related work

Bayesian approaches have been used in both diagnostic (within-task) and assessment (across-task) student models. For example, ANDES [Conati, Larkin, and Van Lehn 97] uses a belief network to represent alternate plans that may be used to solve physics problems. Student actions are used to update the probabilities of the respective plans.

[Collins et al 96] apply Bayesian Nets to granularity hierarchies [McCalla and Greer 94]. Assessment is the main purpose rather than diagnostic student modeling. A utility measure is used to choose the best query as the one that maximizes the change in expected probability for some target node. Bayesian updating is used to propagate values from evidence to higher-level nodes. The model used does not allow for a probability distribution of skills over more than one level. Instead, each skill is considered either mastered or not and has associated with it a single measure of its probability of being mastered. For experiments with small networks of 11 or 15 nodes 122 to 1345 conditional probabilities were required.

The approach presented here is an assessment approach, unlike that used in ANDES. It differs from the approach mentioned in the last paragraph and the localized computation approach of [Reyes 96], also used for assessment, in its restriction to just one level of propagation. But, in turn, it is much simpler and requires far fewer conditional or a priori probabilities (e.g., 7 in this paper's earlier example compared to a minimum of 122 in the last example above). Finally, neither of the assessment approaches models a skill distribution, instead only mastery (student-knows(x)) or non-mastery ($\neg$ student-knows(x)) is modeled. Essentially the student is believed to be in a state of perfect knowledge or complete ignorance of a concept or skill and the probability measure represents the likelihood of that state being the correct one given what the tutor knows. In contrast, the model presented in the paper represents student skill as a probability distribution.

Conclusions

The primary conclusion is that Bayesian modeling can be practically applied to intelligent tutoring systems: if complete belief network propagation is not required and if performance data can be categorized by skill levels, then only a small number of model parameters are required and a linear time updating can be performed. The net result is to make the Bayesian modeling approach more readily accessible as a student modeling approach for a wide variety of intelligent tutoring systems where knowledge is inferred from noisy data.

Acknowledgments

This work was performed for AL/HRA under funding from DARPA's CAETI program. I would like to thank Dr. Joe Mattoon for acting as program monitor and Neil Jacobstein for originally proposing the Desktop Associate project.

References

[Clancey 87] Clancey, W. J. Knowledge-based Tutoring—The GUIDON Program. MIT Press.

[Collins, Greer, and Huang 96] Collins, J.A.; Greer, J.E.; and Huang, S.H. "Adaptive Assessment Using Granularity Hierarchies and Bayesian Nets". Lecture Notes in Computer Science 1086. Proceedings of the Third International Conference, ITS '96. Frasson, Gauthier, and Lesgold (eds.), Springer, 1996, pp. 569-577.

[Conati and VanLehn 96] Conati C., and VanLehn K. POLA: A student modeling framework for probabilistic on-line assessment of problem solving performance. Proceedings of UM-96, Fifth International Conference on User Modeling.

[McCalla and Greer 94] McCalla, G.I. and Greer, J.E. "Granularity-Based Reasoning and Belief Revision in Student Models" Student Models: The Key to Individualized Educational Systems, J. Greer and G. McCalla (eds.), New York: Springer Verlag, 1994, pp. 39-62.

[Murray 97] Intelligent Tools and Instructional Simulations—the Desktop Associate, Final Report. Teknowledge Corporation. Submitted to Armstrong Laboratory, Aircrew Training Research Division October 1997. Contract Number N66001-95-D-8642/0003.

[Reyes 96] Reyes, J. "A Belief Net Backbone for Student Modeling". Lecture Notes in Computer Science 1086. Proceedings of the Third International Conference, ITS '96. Frasson, Gauthier, and Lesgold (eds.), Springer, 1996, pp. 596-604.

[Russell and Norvig 95] Russell, S.; and Norvig, P. Artificial Intelligence, a Modern Approach. Prentice Hall. 1995.

[VanLehn 97] Van Lehn, K. Personal communcation.

Student Modeling from Conventional Test Data:
A Bayesian Approach Without Priors

Kurt VanLehn, Zhendong Niu, Stephanie Siler and Abigail S. Gertner

Learning Research and Development Center
University of Pittsburgh
Pittsburgh, PA 15260
VanLehn@cs.pitt.edu, niu+@pitt.edu, siler+@pitt.edu, gertner+@pitt.edu

Abstract. Although conventional tests are often used for determining a student's overall competence, they are seldom used for determining a fine-grained model. However, this problem does arise occasionally, such as when a conventional test is used to initialize the student model of an ITS. Existing psychometric techniques for solving this problem are intractable. Straight-forward Bayesian techniques are also inapplicable because they depend too strongly on the priors, which are often not available. Our solution is to base the assessment on the *difference* between the prior and posterior probabilities. If the test data raise the posterior probability of mastery of a piece of knowledge even slightly above its prior probability, then that is interpreted as evidence that the student has mastered that piece of knowledge. Evaluation of this technique with artificial students indicates that it can deliver highly accurate assessments.

Introduction

Diagnostic testing uses conventional test formats (e.g., items with multiple choice or numerical answers) but assumes that a student's competence can be characterized by a set of several subskills or factors. For instance, competence in multi-digit addition might be characterized with the subskills of carrying, processing columns without carries, and other subskills as well.

In its simplest form, a diagnostic test scoring algorithm inputs binary answer data (i.e., 1 if the question was answered correctly, 0 if answered incorrectly) and outputs a level of mastery for each of the subskills. Existing algorithms (e.g., DiBello et al., 1995; Samejima, 1995; Tatsuoka, 1990, 1995) enumerate all possible subsets of subskills that have distinguishable patterns of answers. The algorithms examine each subset and pick the one that best fits the answer data.

An unusual application of diagnostic testing arose during the development of the Andes physics tutoring system (VanLehn, 1996; Conati, Gertner, VanLehn & Druzdzel, 1997). Andes has a student modeler that uses Bayesian techniques to calculate the probability of mastery of each of about 350 rules. Because it is a Bayesian, it requires for each rule a prior probability, that is, the probability that a randomly drawn student from the population will have already mastered that rule before using Andes. In order to find these prior probabilities, we planned to use diagnostic testing. That is, we planned to treat each of the rules as a distinct "subskill" or "factor," then use diagnostic testing to find out which "subskills" each student had mastered. By counting how many times each rule/subskill was mastered, we could estimate the prior probability of that rule in the population.

The test, which was developed by the physics instructors associated with the project, had 34 items, all of which had multiple choice or short-answer formats. We determined which of the Andes rules were required for correctly answering each problem. Overall, 66 rules were used at least once during the test.

Unfortunately, 66 "subskills" are much more than typically used in diagnostic testing. The existing scoring techniques would have to examine as many as 2^{66} subsets of rules in order to tell which subset best fit a given student's answers. This made existing scoring techniques inapplicable, so we had to develop a diagnostic test scoring algorithm that would infer, given a student's binary answer data, whether or not the student had mastered each of the 66 rules.

If such an algorithm can be found, then it could be used for other purposes besides determining priors for Andes student modeling. For instance, we could routinely give a student who was about to use Andes a short multiple-choice test. The results of the test could be used to initialize the student's model.

The algorithm needs to be told which rules (or subskills, etc.) are required for correctly solving each problem. If the problem can be solved with two or more correct strategies, then it may be necessary to use a disjunction in such a specification. For instance, if one strategy requires rules 1, 2 and 3, and the other strategy requires rules 3, 4 , 5 and 6, then one would have to specific that correctly solving the problem requires knowing rule 3 and either rules 1 and 2 or rules 4, 5 and 6.

However, items are usually written to have just one correct solution, although students may always invent ones that the authors did not anticipate. Psychometricians often assume that items have just one correct solution, which allows them to use a simplified representation, called a Q-matrix (Tatsuoka, 1990), for the relationship between knowledge and problems. In a Q-matrix, the columns are problems, the rows are pieces of knowledge, and cells are 1 if the piece of knowledge is required by the problem and 0 is if the knowledge is not required for solving that problem. Although a Q-matrix cannot accurately represent problems with multiple correct solution strategies, it has been found adequate for most tests, including the one we have used for testing.

The general problem can be stated as follows: Given

- a test with N items;
- a knowledge base of M rules (we will use "rule" to stand for any kind of unitization of knowledge);
- a M by N Q-matrix;
- an N-long binary vector indicating which test items the student answered correctly,

output a M-long real-numbered vector indicating the probability of mastery of each rule.

Research approach/method

Our approach was empirical: Try several diagnostic test scoring methods and evaluate them using artificial students. An artificial student is a function that, when given a set of mastery levels for the rules, produces a binary answer data vector. To use an artificial student for evaluation, the answer vector is fed into the test scoring method, which then predicts the mastery levels for each rule. If the predictions match the original mastery levels, then the test scoring method is accurate.

Although we would have preferred to evaluate the scoring methods with human students, that would require knowing with certainty what their levels of mastery were on each of the 66 rules.

In principle, artificial students should be based on real cognitive models. They should model forgetting, priming, guessing, cheating and all the other things students do during tests. However, we used a simpler framework that only modeled inadvertent mistakes (slips) and guessing. In our artificial students:

- P(the problem's answer is correct | all rules required for answering it are mastered) = 1 – slip.
- P(the problem's answer is correct | at least one rule required for answering it is not mastered) = guess / number of possible answers for this problem.

That is, the model has two global parameters: the probability of a slip and the probability of a guess. Once a person has decided to guess, whether they get the problem correct is inversely proportional to how many possible answers that multiple choice problem has. Since the equations above only give the probability of a problem's answer being correct, the probabilities are used as odds in a random number generator to generate the actual binary answer vector.

For evaluating the proposed assessments, we needed a collection of artificial students. We generated a collection of 201 artificial students with slip = .1 and guess = .3 by first randomly generating a level of competence C, then randomly generating rule masteries such that P(mastery of a rule) = C. That is, artificial students with high C had many rules mastered and student with low C had few rules mastered.

After the artificial students have been assessed and predictions about their mastery levels have been obtained, we need to measure the degree of match between the predicted and actual mastery levels. We evaluated the match separately for each rule, since we wanted to see if some rules were easier to assess than others. For each rule, we counted the number of artificial students where (A) the rule was actually mastered, (B) the rule was predicted to be mastered, and (C) the rule was both predicted to be mastered and actually mastered. Then:

- Accuracy is C/B. It should be as close to 1 as possible.
- Coverage is C/A. This should also be as close to 1 as possible.

Originally, we sought to maximize accuracy alone. However, when we were adjusting parameters (as described below), we found that accuracy reached a plateau rather than a peak as we varied the parameter values. We needed some way to select a parameter value among those which tied for producing the maximum accuracy. Thus, we adopted coverage as a desirable but secondary feature. To make parameter tuning easier, we define utility = coverage + 2*accuracy, which gives accuracy twice as much weight as coverage. We later considered the effects of replacing the "2" with

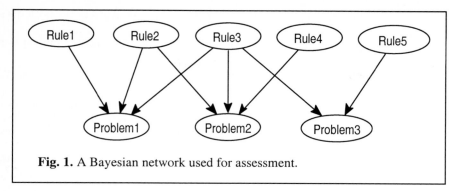

Fig. 1. A Bayesian network used for assessment.

other values in order to see if varying the relative importance of coverage and accuracy made any difference in our findings (see below).

Failures

We tried several obvious schemes but rejected them for various reasons. However, the scheme we ultimately accepted is based on what we learned from our failures, so we will discuss them first.

Noisy And

The first test scoring method we considered was based directly on the causality, as we perceived it. Mastery of rules *causes* problems to be answered correctly or not. Thus, we constructed a Bayesian network (Pearl, 1988) with nodes for problems and rules, and links from the rules to the problems (the causal direction). That is, a problem's node's parents were the nodes representing rules that were required for answering the problem correctly. For instance, in Figure 1, rules 1, 2 and 3 are required by problem 1, so they are the parents of problem 1 in the network. The conditional probability table of the problem's node is:
- P(answer correct | all rules required for answering it are mastered) = 1 − slip.
- P(answer correct | at least one rule required for answering it is not mastered) = guess / number of possible answers to that problem.

This is similar to a noisy And (Pearl, 1988), hence the name. It is also the same function as used in the artificial students, but the slip and guess parameters can be changed in order to optimize the performance of the assessment function.

Unfortunately, because the rule nodes are roots of the network, this approach requires assigning a prior for each rule node. In our application, the population priors are not known. Bayesians often use 0.5 for a prior when they don't know the actual prior. However, we discovered that for most rules, the posterior depended strongly on the choice of prior. For 46 of the 66 rules, when we tried the priors of .3, .5 and .8, the posterior was within ±0.05 of the prior. For the remaining 20 rules, the posteriors were relatively insensitive to the priors.

What seems to be happening with the 46 rules that are overly sensitive to the prior is the following:

- If a problem is incorrect, then *any* rule required by it could be unmastered. Thus, the network passes out blame rather thinly.
- If a problem is correct, then either the student guessed or all the rules must be mastered. Thus, even a little evidence of nonmastery of one of the rules will cause the network to infer that the student is guessing, which attenuates the credit the network passes out.

Although the above is just our interpretation of what happens, it is a fact that the network passes out credit and blame rather thinly. For most rules, it seems to take a lot of consistent evidence before the noisy-And network is willing to change the prior probabilities much.

Noisy And with second order probabilities

Since the influence of the priors was so strong, we sought to unbias the network using second order probabilities (Neopolitan, 1990), which are thought to be a way of representing ignorance of priors. Each rule node was given a new parent with 5 values, 0 through 4, which were given a uniform prior probability distribution (each value had a prior of 0.2). The rule's conditional probability table was $P(rule|parent=N) = 0.25*N$, where N is one of the parent's values. In other words, this network is saying that it is equally likely that the rule node could have a "prior" of either 0, 0.25, 0.5, 0.75 or 1.0

This made no difference. Assessments given to students were exactly the same as those given by 0.5 priors in the preceding, simpler noisy-And network.

A noisy Or network

To obviate the need for priors, we tried reversing the links in the Bayesian network. Each rule became a noisy Or (Pearl, 1988), with problems as the parents. That is, if any of the problems that required a rule was answered correctly, then the rule was probably mastered.

However, this meant that the rules were conditionally independent given the evidence, which just isn't true. For example, suppose rules R1 and R2 are required by problem P, and P is incorrect. Finding out that R1 is mastered should convince you that R2 is not mastered. But because R1 is d-separated from R2 by P, they are conditionally independent in the network. Thus, evidence about R1 will not influence the probability of mastery of R2 the way it should.

Counting

In desperation, we tried an extremely simple solution. We kept a score for each rule. We incremented the score by 1 when a problem requiring the rule is correct. We decremented the score by 1/N when a problem was incorrect and required N rules to solve it correctly. The intuition is that if the problem is correct, then the rule must be mastered. If it is incorrect, then at least one of the N rules required by it is incorrect, but since we don't know if it is this one, we blame each rule equally.

Because rules participate in differing numbers of problems, the ranges of the scores can vary widely. Each rule needs a threshold that is unique to that rule. If the rule's score is above the threshold, the rule is predicted to be mastered.

In order to find values for all 66 thresholds, we used the artificial students to generate scores on rules. For each rule, we adjusted its threshold to maximize the rule's utility.

We discovered that the best threshold was almost always the minimal possible score for that rule. That is, a rule was considered mastered if any of the problems it participated in were correct. This means that the counting technique is working exactly like the noisy Or, without the noise. Therefore, it also misrepresents the dependencies.

A success

Of all the methods we tried, the noisy-And seemed the most plausible since it approximated the causality and it represented the conditional dependencies correctly. The only problem was that most of the rules were overly sensitive to their prior probabilities. In fact, they had posterior probabilities that were within .05 of their prior probabilities.

We examined the 20 rules where priors were not affecting the posteriors. In all cases, there was at least one problem that required either only that rule, or that rule and one other. That is, there was at least one problem where the rule was used in isolation (or nearly in isolation). Conversely, all rules that were used in isolation (that is, one of the problems they appeared in had only one or two required rules) were relatively unaffected by the priors. In Figure 1, rules 3 and 5 are "used in isolation" because they are used in problem 3, which has only two rules required for correctly solving it.

Finding that rules used in isolation were insensitive to the priors suggested that it was the test that was responsible for lack of sensitivity, and not the assessment method itself. This renewed our faith in the noisy And method.

When the noisy And apportions credit and blame, it usually spreads them thinly among the rules, so that it hardly moves the rules' probabilities from their priors. This suggests looking at the difference (change) in probability as a way to compensate for the small amount of credit/blame being handed out.

To implement this key insight, we modified the assessment function by giving each rule a threshold that was just above the prior. If the rule's posterior is above the threshold, then the rule is predicted to be mastered. The intuition is that in such cases, the rule is receiving credit (albeit not much) for the student's correct answers, and is

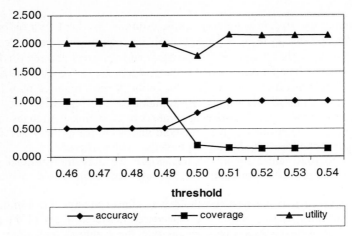

Fig. 2. Choosing a threshold to maximize utility

thus probably known. Because the thresholds are functions of the priors, it shouldn't make any difference what priors are used. Thus, the predictions should be independent of the priors.

Setting the thresholds

For each rule, we tried varying the threshold slightly around the prior. Figure 2 shows the result of varying the threshold on a typical rule (not one of the ones that appears in isolation) from –0.04 to +0.04 in steps of 0.01 about the prior, which was 0.5 in this case. As can be seen, the coverage varies from 1 to 0 while the accuracy varies from 0.5 to 1. Utility, which was defined as coverage + 2*accuracy, peaks at 0.51, so that is the threshold chosen.

Notice that plateau in accuracy. If we tried to use accuracy alone in order to select a threshold, all values for the threshold above 0.51 would be tied. However, by adding in a little bit of coverage to the utility function, we can make it peak. For this particular rule, if utility is defined as coverage + M*accuracy and M>1.8, then there is a peak at 0.51. The peak is at 0.50 if 1.6<M<1.8. There is no peak in utility if M<1.6. Instead, there is a plateau from 0 to 0.49. Since every rule's curve was similar to this one, values for M of 2 or more (i.e., accuracy is twice as important as coverage) caused the peak in utility to be slightly above the prior. Values of M between 1 and 2 would cause utility to peak at the prior itself, whereas values of M less than 1 (i.e., coverage is more important than accuracy) yielded plateaus rather than peaks. We defined utility with M=2 since that tended to maximize accuracy without affecting coverage very much (see Figure 2).

The rules that appeared in isolation had flat curves for accuracy and coverage in the vicinity of the prior, so we gave them thresholds that were the priors themselves. Their accuracy and coverage were both close to 1.

Setting the prior, slip and guess parameters

The new noisy And has three global parameters, namely the prior, the slip and the guess. To find values for these parameters, we searched the parameter space for values that would maximize utility given an initial set of 201 artificial students.

The procedure was to select values for the 3 global parameters, run the noisy And, collect posteriors on each rule for each student, select rule thresholds that maximized utility for that rule, then sum the overall utility.

We found that prior = 0.5, guess = 0.3 and slip = 0.01 yield maximal values. However, we also found that utility was relatively insensitive to all three values.

Varying the set of artificial students

However, we worried that these results could be idiosyncratic to the particular set of 201 artificial students used to produce them. Therefore, we generated new sets of artificial students, and compared the utilities obtained by assessing them to the utilities obtained from the original 201 students.

The first set was 400 artificial students generated with the same values for the guess and slip parameters. Predicted levels of mastery were generated for each of the 400 student's rules, and the prediction's accuracy, coverage and utility were calculated. The mean utility for the 400-student set was 2.465, and the mean utility for the original 201-student set was 2.372. Although statistically reliable (T-test, p<.0001) due to the large number of data points, the difference in means was only 4%. The next set was 201 artificial students generated by raising the value of the slip parameter to 0.1. Again, there was a small (1%) but reliable difference (p < .01). Similarly, lowering guess to 0.1 and keeping slip at 0.1 generated a small (1%) but reliable difference (p < .001).

Thus, the results seem relatively insensitive to the specifics of the set of artificial students used for evaluation. Regardless of how the artificial students use to evaluate the test scoring method were generated, the test scoring method yielded high accuracy and moderate coverage.

Discussion

The problem discussed here is to infer the posterior probability of mastery of a set of N rules given a test with M items, where each item has been scored as correct or incorrect. We are given a Q-matrix, which indicates which rules are required for correct answers to each problem.

Since we do not have prior probabilities of mastery, it seemed initially that we could not use the Noisy-and approach. However, we were unable to find a method that both represented the conditional dependencies that exist and did not require priors until we noticed that the posterior probabilities of the noisy And did vary in response to the data, but just did not move far from the priors. The network was passing out credit and blame rather thinly. Thus, we used priors, but looked for small changes away from the prior. If a rule's posterior is above the prior by an amount specified by a rule-specific threshold, then the rule was interpreted as being mastered. Artificial students were used to select thresholds that maximized accuracy and coverage.

We discovered that there were essentially two kinds of rules on the test. The rules used in isolation were accurately assessed by virtually any combination of parameters. For the other rules, the coverage and accuracy traded off, as shown in Figure 2. Thresholds were picked so that the accuracy was always over 90% and often close to 100%, but the coverage was around 25%.

According to this evaluation, if the assessment says that the student has mastered a rule, then it is probably right. On the other hand, if it says that the student has not mastered a rule, then it will often be wrong. The latter should thus be interpreted as "insufficient evidence to conclude mastery exists" instead of "non mastery." We experimented with Bayesian network-based methods for discriminating between lack of evidence and evidence of non-mastery, but failed to find one that worked. This would be a good topic for future work.

Bayesian methods have always had difficulty working with applications where priors are not available. As textbook authors (e.g., Neopolitan, 1990) are fond of pointing out, a prior of 0.5 on a true/false variable does not represent ignorance, but instead represents certain knowledge that the variable in is true 50% of the time in the population. Second order probabilities (Neopolitan, 1990), Dempster-Shafer (Pearl, 1988; Neopolitan, 1990) and other techniques have been used to represent ignorance, but they have drawbacks of their own. As far as we know, using the difference between priors and posteriors has never been tried before as a means of making predictions insensitive to the priors. It only applies when the outcome nodes (the ones whose posteriors are important) are the same as the nodes whose priors are unknown. However, such networks are common in diagnostic applications such as student modeling. Empirical testing with artificial data suggests that our technique is successful for our application, but more work is needed to understand the properties of this solution.

We embarked on this research in order to use a diagnostic test to provide priors for Andes' Bayesian network. Having evaluated the proposed diagnostic testing method and finding that it produces accurate results with artificial students, we have analyzed the test data from the 178 human students, found out which rules were mastered by which students, and thus obtained the priors that Andes' needs. Ironically, the method that we proposed here could be used with Andes itself, thus removing the need for priors. Our next step may be to try this and evaluate it with either artificial students.

Acknowledgements

This research is supported by ARPA's Computer Aided Education and Training Initiative under grant N660001-95-C-8367, by ONR's Cognitive Science Division under grant N00014-96-1-0260 and by AFOSR's Artificial Intelligence Division under grant F49620-96-1-0180. We would like to thank the rest of the Andes group for their help.

References

Conati, C., Gertner, A., VanLehn, K. & Druzdzel, M. (1997). On-line student modeling for coached problem solving using Bayesian networks. In A. Jameson, C. Paris & C. Tasso, *User Modeling: Proceedings of the Sixth International conference, UM97*. New York: Springer Wein.

DiBello, L. V., Stout, W.F. & Roussos, L. A. (1995) Unified cognitive/psychometric diagnostic assessment likelihood-based classification techniques. In P. D. Nichols, S. F. Chipman & R. L. Brennan (Eds.) *Cognitively Diagnostic Assessment*. Hillsdale, NJ: Erlbaum.

Neopolitan, R. E. (1990). *Probabilistic Reasoning in Expert Systems: Theory and Algorithms*. New York: Wiley.

Pearl, J. (1988). *Probabilistic Reasoning in Intelligent Systems: Networks of Plausible Inference*. San Mateo, CA: Morgan-Kaufman.

Samejima, F. (1995). A cognitive diagnosis method using latent trait models: Competency space approach and its relationship with DiBello and Stout's unified cognitive-psychometric diagnosis model. In P. D. Nichols, S. F. Chipman & R. L. Brennan (Eds.) *Cognitively Diagnostic Assessment*. Hillsdale, NJ: Erlbaum.

Tatsuoka, K. K. (1990). Toward an integration of item-response theory and cognitive error diagnoses. In N. Fredericksen, R. L. Glaser, A. M. Lesgold & M. G. Shafto (Eds), *Diagnostic Monitoring of Skill and Knowledge Acquisition*. Hillsdale, NJ: Erlbaum.

Tatsuoka, K. K. (1995). Architecture of knowledge structures and cognitive diagnosis: A statistical pattern recognition and classification approach. In P. D. Nichols, S. F. Chipman & R. L. Brennan (Eds.) *Cognitively Diagnostic Assessment*. Hillsdale, NJ: Erlbaum.

VanLehn, K. (1996). Conceptual and meta learning during coached problem solving. In C. Frasson, G. Gauthier and A. Lesgold (Eds.) *ITS96: Proceeding of the Third International Conference on Intelligent Tutoring Systems*. New York: Springer-Verlag.

Toward a Unification of Human-Computer Learning and Tutoring

Henry Hamburger and Gheorghe Tecuci

Department of Computer Science, MSN 4A5, George Mason University
4400 University Dr., Fairfax, VA 22030-4444, USA
{henryh, tecuci}@gmu.edu

Abstract. We define a learning tutor as being an intelligent agent that learns from human tutors and then tutors human learners. The notion of a learning tutor provides a conceptual framework for integrating the fields of intelligent tutoring-learning environments and machine learning-based knowledge acquisition. We present the conceptual framework of a learning tutor that adapts and integrates major portions of two existing successful systems, one of each kind, originally built separately by the respective authors. It is being developed and applied to the domains of software use and chemistry.

1 An Approach to Unification

Machine Learning-based Knowledge Acquisition (MLKA) systems and Intelligent Tutoring-Learning Environments (ITLE) are engaged in the same activity except for a role reversal: one system learns from humans and the other helps humans learn. Nevertheless, the two kinds of systems, as well as the fields of Machine Learning and Intelligent Tutoring Systems, have grown up separately and remain largely independent (but see [1]).

We have begun to investigate, elucidate and integrate the areas of potential symbiosis of MLKA and ITLE, with a view to facilitating the transfer of knowledge from one field to the other. Our interest is partly at the knowledge level, but we are at least equally concerned with the concrete goal of implementing a unified system with practical benefits. One of us has built a large system, Disciple, that learns ([12], [13], [14]). The other of us has built one, FLUENT, that tutors ([6], [10]). That experience and the actual software produced are contributing to the current work described here. Both projects have put considerable effort into tool-building. In the present work, we continue to build development tools usable by teachers as well as by researchers, enabling teacher-experts to be directly involved in improving educational software.

Our central integrative concept and implementation project is the Learning Tutor (LT), defined as an intelligent agent that can be directly taught by a human and can then tutor human students. Such an agent can serve as an asynchronous communication channel between a human tutor and an unlimited number of human students, one at a time. In the first phase of communication, the agent behaves as an interactive MLKA system, learning directly from a human tutor the domain knowledge and the tutorial knowledge. Then, using the domain and tutorial knowledge, the agent assumes the opposite role, functioning as an ITLE. A key desideratum for an LT is natural communication. The communication in each of the two phases is natural to the extent that it resembles human tutorial communication. Thus an LT needs natural language processing and a highly flexible two-way graphics communication capability, both functioning under the guidance of a tutorial discourse framework. The actual construction of an LT drives our comparative study of communication and representation strategies in MLKA and ITLE systems. Both fields provide insights into the appropriate characteristics for a shared internal knowledge representation that serves the operations of learning, tutoring and communicating meaningfully with both human parties, in both linguistic and graphical media. For the representation to be appropriate for communication, it must support the elementary teaching moves of both the human teacher and the agent teacher. Results in human learning and human-computer interaction complement ITLE work as guidance for communication. Results in MLKA allow to overcome the knowledge acquisition bottleneck in the construction of domains, curricula and examples for systems that support human learning.

The paper is organized as follows. The next section takes note of some relevant developments in MLKA and ITLE and how they influence our approach. Section 3 presents the architecture of the LT. Within that context we then elaborate on the communication issues mentioned above. Section 5 is a discussion of our choices of software and chemistry as domains in which the LT operates, and presents a graphical tool that enables a non-programmer to build concept-based animations, which are seen to have the potential for a key role in the LT's communicative capabilities.

2 Relevant Developments in MLKA and ITLE

Developments in both MLKA and ITLE make the notion of an LT both timely and promising. We briefly spotlight, in MLKA, apprenticeship learning, multistrategy learning, and programming by demonstration, and, in ITLE, shared control, enriched interfaces and knowledge tuned to tutoring. These developments have clarified the nature of the knowledge and communication that are needed for an effective LT.

Apprenticeship learning is a type of knowledge acquisition and learning in which a learning agent acts as an apprentice to a human expert. The agent assimilates new knowledge from the human expert, by observing and analyzing the way the expert solves problems, as well as by interacting with the expert. ([9], [12], [16]). Multistrategy learning refers to a type of learning in which the learner integrates different learning strategies to take advantage of their complementary nature and to perform learning tasks that are beyond the capabilities of monostrategy learners [8]. Programming by demonstration [5] refers to a type of programming in which a computer system is taught how to perform a task by graphically showing it examples of task performance and explaining them. Disciple embodies elements of all these approaches, allowing a user to build an agent much as one would teach a human apprentice, by giving the agent specific examples of problems and solutions, explanations of these solutions, and supervising the agent as it solves new problems.

One ITLE development important to LT grows from the dialogue on who is in charge. A directive tutor keeps students on the solution path, but a constructive learner learns by wandering in the field of study. Collins and Brown [4] would even wish students to "flounder" in their problem-solving, as a preliminary phase to constructing their own knowledge. Anderson has warned of the potential frustration in floundering, but he agrees that students must learn problem-solving rules by use, not simply by being told [2]. The enriched interface began in the work of Hollan et al. [7], with their conceptually valid visual representation of a simulation. Generic tools for building such interfaces were later developed by Towne and Munro [15]. Pedagogically tuned knowledge was Clancey's [3] response to a problem that unexpectedly arose when the knowledge base of an expert system was first imported into the expertise component of an ITLE. Knowledge in an expert system is judged by its performance in its domain.

When that performance-oriented knowledge is called on to support communication in tutoring, there is no guarantee that it will make sense to novices. The FLUENT system has been directly responsive to the first two of these developments, offering the learner the opportunity to take charge of some parameters that determine system behavior and to relinquish control of others to the electronic tutor. In this way the student can get appropriate guidance without losing ultimate control. Our potential for interfaces arises from the tools described in the section 5.1. Our approach to pedagogical knowledge has been to develop a complex data structure called a tutorial schema, built out of interaction types, linguistics viewpoints and domain plans ([6], [10]).

3 The Unified Architecture of the Learning Tutor

A key aspect of our strategy of unification is to specify the different kinds of knowledge required in the various components of an ITLE and then to arrange for that knowledge to be directly acquired from a human tutor by MLKA methods. This approach leads to the LT architecture shown here as Fig. 1.

Various components of the typical MLKA and ITLE are shared inside the LT as follows. The MLKA Engine, the Domain Knowledge and the Inference Engine constitute a multistrategy apprenticeship learning system, the role of which is to learn the expertise knowledge from the human tutor. Of these three parts, the latter two constitute what is known as the expertise module of an ITLE. Domain knowledge must go beyond performance adequacy; it must be pedagogically appropriate. This is a new demand for LT construction, not previously faced by the independent field of Knowledge Acquisition. Thus our strategy for the problem of obtaining pedagogically appropriate domain knowledge can involve altering the human's stance. The human in this interaction must now be both a tutor and an expert at the same time. This tutor-expert must interact with a view to getting things not only correct but also comprehensible. Just as one communicates knowledge differently to a beginning student than to a colleague, so must the tutor-expert interact differently with an LT than an expert does when imparting a domain to an expert system. During the agent's learning process, the MLKA Engine continuously extends and improves the Domain Knowledge until its domain quality and pedagogical form are both good enough to serve as the expertise for tutoring.

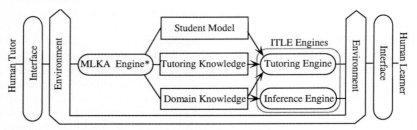

Fig. 1. An architecture for the Learning Tutor. Lines indicate two-way flow of information, arrows one way. *The MLKA Engine has submodules for its various responsibilities as outlined in the text.

In addition to this more extensive domain knowledge, the system also must acquire explicitly pedagogical knowledge (as opposed to pedagogically appropriate domain knowledge) for the tutorial component. In FLUENT such knowledge takes the form of tutorial schemas provided directly by a teacher-expert working with a tool. In the Disciple approach, the MLKA Engine, the Tutoring Knowledge and the Tutoring Engine in Fig. 1 are viewed as a multistrategy apprenticeship learning system the role of which is to acquire tutoring knowledge. The tutor has two top-level subcomponents, one involving curriculum (choosing problems to pose to the student) and one to communicate assistance in ways that are responsive to both the problem state and the student (as represented in the student model). Curriculum knowledge includes such aspects as degrees of difficulty and the prerequisite relationships among the various concepts and problems. It is straightforward to acquire this kind of information. As for communication, the approach is to call upon the tutor-expert for the rationale behind choosing a particular form of communication in a particular situation. This is done via a structured dialog using the LT's communication language. Such a scenario involves alternation, within a MLKA session, between acquiring domain knowledge and acquiring pedagogical knowledge.

Yet a third relationship between the two agent roles concerns both domain and tutorial modules, as follows. Each concept or rule from the Domain Knowledge is annotated with information indicating how it has been learned from the human's tutoring moves. The annotations include examples from which the rule or concept has been learned, as well as the various explanations or hints provided by the human tutor. The resulting material then becomes an augmentation to the Tutoring Knowledge of the ITLE. The LT attempts to teach the human learner similarly to the way it was taught by the human tutor, by using these knowledge annotations from the human tutor.

A fourth connection is that deploying MLKA techniques within the ITLE supports the important ITLE function of student modeling. Inferring an accurate student model has long been a main and difficult research goal in Intelligent Tutoring Systems. Our approach of using MLKA to evolve the student model renders this task much more manageable. Indeed, it allows the LT to verify or extend the student model by engaging in a dialog with the student like that with the tutor. This approach thus takes into account Self's [11] maxim - not to guess what the student knows but let her tell you - yet remains responsive to the individual student.

4. Communication

In order to create natural and compatible communication links among the human tutor, the LT and the human student, all the interactions are based on a common communication repertoire that expresses various types of teaching moves. In Disciple these include providing examples, hints, explanations, problems, definitions, taxonomic and other facts, corrections, and confirmation of partial corrections. These various forms of communication have both a spatial and a verbal component, notably the diagrams that are so essential to technical communication. In our work, the problem-solving communication between the human tutor or student, on one side, and the LT on the other side, involves knowledge-based, interactive, animated diagrams in addition to textual and symbolic interaction.

Since FLUENT is a conversational system, it too has contributions to make to communication in the LT. Specifically, we are incorporating the notions of views, interaction types and tutorial schemas, described at some length in the work cited above. An interaction type is a short sequence of specified types of linguistic and spatial moves by specified parties. In the Movecaster interaction type, for instance, the student makes an action occur and the system describes it.

Linguistic move types within an interaction type include Disciple's communication repertoire mentioned above as well as FLUENT's questions, command and statements. The latter are elaborated by linguistic viewpoints or views, which enable the natural language generation system to take account of some discourse phenomena. They distinguish, for example, between actions and the results of those actions, as in "You picked up the box." vs. "You are (now) holding the box."

Tutorial schemas allow a teacher-expert to organize interaction types into a coherent educational session, coordinated with meaningful, visible ongoing changes in the underlying microworld situation. The situation is coherent because its activities are guided by plans that make sense in the particular domain. Technically a plan is a flexible tree of subplans and ultimately actions, with constraints on time-sequence where appropriate. The roles in a plan are class-constrained variables, analogous to function arguments. Execution of plans skips any subplans or actions whose goals are currently met. The simplest tutorial schema is just a plan and an interaction type. More generally it can be a sequence of pairs, each consisting of a plan and a regular expression of interaction types.

5. Two Domains

We have begun to develop the LT to learn and teach material in two domains. The first domain is the use of a software tool, in particular our own tool for creating concept-based diagrams and animations. Besides providing a domain, this tool also supports the learning of other domains, especially technical ones like our second domain, chemistry. Both of these topics are useful, well-understood and problem-oriented. Moreover, the two are distinct enough to push the work toward general applicability.

ITLEs have been most successful in technical education, and we see our work as building on that success. Rapid technology-driven changes in the subject matter of many fields have created a need for educational systems that are rapidly produced and easily updated, yet retain the high pedagogical quality of the best ITLEs. The unified LT approach can provide precisely such a capacity by permitting collaboration with humans in both the learning and the teaching phases.

5.1 Learning to Use Concept-Based Animation

Developed in the context of the FLUENT project, our concept-based graphics and animation tool provides some 100 operations for creating sketches and incorporating them into animations. Even a non-programmer can create animations, define classes and create class instances that inherit the animations of its class. It is also straightforward to specify that certain animated events occur when objects of two particular classes come into contact. A teacher can thus establish an entire microworld that then permits a student to control the combination of events to produce meaningful, continuing situations.

The present and future importance of learning to use software is clear. Moreover, our particular choice of diagram and animation software supports the learning of an important communication ability. Though often taken to be a verbal skill, communication also has a spatial component – the picture that is worth many words. This is particularly true in technical communication, where diagrams are ubiquitous.

Clarity of diagrams is an issue for textbooks, financial reports, appliances manuals and indeed within the software of ITLE systems, where it relates to the important issue of cognitive fidelity of the interface.

The role of diagram software in a presentation is analogous to that of a human language in an ordinary conversation. To converse meaningfully, you need something to say and a language to say it in. Similarly, to make a presentation with diagrams, including animated ones, you need both domain knowledge and diagram ability. These two kinds of knowledge are thus complementary. Since it is easier to learn one thing at a time, the learning and teaching by machine and human should proceed counter-clockwise through Fig. 2, from the upper left. The left side of the figure has the machine (M) learning a domain from a human teacher-expert (T) in the usual MLKA manner. M's learning to diagram can then be grounded in this new knowledge. Proceeding in a complementary manner, the human student (S) can then acquire diagram skill from the agent in a simple, familiar domain. That knowledge can then support a partly graphical communication in which the human learner acquires new domain knowledge.

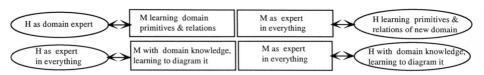

Fig. 2. Four kinds of knowledge communication
between human (H, in ovals) and machine (M, in boxes)

We expect our approach to LT and its application to a drawing tool to contribute to the way people learn to use new software packages. Currently users invest a large amount of time learning a software package. Existing help facilities are based on the idea of letting a user seek needed information, with emphasis on ease of search. However, the user must know what to look for. In contrast, the LT approach is to let the user learn about the software package while trying to solve a specific problem with it. This is possible because the LT has been trained by an instructor by solving problems similar to the user's problem. Therefore, when the user attempts to solve a problem, the LT can suggest a solution, can guide the user through a customized manual, or can give advice on how to solve the problem.

The following are the key properties of our concept based animation tool:
• There are many operations on points, segments, parts and figures.
• There is symbolic as well as visual control of the graphics.
• Animations include symbolic information along with key frames.
• The graphics and animation are linked to a conceptual representation.
• A builder-user can build animations, classes, objects, concepts and linkages.
• An end user or the system can activate the currently meaningful animations.

Fig. 3 shows the major kinds of graphical and conceptual entities that have been implemented and the important relationships between them. As an example of how to interpret the linkages in Fig. 3, the arrow from FIGURE on the graphical side to OBJECT on the conceptual side means that an object corresponds to the figures that depict it in various states. Similarly, an action may correspond to different animations, depending on the state of its object. As a specific example of one action (on the conceptual side) having more than one animation, the person in Fig. 4 has shapes that face left, right or out from the screen. It can switch among their states by animations for actions of turning and it has other animated actions like walking, which are animated differently depending on which way the person is facing.

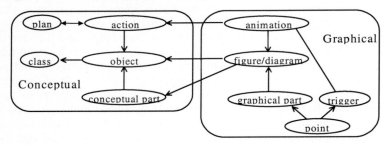

Fig. 3. Graphical and conceptual aspects of representation. An arrow means that several instances of the type at its tail may correspond to a head instance. The two-way arrow is a many-many mapping, and the line a one-one mapping.

The linkage to underlying conceptual representation is crucial to meaningful manipulation of the animated figures and to reasoning about their actions. Together the graphics, animations, knowledge, reasoning and their mutual relationship support the acquisition and communication of knowledge. As an example of the conceptual-graphical link, teachers and learners can: (i) associate graphical constructions to classes, (ii) parameterize the properties of classes, and (iii) create instances of those classes, having particular values for selected parameters. Another linkage of equal importance is that between teacher and students, via the software. One key to this linkage is the trigger, a region associated with a figure that the user can click to activate a particular action for the object corresponding to that figure. By providing a trigger for an animation, the creator of the diagram enables its user to initiate and control an action that updates the properties of the underlying conceptual object. A teacher can create an animation trigger that students can use to control animations and hence the underlying microworld that they are learning about.

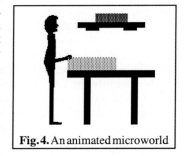

Fig. 4. An animated microworld

5.2 Chemistry

Chemistry suits our purposes because it has rich, precise knowledge structures involving both symbolic and numerical computation, that are well suited to learning via our knowledge-based, interactive, animated diagrams, which are jointly manipulable by a person and a machine. Some of the Chemistry topics have the additional desirable property of having two or more different visual representations. There are alternative visualizations for such concepts as element categories and molecule geometry and for various categories of chemical and physical processes. The geometry of molecules, for example, can be represented and communicated as wireframe, ball and stick, or spacefilling models, each with its own advantages for manipulation, envisioning and problem-solving.

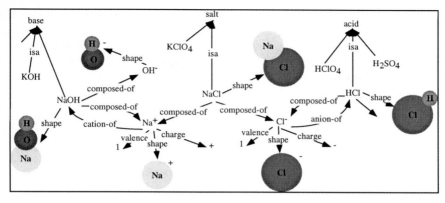

Fig. 5. Part of the agent's knowledge of chemistry

We now illustrate the use of the LT in the chemistry domain, showing how a chemistry teacher could teach the agent, through examples and explanations, and how the agent could then teach a student, imitating the way in which it was taught by the teacher. Let us assume that the agent already has some knowledge about chemical compounds, part of which is represented in the semantic network in Fig. 5.

To teach the agent how various substances react, the teacher provides a specific example of a chemical reaction (such as NaOH + HCl → H₂O +NaCl), informing the system about the reaction in several different ways. One way is to interact with the explanation interface of Disciple, explaining to the agent the result of the reaction in terms that are known to the agent, that is, in terms of the concepts and the features from the semantic network shown in Fig. 5:

NaCl is composed of Na⁺ (a cation of NaOH) and of Cl⁻ (an anion of HCl)

H₂O is composed of OH⁻ (a component of NaOH) and of H⁺ (a component of HCl)

The teacher can also use the drawing tool presented in the preceding section to create a concept-based diagram and an animation, and to annotate them using free text, as exemplified in Fig. 6. The animation of course runs smoothly through interpolations between the frames shown in Fig. 6.

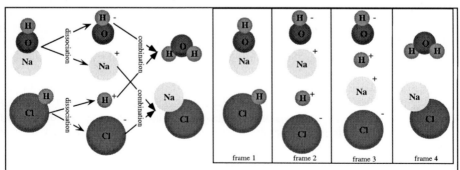

NaOH reacts with HCl to produce NaCl and H₂O. The reaction has two parts:
- NaOH dissociates into OH⁻ and Na⁺, while HCl dissociates into H⁺ and Cl⁻.
- OH⁻ combines with H⁺ to produce H₂O, while Na⁺ combines with Cl⁻ to produce NaCl.

Fig. 6. Teacher's diagram, animation and the textual annotation of a chemical reaction

At this point, the teacher may give the agent additional examples of reactions (such as, $KOH + HClO_4 \rightarrow H_2O + KClO_4$) that are used to generalize the rule. Or, the agent may use analogical reasoning to hypothesize reactions similar to the one received from the teacher, who will be asked to analyze them. These additional examples (or counter-examples) of chemical reactions are generalized by the learning tutor, using the knowledge from the semantic network in Fig. 5, to get generalized results like the three listed next, and ultimately to form a general reaction rule, as shown in Fig. 7.

> NaOH and KOH are generalized to any base (see the upper left side of Fig. 5)
> HCl and $HClO_4$ are generalized to any acid
> Na^+ and K^+ are generalized to any metal ion.

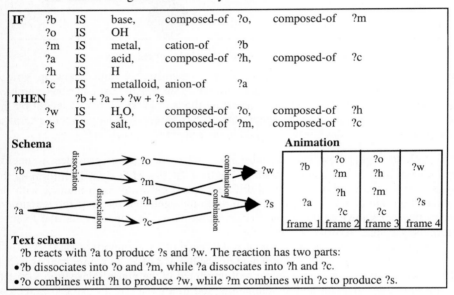

Fig. 7. A general reaction rule

The generalized rule at the top of Fig. 7 states that a base reacts with an acid to produce water and the appropriate salt. This formal representation of the rule allows the agent to perform various types of reasoning but it is not learner friendly. That is, it is an expert-style, performance-oriented rule, not fit for pedagogical purposes. To tutor the student the LT will use rule's annotations. For instance, the agent may imitate, at a conceptual level, the way it was taught by the teacher. For this it is enough to generate instances of the rule in the context of the semantic network in Fig. 5. This will provide examples of chemical reactions (such as, $KOH + H_2SO_4 \rightarrow H_2O + KHSO_4$), illustrated with diagrams and animations similar to those in Fig. 6. Another possible use of the rule is in generating test questions [13] or in verifying chemical reactions specified by the student.

6. Goals

Both MLKA and ITLE can benefit from the attempt to transfer knowledge between them. Our strategy is to design a general theoretical framework for the learning and tutoring processes and to refine it as we implement a system that can support learning and tutoring in disparate domains. We aspire to a more comprehensive and unifying view that can contribute to the development of new educational techniques and insight. Within this long-term goal are these subgoals: 1) Comparative analysis of MLKA and ITLE, with consideration of integration and transfer of techniques, human-machine communication and knowledge representation to support the demands of reasoning, learning and communication. 2) ML-based KA methods for enabling an LT to acquire domain expertise, pedagogical strategies and student models. 3) Prototypes of two LTs.

Acknowledgments: Part of this research was done in the Learning Agents Laboratory which is supported by the AFOSR grant F49620-97-1-0188, as part of the DARPA's HPKB Program, by the DARPA contract N66001-95-D-8653 and by the NSF grant CDA-9616478.

References

1. Aïmeur, E. Frasson, C.: Eliciting the learning context in co-operative tutoring systems. In: Proc. of the IJCAI-95 Workshop on Modeling Context in Knowledge Representation and Reasoning (1995)
2. Anderson, J.R. Pelletier, R.: A development system for model-tracing tutors. In: Birnbaum L.(ed.): *Proc. of the Int. Conf. on the Learning Sciences, Evanston, Illinois*. Charlottesville, VA: Assoc. for the Advancement of Computing in Education (1991)
3. Clancey, W.J.: *Knowledge-Based Tutoring: The GUIDON Program.* MIT Press (1987)
4. Collins, A. Brown, J.S.: The computer as a tool for learning through reflection. In: Mandl H. and Lesgold A. (eds.): *Learning Issues for Intelligent Tutoring Systems.* Berlin: Springer-Verlag (1988)
5. Cypher, A. (editor), *Watch what I do: programming by demonstration.* MIT Press. Cambridge. MA (1993)
6. Hamburger, H.: Structuring two-medium dialog for language learning. In: Holland M., Kaplan J., Sams M. (eds.) *Intelligent Language Tutors: Balancing Theory and Technology.* Hillsdale, NJ: L. Erlbaum Associates (1995)
7. Hollan, J.D., Hutchins, E.L., Weitzman, L.: Steamer: an interactive, inspectable simulation-based training system. *AI Magazine,* 5, (1984) 15-28
8. Michalski, R.S., Tecuci, G. (eds.): *Machine Learning: A Multistrategy Approach Volume 4,* Morgan Kaufmann Publishers, San Mateo, CA (1994)
9. Mitchell T.M., Mahadevan S., Steinberg L.I.: LEAP: A Learning Apprentice System for VLSI Design. In: Kodratoff Y. and Michalski R.S. (eds.): *Machine Learning,* vol III, Morgan Kaufmann, San Mateo (1990)
10. Schoelles, M., Hamburger, H.: Teacher-usable exercise design tools. In: Frasson C., Gauthier G., Lesgold A. (eds.) *Intelligent Tutoring Systems: Proceedings of the Third International Conference, ITS '96, Montreal.* Berlin: Springer (1996)
11. Self, J.A.: Bypassing the intractable problem of student modeling. In: Frasson C., Gauthier G. (eds.): *Intelligent Tutoring Systems: At the Crossroads of Artificial Intelligence and Education.* Norwood, NJ: Ablex Publ. Co (1990)
12. Tecuci G., Kodratoff Y.: Apprenticeship Learning in Imperfect Theory Domains. In: Kodratoff Y., Michalski R.S. (eds.): *Machine Learning: An Artificial Intelligence Approach,* vol. 3, Morgan Kaufmann, (1990) 514-551
13. Tecuci G. Keeling H.: Developing Intelligent Educational Agents with the Disciple Learning Agent Shell. In this volume (1998)
14. Tecuci G.: *Building Intelligent Agents: An Apprenticeship Multistrategy Learning Theory, Methodology, Tool and Case Studies,* Academic Press, London (1988)
15. Towne, D.M., Munro, A.: Two approaches to simulation composition for training. In: Farr M., Psotka J. (eds.): *Intelligent Instruction by Computer: Theory and Practice.* Washington: Taylor and Francis (1992)
16. Wilkins D.C.: Knowledge Base Refinement as Improving an Incorrect and Incomplete Domain Theory. In: Kodratoff Y., Michalski R.S. (eds.): *Machine Learning: An Artificial Intelligence Approach.* Vol. III. San Mateo, CA: Morgan Kaufmann (1990)

Developing Intelligent Educational Agents with the Disciple Learning Agent Shell

Gheorghe Tecuci and Harry Keeling

Department of Computer Science, MSN 4A5, George Mason University
4400 University Dr., Fairfax, VA 22030-4444, USA
{tecuci, hkeeling}@gmu.edu

Abstract. Disciple is an apprenticeship, multistrategy learning approach for developing intelligent agents where an expert teaches the agent how to perform domain-specific tasks in a way that resembles how the expert would teach an apprentice. We claim that Disciple can naturally be used to build certain types of educational agents. Indeed, an educator can teach a Disciple agent which in turn can tutor students in the same way it was taught by the educator. This paper presents the Disciple approach and its application to developing an educational agent that generates history test questions. The agent provides intelligent feedback to the student in the form of hints, answer and explanations, and assists in the assessment of student's understanding and use of higher-order thinking skills.

1 Introduction

Disciple is an apprenticeship, multistrategy learning approach for developing intelligent agents where an expert teaches the agent how to perform domain-specific tasks in a way that resembles how the expert would teach an apprentice, by giving the agent examples and explanations, as well as by supervising and correcting its behavior [11]. It integrates many machine learning and knowledge acquisition strategies taking advantage of their complementary strengths to compensate for their weaknesses [5, 9, 10]. As a consequence, it significantly reduces the involvement of the knowledge engineer in the process of building an intelligent agent. A type of agent that can be built naturally with Disciple is an educational agent (i.e. an agent that assists an educator in an education-related task). Indeed, an educator can teach a Disciple agent and then this agent can tutor students in the same way it was taught by the educator. Therefore, such an application of Disciple illustrates an approach to the integration of machine learning and intelligent tutoring systems [1, 8].

This paper is organized as follows. Section 2 introduces the architecture of Disciple. Section 3 presents the test generation agent built with Disciple. Section 4 describes the process of building the agent. Section 5 presents experimental results and Section 6 summarizes the evidence in support of the claims of the Disciple approach.

2 Disciple Learning Agent Shell

The current version of the Disciple approach is implemented in the Disciple Learning Agent Shell, the architecture of which is presented in Fig. 1. The Disciple shell has four main domain independent components shown in the light gray area of Fig. 1:
  • a knowledge acquisition and learning component for developing the knowledge base (KB), with a domain-independent graphical user interface;

- a problem solving component that provides basic problem solving operations;
- a knowledge base manager which controls access and updates to the KB;
- an empty KB to be developed for the specific application domain.

The two components in the dark gray area are the domain dependent components that need to be developed and integrated with the Disciple shell to form a customized agent that performs specific tasks in an application domain. They are:
- a specialized problem solver that provides the specific functionality of the agent;
- a domain-specific graphical user interface.

In the case of the test generation agent that is presented in this paper, the specialized problem solver is the test generator that also builds and maintains a student model. Two domain specific interfaces were built to facilitate the communication between the history expert/teacher and the agent, and between the agent and the students.

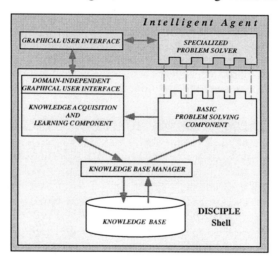

Fig. 1. The architecture of the Disciple shell

3 A Test Generation Agent for Higher-Order Thinking Skills

The developed Disciple agent generates history tests to assist in the assessment of students' understanding and use of higher-order thinking skills. An example of specific higher-order thinking skill is the evaluation of historical sources for relevance, credibility, consistency, ambiguity, bias, and fact vs. opinion [2,3,4,6]. To motivate the middle school students, for which this agent was developed, and to provide an element of game playing, the agent employs a journalist metaphor. It asks the students to assume the role of a journalist who has to complete assignments from the Editor. One assignment could be to write an article on the experience of African American women during the Civil War. Within this context, the students are given source material and asked various questions that would require them to exercise the skill of evaluation. In these assignments, students are asked to apply higher-order thinking skills in much the way journalists do when they complete their assignments and prepare stories for publication.

The agent dynamically generates a test question, based on a student model, together with the answer, hints and explanations. An example of a test question is shown in Fig. 2. The student is asked to imagine that he or she is a reporter and has been assigned the task to write an article for Harper's Weekly during the pre Civil War period on slave culture. He or she has to analyze the historical source "Group of Slaves" in order to determine whether it is relevant to this task. In the situation from Fig. 2 the student answered correctly. Therefore, the agent confirmed the answer and provided an explanation for it, as indicated in the lower right pane of the window. The student can also request a hint, which in this case is the following one: "To determine if the source is relevant to your task investigate if it illustrates some component of slave culture, check when it was created and when Harper's Weekly was issued."

The agent has two modes of operation: final exam mode and self-assessment mode. In the final exam mode, it generates an exam consisting of a set of test questions. The student has to answer one test question at a time and, after each question, he or she receives the correct answer and an explanation of the answer. In the self-assessment mode, the student chooses the type of test question to answer, and may request a hint to answer the question, the correct answer, and the explanation of the answer.

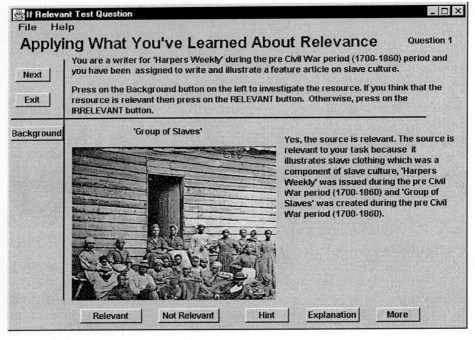

Fig. 2. A test question, answer and explanation generated by the agent[1]

---

[1] Picture reproduced from LC-B8171-383, Library of Congress, Prints & Photographs Div.

4 Building the Test Generation Agent

To build the test generation agent the teacher (possibly assisted by a knowledge engineer) first develops the knowledge base of the agent. Then, the knowledge engineer builds the test generation engine and the student's interface.

The KB of any Disciple agent should contain an ontology [7] and a set of rules. The ontology contains descriptions of historical concepts (such as "slave culture"), historical sources (such as "Group of Slaves" in Fig. 2), and templates for reporter tasks (such as "You are a writer for a PUBLICATION during a HISTORICAL-PERIOD and you have been assigned to write and illustrate a feature article on a SLAVERY-TOPIC."). Using these descriptions, the agent communicates with the students through a stylized natural language, as shown in Fig. 2.

Fig. 3 shows an example of a relevancy rule. It is an IF-THEN rule where the condition specifies a general reporter task and the conclusion specifies a source relevant to that task. The condition also incorporates the explanation of why the source is relevant to the task. Associated with the rule are the natural language templates corresponding to the task, explanation and conclusion of the rule. These templates are automatically created from the natural language descriptions of the elements in the rule. One should notice that each rule corresponds to a certain type of task (WRITE-DURING-PERIOD, in this case). Other types of tasks are WRITE-ON-TOPIC, WRITE-FOR-AUDIENCE, and WRITE-FOR-OCCASION. Therefore, for each type of reporter task there will be a family of related relevancy rules. The rules corresponding to the other evaluation criteria, such as credibility, accuracy, or bias, will have a similar form.

IF

?W1	IS	WRITE-DURING-PERIOD, FOR ?S1, DURING ?P1, ON ?S2
?P1	IS	HISTORICAL-PERIOD
?S1	IS	PUBLICATION, ISSUED-DURING ?P1
?S2	IS	SLAVERY-TOPIC
?S3	IS	SOURCE, ILLUSTRATES ?S4, CREATED-DURING ?P1
?S4	IS	HISTORICAL-CONCEPT, COMPONENT-OF ?S2

THEN

RELEVANT HIST-SOURCE ?S3

Task Description: You are a writer for ?S1 during ?P1 and you have been assigned to write and illustrate a feature article on ?S2.

Explanation: ?S3 illustrates ?S4 which was a component of ?S2, ?S1 was issued during ?P1 and ?S3 was created during ?P1.

Operation Description: ?S3 is relevant

Fig. 3. A relevancy rule

4.1 Building the Agent's Ontology

The process of building the agent's ontology starts with choosing a module in a history curriculum (such as Slavery in America) for which the agent will generate test questions. Then the teacher identifies a set of historical concepts that are appropriate and necessary to be learned by the students. The teacher also identifies a set of historical sources that will enhance the student's understanding of these concepts and that will be used in test questions. All these concepts and the historical sources are represented by the history teacher in the knowledge base of the agent, by using the various editors and browsers of Disciple. One is the Source Viewer that displays the historical sources. Another is the Concept Editor that is used to describe the historical sources. The historical sources have to be defined in terms of features that are necessary for applying the higher-order thinking skill of evaluation. For instance, a source is relevant to some topic if it identifies, illustrates or explains the topic or some of its components. In particular, "Group of Slaves" in Fig. 2 is defined as being a photo. It illustrates the concepts slave clothing, child slave, female slave, male slave and field slave. Other information is also represented, such as the audience for which this historical source is appropriate and when it was created.

4.2 Teaching the Agent to Judge the Relevance of a Source to a Task

After the semantic network is defined, the teacher has to teach the agent how to judge the relevancy (as well as the credibility, accuracy, and the other evaluation criteria) of a source with respect to various reporter tasks. Fig. 4 presents the phases of this teaching process.

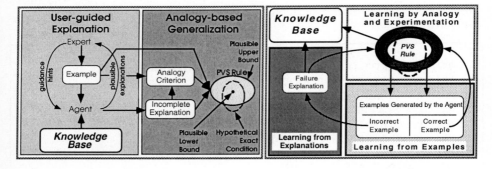

Fig. 4.   (a) Rule Learning   (b) Rule Refinement

First, the teacher gives to the agent an example consisting of a task and a historical source relevant to that task, as illustrated in Fig. 5. Next, the teacher has to help the agent understand why the source is relevant to the task. Rather than giving an explanation to the agent, the teacher will guide the agent to propose explanations and will select the correct ones. For instance, the teacher may point to the most relevant objects from the input example and may specify the types of plausible explanations to be searched for. From these interactions, it was concluded that the source HUMAN-FLESH-AT-AUCTION is relevant to the task of writing an article for CHRISTIAN-RECORDER, during POST-CIVIL-WAR, on SLAVE-LIFE because:

- HUMAN-FLESH-AT-AUCTION illustrates SLAVE-SELLING which was a component of SLAVE-LIFE
- CHRISTIAN-RECORDER was issued during POST-CIVIL-WAR
- HUMAN-FLESH-AT-AUCTION was created during POST-CIVIL-WAR

Fig. 5. Initial example given by the teacher

One may notice that this explanation is similar to the explanation from the test question in Fig. 2. This illustrates a significant benefit to be derived from using the Disciple approach to build educational agents. That is, the kind of explanations that the agent gives to the students are similar to the explanations that the agent itself has received from the teacher. Therefore, the agent acts as an indirect communication medium between the teacher and the students.

The found explanation is generalized by the agent to an analogy criterion. Then the analogy criterion and the example are used to generate a rule with two conditions: a plausible lower bound condition which is very specific, covering only the example in Fig. 5, and a plausible upper bound condition which is very general, covering examples that are analogous with the initial example. To improve this rule, the teacher will invoke the rule refinement process represented in Fig. 4b, asking the agent to generate examples similar with the one in Fig. 5. Each example generated by the agent is covered by the plausible upper bound and is not covered by the plausible lower bound of the rule. The example (which looks like the one in Fig. 5) is shown to the teacher who is asked to accept it as correct or to reject it, thus characterizing it as a positive or a negative example of the rule. A positive example is used to generalize the plausible lower bound of the rule's condition. A negative example is used to elicit additional explanations from the expert and to specialize both bounds, or only the plausible upper bound. This process will continue until either the two bounds of the rule become identical or until no further examples can be generated. The final learned rule is the one from Fig. 3.

4.3 Developing the Test Generation Engine

One of the agent's requirements was that it also generates hints and feedback for right and wrong answers (see Fig. 6). The Hint is the part of the Explanation that refers only to the variables used in Task Description. The Right Answer is generated from the Operation Description and the Explanation, and the Wrong Answer is a fixed text.

Hint: To determine if the source is relevant to your task investigate if it illustrates some component of ?S2, check when it was created and when ?S1 was issued.

Right Answer: Yes, the source is relevant. The source is relevant to your task because it illustrates ?S4 which was a component of ?S2, ?S1 was issued during ?P1 and ?S3 was created during ?P1.

Wrong Answer: No, the source is not relevant. Investigate this source further and analyze the hints and explanations to improve your understanding of relevance. You may consider reviewing the material on relevance. Then continue testing yourself.

Fig. 6. Additional templates associated with the rule in Fig. 3

We have developed a test generation engine that generates four types of test questions:
- IF RELEVANT: Show the student a writing assignment and ask whether a particular historical source is relevant to that assignment;
- WHICH RELEVANT: Show the student an assignment and three historical sources and ask the student to identify the relevant one;
- WHICH IRRELEVANT: Show the student an assignment and three historical sources and ask the student to identify the irrelevant one; and
- WHY RELEVANT: Show the student an assignment, a source and three possible reasons why the source is relevant, and ask the student to select the right reason.

To generate an IF RELEVANT test question with a relevant source, the agent simply needs to generate an example of a relevancy rule. This rule example will contain a task T and a source S relevant to it, together with a hint and an explanation. However, if the student requires all the possible reasons for why the source S is relevant to the task T, then the agent will need to find all the examples containing the source S and the task T of all the relevancy rules from the family of rules corresponding to the task T. To generate an IF RELEVANT test question with an irrelevant source the agent has to first generate a valid task T by finding an example of a relevancy rule R. Then it has to find a historical source S such that the task T and the source S are not part of any example of any rule from the family of rules corresponding to the task T.

The methods for generating WHICH RELEVANT and WHICH IRRELEVANT test questions are based on the methods for generating IF RELEVANT test questions. First an IF RELEVANT test question with a task T and relevant source S is generated. Then additional relevant or irrelevant sources are looked for, as described above.

The method for generating WHY RELEVANT test questions starts with generating an example E_1 of a relevancy rule R_1. This example provides a correct task description T, a source S relevant to T, and a correct explanation EX_1 of why the source S is relevant to T. Then the agent chooses another rule that is not from the family of the relevancy rules corresponding to T. Let us suppose that the agent chooses a credibility rule R_2. It then generates an example E_2 of R_2, based on E_1 (that is, E_2 and E_1 share as many parts as possible, including the source S). The agent also generates an explanation EX_2 of why S is credible. While this explanation is correct, it has nothing to do with why S is relevant to T. Then, the agent repeats this process to find another explanation that is true but explains something else, not why S is relevant to T.

Similar test questions could be generated for each evaluation skill such as, IF CREDIBLE test questions or WHY CREDIBLE test questions.

5   Experimental Results

The ontology of the test generation agent includes the description of 252 historical concepts, 80 historical sources, and 6 publications. The KB also contains 54 relevancy rules grouped in four families. These rules have been learned from an average of 2.17 explanations (standard deviation 0.91) and 5.4 examples (standard deviation 1.37), which indicates a very efficient training process.

We have performed five experiments with the test generation agent. The first three experiments tested the correctness of the knowledge base, as judged by the domain expert who developed the agent, and by a domain expert who was not involved in its development. The fourth and the fifth experiments tested the quality of the test generation agent, as judged by students and by teachers.

The results of the first three experiments are summarized in Table 1. IF RELEVANT test questions were randomly generated by the agent and answered by the developing expert (in the first experiment) and by the independent expert (in the second and the third experiment). The agreements or the disagreements between the expert and the agent were recorded and the percentage of the correct answers of the agent (the accuracy) was computed. These experiments have revealed a much higher predictive accuracy in the case of IF RELEVANT test questions where the source was relevant. We have analyzed each case where both the developing expert and the independent expert agreed that the agent failed to recognize that a source was relevant or irrelevant to a certain task. In most cases it was concluded that the representation of the source was incomplete. This analysis suggested that the representation of the sources should be guided by the following "projection" principle which, if followed, would have avoided many of the agent's errors: *Any historical source must be completely described in terms of the concepts from the KB.* This means that if the knowledge base contains a certain historical concept, then any historical source referring to that concept should contain the concept in the description of its content.

Table 1. Evaluation results

Reviewer	Total number of reviewed questions	Number of IF questions with relevant sources	Number of IF questions with irrelevant sources	Time spent to review all the questions	Accuracy on IF questions with relevant sources	Accuracy on IF questions with irrelevant sources	Total accuracy
Developing expert	406	202	204	5 hours	96.53%	81.86%	89.16%
Independent expert	401	198	203	10 hours over 2 days	95.45%	76.35%	85.76%
Independent expert	1,524	198+1,326	–	22 hours for 1,326 questions	96.19%	–	–

We have also conducted an experiment with a class of 21 students from the 8th grade at The Bridges Academy in Washington D.C. The students were first given a lecture on relevance and then were asked to answer 25 test questions that were dynamically generated by the agent. Students were also asked to investigate the hints and the explanations. To record their impressions, they were asked to respond to a set of 18 survey questions with one of the following phrases: very strongly agree, strongly agree, agree, indifferent, disagree, strongly disagree, and very strongly disagree. Fig. 7 presents the results from 7 of the most informative survey questions.

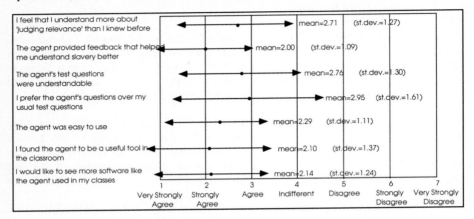

Fig. 7. Student survey results

Finally, a user group experiment was conducted with 8 teachers at The Public School 330 in the Bronx, New York City. This group of teachers had the opportunity to review the performance of the agent and was then asked to complete a questionnaire. Several of the most informative questions and a summary of the teachers' responses are presented in Fig. 8.

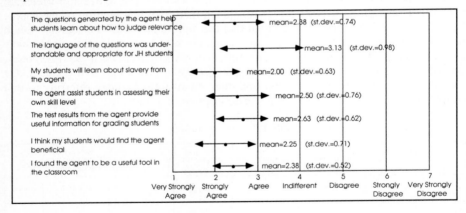

Fig. 8. Teacher survey results

6 Conclusions

We have presented the Disciple approach and its application to the development of an educational agent. We have provided experimental evidence that the process of teaching the agent is natural and efficient, and that it results in a knowledge base of high quality and in a useful educational agent. The agent provides the educator with a flexible tool that lifts the burden of generating tests for large classes, tests that do not repeat themselves and take into account the instruction received by each student. Because the agent is taught by the educator through examples and explanations, and then it is able to provide similar examples and explanations to the students (as part of the generated tests), it could be considered as being a preliminary example of a new type of educational agent that can be taught by an educator to teach the students [8]. Although not discussed in detail in this paper, this work also shows an automated computer-based approach to the assessment of higher-order thinking skills [2,3], as well as an assessment that involves multimedia documents [6]. Both of these represent very important goals in the current education research. We are currently using Disciple to develop a statistical analysis assessment and support agent.

Acknowledgments

This research was done in the Learning Agents Laboratory at George Mason University. Tomasz Dybala and Kathryn Wright contributed to the development of Disciple. Lynn Fontana, Rich Rosser, and David Webster assisted in the initial development of the KB. Lawrence Young, who holds an MS in History Education, acted as the independent expert. The research of the Learning Agents Laboratory is supported by the AFOSR grant F49620-97-1-0188, as part of the DARPA's High Performance Knowledge Bases Program, by the DARPA contract N66001-95-D-8653, and by the NSF grant No. CDA-9616478.

References

1. Aïmeur, E., Frasson, C.: Eliciting the learning context in co-operative tutoring systems. IJCAI-95 Workshop on Modeling Context in Knowledge Representation and Reasoning (1995)
2. Beyer, B.: Practical Strategies for the Teaching of Thinking. Allyn and Bacon, Inc. Boston, MA. (1987)
3. Beyer, B.: Developing a Thinking Skills Program. Allyn and Bacon, Inc. Boston, MA. (1988)
4. Bloom, B.: Taxonomy of Educational Objectives. David McKay Co., Inc. New York. (1956)
5. Buchanan, B. G. and Wilkins, D. C. (eds.): Readings in Knowledge Acquisition and Learning, Morgan Kaufmann, San Mateo, CA. (1993)
6. Fontana, L., Debe, C., White, C., Cates, W.: Multimedia: Gateway to Higher-Order Thinking Skills in Progress. In Proceedings of the National Convention of the Association for Educational Communications and Technology (1993)
7. Gruber, T. R.: Toward principles for the design of ontologies used for knowledge sharing. In Guarino, N. and Poli, R. (eds.): Formal Ontology in Conceptual Analysis and Knowledge Representation, Kluwer Academic (1993)
8. Hamburger H. and Tecuci G.: Toward a Unification of Human-Computer Learning and Tutoring, in this volume (1998)
9. Michalski, R.S. and Tecuci, G. (eds.): Machine Learning: A Multistrategy Approach Volume 4, Morgan Kaufmann Publishers, San Mateo, CA. (1994)
10. Tecuci, G. and Kodratoff, Y. (eds.): Machine Learning and Knowledge Acquisition: Integrated Approaches, Academic Press, London (1995)
11. Tecuci G.: Building Intelligent Agents: An Apprenticeship Multistrategy Learning Theory, Methodology, Tool and Case Studies, Academic Press, London (1998)

An Instructor's Assistant for Team-Training in Dynamic Multi-Agent Virtual Worlds

Stacy C. Marsella & W. Lewis Johnson

Information Sciences Institute / Univ. of Southern California
4676 Admiralty Way, Marina del Rey, CA 90292
{marsella, johnson}@isi.edu

Abstract. The training of teams in highly dynamic, multi-agent virtual worlds places a heavy demand on an instructor. We address the instructor's problem with the PuppetMaster. The PuppetMaster manages a network of monitors that report on the activities in the simulation in order to provide the instructor with an interpretation and situation-specific analysis of student behavior. The approach used to model student teams is to structure the state space into an abstract situation-based model of behavior that supports interpretation in the face of missing information about agent's actions and goals.

1   Introduction

Teams of people operating in highly dynamic, multi-agent environments must learn to deal with rapid and unpredictable turns of events. Simulation-based training environments inhabited by synthetic agents can be effective in providing realistic but safe settings in which to develop skills these environments require (e.g., [14]). To faithfully capture the unpredictable multi-agent setting, virtual world simulations can be inhabited by multitudes of synthetic agents which ideally exhibit the same kind of complex behaviors that human participants would exhibit. For example, Distributed Interactive Simulation (DIS) training sessions involve student teams interacting with potentially thousands of synthetic and human agents within a very dynamic battlefield simulation [14].

However such virtual environments present a problem for the instructor who must evaluate and control rapidly evolving training sessions. Information from any one student's perception of events may be unavailable and agents (human or synthetic) may not be able to explain their own motives. Furthermore, abstracting from the behavior of individuals to the behavior and goals of teams requires additional effort. Conversely, there may be too much low level information for the instructor to absorb and interpret. And as the number of interacting agents grows, the difficulty increases. Accordingly, it may be difficult to determine what teams are doing and why they are doing it.

We address the instructor's problem with a synthetic assistant, the Puppet-Master, which provides a high-level interpretation and assessment of the teams. As the teacher's automated assistant, the PuppetMaster dynamically assigns probes that monitor student teams and synthetic agents in the simulation. The situation in the virtual world is then assessed from the perspective of high level training objectives. The assessment includes events, trends and aggregate reporting over multiple entities (e.g., for revealing teamwork). The resulting evaluation is used to compose presentations that reduce the instructor's effort during the exercise and assists the instructor's review with students after the exercise.

The central concern of this paper is how the PuppetMaster forms its assessment of student teams. The dynamics and pedagogical goals for the domains we have been considering present a considerable challenge for student assessment. In dynamic environments, such as DIS battlefields, there are multiple tasks and multiple agents/teams performing those tasks. Moreover, there is no overall plan of action either at the individual or team level that can be guaranteed to achieve the goal; events can enfold in such a way that obviates any plan. Student teams must learn to operate in both goal-directed and reactive fashions. To assess how well a team is doing, it is critical to appropriately model the students' loosely scripted interactions with the world, in the face of changing plans, partial information and irrelevant information. And instructional support needs to foster development of initiative and the ability to react or replan appropriately.

This can present a problem for modeling students and/or their task performance [15, 2, 10, 4, 1] as well as more generally plan recognition[11, 5]. For instance, student monitoring is often tied to detailed modeling of the task and matching of actions or events. Such approaches tend to have most ready application when the skill to be acquired can be fully modeled in terms of what specific actions need to be taken and the order in which they should be taken. Approaches to modeling in more dynamic settings (e.g., [4]) do weaken somewhat how actions and goals are fitted into a plan. But the pedagogical intent to do a detailed fitting or causal analysis remains along with the presumption of access to all the information and action modeling that supports that analysis. Related work in agent tracking (e.g., [13]) infers plans that are a mix of plan-based and reactive procedures but also presumes detailed modeling of an agent's actions. Finally, there also needs to be a way to aggregate the modeling of an individual agent's behavior into the modeling of team behavior.

To model student teams, we have adapted an approach from reactive planning research, the Situation Space [12, 7]. A situation space structures states of the world into classes of problem solving histories whereby an agent's recognition of its *current situation* guides its goal-directed behavior. The PuppetMaster models both reactive and goal driven behaviors within the framework of a situation space model of the entire student team. The *current situation* provides a top-down focus for monitoring, inferring missing information and assessing behavioral trends.

2   The Need

We explored the design of our instructor's assistant in virtual world simulation for training military tank platoons. The entities in this simulation environment include teams of trainees in tank simulators as well as synthetic forces generated by software such as the ModSAF (Modular Semi-Autonomous Forces) program [3]. There are four tank simulators in a typical platoon exercise, each manned by four students, and approximately fifty synthetic forces. Army instructors manage the exercise, performing the roles of superior officer (e.g., issuing orders) and adversary (e.g, dynamically creating and tasking opposing forces). After the exercise, instructors provide feedback to students.

An exercise for a tank platoon might involve traveling in *wedge* formation to a location in order to occupy a position which blocks the opposing force. While in a wedge formation, there are guidelines as to how the individual tanks follow each other, keep each other in sight, etc. As the platoon travels to the position along the virtual terrain, it may encounter friendly or opposing forces to which it has to respond appropriately. These forces can be either synthetic or human agents and encounters with them can rapidly unfold in unpredictable ways. Likewise, the platoon may encounter terrain features that can slow down and/or damage its vehicles. Thus, the multi-agent dynamic qualities of the simulation can rapidly impact what needs to be done to satisfy the broadly scripted exercise, as well as whether it can be satisfied.

Based on our observations of these exercises, instructors do not micromanage or even micro-evaluate the students. For instance, they don't analyze student behavior on an action-by-action basis unless the effect of a student's actions is entirely anomalous in the current situation. Additionally, there are also individual differences in how instructors evaluate specific skills in the training context.

These characteristics are consistent with the nature of the domain and the skills that need to be acquired. Because of the dynamic, multi-agent domain, there is no guaranteed plan for achieving the goals set out for the students. Without such a plan, or other agreed upon objective basis, micro-evaluation at the level of each and every individual action is problematic. Furthermore, understanding the rationale for every action may require modeling the domain from the perspective of every student, e.g., down to the level of every rock which must be circumnavigated to avoid tread damage. Also, because of the dynamic domain, it is necessary to foster the development of initiative in the teams consistent with situation-appropriate goals and behaviors.

Although instructors do an excellent job of managing training exercises, the tools that they have at their disposal are severely lacking. Instructors are often forced to write notes to themselves on paper as the exercise proceeds, and must rely on subjective impressions. Also, as an exercise unfolds over time, relevant information concerning transient events or trends may be missed.

Instructors need to know how well the platoon is maintaining their formation over time, which requires analysis of the formation over time, when it is appropriate. A formation that is appropriate when traveling may be inappropriate when engaging the enemy. If the formation is poor, an analysis from the team's perspective is necessary. Is it a problem in maintaining visual contact, difficulty navigating the terrain, or problems with the vehicles? If the enemy is nearby, is the team in a position to spot them or be spotted by them?

The information necessary to address these concerns is present in the simulation, if one looks in the right place at the right time. The goal of the PuppetMaster is to extract the information from the simulation automatically and to analyze it both from the team's and instructor's perspectives, allowing the instructor to focus on where to provide instructional feedback.

3   Situation Spaces in the PuppetMaster

The PuppetMaster works within the Probes system which includes virtual world monitors and a display manager. Based on a description of the training objectives of each exercise, the PuppetMaster dynamically assigns the monitors (typically embedded in instrumented ModSAF agents) depending on what information is required to recognize and analyze the current phase of the exercise. These monitors collect the requested data and report back, on a regular basis, or when interesting events occur, or in response to queries from the PuppetMaster. The PuppetMaster uses the data it receives to interpret and assess the training exercise. Output to the instructor is controlled by a display manager. PuppetMaster's understanding of the training exercise is organized around a Situation Space. It uses the Situation Space to control monitoring, form an assessment of the team and selectively report the assessment.

As developed in reactive planning research, Situation Spaces structure states of the world into situations and links between situations. The behavior of the agent is organized around its current situation which determines the (sub)goal(s) it should try to achieve (or maintain) as well as how to monitor the world. In turn, monitoring determines whether traversal to a new situation has occurred. Traversal could be caused by successful achievement of a (sub)goal or unexpected turn of events which could be advantageous or dis-advantageous. Paths through the situation space represent alternative abstract partial plans which incorporate both goal-directed behavior as well as goal-directed responses to unforeseen events.

To make these ideas more concrete, consider the situation space depicted in Fig. 1 for the simplified example problem presented earlier. Recall the problem is to travel in a wedge formation to a blocking position, responding to encounters with the opposing force en route. The current situation at the start of the exercise is assumed to be "Traveling" (Wedge Formation). When a platoon is in this situation, their goals include traveling along some route towards the blocking position, and maintenance goals of maintaining a wedge formation and scanning for the enemy. As they pursue these goals, expected or un-expected transitions can occur that must be monitored. For instance, the students must monitor for reaching their objective, based on the transition to the Goal situation. Also, they must monitor for contact with other forces. This could cause a transition to an "Action on Contact." The goals in this new situation would include assessing the threat, targeting opposing forces and insuring one is not an easy target. When in the Action on Contact situation, transitions to "Disabled" or back to "Traveling" must be monitored.

Several characteristics of Situation Spaces can be gleaned from this example. There can be an indefinite number of paths through the space. This allows it to compactly express the dynamic characteristics in these training environments whereby students can undergo repeated and unexpected encounters. The necessary reactivity is modeled within an overall goal-directed declarative plan. And the set of possible plans is modeled at a high level, with each situation modeling many possible problem solving histories.

In addition to their value in planning, situation spaces are a good declarative model around which to organize analysis of team behavior in a dynamic world. To serve that end, we transformed them from an aid for planning to an aid for analysis of team behavior.

3.1   Situation Spaces from an Instructor's Perspective

We made two moves to use Situation Spaces to analyze team behavior. First, we transformed the goals indicated by a situation from goals-to-be-achieved to analyses-to-be-performed. For instance, the goal associated with traveling in a wedge, along a route to the blocking position, becomes an analysis goal to determine how well the team is traveling. Similarly, the Action On Contact goals of "targeting" and "avoid being an easy target" become how well they are targeting and avoid being targeted.

The other move we made was to allow for multiple perspectives. This move is necessary because the student team may have a different perspective from the PuppetMaster as to what the current situation is, and such discrepancies provide key pedagogical assessments. For instance, the students may transition to an Action On Contact situation and fire at what they think is the opposition, but actually are distant rocks. Meanwhile, the PuppetMaster, due to its larger perspective, will know that the transition to action on contact was a mistake. Conversely, a viable enemy threat may exist which the students have not seen.

A consequence of maintaining multiple perspectives is that, for those transitions that could result in bifurcation of perspective, there needs to be a transition arc for each perspective. For the transition from the Traveling to the Action On Contact situations there need to be 2 arcs, one for pedagogical perspective and one for team perspective. (Figure 1 shows only one of the arcs.)

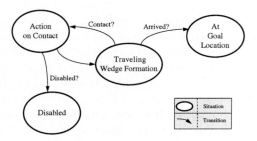

Fig. 1. Example Situation Space.

Another consequence of multiple perspectives is the need to determine which situation is the appropriate basis for monitoring and reporting analyses. We have found it sufficient to report analyses based on the team perspective, for several reasons. Reporting an analysis of the team from a perspective different from that guiding their behavior tends to generate marginally useful information. In contrast, analyzing team behavior from their perspective generates the information needed to infer the point at which they finally transition into the "correct" situation. For instance, when the team is traveling in a wedge, there are certain behaviors they are supposed to exhibit such as constantly scanning their turrets and following each other at a certain distance. These behaviors are not typically appropriate during active engagements so their cessation is a key indicator for inferring transition of the team perspective. On the other hand, the pedagogical perspective is key in analyzing failures of the team in assessing their situation.

Our experience is that the bifurcation into two perspectives persists only for very short periods of time. There are several reasons for this. The situation space is at a very high level of abstraction so a bifurcation tends to indicate a dramatic misread of the environment. In addition, given the pressure that the domain exerts on the team's behavior, such a misread is likely not to persist for long. For example, incoming rounds are a solid indicator to the team that those "rocks" off in the distance are actually the opposition firing at them.

Allowing for these two perspectives has proved sufficient to date in characterizing the state of a platoon exercise. However, we could go further. Recall there are four tanks in a platoon. One might break the team perspective into individual tank perspectives, thus having PuppetMaster track what it considers to be each tank's perspective on the current situation. Now discrepancies between tank perspectives reflect factors such as breakdown in coordination.

This move towards multiple perspectives assumes that the perspectives share the same situation space. However, if there were multiple platoons being assessed, performing different missions, then different situation spaces would be more appropriate. Conversely, we may model a single agents overall behavior as being composed of distinct situations in multiple situation spaces. These points beg the question of composition over situations which would need further study.

In Probes, a situation space is defined as a set of situations, with each situation being a 3-tuple consisting of:

- List of predicate functions for transitions of situation perspectives
- Set of evaluation functions for forming an assessment
- Initialization function which invokes monitors pertinent to the situation.

The Army's instructional material, reinforced by our observations of actual training sessions, provided the high-level structure of the situation space (types of situations, transitions and evaluations). From there, the actual transition, evaluation and initialization functions were defined. Across all the exercises for platoon training, the instructional material was laid out in a modular fashion that shared exercise goals, situations and assessment criteria. This suggests that the application of situation spaces across the full suite of platoon exercises could be semi-automated with considerable reuse of transition and evaluation functions.

3.2   Situation-Based vs. Event-Based Modeling

Structuring the state space into a situation space achieves several ends. Monitoring can be organized top-down around the situation, which in turn usefully constrains interpretation and assessment. Behavioral trends can be monitored and assessed according to their appropriateness within a situation. Changes in behavioral trends within a situation can be used to infer missing information, such as whether the platoon has spotted the enemy and is going into action on contact. Unnecessary details about the state of the world are not monitored. And the transitions between situations provide a principled basis of coupling analysis of planned and reactive behaviors.

A key feature of the approach is that the high level analysis appropriate to the situation is based mainly on partial state descriptions and trends in those descriptions. This is quite different from work on student modeling and plan recognition which use a complete action model as the basis of checking/inferring a plan with an agent's actions. For instance, recognizing that a platoon is trying to travel in a wedge formation would be at best difficult if the recognition was based on the low level actions that the 16 crew members in the 4 tanks were executing. And evaluating this team behavior is best done at the level of the abstract, partial state descriptions, especially trends in those descriptions, and not at the level of individual discrete actions these various team members are performing. The relation between the levels is not strongly fixed. Moreover, recognition and evaluation is best done at the level at which this joint behavior has consequences in this dynamic environment. Still, causal analysis at the level of individual actions would be of diagnostic utility but only in the context of the higher level analysis and not as a way of deriving the higher level analysis. Some form of constrained plan recognition, for example, may be useful for determining why a wedge formation is falling apart.

4   Example

Let's now consider an example run of the Probes system. In the following example, the team is training on the exercise discussed earlier, traveling in a wedge to a blocking location. Blue is the platoon being assessed whereas Red is the opposition. Here, both sides are comprised of synthetic agents being run by ModSAF, but in an actual exercise Blue would be human crews in simulators.

Probes provides instructors with a coordinated set of presentations. Figure 2 shows two presentations: the situation space for the exercise on the left, with the current situation (team perspective) highlighted. On the right is a log of high-level events and assessments. The PuppetMaster automatically determines which situation is currently in force, by monitoring activities in the simulation. Probes also uses synthesized speech to announce situation transitions.

The exercise analysis log records events and analyses that are likely to be relevant to the current situation. Note that during "Situation Travel (Wedge)" (traveling in wedge), the PuppetMaster reports that vehicles in the platoon are in a poor wedge formation. In contrast, when Situation Act occurs (i.e., Blue is

Fig. 2. Probes' Situation Presentation.

in an Action on Contact) PuppetMaster starts reporting that the platoon is still in a wedge when it should probably be going "on line", in effect modifying their formation in a fashion consistent with the exigencies of an active engagement. At this point it stops assessment of the wedge alignment, since the wedge formation is no longer appropriate for the current situation.

These analyses rely on trends in partial state descriptions, in particular, persistence in the relations between tanks over time. The analyses are not trying to evaluate (or infer) travel in a wedge by reasoning about the actions which the four tanks are executing (or the 16 crew members).

The log also reports when Red spots Blue. PuppetMaster's monitoring can access state information internal to the synthetic agents which reveals tactics and situation assessments. When Red spots Blue, their internal assessment recognizes a threat and, based on that assessment, the PuppetMaster's pedagogical perspective transitions to Action on Contact ("ActualSit Act"). The pedagogical perspective also would have transitioned if Blue's team perspective had transitioned and the transition was valid (e.g., the opposing force did not turn out to be rocks). In the case of the Blue forces (especially when they are human crews), PuppetMaster infers their intent based on the current situation, the objectives of the exercise and trends in the partial state descriptions that are being monitored. For instance, if Red can (potentially) be spotted and is in range, plus Blue has turrets aiming at Red, breaks out of wedge formation, or flattens the wedge, then a situation transition for Blue's perspective can be inferred.

As the situation changes, Probes displays statistics about the unit's performance as appropriate to the current situation. Figure 3 depicts two displays specific to the poor wedge formation. On the left is an "Analysis Details" window, which the instructor accesses by clicking on the poor wedge notification in the event log. This causes Probes to do some shallow reasoning and reveal relevant factors such as local terrain conditions, damage to the vehicles, etc. On the right is a wedge evaluation gauge which pops up automatically when the platoon is in a wedge and depicts the distances between tanks and the overall depths of the wedge. Ideally, Probes analysis can be coupled to a 3D (stealth) view of the virtual world and we have experimented with ways of annotating the 3D display with relevant analysis data.

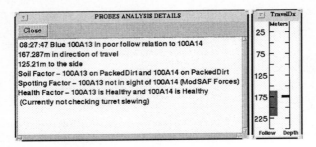

Fig. 3. Probes' presentation of specific details concerning flawed wedge formation.

5   Status

The Probes system has been fully implemented, with all the capabilities illustrated in the "Example" section. We are currently pursuing collaborations that will allow us to evaluate Probes in various training contexts.

Our research is also focusing on techniques for automating the construction of situation spaces, including the use of a scenario generation as a front-end to the situation space construction [9] and decision tree induction for deriving evaluation functions [8]. We are studying the implications of applying situation spaces to more complex teams of students where individual students would be best modeled as distinct situation spaces. In particular, we are concerned with how to formalize the relation between these situation spaces. Work in formal models of teamwork (e.g., [6]) may potentially be useful here.

We expect the design will have applicability to domains that share the unpredictable nature of training of tank platoons. Currently, the applicability of the method is being evaluated in other domains.

6   Concluding Remarks

Simulation-based training of teamwork skills for dynamic, unpredictable multi-agent settings present special challenges from a pedagogical standpoint. It is our view that the instructor can benefit immensely from an assistant that is an intelligent interpreter of events in the simulation. Further, only an automated assistant can play this role: human agents have great difficulty even assimilating the information coming from all the agents' viewpoints and as a consequence have difficulty assessing that information. To be useful, such an assistant also needs to be able to interpret events from a viewpoint of instructional objectives. Finally, it must be able to handle missing information as well as different kinds of agent architectures.

We have developed the PuppetMaster that can assess a training session from the standpoint of instructional objectives. This assistant uses a situation-based approach to modeling behavior that is consistent with the information it has available and the analyses it needs to perform.

Additional Details: http://www.isi.edu/~marsella/pp/

Acknowledgements: The authors wish to acknowledge the assistance of Robert Balzer's group at ISI. This work was funded by DARPA Computer Aided Education and Training Initiative. Opinions expressed are those of the authors and not of the funding agencies or the US Government.

References

1. Alexe, C. & Gecsei, J. A Learning Environment for the Surgical Intensive Care Unit. In Frasson, C., Gauthier, G. & Lesgold, A. (Eds), *Intelligent Tutoring Systems, ITS '96 Proceedings*. Berlin:Springer, 1996. 439-447.
2. Anderson, J.R., Boyle, C.F., Corbett, A.T. & Lewis, M.W. R. Cognitive Modelling and Intelligent Tutoring. In *Artificial Intelligence*, 42(1), 1990. Pp. 7–49.
3. Calder, R.B., Smith, J.E, Courtemanche, A.J., Mar, J.M.F. & Ceranowicz, A.Z. ModSAF Behavior Simulation and Control. In *Proc of the 3rd Conference on Computer-Gen. Forces and Behavioral Representation*. Orlando, Fla: Univ. of Central Fla. Inst. for Simulation and Training, 347-356.
4. Hill, R. & Johnson, W.L. Situated plan attribution for intelligent tutoring. In *Proc. of the Nat. Conf. on AI*. Menlo Park, CA: AAAI Press, 1994.
5. Kautz, H. & Allen, J.F. Generalized Plan Recognition. In *Proceedings of the National Conference on Artificial Intelligence*. Menlo Park, CA: AAAI Press, 1986.
6. Levesque, H.J,, Cohen, P.R. & Nunes, J.H.T. On Acting Together. In *Proc. of the Eighth Natl. Conf. on AI*. Los Altos: CA, Morgan Kaufman, 1990. Pp 94–99.
7. Marsella, S. C. & Schmidt, C.F. Reactive planning using a "Situation Space". In Hendler, J. (Ed.) *Planning in Uncertain, Unpredictable, or Changing Environments (Working Notes 1990 AAAI Spring Symp.)*. Available as SRC TR 90-45 of the Systems Research Ctr, Univ of Maryland, College Park, MD. 1990.
8. Murthy, S. K., Kasif, S. & Salzberg, S. A System for Induction of Oblique Decision Trees. In *Journal of AI Research*, 2, 1994, Pp. 1-32.
9. Pautler, D., Woods, S. & Quilici, A. Exploiting Domain-Specific Knowledge To Refine Simulation Specifications. Proc. of the Twelfth IEEE International Conf. on Automated Software Engineering, Nevada, November 1997. Pp 117-124.
10. Rickel, J. & Johnson, J.L. Integrating Pedagogical Capabilities in a Virtual Environment Agent. In Johnson, W.L. (Ed.) *Proc. of The First International Conference on Autonomous Agents*. New York: The ACM Press, 1997. Pp 30–38.
11. Schmidt, C.F., Sridharan, N.S. & Goodson, J.L. The plan recognition problem: an intersect. between psychology and artificial intelligence. AI, 11(1,2), 1978. 45–83.
12. Schmidt, C.F., Goodson, J.L., Marsella, S.C., Bresina, J.L., Reactive Planning Using a Situation Space. Proc of 1989 AI Systems in Govern. Conf, IEEE, 1989.
13. Tambe, M. & Rosenbloom, P. Architectures for Agents that Track Other Agents in Multi-Agent Worlds. In Wooldridge, M., Muller, J.P. & Tambe, M.(Eds) *Intell. Agents II, Agent Theories, Arch., and Lang.* Berlin:Springer-Verlag, 1996. 156–170.
14. Tambe, M., Johnson, W.L., Jones, R., Koss, F., Laird, J.E., Rosenbloom, P.S. & Schwamb, K. Intelligent Agents for interactive simulation environments. *AI Magazine*, 16(1), 1995.
15. VanLehn, K. Student Modelling. In Polson, M.C. & Richardson, J.J. (Eds.), *Intelligent Tutoring Systems*. Hillsdale, NJ: Lawrence Erlbaum, 1988. Pp. 55–78.

Visual Emotive Communication in Lifelike Pedagogical Agents

Stuart G. Towns[1], Patrick J. FitzGerald[2], and James C. Lester[1]

[1] Department of Computer Science
North Carolina State University
Raleigh, NC 27695
{sgtowns, lester}@eos.ncsu.edu
[2] Department of Design and Technology
North Carolina State University
Raleigh, NC 27695
pat_fitzgerald@ncsu.edu
http://multimedia.ncsu.edu/imedia/

Abstract. Lifelike animated agents for knowledge-based learning environments can provide timely, customized advice to support leaners' problem-solving activities. By drawing on a rich repertoire of emotive behaviors to exhibit contextually appropriate facial expressions and emotive gestures, these agents could exploit the visual channel to more effectively communicate with learners. To address these issues, this paper proposes the *emotive-kinesthetic behavior sequencing* framework for dynamically sequencing lifelike pedagogical agents' full-body emotive expression. By exploiting a rich behavior space populated with emotive behaviors and structured by pedagogical speech act categories, a behavior sequencing engine operates in realtime to select and assemble contextually appropriate expressive behaviors. This framework has been implemented in a lifelike pedagogical agent, COSMO, who exhibits full-body emotive behaviors in response to learners' problem-solving activities.

1 Introduction

Recent years have witnessed significant advances in intelligent multimedia interfaces that broaden the bandwidth of communication in knowledge-based learning environments. Moreover, because of the potential benefits of both agent-based technologies and anthropomorphic interfaces, concerted efforts have been undertaken to develop pedagogical agents that can play an important role in learning environment architectures [4, 5, 7, 13, 16] In particular, *animated pedagogical agents* [12, 14] that couple advisory functionalities with a strong lifelike presence offer the promise of providing critical visual feedback, which raises the intriguing possibility of creating learning environments inhabited by pedagogical agents in the form of intelligent lifelike characters.

Engaging lifelike pedagogical agents that are visually expressive could clearly communicate problem-solving advice and simultaneously have a strong motivating effect on learners. If they could draw on a rich repertoire of emotive behaviors to exhibit contextually appropriate facial expressions and expressive gestures, they could exploit the visual channel to advise, encourage, and empathize with learners. However, enabling lifelike pedagogical agents to communicate the *affective* content of problem-solving advice poses serious challenges. Agents' full-body emotive behaviors must support expressive movements and visually complement the problem-solving advice they deliver. Moreover, these behaviors must be planned and coordinated in realtime in response to learners' progress.

To address these issues, this paper proposes the *emotive-kinesthetic behavior sequencing* framework for dynamically sequencing lifelike pedagogical agents' full-body emotive expression. Creating an animated pedagogical agent with this framework consists of a three phase process:

1. **Emotive Pedagogical Agent Behavior Space Design:** Creating a behavior space populated with emotive behaviors with full-body movements including facial expressions with eyes, eyebrows, and mouth and gestures with arms and hands.
2. **Speech Act-Based Behavior Space Structuring:** Constructing a behavior space in which pedagogical speech acts are associated with their emotional intent and their kinesthetic expression.
3. **Full-body Emotive Behavior Sequencing:** Creating an emotive-kinesthetic behavior sequencing engine that operates in conjunction with an explanation system to dynamically plan full-body emotive behaviors in realtime by selecting relevant pedagogical speech acts and then assembling appropriate visual behaviors.

This framework has been used to implement COSMO (Figure 1), a lifelike pedagogical agent with realtime full-body emotive expression. Cosmo inhabits the INTERNET ADVISOR, a learning environment for the domain of Internet packet routing. An impish, antenna-bearing creature who hovers about in a virtual world of routers and networks, he provides advice to learners as they decide how to ship packets through the network to specified destinations. Previous work with the COSMO project focused on techniques to enable lifelike agents to dynamically create deictic references to particular objects in learning environments [15]. Here, we propose the emotive-kinesthetic behavior sequencing framework and illustrate its use in COSMO's realtime emotive behavior sequencing as it corrects learners' misconceptions detected in the course of their problem-solving activities.

2   Pedagogical Agents

As a result of developments in *believable* intelligent agents [2], the intelligent tutoring systems community is now presented with opportunities for exploring new technologies for *pedagogical agents* and the roles they can play in communication. Work to date on pedagogical agents is still in its infancy, but progress is being made on two fronts. First, research has begun on pedagogical agents that can facilitate the construction of component-based tutoring system architectures and communication between their modules [13, 16], provide multiple context-sensitive

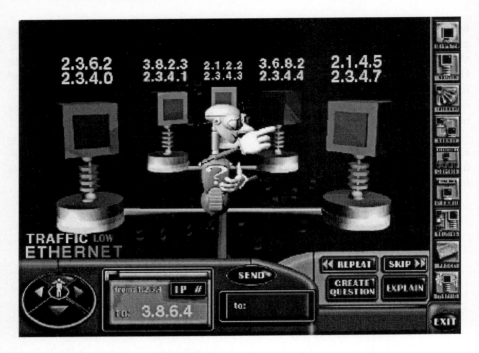

Fig. 1. Cosmo and the INTERNET ADVISOR learning environment

pedagogical strategies [7], reason about multiple agents in learning environments [5], and act as co-learners [4]. Second, projects have begun to investigate techniques by which animated pedagogical agents can behave in a lifelike manner to communicate effectively with learners both visually and verbally [1, 12, 14] It is this second category, lifelike animated pedagogical agents, that is the focus of the work described here.

Lifelike pedagogical agents hold much promise because they could play a central communicative role in learning environments. Through an engaging persona, a lifelike pedagogical agent could simultaneously provide students with contextualized problem-solving advice and create learning experiences that offer high visual appeal. Perhaps as a result of the inherent psychosocial nature of learner-agent interactions and of humans' tendency to anthropomorphize software, recent evidence suggests that an ITS with a lifelike character can be pedagogically effective [9] while at the same time can have a strong motivating effect on learners [8].

> **Situated Emotive Communication:** Lifelike agents' emotive behaviors must support the goal of facilitating students' learning. The behaviors must therefore be situated, i.e. agents should exhibit their behaviors directly in support of problem solving.

Although work is underway on two projects on lifelike pedagogical agents, neither has focused on runtime inference techniques for providing visual feedback via the exhibition of continuous full-body emotive behaviors. The STEVE (Soar Training Expert for Virtual Environments) project has produced a full complement of animated pedagogical agent technologies for teaching procedural knowledge. Although the STEVE agent can create on-the-fly demonstrations and explanations of complex devices and its creators are beginning to examine more complex animations [11], its focus to date has been on the realtime generation of behaviors using a non-emotive agent. The DESIGN-A-PLANT project [14] has produced effective animated pedagogical agent technologies that are the creation of a multidisciplinary team of ITS researchers and animators, but it also has not yet addressed realtime inference about the creation of full-body emotive behaviors.

3   Emotive-Kinesthetic Behavior Sequencing Framework

To enable a lifelike pedagogical agent to play an active role in facilitating learners' progress, its behavior sequencing engine must be driven by learners' problem-solving activities. As learners solve problems, an explanation system monitors their actions in the learning environment (Figure 2). When they reach an impasse, as indicated by extended periods of inactivity or sub-optimal problem-solving actions, the explanation system is invoked to construct an explanation plan that will address potential misconceptions. By examining the problem state, a curriculum information network, and a user model, the explanation system determines the sequence of pedagogical speech acts that can clearly repair the misconception and passes the types of the speech acts to the emotive-kinesthetic behavior sequencing engine. By assessing the speech act categories and then identifying full-body emotive behaviors that the agent can perform to communicate the affective impact appropriate for those speech act categories, the behavior sequencing engine selects relevant behaviors and binds them to the verbal utterances determined by the explanation system. The behaviors and utterances are then performed by the agent in the environment and control is returned to the learner who continues her problem-solving activities.

3.1   Emotive-Kinesthetic Behavior Space Design

To exhibit full-body emotive behaviors, a pedagogical agent's behavior sequencing engine must draw on a large repertoire of behaviors that span a broad emotional spectrum. For many domains, tasks, and target learner populations, agents that are fully expressive are highly desirable. To this end, the first phase in creating a lifelike pedagogical agent is to design an *emotive-kinesthetic behavior space* that is populated with physical behaviors that the agent can perform when called upon to do so. Because of the aesthetics involved, an agent's behaviors are perhaps best designed by a team that includes character animators. Creating a behavior space entails setting forth precise visual and audio specifications that describe in great detail the agent's actions and utterances, rendering the actions, and creating the audio clips.

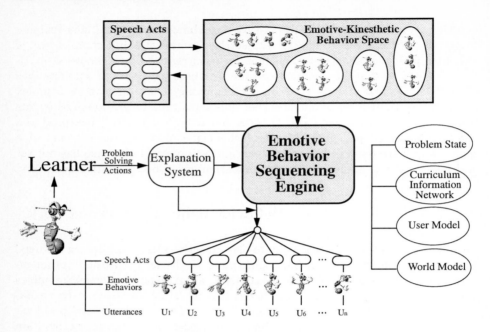

Fig. 2. The Emotive-Kinesthetic Behavior Sequencing Architecture

Stylized Emotive Behaviors. It is important to draw the critical distinction between two approaches to animated character realization, life-quality vs. stylized [3]. In the *life-quality* approach, character designers and animators follow a strict adherence to the laws of physics. Characters' musculature and kinesthetics are defined entirely by the physical principles that govern the structure and movement of human (and animal) bodies. For example, when a character become excited, it raises its eyebrows and its eyes widen. In contrast, in the *stylized* approach, a consistency is obeyed yet the laws of physics (and frequently of human anatomy and physiology) are broken at every turn. When a character animated with the stylized approach becomes excited, e.g., as in the animated films of Tex Avery [3], it may express this emotion in an exaggerated fashion by rising from the ground, inducing significant changes to the musculature of the face, and bulging out its eyes.

Expressive Range. To be maximally entertaining, animated characters must be able to express many different kinds of emotion. As different social situations arise, they must be able to convey emotions such as happiness, elation, sadness, fear, envy, shame, and gloating. In a similar fashion, because lifelike pedagogical agents should be able to communicate with a broad range of speech acts, they should be able to visually support these speech acts with an equally broad range of emotive behaviors. For example, they should be able to exhibit body language that expresses joy and excitement when learners do well, inquisitiveness for uncertain situations (such as when rhetorical questions are posed), and disappointment when problem-solving progress is less than optimal.

3.2   Behavior Space Structuring with Pedagogical Speech Acts

An agent's behaviors will be dictated by design decisions in the previous phase, which to a significant extent determine its personality characteristics. Critically, however its runtime emotive behaviors must be somehow modulated to a large degree by ongoing problem-solving events driven by the learner activities. Although, in principle, behavior spaces could be structured along any number of dimensions such as degree of exaggeration of movement or by type of anatomical components involved in movements, experience with the implemented agent suggests that the most effective means for imposing a structure is based on *speech acts* and is inspired by foundational work on affective reasoning [6]. By creating emotive annotations that connect pedagogical speech acts to relevant physical behaviors, behavior spaces can be augmented with representational structures that enable an emotive behavior sequencing engine to identify relevant behaviors at runtime. To illustrate, the COSMO agent deals with cause and effect, background, assistance, rhetorical links, and congratulatory acts as follows:

- *Congratulatory:* When a learner experiences success, a `congratulatory` speech act triggers an `admiration` emotive intent that will be expressed with behaviors such as applause, which depending on the complexity of the problem will be either restrained or exaggerated. The desired effect is to encourage the learner.
- *Causal:* When a learner requires problem-solving advice, a `causal` speech act posed rhetorically triggers an `interrogative` emotive intent that will be expressed with behaviors such as head scratching or shrugging. The desired effect is to underscore questioning.
- *Deleterious effect:* When a learner experiences problem-solving difficulties or when the agent needs to pose a rhetorical question with unfortunate consequences, `disappointment` is triggered which will be expressed with facial characteristics and body language that indicate sadness. The desired effect is to build empathy.
- *Background* and *Assistance:* In the course of delivering advice, `background` or `assistance` speech acts trigger `inquisitive` intent that will be expressed with "thoughtful" restrained manipulators such as finger drumming or hand waving. The desired effect is to emphasize active cognitive processing on the part of the agent.

To create a fully operational lifelike agent, the behavior space includes auxiliary structuring to accommodate important emotive but non-speech-oriented behaviors such as dramatic entries and exits from the learning environment. Moreover, sometimes the agent must connect behaviors generated by two separate speech acts. To achieve these `rhetorical link` behaviors, it employs subtle "micro-movements" such as blinks or slight head nods.

3.3 Dynamic Emotive Behavior Sequencing

To dynamically orchestrate full-body emotive behaviors that achieve situated emotive communication, complement problem-solving advice, and exhibit real-time visual continuity, the emotive behavior sequencing engine selects and assembles behaviors in realtime. By exploiting the pedagogical speech act structuring, the sequencing engine navigates coherent paths through the emotive behavior space to weave the small local behaviors into continuous global behaviors. Given a communicative goal G (such as explaining a particular misconception that arose during problem solving), a simple overlay user model, a curriculum information network, and the current problem state, it employs the following algorithm to select and assemble emotive behaviors in realtime:

1. **Determine the pedagogical speech acts $A_1 \ldots A_n$ to achieve G.** When the explanation system is invoked, it employs the by-now-classic techniques from the explanation community to determine a set of relevant speech acts.[1] For each speech A_i, perform steps (2)–(5).
2. **Identify a family of emotive behaviors F_i to exhibit when performing A_i.** Using the emotive annotations in the behavior speech act structure, index into the behavior space to determine a relevant family of emotive behaviors F_i.
3. **Select an emotive behavior B_i that belongs to F_i.** Either by using additional contextual knowledge, e.g., the level of complexity of the current problem, or simply randomly when all elements of F_i are relevant, select an element of F_i.
4. **Select a verbal utterance U_i that is appropriate for performing A_i.** Using a audio library of voice clips that is analogous to physical behaviors, extract a relevant voice clip. The voice clip may be either *connective* (e.g., "but" or "and"), *phrasal* (e.g., "this subnet is fast,"), or *sentential* (i.e., a full sentence).
5. **Coordinate the exhibition of B_i with the speaking of U_i.** Couple B_i with U_i on the evolving presentation timeline.
6. **Establish visual continuity between $B_1 \ldots B_n$.** Examine the final frame of each B_i, compare it with the initial frame of each B_{i+1}, and if they differ, introduce transition frames between them.

The resulting behaviors are then presented directly in the learning environment and control is immediately returned to the learner. The net effect of the sequencing engine's activities is the learner's perception that an expressive lifelike character is carefully observing their problem-solving activities and behaving in a visually compelling manner.

4   An Implemented Full-Body Emotive Pedagogical Agent

The emotive-kinesthetic behavior sequencing framework has been implemented in COSMO, a lifelike (stylized) pedagogical agent that inhabits the INTERNET ADVISOR learning environment. Cosmo and the INTERNET ADVISOR environment are implemented in C++ using the Microsoft Game Software Developer's

---

[1] For example, the particular class of explanations focused on in the current implementation were inspired by McCoy's seminal work on discourse schemata for correcting misconceptions [10].

Kit (SDK). Cosmo's behaviors run at 15 frames/second with 16 bits/pixel color on a Pentium Pro 200 Mhz PC with 64 MB of RAM. Cosmo, as well as the routers and subnets in the virtual Internet world, were modeled and rendered in 3D on SGIs with Alias/Wavefront. The resulting bitmaps were subsequently post-edited with Photoshop and AfterEffects on Macintoshes and transferred to PCs where users interact with them in a $2\frac{1}{2}$D environment. Cosmo has a head with movable antennae and expressive blinking eyes, arms with bendable elbows, hands with a large number of independent joints, and a body with an accordion-like torso. This allows him to perform a variety of behaviors including pointing, blinking, clapping, and raising and bending his antennae. His verbal behaviors (recorded by a voice actor) include 200 utterances ranging in duration from 1–20 seconds.

Students interact with COSMO as they navigate through a series of subnets to learn about network routing mechanisms. Given a packet to escort through the Internet, they direct it through several networks connected by routers. At each subnet, the learner uses factors such as address resolution, subnet type, and traffic congestion to decide whether they should send their packet to a router on the current subnet, or should view adjacent subnets. Learners' journeys are complete when they have successfully navigated the network and have delivered their packet to the proper destination.

Suppose a student has just routed her packet to a fiber optic subnet with low traffic. She surveys the connected subnets and selects a router which she believes will advance it one step closer to the packet's intended destination. Although she has chosen a reasonable subnet, it is suboptimal because of non-matching addresses, which will slow her packet's progress. The emotive behavior planner chooses speech acts and then relevant emotive behaviors as follows. First, it uses its deictic behavior planner [15] to refer to the onscreen subnet information and direct COSMO to say, "You chose the fastest subnet." It then directs him to perform a micro-movement, exhibiting a blink, as he says, "Also, ..." Following that, he refers to the traffic information ("...it has low traffic.") Then, the emotive behavior planner selects a congratulatory and enthusiastic applauding behavior to indicate the learner made a great choice on those factors. As COSMO then poses a rhetorical question ("But more importantly, if we sent the packet here, what will happen?"), the emotive behavior sequencer directs him to scratch his head inquisitively. Next, because the packet will not arrive at its intended destination (a deleterious effect) since the learner chose a poor address, the behavior sequencer directs him to behaved disappointedly by using a sad facial expression, slumping body language, and dropping his hands as he says, "If that were the case, we see it doesn't arrive at the right place." After another remark, he employs a restrained manipulator in the form of finger tapping as he explains the role of addresses in internet routing. Finally, he points out a better choice, which the learner enacts.

The emotive-kinesthetic behavior sequencing framework has been "stress tested" in a very informal focus group study in which 10 students interacted with COSMO for approximately half an hour each[2]. The subjects of the study (7 men and 3 women with ages ranging from 14 to 54) expressed genuine delight in interacting with COSMO. Their typical reaction was that he was fun, engaging, interesting, and full of charisma. Although a few subjects voiced the opinion that COSMO was overly dramatic, almost all exhibited particularly strong positive responses when COSMO performed the exaggerated congratulatory behaviors. In short, they seemed to find him very entertaining and his advice very helpful.

5   Conclusions and Future Work

Because of their strong lifelike presence, animated pedagogical agents offer significant potential for playing the dual role of providing clear problem-solving advice and keeping learners highly motivated. By endowing them with the ability to exhibit full-body emotive behaviors to achieve situated emotive communication, to complement problem-solving advice, and to exhibit realtime visual continuity, an emotive behavior sequencing engine can select and assemble expressive behaviors in realtime. In the emotive-kinesthetic behavior sequencing framework for dynamically planning lifelike pedagogical agents' full-body emotive expression, a behavior sequencing engine can navigate a behavior space populated with a large repertoire of emotive behaviors. By exploiting the structure provided by pedagogical speech act categories, it can weave small expressive behaviors into larger visually continuous ones that are then exhibited by the agent in response to learners' problem-solving activities.

This work represents a small step towards the larger goal of creating fully interactive and fully expressive lifelike pedagogical agents. To make significant progress in this direction, it will be important to develop a comprehensive theory of pedagogical speech acts and leverage increasingly sophisticated computational models of affective reasoning. We will be pursuing these lines of investigation in our future work.

Acknowledgements

Thanks to Dorje Bellbrook, Tim Buie, Charles Callaway, Mike Cuales, Jim Dautremont, Amanda Davis, Rob Gray, Mary Hoffman, Alex Levy, Will Murray, Roberta Osborne, and Jennifer Voerman of the North Carolina State University IntelliMedia Initiative for their work on the behavior sequencing engine implementation and the 3D modeling, animation, sound, and environment design for the INTERNET ADVISOR. Support for this work was provided by the following organizations: the National Science Foundation under grants CDA-9720395 (Learning and Intelligent Systems Initiative) and IRI-9701503 (CAREER Award

---

[2] The study simultaneously studied two aspects of the agent's behavior sequencing: its ability to generate unambiguous deictic references, which also yielded encouraging results, and the overall effects of his emotive behaviors.

Program); the North Carolina State University IntelliMedia Initiative; Novell, Inc.; and equipment donations from Apple and IBM.

References

1. Elisabeth André and Thomas Rist. Coping with temporal constraints in multimedia presentation planning. In *Proceedings of the Thirteenth National Conference on Artificial Intelligence*, pages 142–147, 1996.
2. Joseph Bates. The role of emotion in believable agents. *Communications of the ACM*, 37(7):122–125, 1994.
3. Shamus Culhane. *Animation from Script to Screen*. St. Martin's Press, New York, 1988.
4. P. Dillenbourg, P. Jermann, D. Schneider, D. Traum, and C. Buiu. The design of MOO agents: Implications from an empirical cscw study. In *Proceedings of Eighth World Conference on Artificial Intelligence in Education*, pages 15–22, 1997.
5. Christopher R. Eliot and Beverly P. Woolf. A simulation-based tutor that reasons about multiple agents. In *Proceedings of the Thirteenth National Conference on Artificial Intelligence*, pages 409–415, 1996.
6. Clark Elliott. *The Affective Reasoner: A Process Model of Emotions in a Multi-agent System*. PhD thesis, Northwestern University, 1992.
7. Claude Frasson, Thierry Mengelle, and Esma Aimeur. Using pedagogical agents in a multi-strategic intelligent tutoring system. In *Proceedings of the AI-ED '97 Workshop on Pedagogical Agents*, pages 40–47, 1997.
8. James C. Lester, Sharolyn A. Converse, Susan E. Kahler, S. Todd Barlow, Brian A. Stone, and Ravinder Bhogal. The persona effect: Affective impact of animated pedagogical agents. In *Proceedings of CHI'97 (Human Factors in Computing Systems)*, pages 359–366, Atlanta, 1997.
9. James C. Lester, Sharolyn A. Converse, Brian A. Stone, Susan E. Kahler, and S. Todd Barlow. Animated pedagogical agents and problem-solving effectiveness: A large-scale empirical evaluation. In *Proceedings of Eighth World Conference on Artificial Intelligence in Education*, pages 23–30, Kobe, Japan, 1997.
10. Kathleen F. McCoy. Generating context-sensitive responses to object-related misconceptions. *Artificial Intelligence*, 41:157–195, 1989 1990.
11. Jeff Rickel. Personal communication, January 1998.
12. Jeff Rickel and Lewis Johnson. Integrating pedagogical capabilities in a virtual environment agent. In *Proceedings of the First International Conference on Autonomous Agents*, pages 30–38, 1997.
13. Steven Ritter. Communication, cooperation, and competition among multiple tutor agents. In *Proceedings of Eighth World Conference on Artificial Intelligence in Education*, pages 31–38, 1997.
14. Brian A. Stone and James C. Lester. Dynamically sequencing an animated pedagogical agent. In *Proceedings of the Thirteenth National Conference on Artificial Intelligence*, pages 424–431, Portland, Oregon, 1996.
15. Stuart Towns, Charles Callaway, Jennifer Voerman, and James Lester. Coherent gestures, locomotion, and speech in life-like pedagogical agents. In *Proceedings of the Fourth International Conference on Intelligent User Interfaces*, pages 13–20, San Francisco, 1998.
16. Wen-Cheng Wang and Tak-Wai Chan. Experience of designing an agent-oriented programming language for developing social learning systems. In *Proceedings of Eighth World Conference on Artificial Intelligence in Education*, pages 7–14, 1997.

Incorporating Personality into a Multi-Agent Intelligent System for Training Teachers

Jianwen Yin, Magy Seif El-Nasr, Linyu Yang, and John Yen

Center for Fuzzy Logic, Robotics, and Intelligent Systems
Department of Computer Science
Texas A&M University
College Station, Texas 77843-3112

Abstract. This paper presents a system prototype for training a teacher based on two objects: the topic and students. In the system prototype, a concept model is defined to provide many topics needed to train teachers. Moreover, the Virtual Classroom Environment (VCE) is built to provide a multi-agent environment for teaching. In the VCE, students with many different personalities and motivations can communicate with each other as well as the teacher. The teacher can use various teaching techniques provided by the system to teach students specific topics in the VCE. The teacher can also test the students at the end of each class. Furthermore, the teacher can also ask the system to give an evaluation of the teaching process. The system will evaluate the user based on the result of the test(s) and the statistics of the whole teaching process throughout the class. The user can gain his/her teaching experience by analyzing the evaluation.

1 Introduction

Most of the existing Intelligent Tutoring Systems (ITSs) focus on training only one individual user. However, group training is also very useful, in case such as training a group of students to cooperate with each other. In this case, some of the students in the group could be real human beings, and others could be synthetic agents. Thus, the issue to be raised is: how to extend ITS architecture into a multi-agent intelligent training system? Personality plays a decisive role in student's actions, it determines whether a student is eager to learn or willing to collaborate. It further determines how the teacher can control the class and teach. Thus, the other challenging issue to be raised is: how to incorporate personality into software agents that simulate a more realistic student model. This paper presents a Multi-Agent Intelligent Teacher Training System (MAITTS).

MAITTS is a kind of ITS, in which teaching is the given domain. Training a teacher is considered one of the most challenging and time-consuming tasks. Training systems that involve training a user to do some maintenance tasks are easy to develop; since maintenance tasks often involve a specific number of steps, and maintenance is a well-defined domain, there are many experts who can define different training lessons. However, teaching is not a well-defined domain. Questions, such as: what constitutes a good teacher, what lessons we should give a teacher and how we should order these lessons, are still open. As of now we know of no one who could give a clear-cut answer to these questions. You can still go up to a teacher, whom you think is a good teacher, and ask him/her to write down some training lessons to train other people to teach as he/she does. The answer is often "teaching is an experience that you cannot put on paper." However, we have reasons to believe that qualities of a good teacher often include experience with different personalities. Furthermore, it involves communication and motivational ability. More than that, it also involves understanding the students, which is an obstacle that presents a big challenge to the Intelligent Tutoring System. We propose a training system that models a classroom. The trainee (our user) will use the system to interact with the students (our social agents). Our social agents will be developed to have various personality and intellectual abilities. Some of them are troublemakers and some of them are not. Some of them have fear of speaking up and some of them do not. In other words, we will try to simulate a set of personality traits that the trainee will face in his/her real classes.

Intelligent Tutoring systems rely on a collection of lessons that is given in a certain order. However, as mentioned above, developing a good teacher cannot be done with lessons. It is rather an experience that has to be handed to the trainee. Furthermore, tutor-training programs today rely on one-way seminars that are given by experienced tutors. However, seminars show little improvement, if any. Training is best done when the trainee is faced with a situation that calls for an action. When faced with a situation, the trainee will then develop some reactions or alternative courses of actions. Failure, in this case, is better demonstrated and learnt by the trainee. As Nietzche said, "what does not destroy me, makes me stronger." Thus, the trainee will be building up experiences through various situations.

2 Backgrounds

ITSs are very popular among researchers nowadays. The theory, technology and practice of ITSs are introduced in [1]. The area of human-like agents is another popular area, which has been under research for many years. Emotions and models of emotion have been described in [8, 12]. By 1994, an effort was made by Masuyma to formulate the human emotions into a set of rules [10]. An attempt was made by S. Sugano and T. Ogata [15] to simulate human mind through an electrically wired robot. A prototype of the human decision-making process using emotion was developed by Inoue et al. [9], they used neural networks to simulate behaviors given some environmental information. By the 1990's, researchers on the agent technology began working on modeling emotions. J. Bates is building a believable agent (OZ project) [3, 4, 5, 13] using the model described in [11]. The MIT lab is also producing an emotional multi-agent project [2].

There were a lot of personality frameworks that were presented in the AAAI Symposium 1997 [7, 6, 14]. Christopher Dryer developed a group of agents that delegate work and communicate with each other according to a certain organizational structure [7]. Each agent has a different personality based on its position in the hierarchy and its task(s). Additionally, Castefranchi et al. have developed another system that constitutes of social agents with different personalities. The personalities were developed according to several categories, including helpful agents and selfish agents [6]. Another system, which was quite similar to Castefranchi's system, is a system developed by Paola Rizzo et al. [14]. This system treats different types of personalities on the scale of goal priorities. Thus, if an agent is a selfish agent, then it will have high priority on goals such as self-image.

3 The Architecture of a Multi-Agent Intelligent Teacher Training System

3.1 Overview of the System

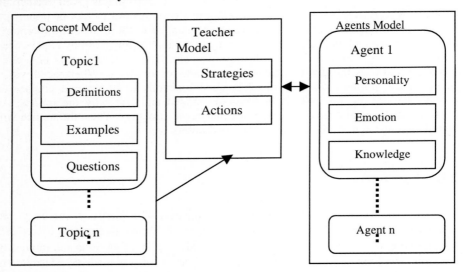

Fig. 1. System Architecture

Figure 1 illustrates the architecture of a Multi-Agent Intelligent Teacher Training System (MAITTS). As the figure illustrates, the system consists of three major components: the concept model, the teacher model and the agents model. The teacher model (or user model) consists of several teaching strategies and actions. The teacher may use the teaching strategies provided by the system. These strategies can be listed as, but not limited to the following: giving definitions, giving examples or asking questions. The action box, shown in the figure, represents actions that the teacher may take within the session – actions such as pointing to a student, shouting at a student, etc. The concept model consists of some hierarchically organized topics. These topics define the concepts that the user (teacher) will teach in the class. Furthermore, each topic consists of definitions, examples and questions. The agent model represents a Virtual Classroom Environment (VCE) consisting of many students (classroom agents) with different personalities. Each classroom agent has its own personality, its current emotion and its own knowledge, which include the common knowledge of the topics and the knowledge accumulated through learning. Furthermore, each classroom agent will have a certain behavior that is mapped from his/her internal state. Additionally, each agent will form his/her own opinion of the teacher and every other agent.

A comparison between the components in MAITTS and the components in the traditional ITS and Multi-Agent ITS is shown in Table 1. The classroom agent in MAITTS is the counterpart of the agent in Multi-Agent ITS, and the VCE in MAITTS is the counterpart of the Environment Model in Multi-Agent ITS. Both of them map to the System Model in traditional ITS. The Concept Model in MAITTS is the counterpart of the Expert Model in Multi-Agent ITS and traditional ITS. The Teacher Model is the counterpart of the User Model in Multi-Agent ITS and traditional ITS. And finally, the Evaluation Feedback is the counterpart of the Coaching Model in traditional ITS.

Table 1. Comparision between MAITTS , ITS and Multi-Agent ITS

ITS	Multi-Agent ITS	Multi-Agent Intelligent Teacher Training System
System Model	-Agent 1 -Agent 2 . . -Environment Model	- Classroom Agent 1 - Classroom Agent 2 . . . - Virtual Classroom Environment
Expert Model	-Expert Model A -Expert Model B . .	Concept Model
User Model	-User 1 Model -User 2 Model . .	Teacher Model
Coaching Model		Evaluation Feedback

3.2 Detailed description of the system

The communication between an agent and the teacher involves more than just an arrow. In order to get the feel of how the system is laid out and how the various components interact with each other, we present the detailed relationship of the components in figure 2. Figure 2 shows the detailed description of the teacher model and the agents' model. The teacher is confronted with some predefined set of actions that he/she can take on a specific environment. The actions that a teacher takes will have some impact on the motivational process of each student. This motivational process will have an impact on the agent's learning process as shown in the figure. Students (agents) will first perceive events that the teacher introduces to the environment and then an action is produced through the motivational process and the personality of each agent. This action is then embodied in the form of animation or a text box that makes the user/teacher aware of the reaction of each student. Thus, if a student is confused, a facial expression can be generated for this student. Through animation, facial expressions or even text box, the teacher will then have some feedback on the teaching techniques or actions that he/she used.

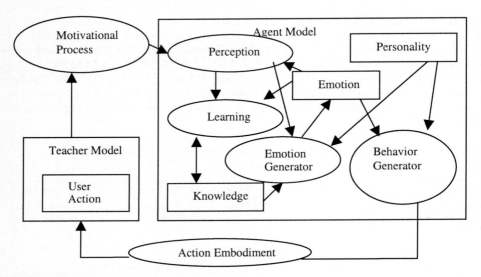

Fig. 2. Detailed design of components

3.3 Agent Model

The Classroom Agent Model is shown in figure 2. A classroom agent (student) can have its own personality, its current emotion and its knowledge. Furthermore, the personality of the classroom agent will determine its behavior and its emotion. The behavior of the classroom agent gives some feedback to the teacher. Moreover, the emotion plays an important role in the Classroom Agent Model. If the classroom agent perceives an event that motivates him/her, positive emotions will be generated, which will promote its learning. However, if the classroom agent perceives an event that dismotivates him/her, negative emotions will be generated, which will inhibit its learning. Emotions are represented with several internal states, including depression and frustration. These emotional states can affect the motivational level and boredom level, which in turn affect the agent's perception and learning. A discussion about how personality may affect motivational levels and learning is represented in section 4.

4. Incorporating Personality into Classroom Agents

Figure 3 is a personality-dependent student learning model; the contents in the left two boxes of the figure are just examples. From this figure, we can say that personality determinates the student's motivation and his/her ability to learn. The user of the system can learn how to control a class and motivate the students with different personalities through communicating with them.

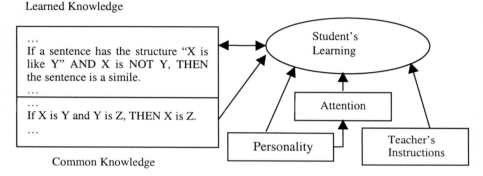

Fig. 3. Personality-dependent Student Learning Model

The source of learning is from the teacher's instructions. These instructions will increase or decrease the students' motivational levels according to the students' personalities. In turn, these motivational levels will determine the attention of each student. The attention will then affect learning through perception of different instructions from the teacher. This concept will be detailed by an example in section 5.

5. A Prototype Implementation

5.1 Concept Model

The concept model of MAITTS is implemented as hierarchically organized topics. Topics are represented through facts and rules. As explained in figure 3, a student can either learn new facts and rules from the teacher's instructions or learn new facts through reasoning. In our system, we have implemented one topic. To choose an appropriate example topic is very important in our implementation. The topic should be representative and not too complicated to describe. Based on this principle, we chose poetry writing as our topic. Some examples in the concept model are:

Rules such as:
- If a sentence has the structure " X is like Y" AND X is NOT Y, THEN the sentence is a simile.

- If a sentence has the structure " X is Y" AND X is NOT Y, THEN the sentence is a metaphor.
- If X is Y AND Y is Z, THEN X is Z.
  Facts such as:
- Jimmy is a man.
- Both man and woman are human beings.
- Human beings are not animals or plants.
- Magy is a woman.
- Rose is plant.

We assume all agents have a priori knowledge about the topic taught. According to our personality-dependent student learning model introduced in figure 3, the knowledge can be updated by learning from the teacher's instructions. However, the question of whether a student can learn also depends on the student's personality; for example how smart and diligent he/she is. In the real world, a person's knowledge is infinite and thus we will not be able to represent a very complete and accurate knowledge base. Nevertheless, we think it is appropriate to relate the a priori knowledge to the examples that the teacher gives in the class. If the student pays attention to the teacher and grasps all the rules and facts listed above, then he/she can reason that "Magy is a rose" is a metaphor based on the facts 2, 3, 4, 5 and rules 2, 3. An "idiot savant" cannot do the reasoning as shown in the previous sentence, even though he/she pays attention to the teacher all the time. He/she can learn that "Magy is a rose" is a metaphor only if the teacher directly says, "'Magy is a rose' is a metaphor."

We constructed the knowledge base to hold the minimum amount of information that is needed for our model to work. We think that the knowledge can be easily updated with other domain specific examples or knowledge that students in other systems might have.

5.2 Personality Types

The VCE is a virtual classroom environment with randomly arranged, n, students; in our system, we implemented 6 personality types in the VCE. Our personality types are as follows:

Nerd (Jane): withdrawn has difficulty communicating with people. Major goal is studying and education. He is always with his laptop. He goes by the book and does as told. He doesn't care about his image or how people perceive him, very easily motivated, discouraged when people make fun of him/her, encouraged when the teacher asks him to do something. *Spiteful Bully(Thomas):* makes fun of weaker people (Nerd and the Idiot), loves to see other people in trouble, doesn't care about his image or how people perceive him, does not help people, his entertainment is to watch people in trouble and make jokes on them, he does not abide by any social norms. He is encouraged when the teacher gives an example that makes fun of a person, and he gets bored very easily. *Trouble Maker (Mark):* main goal is to be funny and dominant around the crowd, enjoys making jokes on people, cares about how people perceive him/her, hates education and learning, like to socialize and tell jokes, abide by social rules (but not when it contradicts with his major goals), likes to get his goals the easiest way possible, helps people (if it does not contradict with his higher goals), motivated when given attention in the class, and gets bored easily if he doesn't understand and feels that other people do. *Thinker (Elliot):* he thinks a lot before his next action, brave -stands up for his actions and standards, cares a lot about his/her image, helps people if he can, always asks questions, discouraged if the teacher goes into a one-way teaching, and he doesn't like off-topic discussions. *Idiot (Bart):* he is withdrawn from the crowd, pulls up big words to impress other people but he doesn't know what they really mean, always paranoid when people talk about idiots, doesn't think about what is being said, always assumes that the teacher is right, discouraged when people make fun of him and discouraged when the teacher puts him on the spot by asking him questions or shouting at him. *Followers (Mary):* she follows the dominant personality, care about her image a lot so she doesn't try to put herself on the spot, doesn't have an opinion of her own - she instead shapes her opinion by what the group agrees on, or what the dominant character agrees on.

We chose these characters because the project was meant to train the user to control the class. Thus, we thought that the best way to train a person is to present him with a challenge. We tried to put some difficult personalities to teach, however, in order to make the experience more pleasurable for the user, we also made up many extreme personalities that you normally would not see in one class. So our slogan is 'if the user can teach this class, he/she can teach anything!'

5.3 Feedback to teachers

After the teacher teaches the class, he/she can get a feedback from the system. The feedback is generated by the system based on the statistics and testing results. The feedback tells whether the teacher can control the class, whether he/she can motivate the students enough to learn or bore them to death, etc. By analyzing the feedback, the teacher can gain his/her experience and improve his/her teaching skills. The feedback is given based on some information collected during the teaching process. This information include: information of how many questions have been asked, how many of them have been answered correctly, how many students are listening to the teacher, and how many students are sleeping, etc.

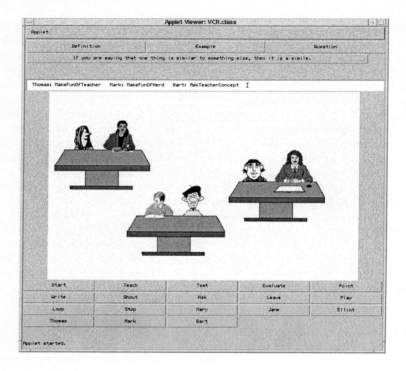

Fig. 4. GUI of MAITTS

6 Conclusion & Future Work

The concept of a good teacher is a fuzzy concept. The domain of teaching is not well defined, but the goal of a teacher is clear. It is (1) to control the class, (2) to motivate the students to learn, and (3) to have the explanation and convincing power. These three factors play an important part in the feedback process. Thus, instead of teaching a user how to teach, we let the user experience teaching a virtual class with virtual students, and then tell him/her what they did wrong through feedback.

Two important issues have been raised and fully discussed in this paper, namely Multi-Agent ITS and using personality agents in the student models. We think that the addition of these two features have had a great impact on our work. Furthermore, they provided one more thread in the fully grown web of ITS.

Since this is an ongoing research, we still have some points to improve and research. One possibility of improvement is to extend the model from training a teacher how to teach a class to training a group of student on how to collaborate with each other. The group of students can learn how to collaborate by communicating with classroom agents with different personalities. The knowledge representation is another point that we can improve, even through it is not the main concern of this research. Moreover, topics can be added to make the system suitable for different subjects.

References

1. Goodkovsky,V.A.& Kazennov, A.Y.: Intelligent Tutoring Systems: Theory, Technology and Practice. In P.Brusilovsky, V.Stefanuk (Eds.). Proceedings of the EAST-WEST conference on emerging computer technologies in education , . Moscow: ICSTI. (1992)123-127
2. J. Velasquez. Modeling Emotions and Other Motivations in Synthetic Agents. *Proceedings of the AAAI Conference 1997*, (1997) 10-15
3. J. Bates. The Role of Emotion in Believable agents. *Communications of the ACM*, vol. 37, no. 7, (1992)122-125
4. J. Bates, A. Bryan Loyall and W. Scott Reilly. An Architecture for Action, Emotion, and Social Behavior. Technical Report CMU-CS-92-144, School of Computer Science, Carnegie Mellon University, Pittsburgh, PA, (1992)
5. J. Bates, A. Bryan Loyall and W. Scott Reilly. Integerating Reactivity, Goals and Emotion in a Broad Agent. Technical Report CMU-CS-92-142, School of Computer Science, Carnegie Mellon University, Pittsburgh, PA, (1992)
6. Cristiano Castefranchi, F. de Rosis and Rino Falcone. Social Attitudes and Personalities in Agents. *AAAI Fall Symposium '97,* (1997)
7. Christopher Dryer. Ghosts in the Machine: Personalities for Socially Adroit Software Agents. *AAAI Fall Symposium 1997,* (1997)
8. Daniel Goleman. *Emotional Intelligence.* Bantam Books: New York, (1995)
9. K.Inoue, K.Kawabata and H. Kobayashi. On a decision making system with emotion. *IEEE Int Workshop on Robot and Human Communication,*(1996)461-465
10. E. Masuyama. A Number of Fundamental Emotions and Their Definitions. *IEEE International Workshop on Robot and Human Communication,* (1994)156-161
11. A. Ortony, G. Clore and M. Foss. The Referential Structure of the Affective Lexicon. *Cognitive Science,* Vol. 11, (1987)341-364
12. R. Pfeifer. Artificial Intelligence Models of Emotions. *Cognitive Perspectives on Emotion and Motivation.* ,(1988)287-320
13. W. Reilly and Joseph Bates. *Building Emotional Agents.* Technical Report CMU-CS-92-143, Carnegie Mellon University:PA, (1992)
14. Paola Rizzo, Maneula Velosa, Maria Miceli and Amedeo Cesta. Personality-Driven Social Behaviors in Believable agents. *AAAI Symposium 1997, (1997)*
15. Shigeki Sugano and Tesuya Ogata. Emergence of mind in robots for Human Interface - research methodology and robot model . *Proc. International Conference on robotics and Automation IEEE,* (1996)
16. Digman, J.M. Personality Structure: Emergence of the Five-Factor Model. Annual Review of Psychology, 41, (1990)417-440

The Intelligent Helpdesk:
Supporting Peer-Help in a University Course

Jim Greer, Gordon McCalla, John Cooke, Jason Collins, Vive Kumar,
Andrew Bishop, Julita Vassileva

ARIES Laboratory, Department of Computer Science, University of Saskatchewan,
Saskatoon, S7N 5A9 CANADA
Email: {greer,mccalla,jiv}@cs.usask.ca

Abstract. Universities, experiencing growths in student enrollment and reductions in operating budgets, are faced with the problem of providing adequate help resources for students. Help resources are needed at an institution-wide and also at a course-specific level, due to the limited time of instructors to provide help and answer questions. The Intelligent IntraNet Peer Help Desk provides an integration and application of previously developed ARIES Lab tools for peer help to university teaching. One of its components, CPR, provides a subject-oriented discussion forum and FAQ-list providing students with *electronic* help. Another component, PHelpS, suggests an appropriate peer to provide *human* help. In both cases it is *peer* help, since the help originates from students themselves. The selection of the appropriate help resource (electronic or human) is based on modelling student knowledge and on a conceptual model of the subject material.

1 Introduction

Universities are faced with the difficult problem of providing adequate help resources for their members, i.e. the staff, faculty and students. Help resources are needed at an institution-wide and also at a course-specific level, due to the limited time of instructors to provide help and answer questions. Computer technology offers several approaches to facilitating and providing the necessary personalized help resources that can be made available to a mass audience. By deploying IntraNets in universities different kinds of resources (lecture notes, exercises, quizzes, syllabi, etc.) can be made available on request to any student. There are numerous positive examples of implementing on-line course materials and discussion groups at other universities, for example, the Virtual-U Project [14], WebCT [8], and Quorum [3].

However, merely providing access to appropriate material via a network doesn't solve the problem of providing help. One way to decrease the load of teachers is to provide conditions for students to help each other. Peer help has many pedagogical advantages [12]. First, it promotes the socializing of students in the context of work and increases their motivation by giving social recognition for their knowledge and helpfulness. Second, peer help is deeply situated in a shared context and can therefore provide a stronger learning experience for the person asking for help. Third, it is a way to make learning happen "just in time", i.e. when the problem arises. Fourth, it promotes processes of self-explanation [5] and reflection in the helper, and in this way "reciprocal" learning takes place. Fifth, it is cost effective, since it uses the learners themselves as a teaching resource. And finally, it facilitates social interaction in a group of learners and helps to create knowledge-anchored personal relationships among them.

Peer-help happens naturally within small groups of learners. When the group of learners is too large or distributed, however, obstacles arise. In a university environment this is often the case. For example, the Department of Computer Science at the University of Saskatchewan offers an introductory service course in computer science (CMPT 100) for students from various faculties (commerce, arts & science, nursing, agriculture, etc.) which involves about 600 students per academic term. Learners who need help may not know whom to ask, since they may not be able to identify which student is knowledgeable; in fact they may not even know the other learners. In addition, many student questions relate to their assignments or laboratory activities, arising while they are working at their computers at home or in the labs. These factors combine to make peer help more challenging to provide. If the students did know a potential helper, they wouldn't know whether or not the helper was currently available, which means a loss of time and a loss of the immediate context in which the problem has arisen. Computer technology can be applied to help overcome some of these problems facing peer help. There are many Computer Supported Collaborative Work (CSCW) tools that facilitate communication among peers. However, they rarely ever provide personalized help on demand. We have been developing cognitive tools that support peer help in the context of university teaching in an individualized way and just in time. The tools can provide support in several ways:

- by providing an appropriate "discussion facility" where people can ask subject-related questions and give answers, discuss problems of common interest either synchronously (like a chat-facility), or asynchronously (like a newsgroup-facility);
- by finding appropriate peer helpers who are knowledgeable and likely to be able to answer a learner's question;
- by providing a shared workspace for helper and helpee where they can share the context of the problem;
- by helping the helper better understand the problem of the person asking for help and suggesting a pedagogically appropriate way of helping. For example, sometimes it is pedagogically better not to give any help, but to encourage the learner to try harder to solve the problem alone.

In this paper we focus on the first two ways of supporting peer help. The last two ways are the topics of other ongoing research projects in our lab and are not discussed here. The discussion facility, called the Cooperative Peer Response (CPR) system, provides a suite of WWW-based tools to facilitate cooperative learning, peer help, and expert help within a University course. The CPR discussion forum encourages peer help; it has been deployed in a number of University courses and has proven to be an effective learning support tool.

The second tool, called the Peer Help System (PHelpS) provides a facility for locating somewhere on the network a peer helper who is ready, willing, and able to provide help to a particular help request. A PHelpS prototype has been deployed in a distributed workplace environment [10] and preliminary experiments suggest that it is an effective training and performance support tool.

CPR and PHelpS, together with various related spin-off projects, have led to an attempt to integrate several cognitive tools into a new style of Intelligent IntraNet Peer Help-Desk facility. Such a Help-Desk draws together a variety of cognitive tools, particularly tools for peer help, into a comprehensive environment to support many styles of learning. The advantage of using an IntraNet instead of the Internet is that access is restricted to only those students attending the course, so that they can communicate with their peers and teachers. In this way students are protected from possibly disturbing comments made by occasional "visitors", who are not involved in the course. This makes it easier to track down what students are doing and to collect information about the topics that were discussed. This information is used both for improving the peer-help facility and as feedback to teachers to adapt the course accordingly. It also eliminates some concerns about the privacy of user information gathered during students' work with the system.

This paper outlines the design of the Intelligent IntraNet Help-Desk. It does not focus on the architecture of the proven peer-help tools (PHelpS and CPR) that act as its structural skeleton, since they are described in detail elsewhere [6, 10], but rather focuses on the integration of these tools in the context of university teaching.

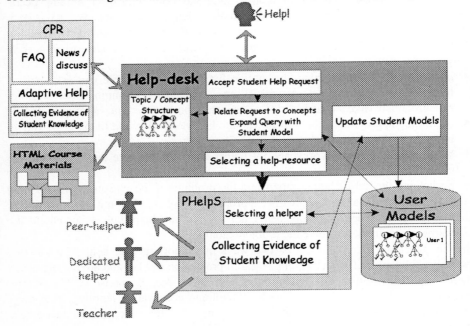

Fig. 1. Architecture of the Integrated Help-Desk

2   The Intelligent IntraNet Help-Desk: An Integration of Cognitive Tools

The help-desk provides individualized on-line multi-modal peer-help, as shown in Figure 1. In this integrated system, CPR acts as a medium for multiple users to communicate with one another in electronic and asynchronous ways and provides a resource for adaptive help. The role of PHelpS is to select an appropriate human helper when necessary and to facilitate the subsequent direct communication between the peers.

The Intelligent IntraNet Help-Desk accepts and interprets help-requests coming from students. Help requests can be made directly, or while browsing through the course materials, or while working with CPR. The Help-Desk locates an appropriate help-resource (e.g. related FAQs, a discussion thread related to the help-request, or web-pages addressing the concepts involved in the help request) or a knowledgeable peer-helper. Next we shall discuss the Help-Desk, which is the central component in Figure 1.

2.1   Knowledge Representation

Central to the intelligence of the HelpDesk is a knowledge base representing course topic and concept structure. This knowledge base is needed in order to "understand" the student's help-request so as to match it to relevant articles and discussion threads in CPR and to find peers with the knowledge to deal with the request. We decided to use a two-layered knowledge representation, similar to the one used in BIP [2]. On the first, coarser "topic level", the organization of the course and the activities taking place during it are represented (lectures, chapters or sub-chapters, exercises, labs, assignments, tests). The deeper concepts addressed by the topics taught in the course are represented on the second level. Several topics can relate to one concept (for example, several lectures, exercises or assignments may relate to various aspects of recursion). Similarly one topic may address several concepts (for example a lecture on web searching might refer to concepts such as "browsing' or "search strategies"). The topic-concept structure is shown in Figure 2. We shall discuss it again in more detail later.

2.2   Student Modelling

One of the limitations of cognitive models (which sometimes discourage people from using them for instructional purposes) is the absence of elaborate analytic models of group learning. Therefore, it difficult if not impossible to fully apply existing cognitive theories of group learning in the construction of intelligent learning or help environments. Despite this, we believe that partial solutions should be sought. In the Help-Desk we have applied two simple and well-known representation techniques for student modelling: a numeric overlay and a profile of several general parameters. Two types of evidence are used to update the student models: direct and indirect. The direct evidence comes from observed students' actions. During students' work with the web-based materials, with CPR and with PHelpS, the Help-Desk collects evidence about student knowledge and updates the individual student models. There are at least 10 sources of direct evidence about the student, which can be used: the history of studied topics in the course, the assignment marks of students, explicit testing on topics, the student's self-assessment (see the personal check-marks in Figure 4) , the teacher's assessment (see the lecturer check-marks in Figure 4), votes in the newsgroup in CPR (about which answers are good), posted questions and answers in CPR, observation of CPR browsing (threads visited, participation), observation of browsing in the web-based course materials, feedback about the student, given by the peer helper, feedback about the peer-helper, given by the student.

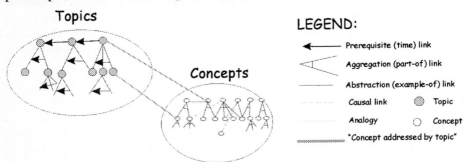

Fig. 2. The concept-topic structure

Every student model has two parts. The first part contains general information about the student, such as name, alias (if he / she wishes to have one for privacy reasons) and several parameters providing a general evaluation of the student. These include general helpfulness, general knowledgeability, overall willingness to help, and history data (e.g. how active he / she has been in general and how many times he / she has given help recently). These general parameters contribute to the calculation of the score for every student when a peer-helper has to be selected by PHelpS.

The kernel of the student model is a numeric overlay over the concept-topic structure. This overlay model provides information about how much the student knows about each concept and topic. The Help-Desk uses it in order to better "understand" the student's help-request, i.e. to place it in the right context (of the current topic) and to expand it eventually with related concepts, which are considered not known by the student (according to the student model).

The indirect evidence for updating the student models is gathered from directly observing evidence about knowledge of certain concepts and topics and propagating it to related concepts and topics. In order to make this clear we explain the concept-topic structure in more detail (see Figure 2). The topic structure includes prerequisite links (what *should be taught* before what) and temporal links (which topic *was actually taught* before which). Each topic can be broken down into sub-topics to decompose the structure further. In this way the topic structure is represented in an aggregation hierarchy (AND/OR graph) of concepts ordered according to prerequisite links and temporal links.

Each of the topics may be connected to multiple concepts in the concept structure. Concepts represent the teaching goals, i.e. the elements of knowledge that the student has to develop as a result of taking the course. Concepts can be related to other concepts through various semantic links, including abstraction and aggregation (which in turn may use AND/OR clustering semantics), causal links, analogy links, and prerequisite links.

Why do we need a two-layered knowledge representation? The topic–structure provides a natural way to represent the position of a student in a course. However, it is not fine-grained enough to represent the differences in knowledge/ understanding among peers who are taking the same course. All it can state is the historical fact that the students have attended a certain lecture or have done a certain assignment. A finer distinction is needed in order to find capable peer-helpers, which reflects the knowledge of students and their ability or understanding. This distinction can only be found at the concept level, since every topic, sub-topic, assignment and test are related to a (set of) concept(s). Another advantage of maintaining a concept level is the possibility to take into account the various semantic links among concepts and to propagate knowledge values in user profiles through the concept network. In this way the system knows not only what the student has been taught, but by observing knowledge about one concept (e.g. good performance on a test), the system is also able to deduce that the student is likely to have knowledge on a related concept. In this way the knowledge value on one concept can be propagated to related concepts. As a result, a help-request addressing a given concept may be directed to a helper who hasn't exactly demonstrated knowledge on this concept, but is expected to have it because of having successfully mastered a closely related concept.

Knowledge propagation can happen among concepts or among topics and also between the two levels (from topics to concepts). Following the prerequisite links at the topic level, the system can conclude that if a student is currently working on topic B which has topic A as a prerequisite, the student has some knowledge of A (see Figure 3). Following temporal links, the system can conclude that if a student is currently working on topic C that was preceded by B, the student should have some knowledge of B.

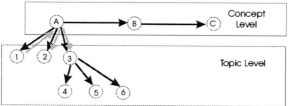

Fig. 3. Propagation of knowledge values among topics and concepts

Following the topic-concept links, the system can conclude, that if a student has learned topic A with related concepts 1, 2 and 3, the student has some knowledge of these concepts. Propagation in the opposite direction is also possible. For example, if there was strong evidence that the student knows concept 1, which is related to topic A, which is related to two other concepts, 2 and 3, the system can conclude that the student has learned topic A, and is also knowledgeable about concepts 2 and 3 (the gray arrows in Figure 3).

Following the semantic links among concepts, one can also make some conclusions about general knowledge levels. For example, if the student knows concept 3, which is an abstraction of 5, 6 and 7, the system can conclude that the student knows at least one of the examples 5, 6 or 7.

For our early experiments, the propagation techniques have been tailored specifically for the concept structure of the CMPT 100 course. We intend to generalize these techniques by overlaying Bayesian belief networks on these concept structures in the future. The updating and propagation of knowledge values through the topic and concept level of all student models takes place all the time, also while the student is not on-line. In this way the models are always kept up-to-date, and when a help-request is posed or a peer-helper is required, the system can react quickly. One important decision we took is to make the student models inspectable by both students and teachers. In this way the unavoidable imprecision and errors that can happen in diagnosis (i.e. in the interpretation of direct evidence and propagation) can be corrected by a human.

2.3   Help-Desk Operation

The student requests help about a certain topic by clicking on a question mark associated with a particular topic, subtopic, or activity (see Figure 4). The help-request is expanded with related concepts and topics which he or she is believed not to know (according to the student model) and is passed further to CPR in order to recommend a thread or posting in the FAQ, which corresponds to the concepts related to the query. If no such resource is available in CPR, or if the student has chosen explicitly to request a human helper, the expanded request is passed on to PHelpS to find an appropriate peer-helper.

PHelpS finds a peer (student) who is currently on-line, and who is knowledgeable about the concepts related to the help request. The identification a peer is carried out by an applet, which is downloaded automatically for every registered user when he /she starts his / her browser. This applet periodically sends messages to the server indicating that the person is still on-line and active. When the peer-matching algorithm has identified some active user as a good potential helper, PHelpS contacts this student by starting another applet. It presents to the helper the topic about which help was requested and the list of the related topics and concepts, which the HelpDesk believes the student asking for help does not know, and opens a chat window. In this window, the helper can answer the question or explore some follow-up questions with the student requesting help. If such a dialogue is established and carried through to conclusion, then the Help-Desk presents an evaluation form to both the student who asked for help and the helper so that they can both provide feedback on the quality of help and the level of knowledge of each other. This feedback is used to update the models of the helper and the student requesting help.

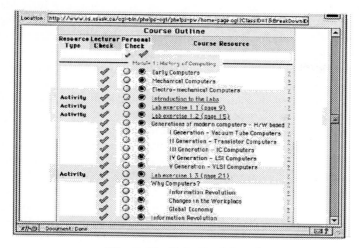

Fig. 4. The Help-Desk Interface

3   Comparison with Other Work

There have been numerous approaches in the field of AI and Education aimed at providing peer help for the learner. Most of them, however, try to create an artificial peer, i.e. an intelligent component or agent, who collaborates with the learner, an approach that was originally proposed by Self in 1986 [13]. Examples of such artificial peers are Dillenbourg & Self's [7] artificial co-learners, Chan & Baskin's learning companions [4], and Aimeur & Frasson's "troublemaker"[1]. All of these systems are focussed on collaborative problem solving (and consequently have a very restricted domain of application). They generate help and utterances themselves (using their knowledge bases) and decide when to interfere (using their pedagogical strategies). In this sense they are classical "Intelligent Tutoring Systems".

Our approach to providing peer help differs significantly from these classical approaches. First, the subject domain of the Help-Desk can be as broad as needed; the only requirement is the existence of some kind of domain structuring (into topics, concepts, tasks or skills) to which help-requests can be indexed. Second, there is minimal *fully automatic* generation of computer-based help, so the system can perform with a less extensive knowledge base and less sophisticated reasoning mechanisms. All the help entries are generated by the students themselves, by means of posting questions and answers to the discussion groups in CPR and by providing direct help via PHelpS. Third, the system doesn't interfere with the help dialogue and doesn't make pedagogical decisions. It is activated only by an explicit request from the student. In this way the Intelligent IntraNet Peer Help-Desk naturally involves human intellect at precisely those points that are currently considered as the "Achilles' heels" of AI-based learning environments: the diagnosis of a student's knowledge, pedagogical decision-making, and generating the instructional content.

The Intelligent IntraNet Peer Help-Desk can be compared with other student model-based approaches for selecting an appropriate human helper. Hoppe's [9] COSOFT is the first ambitious project to address several issues related to the use of student modelling in order to parameterize human-human collaboration. Later Mühlenbrock et al. [11] pursued this research further. The questions raised by Hoppe in 1995 include the composition of a learning group from a known set of students, and especially the selection of a peer-helper, the identification of problems to be dealt with in a collaborative session or the selection of tasks that are adequate for a given learning group. Hoppe's approach has been primarily targeted at exploring possible improvements to group student modelling to support human collaboration. It focuses on a limited domain since it employs classical ITS diagnosis, representation and matching. In addition it is intended to support only human-human collaboration, but not to be integrated with an automatic advice or help utility. Our Help-Desk uses the same student models both for selection of human partners and for providing electronic help (based on the FAQ facility). Unlike COSOFT, the student modelling approach employed in our Help-Desk doesn't rely so much on computer diagnosis, but on human feedback. This makes it easily transferable to new domains. The modification of PHelpS (which is a task-based help system designed to work in procedural workplace domains) to a concept / topic-based help system designed to work in a post secondary course environment took about four weeks of work for one programmer. We expect that changing to a different topic/concept structure for a different domain will take even less time.

4   Conclusion and Future Work

The Intelligent Intranet Helpdesk is being currently employed to support peer-help among the 480 students in the CMPT 100 introductory computer science course for non-majors at the University of Saskatchewan. Data about the discussion groups facility (CPR) usage and about interactive peer-help sessions mediated via PHelpS are being collected. Helpers and helpees have to fill out a short questionnaire after each peer-help session mediated by the system. We will analyse
- the correlation between the system's choice for best peer helper (based on the student models of the helper and helpee) and the quality of the help provided (based on the evaluation of the helpee);
- the quality of the system's representation of a student's (helpee's) knowledge based on the feedback of the peer helper;
- the overall picture of students' success on tests and assignments in comparison with results from previous semesters when no HelpDesk was available.

The results obtained will be used to tune the user modelling techniques and to improve the peer-matching scheme of the HelpDesk. In future, we will be pursuing a development of the HelpDesk "in depth" (using more artificial intelligence techniques to amplify the abilities of the HelpDesk in diagnosis, pedagogy and collaboration support). We believe this provides us with a broad and interesting research perspective, that should result in the construction of flexible, usable, robust and sophisticated tools to support human learning that are characterized by their ability to react to individual differences among learners.

Acknowledgement. This research was carried out under the auspices of the Canadian Telelearning Network of Centres of excellence, project 6.2.4.

References

1. Aimeur E. & Frasson, C. Analysing a New Learning Strategy according to Different Knowledge Levels". *Computer and Education, An International Journal*, (1996) **27**, 2, 115-127.
2. Barr A, Beard, M., Atkinson, R.C. The Computer as a Tutorial Laboratory: the Stanford BIP Project. *International Journal of Man-Machine Studies*, (1976) **8**, 567-596.
3. Canas, A., Ford, K., Hayes P., Brennan, J., Reichherzer, T. Knowledge Construction and Sharing in Quorum, in Greer J. (Ed.) *Artificial Intelligence and Education, Proceedings AIED'95*, (1995) AACE, 218 – 225.
4. Chan T.W. & Baskin A. Learning Companion Systems. In C. Frasson & G. Gauthier (Eds.) *Intelligent Tutoring Systems: On the Crossroads of AI and Education.* (1990) Ablex, NJ, 6-33.
5. Chi, M.T.H., de Leeuw, N., Chiu, M.H., La Vancher, C. *Eliciting self-explanations improves understanding. Cognitive Science* (1994) **18**, 439-477.
6. Collins, J. Greer, J., Kumar, V., McCalla, G., Meagher P., Tkach, R. Inspectable User Models for Just in Time Workplace Training. In A. Jameson, C. Paris, C. Tasso (Eds.) *User Modelling, Proceedings of the UM97 Conference*, (1997) Springer Wien New York, 327-337.
7. Dillenbourg, P. & Self, J. A Computational Approach to Socially Distributed Cognition. *European Journal of Psychology of Education*, (1992) Vol.**VII** (4), 353-372
8. Goldberg M. WebCT – Word Wide Web Course Tools (1997) (Web-Page) http://homebrew1.cs.ubc.ca/webct/
9. Hoppe, H.-U. The Use of Multiple Student Modelling to Parameterise Group Learning, in J. Greer (Ed.) *Artificial Intelligence and Education, Proceedings of AIED'95*, (1995) AACE, 234-241.
10. McCalla, G., Greer, J., Kumar, V., Meagher, P, Collins, J., Tkatch, R., Parkinson, B. A Peer Help System for Workplace Training. In B. duBoulay and R. Mizoguchi (Eds.) *Artificial Intelligence and Education, Proceedings of AIED'97*, (1997) IOS Press: Amsterdam, 183-191.
11. Mühlenbrock M., Tewissen F., Hoppe H.U. A Framework System for Intelligent Support in Open Distributed Learning Environments, In B. duBoulay and R. Mizoguchi (Eds.) *Artificial Intelligence and Education, Proceedings of AIED'97*, (1997) IOS Press: Amsterdam, 191-198.
12. Pressley, M., Wood E., et al. Encouraging mindful use of prior knowledge: Attempting to construct explanatory answers facilitate learning, *Educational Psychologist*, (1992) **27**, 91-109.
13. Self, J. The application of machine learning to student modelling. *Instructional Science*, (1986) **14**, 327-388.
14. Virtual-U. Simon Fraser University, Virtual-U Research Project (Web-Page) (1997) http://virtual-u.cs.sfu.ca/vuweb/

On the Notion of
Components for Intelligent Tutoring Systems

Vladan Devedzic [1], Danijela Radovic [2], and Ljubomir Jerinic [3]

[1] Department of Information Systems, FON - School of Business Administration,
University of Belgrade, PO Box 770, Jove Ilica 154,
11000 Belgrade, Yugoslavia
devedzic@galeb.etf.bg.ac.yu
[2] Technical Faculty Cacak, Svetog Save 65,
32000 Cacak, Yugoslavia
danijela@tfc.tfc.kg.ac.yu
[3] Institute of Mathematics, University of Novi Sad, Trg Dositeja Obradovica 4,
21000 Novi Sad, Yugoslavia
jerinic@uns.ns.ac.yu

Abstract. The concept of software components has received relatively little attention so far by the researchers in the field of AIED. This paper is an attempt to bring more light on this important concept and to describe the benefits that component-based ITSs can bring to the field. Surprisingly enough, there is still no consensus on the notion of component among AIED researchers. There are many open questions and unclear issues. By carefully structuring the description of software components in general, as well as by showing some examples of components for ITS design, the paper presents several important related issues, like functionality of components, their granularity, generality, interoperability, and reusability. Special attention is given to the architectural and communication considerations, as well as to the relation between components and ontologies for ITS design.

1   Introduction

The purpose of this paper is threefold:
1. It is supposed to describe from different viewpoints (architectural, design, software engineering, and utility) the concept of software *components* that may be useful for development of Intelligent Tutoring Systems (ITSs).
2. It is also intended to be a survey of important problems, questions and issues related to such components.
3. It should draw the reader's attention to the possibilities that component-software technology can offer to the field of ITSs.

Although the concept of components has been largely used in the area of software engineering during the last decade (see, for example, [1]), it is only since recently that it draws significant attention in the community of researchers working in the area of Artificial Intelligence in Education (AIED). Exceptions from this rule include relatively few people from the AIED community (some examples are the work of Murray [6] and Munroe et al. [5]).

The paper has been inspired by an informal discussion on the topic of software components, held during the AIED'97 conference in Kobe, Japan[1]. Starting from some conclusions of that discussion, as well as from the relevant literature both in the area of ITSs and from the area of software engineering, and from our own previous work, we have elaborated on the idea of software components for ITSs and organized the paper as follows. First the usual process of ITS development is overviewed, with some comments on its inherent difficulties. Then some requirements are enumerated that would significantly alleviate the process of ITS development. This is followed by a description and a discussion of the concept of software component and the most important issues related to it. Examples of software components that we have identified in our own work are also shown. Architectural and communication aspects of components for ITSs are shown next. The Discussion Section comments on the relationship between the concept of components and component of ontologies for ITS design. Finally, some conclusions and open questions are presented.

2   The process of ITS development

2.1   How do we usually develop ITSs?

Traditional ITSs are concentrated on the domain knowledge they are supposed to present and teach; hence their control mechanisms are often domain-dependent. More recent ITSs pay more attention to generic problems and concepts of the tutoring process, trying to separate architectural, methodological, and control issues from the domain knowledge as much as possible (see, for example, [5]). In other words, there are interactive and integrated development tools for building ITSs, i.e. for helping the developer plug-in some domain knowledge and test the prototype system, and then gradually and incrementally develop the final system. Such integrated tools are often referred to as *shells* (e.g., ITS shells, or ILE shells, or IES shells, etc.), which usually require a knowledge engineer in order to be fully used, or *authoring tools*, which can be also used by human instructors who do not necessarily have knowledge engineering experience. Still more recent ITSs are developed for collaborative learning, and often use Internet/WWW/agents technology in order to provide comfortable, user-oriented, distributed learning and teaching facilities [2].

The ITS models used in most of these systems, shells, and authoring tools, as well as the corresponding knowledge models, differ only to an extent. However, the design methodologies employed vary a lot, and sometimes even remain blurred for the sake of the system functionality alone. On the other hand, using a shell for developing an ITS brings more systematic design, but can also become a limiting factor if the shell

---

[1] The discussion has been organized as a part of the workshop "Issues in Achieving Cost-Effective and Reusable ITSs". The core or the discussion group included six people from AIED community working in different fields (Ana Paiva, Pamela Woods, Kiyoshi Nakobayashi, Ulrich Hoppe, Martin Muhlenbrock, and Vladan Devedzic). Later on, another fifteen researchers (approximately) from the AIED community have joined the discussion.

doesn't support a certain knowledge representation technique or design strategy that may be needed in a particular system.

Many researchers have also noted that current ITSs are usually built from scratch (see, for example, [4]). Moreover, knowledge embedded in ITSs does not accumulate well, and specifying functionalities of software modules of current ITSs often implies a lot of difficulties.

2.2   What would be nice when we develop ITSs?

It would be very nice:
1. if we could *easily assemble* our ITSs, shells, authoring shells, agents, etc., *from existing and pretested pieces of software*, without the need to develop and implement them from scratch;
2. if we could have our shells and toolkits offering us *only the tools and options that we really need*; we don't want our shells and toolkits to lack a tool or an option that we really need in a given project, but we also do not need a whole bunch of unnecessary tools and options from them;
3. if we could *easily replace* any piece of software in an ITS by a similar (and possibly new) one, without any serious harm to the rest of the system; this would allow us, for example, to experiment with several versions of our system, each one having a certain functionality implemented in a different way (i.e., by a different piece of software);
4. if in order to develop a new piece of software that we find out to be necessary in our project (and it happens frequently) we could *have some other piece of software to start with*; the other piece of software should, of course, be logically and functionally similar to the desired one whenever it is possible;
5. if the existing pieces of software could be *logically organized and catalogued* in a repository (or repositories), such that we can easily access and check the pieces by means of a DBMS;
6. if we could *easily enlarge* the repository with new software we develop during our project, for later use in another similar project;
7. if we could *automatically refresh and update* the repository time after time, putting in it some new pieces and deleting some pieces of software that are no longer needed, based on the functionality and use-statistics information;
8. if the *access* to the repository could be as easy as possible, e.g. through Internet or an Intranet; in other words, if we could easily get, put, organize, and update software in a remote repository;
9. if pieces of software in such repositories were fully *interoperable*, i.e. able to execute on multiple platforms and to be easily combined with software developed by somebody else, in another programming language, etc.; in this way, when assembling an ITS, a shell, an agent, or another system, we wouldn't feel constrained by the hardware we use, the operating system installed on it, and so on.

In short, it would be very nice if we could concentrate more on *design* of ITSs, and automate their implementation and maintenance as much as possible. It would be very nice if we could dedicate our work mostly to cognitive aspects, learning and teaching issues, and effectiveness of ITSs, and having most of the software changes in them done quickly.

Component-software technology offers some possibilities that can be employed if we want the above requirements to be satisfied when we develop ITSs. "Component software addresses the general problem of designing systems from application elements that were constructed independently by different developers using different languages, tools, and computing platforms" [1]. The idea is to build ITSs through an assembly of reusable, pretested, and independently upgradable software components.

3   What is a component?

Although this simple question might look easy to answer, the informal discussion among several researchers from the AIED community mentioned in the Introduction has shown that consensus is not easy to reach on that subject. What follows is not a strict definition of the concept of *component*, but it offers an intuitively clear understanding to start with:

> *A component is a piece of a larger system that can be put in, taken out, and used together with other components to contribute to the global system's behavior ...*[2]

In case of an ITS, the above description of a component immediately raises several other questions[3], like:

* Are components, for example, a lesson, a topic, an objective, an exercise, a didactic tool, and a pedagogical point?
* Is an agent a component?
* Can a data object be a component?
* Are components services or...?
* Can we buy a software component in a software shop? If so, how are the components classified there?

In order to try to answer questions like these, we have to consider several major issues first. The issues considered here are not the only ones that can be associated with the notion of components. However, these are considered to be necessary for a component specification.

3.1   Functionality

Any software component must be first considered from its functionality aspect; that is, *what it does* as a component of a larger (global) system, *how it contributes* to the overall system behavior? In other words, regarded as a standalone piece of software, what does it expect at its input, what output does it produce, and what conditions must be met in order to produce the expected output? For example, if a *lesson* is a

---

[2] This is exactly the conclusion that has been reached by the core of the group mentioned above.
[3] Questions like these have been put during the discussion in Kobe, but have remained unanswered!

component, what is it supposed to do in an ITS, and what are its I/O aspects as a software component?

However, it is already mentioned that specifying functionalities of components is not easy. We agree with the opinion of Ikeda et al., that functionality of components should be described in terms of a common vocabulary [4]. However, the work on building such a vocabulary in the area of ITS is still underway.

3.2   Granularity

Each component is also featured by its granularity; that is, there are *smaller and larger* components, *simple and complex* components, *atomic and aggregate* components. In other words, simple components can be combined into a larger one in order to get a distinctly new (more complex) functionality. For example if there were components describing *topics*, they could be combined (together with some other components) into a *lesson* component.

3.3   Generality

There are more general and more specific components. Some components can be derived from more general ones by specifying additional features and/or functionalities. There are components that can be used in many different ITSs, while other components can be used only in a specific kind of ITSs. For example, and quite informally and intuitively, if a *lesson* is a component, we can think of an *easy lesson* as being derived from the lesson component.

3.4   Interaction and interoperability

Although each component has its standalone functionality, it usually communicates with other components of a larger system. It is therefore important to agree upon an appropriate communication protocol for information exchange between components. This includes specification of data formats for input/output, timing and synchronization, conditions for interaction (if any), etc., and is of particular importance in distributed heterogeneous environments [11].

3.5   Reusability

This is one of the most important issues related to components for ITSs. In order to achieve full reusability of such components, *generic*, context-free components should be developed first, and then they can be tuned to a particular application [4]. For example, if *lesson* is a generic component, the component *lesson with theorems* could be easily derived from it [3].

3.6   Specification of components

Components are defined by their functionality in the first place. For example, if we think of a certain *exercise* in a particular ITS, then its functionality (assessment of the student's knowledge of a specific topic) defines it as a component sufficiently enough to be easily differed from other kinds of components, like *lessons, topics, objectives,* etc.

However, components also have their properties, i.e. their *attributes* and their *functions*. For the *exercise* component, obvious attributes are its *difficulty*, its *result*, and its *prerequisites*. Its important functions are the possibilities to *show true result* (on request from the student or from the pedagogical module) and *show hint* (if available). Full specification of any such a component must include complete lists of its externally accessible attributes and its functions that can be used by other components in order to achieve the component's desired functionality.

3.7   Types of components

Types of components can be defined based on the types of their functionalities. The purpose of some components is to help assemble an ITS, regardless of the domain of knowledge that the students are supposed to learn from that ITS. These components are *system components*. They can be further divided into knowledge base components, student model components, and pedagogical components (see the next Section).

We can also think of components that have domain-dependent functionalities which are essential for building an ITS in a given domain, but can be useless for ITSs in other domains. Such components are *domain components* (e.g., *algebraic equation* component).

Finally, there are components whose primary purpose is to help communicate appropriate data and knowledge contents between ITSs and their users. They are called *interface components* (e.g., *chart* and *diagram* components).

4   Examples of components for ITSs

In order to illustrate the above considerations, this Subsection enumerates some software components for ITSs that we have identified as generic components in our GET-BITS model of ITSs (see [3]. The components are listed in Table 1. The lists of components are not exhaustive. They are created for specific parts (modules) of any ITS (knowledge base (expert module), student model, and pedagogical module). Note that we haven't considered components for ITS user interfaces yet. More in-depth treatment of some of the components from Table 1, as well as of their functionality, granularity, complexity, levels of abstraction, etc., can be found elsewhere (e.g., [3], [8]).

Table 1. Partial lists of software components for ITSs (by ITS modules) in the GET-BITS model

Knowledge base components	Student model components	Pedagogical components
Lesson	Motivation	Teaching strategy
Topic	Concentration	Teaching operator
Exercise	Capacity	Teaching planner
Explanation	Misconception	Path selector
Question	Performance	Model of task difficulty
Example	Current knowledge	Hint generator

5   How to put components together?

In order to make possible to assemble an ITS from them, components must have functions that support the integration of the other (sub)components. There are two basic types of such functions:
1. functions providing means for data exchange between components;
2. functions providing means for aggregation of components.
In order to be able to specify such functions for any particular component, two kinds of considerations are necessary: architectural and communication aspects.

5.1   Architecture

This is still an open question. Although significant amount of work has been done on software architectures for component-based systems in general (e.g., [11]), this kind of work in the context of ITSs has just begun (some examples can be found in [2], and [10]).

In our own work, we have come to the conclusion that in order to provide efficient means of building component-based ITSs, *layered* software architectures are needed. Examples of such architectures can be found in [3] and [9]. Layers are sets of classes on the same level of abstraction. One extension of the concept of layered software architecture, particularly relevant for our work, is the orthogonal architecture [9]. In the orthogonal architecture, classes (objects) are organized into layers and threads. Threads consist of classes implementing the same functionality, related to each other by the using relationship.

The architecture adopted in our GET-BITS model of ITSs has several modifications of the original orthogonal architecture, made in order to adapt it for development of component-based ITSs [3]. The most important one is that unlike the original orthogonal architecture, threads do not necessarily start from the same class, and they also do not end at the same set of classes. Threads are "vertical", in the sense that their classes belong to different layers. Layers are "horizontal", and there is no using relationship among the classes in the same layer. Hence modifications within a thread do not affect other threads. Layers and threads together form a grid. By the position of a class in the architecture, it is easy to understand what level of abstraction and what functionality it implements. Layers in our architecture are shown in Figure

1. The architecture itself is highly reusable, since it is shared by all programs in a certain domain which have the same layers, but may have different threads.

Layer	Objective	Semantics
Layer 1	Integration	Multiple agents or systems
Layer 2	System	Single agent or system
Layer 3	Blocks	System building blocks
Layer 4	Units	Units of primitives
Layer 5	Primitives	Parts of units

Fig. 1. Layers in the architecture of component-based ITSs adopted in the GET-BITS model

5.2   Communication - How do these components communicate?

The idea of having a component-based ITS implies that its components will be developed independently, in (possibly) different languages, on (possibly) different machines, and using (most probably) different software development tools. Yet we have to put them all together, to make them communicate not only among themselves, but also with possibly quite different applications (like traditional databases, for example). If this is to be provided efficiently, some standards must be conformed to. Fortunately, such standards exist already. They specify standard interfaces for transparent object (component) communication, both on a single machine and in heterogeneous distributed environments. The most widely accepted standard in this regard to date is the CORBA standard developed by the Object Management Group (OMG) [11]. In the area of ITS, one of the first successful implementation in this sense has been the recently developed architecture for intelligent collaborative educational systems, proposed by Suthers and Jones [10].

6   Discussion

Two important facts come from the above Sections:
* specification of components for ITSs must be preceded by an agreement on a common vocabulary in the domain;
* components must be organized around certain taxonomy.

These facts bring us to the important question on the relation between components and ontologies. In our view, there is a significant commonality between these two concepts, although they are not the same. Questions that must be answered precisely are:

1. What is the correspondence between components and ontologies?
2. Can ontologies be components and vice versa?

As for the first question, both components and ontologies require common vocabulary and a certain organizational structure. On the other hand, ontologies are conceptually more abstract, in the sense that they define abstract concepts and relations between them in a problem domain, such as ITS. Components are more "down on Earth" things, being real software implementations of concepts and their functionalities at a certain level of abstraction and at a certain place in the overall software architecture. Ontologies are, in a sense, a basis for component development, since it is ontologies that define a certain conceptual relationship between components, i.e. the kind of relations and communication between software components (see also [10]).

The second question, in our opinion, requires more elaboration. As for now, it looks more or less obvious that components can be *parts* of ontologies. Ontologies are formalized structures (e.g., hierarchies and grids), and usually nodes or intersections of such structures represent concepts that can have more or less precisely defined functionalities in terms of the vocabulary of the problem domain. It is also possible to develop a component that fully corresponds to certain ontology. For example, in the Eon system [7], there are "ontology objects". They are data objects, each of which defines a conceptual vocabulary for a part of the system. Topic Ontology objects are concrete examples of ontology objects for which a corresponding software components can be developed. We also envision development of other software components corresponding to certain ontologies as a whole. It should be also noted that our experience shows that at a certain level of abstraction components need not necessarily fully correspond to ontologies or parts of ontologies. There are components shared by different domains and different ontologies.

7   Conclusions

Software components for ITS design, in the software engineering sense of the term, have started to attract increasing attention among the researchers in the field. Component-based design of ITSs can bring a number of benefits do the developers, including enhanced reusability, ease of development, modifications, and maintenance, enhanced interoperability, and further practical support for knowledge sharing (together with ontologies). There is a large degree of correspondence between components and ontologies, and both require agreement on the vocabulary of the domain of ITS, the work that is always underway by several researchers and research groups.

As the development of components for ITS design has begun only recently, further research efforts are needed in order to get the full spectrum of benefits from component-based ITSs. Recent efforts have managed to bring some results regarding the architectures for component-based ITSs and initial taxonomies of such components. These results, however, only touch some of the basic infrastructure, interoperability, and reusability issues. There are several remaining open questions that need to be investigated further. One of the most important is the question of the contents of components. If we agree upon these contents, we will be able to answer questions like: "Can a lesson containing such-and-such topics be a component?" (this question, put during an informal discussion among AIED researchers, has remained unanswered and has shown that consensus is very hard to reach). Another interesting open question concerns the relationship between software components and ontologies, which still needs to be precisely defined.

8   Acknowledgement

The authors would like to thank all the participants to the discussion on the topic of software components, held during the AIED'97 conference in Kobe. Many of their thoughts and expressions have been very useful and have helped shape up the ideas presented in the paper.

References

1. Adler, R.M.: Emerging Standards for Component Software. IEEE Computer, March (1995) 68-76
2. Brusilovsky, P., Ritter, S., Schwarz, E.: Distributed Intelligent Tutoring on the Web. In: du Boulay, B., Mizoguchi, R. (eds.): Artificial Intelligence in Education", IOS Press, Amsterdam / OHM Ohmsha, Tokyo (1997) 482-489
3. Devedzic, V., Jerinic, Lj.: Knowledge Representation for Intelligent Tutoring Systems: The GET-BITS Model. In: du Boulay, B., Mizoguchi, R. (eds.): Artificial Intelligence in Education. IOS Press, Amsterdam (1997) 63-70
4. Ikeda, M., Kazuhisa, S., Mizoguchi, R.: Task Ontology Makes It Easier To Use Authoring Tools. Proc. of The 15th IJCAI, Nagoya, Japan (1997) 453-460
5. Munroe, A., Pizzini, Q., Towne, D., Wogulis, J., Coller, L.: Authoring Procedural Training by Direct Manipulation. USC working paper WP94-3 (1994)
6. Murray, T.: Toward a conceptual vocabulary for intelligent tutoring systems. Working paper available at http://www.cs.umass.edu/~tmurray/papers.html (1996)
7. Murray, T.: Authoring Knowledge Based Tutors: Tools for Content, Instructional Strategy, Student Model, and Interface Design. Submitted to the Journal of the Learning Sciences, http:// www.cs.umass.edu/~tmurray/ (1997)
8. Radovic, D., Devedzic, V., Jerinic, L.: Component-Based Student Modeling. Proc. the Workshop on Current Trends and Applications of Artificial Intelligence in Education, Mexico City, Mexico (1998) 73-82
9. Rajlich, V., Silva, J.H.: Evolution and Reuse of Orthogonal Architecture. IEEE Tr. on Software Engineering 22 (1996) 153-157
10. Suthers, D., Jones, D.: An Architecture for Intelligent Collaborative Educational Systems. In: du Boulay, B., Mizoguchi, R. (eds.): Artificial Intelligence in Education", IOS Press, Amsterdam / OHM Ohmsha, Tokyo (1997) 55-62
11. Vinoski, S.: CORBA: Integrating Diverse Applications Within Distributed Heterogeneous Environments. IEEE Comm. Mag. 14 (1997) 28-40

An Intelligent Tutoring System for Teaching Formal Languages

Vladan Devedzic [1] and John Debenham [2]

[1] Department of Information Systems, FON - School of Business Administration
University of Belgrade, POB 770, Jove Ilica 154,
11000 Belgrade, Yugoslavia
Email: devedzic@galeb.etf.bg.ac.yu
[2] Key Centre for Advanced Computing Sciences
University of Technology, Sydney, PO Box 123
Broadway, NSW 2007, Australia
Email: debenham@socs.uts.edu.au

Abstract. The paper describes design of the FLUTE system, an intelligent tutoring system in the domain of formal languages and automata. The basic idea of the FLUTE system is a systematic introduction of students into the system's domain, in accordance with both the logical structure of the domain and individual background knowledge and learning capabilities of each student. Other intelligent tutoring systems in that domain are not described in the open literature. The knowledge in the FLUTE system is represented using a recently developed object-oriented model of intelligent tutoring systems, called GET-BITS. A brief overview of the model is also included. The contents that should be presented to the student during tutoring sessions are discussed and logical organization of such contents within the system is described. The system implementation is based on a number of design patterns and class libraries developed in order to support building of intelligent systems. The system is analyzed in the paper from the pedagogical point of view. Every concept that a student has to learn during a session with FLUTE, the system illustrates by a number of examples. This makes the tutoring process more dynamic and facilitates learning.

1   Introduction

A major problem for many students of computer science in adopting and mastering the material taught in the courses of formal languages and automata is a large number of abstract, complex, specific, and seemingly very similar concepts they have to learn. This leads to potential monotony and difficulties in capturing the essence and diversity of the concepts when the material is presented in the traditional way.

In order to make learning formal languages and automata more attractive for students and make the abstract material more concrete, development of an intelligent tutoring system (ITS) called *FLUTE* (**F**ormal **L**anguages and a**UT**omata **E**ducation) has been started. The system design is based on the *GET-BITS* model of ITS (**GE**neric **T**ools for **B**uilding **ITS**) [4].

This paper presents the design of the FLUTE system and analyzes the system's functionality from the pedagogical point of view. Section 2 defines the problem more precisely, and Section 3 briefly overviews the GET-BITS model. In Section 4 the architecture of the FLUTE system is described and it is shown how different parts of knowledge are effectively represented and built in the knowledge base. Sections 5 through 7 present the analysis of the FLUTE system, showing its advantages and limitations.

2   Problem Statement

It is an ultimate goal of any ITS to make the learning process in the corresponding domain most effective. Careful selection of the contents, kinds and structure of knowledge, information and data to be built into the ITS is of an extreme importance in achieving that goal. In that sense, this paper describes:

1. the overall architecture of the FLUTE system from the knowledge and data organization perspective;
2. the structure of domain knowledge built in the system; all the important contents the student has to learn are specified, as well as possible paths he can take in learning;
3. how the domain knowledge is related to the necessary pedagogical knowledge and the student models;
4. how the GET-BITS model is used in designing the system from the software engineering perspective; and
5. the role of numerous examples in illustrating each topic;

3   Previous Work

Other similar ITS in the domain of formal languages and automata are not reported in the open literature. However, design of several other successful ITS in different domains of computer science, e.g. [8], [10], as well as of some other ITS from related areas [2], [9], has helped in designing the FLUTE system. In formulating the domain knowledge that should be built into the FLUTE system several textbooks on formal languages and automata, such as [7] or [12], were consulted. The structures of some relevant university courses and the experience of several human instructors teaching formal languages at the university level were also considered. Since one of the project ideas was that the FLUTE system should be practically oriented, i.e. to represent knowledge that can be practically applied, literature on compilers and compiler writing [5] has been used too.

The ITS models used in these systems, as well as the corresponding knowledge models, differ only to an extent. However, the design methodologies employed vary a lot, and sometimes even remain blurred for the sake of the system functionality alone. On the other hand, using a shell for developing an ITS brings more systematic design, but can also become a limiting factor if the shell doesn't support a certain knowledge representation technique or design strategy that may be needed in a particular system.

In order to eliminate the shortcomings of these two approaches, the GET-BITS model of ITS has been used in designing the FLUTE system. GET-BITS is an object-oriented domain-independent model of ITS [4]. It is based on a number of design patterns [6] and class hierarchies that have been discovered for ITS teaching and learning processes. In support of the patterns, appropriate C++ class libraries have been developed. The class hierarchies start from the universal, abstract, and unifying concept of *knowledge element* [4]. It reflects the possibility of representing all data, information and knowledge in an intelligent system in a unified way [3]. Many meaningful subclasses that are needed for building a wide range of ITS are derived directly or indirectly from the knowledge element class (concepts like lessons, questions, tasks, answers, rules, plans, assessments, exercises, etc.). However, classes for knowledge representation are not the only tools needed to build an object-oriented ITS. Apart from knowledge of various kinds, in each such ITS there must also exist some control objects that functionally connect the system's modules, handle messages, control each session with the system, monitor student's reactions, etc. In other words, such objects provide control and handle dynamics of ITS. GET-BITS also specifies classes of these control objects.

4   Architecture of the FLUTE System

The architecture of the FLUTE system is shown in Figure 1. Note that the figure only stresses the details relevant for this paper, i.e. the *nature* and *kinds* of knowledge and data in the system. It doesn't show explicitly the active components of the modules (things like planners, inference mechanisms, example generators, exercise generators, etc.) and submodules of the individual modules. Student administration module, also omitted from Figure 1, maintains a database of students (users of the FLUTE system), records the current status of their knowledge and progress, handles student registration, and can be accessed directly through the user interface module.

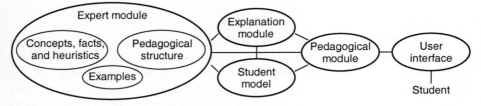

Fig. 1. Architecture of the FLUTE system

4.1   Expert Module

It is obvious from Figure 1 that there are three distinct parts in the model of domain knowledge used in the FLUTE system. The first part contains all of the concepts, topics, facts and domain heuristics the student has to learn. A meaningful subset of such items can be logically organized as a *lesson*. Items in a lesson are closely coupled but they can refer to items in other lessons. Some important attributes of each lesson are sets of objectives and goals, sets of topics, concepts, facts, theorems, etc. taught in that lesson, a set of the corresponding teaching rules, and a set of associated problems (tests, questions and exercises). An example is shown in Table 1 and Figure 2.

A major difficulty in mastering the basics of formal languages and automata is the domain's inherent abstractness. The best way to overcome it is to use a number of examples to illustrate all the concepts, principles and theory of the domain. Hence an essential component of domain knowledge is a database of *examples* (see Figure 1), which are systematically associated with every topic, concept, etc. that a student has to learn during a session. Presenting examples to the student is under the control of the system's pedagogical module. This makes the tutoring process more dynamic and facilitates learning.

It should be noted in Figure 1 that the pedagogical structure of the domain is considered a part of the domain knowledge rather than a part of the pedagogical module. This makes possible to separate all of the domain-dependent knowledge, stored within the expert module, from the other kinds of knowledge (i.e., from domain-independent pedagogical and explanation strategies and student model). Pedagogical structure of the domain is defined in FLUTE as a set of directed graphs showing explicitly precedence relationships of knowledge units within each lesson and among the topics of different lessons.

Table 1. Hierarchy of items in a lesson

Level	Item	Example
1	Lesson	Derivation trees
2	Objective;	Redundancy of grammars;
	Goal	Obtaining reduced grammar
3	Topic	Redundant grammar
4	Concept;	Inactive (dead) symbol;
	Fact;	Redundant grammar contains unnecessary nonterm.symbols
	Theorem	Pumping lemma

Such a *dependency graph*, defining the entire domain of the FLUTE system, is shown in Figure 3. It defines subjects of learning and possible learning paths in the domain. Wherever there is a fork on the path the learning process can go either way. Wherever there is a join of two paths, the learning process cannot be continued unless the student has proved to master the knowledge along both paths (this is checked by the pedagogical module and is recorded in the student model). There are four *knowledge levels*: preliminaries, basic level, senior level, and advanced level. They must be passed in strict sequence. One of the parameters of the student model is the knowledge level, reflecting the student's background knowledge. The student is periodically and automatically tested by the pedagogical module to prove his knowledge level.

Rule D98:	If a context-free grammar is reduced,
	Then it contains no inactive symbols.
Problem P112:	Find a reduced grammar that is
	equivalent to the context-free grammar ~E123
Example E123:	G = ({S,A,B,C}, {a,b,c}, S, F), F = {...}

Fig. 2. A rule, a problem, and an example grammar

A set of lessons is associated with every subject in Figure 3. For example, the subject of context-free grammars (CFG) is taught in the following set of lessons: derivation trees, normal forms, linear CFG, regular expressions and special types of CFG. Lessons of such a set are also treated as nodes of a dependency graph, hence precedence relationships for teaching lessons related to a subject are specified explicitly.

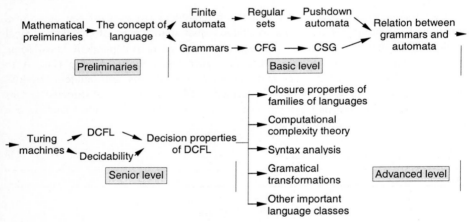

Fig. 3. Pedagogical structure of the domain (CFG - Context-Free Grammars; CSG - Context-Sensitive Grammars; DCFL - Deterministic Context-Free Languages)

4.2   Student Model

Student model in FLUTE is an object of a class derived from the GET-BITS *StudentModel* class. Its attributes are designed to reflect:

- the state of the student's *current knowledge* (a combination of one of the four knowledge levels and one or more "points" on a path (paths) on that level);
- the student's *current progress* in learning a particular lesson ("point(s)" in the lesson's dependency graph);

- *timing* and *frequency* of trying various exercises and asking for hints, explanations, and help;
- the student's *performance* in answering the system's questions and solving problems (grades and timing, as well as the ratio of correct and incorrect answers); an important part of it is a degree of remembering "old" lessons (answers to questions from the lessons learned during previous sessions);
- the student's *learning behavior* (frequencies of following correct/incorrect paths in learning a topic or a concept);
- measures of how continuously and how frequently the student learns from the system;
- measures of the student's initiative in working with the system (e.g., how many times the student has tried the restricted option of including a new example in the knowledge base).

The values of the attributes are calculated from applying a set of rules and simple functions from the pedagogical module to a set of parameters that the system acquires and updates automatically during each session. Some of the parameters are indicated in parentheses in the above descriptions of the attributes. The student model is saved after each session and is used in the beginning of the next session. A new student (having a session with FLUTE for the first time) is given a set of exercises and tests before the tutoring process starts, in order to estimate his background knowledge and determine initial values of the attributes of the student model.

The student model is updated and maintained by the system. Only the users with special privileges (human instructors) can modify the student model themselves.

4.3   Pedagogical Module

FLUTE always operates in one of the following three modes of operation: teaching, examination, and consulting. It is actually the pedagogical module that operates in one of these three modes.

When operating in the *teaching mode*, the pedagogical module presents a lesson to the student. In the beginning of presentation, a dedicated rule-based planner (called the *lesson presentation planner*) develops an initial plan of teaching actions. The plan is based on the contents of the lesson being presented, the relevant dependency graphs and the student model. The plan actually represents a detailed outline of the lesson presentation. The strategy of Raymond and Pilon [11] is used for guiding the plan generation: each objective of the lesson being presented is decomposed into a number of *transparencies*, each one of them roughly corresponding to one concept, fact, or theorem. Each transparency is set up of several *pedagogical points*, covering the item contained in that transparency. Starting from the initial plan, the lesson presentation planner generates sub-plans for presenting the lesson's objectives, topics, concepts, etc. Interaction with the student in teaching mode is provided through a set of buttons and dialog boxes. Depending on the student's reactions, the student model is regularly updated (attributes like current progress, learning behavior, average speed of mastering lessons, etc.) and the sub-plans and possibly the entire lesson presentation plan can be changed if necessary.

In the *examination mode*, FLUTE's pedagogical module can generate problems and exercises for the student, offer hints and suggestions for problem solving, and conduct a more complex assessment of his knowledge through a systematic series of tests and examinations. After each examination session, no matter how complex it was, the pedagogical module updates the relevant attributes of the student model (grades, answering speed, current progress, etc.) and generates a plan of remedial actions and presents it to the student in the form of suggestions for further sessions and learning. All of the questions, problems, and exercises are designed as parts of the corresponding examples in the database of examples in the expert module. The pedagogical module differs between illustrative examples (used mostly in teaching and consulting modes) and test examples, and can store and retrieve past exams and tests on student's request.

The *consulting mode* is the one in which FLUTE answers the student's questions, explains domain concepts and heuristics, repeats required parts of any lesson corresponding to the student's current knowledge (as recorded in the student model), refines problem solutions, provides hints for further learning, etc. In this mode, the pedagogical module frequently transfers its control to the explanation module. The consulting mode is entered strictly on request. The pedagogical module can alter the values of some attributes of the student model in this mode as well, but the timing functions are turned off. The student's initiative is considered most relevant in this mode and is calculated by dedicated functions. Under the control of a human instructor, the student can extend the example database by a new example. Although there is no automatic recognition of the type, quality and relevance of the newly included example, this is a very useful way of extending the system's knowledge during the sessions themselves.

The core of knowledge built in the pedagogical module are the following sets of rules:
- lesson presentation rules (rules of the lesson presentation planner)
- remedial rules (rules of the remedial actions planner)
- diagnostic rules (for evaluating the student's knowledge and understanding of topics, concepts, etc.)
- student model rules (for updating the student model)
- didactic rules (defining the presentation's "look-and-feel" (pointing, highlighting, underlining,...))
- control rules (a kind of meta rules for the overall control of the pedagogical module operation)

Figure 4 shows an example of a diagnostic rule (PD8) and of a control rule (PC6):

Rule PD8:   If test-score > 55 then set passed-test.
Rule PC6:   If passed-test then calculate grade.

Fig. 4. Examples of pedagogical rules

5   Assumptions and Constraints

FLUTE is designed as a single-user system, i.e. as an individual learning tool.

Once a student reaches a certain knowledge level and the system assigns him certain current knowledge and progress indicators, it is assumed that the students knows *everything* (i.e., he can apply every domain-dependent rule) before the corresponding point on the relevant dependency graphs. It depends on the pedagogical module to decide when and how to check the students current knowledge and whether to return him to a previous point or level if his performance is not satisfactory.

FLUTE is neither multimedia system nor a hypertext system, although in the analysis below it is compared to some multimedia and hypertext supported ITS.

Only the first two knowledge levels from Figure 3 are currently implemented (see [4] for implementation details), and the rules of the pedagogical and explanation modules are still subject to change. To develop the whole system is an extremely complex task, and it should be noted that several potentially useful add-ons (parsing and analysis of newly included examples, case-based reasoning, analogical reasoning, concept generalization,...) were omitted from the current design for the sake of reduced complexity.

6   Evaluation Criteria

Pedagogical aspects and design suitability are the most important criteria used in the next Section for analysis and evaluation of the FLUTE system in comparison with some other ITS. The other criteria used are design flexibility (modularity, reusability and portability), ease of use, and flexibility of the student model.

7   Analysis and Evaluation

FLUTE is not a replacement for human instructor. It is a tool that helps students in learning about formal languages and automata. It doesn't simply transfer all of the built in knowledge to the student - the idea is that it helps the student *gradually develop* his knowledge in that domain. The built-in knowledge is, of course, limited. Therefore selected knowledge items in the knowledge base (lessons, topics, concepts, and examples) contain pointers to some references which are shown to the student when the pedagogical module decides it could be helpful or when it exhausts the other teaching possibilities.

When FLUTE is compared to some other ITS that have been used as referent systems in designing it ([2], [8], [9], [10]), its advantages come from:

- the systematic object-oriented design, based on the GET-BITS model;
- its explicit, highly modular, and extremely flexible model of domain knowledge; it is open and easy for extensions, since several new inputs can be added to any

dependency graph; occasionally a new output from a graph can be generated (for example, another advanced topic can be added in the advanced level in Figure 3);
- its strong, knowledge-based lesson presentation and didactic components (the way and time it shows lesson outlines, objectives, transparencies, etc., always depends on the student's recent reactions and the student model);
- its knowledge-based and student-model-based deduction on the moments when the student must undergo exercises regarding both current lesson and past lessons;
- several different ways and levels of assessments of the student's knowledge (questions, exercises, tests, etc.);
- supporting timing functions in the examination and teaching modes, which is reflected in the student model;
- the way it switches between three different modes of operation, both on the user's request and automatically, when the pedagogical module decides it is necessary;
- its user-oriented, separate explanation module;
- the way it treats examples (the role of examples is stressed in all three modes of operation, which makes the learning process much easier and more attractive); and
- its more refined student model, allowing for more appropriate representation of student's knowledge and learning capabilities.

FLUTE's pedagogical module has been designed starting from the variants of the coach model, but with additional features described in Section 4.

Most apparent limitations and deficiencies of FLUTE's design w.r.t. the design of the other ITS mentioned above are the lack of hypertext support, the lack of histories of past lessons, learning, and assessments in the student model, and weak example classification.

8   Conclusions

Design of FLUTE, an intelligent tutoring system in the domain of formal languages and automata, is featured by an explicit, flexible and easily extensible model of domain knowledge, three modes of operation (teaching, examination, and consultation), highly refined student model, and an extensible database of examples that facilitate both learning and tutoring processes. Domain-dependent pedagogical knowledge is included in the expert module, rather than in the pedagogical module, and the explanation facility is separated from the pedagogical module and constitutes a separate module in the system's architecture. The main advantages of such design are improved lesson presentation and knowledge maintenance, as well as more explicit distinction between different pedagogical features. The design is based on GET-BITS, an object-oriented model of intelligent tutoring systems, and can be used for developing other intelligent tutoring systems as well.

There are several directions in future research and further development of the FLUTE system:
- development of appropriate techniques for knowledge simplification and maintenance, since the knowledge base in the expert module is upgraded time after time;

- development of an automatic classifier of the examples in the database; such a classifier should be based on both the domain knowledge and the pedagogical knowledge;
- development of a case-based generator of new problems for students, starting from the database of examples and incomplete input data.

References

1. Adler, R.M.: Emerging Standards for Component Software. IEEE Computer, March (1995), 68-76
2. Chee, Y.S., Xu, S.: SIPLeS: Supporting Intermediate Smalltalk Programming through Goal-based Learning Scenarios. In: du Boulay, B., Mizoguchi, R. (eds.): Artificial Intelligence in Education. IOS Press, Amsterdam (1997) 95-102
3. Debenham, J.K.: Unification of Knowledge Acquisition and Knowledge Representation. Proc. of The International Conference on Information Processing and Management of Uncertainty in Knowledge Based Systems, IPMU'96, Granada, Spain (1996) 897-902
4. Devedzic, V., Jerinic, Lj.: Knowledge Representation for Intelligent Tutoring Systems: The GET-BITS Model. In: du Boulay, B., Mizoguchi, R. (eds.): Artificial Intelligence in Education. IOS Press, Amsterdam (1997) 63-70
5. Fischer, C.N., LeBlanc, R.J.: Crafting a Compiler. Benjamin/Cummings Publishing Company, New York (1988)
6. Gamma, E., Helm, R., Johnson, R., Vlissides, J.: Design Patterns: Elements of Reusable Object-Oriented Software. Addison-Wesley, Reading, MA (1994)
7. Hopcroft, J.E., Ullman, J.D.: Introduction to Automata Theory, Languages and Computation. Addison-Wesley, Reading, MA (1979)
8. Johnson, W.L.: Understanding and Debugging Novice Programs. Artificial Intelligence 42 (1990) 51-97
9. Kong, H.P.: An Intelligent, Multimedia-Supported Instructional System. Expert Systems with Applications 7 (1994) 451-465
10. Matsuda, N., Kashihara, A., Hirashima, T., Toyoda, J.: An Instructional System for Behavior-Based Recursive Programming. In: du Boulay, B., Mizoguchi, R. (eds.): Artificial Intelligence in Education. IOS Press, Amsterdam (1997) 325-330
11. Raymond, J., Pilon, D.: Software Tools for Computer-Aided Lecturing. IEEE Transactions on Education 37 (1994) 23-30
12. Revesz, G.E.: Introduction to Formal Languages. McGraw-Hill, New York (1983)

Elaborating Models of Algebraic Expression-Writing

Mary A. Mark, Kenneth R. Koedinger, and William S. Hadley

School of Computer Science, Carnegie Mellon University, Pittsburgh, PA 15213
mary.mark@cs.cmu.edu, ken.koedinger@cs.cmu.edu, bh23@andrew.cmu.edu

Abstract. This paper discusses the refinement of the algebraic expression-writing rules for the PAT Algebra I tutor, between 1992 and 1997. Direct observation of students in class, step-by-step PAT tutor protocols tracing student behavior, and statistical analysis of protocol data, have all informed our understanding of students' skills, and our refinement of this part of PAT's production model.

1 Introduction

Since 1992, the Pittsburgh Advanced Cognitive Tutor Center has been developing an intelligent tutoring system for algebraic problem solving, the PAT Algebra I tutor. First used in one grade nine algebra classroom, the PAT Algebra I tutor is now used in about 40 schools. The tutor has been designed to complement the PUMP algebra curriculum used in grade nine algebra classes (cf. [3]). Both are designed to address math reform concerns of the National Council of Teachers of Mathematics [8]. They focus on the mathematical analysis of real world situations, and the use of multiple representations for problem-solving [6].

Much of the PAT development effort has focused on breadth, providing materials for a full curriculum year. The current tutor curriculum includes over 15 lessons of multiple sections, drawing on over 400 problem situations. The complete production model contains 56 production sets, and 623 production rules.

As reported elsewhere, the overall impact of PAT tutoring is positive [6], [7]. We have also examined specific aspects of PAT tutoring in some detail. This paper describes the development of the PAT production rules for expression-writing from 1992 to 1997. A brief description of the PAT tutor's interface and behavior places expression-writing in the context of other algebraic problem solving skills modeled in PAT. We then discuss development of the expression-writing model from our initial modeling as a single skill to our current characterization of expressions in terms of features of operators and arguments which cause students difficulty. These changes in the model are supported by formative analyses of students' expression-writing success. These analyses also provide evidence that students are learning to write expressions as they use the tutor. Finally, we suggest future directions for development.

2   The PAT Algebra I Tutor

Daily, people deal with situations that draw on algebraic and quantitative reasoning skills. Checking the amount of a paycheck, estimating the discount applied to an on-sale purchase, and choosing between long-distance telephone services, are three examples of real-world situations in which algebraic skills are useful. The PAT tutor tries to help people to learn and apply mathematical problem-solving skills in the context of such real-life situations. To solve a PAT problem, students read a textual description of a situation with related questions. They represent the situation using tables, graphs, and symbols as tools to answer questions. Multiple representations are a major focus of the tutor.

Figure 1 shows a partial solution for a problem involving a single linear equation, from Lesson 1 of the PAT Algebra I curriculum for the 1996-1997 school year. The lesson focuses on constructing a table by finding solutions to questions and writing an expression.

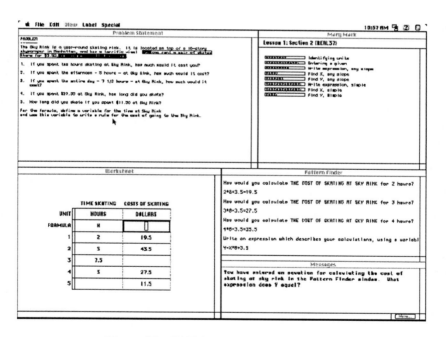

Fig. 1. The PAT Algebra I Tutor, Lesson 1

The top-left corner of the tutor screen shows a problem situation: the cost of skating at Sky Rink, based on a flat fee for renting skates, and a per-hour fee for the time spent at the rink. Students investigate this situation using tools such as a spreadsheet (the "Worksheet" window) and a tool for identifying algebraic expressions by elaborating patterns (the "Pattern Finder" window).

Students construct the Worksheet (lower-left of Figure 1) by identifying relevant quantities in the situation, labeling columns, entering appropriate units, writing an algebraic expression, and answering the questions in the problem description. The Pattern Finder window (center-right) can be used at any time. Students who have difficulty writing expressions are encouraged to examine progressions of concrete instances of arithmetic expressions, and look for underlying patterns indicating the form of the expression. The Pattern Finder design was informed by previous prototype research in which students who were encouraged to work out concrete instances prior to expression-writing performed better on expression-writing during training, and learned more from pre-test to post-test, than students in a control group who were encouraged to write the expression first and then answer concrete instances by evaluating the expression [5].

On average, students spend about twelve minutes solving such a problem. The tutor monitors their activities and provides feedback through *model tracing* (cf. [1]) to individualize instruction. With both correct and buggy rules, the tutor can often indicate what is wrong with the answer or suggest a better alternative.

Another way of individualizing instruction is to offer help on request. The tutor selects help messages by using the production system to identify a desirable next activity, based on the student's current focus of activity, the overall status of the student's solution, and internal knowledge of interdependencies between problem-solving activities. Multiple levels of help provide more detailed information for repeated requests. The "Messages" window in Figure 1 shows the result of a help request. The current focus of attention is the worksheet cell for the expression, selected under the column entry for 'costs of skating'. Based on information about the problem state, especially other tasks completed, the student is encouraged to relate the Pattern Finder solution to the desired worksheet expression: "You have entered an equation for calculating the cost of skating at Sky Rink in the Pattern Finder window. What expression does Y equal?" If the Pattern Finder had not been used, different help would be given, prompting the direct construction of an expression based on information from the problem statement e.g. "Read the problem statement to see how to calculate the cost of skating at Sky Rink. The expression for the cost of skating at Sky Rink depends on the number of hours skated." or, more explicitly, "To write an expression for the cost of skating at Sky Rink, enter 8 times the number of hours skated, plus 3.50. Use a variable to represent the number of hours skated."

PAT also monitor students' learning across problems, supporting learning through *knowledge tracing*. The Skillometer window displays the tutor's assessment of the student's acquisition of problem solving skills. The tutor can identify individual areas of difficulty and present problems targeting skills which are not mastered [2]. Self-paced advancement through sections and lessons of the curriculum is also accomplished through knowledge tracing.

For model tracing and knowledge tracing to be effective, the cognitive model must capture aspects of the problem that the student finds difficult, and differentiate these from aspects of the problem which the student finds easy. Otherwise, the tutor will be unable to focus remediation on those areas where the student needs work. The model must also differentiate easy from difficult skills to ensure that a student is not being advanced past areas of difficulty without detection. The cognitive model is the heart of the tutor: its ability to make such discriminations is essential.

3   Models of Expression-Writing

Writing algebraic expressions is an important and difficult skill for students. The ability to capture the complexities of a mathematical relationship and represent them in an elegant algebraic form is seen by teachers as an indicator of students' understanding of the specific situation and the underlying mathematical relationships. The ability to translate a quantitative problem situation into algebraic symbols is important for using real-world tools to solve real-world problems [5].

To experts, writing an algebraic expression like "8.0 ∗ x + 3.50" seemed a fairly obvious process: you read the problem statement, identified the changing quantity and rate of change in the problem, checked for an initial value, and put the appropriate numbers in the appropriate places in the formula. Novice students entered many unexpected answers. Through observations in class and examination of protocol data we examined what students were doing and tried to determine what they were and were not learning about expression-writing.

The data presented here was collected in the 1996-1997 school year, at Langley High School, Pittsburgh, PA. Langley is a typical urban school, mixing lower and middle class families. About 50 % of students are from single parent families, 60% come from families with sufficiently low incomes to qualify for the free reduced lunch program, and 50% are minority students. Student attendance is volatile, with high absenteeism (30%) and student mobility (20%).

Data collection occurred while developing and deploying the tutor in grade nine classes as part of the regular class schedule. The PAT tutor saved protocol files recording student actions and productions fired. The tutor curriculum was designed to meet classroom constraints for instructional time available and material to be covered. This client-centered approach meant that the curriculum was not ideally suited to testing some of our hypotheses about expression-writing.

We have chosen to present the 1996-1997 Lesson 1 data, as representative of the abilities of incoming grade nine students; and to discuss it in terms of cognitive models from present and previous years, to illustrate the expressiveness of the cognitive models developed from 1992 to 1997. Reanalyzing one data set rather than data from each year also excludes the possibility that different analyses reflect changes in the population, teacher, or tutor versions of different years, unrelated to changes in the expression-writing model.

1992-1994: In its first year the PAT tutor was used in selected classes for short periods of time. Development focused on introducing new tutor components and increasing curriculum coverage. Model tracing was used within sections, but knowledge tracing was not yet used. In the second year, we introduced knowledge tracing, and began to analyze student data and review our design. Development involved many target skills besides expression-writing, including numerical solution of result-unknowns and start-unknowns, quantity and unit identification, table building, graphing skills, equation solving, etc.

Initially, expression-writing was modeled as a single skill. Students were not very successful at writing expressions. They succeeded on their first attempts at writing expressions only 39% of the time, across all problems in Lesson 1. In comparison, when solving result-unknown questions, e.g. "If you skated at Sky Rink for two hours, how much would it cost you?", students were correct 71% of the time on their first attempt at answering the first result-unknown in a problem.

Furthermore, when treated as a unitary skill, student profiles and accuracy curves for groups of students showed that students did not succeed consistently in writing expressions. In the following student profile, "Student AB" succeeds in 11 of 21 first attempts at writing an expression. Zero values indicate failures; -1 indicates help requests; and positive values indicate the elapsed time to enter the correct answer measured in seconds. Successes and failures intermix apparently randomly, although more successes occur in the second half of the curve.

```
("Student AB" (IDENTIFY-EXPRESSION WORKSHEET-TUTOR-MODE)   11   21
    38.016    10.945     0.000    -1.000     0.000     0.000    10.337
    -1.000    11.189     0.000    11.172     0.000     0.000     0.000
    61.257     0.000    19.762     8.839    47.127    40.550    18.833)
```

1994-1995: Based on classroom and tutor protocols, we refined our model to categorize expressions based on their mathematical formula. Students were required to write an expression of the form MX+B, where M is the slope and B the y-intercept. Depending on the sign of the slope and intercept values, and whether the intercept was zero or non-zero, six different forms were identified: MX, MX+B, MX-B, -MX, -MX+B, and -MX-B. Forms involving negatives were rare and were reserved for later lessons involving graphing. Lesson 1 therefore focuses on the three most common variants: MX, MX+B, and MX-B.

Reanalysis of the student data suggests that rewriting production rules to capture differences between forms helps to more accurately identify students' strengths and weaknesses. The previous accuracy profile becomes far more comprehensible: "Student AB" demonstrates considerable success with MX forms, but succeeds only 50% of the time when writing expressions with positive non-zero intercepts (MX+B forms), and 25% of the time when dealing with negative intercepts (MX-B forms). The student succeeds more often in the second half of each curve, suggesting that learning may be occurring.

```
("Student AB" (FORM=MX IDENTIFY-EXPRESSION)      7   11
    10.945     0.000    10.337    -1.000    11.189     0.000
    11.172     0.000    47.127    40.550    18.833)
("Student AB" (FORM=MX+B IDENTIFY-EXPRESSION)     3    6
    38.016     0.000     0.000    61.257     0.000     8.839)
("Student AB" (FORM=MX-B IDENTIFY-EXPRESSION)     1    4
    -1.000     0.000     0.000    19.762)
```

A single factor ANOVA statistically tested the relationship of form to student success (Figure 2). Twenty-four problems from Lesson 1 were examined, not including a demonstration problem. Thirteen problems were of form MX, seven were MX+B, and four were MX-B. The success rate for writing the expression for each problem was defined as the percentage of students who correctly wrote an expression for that problem on their first attempt at doing so. From 16 to 63 students attempted each problem, averaging 42.375 students per problem.

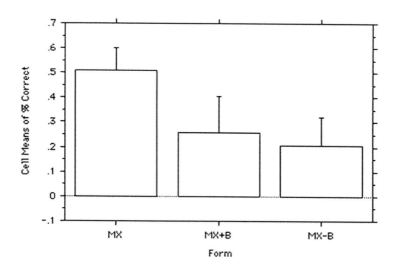

Fig. 2. Expression-Writing Success For Problems Categorized By Form

The mean success rate for MX problems was 50% ($sd = .149$); for MX+B, 25% ($sd = .159$); and for MX-B, 20% ($sd = .072$). Differences between forms were statistically significant ($F(2, 22) = 11.0, p < .0006$). Scheffe's S post-hoc comparisons indicated that MX problems were easier than MX+B ($p < .004$) and MX-B problems ($p < .005$). No significant difference was reported between MX+B and MX-B problems. Unfortunately, the data available for MX-B problems was limited, as only four MX-B problems were included in Lesson 1.

At the end of the 1994-1995 school year, the production model was refined to categorize expressions in these categories, and to use these production rules in knowledge-tracing when assigning new problems. Lessons and sections were reorganized to vary students' exposure to different forms. Buggy productions were added to identify cases where a student was omitting or mis-identifying the slope or intercept of the expression: e.g. "How many dollars do you start with when you calculate the cost of skating at Sky Rink?" Feedback was designed to prompt students to distinguish between these parts of the expression, for example, if the two numbers were reversed, "Which number should be the slope and which should be the intercept?" Incorrect entry of number signs was also diagnosed by buggy productions: e.g. "Does the height of a tree increase or decrease as the time that the tree has been growing increases?"

1995-1996: Organizing expressions by form did not completely explain why students found some problems harder than others. When we compared problems in terms of expression-writing difficulty, there were still anomalies which were easier or harder than expected. We looked for features of difficult and easy problems and characteristic student errors indicating possible areas of difficulty.

Features of expressions which seemed to give students difficulty included large numbers, decimals, and fractions. These aspects of expression-writing were reified as: (1) the size of the numbers involved, operationally defined as small (-100 ¡ x ¡ 100) and large (greater than or equal to +/-100) ; and (2) the type of the number involved, with integer values categorized as simple numbers and non-integers as difficult numbers. An expression was classified as difficult if it included difficult numbers; and as large if it included large numbers. The production model and the tutor curriculum were modified to incorporate these categories into productions and knowledge-tracing.

It was also difficult for students to write expressions in which numbers had to be transformed. Textual descriptions of numbers such as "8 and one-quarter", which could be written as either a decimal, "8.25"; or an expression, "8+1/4", caused many errors. Students had difficulty with unit conversions even for such presumably familiar conversions such as entering "1/4 of an hour" as a value in minutes. Students failed sometimes because they did not realize that a conversion was needed, but more often because they did not know how to make the transformation. Asked directly how many minutes were in an hour, a student might answer, "50? 100?" Buggy productions were implemented to model-trace failures in conversion and provide feedback: e.g. "You need to calculate the rate of change in the expression for 'the height of the river' in feet, not in inches. Divide by 12 to get an amount in feet. " However, because problems involving textual conversions were hard to identify a priori, given the representation of problems in the tutor, conversions were not modeled explicitly for knowledge-tracing. Conversion is a desirable area for future research.

A regression analysis of all possible learning events in Lesson 1 for the 1996-1997 year suggests that this further categorization of expression-writing skill is useful in predicting student success and failure. A regression model was performed in which correctness on the first attempt at writing the expression was the dependent variable. The problem position (the nth problem assigned to a student, n=1...20), the algebraic form of the problem (MX, MX+B, or MX-B), and the difficulty of the numbers involved (integer or decimal) were the independent variables. The model yielded statistically significant effects of each of these variables (R=.3168). The regression equation is as follows:

$$\%Correct = 43.7 + 0.9*POS - 28.0*FORM2 - 34.8*FORM3 - 16.0*DEC \quad (1)$$

where POS is the problem position (1-20); FORM2 is 1 if the problem is an MX+B problem and 0 otherwise; FORM3 is 1 if the problem is an MX-B problem and 0 otherwise; and DEC is 1 if the problem has any decimal arguments and 0 if they are all integers. A possible learning event was defined as a student's first attempt at writing an expression for a problem. At each possible learning event, a student could succeed or fail in writing the expression. The three effects can be described as follows (see Figure 3):

Expression form effect: ($p < .0001$) MX problems are easiest (M $=$ 44%), MX+B are harder by 28% (M $=$ 16%), MX-B are slightly harder by 35% (M $=$ 9%).

Number type effect: ($p < .0003$) Problems with integer arguments are easier (M $=$ 31%) and problems with decimal arguments are 16% harder (M $=$ 15%).

Learning effect: ($p < .03$) On average students are getting about 1% better on each expression writing experience. For example, as predicted by the model, students are about 44.6% correct on their first MX integer problem, but 61.7% correct by their twentieth MX integer problem. On the MX+B decimal problems, students start at 0.6% on the first problem and reach 17.7% by the twentieth problem.

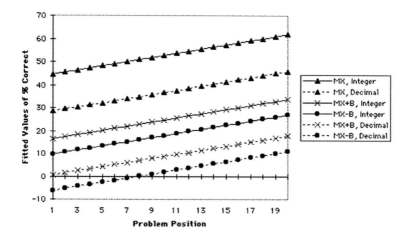

Fig. 3. Fitted Regression Analysis of Learning Events, by Form and Integer Difficulty

Interestingly, even though previous analysis did not show significant differences between MX+B and MX-B forms, defining the form in terms of MX, MX+B, and MX-B proved to be a stronger predictor of success in the regression than defining form in two categories, MX and MX+-B (not shown). This suggests that sign is important in determining the difficulty of the form, as well as the presence or absence of a non-zero intercept. The number of problems with negative numbers in the curriculum should be increased to more effectively test this hypothesis. The second strongest indicator of student success on specific problems was number type. Integers were easier to deal with than non-integer numbers. Again, this supported our hypothesis.

The other possible predictor of problem difficulty which we examined was number size. We did not find a significant effect of number size in the regression. Unfortunately, Lesson 1 included very few problems with large numbers, limiting our ability to examine this. Our original categorization may be either inadequate or inappropriate. One possibility is that "large" numbers like 2067959 are harder for students, while "large" numbers involving patterns or repeating digits, like 8000, are not much harder than "small" numbers like 80. Examination of the "large" problems in the 1996-1997 data set suggested this possibility, but better problem selection is needed to assess this properly.

The regression shows a small increase (approximately 1%) in the probability that students will get the nth+1 problem correct on their first attempt, compared to the nth problem. While this is evidence that students are learning as they work through the lesson, students are obviously still having a lot of trouble writing algebraic expressions for word problems after finishing this first lesson. One explanation for students' difficulties is that these are disadvantaged urban students, with extremely poor background knowledge and skills. Incoming grade nine students at Langley scored near chance on an Iowa Algebra readiness test. Students are also exposed to many new skills at once in the first lesson: they have more opportunities to learn these skills as they work through the curriculum.

The regression analysis has potential implications for curriculum redesign. Assigning short sequences of problems with few remedial problems may mean that students don't get enough exposure to master expression-writing. Presenting one type of problem at a time may lead to acquisition of superficial "rules" which do not generalize well [5], such as "pick the first number you see and multiply it by x". Mixing types of problems in longer sequences may better support learning.

Since students are substantially better at generating numerical answers for these problems (71%) than at writing abstract expressions (39%), students clearly are not using the expression to generate the result-unknown answer (cf. [5], [4]). Further investigation of students' understanding of and ability to generate symbolic representations is highly desirable. At least when the quantities and relationships involved are fairly simple, students may understand the relationships in the problem situation, but not be able to generate symbolic representations of them. Deeper understanding of the relationships between skills, and the strategies that students use to solve problems, are also desirable, and may facilitate the development of tools to support the acquisition of more difficult skills by relating them to existing student knowledge.

4   Conclusions

Since 1992, we have been refining the PAT Algebra productions to more closely model students learning. Expression-writing skills have been a rich focus of development. Students must identify relevant operators, quantities, and units as they read the problem situation, and generate a symbolic representation expressing the relationships involved in algebraic notation. In addition to determining whether a correct expression is entered, the tutor can now identify answers involving the presence, absence, and possible reversal of the slope and intercept values; the reversal of number signs, the use of incorrect operators, and failures to convert quantities involving units of measurement. In addition to its model-tracing capabilities, the tutor assigns remedial problems based on features of the expression such as the form of the equation and whether or not the numbers involved are integers or fractions and decimals. Data analysis indicates that these aspects of problem complexity are predictors of expression-writing difficulty and student success. The hypothesis that number size would relate to expression-writing difficulty was poorly tested and should be reexamined.

When form and number type are factored out in a regression analysis, evidence remains that students are learning to write expressions as they use the tutor, although the rate at which they learn is slow. It is important to place this result in context by remembering that expression-writing is one of many skills targeted by the PAT Tutor. Although the effect of Lesson 1 on students' acquisition of expression writing skills is modest, large overall effects of PAT's multiple lessons across a whole array of skills are heartening [6]; [7].

References

1. Anderson, J.R., Boyle, C.F., Corbett, A.T., Lewis, M.W.: Cognitive modeling and intelligent tutoring. Artificial Intelligence, 42 (1990), 7-49.
2. Corbett, A.T., Anderson, J.R., Carver, V.H. and Brancolini, S.A.: Individual differences and predictive validity in student modeling. In A. Ram & K. Eiselt (eds.) The Proceedings of the Sixteenth Annual Conference of the Cognitive Science Society. Hillsdale, NJ: Lawrence Erlbaum (1994)
3. Hadley, W.S.: CMU PACT Center Mathematics Curriculum, 1997-1998. Pittsburgh, PA: PACT Center, Carnegie Mellon University (1997)
4. Heffernan, N. T., Koedinger, K. R.: The composition effect in symbolizing: The role of symbol production vs. text comprehension, Proceedings of the Nineteenth Annual Meeting of the Cognitive Science Society . Mahwah, NJ: Erlbaum (1997)
5. Koedinger, K. R., Anderson, J. R.: Illustrating principled design: The early evolution of a cognitive tutor for algebra symbolization. To appear in Interactive Learning Environments.
6. Koedinger, K. R., Anderson, J.R., Hadley, W.H., Mark, M. A.: Intelligent tutoring goes to school in the big city. International Journal of Artificial Intelligence in Education, 8 (1997), 30-43
7. Koedinger, K. R. Sueker, E.L.F.: PAT goes to college: Evaluating a cognitive tutor for developmental mathematics. In Proceedings of the Second International Conference on the Learning Sciences, Charlottesville, VA: Association for the Advancement of Computing in Education (1996)
8. National Council of Teachers of Mathematics: Curriculum and Evaluation Standards for School Mathematics. Reston, VA: The Council (1989)

AVATAR: An Intelligent Air Traffic Control Simulator and Trainer

Catherine Ann Connolly,[1] 1Lt Jay Johnson[2] and MSgt Chuck Lexa[2]

[1] Galaxy Scientific Corporation
7334 Blanco Rd., Suite 206
San Antonio, TX 78216
(210) 979-9161
cconnolly@galaxyscientific.com

[2] USAF Research Laboratory
7909 Lindburg Dr.
Brooks AFB, TX 78235-5352
(210) 536-2034

Abstract. A continuum of simulation-based training systems currently exists and can be distinguished not only by their level of fidelity or graphical realism, but also by their level of intelligence. Intelligence in this case, is considered to be the ability of a system to diagnose and provide adaptive instruction and remediation. In this paper we discuss an intelligent air traffic control simulator and trainer called the Advanced Virtual Adaptive Tutor for Air Traffic Control Readiness (AVATAR). Unlike most of today's simulations, AVATAR is based upon theoretically grounded instructional strategies and uses intelligent technologies that enable the system to diagnose, instruct, and remediate students based upon their performance while providing dynamically interactive simulation. A discussion of instructional deficiencies within current training simulations is presented as well as information about the instructional strategies and intelligent technologies used within AVATAR to overcome those shortcomings.

1 Introduction

As technology in the field of computers has advanced, so has the ability to generate relatively low cost, high fidelity simulations for training. Simulations offer a unique training environment that has the benefit of allowing students to perform a task without fear of harming the real world equipment or themselves (Shute & Psotka, 1996). These systems also offer the possibility of an instructor to divide a complex task into smaller, simplistic components (part-tasks). In addition, simulations provide an environment where team members can learn to collaborate. The benefits of using simulators for training are numerous and a relative explosion in the development and use of them has occurred over the last decade.

Reasons for the increased use of simulations is due in part to the advances made in computational power and the use of object-oriented architectures. Previous computers were both cost-prohibitive and severely limited in their ability to mimic the complex interactions of real world systems. Today, however, computers are more cost-effective and have the increased power to simulate complex systems. Early simulation development efforts were aimed at harnessing this newfound power in computers. Most of the development effort focused on providing high fidelity environments in which the student(s) could practice a particular skill or task often under varying conditions. A real tradeoff was made between the use of computational power for instruction and providing high-fidelity simulation. Fidelity can be generally defined as the degree of similarity between the simulated and operational environments (Hays & Singer, 1989). Despite the simplicity of its definition, fidelity is a very complex variable and constitutes both physical and functional similarities between real world and simulated environments.

Unfortunately much of these early efforts to develop high-fidelity simulations have gone largely without reward. A meta-analysis by Hays, Jacobs, Prince and Salas (1992) of flight training simulator effectiveness studies revealed that positive training outcomes may be realized using simulators that do not have a high physical resemblance to the operational aircraft. Moreover, the authors found that the effectiveness of the simulator appears to vary according to the training method used. It is still more unfortunate that the focus of simulation development disregards these findings and continues to emphasize and promote high fidelity as the main goal in the system. It is disconcerting to assess the relative direction that these systems are currently taking. While advances in other computing areas such as graphic art and distribution via the world-wide web is being embraced by the simulation community, advances in other areas such as adaptive remediation and instruction in intelligent tutoring systems, have been largely ignored.

Another common problem with current simulation systems is that they are generally hard-coded. In other words, the systems are programmed to look and perform in a specific manner. Any changes to the real world system would need to be incorporated into the simulation at an enormous cost. What is needed is an ability to modify the simulated environment in a cost effective and time-efficient manner.

We believe that the focus of development efforts should be on incorporating intelligent technologies into these simulators rather than emphasizing the relative fidelity of the systems. Likewise, we would like to see training simulations, much like computer-based training (CBT) systems, evaluated and categorized along a continuum based on their inherent features including those capabilities that make a system intelligent. Although this list is by no means comprehensive, some of the capabilities that we feel are most important and are severely lacking in most of today's training simulators include:

- Dynamic and interactive simulation based upon student's responses.
- Environments that allow real world collaboration among team members.
- Ability of the instructor to intervene and interact with the student.
- Ability to monitor, track, and diagnose the student's performance.

- Ability to provide adaptive instruction.
- Ability to provide adaptive remediation.
- Ability to cost-effectively generate new environments (Authorability).

This paper presents the newly developed Advanced Virtual Adaptive Tutor for Air Traffic Control Readiness (AVATAR). AVATAR, seen in Figure 1, represents an initial step toward the integration of intelligent technologies into training simulators. This training simulator unlike many of its contemporaries provides high-quality and dynamic simulation as well as the ability to diagnose student errors, provide adaptive instruction and remediation as well as author new environments. This paper presents the instructional strategies and intelligent features of the AVATAR simulator that attempt to overcome some of the deficiencies of contemporary systems listed above. The goal of this paper is to demonstrate how instructional strategies and ITS technologies can be implemented into simulation systems effectively.

2   Overview of AVATAR

Intelligent technologies coupled with theoretically grounded instructional strategies provide the backbone of AVATAR. This adaptive training simulator teaches air traffic control students control tower procedures and operations, ground and local coordination, and phraseology. This system, unlike most of the current simulations where the instructional strategy and any form of diagnosis and remediation is left to the instructor on hand, is based upon a classification scheme of error recognition which defines types and criticality of errors.

As students dynamically interact with the simulation, the system monitors and diagnoses their verbal (commands to the pilots) and console panel performance (selection of appropriate frequencies). The diagnosis of errors is handled much like a buggy library approach (Brown and Burton, 1978). However, AVATAR is somewhat unique in that it allows students to commit some types of errors without receiving immediate remediation. This ability is handled in part, by the error classification scheme mentioned above. Once an error has been diagnosed by the system, adaptive instruction and remediation in the form of an auditory or visual message is presented to the student. The instructions and remediation presented depend upon type of error and criteria preset by the instructor and within the system. This feature allows the student to gain insight from their own errors and develop critical reasoning skills to predict future errors on their own. If the student however, continues to commit the same error, remediation will appear once the criteria threshold set by the instructor has been reached. AVATAR is also designed so that the instructor has the ability to over-ride the system and provide immediate instruction and remediation as deemed necessary.

AVATAR acts much like a coached practice environment by combining apprenticeship training with intelligent instruction. Shute and Psotka (1996) outlined the benefits of these types of environments as providing greater learner initiative through hands-on learning, experientially anchored knowledge, and coaching within an applicable context. We also believe that by providing the flexibility to change both the criteria and the scenario in real-time provides even greater power as an instructional tool.

Fig. 1. Screen display of AVATAR.

2.1 Dynamic & Adaptive 3D Simulation

AVATAR utilizes a script to initially drive each training scenario. Each script is generated by an air traffic control (ATC) subject matter expert. The difficulty of the script can vary from basic control tower operations to complex airport activity. The scripts define the type of approach or takeoff each aircraft will accomplish and what time it should start in the scenario. It's then up to the characteristics of the aircraft to complete its task given by the script. There are expected responses to accomplish a particular task such as an aircraft doing a downwind approach landing. Beyond these responses, the student controller can dynamically alter the aircraft's path to accomplish the proper spacing by using commands to do things such as extend the path on downwind or to fly in a circle.

The student interacts with the scenario utilizing a speaker-independent voice recognition software package. This system does not require any voice recognition training and has shown an initial recognition accuracy rate of about ninety-eight percent. Using this voice recognition system allows the student to use and practice the standard air traffic control phraseology used in the real world. The phrase the student gives is validated by the system to ensure it's a correct phrase. It is then translated into a command and sent to the intelligent tutor where it is verified for content such as proper hold areas, runways and taxiways. If an error is made, verbal remediation is given to the student indicating which type of error occurred. Each error is recorded by the system according to the student identification for later debriefing by the instructor.

In addition to the voice recognition, new students are provided with cue cards displayed on the screen below the simulation with the exact phrase to be said. As the student progresses and becomes more proficient, the instructor has the capability to turn these cue cards off. When the cue cards are turned off, the student will still receive the verbal remediation. If the same mistake is made two times, the cue card is turned back on for that phrase. This capability allows students to become accustomed to the environment, taste the success of learning the proper phraseology before having to generate it themselves. In addition, by providing the verbal cues the cognitive workload is shifted from the verbal phraseology demands and allows the ATC to focus on other critical tasks such as monitoring the airspace and ground movements.

The instructor also has the capability to dynamically alter many items in the airport environment as well as some aspects of aircraft in the scenario. These include the ability to alter the wind speed, wind direction, turn the remediation and instructional cue cards on and off, and alter the altimeter. If a student is progressing well and the scenario is getting too easy, the instructor can increase the complexity by introducing the next aircraft in the script file into the scenario prior to its scheduled time. In contrast, if the student is having difficulty, the instructor can remove aircraft from the scenario. We believe that this ability to adapt the instruction based on their individual differences in ability prior and during the simulation provides incredible flexibility for both the instructor and the student.

2.2 System Authoring Capabilities

AVATAR was developed in part by using the Virtual Interactive Intelligent Tutoring System Development Shell (VIVIDS). VIVIDS is an authoring tool used by instructional developers and subject matter experts to produce and maintain simulation-based adaptive training systems that are delivered via virtual environments. The purpose of the software is to allow for the combining of virtual and two-dimensional worlds with adaptive instruction. This advanced technology benefits users by:

- Providing the capability to produce automated simulation-based training on personal computers.
- Reducing the risk of physical harm to trainees while they learn to perform tests in hazardous environments.
- Reducing training costs.
- Increasing efficiency of trainee time by reducing the number of students waiting to practice on expensive simulators or other training devices.
- Increasing portability of training.
- Helping maintain student flow during downsizing.
- Reducing the costs of maintaining and updating automated training systems.

In addition to this initial development cycle, VIVIDS will allow ATC subject matter experts and/or instructors the ability to rapidly develop simple to complex scenarios. These scenarios are the foundation for the instructional lessons. The clean course developer/instructor interface eliminates the need to "hard code" the scenarios and allows the instruction to be developed by completing a series of point and click procedures. Once the scenario / lesson has been generated, it is saved as a file so that it can be quickly modified to specific training needs.   Figure 2 illustrates the instructor's interface that enables them to monitor and change the scenario 'on the fly' while the student is performing the task in AVATAR.

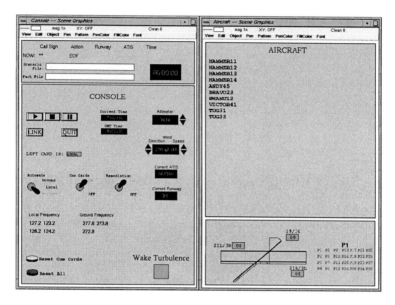

Fig. 2. Instructor Interface during AVATAR simulation.

2.3 Intelligent Instructional Model

As mentioned earlier, the system has the ability to provide monitor, track and provide adaptive remediation and instruction based upon the student's performance and the instructional objectives. The system has been developed such that at any given moment during a scenario, information about the location, direction, classification of aircraft including speed, weight, and landing/departing requirements (e.g. runway length required for departure) are not only tracked, such as in a buggy library, but are actually forecasted. That is, the information that the system gathers moment to moment is compared to the rules set forth by the ATC environment. The system then uses this moment to moment simulation-based information to predict all possible correct actions/information that the student might supply. Unlike some domains for which ITS have been developed, there are specific rules within the ATC environment that are procedurally correct or incorrect. Whenever the student supplies commands that are in conflict with the system's predicted list of correct actions, the system analyzes whether this conflict results in a critical error (e.g. planes would crash) or a non-critical error. Critical errors are immediately instructed and remediated in the form of a verbal error message. For example, the system will indicate to the student that runway 21 is currently in use and not available for landing. If the student does not provide the correct runway landing information after getting this error message, adaptive remediation will appear in the form of a visual cue card on the screen indicating what the appropriate runway instructions should be. If the error is analyzed to be non-critical then the system can provide remediation immediately or tallies it and provides remediation once the instructor's criteria threshold has been met. Again, the instructor has the ability to set the criteria level for the number of various categories of errors.

In order to develop the system's ability to monitor, track, and remediate the student and their performance, a classification scheme had to be developed. This error classification scheme was developed based upon many factors including a cognitive task analysis, the current standards used for rating performance within the static and simulation laboratories at the training school located at Keesler AFB, as well as gathering information and input from the subject matter experts themselves.

Five types of errors were derived from the assessment; coordination, procedural, phraseology, communication and other. Future versions of AVATAR will also include a time delay error in which the student will be monitored and instructed if they took more time than necessary to supply the correct information. The goal of the classification scheme was two-fold; to provide the system with the ability to effectively diagnose and remediate the student based on the type and criticality of the error and to provide an instructionally useful archive following the student's performance on each scenario. This performance archive, called a "Debrief," in keeping with the AVATAR environment, is an automated tracking tool that can be used by the instructor to rate the student's performance as well as use it to remediate the student face-to-face on the number and types of errors that they had made. This performance archive will also enable the instructor to monitor the students' learning curves across the course.

2.4 Collaborative and Integrated Team Training Solution

In a real world control tower, there are several people interacting with each other to accomplish the task of controlling the aircraft on the ground and in the surrounding air space. The local control position has authority over all active runways and all aircraft in the air. The ground control position has control of all aircraft on the taxiways around the airport and must move these aircraft to and from runways for takeoffs, landings and parking. The third position, the flight data position, interacts with the local controller and passes information to base operations and to off-site radar controllers. AVATAR provides training for the local and ground control positions mimicking the real world environment. Although specific training is not available in the current system for the data flight position, a person manning this position has the ability to verbally interact with the local and ground controller. The ability of the data flight position to interact with either the local or ground controller is consistent with real world ATC environments.

The students must interact with the system as well as interact with each other to ensure aircraft safety and completion of the aircraft's mission. If the student doesn't react to a required response, the system will wait a certain period of time depending on what is happening, and it will then prompt the student to take action. The system also provides the capability for the instructor to turn off remediation to allow AVATAR to be used as a testing tool. This will also prevent the cue cards from appearing if the student makes the same mistake twice.

2.5 AVATAR Platform

AVATAR consists of several integrated components. The rendering of the images is performed using a Silicon Graphics (SGI) Octane or Onyx Infinite Reality. The voice recognition and the instructor's panel are run on an SGI Indy. The instructor's panel was developed using VIVIDS, an ITS shell developed by Behavioral Technology Laboratories at the University of Southern California under sponsorship of the U. S. Air Force Research Laboratory. The software for the voice recognition is based on Hark software, allowing two students to be controlled by one computer. The student console contains switches and lights for training frequency management and precision approaches. There is also a PC at the student console that will display airport environment information as well as a radar screen (DBRITE) showing location of aircraft in a 20-mile area.

3   Field Implementation and Evaluation

The system was initially developed to test the implementation of specific instructional strategies and capabilities derived from the VIVIDS authoring tool and those founded in the Training Research and Automated Instruction (TRAIN) laboratory. Once the proof of concept was successful, emphasis was placed on developing a transitional software application that could not only provide the basis for a virtual reality testbed, but also fulfill the training deficiencies of an Air Force training unit. For over a year, the Mission Critical Skills Division has been in direct contact and cooperation with the 81st Training Wing, Keesler AFB MS. The 81st TRW is responsible for the Air Force's initial air traffic control training.

AVATAR will be implemented into selected 81st TRW courses on March 2, 1998. The effectiveness of the tutor and its instructional strategies will be evaluated and efforts will continue to complete a product specifically designed to replace the current training method. The overall goal will be to train with a consistency that surpasses today's standards.

4   Conclusion

This paper has described why simulations have and will continue to become increasingly useful for training. We have also begun to identify some deficiencies that current training simulators lack in order to be used as a more effective instructional tool. AVATAR was presented as an example of how instructional design principles and strategies, as well as intelligent technologies can be incorporated into a training simulator successfully. We would like to propose that the future evaluation of training simulators be based more upon their use of these capabilities rather than by their ability to mimic real world systems. It is our hope that the efforts such as those undertaken with the AVATAR project to incorporate intelligent capabilities in the form of adaptive instruction and remediation will continue. Just as we have seen a progression over the years for CBT in terms of their intelligence, we would like to see this progression occur in the area of training simulators.

Acknowledgements

Funding for AVATAR was supported by the Advanced Training Technology Branch of the Air Force Research Laboratory located at Brooks AFB Texas. We are indebted to the AVATAR development team for their excellent work including; TSgt Sean Mitchem, SSgt John Iler, SrA Dave Acton, SrA Alex Applegate, SrA Shawn Pomeroy, and A1C Ed Abshire. In addition, we would like to thank Dr. Wes Regian the Branch Senior Scientist, Mr. Jim Fleming AVATAR's Program Manager, and MSgt James Kurth , SSgt Dan Smith, SrA Michael Nemeth, SrA James Marvin for their technical assistance. Lastly, we would like to express our appreciation to the U.S. Air Force Air Education and Training Command, 334 Training Squadron at Keesler AFB MS, and the people there that contributed to this project including Bob Davis, TSgt Watson, Capt Kevin Melton, CMSgt Wright, Lt Col Payne and Lt Col Strange. The opinions expressed are those of the authors and do not reflect the policy of any government agency.

References

Brown, J. S., & Burton, R. R. (1975). Multiple representation of knowledge for tutorial reasoning. In D. G. Bobrow and A. Collins (Eds.), Representation and understanding (pp 311-349). New York: Academic Press.

Hays, R. T., Jacobs, J. W., Prince, C. and Salas, E. (1992). Flight simulator training effectiveness: A Meta-Analysis. Military Psychology, 4(2), 63-74.

Hays, R. T., & Singer, M. J. (1989). Simulation fidelity in training system design: Bridging the gap between reality and training. New York, NY: Springer-Verlag.

Shute, V. J., and Psotka, J. (1996). Intelligent Tutoring Systems: Past, Present and Future. In D. Jonassen (Ed.), Handbook of Research on Education Communication in Technology: A

Project of the Association for Education Communication. New York, NY: MacMillan, 570-600.

Towne, D. M., & Munro, A. (1992). Two approaches to simulation composition for training. In M. J. Farr & J. Psotka (Eds.), Intelligent instruction by computer: Theory and practice (pp. 105-125). Washington, DC: Taylor and Francis.

VIVIDS   0.1   Release   Notes.   Support   for   Virtual   Environments. Http://btl.usc.edu/VIVIDS/vivRelNote01.htm.

Weaver, J. L., Bowers, C. A., Salas, E., Cannon-Bowers, J. A. (1995). Networked simulations: New Paradigms for team performance research. Behavior Research Methods, Instruments & Computers, 27 (1), 12-24.

An Advanced Embedded Training System (AETS) for Tactical Team Training

W. Zachary[1], J. Cannon-Bowers[2], J. Burns[3], P. Bilazarian[4], and D. Krecker[4]

[1]CHI Systems, Inc., 716 N. Bethlehem Pike, Suite 300, Lower Gwynedd, PA
wayne_zachary@chiinc.com; http://www.chiinc.com
[2]Naval Air Warfare Center-Training Systems Division, Orlando, FL
janis_cannon-bowers@ntsc.navy.mil; http://www.ntsc.navy.mil
[3]Sonalysts, Inc., Orlando, FL
burns@sonalysts.com; http://www.sonalysts.com
[4]Lockheed Martin Advanced Technology Laboratories, Camden, N.J.
{pbilazar, dkrecker} @atl.lmco.com; http://www.atl.lmco.com

Abstract. The Advanced Embedded Training System (AETS) applies intelligent tutoring systems technology to improve tactical training quality and reduce manpower needs in simulation-based shipboard team training. AETS provides layers of performance assessment, cognitive diagnosis, and instructor-support on top of the existing embedded mission simulation capability. Detailed cognitive models of trainee task performance are used to drive the assessment, diagnosis and instructional functions of the system.

1 Introduction and System Rationale

The development of automated instruction has proceeded through several stages, beginning with simple computer-aided instruction (CAI) systems in the late 1950s which provided strictly didactic material in rigid instructional sequences. Dominant themes in the last two decades have been the emphasis on providing dynamic environments for applying and practicing problem-solving knowledge (problem-based learning), focusing diagnosis on the underlying knowledge state of the student rather than observed behavior alone (student modeling and cognitive diagnosis), and adapting the instruction to the student's evolving knowledge state (adaptive tutoring). The dominant paradigm recently has been "cognitive apprenticeship"([1]), in which the computer acts as an adaptive coach to the student (the apprentice) who works through a series of problem-solving exercises. Current intelligent tutoring systems (ITS) mainly fall into this category.

All of these research-oriented ITS were built in problem domains which share several features. The domains involved little indeterminacy (cases in which multiple knowledge paths can lead to the same action), the relevant knowledge was comparatively closed and could be represented by relatively few rules, and the problem-solving activities were individually-based (rather than team-based) and involved non real-time problems that could be easily stopped and restarted. Unfortunately, tactical domains possess none of these features. There is great indeterminacy, the problems and required knowledge are complex and open, the problem solving is team-based, and the problem environment is fast-paced. Perhaps because of these reasons, classical intelligent tutoring systems technology has been slow to emerge into the tactical world.

A major attempt to solve these problems, however, has been made in the Advanced Embedded Training System (AETS), a Navy Science & Technology Advanced Technology Demonstration project to apply ITS technology to shipboard team training (see [2]). [1] AETS used the concepts of intelligent tutoring-problem-based learning, cognitive diagnosis, student modeling, and focused, adaptive tutoring-but found that new technologies had to be developed to deal with the indeterminacy, open knowledge spaces, team problem solving, and real-time nature of tactical domains. This paper overviews AETS architecture and operation, with focus on these new technologies.

1.1   The Task Domain

The Navy's Aegis command and control system has an embedded simulation mode, in which a mission simulation is 'worked' using the actual tactical workstations on the ship. When a tactical team currently receives team training via embedded simulation, however, all performance measurement, diagnosis, feedback, and instruction is performed by human instructors, often in a labor-intensive manner (up to one instructor per student), and with a great deal of inconsistency across instructors and ships. The AETS was undertaken to improve this process by using ITS technology to make simulation-based team training less instructor-intensive, more thorough, and more consistent, by supporting, but not removing human instructors.

AETS focuses on the Air Defense Team (ADT), one of several (albeit one of the most important) teams functioning in an Aegis ship's Combat Information Center. The job of the ADT is to protect own-ship and other assets (e.g., an aircraft carrier) from air attack. This job can be very difficult under conditions of low-intensity conflict, such as the Persian Gulf, where the skies are filled with commercial aircraft, industrial aircraft (e.g., helicopters moving to/from oil drilling platforms), and military aircraft from multiple countries, many of which are hostile to one another and to US forces, and where the threat of terrorist attack is also omnipresent. The activities of the ADT revolve around representations of airborne objects (i.e., fixed-wing aircraft, rotorcraft, or missiles) in the space around the ship. These objects are generically called 'tracks', and are displayed as icons on a geographical display at each person's workstation. The major source of track data is the powerful radar on-board the Aegis ship, but there are other sources, including radars on surveillance aircraft, other shipboard sensors (e.g., one detecting electronic emissions from a track); sensors on other ships, ground forces, and other intelligence sources. A track may be known from just one or from multiple data types. In some cases, different data sources may create different tracks that, in 'ground truth', represent the same object.

[1] This work was performed under contracts N00014-96-C-0051, N61339-97-C-0405, and N61339-96-C-0055. The views expressed are those of the authors and do not reflect the official positions of the organizations with which they are affiliated or of the sponsors. The authors wish to acknowledge the support and contributions of RADM George Huchting and Susan Chipman, and the many members of the project team.

At the same time, single tracks can represent multiple objects, such as close flying aircraft. The air defense team as a whole is responsible for:

- disambiguating and interpreting information about each air track;
- determining if a track represents a potential threat to own-ship or a defended asset;
- taking a variety of actions to neutralize or minimize any potential threat.

The space of actions that can be taken is large. The ADT may, for example, send verbal warnings calling for a track to change course. In some cases, the team may direct friendly aircraft to try to get visual identification on a track, to challenge the track, to escort it away from the own-ship, or, in some cases, launch a missile to attack and destroy the track. Internally, team members will verbally pass information they have inferred or received to other members of the team; these internal messages are important in correlating data across sources and helping the team share a common mental model of the airspace.

2   AETS Architecture

The architecture of the AETS was designed to fulfill four main goals:
1. automate the capture and analysis of data on trainee problem-solving;
2. conduct automated, intelligent performance assessment and diagnosis of those data;
3. provide on-line instruction and feedback based on assessment and diagnosis; and
4. support a reduced human training staff in providing improved post-exercise debriefs.

Figure 1 depicts the overall functional architecture of the AETS. The center row of the figure highlights four generic components that work in parallel. Three fully automated components supplement and support a fourth interactive component (far right) that allows a human instructor to record observations and initiate feedback. The instructor receives information from the automated components, makes notes on his direct observations, and communicates with trainees using a hand-held device known as ShipMATE (Shipboard Mobile Aid to Training and Evaluation).

The primary interactions with the team being trained are shown at the four corners of Figure 1. A training session begins with a pre-exercise briefing on the training scenario. After the briefing, the existing simulation capability of the Aegis-class ship plays out the scenario on the team's workstation consoles. The team's responses are observed both by the automated system and by the instructor. During the scenario, real-time automated and instructor-initiated feedback is sent to the trainees. Shortly after the end of the scenario, the instructor uses ShipMATE to present a post-exercise debriefing, using automatically generated reports and his own computer-assisted performance assessment.

The automated data capture component observes and aggregates the actions of each trainee in multiple modalities. It captures all keystroke sequences and aggregates them automatically into higher level functional interactions with the workstation. In parallel, the system records all trainee speech communications, recognizing and analyzing them into semantic components that define the source, destination, message type, and objects and relationships mentioned. Also, in parallel, each trainee's eyes are tracked, and the eye-movement data are analyzed to assess what the trainee viewed, when, and for how long. The output of the automated data capture component is three streams of observed high level actions (HLAs) for each trainee. The combination of keystroke, speech, and eye HLAs provides a coherent record of what the trainee is doing during the exercise.

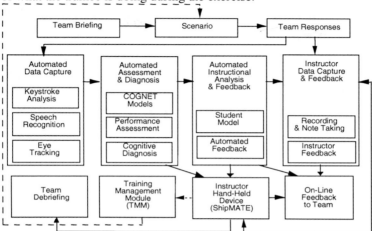

Fig. 1. AETS Functional Architecture

The automated assessment and diagnosis component dynamically compares this picture of <u>what</u> the trainee is doing with a model-based specification of what the trainee <u>should be</u> doing. An executable cognitive model of each trainee position passively observes the information provided to the trainee and identifies HLAs that an experienced operator would be expected to take at that point in the exercise. The model also identifies the knowledge and skill elements needed to generate the expected behavior and training objectives associated with the expected HLAs. Performance assessment and cognitive diagnosis are two stages of automated analysis of the trainee's behavior. Performance assessment compares observed HLAs of the trainee to expected HLAs generated by the model to determine if the recommended behavior occurred. Results are summarized by the calculation of overall numeric and qualitative scores. Cognitive diagnosis relates performance assessment results to knowledge and skill elements identified by the cognitive model and makes inferences to determine what knowledge and skills are (and are not) demonstrated in the observed behavior.

The automated instructional analysis and feedback component has two interrelated functions. First, it maintains a dynamic student model for each trainee. The student model records inferences about the trainee's mastery of training objectives, as evidenced by automated performance assessment results. The second function is the generation of real-time automated feedback. Feedback is triggered by automated performance assessment results and involves first selecting an instructional opportunity and then selecting a feedback template. Instructional selection depends on the qualitative result of a current performance comparison, how recently the trainee received feedback on the associated training objective, and the priority of the training objective. The structure and modality of the feedback depend on a feedback template, which is selected according to the training objective involved and its mastery by the trainee. Feedback, which is provided through a limited display window and/or highlighting of console display elements, is judiciously limited to avoid intrusion onto task performance. This component also provides the instructor with operator performance summaries for use in debriefing.

Instructor data capture and feedback is an interactive software component supporting the instructor and running on a hand-held computer called ShipMATE. ShipMATE provides a medium for the automated components to communicate information to the instructor, who can decide how (and if) to use it. ShipMATE also allows the instructor to save voice comments and digital ink notes about trainee performance and to generate real-time feedback and post-exercise debriefs. ShipMATE facilitates instructor-generated feedback to trainees through a database of feedback templates that the instructor can call up and transmit. For post-exercise debriefing, ShipMATE constructs a variety of reports from automated performance, diagnosis, and instructional information and allows the instructor to select, organize, and present or replay captured information.

2.1   Cognitive Modeling

AETS depends on embedded cognitive models of each of the trainees. These models must generate, dynamically and in real time, expert-level solutions to the simulated missions being worked by the team being trained. Creating such models proved in itself a major challenge. The models were developed using the COGNET representation [3]. This framework was highly appropriate to the need, having been designed specifically for modeling and analysis of real-time, multi-tasking domains. Moreover, partial COGNET models of the ADT already existed [4], along with a software system to execute the models as needed within AETS.

Figure 2 shows the architecture of the COGNET model of each team member. There are three separate processes organized into two levels of processing, the 'reasoning kernel', which simulates the cognitive processes, and the 'shell' which simulates the perceptual and motor processes, and manages the sensory and motor interactions with the external environment. The perceptual process, which internalizes sensed information, is instantiated as a set of spontaneous-computation (i.e., self-activating) rules that capture the relevant perceptual knowledge about how to internalize sense information and relate it to the evolving mental model of the situation. These rules are fired as relevant perceptual cues are received from the environment. In parallel, a cognitive process activates and executes complex chunks of procedural knowledge (called cognitive tasks). These tasks are activated according to the current context provided, as defined by an internal model of the external situation. This internal model, expressed as declarative knowledge, is represented as a multi-panel blackboard structure and is stored in an extended working memory. Each panel is subdivided into levels, or categories, on which hypotheses (representing individual knowledge elements) are dynamically posted and unposted (as the situation changes). The cognitive tasks are activated in a context sensitive manner, based on the current blackboard contents. Often, tasks must compete for the attention, as one context (pattern of blackboard information) can cause multiple cognitive tasks to be activated. As the cognitive tasks execute, the simulated operator develops and executes plans for solving the problem and/or pieces of his ADT role. The cognitive tasks may also change the blackboard (e.g. make inferences), as well as activate specific action processes (typically speaking and/or workstation actions). These processes generate specific operator acts in the external world, through the (also parallel) operation of the motor processing system. The cognitive tasks are represented as GOMS-like goal hierarchies with a formally defined operator set.

In AETS, the embedded cognitive models need to generate diagnostically useful predictions of trainee actions at both behavioral and cognitive levels. This predictive use of the models required adaptation of the models, in two ways. First, their action space had to be abstracted. As discussed above, the predicted behaviors had to be defined at an abstract level, above that of simple keystrokes; these abstracted behaviors are the HLAs discussed above. These abstract HLAs were not a natural product of either the modeling effort or the cognitive task analysis on which the models were based. Instead, they required a separate effort to define them conceptually, and to embed them into the model structure.

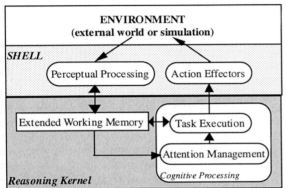

Fig. 2. Executable COGNET model processing structure

A second adaptation was required to allow a cognitive diagnosis of the trainee in cases where the trainee's behavior diverged from the recommended path. The models were augmented to create a trace of the knowledge elements involved in producing each behavior expected of the trainee, beginning with the relevant perceptual stimuli. The main problem in creating this knowledge trace was computational. Each perceptual stimulus received by the model could lead to an unknown number of possible future behaviors; the cognitive architecture was modified to build and maintain each of these possible threads in real-time, and in a way that provided a valid trace of the cognitive processes involved. To solve this problem, multiple possible means of recording and tracing the reasoning threads were developed, and assessed both for theoretical reasonableness (in human information processing terms) and computational efficiency.

Because these cognitive models had to be able to perform complex tactical tasks at an expert level, they are relatively complex. The model of the team coordinator, called the Anti-Air Warfare Coordinator or AAWC, for example, includes more than 25 cognitive tasks, with more than 500 lower level goals and subgoals, and several thousand instances of individual cognitive or action operators. Its 'mental model' includes 15 blackboard panels, with more than 90 individual levels and more than 500 hypotheses active on this blackboard at a typical moment. Its perceptual system includes more then 100 perceptual rules, and its action system more then 300 domain-specific action types. In addition, to simplify the complex action space, a total of 65 HLAs were defined. Of these, three were eye-movement actions, 24 were keystroke/workstation-based actions, and the remainder were speech actions.

2.2   Performance Assessment

The AETS conducts automated performance assessment both at the action level and at the event level. This section describes some of the challenges and solutions involved.

At the action level, the AETS compares observed actions taken by a trainee with expected actions generated by a cognitive model. A meaningful and efficient comparison depends on a common taxonomy of observed and expected actions. The granularity cannot be too fine, or the actions would lack independent significance. Nor can it be too coarse, or data capture would miss important actions. The AETS solution defines a list of high-level action (HLA) types with specific attributes that vary from one instance to another. Keystroke HLAs define keystroke sequences that accomplish meaningful functions, speech HLAs correspond to entire message communications, and eye HLAs represent dwells on certain parts of the console. In each case, the HLA type defines the basic action, while variable attributes hold specific information entered, spoken, or seen.

There are a variety of challenges in the recognition and evaluation of HLAs. While keystrokes can be definitively captured, current technology does not support foolproof speech recognition or eye tracking. Consequently, a confidence measure is associated with observed speech actions so that low confidence recognition can be discounted in evaluation. Similarly, some eye HLAs relate to small regions of the console rather than to the precise data displayed there. Evaluation difficulties arise from the multiplicity of ways in which HLA attributes may be set (or left unset). Matches between observed and expected actions are scored based on a classification of attributes into key and non-key categories. The overall positive/negative evaluation depends on how key attributes match. Non-key attributes only affect a finer gradation of scoring.

The AETS supports an Event-Based Approach to Training (EBAT) by collecting and evaluating sets of expected actions related to critical scenario events. For complex scenarios in which many different events simultaneously demand the trainee's attention, a central difficulty for EBAT is distinguishing which actions relate to which events. The AETS solution selects from the scenario a number of instructionally critical events and specifies for each one a time window for responses and a response identifier (or condition). Following the occurrence of a critical scenario event, the AETS collects all the model-generated expected actions that fall within the time window and match the response identifier (typically a track number). When the time window expires, a composite evaluation aggregates the trainee scores over the collection of expected actions.

2.3   Cognitive Diagnosis: Recognition-Activated Model Assessment

Classical ITSs typically work in relatively deterministic knowledge spaces, and so are able to diagnose cognitive state at a very fine grain by processing each observable low-level action. AETS, in contrast, had to work in an indeterminate space. While the COGNET models generate the high level actions that the trainee needs to perform, there are typically many reasoning sequences for generating each of those actions from low-level knowledge elements in them. To solve this problem, the RAMA algorithm was developed. RAMA (Recognition-Activated Model Assessment) does not try to perform cognitive diagnosis continuously, but only periodically, when the behavioral assessment component recognizes that the trainee either has or has not taken some recommended HLA. This recognition activates a bayesian inference process [5] that assesses all the knowledge that could have been used to generate the current recognized event from the likely knowledge state of the last recognized event. RAMA works on the knowledge traces produced by COGNET, (see above), and operates as follows:

from any given point in the problem-solving process where an operator action has been recognized to have been taken (or not taken):

- Process the cognitive model forward to (the next expected) High Level Action (HLA); note the trace of the knowledge states used along the way and call it the current knowledge trace;
- Wait for the performance monitoring system to observe the HLA or conclude that trainee did not perform it;
- If HLA was taken correctly, update the system's belief that trainee understands and has used correctly the intermediate knowledge states in the current knowledge trace;
- If HLA was not taken correctly, update the system's belief that one or more of the intermediate knowledge states in the current knowledge trace was not understood or used correctly by the trainee.

Through this periodic bayesian processing approach, RAMA is able to build, over time, a coherent model of the trainee's state of acquisition of each element of knowledge in the COGNET model.

2.4   Feedback, Instruction, and Team Training Support

The AETS mixes both individual feedback/instruction and team training, and uses both automated and human delivery methods. The interface to the AETS is provided through two elements, a Training Management Module (TMM) and the Shipboard Mobile Aid for Training and Evaluation (ShipMATE). Viewing the scenario as the "curriculum", the TMM (currently under development) is being designed to support semi-automated training materials preparation. When complete, the TMM will allow an instructor to review team performance profiles (based on historical data) in order to define training objectives. Once this has been done, the instructor will be presented with candidate events that support the training objectives and they can then place their scenario anywhere in the world. Once the context has been established, the TMM will populate the scenario with the selected events complete with requisite contextual information and with linkages to performance measurement systems.

Providing a tool such as the TMM enables automated individual feedback/instruction that is delivered at the trainee's workstation using objective-based templates that are dynamically tailored to the specific context. Therefore, the automated performance measurement and diagnosis elements of the AETS receive much of the TMM measurement specifications. In order to integrate the instructor into the AETS, ShipMATE is used to take advantage of their expertise and observational skills. This portable PC is "networked" with the AETS and allows a mobile instructor to observe and collect data on multiple trainees at the same time. ShipMATE also provides tools for the instructor to formulate and deliver training to the trainer, either verbally or through the trainee's workstation and it supports allocation of complex measurement tasks to the most sophisticated component of the

AETS-the human. For example, team process assessment and diagnosis requires application of a measurement scheme that relies on human observation of team communications-ShipMATE hosts this tool.

Following the exercise, instructors will use ShipMATE to prepare individual and team level feedback. ShipMATE enables this by allowing for rapid review and reduction of instructor-based and automated measurement system data. ShipMATE is also designed to support presentation of debrief materials both for individuals and for the team.   Through the dynamic link to the automated components of AETS, performance measurement data collected and reduced by instructors can be fed back to the TMM to update performance records in anticipation of subsequent training evolutions.

3   Implementation Status of AETS

AETS is being implemented and evaluated in three phases. Phase one, completed in 1997, developed the system's communication and computing infrastructure and integrated an initial system prototype for only two watchstanders, using a mix of real and placeholder components.   The automated data capture component and the instructor data capture component were fully functional in this initial prototype, while the automated assessment and diagnosis was only partially implemented, with no active cognitive diagnosis. The automated instructional analysis and feedback system was represented only by a placeholder component. Phase two expanded the system to include fully functional prototypes of all components of the architecture, and a team of four watchstanders. The integration of the Phase two AETS, still in a laboratory context, is followed by an initial assessment of the effectiveness of the system, at the time of the writing of this paper. Phase three will, in calendar 1999, upgrade and expand all components of the Phase two system and demonstrate the system's ability to communicate with operational equipment.

4   Conclusions

Although it is too early to assess the operational value, there are already several clear implications and lessons learned from this large and ambitious project:

Hybrid approaches work. There is no 'pure' ITS architecture that can or should be directly applied to create an ITS in a complex, real-world environment such as Aegis . Rather, system details and architecture must be fit to the constraints and opportunities of the application environment. A flexible architecture and advanced system integration methods can integrate the diverse pieces into a hybrid whole.

Use architectural redundancy. The fluid nature of this task domain, and the difficulties of observing trainee performance (digitally) forced AETS not to rely on any one source for all its data, and hence required multiple data paths in its architecture. These multiple paths (e.g., collecting data separately from eyes, hands, and voice) allowed the data sources to be used alone if necessary, yet add value to one other when all were available, and allowed AETS to perform just behavioral diagnosis if cognitive analysis could not be performed at any time.   By anticipating these concessions to the complexity and uncertainty in real-time and real-world domains in its architecture, AETS was able to make a virtue of necessity.

Embedded training is an ideal home for ITS. Complex real-time systems like Aegis are increasingly being built with embedded simulation capability. Using this capability provides a platform that allows the ITS to train in the actual work environment and eliminates the (often costly) need to create/simulate workstations, interfaces, and/or underlying systems. However, it also focuses attention on system integration issues, and requires the ITS to be designed to the software interfaces provided by the host environment. Although the embedded ITS designer ultimately has little control of the training environment and must compromise constantly, the payoff of the embedded training context is clear -- virtually instant fieldability.

Embedded ITS like AETS can ultimately provide a continuous learning environment through a seamless web of training, practice, and performance, all using a common workstation and a common set of performance standards and measures. With reduced need for off-site training facilities and on-site instructors, embedded ITS can not only provide better training, but also better training at reduced cost.

References

[1] Collins, A., Brons, J., & Newman, S. (1989) Cognitive apprenticeship: teaching the craft of reading, writing, and mathematics. In Resnick, L. (Ed.), Knowing, learning and instruction: Essays in honor of Robert Glaser. Hillsdale, N.J.: Lawrence Erlbaum Assoc.

[2] Zachary, W., & Cannon-Bowers, J. (1997) Guided Practice -- a New Vision for Intelligent Embedded Training. Proc. of Human Factors & Ergonomics Society 41st Annual Meeting. Santa Monica, CA: HFES, pp. 1111-1112.

[3] Zachary, W., Ryder, J., Ross, L., & Weiland, M. (1992) Intelligent Human-Computer Interaction in Real Time, Multi-tasking Process Control and Monitoring Systems. In M. Helander & M. Nagamachi (Eds.). Human Factors in Design for Manufacturability. NY: Taylor & Francis, pp. 377-402.

[4] Zachary, W., Ryder, J., & Hicinbothom, J. (in press) Cognitive Task Analysis & Modeling of Decision Making in Complex Environments. In J. Cannon-Bower & E. Salas (Eds.), Decision Making Under Stress, Wash, DC: APA.

[5] Martin, J. & VanLehn, K.. (1995) Student assessment using bayesian nets. International Journal of Human Computer Studies, 42:575-591.

Creating More Versatile Intelligent Learning Environments with a Component-Based Architecture

Steven Ritter[1], Peter Brusilovsky[2], and Olga Medvedeva[1]

[1] Department of Psychology, Carnegie Mellon University
Pittsburgh, PA 15213, USA
{sritter, medol}@andrew.cmu.edu

[2] School of Computer Science, Carnegie Mellon University
Pittsburgh, PA 15213, USA
plb@cs.cmu.edu

Abstract. In this paper we show that, with an appropriate component-based architecture, new functionality can be added to an Intelligent Tutoring System (ITS) with minimal effort. In particular, we show that an explanation function can be added to a component-based ITS which was originally designed to support activity in a learning-by-doing environment. We support these two claims by presenting our recent efforts to extend the Java Algebra Tutor, a variant of the PAT algebra tutor, with a generic example explanation module.

1   Introduction

A human tutor performs several different activities in the teaching process. For example, when teaching some math topic in the classroom a human tutor may:
- explain the core knowledge on the topic
- tell how this knowledge can be applied to solving problems in the given area
- provide examples of problem solving (perhaps by solving several problems on the blackboard and explaining each step of the solution)
- support a student in the process of problem solving by providing hints and corrections
- suggest a relevant example from past experience
- analyze student solutions and explain errors
- suggest the next most relevant activity for the student to participate in, taking into account student learning goals and experience

For an ITS to approach the flexibility and generality of a human tutor, it will need to support at least these kinds of activities, in ways that adapt to individual students' needs and abilities. Adaptive hypermedia systems [2] can present the core knowledge. Problem solving support systems [6] can help the student in the process of problem solving. Solution analyzers [15] can explain errors and deduce misconceptions. Problem sequencing systems [7] can analyze the student model and select the most relevant activity. However, no existing single ITS can intelligently perform more than a few of the activities listed above.

There is a very practical reason for this lack. Existing "single-purpose" ITSs are a natural result of the traditional approach to ITS development. With this approach, developing an ITS which can support two or three different activities doubles or triples the research and development time. Very few ITS research groups or developers can afford this effort. At the same time, to be useful, ITSs have to support some reasonable part of the teacher's or/and student's work. Otherwise, the benefit from using one more system is not worth the burden of installing and learning it.

This problem was analyzed by Brusilovsky [1] in his talk at the AI-ED'95 conference. The author claimed that the problem can be resolved with a new approach to ITS development and a new architecture based on re-usable interacting components. With such a component-based architecture, new functionality could be added to an ITS with minimal effort through re-use of the existing components in another context. At the same conference, Ritter and Koedinger [12] suggested one promising component-based architecture. This architecture has since been applied to the development of several component-based ITSs [11; 13].

In this paper we present another component-based ITS built along the lines of Ritter and Koedinger's [13] architecture. This system provides both interactive problem solving support and step-by-step example presentation in basic algebra. The example presentation functionality was added to the core problem-solving support engine with minimal programming by re-using existing modules in another context. One of the goals of this paper is to demonstrate how new functionality in the given component-based architecture can be added by re-using existing components. To achieve this goal, we provide some basic background on Ritter and Koedinger's [13] plug-in architecture, briefly present the original problem-solving support system and describe how the example explanation component was built by re-using the modules of the original system.

2   The Java Algebra tutor

The Java Algebra Tutor is a variant of the Practical Algebra Tutor (PAT), described in [6]. The tutor assists students in solving word problems described by one or two linear equations. Students solve these problems by completing a spreadsheet and graph describing the problem situation and by solving equations related to the problem situation. The system encourages active learning-by-doing. Students can ask for hints at any step of the process, and the system provides immediate feedback on the appropriateness of each student action. The Java Algebra Tutor currently implements only the spreadsheet portion of the system.

PAT contains an expert system capable of solving the problems that are posed to students. As students take steps to complete the problem (for example, by filling in cells in the spreadsheet), the tutor considers whether or not those steps are consistent with a solution that it would follow. If not, the tutor checks to see if the step is consistent with a common error (or "bug"). In such cases, the tutor is able to provide instruction tailored to that bug. Since the tutor is tracking the student's solution at each step, the tutor is able to give help associated with the student's solution path at any time.

In addition to providing help and identifying errors, the tutor continually assesses the student's progress. Each of the rules in the underlying expert system represents a skill that the student needs to master in order to solve the problem. Each skill is either mastered or not, and the tutor maintains, for each student, the probability that the student has mastered the skill. These probabilities are displayed graphically on the "skillometer," which provides the student with information about his or her progress along each of the component skills in the curriculum.

The Java Algebra Tutor contains a compiled version of the expert system's rules, as they apply to the current problem situation. Instead of pattern matching against rules in the expert system, the tutor simply matches student inputs and branches along predetermined paths. This compiled version of the system provides better response time with a lower memory requirement, while still preserving the entire behavior of the model-tracing system. From the user's point of view, there is no difference between the systems.

3   Presenting examples while teaching problem solving skills

While the Java Algebra Tutor provides support for students' problem-solving activities, examination of its initial use made it clear that more specific declarative support for the activity was needed. This is especially important when the instruction is being delivered over the World-Wide Web. Unlike in the classroom context, students accessing the tutor over the World-Wide Web do not have a teacher or other student to guide them in working through a new problem type, and students are much more likely to jump around the curriculum, thus getting less practice on multiple problems of the same format. These students find it tedious to be thrown into the middle of a problem-solving situation, with the only guidance being the ability to ask for help at each step along the way. To provide some declarative instruction, [3] developed a link between an online tutor for algebra and declarative instruction delivered through InterBook [2].

Still, the addition of declarative instruction through InterBook represents only one step towards more flexible presentation of domain knowledge. An obvious next step would be to add the ability for students to follow complete examples of problem solving using the exact tools they will be asked to use to solve problems. Ideally, these examples would be personalized to reflect each student's level of skill. We can distinguish three basic methods of presenting the information required to master a skill: learning from declarative information, learning by doing, and learning by example. These methods of learning may involve different cognitive mechanisms [14] and can be seen as complimentary. They may account for forming different components of a complex skill [8]. An effective tutor (human or computer) should apply all the three in combination.

Despite a growing body of work on learning from examples in the psychological literature [c.f. 5; 16], learning from examples has received relatively minor attention in the ITS area. ITS researchers acknowledge the role of learning from examples in problem solving [9], but existing ITSs rarely support this method. The ones that do offer an example when it is required [4; 10; 17], typically leave the student alone to explore the examples. We do not know any ITS which provides step-by-step examples in a way that is sensitive to individual students' abilities.

In this paper, we show how this step-by-step example presentation can be added with minimal effort to any system which includes problem solving expertise and an appropriate component-based architecture. Moreover, as we will show later, our example presentation module itself could be re-used to present examples in different domains, thus reducing the efforts to implement this important functionality.

4 Example presentation in PAT-Java

To add example presentation to PAT-Java, we have developed a small example-presentation module which performs its duties mainly by communicating with existing components such as the Tutor and the Spreadsheet. The module interacts with the student through a small dialog (Figure 1) which appears when the student select an example to learn.

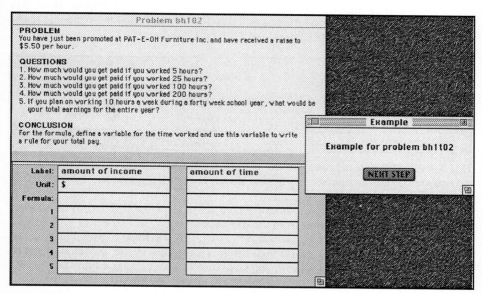

Fig. 1. PAT-Java example presentation interface. The problem-solving window with the spreadsheet is now controlled by the example presentation module. The system is ready to present the next problem-solving step to the student.

Once the student has selected a problem on which to receive an example solution, the student presses the NEXT STEP button (Figure 1). Each step of the example consists of two substeps. On the first substep, the system prepares the student for the next step. It highlights the next cell to be filled and tells the student what is supposed to be entered on this step. This information is presented using an existing interface component: the help window used to present all help text in the Java Algebra Tutor.

This window includes two buttons, labeled >>> and <<<, which allow the student to request more or less detailed explanations of why a particular step is appropriate (Figure 2). At this point, the cell to be filled is still highlighted, but empty.

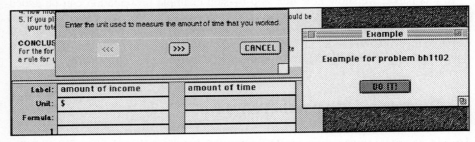

Fig. 2. The display after the student pushes NEXT STEP, and the system starts to explain a step in the solution.

When the NEXT STEP button is pushed, its text changes to DO IT! To start the second substep, the student has to push the DO IT! button. After that, the system simply performs the problem solving step, i.e., fills the current cell. (Figure 3). At this point, the DO IT! button is converted back to say NEXT STEP, and the system is ready to present the next step to the student.

CONCLUSION
For the formula, define a variable for the time worked and use this variable to write a rule for your total pay.

Example

Example for problem bh1t02

Label:	amount of income		amount of time	
Unit:	$		hour	
Formula:				

NEXT STEP

Fig. 3. After the student pushed the DO IT button, the explained step is performed and all changes are made in the interface. The system is ready to explain next problem-solving step.

By providing a progressively more detailed set of explanations and by separating the demonstration of the action from the explanation itself, we expect to give them a better understanding of each problem-solving step. We also hope to promote students' self-explanations [5] as they go through the problem. That is, we expect students to rely more and more on their own explanations of the actions suggested by the example presentation module and less on the accompanying text.

The sequence of steps presented to the student adapts to the student's knowledge level in the following way. If a student has demonstrated, through prior problem solving, that he or she has the ability to complete a particular step, then the system will immediately perform that step, without the student needing to intervene by pressing the NEXT STEP or DO IT! buttons. For example, if a student has demonstrated the ability to correctly complete the column labels in the spreadsheet, the example presentation module will fill in those labels, without any explanations being provided, before demonstrating to the student how to enter the unit of measure.

5   Example presentation in a component-based architecture

5.1   Lightweight tutoring agents: a component-based architecture

Ritter and Koedinger [12; 13] proposed a "plug-in" architecture for intelligent tutoring systems. The primary purpose of the architecture was to allow the incorporation of commercial, off-the-shelf software into a tutoring environment. This was accomplished by enforcing a distinction between the tutoring knowledge and the tools which students use to solve problems. In this context, the "tool" was defined as the program that the user sees (such as a spreadsheet, word processor or simulation environment), and the "tutor agent" was defined as the program that contains the tutoring knowledge and is able to evaluate and offer advice to the student using the tool. The plug-in architecture provides the ability to monitor the student's behavior at an appropriate level and the ability to provide feedback to students in a flexible manner, so that the tutor agent does not need to be aware of many of the details of the tool. Some messages in this "plug-in" architecture are presented in Table 1. In the Java Algebra Tutor and the example presentation module, we are taking advantage of the "plug-in" architecture for a very different purpose. Instead of incorporating off-the-shelf tools, the Java Algebra Tutor uses a custom-built spreadsheet module. Still, the design of the tutor agent component isolates the appropriate elements of the system in a way that allows a novel component, the example presentation module, to use the tutor agent for its own purposes.

5.2   Example presentation

This system provides an illustration of how it is possible, in a well-defined component architecture, to re-use the system's knowledge in an unanticipated context. The tutoring component, which is the part of the system responsible for deciding which step to take next, what help text to give for it and which skills are involved in taking that step, is the exact same program that is used in the learning-by-doing system. The example presentation module system is opportunistically taking advantage of some of the features of the tutoring component that result from it following Ritter and Koedinger's [13] plug-in architecture. In this section, we describe some aspects of the architecture that make this possible.

Message	Parameters	Handled by	Meaning
start problem	initial, goal state	tutor agents	start an activity
process tool action	selection, action, input	tutor agents	student performed some action
process help request	selection, input	tutor agents	student asks for hint
process done		tutor agents	student indicates problem complete
get next step		tutor agents	request for next step in solution
perform user action	selection, action, input	tool	perform some action
get user value	object, property, datatype	tool	request for some value of tool property

Table1. Subset of messages defined in the plug-in architecture in [13].

The plug-in tutoring architecture defines a strict distinction between a tool, which is the component of the system with which the user interacts in order to solve a problem, and the tutor agent (also called tutoring component) which is the part of the system that is responsible for guiding the student in the problem solving process and evaluating the student's abilities in the domain. The plug-in architecture defines a set of messages that allow the tool to communicate the semantics of student actions to the tutor agent and a set of messages that are sent from the tutor agent to the tool in order to give feedback to the student and initialize the state of the tool. The plug-in architecture also defines messages that can be used to query the state of the tool and tutor agent.

The basic algorithm used by the example presentation module is as follows:

1. The example presentation module tells the tutor agent to create a new student (whose name is "demonstrator") and to direct all feedback about that student to itself. Although this action is outside of the plug-in architecture as described in [13], this is the same procedure used by the "curriculum manager" (described in that paper) when a student logs in to the system. From the tutor agent's perspective, a new student named "demonstrator" has decided to use the system. There are now two students using the system, the real student and the example presentation module.

2. The example presentation module selects a problem to demonstrate to the student and sends a "start-problem" message to the tutor agent, indicating that this is the problem that the student named "demonstrator" will be using.

3. The example presentation module displays a NEXT STEP button to the student. When the student presses that button, the example presentation module sends a "get-next-step" query to the tutor agent. This query returns a description of the semantics of the next action that the user should perform. Specifically, each step is described as a selection, action, input triple (roughly corresponding to a direct object, verb and indirect object). For example, when the example presentation module sends the first "get-next-step" query, the tutor agent might reply with selection="cell R1C1 in the spreadsheet", action="type", input="Time", meaning that it would recommend that the student type the word "time" into cell R1C1 of the spreadsheet. We have expanded the semantics of the "get-next-step" query so that, in addition to the selection, action, input triple, it returns a list of the skills that

are involved in this action. In this case, the "get-next-step" query would return the information that the single skill called "Enter column label" would be affected by the recommended action.

4. If the student has not yet demonstrated mastery of the skills needed to perform the next step (e.g., in this case, the student has not mastered the "Enter column label" skill), the example presentation module sends a "process-help-request" message to the tutor agent, passing along the recommended selection as the item on which to give help. From the tutor agent's perspective, the student named "demonstrator" has just asked for help on that item, so it returns the help text that the student would see in that situation. The example presentation module displays that help text to the real student.

5. The NEXT STEP button changes to a DO IT! button. When the user presses this button, the example presentation module sends a "process tool action" message to the tutor agent, passing along the recommended selection, action and input that it received in step 3. From the tutor agent's perspective, this message is an indication that the student has performed the action in the tool. In our example, the tutor agent believes that the student just typed the word "Time" into cell R1C1 of the spreadsheet. Since the student has not actually interacted with the spreadsheet, the example presentation module also sends a message to the spreadsheet ("perform-user-action"), telling it to change the value of cell R1C1 to "Time." If the student had already demonstrated mastery of the skills required to perform the step recommended in step 3, the example presentation module would automatically send the "process tool action" step to the tutor agent (and the "perform-user-action" message to the tool), without any student intervention. This would have the effect of automatically filling in those steps that the student is presumed to already know how to perform. In this way, the system adapts to the student's skill level, only demonstrating those steps that the student does not yet understand.

Steps 3 to 5 are repeated until the tutor agent indicates that the student has completed the problem. It should be apparent that (with the exception of a few elements of its user interface) the example presentation module is completely general. The algorithm described is in no way specific to the Java Algebra Tutor, algebra, or to tutors using a spreadsheet tool. The example presentation module does not need to interpret the semantics of the recommended student step; it just passes it back on to the tutor agent as the student's action. Similarly, it doesn't need to know the semantics of the help text or the skills affected by student actions; it just needs to be able to display the help text and access student model information for the skills it is told about. Thus, the example presentation module can be used with any tutor agent and tool following the plug-in architecture.

The algorithm used by the example presentation module is similar to one described in [11]. In that paper, a system component queried the tutor agent (one used to teach equation solving) repeatedly to discover a recommended problem solution. However, instead of using that solution path to demonstrate an example to the student, that system used the information to compare the recommended solution to that performed by the student, as a way of identifying places where the tutor agent was deficient. Both of these cases demonstrate that, although tutor agents are written with the primary purpose of providing instruction in a learn-by-doing system, when they are implemented as components with appropriate interfaces, their knowledge can be reused in novel and interesting ways. In this architecture, knowledge re-use is different from knowledge sharing. Different components do not (necessarily) have access to the same knowledge base, as they would in a typical blackboard system. Instead, each component is assumed to maintain its own knowledge, but it is able to communicate aspects of its understanding when queried.

6   Summary and future work

In this paper we have tried to demonstrate that new functionality can be relatively easily implemented in an ITS built with a component based architecture, such as the "plug-in" architecture [13]. In particular, we have tried to show how to implement an example explanation module in a system with problem-solving expertise. We hope that the ideas and the real-world example presented in this paper will encourage other ITS developers to use a component based architecture and to consider an example explanation module as an extension of existing problem solving support systems.

Among our own plans is to continue the work on component architecture for ITSs. We hope to experiment with more components and to develop a tool kit for building component based ITSs with Java on the Internet. This model for example presentation can be made much more adaptive. Currently, the system has two options for explaining each step of the example. If the skills behind the step are mastered, the system will not stop to explain the step at all. If the skills are not yet mastered, the step will be explained in two substeps. There are several ways of improving on that. First, we can manipulate the granularity of a step explanation to a greater extent. For some simple steps already seen before, one substep is enough. For some complex steps which are new for the student, even two sub-steps and brief explanations may be not enough to understand why something was done by the system. Second, the text and vocabulary of the explanation generated for each substep could be adapted to the student's knowledge. Third, the order of showing the steps may be adapted to the student's background knowledge. For example, we might recommend that an algebra novice fill in the formula cell at the very end, so that completed rows in the spreadsheet can support inductive inference of the formula. On the other hand, a student who already understands formulas would be instructed to fill in the formula cell before calculating the answers, so that the system will calculate using the formula and the entered givens (as a spreadsheet does).

Acknowledgments

This work was supported by the National Science Foundation and the Advanced Research Projects Agency under Cooperative Agreement CDA-940860, and by a James S. McDonnell Foundation grant to Peter Brusilovsky.

References

1. Brusilovsky, P.: Intelligent learning environments for programming: The case for integration and adaptation. In: Greer, J. (ed.) Proc. of AI-ED'95, 7th World Conference on Artificial Intelligence in Education, Washington, DC, AACE (1995) 1-8
2. Brusilovsky, P., Eklund, J., and Schwarz, E.: Web-based education for all: A tool for developing adaptive courseware. Computer Networks and ISDN Systems. **30**, 1-7 (1998) 291-300
3. Brusilovsky, P., Ritter, S., and Schwarz, E.: Distributed intelligent tutoring on the Web. In: du Boulay, B. and Mizoguchi, R. (eds.) (Proc. of AI-ED'97, 8th World Conference on Artificial Intelligence in Education) IOS, Amsterdam (1997) 482-489
4. Brusilovsky, P. L.: Intelligent Tutor, Environment and Manual for Introductory Programming. Educational and Training Technology International **29**, 1 (1992) 26-34
5. Chi, M. T. H., Bassok, M., Lewis, M. W., Reimann, P., and Glaser, R.: Self-explanations: How students study and use examples to solve problems. Cognitive Science **13** (1989) 145-182
6. Koedinger, K. R., Anderson, J. R., Hadley, W. H., and Mark, M. A.: Intelligent tutoring goes to school in the big city. In: Greer, J. (ed.) Proc. of AI-ED'95, 7th World Conference on Artificial Intelligence in Education, Washington, DC, AACE (1995) 421-428
7. McArthur, D., Stasz, C., Hotta, J., Peter, O., and Burdorf, C.: Skill-oriented task sequencing in an intelligent tutor for basic algebra. Instructional Science **17**, 4 (1988) 281-307
8. McKendree, J. and Anderson, J. R.: Effect of practice on knowledge and use of basic Lisp. In: Carroll, J. M. (ed.) Interfacing Thought: Cognitive Aspects of Human-Computer Interaction. Bradford Books/MIT Press, Cambridge (1987)
9. Pirolli, P. L. and Anderson, J. R.: The role of learning from examples in the acquisition of recursive programming skills. Canadian Journal of Psychology **39** (1985) 240-272
10. Recker, M. M. and Pirolli, P.: Student strategies for learning programming from a computatioinal environment. In: Frasson, C., Gauthier, G. and McCalla, G. I. (eds.) Intelligent Tutoring Systems. (Proc. of Second International Conference on Intelligent Tutoring Systems, ITS'92, Montreal) Springer-Verlag, Berlin (1992) 382-394
11. Ritter, S.: Comminication, cooperation and competition among multiple tutor agents. In: Boulay, B. d. and Mizoguchi, R. (eds.) Artificial Intelligence in Education: Knowledge and Media in Learning Systems. (Proc. of AI-ED'97, 8th World Conference on Artificial Intelligence in Education, Kobe, Japan) IOS, Amsterdam (1997)
12. Ritter, S. and Koedinger, K. R.: Towards lightweight tutoring agents. In: Greer, J. (ed.) Proc. of AI-ED'95, 7th World Conference on Artificial Intelligence in Education, Washington, DC, AACE (1995) 91-98
13. Ritter, S. and Koedinger, K. R.: An architecture for plug-in tutor agents. Journal of Artificial Intelligence in Education **7** (1996) 315-347
14. Schmalthofer, F. and Kuehn, O.: The psychological process of constructing a mental model when learning by being told, from examples, and by exploration. In: Ackermann, A. and Tauber, M. (eds.): Informatics and Psychology. Schuerding Proceedings (1989)
15. Sleeman, D. H.: An attempt to understand student understanding in basic algebra. Cognitive Science **8** (1984) 387-412
16. VanLehn, K., Jones, R. M., and Chi, M. T. H.: A model of the self-explanation effect. Journal of the Learning Sciences **2**, 1 (1992) 1-60
17. Weber, G.: Individual selection of examples in an intelligent learning environment. Journal of Artificial Intelligence in Education **7**, 1 (1996) 3-31

Goal-Based Autonomous Social Agents: Supporting Adaptation and Teaching in a Distributed Environment

Julita Vassileva

ARIES Laboratory, Department of Computer Science, University of Saskatchewan,
1C101 Engineering Bldg, 57 Campus Drive, Saskatoon, S7N 5A9 Canada
Email: jiv@cs.usask.ca

Abstract. This paper proposes a theoretical framework that allows goal-based agents attached to networked applications and learning environments to support users' work and learning. Users, learners, applications and learning environments are represented by autonomous goal-based social agents who communicate, cooperate, and compete in a multi-system and multi-user distributed environment. This allows for a uniform approach to support the user while working, by adaptation to the user's goals, preferences, level of experience and available resources; as well as teaching the user using various teaching paradigms (consrtuctivist or instructivist). In addition it allows one to take into account the user's /learner's motivation and affect; as well as enabling a coherent discussion of teaching strategies.

1 Trends in the Development of Adaptive and Teaching Systems

Two major trends can be observed in the development of learning environments, which follow from the rapid development of networking and communication technologies:

- An integration of working and learning environments.
- No virtual difference between humans and application agents

Nowadays nearly all commercial applications (most prominently CorelDraw, Toolbook etc.) are equipped with training programs, which provide an introduction into the main features and basic working techniques, as well as with on-line help, which is in some cases context-sensitive and even adaptive (MS-Office 97). This means that the user is working and learning at the same time, and can switch from "working" mode to "learning" mode at will. It is easy to switch from some type of teaching or demonstration, which will help the user learn about something specifically needed at the moment, and then switch back to the "working" mode to try and use the newly acquired knowledge in practice.

From the other side, learning environments specifically designed for educational purpose in some subject are often inspired by constructivist and Vygodskian theories of learning, which focus on context-anchored learning and instruction, that takes place in the context of solving a realistic problem. There is a tendency in learning environment design philosophies towards integrating work and learning; work being the source of problems and motivation for learning.

In general, one can observe a convergence between working environments and learning environments. For example, instead of adapting to sub-optimal learner behavior, the system may decide to *teach* the learner (instruct, explain, provide help, etc.) how to do things correctly, i.e. to make the user adapt to the system by learning. In reality every adaptation is bi-directional. Every participant in an interaction process adapts to the other participant(s). The system learns about the user and adapts to him/her; the user learns about the system and adapts accordingly. An adaptive system should support the user's learning about the system [8]. It has to be able to decide whether to adapt to the user or to teach something instead (i.e. to make the user adapt to the system). It must decide whether to be reactive or proactive. In this way the system will be an active participant in the interaction, an autonomous agent, which can decide in the course of interaction and not just follow embedded decisions made at design time (normative decisions).

An attempt to build such a system which can take decisions about whether to teach or to coach the student depending on the context of interaction and state of student model has been designed and implemented using reactive planning techniques [8]. However, we feel that such a pedagogically "competent" system has to be able to negotiate its decisions with the learner and not just impose them, since no mater what expertise is underlying these decisions, there is always uncertainty about the correctness of this knowledge and about the student model.

Therefore we decided to model the pedagogical component in an intelligent learning environment as an autonomous agent that pursues certain teaching goals. These goals can be cognitive (subject- and problem-specific), motivational, and affective (learner- and subject-specific). We call these agents "Application agents", since they are associated with an application which can be in a special case, a learning environment. Since the user / learner is also an autonomous agent pursuing his / her own goals, the decision of which and whose goals will be pursued (the pedagogical agent's or the learner') is made interactively, in a process of negotiation and persuasion.

In pursuing its goals, an application agent uses explicitly its relationship with the user/ learner. It can modify the parameters of the relationship, so that it can adopt user goals or learner goals and provide resources for them (achieving in this way explorative learning), infer and adapt to the learner's goals (to provide adaptive help or coaching) or try to make the learner achieve the teaching goals of the agent (to instruct the user / learner how to do something).

The second major trend in the development of teaching systems is that there is no virtual difference between humans and application agents. It is no longer necessary that the teaching system is an almighty teacher knowing the answer to any question that may during the interaction /learning session. Networking provides a possibility to find somewhere else a system or a human- partner who can help the learner with his/her problem and explain him/her themes that the system itself can not. This trend can be seen in the increasing work on collaborative learning systems, which are able to find appropriate partners for help or collaboration, to form teams and support goal-based group activities [1], [2]. For this purpose, it is imperative that teaching systems (and other computer applications providing adaptive help) be able to communicate information about their users (user models) and about their available resources and goals in order to find an appropriate partner. We can imagine application agents, attached to every application or learning environment, which have an explicit representation of the user's or application's goals, plans, and resources. These agents communicate and negotiate among themselves for achieving their goals. This means that we need an appropriate communication language about goals and resources, which would allow these agents to share information. This communication has to be on a higher level than the level of knowledge communication (as in KQML or KIF), since it has a different purpose. While KQML and KIF have to define how the agents communicate their knowledge, this higher level of communication has the purpose to define who will be contacted, about what, when and how communication will take place (i.e. in which direction etc.).   This level of communication has to be also transparent for humans, since some of the partners may be human-agents.

2   Goal-Based Agents

We propose creating "application agents" associated with applications, tutors, coaches and learning environments (see Figure 1). These agents will possess an explicit representation of the goals for which the application has resources and plans. Usually, these goals are embedded implicitly in the application at design time and can be *achievement goals* (for example, creating a table in Word), *typical user tasks* (which the application supports), and *user preferences* (normally also embedded at design time). Teaching applications have normative *teaching goals* (i.e. what the application is supposed to teach), which can be further classified into content goals, presentation goals / tasks, psycho-motor and affective (motivational) goals. Every application is provided, at design time, with resources and plans for achieving these goals (data, knowledge, functions of the application).

Human agents also possess goals, resources and plans. Classifications of human goals have been proposed by Schank & Abelson [5] and later by Slade [6]. Slade also proposes various dimensions for goals, like polarity, persistence, frequency, deadline etc., which influence the goal-importance. Human resources can be divided into two categories: tangible (money, time, objects, skills, credentials, rank etc.) and cognitive (memory, attention, knowledge, affects, moods). The resources can be classified with respect to whether they are perishable, expendable, interchangable, transferable etc.

Humans communicate their goals, available resources and plans to their "personal agents", which serve as mediators in search for other application agents or personal agents that can provide resources and plans for achieving the goals of the human users. In this way, a human user and a software application appear in a symmetric position, they possess goals, resources and plans, and they can adopt each other goals (i.e. help each other achieve their goals) mediated by the "pedagogical agents" and the "personal agents" (see Figure 1.)

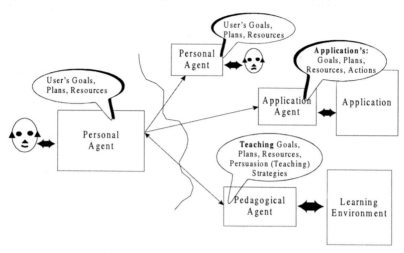

Fig. 1. Personal and Application Agents

3   A Goal-Theory of Agents

According to Slade's [6] theory of goals, the behavior of a goal-based agent (for example, humans) follows the principles:

<u>Principle of Importance</u> *The importance of a goal is proportional to the resources that the agent is willing to spend in pursuing this goal.*

Humans possess not only tangible resources, like money, time, hardware configuration, etc., but also cognitive resources, like attention, memory, affect, moods etc. In order to infer each other's goals, the agents use the following

<u>Principle of Investment</u> *The importance of an active goal is proportional to the resources that the agent has already expended in pursuit of that goal.*

The place of the human-agents specific resources (attention, affects and moods) in the goal framework is explained below.

<u>Motivation</u> *An agent's motivation to pursue a given goal is equivalent to the importance of the goal for the agent.* So, the motivation of an agent to pursue a given goal is proportional to the resources that the agent is willing to spend in pursuing that goal.

Attention *is the amount of processing time spent by the agent in pursuing some goal.* The importance of a goal is proportional to the attention / amount of processing time which the agent is willing to expend in pursuit of that goal.

Affects *The importance of a goal is proportional to the degree of affective response to the status of that goal.* This means that the difference among happiness, joy and ecstasy relates to the importance of the goal that is achieved or anticipated. Happiness does not depend only on the world, but also on one's idiosyncratic goal hierarchy. Knowing the human's emotion (via an appropriately designed interface e.g. buttons allowing the user to directly communicate his / her emotion), the personal agent can infer the importance of the goal, on which the user has just failed or succeeded. Knowing the importance of the user's goal, the system can predict the affective response to goal-achievement or -failure.

Moods *Goal persistence is reflected in persistent affective states, or "moods".* The intensity of the mood reflects the importance of the related goals. An agent is in a good mood when after having achieved an important persistent goal. According to the principle of importance, the agent might be prepared to expend considerable resources to achieve this goal. Now these resources are free for other goals. So an agent in a good mood effectively has excess resources that could be used for new goals. An agent in bad mood has a lack of resources, and as such will be much less open to the pursuit of any new goals. This fits with our everyday experience. There is a heuristic that suggests that people try to put someone in a good mood before delivering bad news or making a request. This can be used in order to decide whether a system should teach the user (i.e. make him/her adopt the system's teaching goal) or whether it should adapt to the user (i.e. the system adopts the user's goal).

4   Relationships

An agent must act in a world populated by other agents. Many of an agent's goals require the help of another agent. In this way, relationships among agents can be viewed as another kind of resources for achieving goals.

Principle of Interpersonal Goals Adopted goals are processed uniformly as individual goals, with a priority determined by the importance and context of the relationship.

Parameters of Relationships: Inter-agent relationships can be characterized by the following parameters:
Type of the other agent involved in the relation:
− Human
− Computer

Type of Goal Adoption
− Goal Assignment
− Goal Inferring (adapting)
− Goal Development (teaching)

Symmetry of Relationship
- Asymmetric: dominated
- Asymmetric: dominating
- Symmetric

Sign of Relationship

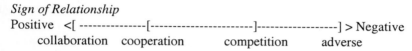

Positive <[---------------[----------------------]------------------] > Negative
    collaboration   cooperation   competition   adverse

The *importance* and the *context* of the particular relationship for a given agent determine both what goals the agent will adopt and what importance will be assigned to these goals. The principle of importance applies to adopted goals, meaning that an agent will expend resources in pursuit of an adopted goal in proportion to the importance of the adopted goal. The same applies to cognitive resources. For example, the agent will spend more attention (time thinking) about the interests or problems of a close friend than those of an acquaintance.

If an agent A wants that another agent B adopts A's goal as an important goal, it uses persuasion strategies. These are inter-agent planning strategies that aim at increasing the relative goal importance for another agent of an adopted goal. Persuasion strategies may, for example, exploit the importance of the relationship between A and B ("if you don't do this for me, I won't play with you anymore"), they can increase the importance of the goal B by bargaining resources, or offering that A will achieve a goal of B in exchange ("if you do this for me, I will do that for you"). A set of persuasion strategies was proposed by Schank & Abelson [5]. Persuasion strategies are particularly important when the type of goal adoption is "Goal Development", i.e. when agent A has a teaching goal and it wants that agent B adopts this goal as an important goal (thus B will be motivated to achieve the goal, i.e. to learn). We can consider some teaching strategies used by human teachers as a special case of persuasion strategies aimed at motivating the student to achieve some teaching goal. One can easily find parallels between the conditions for successful persuasion formulated by Slade [6] and some conditions for successful teaching. Slade's conditions are the following:
- the agent B should be aware of A's goal,
- B has to be in possession of resources and plans for pursuing A's goal,
- the relationship between A and B has to be perceived as important by B,
- B must not have any important goals that conflict with A's goal (i.e. with respect to some resource),
- the goal of A has to be intrinsically important.

For example, the first condition states that the student has to know exactly what is the goal he /she is trying to achieve. The second condition states that the student has to have the necessary prerequisite knowledge and cognitive resources free at the moment in order to be able to pursue a given teaching goal.

Another important characteristic of a relationship is its closeness. The closeness of relationship denotes how well the agents understand (are aware of) each other's goals. When talking about closeness, we always mean closeness from the point of view of a certain agent: it can well be the case that one agent understands the goals of the other one well, but the second one is not aware of the goals of the first one. Agents learn about each other's goals from three main sources:
- Normative knowledge about other agents' goals (stereotypes embedded at design time)
- Statement of a goal by an agent (direct goal communication via some language)
- Inferred knowledge arising from observation of an agent's behavior (diagnosis as in user modeling systems).

The closeness of the relationship between a human user and his / her personal agent should be as high as possible. This means that a personal agent must use not only normative and directly communicated knowledge about the user's goals, but should be able to infer user goals from his /her behavior (methods for diagnosis in user modeling and plan recognition could be applied), as well as infer the user's affect and moods (communicated in some way from the user to his /her personal agent).

Definition: *An agent, who is able to represent explicitly, reason about and modify the parameters of its relationships with other agents, when it is able to create and destroy relationships according to its goals, is called a social autonomous goal-driven agent*.

Personal agents and application agents (which can be pedagogical agents if the application is a learning environment) are examples of social autonomous goal-driven agents.

A personal agent can be related with the human user with an asymmetric goal-assignment type of relationship (i.e. the application receives and executes commands from the user). In this case, the personal agent searches among the available relationships with application agents the one that is most appropriate for achieving the current user's goal. If no such relationships are available, it will contact a broker-agent that has a large number of relationships to various application agents (including pedagogical agents). The broker will find and contact an application agent that can fulfill the goal. The personal agent will negotiate with the application agent (see Figure 1) in order to find reasonable conditions for obtaining the service. When agreement is achieved, the application agent adopts the user's goal and provides its normative resources and plans for achieving the user's goal.

Pedagogical agents have a set of normative teaching goals and plans for achieving these goals as well as persuasion plans (i.e. teaching strategies) and associated resources in the learning environment. The persuasion plans can involve a modification of the parameters of the relationship between the pedagogical agent and the user. For example, it can change the sign of the relationship from collaborative to competitive (game-like) or to cooperative (simulating a peer-learner), or the symmetry of the relationship from user-dominated (a constructivist type of learning environment), to symmetric (coach), or pedagogical agent dominated (insturctivist tutor).

If a personal agent is able to reason about and modify the relationship with the user, it can decide not only to fulfil the user's orders, but also to change the relationship to become more symmetric, or to take initiative and teach the user something suggested by the corresponding application agent. For this to happen, the personal agent should have adopted a goal from a pedagogical agent of some learning environment (who has managed to persuade the personal agent that it is in possession of resources and plans for pursuing a teaching goal related to the current goal of the user). In this case, the personal agent has to make a decision between two conflicting goals (the achievement goal of the user and the adopted teaching goal from the pedagogical agent of the learning environment). In order to be able to make decisions, the personal agent needs to be able to reason about the relative importance of the goals and to plan resources.

5   An Architecture for Autonomous Goal-Based Social Agents

Ideally, an autonomous cognitive agent will possess a reactive, reasoning, decision-making and learning capability. Therefore it has to contain processes implementing these capabilities. We propose an architecture for autonomous goal-based social agents (see Figure 2) which contains the following components:

- *Explicit Representation of Goals, Plans, Resources and Actions* available to the agent (Elements);
- *Explicit Representation of the Agent's Relationships* with other agents and ensuring that all the parameters of the relationship can be manipulated by the agent (Relationships);
- *Internal Processes* which can be applied to the elements, but also on the parameters of the relationships of the agent and for enforcing inter-agent goal-adoption (Processes).

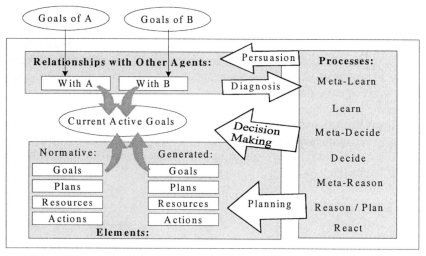

Fig. 2. An Architecture of Intelligent Personal /Application Agent.

A personal agent with this architecture should have the following properties:
- *Taking into Account User Motivation, Emotions, and Moods.* According to the principle of importance, the motivation can be naturally taken into account by assessment of the relative importance of goals.
- *Unified Model of Collaborative, Cooperative, Competitive, and Adverse Behavior.* A truly adaptive system should be able to modify its type of relationship with the user. The explicit representation of the sign of the relationships will allow the agents to reason and dynamically modify their behavior with respect to other agents.
- *The Agent Decides about the Style of Behavior* (passive or proactive) it will have with other agents (and with the user).

An agent defined in this way fulfils Nwana's [4] definition of a "smart" agent and is an ideal to which one could strive. However, to bring this architecture to a computational framework, one has to find new techniques for reasoning and decision-making about inter-agent relationships.

We are currently working on the implementation of this agent-based framework as a basis for the Intelligent Helpdesk (I-Help) project [3]. Students and applications (discussion forum, a WWW-based pool of teaching materials and an on-line help system) in this architecture are represented by agents who can communicate among themselves by exchanging messages about their goals, needs and available resources. This implementation is in JAVA, the agents are implemented as threads communicating with messages via TCP/IP on the Internet. We are defining a taxonomy of goals and resources for a selected domain, which is to be used by the agents. As a first version, the agents will communicate with a broker-agent who keeps information about the goals and resources the agents need or have to offer. Gradually, the agents will develop relationships, which will allow them to select "partners" without contacting a central service. As a start, the agents will be kept "slim", i.e. unintelligent. They will "borrow" reasoning, planning, persuasion and negotiation services (advice) from existing planning systems or specially developed for this purpose applications, represented in the frameworks by their application agents. Starting with a minimal communication scheme, we will extend the "intelligence" of agents by adding capabilities of reasoning about goals, inferring the importance of the goals of other agents, decision making and inter-agent planning (persuasion). The basic agent architecture can be completely unintelligent and serve purely communicative functions; i.e. not including any reasoning, planning, decision-making and learning capabilities. However, when it is necessary and possible, one can further develop these capabilities in any single agent, without adversely affecting the general scheme of interaction.

6   Summary

We are proposing an agent-based framework for supporting adaptation and teaching/learning in a distributed environment. Every application (working or teaching system) is provided with an agent, called "application" or "teaching" agent which possesses an explicit representation of the goals of this application (achievement goals or teaching goals), the available resources, plans and relationships. Human users are provided with "personal" agents, which contain representation of the user's goals, available resources, plans and relationships (stored in a user model; inferred or assigned directly by the user). The representation of goals, resources, relationships and plans is based on a special taxonomy, using Slade's theory of goals [6]. When a user faces a problem and needs a specific adaptation in his/her working or learning environment, the personal agent searches for an appropriate adaptive application or a teaching program in the distributed environment (e.g. Internet). This is done by negotiating with the application agents and teaching agents of other applications or with the personal agents of other human users to find one that is appropriate, available, and willing to help.

Acknoweldgement: Special thanks to Jim Greer for comments on earlier drafts of this paper.

References

1. Hoppe H.U. The use of multiple student modeling to parameterize group learning. In Artificial Intelligence and Education: Proceedings of AI-ED 95, AACE, (1995), 234-241.
2. Collins J., Greer J., Kumar, V., McCalla, G., Meagher P., Tkatch, R. Inspectable User Models for Just-In-Time Workplace Training, in User Modeling, Proceedings of UM97, Springer (1997) Wien NewYork, 327-338.
3. Greer, J., McCalla, G., Cooke, J., Collins, J., Kumar, V., Bishop, A., Vassileva, J. The Intelligent Helpdesk: Supporting Peer-Help in a University Course, Proceedings ITS'98 (this volume), (1998) , Springer Verlag: Berlin-Heidelberg.
4. Nwana H. (1996) Software Agents: An Overview, *Knowledge Engineering Review*, 11, 1-40.
5. Schank, R., Abelson, R. *Scripts, Plans, Goals and Understanding*. Lawrence Erlbaum Assoc., (1977) Hillsdale, NJ.
6. Slade, S. *Goal-Based Decision Making: An Interpersonal Model*. Lawrence Erlbaum Associates Inc. (1994) Hillsdale, NJ.
7. Vassileva J. Reactive Instructional Planning to Support Interacting Teaching Strategies, in *Proceedings of the 7-th World Conference on AI and Education*, 334-342, (1995) AACE: Charlottesville, VA.
8. Vassileva, J. A task-centered approach for user modeling in a hypermedia office documentation system, *User Modeling and User Adapted Interaction*, (1996) **6**, (2-3), 185-223.

Curriculum Sequencing in a Web-Based Tutor

Mia K. Stern and Beverly Park Woolf

Center for Knowledge Communication
Computer Science Department
University of Massachusetts
Amherst, MA 01003
USA
{stern,bev}@cs.umass.edu

Abstract. In this paper, we discuss using a student model in a web-based course to sequence the curriculum. Since the teaching in a web-based course is usually non-linear, dynamic curriculum sequencing is important as there is not a linear path that will be appropriate for all students. Thus a student model needs to be constructed which can guide students through the non-linear curriculum. This student model is built on the student's quiz performance and on how well he studies the material. The student model is used to judge how well a topic has been "learned", which can then be used to determine which other topics are ready to be learned. In this paper, we discuss how the student model is constructed and used for curriculum sequencing.

1 Introduction

MANIC (Multimedia Asynchronous Networked Individualized Courseware) [6][7] is an intelligent tutoring shell used for delivering a variety of courses over the World Wide Web. The goal of MANIC is to deliver any existing lecture course via the Web. Currently, seven courses are being taught using the MANIC software (six in computer science and one in art history).

Traditional lecture courses are necessarily linear, due to the constraints of that mode of teaching. However, there is no reason to apply this restriction to an on-line version of the same course. Thus, we are investigating ways to convert linear lecture-based courses to on-line customized courses in which the domain is non-linear.

Currently, MANIC courses are presented using both audio from the lecture courses as well as the slides shown in class. Students can listen to audio from a lecture, and while it is being played, the corresponding slide is synchronously displayed. Students can also simply view the slides without listening to the audio, using the provided "next" and "previous" buttons, as well as the table of contents. See [6] for more details on how students interact with MANIC.

The non-linear version of MANIC stores topics in a simple semantic network, with link types indicating the relationship between a topic and its pretopics (connected topics preceding the topic in the semantic net). Links currently represent *prerequisite*, *corequisite*, *related*, and *remedial* relationships, similar to the link types used by Intelligent Guide [5]. It should be noted that remedial topics are treated as special topics. These topics are not required to be learned by all students; they are only taught to those students who need to see the material.

Furthermore, each topic is divided into subtopics, which are smaller grained units that allow the tutor to reason at a finer level. When a subtopic is displayed to the student, the actual content is dynamically generated based on the student model. The techniques for this adaptive content are not presented in this paper.

In non-linear domains, users can find themselves "lost in hyperspace" [4]. An intelligent guide can be useful in avoiding this problem. To this end, we have developed a tutor that uses a student model to judge what the student knows and can use this model to guide the display of material.

In this paper, we discuss how the student model is used to guide the student through the non-linear domain. We first discuss the motivation for this technique. We then discuss the data the student model gathers about each student, and how it makes a judgment on how well a topic is "learned." We next discuss how these rankings are used to judge how ready topics are to be learned. We conclude with a discussion on possible ways to improve on these methods.

2   Motivation for Sequencing Curriculum

Curriculum sequencing can be seen as a two part process: deciding on relevant topics based on the current student model, and then selecting the best one [1]. In this paper, we discuss our approach to both of these tasks within the MANIC framework.

A student is "ready to learn" a topic only if he has performed sufficiently well on its pretopics. The problem thus decomposes into determining:

- How well the student has performed on a topic's pretopics and on the topic itself
- How to combine the ratings for all the pretopics, as well as the rating for the current topic

The first item corresponds to how well a topic is "learned." In traditional intelligent tutoring systems, this can be judged by examining how a student performs on quizzes and tests about the topic. In MANIC, we also make judgments based on quiz performance, as quizzes are given upon completion of each topic. However, additional information is used to construct the student model. For example, the student's access patterns for viewing the course material, including how much time he has spent studying a topic, whether the corresponding audio was played and if topics were reviewed multiple times are combined into a rating about how well a topic is learned.

For example, say we have two students, both of whom are working on a given topic, and neither student performs well on a quiz on that topic. The first student spent 5 minutes studying the associated material while the second student spent 2 hours studying the material. Clearly, we need to differentiate these two students. Thus, we have devised a student modeling rating scheme which takes into account both quiz performance and content access patterns.

The problem of combining ratings on pretopics is important for considering how much weight to give each of them. This weight is influenced by the link type; for example, prerequisite topics are more influential than related topics.

3   How Well is a Topic Learned?

In this section we discuss how each topic is graded, based on direct evidence. Three factors are important in determining the ranking of a topic: how well the student performs on quizzes on the topic, how well it has been studied and how much the topic has been reviewed. These three pieces of evidence are then combined to determine how well a topic has been "learned."

3.1   Quiz Performance

Quizzes give a tutor the most direct information about the student's knowledge. For this reason, quizzes are included in MANIC and are considered the most important piece of information the student model can obtain about the student.

Quizzes in MANIC are dynamically constructed based on the student model. Questions are provided which cover the topics most recently completed, as well as topics that should be reviewed. Furthermore, each question has a level of difficulty (1-4) indicating the level of mastery a student should have to be able to answer the question correctly.

This level of difficulty is also used when updating the student model. Clearly correctly answering a harder question demonstrates a higher ability than correctly answering an easier question. Similarly, failing at a harder question should not be as damaging as failing at an easier question.

The following equations define the quiz question update rules. Equation 1 is used for correctly answered questions; Equation 2 is used for incorrectly answered questions. The results of each question are used to update the quiz value of the corresponding topic.

$$NewValue_{topic} = OldValue_{topic} + OldValue_{topic} * \frac{level\ of\ question}{10} \ . \qquad (1)$$

$$NewValue_{topic} = OldValue_{topic} - OldValue_{topic} * \frac{5 - level\ of\ question}{10} \ . \qquad (2)$$

Each topic has an initial quiz grade (derived from a pre-test). Furthermore, all quiz grades are bounded between 0 and 1.

3.2   Study Performance

The main interaction that students have with a MANIC course is through reading and listening to the course material. Therefore, we need a way to judge how much comprehension the student has gained through these activities.

Previous work in Interbook [2] also updates the student model by using information about whether a user reads a page or not. However, that system simply records if a page has been displayed, without considering if the page was in fact read. In MANIC, we attempt to determine if a student reads and understands the material that is displayed.

Because we have divided topics into various subtopics, the problem essentially becomes judging how sufficiently the subtopics have been studied. Since the current policy is to display at most one subtopic per page, possibly using multiple pages to teach a full subtopic, we need to judge how well all pages for a subtopic have been studied.

The two determining factors in how well a subtopic has been studied are the use of audio and the time spent studying the material. In general, if a page's associated audio is played, the student will gain more information than if just the text is read. However, there is still no indication that the student has understood the information presented either in the audio or in the text.

If the audio for the page has not been played, then we need another way of judging how well the material has been studied. One way to do this is to consider the time spent on the page. Spending too little time, or too much time, reading through a page implies that full comprehension has not been reached. However, these timing data can be extremely inaccurate and should not be relied on heavily. For example, a student may leave the computer and not actually look at or listen to the page. Thus, we cannot distinguish a student who actually spends an hour studying a page from a student who has taken a break for an hour.

Whether a subtopic is sufficiently studied does not warrant a yes or no answer; rather the question is impacted by exactly how much time is spent studying the subtopic. The studied rating on each topic ranges from 0 to 1. If the audio for the subtopic is played, then the rating for that subtopic is the percent of the audio that was played. This assumes that listening to the audio leads to complete understanding, which may not be true. We are looking for alternative measures for judging comprehension in this case.

If the audio is not played, then the rating is dependent on how much time is spent reading the material. Currently, the method we use for rating the amount of time spent is to have an optimal time per page that a student should spend, which is calculated based on the content actually displayed. If the student spends this optimal amount, then the rating for the page is 1. As he moves away from this point, his score decreases, at the rate shown in Figure 1. Of course even with this method, we cannot be certain if the student understands the material.

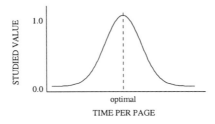

Fig. 1. How studied values are updated based on time read

To compute a study rating for a subtopic, we sum up the scores for each of the pages in that subtopic, and then divide by the number of pages needed to fully explain the subtopic. The number of pages needed per subtopic is a dynamic value, since the material is dynamically generated for each student. However, we can calculate how many pages a student would need if he were to view the whole subtopic to completion. This average is $R_{subtopic}(Studied)$.

Then, to determine how well a topic has been studied, we use Equation 3:

$$R_{topic}(Studied) = \frac{\sum_{i=1}^{NumSubtopics_{topic}} R_{subtopic_i}(Studied)}{NumSubtopics_{topic}}.$$ (3)

If a subtopic is studied more than once, the total time spent on the subtopic is used for $R_{subtopic}(Studied)$.

3.3   Reviewed Topics

The review score on a topic records how many times the student has returned to visit the same topic again. We are interested in recording how frequently a student feels he must review previous material. In general, if he is reviewing frequently, then he is not retaining information sufficiently, and thus he has not learned the material. Of course frequent reviewing might reflect individual differences, which currently we do not take into account. The review score records how many times the student has reviewed, as well as how much of the material he views each time.

The overall reviewed score is composed of two factors: a current time score and an overall score. The overall score starts at 0.1 for each topic. Each time the student reviews the topic, the current time's reviewed score is calculated using Equation 3. This value is then used to adjust the overall reviewed score using the rules in Table 1.

Table 1. Updating rules for review

Current time score	Increase overall value by
≥ 0.8	↑ 50%
$0.5 \leq x < 0.8$	↑ 35%
$0.3 \leq x < 0.5$	↑ 20%
< 0.3	↑ 10%

3.4   Combining these Three Scores

These three scores, quiz performance, study performance and reviewed topics, are very hard to reason about individually, and none alone gives a full picture of the student's knowledge. Therefore, we combine the three scores into a single value, indicating how well the topic is "learned."

The most important score on a topic is the quiz score. If a student has a reasonably high quiz grade (say over 0.8), then he has demonstrated sufficient mastery on the topic, and the other scores do not matter as much. However, if his quiz score is not sufficiently high, the other factors become important, and must be considered when calculating the "learned" score.

A simple way to combine the scores is to do a weighted average, such as:

$$R(Learned) = 0.6 * R(Quizzed) + 0.25 * R(Studied) + 0.15 * R(Reviewed) \ . \quad (4)$$

This formula gives more weight to the quiz scores. However, even if quizzes are not required and students do not take them, it is still possible to create a "learned" score on a topic. The quizzed score can be taken directly from the pre-test. It should be noted, though, that the only way to have a high learned score on a topic is to perform well on the pre-test or on the quizzes; direct evidence of understanding is required.

There is one flaw with Equation 4. If a student has studied a topic and has performed well on the quizzes, but has not needed to review the topic, he will be penalized using Equation 4. Therefore, we propose the following special case when $R_{topic}(Quizzed) > 0.7$ & $R_{topic}(Studied) > 0.7$:

$$R(Learned) = 0.7 * R(Quizzed) + 0.2 * R(Studied) + 0.1 * (1 - R(Reviewed)) \ . \quad (5)$$

Table 2 demonstrates how the "learned" rule can be applied to three students.

Table 2. Learned values for three students

Student	Equation Used	Quizzed	Studied	Reviewed	Total
1	5	0.90	0.90	0.10	0.90
2	4	0.50	0.80	0.70	0.605
3	4	0.30	0.40	0.15	0.3025

4   How to Select the Next Topic

Once each topic's "learned" score has been calculated, a "ready" score for other topics can then be determined. This score determines which topic will be selected next based on two factors: (1) the topic's learned score and (2) the topic's pretopics' learned scores.

The first item is important when considering if a topic needs to be reviewed or does not need to be studied any more. If a given topic's learned score is too low (less than 0.4) to allow the student to move on to another topic, it should be presented again, perhaps being taught differently than it was the first time. Topics for repetition are given higher priority than new topics. On the other hand, if a topic's learned score is sufficiently high (greater than 0.85), then it no longer needs to be studied, and is not considered as a possible topic to study.

The learned scores on the pretopics is important when considering what new topics to present. In order to start a new topic, a student should show sufficient knowledge of its related material. However, in MANIC, we do not necessarily impose a strict threshold on the grades need on each related topic. Consider a topic which is connected to three pretopics (A, B and C). Table 3 illustrates three different students' topic ratings.

If strict thresholds such as those shown in Table 3 are used, then student 1 would not be qualified to start the new topic, but student 2 would be. However, it is not clear that student 2 is any more qualified than student 1 to start the next topic. Therefore, we have decided not to use strict thresholds, but rather to use a more flexible method for determining a "ready" rating for a topic.

Table 3. Three student's rankings

Node	Link Type	Threshold Needed	Student 1	Student 2	Student 3
A	Prerequisite	0.8	0.75	0.81	0.30
B	Prerequisite	0.8	0.99	0.85	0.50
C	Related	0.5	0.99	0.51	0.90

4.1   Adjusting Weights

Each topic's learned score is used to determine the weight on the link between that topic and others in the semantic network. These link weights should take into account the link type because for each different link type, the level of mastery needed to move on in the curriculum may not be the same. For example, a student should demonstrate more knowledge on a strict prerequisite than on just a related topic.

Table 4. Link update rules

Link Type	Threshold needed	Learned value within x of threshold	Updated link value
Prerequisite	0.8	-0.10	0.8
		-0.30	0.6
		-0.50	0.4
		-0.70	0.2
Related	0.5	-0.10	0.7
		-0.25	0.4
		-0.35	0.2
Corequisite	0.65	-0.10	0.8
		-0.30	0.5
		-0.50	0.2
Remedial	0.8	-0.10	0.8
		-0.35	0.5
		-0.60	0.2

We have constructed rules that adjust the link weights to take into consideration the link types, as shown in Table 4. The weights are adjusted based on how close the learned score is to the threshold. If the pretopic's learned score is above the threshold, the adjusted link value is 1. After the conversions, the weights range from 0 to 1, inclusive. By using these kinds of scaling rules, we give more weight to different kinds of relationships. The remedial topic rules are used *only* if the remedial topics have in fact been taught. We are not punishing students who do not need remedial instruction.

4.2   Combining Weights

Once the weights of links are determined, we must then compute the ranking on the topic. This can simply be done by taking an average of the adjusted link weights of the pretopics of the topic in question.

For example, consider a topic that is linked to topics A, B and C, and consider the values for three students on these topics (Table 3). Student 1 is very close to the threshold for topic A and over the threshold for topics B and C. Student 2 is over the threshold for all three topics, and student 3 is under the threshold for topics A and B and over it for topic C. As we would expect, using the rules in Table 4, student 2 has the highest ranking $(1 = \frac{1.0+1.0+1.0}{3})$, followed by student 1 $(0.933 = \frac{0.8+1.0+1.0}{3})$, and finally student 3 $(0.667 = \frac{0.4+0.6+1.0}{3})$.

4.3   Selecting the Next Topic

In MANIC, the student has the option of letting the tutor choose the next topic or choosing it himself. First let us consider the case when the tutor chooses the topic. As we have said in the beginning of this section, topics designated for repetition have a higher priority over new topics to study. Thus if there are any topics to repeat, the one with the lowest "learned" value is chosen as the next topic to study. When a topic is chosen for repetition, it is possible that a remedial topic will be taught first before repeating the topic. This can occur if the "learned" value is less than 0.2 and the topic itself has been sufficiently reviewed by the student. In this case, simply studying the topic again will most likely not result in success.

If no topics need to be repeated, the tutor's goal becomes to guide the student forward through the curriculum. To fulfill this goal, the "next" topics from the topic just studied are evaluated to see if they are ready. If one or more topics have "ready" values over 0.7, the one with the highest value is chosen to be taught. If no such next topic exists, then the semantic net is recursively searched backwards from these next topics, looking for the topic with the highest "ready" value. This policy ensures that topics that can help the student move on to next topics will be taught next, and thus momentum through the curriculum will be preserved.

One flaw with this policy is that link types are not included in the decision to select the next topic. Is it more important to start a topic for which the last topic is a prerequisite, a corequisite, or just related? We will work with domain experts in order to incorporate link types into this decision.

If the student decides to choose the next topic, the tutor presents the topic net to the student, annotated with suggestions on which topics to repeat and/or which new topics to study. The student is informed of which topics have been mastered, which topics should be repeated, and which topics he is ready to start. For each of these topics, the student is given both the "ready" score and the "learned" scores which the tutor has calculated, as a guide for choosing his next topic. This is similar to the adaptive annotation technique used in ELM-ART [3] and Interbook [8].

5   How to Improve these Decisions

Many of the decisions made in MANIC are rather ad hoc, with numbers determined by domain experts and instructors. However, this is not a fault of MANIC alone; may systems rely on *a priori* formulas designed by instructors.

But we are not satisfied with this as a solution. We would like the system to adapt its rules to a more appropriate set by observing how students learn with MANIC. For this reason, we are using machine learning techniques to update the rules used in MANIC.

5.1 Timing Rules

The technique we are using to determine the optimal study time per page is currently applied to all users. However, some students may read slower than others, and thus their optimal time per page may be higher than others.

We would like a method that can determine, based on a student's quiz grades and how much time he has spent on each page, how much time he should spend on a given page. The tutor would then adjust the curve accordingly. If we can be successful at this, the tutor can better assess a student's studying habits.

5.2 Calculating "Ready" Values

The tables presented in Section 4.1 indicating the method for determining if a topic is ready to be studied contain numbers that are intuitive, but have not been proven to be correct. We would prefer numbers that have shown to be correct in practice.

One way to do this is to use a neural net to train the system's rules. With this technique, an expert would create a training set which would include topic networks, with each topic having both their "learned" values and their "ready" values set by the expert. The neural net could then train on these examples to create general rules that would apply to all students. The problem with this method is the amount of work required by an expert to create the training set.

Another technique would enable us to adjust the rules while students are using the system. The learning in this case would be unsupervised, as opposed to the previous technique. The reinforcement would come from observing how students use the system and how they perform on quizzes. For example, if the rules indicate that a student is ready for a topic, but that student does not perform well on a quiz on that topic, then the rules may have incorrectly predicted success, and should thus be updated.

6 Conclusions

In this paper, we have discussed how the student model is used to sequence the curriculum for a non-linear domain. This model is based on three factors: how well the student performs on quiz questions for a topic, how well the topic has been studied, and how much the topic has been reviewed. These individual scores are then combined into a general "learned" score for a topic. Then these learned scores are adjusted, based on link types. Finally, the adjusted values are combined to calculate how ready a student is for new topics to be presented.

The methods described in this paper simply rank the topics. We have not discussed how to teach a topic once it is chosen. Many of the decisions on how to teach (i.e. how to dynamically construct the content of pages) can be made based on the three individual topic scores. For example, a student who has poor quiz grades on a topic and who has not studied the topic for very long should be treated differently than a student with the same quiz grade but who spent 5 times as long studying. The second student should be presented with more background material and more basic information, to try to improve his comprehension.

Furthermore, if the student studies a topic again, the amount the student has reviewed it should influence how it is taught. Displaying the same content each time the student views the topic will not be effective, as it will not provide the student with new information. Each time a student reviews a topic, it should be taught in a different way than it was the last time it was studied.

In the future, we plan to investigate how machine learning techniques described in Section 5 can be used to improve the rules in MANIC. We will also investigate how to use link types when picking the next topic. Finally, we plan a full evaluation of the system to judge if the rules are adequate for the purpose of curriculum sequencing.

Acknowledgments

This work is supported in part by NSF/DARPA and Apple Computer Technology Reinvestment Award (CDA-9408607), by NSF awards (CDA-9502639 and NCR-9508274) and by a University of Massachusetts graduate fellowship. The authors would like to thank James Kurose, Rick Adrion, Jitendra Padhye, Gary Wallace, Jesse Steinberg, and Hu Imm Lee for their contributions to the development of MANIC.

References

1. Brusilovsky, P.: A Framework for Intelligent Knowledge Sequencing and Task Sequencing. In: Proceedings of Intelligent Tutoring Systems (1992) 499–506
2. Brusilovsky, P. and Schwarz, E.: User as Student: Towards an Adaptive Interface for Advanced Web-Based Applications. In: Jameson, A., Paris, C., and Tasso, C. (eds.): User Modeling: Proceedings of the Sixth International Conference, UM97. Springer-Verlag, New York (1997) 177–188
3. Brusilovsky, P., Schwarz, E., and Weber, G.: ELM-ART: An Intelligent Tutoring System on World Wide Web. In: Proceedings of Intelligent Tutoring Systems (1996) 261–269
4. Edwards, D.W. and Hardman, L.: Lost in Hyperspace: Cognitive Mapping and Navigation in a Hypertext Environment. Intellect Books, Oxford (1989)
5. Khuwaja, R., Desmarias, M., and Cheng, R.: Intelligent Guide: Combining User Knowledge Assessment with Pedagogical Guidance. In: Proceedings of Intelligent Tutoring Systems (1996) 225–233
6. Stern, M., Steinberg, J., Lee, H.I., Padhye, J., and Kurose, J.: MANIC: Multimedia Asynchronous Networked Individualized Courseware. In: Educational Media and Hypermedia (1997)
7. Stern, M. and Woolf, B.P. and Kurose, J. F.: Intelligence on the Web? In: Artificial Intelligence in Education (1997) 490–497
8. Weber, G. and Sprecht, M.: User Modeling and Adaptive Navigation Support in WWW-Based Tutoring Systems. In: Jameson, A., Paris, C., and Tasso, C. (eds.): User Modeling: Proceedings of the Sixth International Conference, UM97. Springer-Verlag, New York (1997) 289–300

Vincent, an Autonomous Pedagogical Agent for On-the-Job Training

Ana Paiva* & Isabel Machado**

*IST-Technical University of Lisbon and INESC- Rua Alves Redol 9, 1000 Lisboa
**INESC- Rua Alves Redol, 9, 1000 Lisboa
Emails: Ana.Paiva@inesc.pt & ima@minerva.inesc.pt

Abstract. Animated pedagogical agents are a promising new way to motivate learners that interact with learning environments. However, the majority of the animated agents lack in their autonomy from the learning environment, that is, most of the animated agents are fully embedded in their respective learning environments. In this paper we consider the autonomy of pedagogical agents in two ways: first its autonomy in relation to the control of a user and, and second, its autonomy in relation to the environment. We argue that, to achieve reusability, these two types of autonomy should be considered when developing animated pedagogical agents. To support this argument, we describe a Web-based pedagogical agent called Vincent that embeds these two types of autonomy. Vincent not only combines a set of sensors and actors establishing a communication through messages with several external learning environments, but also determines the best feedback to provide to the learners, having a set of visual and audio behaviors that correspond to emotional attitudes.

1 Introduction

Continuous life-long training is an essential need in any organization and is usually aimed at bringing the work of a trainee up to some criterion of performance, which is appropriate for doing the required job [6]. For logistic reasons such type of training can be more effectively achieved if performed independently from time and place, thus, at a distance. However, distance learning lacks some motivational factors achieved by the presence of the tutors' and the interaction of the other students in the classes. The need for motivational interactions, scaffolding examples, and contextualised feedback, is of furthermore importance for the performance results achieved by the trainee.

Therefore, when developing computer based environments for effectively training at a distance, the designers need to consider, not only the scenario the trainee will be emerged in, but also, how to provide sufficiently stimulating and motivating situations that will make the lack of the tutors and colleagues less important. Thus, for the particular case of the development of distant on-the-job training for footwear industry workers, we had to consider very carefully such motivation factor. To do that, we took the assumption that a synthetic personality, Vincent, whose job is to help the trainees in the learning process, motivating them along each session, would have a positive impact on the trainees. This impact, known as the *persona effect* [9] [10], has already been proved positive for school children.

The other aspect taken into account, when developing Vincent, was its autonomy. Not only its autonomy as an agent that acts based on its goals, but also its autonomy in relation to the environment (see [3] for a discussion on several types of autonomy). The goal was to build a software pedagogical agent that, instead of being fully embedded in the learning environment could be seen as an independent component that interacts with the environments and thus, that can be reused and explored for further learning environments. Since Vincent is a Web based agent, such autonomy becomes more important due to the exponential emergence of Web-based computer based learning applications [2], and this independence can lead to the reuse of Vincent in new systems and domains. As a software component, Vincent was implemented through the use of an architecture, where the sensors and actors establish the relation with the external environments (in this case learning environments) combined with the adoption of communication messages for the interaction between the agent and the environments.

In this paper we will describe the agent Vincent, its properties, architecture and independence from the learning environments, stressing the role played by Vincent as a personality that helps the trainees to overcome difficulties in the training situations.

This paper is organized as follows, first the architecture of a Web-based training system is presented, which combines a set of "micro"-learning environments. Then, the architecture of Vincent is defined and illustrated through some examples. This description is followed by a discussion on the relation between the micro-learning environments and Vincent so that the appropriate interaction is established with the trainee maintaining the autonomy and independence of Vincent. Finally some conclusions are drawn.

2   The TEMAI Family of Micro-Learning Environments

Vincent was originally used in a training system, called TEMAI, which covers the subject "Times and Procedures" taught by the CTC (Technological Shoe-making Center) as a professional training course for employees of diverse shoe-making factories. Although the Web is been extensively used as a mean to deliver computer-based training at a distance (see [2]), its application in industrial settings and on the job training is still yet quite rare. With TEMAI, we developed a highly interactive Web-based training system to be used by shoe-making factories workers.

The training system TEMAI is embedded in a framework provided by the IDEALS project, which is supported by the EEC *"Telematics Applications"* program. The major goal of IDEALS was to install and provide flexible, on-demand, telematics based distance learning and training services in the European market. The IDEALS scenario is composed by a group of Local Training Centers (LTC), spread in several countries and interconnected as a European-wide network, and offers a Modular Training System (MTS) through the World Wide Web (WWW) [8] (see Figure 1). The MTS consists of a client application, running at the trainee's workplace and powerful servers running at the LTCs. One of such servers is the MTS server, which allows the training courses to be provided to the trainees through the Web.

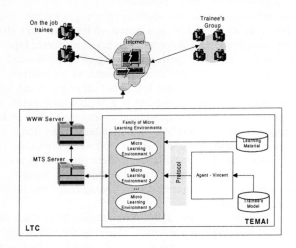

Fig. 1. The training scenario with TEMAI

The training scenarios provided by TEMAI were achieved through the use of what we call "micro-learning environments". These micro-learning environments are used for the construction of exercises allowing the trainee to repeat several exercises of the same type by using the same micro-learning environment (see Figure 2 for an example of a micro-learning environment used within one exercise). For each exercise, the feedback given to the trainee aims not only to encourage him but also to prevent the trainee to be discouraged by the result of his actions. Moreover, the learning process is adapted to the trainee's needs and that is achieved through the use of a probabilistic trainee model [4] kept in a database (as shown in Figure 1). Since TEMAI is embedded in the IDEALS framework, a set of services are also provided to the trainees such as email, audio connection with a tutor, a cafeteria for social interaction, etc.

As shown in Figure 1, the architecture of TEMAI contains a set of micro-learning environments, some learning material that is used for theoretical explanations or for the construction of the exercises, a database with the trainees' state of knowledge and the agent Vincent. There is a clear separation between the micro-learning environments and Vincent (see Figures 1 and 2), which can communicate in between.

In Figure 2 we illustrate one of the micro-learning environments which contains a notebook and a calculator used for the exercises resolution.

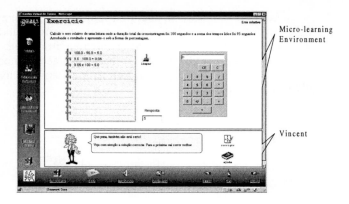

Fig. 2. TEMAI Exercise Example

3   Vincent: The Pedagogical Agent

Endowing interactive learning environments with lifelike characters has been a goal of several research teams for the last few years. The persona effect (see [9] and [10]) states the fact that the presence of a lifelike character in an interactive learning environment can have a positive effect on the trainee's perception of their learning experience. This positive impact has already been demonstrated by Herman the Bug [10], designed for middle school trainees and tested in American schools. In a similar way, the main goal of Vincent is to assist the trainee while solving the exercises, in order to help him in case of any difficulties and make sure the trainee is motivated to learn. Vincent provides interactivity and personalization to the system, giving to trainees the idea of having a friendly tutor that will help him. Since the population of trainees we are dealing with are factory workers, the personality chosen for Vincent is a likeable extrovert character, that helps the trainee when he is in trouble and gets enthusiastic when the trainee performs well. A study on the impact of different agent personalities for different trainees is presented in [7].

3.1 Vincent's architecture

Vincent can, as an autonomous agent, be seen as perceiving the environment (the micro-learning environments and the trainee) and acting on it, having the capability of making inferences about those perceptions, solving problems and determining what actions should he perform to reach his goals [14].

In view of the above definition the agent's architecture must reflect:
- how he perceives the environments the trainee acts upon;
- how he makes decisions; and
- how he acts from the inferences made.

In Figure 3 such architecture is illustrated, and, in a similar way to the actor-based architecture developed by Frasson et al. [5] Vincent contains a sensory and an action modules which handle the interface with the micro-learning environments. However, and in order to combine the animated character of Vincent, the action module is not only responsible for sending requests and information to the learning environments but also to establish an interface with the learner.

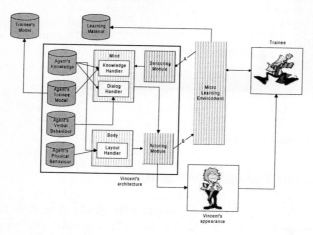

Fig. 3. Vincent's architecture

It is through the sensory module that Vincent performs the following tasks:
- to percept the beginning of the resolution of an exercise by the trainee;
- to percept a request for help;
- to percept when the trainee finishes the resolution of an exercise or when he gives up.

The sensory and action modules communicate with the Body and Mind modules, which are responsible for making inferences and deciding the best pedagogical actions to be performed by Vincent. The major goals of Vincent are: to assist the trainee while solving the exercises, to diagnose the mistakes made; to help him in case of any difficulties and to make sure the trainee is motivated to learn.

To achieve these goals, the behavior of Vincent is divided into two main types:
- **Cognitive behavior**, which is goal oriented and implies deciding what pedagogical actions to take for a particular situation (performed by the *mind* module). This behavior includes: (1) *pedagogical tasks* (such as: encourage the trainee to try to solve the exercise, in particular when he seems to be in a dead end; give hints to help the trainee solving the exercises; if necessary, provide the result of an exercise, taking into account the state of the trainee's motivation and knowledge; decide what is the appropriate feedback message to give to the trainee (if any); (2) *knowledge handling tasks* (such as: change the internal state; update the trainee's model, with the information acquired and inferred about the knowledge's state of the trainee, that is, change the probability of the trainee knowing a particular concept, after he had solved, correct or incorrectly, that

exercise; (3) *diagnostic tasks* which diagnose the mistakes made by the trainee taking into account what the trainee has achieved so far (cognitive diagnosis).
- **Physical behavior**, which include the visual and audio attitudes of Vincent.

To perform the necessary tasks, Vincent keeps an internal knowledge base which takes into account not only the information inferred from the current situation but also from all the activities taken by the trainee, hence, the trainee's model. Such model is kept separately from Vincent in a database that can be accessed by several applications as well as Vincent. Apart from the knowledge's state of the trainee, stored in the database (as a number representing the probability of the trainee knowing a certain topic), Vincent also uses the following information about the trainee's actions: the success reached by the trainee from the resolution of the latest exercises; the number of hints that were given to the trainee while he tried to solve that exercise; how many times the trainee tried to solve the exercise; the result achieved in the exercise and mistakes made by the trainee.

Finally, the *body* module is responsible for changing the agent's appearance, by making animations and simultaneously providing audio messages (chosen by the mind module). Vincent's attitudes change in compliance with the trainee's interactions and are supposed to encourage the trainee to carry on. At present, Vincent has four different animations (see Figure 4) which correspond to four emotional states. These animations are used for different situations combined with several (so far 80) dialogue utterances.

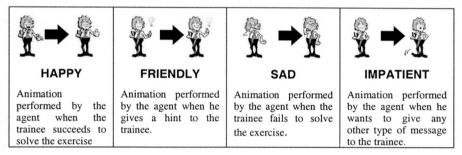

HAPPY	**FRIENDLY**	**SAD**	**IMPATIENT**
Animation performed by the agent when the trainee succeeds to solve the exercise	Animation performed by the agent when he gives a hint to the trainee.	Animation performed by the agent when the trainee fails to solve the exercise.	Animation performed by the agent when he wants to give any other type of message to the trainee.

Fig. 4. Vincent's attitudes

The changes of the attitudes emerge from the behavior of the agent and depend on several factors such as the model of the trainee, the time spent on the exercises, the result obtained by the trainee after solving an exercise, etc. These factors combined measure the "learner's performance" (see Figure 6 for a partial description of a partial state diagram for Vincent's behavior). In Figure 5 another of the micro-learning environments is shown. Such environment is used for students to fill the table in accordance with the exercise made, having also to mark the points in the graphics. As we can observe, the exercise is unsolved and, after waiting for the trainee to act for a while, Vincent becomes impatient. This change of state is expressed in the attitude shown under the form of an animation combined with an audio message.

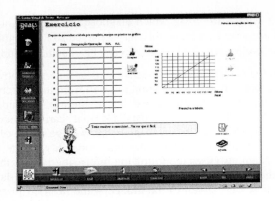

Fig. 5. Exercise – Vincent's attitude

3.2 The Autonomy of Vincent and its Communication with the Micro-learning Environments

According to [3], autonomy is a relational concept that can only be seen in relation to other entities. Therefore, the autonomy of a system must be defined in relation to other systems. To call an agent autonomous we must therefore state in relation to what it is autonomous. Using such relational aspect [3] distinguishes several types of autonomy:

- *Autonomy from the social context* (from other agents, including the user), and
- *Autonomy from the physical context* (from the environment).

The first notion of autonomy, and the more commonly used, considers that agents are autonomous if they act without direct human or other interventions (see [14]). Such type of autonomy can be found in pedagogical agents such as Steve (see [11]) and Herman the Bug.

The second type of autonomy (in the sense [3]) focuses on the agent relation with the environment and considers that an autonomous agent is the one that does not depend on the environment the agent is embedded in. This view of autonomy is contrasted with the notion of adaptation to the environment, that is, agents need to be able to adapt themselves to the changes in the environment. A known problem that considers the balance between these two notions is known as the Descartes problem: how can agent (or human) behavior be responsive and adapted to the environment but also "independent" from the external stimuli that come from that environment?

This second notion of autonomy, as an independence from the environment, is the one we are interested in discussing here. We argue that such property is important for pedagogical agents if we want to consider their reuse in different learning environments. This idea is also explored in [13] that name a tutor agent that meets this property as a "plug-in tutor". However, differently from the tutors presented in [13] and [10], Vincent combines its animated personality with such "plug-in facility".

Thus, with the aim of being reused, Vincent was constructed to act as an independent *component*. To do that we had to establish a communication between the "micro-learning environments" and Vincent. For such communication to be possible, and inspired in [12], a set of constraints were considered:

- The micro-learning environments are observable, i.e., the agent is able to know when its state is modified.
- The micro-learning environments allow agent manipulations, i.e., they have the capacity to fulfill the agent requests. The agent can ask the environment:
  - for information on the domain of the exercise;
  - for information to evaluate the trainees resolution;
  - to demo an exercise resolution (an action).
- The micro-learning environment can be to be questioned by the agent on the state of the environment indicators.

For example, since Vincent's behavior had to be implemented partially independent from the domain, to perform the necessary diagnosis of the trainees' mistakes, he needs to obtain information from the micro-learning environments. It is through such communication that Vincent acquires the domain specific knowledge necessary to perform its pedagogical actions.

The messages send by the agent to the micro-learning environments (indicated in Figure 3 as B) can ask for information (about the student or the status of the environment status) or request to perform actions in the environment (highlight some information or make a demo in the environment). On the other direction, the messages sent to the agent by the micro-environments (indicated as A in Figure 3) contain information concerning both the trainee's actions as well as details of the exercise, domain and status of the environment.

Order	From	To	Action	Description
1	MLE	Agent	Establish Connection	MLE searches for an agent.
2	Agent	MLE	Connection established	Agent registers the MLE as his MLE.
3	Agent	MLE	Ask for exercise information	Requires all information about the exercise: domain and error clues + formula for result calculation
4	MLE	Agent	Return exercise information	Provides all the information required
5	Agent	MLE	Ask for trainee's actions	Agent wants to know if the trainee has already tried to solve the exercise.
6	MLE	Agent	Inform no actions performed	MLE informs that the trainee hasn't tried to solve the exercise
7	Agent	Trainee	Perform an impatient animation + give standard clue	Performs an impatient animation and gives a standard clue.
8	Trainee	MLE	Start to solve the exercise	Trainee begins to solve the exercise.
9	Agent	MLE	Ask for trainee's action	Inquires if any action was performed by the trainee
10	MLE	Agent	Inform some actions	Trainee performed some actions
11	Trainee	Agent	Ask for clue	Trainee clicks the help button
12	Agent	Trainee	Perform a friendly animation + give domain clue	Performs a friendly animation and gives a domain clue
13	Trainee	Agent	Ask for correction	Trainee clicks the correction button
14	Agent	MLE	Ask for result	Ask for the result's value
15	MLE	Agent	Return the result	Return the result's value
16	Agent	Trainee	Perform a sad animation + give error clue	Evaluates the result: **If** exercise incorrect and first correction→ error clue + **else** exercise correct
17	Trainee	Agent	Ask for correction	Trainee clicks the correction button
18	Agent	MLE	Ask for result	Ask for the result's value
19	MLE	Agent	Return the result	Return the result's value
20	Agent	Trainee	Perform a sad animation + demo	Evaluates the result: **If** exercise incorrect and second correction → demo **else** exercise correct

Table 1. Sequence of messages established between the micro-learning environment, Vincent and the trainee.

Table 1 shows a sequence of messages established between the micro-learning environment, Vincent and the trainee (considering the scenario shown in Figure 2).

Finally, and to be adaptive to the trainee, Vincent's behavior depends not only on the states of the communication protocol (as illustrated in Figure 6) but also on the trainee's actions that lead to Vincent's attitudes. These two aspects cause Vincent's internal state to depend on both the communication with the micro-learning environment and on its internal the emotional state. This dependence is illustrated by Figure 6, which shows a partial state diagram for Vincent's behavior (initial phase of Vincent's behavior [4]).

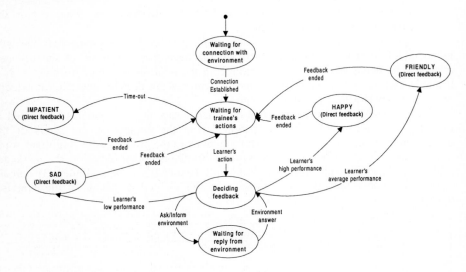

Fig. 6. Vincent's partial behavior (initial phase)

4   Conclusions

Supported by Vincent's architecture, behavior and properties, in this paper we present a new approach for building a Web based autonomous pedagogical agents aiming their reuse in other learning environments. In the approach presented here, and differently from other animated pedagogical personalities ([10], [11]), there is a clear separation between the micro-learning environments and the agent. This independence (seen as an "autonomy from the environment") is of furthermore importance for the future re-use of any of the components of the system.

Although Vincent is only be used in the TEMAI micro-environments' we are already exploring its use in a Physics Web-based intelligent tutoring system for first year university students.

Finally, the Web is been extensively used as a mean to deliver computer-based training at a distance, its application in industrial settings and on the job training is still yet quite rare. With TEMAI and Vincent, we achieved a highly interactive and personalized Web-based training system to be used by shoe-making factories workers.

5 Acknowledgements

This work is a collaboration among many people. We especially thank Sónia Falcão and Tiago Gafeira for developing the structure and basis of this project.

References

1. Assis, A., Santos, J & Paiva A.: Multiple Agents for Multiple Representations. In B. du Boulay and R. Mizoguchi (ed.): Artificial Intelligence in Education: Knowledge and Media in Learning Systems, IOS Press (1997).
2. Brusilovsky, P. et al.: Proceedings of the Workshop on Web based Learning Environments. In the AIED'97 Japan (1997).
3. Castelfranchi, C.: Guarantees for Autonomy in Cognitive Agent Architecture. In M. Wooldridge & N. Jennings (eds.): Intelligent Agents, Springer-Verlag (1995).
4. Falcao, S. & Gafeira, T.: TEMAI- a training system for times and procedures in industrial environments. Technical Report, INESC (1997).
5. Frasson, C., Mengelle, T., Aimeur, E. & Gouardères, G.: An Actor-Based Architecture for Intelligent Tutoring Systems. In C. Frasson, G. Gathier & A. Lesgold (ed.): Intelligent Tutoring Systems, Springer- Verlag (1997).
6. Herriott Watt University: The need for Computer Based Learning, Technical Report (1997).
7. Hietala, P. & Niemirepo, T.: Collaboration with Software Agents: What if the Learning Companion Agent Makes Errors?. In B. du Boulay and R. Mizoguchi (ed.): Artificial Intelligence in Education: Knowledge and Media in Learning Systems, IOS Press (1997).
8. The IDEALS Project Proposal, Technical Report, EEC (1996).
9. Lester, J., Converse, S., Kahler, S., Barlow, S., Stone, B. and Bhoga, R.: The Persona effect: Affective Impact of Animated Pedagogical Agents. In CHI'97 Electronic Publications (1997)
10. Lester, J., Converse, S., Stone, B., Kahler, S. and Barlow, S.: Animated Pedagogical Agents and Problem-Solving Effectiveness: A Large-Scale Empirical Evaluation. In B. du Boulay and R. Mizoguchi (ed.): Artificial Intelligence in Education: Knowledge and Media in Learning Systems, Ed., IOS Press (1997).
11. Rickel, J. & Johnson, L.: Integrating Pedagogical Capabilities in a Virtual Environment Agent. In W.L. Johnson & B. Hayes-Roth (ed.): Autonomous Agents'97, ACM Press (1997).
12. Ritter, S.: Communication, Cooperation and Competition among Multiple Tutor Agents. In B. du Boulay and R. Mizoguchi (ed.): Artificial Intelligence in Education: Knowledge and Media in Learning Systems, IOS Press (1997).
13. Ritter, S. & Koedinger, K.: Towards lightweight tutoring agents. In Proceedings of the Seventh World Conference on Artificial Intelligence in Education, AACE (1995).
14. Wooldridge, M. & N. Jennings: Agent Theories, Architectures, and Languages: A Survey. In M. Wooldridge & N. Jennings (eds.): Intelligent Agents, Springer-Verlag (1995).

LANCA : A Distance Learning Architecture Based on Networked Cognitive Agents

Claude Frasson[1], Louis Martin[1], Guy Gouardères[2], Esma Aïmeur[1]

[1] Université de Montréal, Département d'informatique et de recherche opérationnelle
2920 Chemin de la Tour, Montréal, H3C 3J7, Québec, Canada
[2] Université de Pau, IUT Informatique, Bayonne, France
Phone : 514-343 7019   Fax :   514-343 5834
Email : [frasson, martinl, gouarderes, aimeur]@iro.umontreal.ca

Abstract. The use of Internet as a general vehicle to support distance learning is a recent orientation of learning with multiple positive and negative consequences. The important disadvantage of such an approach is to forget the difference between information and knowledge, between consultation and pedagogy, leading to poor training as a consequence. The need of providing access to information to a larger number of people should not be realized to the detriment of the quality of training.

In this paper we first explain why and how ITS techniques using intelligent agents can be adapted to distance learning. We precise the main characteristics of these agents and their functions in a distributed environment. We then present the architecture of this environment with the role of the different intelligent agents. We show, on an example, how the agents interact with the learner and particularly how a pedagogical agent can switch to a new strategy according to the progression of the learner.

1. Introduction

The use of Internet as a general vehicle to support distance learning is a recent orientation of learning with multiple positive and negative consequences. The advantage is obvious: allow a large number of learners to access to a centralized databank of courses with the ease of Internet. The keen interest for this technology allows rapid access to information based on text, images, video, and applets, without any distinction between advertising information type and course content.

The important disadvantage of such an approach is to forget the difference between information and knowledge, between consultation and pedagogy, leading to poor training as a consequence. The most contradictory aspect is the responsibility of academic authorities which are often not aware of these drawbacks and which encourage the use of such a tool only for reducing training costs. The need of providing access to information to a larger number of people should not be realized to the detriment of the quality of training.

The danger with distance learning is to cut off the learner from the teacher who is no more aware of his/her difficulties, misunderstandings, and the level of knowledge integration and most of all, the motivation of the learner for continuing to acquire the elements of the course. In fact, the main problem encountered in distance learning institutions is the rate of dropping, due to the lack of motivation and help.

Another difficulty is to know the level of understanding of the learner in order to give him/her adapted assistance. This level can be known by submitting the learner to some questions or, even better, to exercises requiring several problem-solving steps. Finally, if distance learning allows learners to proceed at their own pace they cannot provide different strategies, which could be more efficient for discovering and acquiring new knowledge.

All the aspects mentioned above are in the field of Intelligent Tutoring Systems (ITS) but building such a system can be long, particularly if we intend to cover a wide variety of learners profiles. It is quite impossible to anticipate all the difficulties the learner will be faced with, and to adapt learning strategies for each case. We prefer to adopt a constructive approach, which also reflects the tendency in education and according to which knowledge should result from the **interaction** of the learner with his environment. Also, we think that all the questions and solutions related to the problems and given by a learner should serve to other learners, building a common and useful databank. To realize such an approach we have adopted to use *intelligent agents* able to detect the difficulties of the learner and to delegate specific help to be provided. A prototype has been set up and implemented (in Java) in a project, which intends to provide a convivial and efficient telelearning (CETL)[1]. Experimentation involving three countries (Canada, France, and Mexico) is under way.

In this paper we first explain why and how ITS techniques using intelligent agents can be adapted to distance learning. We specify the main characteristics of these agents and their functions in a distributed environment. We then present the architecture of this environment with the role of the different intelligent agents. We show, on an example, how the agents interact with the learner.

2. From ITS to agents based learning

In a recent work [1, 2] we have shown how and ITS architecture can be designed with *intelligent agents*. Various definitions and classifications have been given to intelligent agents, sometimes called software agents [3]. Agents can possess the following properties, depending of the degree of sophistication: reactivity, autonomy, collaborative behavior, knowledge level, temporal continuity, personality, adaptivity, mobility, instructability. A first classification formulated by [4] differentiated intelligent agents according to three parameters: *mobility*, *agency* and *intelligence*. Mobility is the degree to which agents travel through a network. Agency is the degree of autonomy (in terms of interactions) and authority given to an agent (at a minimum an agent can work asynchronously). Intelligence is the degree in which we can gradually deploy preferences, reasoning, planning and learning. At the limit of these last parameters, an agent can learn and adapt to its environment both in terms of objectives and resources available.

---

[1] This project is supported by the ATT foundation

More precisely, in [1] we have shown that ITS agents have to be *reactive* (basic property), *adaptive*, *instructable* and *cognitive*.

Adaptive agents [5] can adapt their perception of situations and modify their decisions by choosing new perceptual strategies, new reasoning methods or new meta-control strategy.

Instructable agents [6, 7] can dynamically receive instructions or new algorithms (for instance new pattern matching algorithms), and can learn or improve their learning according to an history of actions. These properties are very important for educational purposes but are still insufficient for ITS requirements. Indeed, we need to have agents which model human behavior in **learning situations** (cognitive agents).

The *cognitive* aspect of an agent relies upon its capability to learn and discover new facts or improve its knowledge for a better use. Learning can be achieved by a variety of methods (algorithms, i.e. Genetics Algorithms [8], and machine learning, iterative observations). In fact, the three main components of an ITS (the *student model*, the *knowledge model*, and the *pedagogical model*) can be built in the form of intelligent agents.

As indicated above, distance learning has positive and negative impacts.

- The **positive aspects** are of course to provide training and access to knowledge to a higher number of learners than in a conventional training situation (classroom, enterprise). Everybody who can have access to a computer and Internet is then connectable to a wide variety of courses in different sites, provided that these courses are open to the public. Another advantage compared to a book is that course material can benefit from a hypertext format with navigational facilities, images, video demonstration, frequently asked questions, and problems solved.
- The **negative aspects** result from the lack of feedback to the teacher who is no more aware of the understanding stage of the learner. This one is isolated and is likely to be lost and discouraged, a danger, which has been observed in several telelearning institutions. Learners problems are twofold: they can be lost in problem-solving situation if they don't know how to find a solution path to the problem (procedural knowledge or reasoning) or if they don't know some basic concepts or additional information which would be useful to partly guide them towards the solution.

We still think that distance learning should be based on intelligent agents able to operate independently both at a *local level* (close to the learner) and *through the Internet* in order to detect, among the learners in line, who can be associated to facilitate *collaborative learning*. However, four important differences exist with the problematic of ITS:

(1) due to the number of learners to control we need here to adopt a decentralized system with specific software assistants able, for instance, to:
- Reduce tutor implication in repetitive and long tasks such as preparing and giving lectures, correcting exercises, giving several times the same advice.
- Provide local assistance to the learner by detecting mistakes, misunderstandings.
- Provide access to other learners for discussing on a specific topic identified as a difficulty
- Provide multiple pedagogical strategies to gradually improve learning.

(2) The sophistication of agents should be reduced for the benefit of the part concerning the ability of discussion through the network.

(3) The criteria of mobility are crucial in the present situation.

(4) The different types of difficulties of the learners cannot be all determined in advance. The learners should dynamically and progressively build this help themselves.

3. A networked cognitive agents architecture

In addition to the criteria mentioned above, our agents are (1) social, (2) mobile, and (3) they possess feelings. Social agents are able to communicate with other agents for cooperative tasks [9] such as in games and economical environment based on the coordination of agents [10]. Mobile agents, as indicated above, have the ability to move to different sites. For instance, Sulla [11] is a filtering agent on the Web which visits several sites looking at the available information to build an index on the relevant information. Feeling agents aim to have a behavior similar to human.Taking into account these problems and the experience obtained from previous implementation of ITS, we have determined an architecture[2] (Fig. 1) including four networked cognitive agents [12]: a *pedagogical agent*, a *dialog agent*, a *negotiating agent*, and a *moderator agent*.

The pedagogical agent

The role of this agent is to supervise local learning. It provides the learner with a pedagogical strategy to help him/her in a problem-solving situation. It uses:

- a *learner model* initially resulting from requests addressed to the learner, and progressively updated and enriched. The learner model includes various information such as: personal identification, learning preferences, efficiency of specific pedagogical approaches or styles, performance reached in each course and degree of completion,
- a simple *ITS process* (*an analyzer*) that interprets the actions of the learner and compare them to a set of possible solutions,
- several *learning strategies* which can be activated by the pedagogical agent or by the learner.

The pedagogical agent detects the weakness of the learner using the analyzer, and the type of explanation, which fosters the discovery of the solution. It records the trace of the learner's actions in order to improve future help to this type of learner. Finally, it searches for the next pertinent lesson, controls the progress of the learner and, in case of drop of performance, it is able to change the learning strategy.

In the present version of our prototype we have incorporated four learning strategies which support the explanations: the *book*, the *tutor*, the *companion*, and the *troublemaker*. The book is a set of index to the course, related to the understanding of

---

[2] The LANCA architecture is patent pending

a specific concept. The tutor is a directive strategy in which the system gives answers or advice to the learners on request. The companion is a virtual peer able to discuss with the learner, giving some hints or asking questions to highlight the focus of attention of a particular point. The troublemaker derives from a strategy experimented in another project [13, 2]: it is a particular companion who unsettles the learner by proposing solutions which are sometimes truthful but other times erroneous. This tests the student's self-confidence and obliges him to defend his point of view, increasing his motivation.

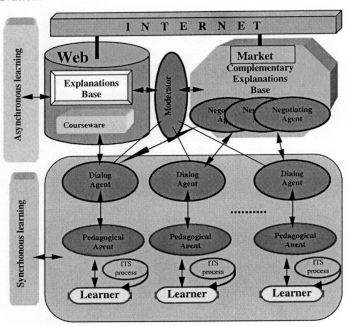

Fig. 1. Architecture of LANCA

The dialog agent

Most current dialog agents involve *service agents* (as Web spiders), which traverse the inter-linked documents making up the Web, constructing an index of the knowledge thus discovered [9]. The difficulty with relying solely upon service agents to find the relevance of an artifact to learner's objectives and profiles is that none of the service agents provide any persistence of state concerning the previous user activity nor analysis of interactions between learners.

The role of our dialog agent is to provide additional help and explanation to the learner particularly when the local explanation of the pedagogical agent is inadequate. It allows integration of different explanations within different communication modes selected according to the needs of user request. The main functions of this agent are the following:

• It manages individual and collective learning sessions adapted to the specified goals from the general courseware (Web) and the personalized needs and requirements of each learner profile.

- In *synchronous* mode it uses a direct chat-room for communicating with other learners via their Pedagogical Agents. Different points of view of the solution can be compared by the learners, contributing to solve conflicts between contradictory explanations using the local ITS.
- In *asynchronous* mode it accesses to a knowledge base through the web interface. The knowledge base includes the courseware, the *explanation base*, the different learner's profiles, and the learning strategies such as the book, the companion, the tutor, and the troublemaker.
- It addresses requests to the negotiating agent for additional help from other learners who might have resolved similar problems (we will see later the details of this principle).
- It asks all the participants to elaborate on which part of the explanation was decisive for reaching the solution.

According to the first goal, the dialog agent has to balance synchronized and unsynchronized communication with learners (or learning groups) with both open and private chat-rooms to support individual and collective learning. When looking at the activities to be performed by the pedagogical agent and the dialog agent we can distinguish *three levels of competence* in their architecture: a *reactive level* to support communications, a *strategic level* to plan and articulate (alternate) Direct and Indirect Learning (for the dialog agent) and the ITS guidance (for the pedagogical agent), a *cognitive level* to learn from the learner's behavior, share the initiative between the learner and his context and improve the agent's behavior (in planing and querying tasks, for instance).

The negotiating agent

Before examining this agent we consider an important point of our system with the improving of the explanations base. When a learner succeeds in an exercise or a task with a good performance he is asked by the dialog agent to be ready to explain again his solution. Then, the dialog agent **records** the explanation, which is stored in the *complementary explanation base, together with the learner profile*. The complementary explanation base is in a *market* of explanations available for the community of learners and managed by negotiating agents who will be able to "sell" them.

The role of the negotiating agent is based on the principle that additional helps are required for the learner who can asks the companion or somebody else on the Web to **discuss** (through email in that case) on a specific topic. However, the time a learner would spend in searching a suitable person would reduce the progression in the course and thus, a specific agent (negotiating agent), present **on the server** and representing the learner, is in charge of this task. The negotiation is based on a protocol that we cannot detail here for a question of available place. The market holds two types of information:

- complementary explanations recorded and transmitted by the dialog agent (available for asynchronous mode),
- information on learner's profiles attached to each negotiating agent. This one is able to know, for instance, that its learner has positively worked on these topics,

with such score, and is ready to give (synchronous mode) an explanation on request from a dialog agent of another learner. Then the proposition and cost of help can be discussed by all the negotiating agents with similar propositions in order to reach an agreement and send the explanation to the waiting dialog agent.

The moderator agent

The role of the moderator is to appreciate and improve the overall functioning of the LANCA system. It aims
- to select among the different explanations given to the learner which was finally efficient (using statistics), and thus updates the knowledge base of explanations using the selected explanation and the learner profile (a couple of index related to the type of learner and the type of positive explanation is created).
- to fix the price of the explanations for the negotiating agents,
- to decide which new explanation that is present in the complementary explanation base can be transferred into the explanations base to serve for further automatic explanations,

If some parts of the moderator can be done automatically (statistics and computation of explanation prices), it is not the case for the evaluation of the efficiency of the explanations. In a first version of our system this aspect if done by a human teacher.

4. An example implemented: the LANCA system

The following prototype of the CETL project illustrates how the agents are distributed. The system is implemented in Java, Javascript and Aglets [14], a mobile agent technology built on top of Java. It is currently experimented between the different partners of the project, in Canada, France, and Mexico.

The course we have developed is stored on the Web and deals with: **How to produce an HTML document?** It includes texts and images describing concepts and procedures attached to this topic, and also several types of exercises of increasing complexity.

Initially, all the agents are on the server. At the registration step, after some questions asked to the learner for obtaining a first version of the student model (profile), or the student model itself, the course is downloaded to the learner together with the pedagogical agent and the dialog agents. According to the characteristics of the learner model, some steps are recommended to the learner who has however the freedom to follow them or not. Fig. 2 shows the whole interface, including a problem-solving situation and a set of strategies brought dynamically by the pedagogical agent and including a tutor, a companion, a troublemaker, and the book, which is an index on the course.

In this figure the tutor is active (the window is enlarged) and tries to interact directly with the learner (in fact the interaction with the learner is not limited to the comment indicated in Fig. 2). Below this set of helps is the **contextual reasoning window**, a means for the learner to interact with the strategy on duty. The contents of this window vary according to the strategy and the actions of the learners in the exercises.

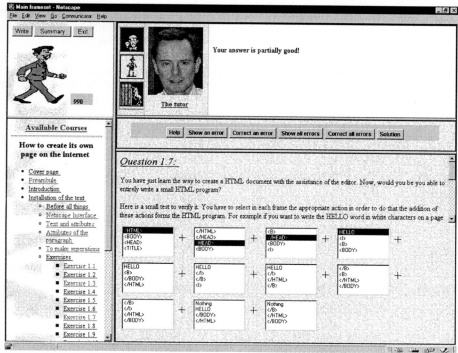

Fig. 2. Answer evaluated

The structure of the exercise allows having several traces and comparing them easily to possible solutions. After the answer of the learner the tutor can **show** him one error or all the errors of his solution, or **correct** one or all the errors, or finally obtain the solution. Of course, the score of the learner will be adjusted accordingly. If the results are inadequate, the pedagogical agent can decide to select a new strategy, for instance a companion (Fig. 3).

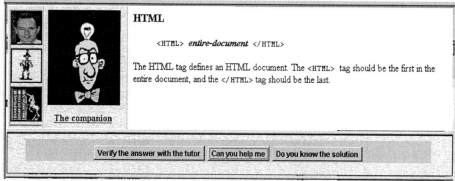

Fig. 3. Comments from a companion

The companion is a simulated learner with approximately the same knowledge level than the learner and who is able to give some parts of the solution or to provoke the principle of self-explanation. This last strategy forces the (good) learner to explain his solution to somebody else and unconsciously, to strengthen his own knowledge.

For learners having a better knowledge level the pedagogical agent can switch to a troublemaker (Fig. 4). This strategy which proved useful for good learners [13] forces them to justify their point of view and reduces their dissonance in case of contradictions.

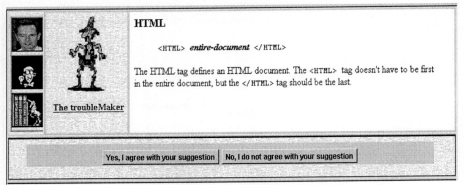

Fig. 4. Using the troublemaker

Here the learner can obtain justification and again choose the correct solution by finally consulting the tutor. However, each consultation (the companion, or the troublemaker, or anybody else on the network) can reduce the score. One important aspect that we cannot detail here for a question of space, is that if the learner looses points by requesting various helps, he can recover new points by providing an explanation which will be useful for another learner. The explanation will be stored in the complementary explanation base.

Conclusion

The architecture and the prototype presented in this article contribute to solve several aspects mentioned in distance learning. They reduce the tutor implication by sending intelligent agents close to the learner, able not only to assist him/her in exercises and concepts understanding but also to capture the learner profile. This profile is used by a pedagogical agent to select a suitable strategy and switch among different strategies at the local level. It is also used by the dialog agent who transfers the information to the negotiating agent in charge of finding adequate synchronous or asynchronous help. The advantage of intelligent (and particularly mobile) agents is to obtain from the local site an image of the learner profile and to allow negotiating agents to search for an adequate help on a market of explanations. Finally, the market is progressively enriched by various explanations, which transit via a complementary base in order to be evaluated and sent to the explanation base. The prototype is currently in experimentation between France, Canada and Mexico. The agents are effectively mobile and we are testing some performance transfer aspects due to the number of images to be sent and the unequal quality of transmission lines.

Acknowledgements

This project is supported by a grant from the ATT foundation that we thank. We want to thank Patrick Messier who has implemented several parts of the prototype, and particularly the analyzer, and who contributed to various fruitful discussions on the agents. Vincent Zemb, from University of Pau, implemented the course. Also, we want to acknowledge the other members of the project, Marc Kaltenbach, Ian Gecsei and Hugo Salguerro (form Mexico) who contributed to several parts of the architecture of the system.

References

1   Frasson, C., Mengelle, T., Aïmeur, E., Gouardères, G.: An Actor-based Architecture for Intelligent Tutoring Systems, ITS'96 Conference, Lecture Notes in Computer Science, No 1086, Springer Verlag, pp. 57-65, Montréal, june 1996

2   Frasson, C., Mengelle, T., Aïmeur, E.: Using Pedagogical Agents In a Multistrategic Intelligent Tutoring System, Workshop on Pedagogical agents in AI-ED 97, World Conference on Artificial Intelligence and Education, Japan, august, 1997

3   Bradshaw, J.,M.: Software agents. AAAI Press, The MIT Press, 1997

4   Gilbert, D., Aparicio, M., Atkinson, B., et al.: Intelligent Agent Strategy. Technical report, Research Triangle Park, IBM Corporation, 1995

5   Hayes-Roth, B.: An architecture for adaptive intelligent systems. Artificial Intelligence: special issue on agents and interactivity, (pp. 327-365), 1995

6   Altermann, R. and Zito-Wolf, R.: Agents, Habitats and Routine Behavior, Thirteen International Conference On Artificial Intelligence, 1993

7   Huffman, S.,: Instructable Autonomous Agents, Ph.D. Thesis, University of Michigan, Dept. of Electrical Engineering and Computer Science, 1994

8   Gouarderes, G.., Canut M.F., Sanchis E.: From Mutant to Learning Agents: Different Agents to Model Learning situations. 14th European Meeting on Cybernetics and Systems Research - EMCSR'98 - Vienna - Austria, Avril 1998

9   Sycara, K., Decker, K., Pannu, A.,Williamson, M., and Zeng., D.: Distributed Intelligent Agents. IEEE Expert, 1996

10 Eriksson, J., Finne, N.,. MarketSpace : an open agent-based market infrastructure. Master Thesis, Computing Science Department, Uppsala University, Sweden, 1997

11 Eichmann, D., Wu, J., Sulla, A.: User Agent for the Web. Technical report, Research Institute for Computing and Information Systems, University of Houston, 1994

12 Frasson, C., Aimeur, E., Gecsei, I., Gouarderes, G., Kaltenbach, M, Salguero, H. S.:Towards Convivial and Efficient Telelearning. ATT report, march, 1997

13 Aïmeur, E., Frasson, C.: Analyzing a New Learning Strategy according to different knowledge levels, Computer and Education, An International Journal, vol 27, no 2, 115-127, 1996

14 Veners, B.: Solve Real Problems with Aglets, a Type of Mobile Agent, JavaWorld, 1997

Poster Papers

The Extension of an Actor Language from Domain-Specific Requirements

Stefano.A. Cerri[1], Antonina Dattolo[2], Vincenzo Loia[2]

[1]Università di Milano, Italy, [2]Università di Salerno, Italy

This work reports about ongoing research that abstracts and generalizes a previously discussed, advanced software architecture, particularly suitable to represent crucial components of Intelligent Tutoring Systems. A distributed ITS framework is extended in terms of social categories of intelligent actors. The basic social entities are discussed, explaining how their activities are organized in a distributed environment performing concurrent computations. In order to highlight the benefits of the architecture, we describe in detail the diagnostic module, considered traditionally at the same time necessary for modeling the student's behaviour and therefore tune the dialogue to the user's needs, but also computationally too complex. We deepen our concerns and present our results showing how to enhance the available tools and languages for needs and problems specific to ITSs. Within this framework, we focused our attention on the design and implementation tools that become a priority: (a) because the underlying primitives imply a mental model of the virtual machine that has a non trivial influence with what the developer will privilege in her/his design and implementation, (b) because the primitives of the tool will eventually map or not onto the real technologies available, such as multiprocessors, interfaces with human agents and the network seen as a world-wide computer. Among the available software design tools, actor languages are certainly the most desirable ones to start with even if they are not easy to use.

A Classification System for Web-Based Training

Terrell N. Chandler, Craig Earon

Galaxy Scientific Corporation, Georgia, USA

This paper presents a six-level classification scheme for Web-Based Training covering features, course development, and course administration. After a brief background review of current trends in distributed training, a classification of Web-Based Training features is presented. Intelligent features such as intelligent tutoring and intelligent agents fall with-in the highest level of the classification scheme. The Smart Center is then described demonstrating the features of a level 4 Web-Based Training site. This is followed by a discussion of the administrative requirements for a Center. The classification schemes for course development standards and course administrative standards are presented within the scope of this discussion.

An Interactive Intelligent Tutoring System with Tutorials Generation and English-Malay Translation Abilities

Noornina Dahlan

University of Sheffield, England

This paper describes an Interactive Intelligent Tutoring System which enables a monolingual user to generate computer-based tutorials in Malay without any programming knowledge; serves as a multiple domain tutor to monolingual English users who are learning Malay; and the system also incorporates an English-Malay translation ability. Based on reviews of previous work, such features are usually incorporated separately in different systems and applications. Therefore, the primary goal of this paper is to describe a prototype of the system; and this paper also highlights the feasibility of integrating these features into one common platform. The implementation of the prototype will be based on paradigms of a flexible and interactive user interface, Intelligent Tutoring System and Natural Language Processing.

WinKE: A Pedagogic Tool for Teaching Logic and Reasoning

Marcello D'Agostino[1], Marco Mondadori[1], Ulrich Endriss[2],
Dov Gabbay[3], Jeremy Pitt[4]

[1]University of Ferrara, Italy, [2]Technical University
Berlin, Germany, [3]King's College London, UK, [4]Imperial College London, UK

WinKE is a new interactive theorem proving assistant based on the KE calculus, a refutation system which combines features from Smullyan's analytic tableaux and Gentzen's natural deduction. It has been developed to support teaching logic and reasoning to undergraduate students. The WinKE process of constructing a proof tree is as faithful as possible to the pen-and-paper procedure. Running under Windows 95, it is easy to use and visually satisfying. The WinKE system features an interactive interface via menus, dialogues, and graphic tools, on-and off-line proof-checking, and is completed by the option to automatically perform proofs (or parts of a proof), and to build up countermodels. User support is provided by bookkeeping facilities, hints, various "undo" utilities, and a detailed on-line help system. The system provides several files with example problems. New ones can be edited directly within WinKE. The interface consists of four windows: the main window providing menus and buttons for quick access to the most basic functions, the graphic window to display and manipulate KE proof trees, a viewer which displays a scaled-down view of the virtual drawing board, allowing to focus on a particular portion of it, and a tool box containing the graphic tools. The design of the interface is close to that of Windows standard software, which makes it very easy to learn how to use the system. WinKE is supportive of an introductory textbook on classical logic, but may also be used independently. References and further information about WinKE as well as the KE calculus can be found at the URL: http://dns.unife.it/dgm/WinKE/.

Thai Learning System on the WWW Using Natural Language Processing and ITS Evaluation

Suyada Dansuwan, Kikuko Nishina, Kanji Akahori

Tokyo Institute of Technology, Japan

Thai Learning System is the Computer Assisted Language Instruction designed to let learners learn the Thai word-order system and let them enter sentences correctly on the WWW. Natural Language Processing enables us to develop the system that parses free-form sentences by learners, finds errors, and gets the informative feedback of the results. Learners have more motivation to learn with this system. The System is the click-button model for learners to handle teaching materials on the WWW easily. Its interface is more the human-oriented. Parsers draw on computational lexicon and structure analyzer to recognize word forms. By utilizing the semantic features of noun phrase constituents, TLS can match to grammatical cases (agent, object, location, etc) and semantic features of the verb. When matching is successful, a noun phrase constituent is eliminated as unsuitable. The sentence is rejected and TLS display indicates the feedback of error processing.

Flexible ILE Development: Case Studies of an Agent-Based Software Engineering Approach

David Duncan[1], Paul Brna[2]

[1]Software Agent Technologies, Scotland, [2]University of Leeds, England

The problem of the increasing cost of constructing Intelligent Learning Environments (ILEs) has been highlighted by a number of researchers. Agent-based software engineering (Genesereth and Ketchpel 1994) has been proposed as the starting point for a methodology for constructing agent-based ILEs. We have developed a methodology, called Flexible ILEs via Agent Systems (FILEAS) which seeks to meet the requirements of researchers by supporting incomplete specification, changes to specification, removal of components, incorporation of existing software and extendibility of component use. A case study was conducted with good ecological validity designed to investigate the strengths and weaknesses of the FIILEAS methodology. The context adopted was the development of an ILE to investigate issues in learning by analogy, and the focus was upon building individual agents. Studies of the kind that have been presented here are rarely made but are needed both to support the research community and to help identify areas for further development of methodologies and tools. The results indicated that the FILEAS methodology would provide much of the flexibility required by ILE researchers. The process of incorporating software was straightforward. Those changes that were required were in the main not too expensive to make. Further work is outlined to carry out an extended case study to examine the methodology.

Declarative Mark-Up Languages as a Tool for Developing Educational Hypermedia

Baltasar Fernandez-Manjon, Antonio Navarro, Juan M. Cigarran, Alfredo Fernandez-Valmayor

Universidad Complutense de Madrid, Spain

Web ever-growing generalization and its use in educational settings is impelling the development of high-quality educational hypermedia applications. Hypermedia systems complexity has promoted the use of abstract hypermedia models to capture the most relevant characteristics of these systems. Current models put the stress on hypermedia components and its hyperlinking structure (e.g. Dexter Model), on-screen presentation (e.g. Amsterdam Model), or on the adaptation of the contents to specific users (e.g. adaptive hyperbooks). These models usually do not address specific aspects that are crucial in the design and maintenance of educational hypermedias, such as the structure and content of the individual components, the structural relations between them, and the conceptual model or educational strategy underlying the application. In our work, we use a descriptive specification, based on the Standard General Mark-up Language (SGML), to simplify the design, development and maintenance of educational hypermedia. We use an SGML based specification for modeling two main aspects of a hypermedia educational application: a) the organization and structure of the application contents, and b) a description that explicitly captures relevant design decisions about presentation and educational features. This kind of description, a "document type definition" in SGML terminology, provides clear and useful design documents that easily relate the work of designers and programmers partially achieving software and platform independence. Also, the specific information about contents simplifies its adaptation to individual users based on an explicit user model. This approach has been used in the development of a hypermedia system designed for teaching text comprehension in a foreign language.

Multi-Agent Based Pedagogical Games

Lucia M.M. Giraffa[1], Rosa M. Viccari[1], John Self[2]

[1]Informatics Institute, UK, [2]University of Leeds UK

MCOE (Multi-agent Co-operative Environment) is a game modelled using a *multi-agent system* architecture composed of a society of agents which work to achieve a common goal: to assist a student to fight against pollution resulting from foreign elements (polluters) and to maintain the equilibrium of the environment [GIR98]. The system has two kinds of agents: reactive (designed and implemented using the object-oriented approach) and cognitive (designed with a mental state approach using the agent model proposed by Móra et al. in [MOR 98]). The agent model used allows us to both formally define the cognitive agent and to execute them to verify the accuracy of the model. The elements of the tutoring agent architecture are: the tutor mental states, the knowledge about what tool to use with each specific foreign elements, the knowledge about energy levels of scenario elements, the rules to help it to decide what action should be taken according to changes of the students' mental states; and sensors for receiving data about the environment.

The SYSTEMIONS: Agents to Design Intelligent Tutoring Systems

Guy Gouarderes[1], C. M. Françoise Canut[2], Eric Sanchis[3]

[1]Université de Pau, France, [2]Université Paul Sabatier, France,
[3]UPS - IUT Rodez, France

Considering the designing steps of ITS and their necessary distributed representation of knowledge, our claim is to make the most of the full potential of new architectures for agents, both at engineering and theoretical levels. The inherent problems of the evolution, the dynamic acquisition and the emergence of knowledge in such systems are underlined and discussed. So, in this paper, a new conceptual scheme for architecturing cognitive agent is proposed based on determinism, rational actor and emergence. Another strong idea is that the term "cognitive agent" can be described as an agent that learns in the same sense in which people learns. So, focus is put both on learning protocols and mutant processes of a new model of agent is proposed: the Systemion.

An Intelligent Learning Environment for Data Modeling

Lynn Hall, Adrian Gordaon

University of Northumbria at Newcastle, UK

A major constraint on the more widespread development and deployment of ITSs lies in their complexity. Knowledge acquisition, knowledge encoding and system architecture design are difficult tasks. In addition, ITSs are often difficult if not impossible to adapt to new domains. Distributed AI offers a potential solution to this problem, offering the possibility of re-using software components. ERM-VLE (Entity Relationship Modelling - Virtual Learning Environment) is a learning environment for entity relationship modelling. The system is based around the MUD paradigm of text-based virtual reality, and exhibits many of the features associated with other intelligent learning environments. It requires learners to be active: they must navigate around in ERM-VLE, collaboratively constructing entity relationship models by manipulating a text-based scenario. The environment is complex. Although the objects to be found within the environment are simple, these objects can be manipulated in a large number of different ways. However, the complexity of the environment is mitigated by the fact that it is also highly structured. Additional support is provided to learners by populating the system with a collection of Intelligent Agents. Some of these agents are domain specific, providing interfaces and pedagogical support specific to the ER modelling task. Other agents are generic, supporting more general aspects of learning within a text-based virtual learning space, such as navigation, communication, and group formation. These generic agents would be re-usable in similar learning environments for domains other than ER modelling. A full postscript version of this paper can be found at http://computing.unn.ac.uk/~cmlh1/cadence/its98.ps

Lessons Learned in Developing Simulation-Based Expert Systems for Troubleshooting Training

Julie A. Jones, Robin Taber

Galaxy Scientific Corporation, Georgia, USA

Simulation-based expert systems have successfully been used in technical troubleshooting training systems for many years. There are two parts to a simulation-based expert system: the simulation and the advisor. The simulation contains knowledge about a technical system. The advisor is a logical inference engine that processes information in the simulation to determine where tests should be made to isolate a fault in the system. When simulation-based expert systems are used for training, they provide advice to students who need help isolating a simulated malfunction. Advances have been made in the sophistication of such simulation-based expert systems over time. However, with advances come tradeoffs for development. This poster will review the features of early, intermediate and recent simulation-based expert systems developed for technical training. This review provides the foundation for discussing some of the key issues involved in the development of such systems. The issues presented include those for both knowledge elicitation and knowledge representation. Sample SBES systems will be demonstrated.

Adult Learning and University Aviation Education

Merrill R. (Ron) Karp

Arizona State University, Arizona, USA

The current aviation arena involves highly complex, technically sophisticated aircraft operating in an increasingly dynamic flight and navigation environment. In order for commercial aviation students to be prepared for careers as pilots, they must undergo very comprehensive theoretical academic education. This study examines appropriate adult learning principles, learning style theory, and cooperative and collaborative learning techniques, and then suggests an integrated learning model to improve long-term retention and enhance application across a broad spectrum of new situations. An essential component of the integrated model is the use of personal computer based flight simulator programs and computer based learning programs to provide immediate application and hands-on learning. While this model focuses on a teaching strategy for theoretical aviation education, it also can be applied to technical education in any learning environment.

610

Integrating the CITS and CSCL Paradigms for the Design of an Effective Collaborative Learning System

Sofiane Labidi, Jeane Silva Ferreira

Federal University of Maranhão, Brazil

We present in this paper our work within the SHIECC project aiming the design and implementation of an effective cooperative learning system in the area of *Total Quality Control*. The proposed system SHIECC is an agent-based software package offering new opportunities in education by integrating collaborative learning with computer, multimedia, and network technologies. Our system has the advantage to provide real-time collaboration. The definition of SHIECC is the result of a lot of investigations of multiple related fields. Specific attention is given to the definition of new cooperative learning strategies and modeling cooperation. A big effort is then done for studying the different kinds of interaction during the different stages within a learning session. We present here the conceptual model of the system, a study on the collaborative learning strategies and our proposal for modeling cooperation between the related heterogeneous agents (humans and software) presenting different roles and characteristics.

Cognitive Diagnosis in ITS Using General Pedagogical Rules

Tang-Ho Le

Universite de Montreal, Canada

This paper presents an approach to cognitive diagnosis in a large-scale ITS. The key ideas are that knowledge is learned only in contexts, i.e. in relation with other knowledge, and that to understand new knowledge the learner has to generate links to old knowledge; if links cannot be generated, impasse occurs. We first describe the learning context in a session, and then summarize some theories about knowledge categorization, knowledge formation and reasoning. Based on these theories, four potential causes of theoretical learning impasses are identified, which are: incoherence of incoming knowledge, insufficient knowledge, misinterpretation of the learning context, and weakness in reasoning. According to the state of the learner's impasse (i.e. the first time, the second time, etc.), we do one of the two kinds of diagnosis as follow: (1) In the shallow diagnosis, the underlying capability category (which results from the content analysis) and the existing links with other capabilities (such as: deviation, generalization, aggregation, etc.) are first verified, and then appropriate didactic resources will be used to help the learner, (2) In the deep diagnosis, the learner's cognitive profile is analyzed to find out the prerequisite capabilities which are weakly acquired or acquired a long time ago; these capabilities are then added to the current plan or a recall resource is used respectively. In the weakness reasoning cases (i.e. prerequisite capabilities are well acquired), reasoning support resources will be used. These resources are created based on the fundamental logical reasoning modes that correspond to deduction, induction and abduction. In our ITS, general pedagogical rules are formulated according to the expertise mentioned above.

Coaching Software Skills on the Job: Laying the Groundwork

Frank Linton, Andy Charron, Debbie Joy

The MITRE Corporation, Massachusettes, USA

We describe the use of a recommender system to enable continuous knowledge acquisition and the individualized coaching of application software skills throughout an organization for an indefinite period of time. We present the results of a year-long naturalistic inquiry into one application's usage patterns based on logs of users' actions. We analyze the data to develop user models, individualized expert models, certainty factors, and instructional indicators. We show how this information could be used to tutor users. We observed sixteen users of Microsoft Word for up to one year. Of the commands used, usage frequencies varied by several orders of magnitude, for example, the ten most-frequently-used commands accounted for 80 percent of all use. The relative frequency of command occurrence is best described by a power curve. Surprisingly, our diverse group of users all tended to learn the same commands in the same sequence, and to use them with the same frequency on the job. Furthermore, the sequence of command acquisition corresponded to the commands' frequency of use. Learning opportunities then, are found at the edge of users' competence and in their areas of anomalous usage. A recommender system can present these learning opportunities to users via an Intelligent Tip mechanism, or present them a Skill Map for more active exploration and learning. With this approach, a group of users automatically creates an evolving set of individualized learning recommendations for each other, continuously becoming more competent at their software-based tasks.

The F-16 C Shop Maintenance Skills Tutor

Christopher Marsh

The MITRE Corporation, Texas, USA

The Air Force identified a need to improve troubleshooting skills for technicians performing flightline maintenance. These skills are normally taught through on-the-job training. This method is both time-consuming and manpower intensive, requiring years of apprenticeship training under experienced maintenance technicians. Today's highly reliable systems fail less often and thus provide fewer opportunities to train technicians on the complex problems. At the same time, the Air Force is combining maintenance specialties and reducing the number of technicians per aircraft. Thus, technicians must have broader knowledge and more general skills. In response to this need, the Human Systems Center at Brooks Air Force Base performed research in Cognitive Task Analysis (CTA) and Intelligent Tutoring Systems (ITS). The CTA research developed techniques to capture troubleshooting strategies used by experts and novices. The ITS research took the results of the CTA to provide a practice environment for working authentic troubleshooting problems while coaching the student with hints and feedback. The results of this research were the Basic Job Skills (BJS) tutors. Prototype BJS tutors showed significant gains in proficiency by novice technicians. The Program Office at the Human Systems Center refined the BJS technology developed in the laboratory and then produced a tutor for teaching technicians troubleshooting skills on F-16 communications systems (C Shop). This tutor is currently being used at Air National Guard wings and will be used as part of an advanced troubleshooting class for the Air Force.

Using Bayesian Networks to Build and Handle the Student Model in Exercise-Based Domains

E. Millán-Valldeperas, J.L. Pérez-de-la-Cruz, F. Triguero-Ruiz

Campus Universitario de Teatinos, Spain

Bayesian networks are a relatively new probabilistic framework for uncertain reasoning that has been object of intense research in the last years. As a consequence, many new algorithms and techniques have been developed. In this paper we suggest how these new techniques could be used to build and handle probabilistic student models that are embedded in Intelligent Tutoring Systems for a particular class of subject domains that we have called *exercise based domains*. First, we make a review of the theoretical background and related work. Then, several issues related to building probabilistic student models are addressed. Specifically, how to construct the bayesian network, and how approximate and goal oriented algorithms can be used to reduce the complexity in updating the student model whenever we want to evaluate a student's answer. Then, we discuss several applications of such student models: adaptive assessment by selecting the most informative item in terms of the sensitivity and specificity of the possible questions to ask, advancement in the curriculum, and intervention. Finally, the disadvantages of using probabilistic student models are presented together with possible ways to overcome them.

SERAC : A Multi-Agent System for the Evaluation and Revision of Knowledge in ITS

Sophie Millett, Guy Gouarderes

LIA - IUT de Bayonne, France

Conceiving an automatic evaluation method loaded in a ITS is the first objective of this paper. This method relies on Reviser Agent that permits knowledge re-engineering from a multi-criteria evaluation (computer, ergonomic...). The second objective is to realise a general approach; so the revision mechanism has to be independent from the evaluation agents that transmit the knowledge. To model this method, we followed three steps. In the first stage, we designed an operational ITS (experimental case) with the help of an object oriented method (from Shlaer and Mellor) and object programming environment (Level5). In the second step, we realised an evaluation of this ITS by human experts to know the malfunctions. In this goal, we used a user task analysis (GOMS method) and an evaluation criteria grid. In the last step, obtained knowledge permits to conceive our automatic evaluation method based on a Reviser Agent (with Scheme and Level5).

MIS-Tutor: An ITS in Support of IS Mastery Learning

Ali Montazemi, Feng Wang

McMaster University, Canada

Increasingly, intelligent tutoring systems (ITS) are expected to enhance learning and teaching processes. This expectation is based on the notion that, by supporting interactive instruction, ITS will encourage students to assume more responsibility for their own learning. ITS, it is argued, can help students learn the elementary and fundamental concepts on which courses are based, thereby freeing faculty to address the more complex and esoteric aspects of course content. Furthermore, ITS aids the assessment of learning more effectively and efficiently than traditional means and also improves feedback of the assessment into educational design. A basic MIS course covers a wide range of fundamental topics. Generally, one objective of the course is to ensure that students learn basic concepts, facts, and methodologies (i.e., students achieve mastery learning). The second objective is to enable students to discover the myriad of complexities that impact on the application of information technology in an organization. We have developed an ITS called MIS-Tutor (MIST) in support of student mastery learning. This enables more class-time to be devoted to the second objective of the course (i.e., student discovery). We have assessed the effectiveness of MIST in support of IS mastery learning over a span of four years with 1,328 students registered in a third-year B.Com.MIS course. Student performance increased from an average of 70% without MIST support (i.e., human tutor only) to an average of 90% when they were supported by MIST and human tutors.

Modeling the Cognitive Effects of Participative Learner Modeling

Rafael Morales, Helen Pain, Michael Ramscar

University of Edinburgh, Scotland

`Participative learner modelling' is characterised by the active and explicit participation of the learner in the modelling task. This definition encompasses several kinds of learner modelling processes, since it does not impose additional restrictions on the sort of the learner's goals, beliefs, or actions. The learner's participation can be of collaboration, negotiation, critique, validation, assessment, etc. The paper outlines an approach to modelling the effects that participative learner modelling may have on the learner's cognitive state. Modelling the learner in this context requires dealing with meta-cognitive issues, such as `awareness' and `reflection', and hence the framework for learner models presented is based on the Dormorbile meta-level conceptual architecture for learner models by John Self, plus a distinction between declarative and procedural encodings of knowledge. It provides a concrete interpretation of what awareness and reflection mean, and how they may be modelled. The stronger requirements imposed by humans on peer interaction make designing systems supporting participative learner modelling harder than designing their more traditional counterparts. We believe, however, that the rich knowledge organisation of a learner model based on the framework laid out in the paper may help to bring closer the ideal of participative learner modelling.

Cognitive Measures for Visual Concept Teaching with Intelligent Tutoring Systems

Andrey R. Pimentel, Alexandre I. Direne

Depto. de Inform'atica – UFPR, Brasil

This work presents a set of cognitive measures for describing radiological image databases. The measures allow an adequate choice of the next image to be presented to the learner when interacting with an ITS (Intelligent Tutoring System) shell that teaches about visual concepts. The goal is to minimise the learning time of radiological concepts and to permit the implementation of a wider variety of long-term, pedagogic strategies. The literature on concept teaching shows very few attempts to produce computer-based material, particularly on visual concept tutoring. Authoring environments have also been rare, showing that ITS for visual concepts are usually not easy to be re-programmed or expanded. We formalise general-purpose measures for dealing with ordering and complexity of image sequences based on the idea of cognitive load of images and teaching sessions. This load derives from the differences of capacities between novice and expert radiologists, which we summarise from the literature in three major dimensions: (1) visual recognition, (2) diagnostic and (3) verbal expressivity. A case study to exemplify the teaching of brain tumor diagnosis through CT-scans has been carried out with the local University Hospital. An implemented software tool, called SEQUENCE, supports part the authoring process for eliciting the cognitive measures and for setting ordering parameters. We are currently using the cognitive measures in ITS for a range of visual domains, as well as discussing their applicability in a significantly different class of domain, such as computer programming.

GURU: A Self-Extending Tutor Model for Pascal Programming

Rhodora L. Reyes, Ruzelle Apostol, Tiffany Kua, Rowena Mendoza,

Carlo Antonio Tan

De La Salle University, Philippines

One of the major components of an ITS is the tutor model. Its primary objective is instruction and remediation. This design is part of a full-blown ITS for Pascal and will focus on the design of the tutor models' domain knowledge and a learning algorithm for its extension. This tutor model is comprised of a set of strategies in teaching basic Pascal programming, a knowledge base consisting of rules specifying the best strategy to utilize, and an algorithm that determines which teaching action (rule) to be deployed given the goals of the system and the current state of the student model. It is usually the case that the domain knowledge is incomplete, thus making the tutor model incapable of using the instructional method appropriate to the learner-user. It is therefore necessary for an effective ITS to embody a learning algorithm, for it to be able to modify its knowledge base through generalization, specialization, and the application of rule probability theory, thereby extending its domain knowledge.

Computational Instructional Design for Construction of Adaptive Tutors in Real Time from Distributed Learning Objects

Kurt Rowley

Command Technologies, Texas, USA

With the advent of the WWW and recent interoperability and ontology initiatives, there are new possible approaches to generating real-time adaptive instruction by drawing from distributed interoperable learning object resources. In order to assemble adaptive tutoring systems appropriate to the needs of individual students, a computational form of instructional design has been developed with a generic instructional vocabulary. The vocabulary facilitates the automatic construction and management of tutoring environments from distributed interoperable components. A demonstration web-based ITS that generates individualized and adaptive instruction in English Composition through the use of an interoperable instructional vocabulary is used for illustration.

Influence of Didactic and Computational Constraints on ILE Design

Nicolas van Labeke[1], Josette Morinet-Lambert[2]

[1]Universite Henri Poincare – Nancy, France, [2]Vandoeuvre les Nancy, France

Our major research aim is to analyse the teachers' needs and to propose a design process taking into account teachers as users. The main characteristics of this project are: 1) the development of *Calques 3D*, a microworld for spatial geometry learning, 2) a pluri-disciplinary work, 3) a framework to lead the negotiation between the different actors, and 4) a production cycle based on a step-by-step upgrading of a prototype. The ILE design has underlined the need of negotiation between the involved partners, since it may result in didactic or computational transpositions of the teaching domain. On the one hand, teachers have often to adapt the domain they teach (e.g. filter, simplification, metaphor, etc.). On the other hand, the software engineers have to restrict the required implementation due to development constraints or ergonomic requirements. This work allows us to focus on three *design rules* induced by the need for maintaining teachers' agreement. First, it appears that any pedagogical choices, even accepted during the design process, could be mistrusted by user-teachers. It implies that an adequate set of *environments parameters* should be implemented in order to allow the teacher to adapt the software according to his usage. Secondly, we consider that each constraint or property added to the teaching domain by the software engineers, for computational reasons, have to be expressed explicitly (e.g. by enhancing graphical interface rules). Finally, adding software features requested by teachers could increase the environment complexity and thus reduce its conviviality. So it appears essential to simplify user-interface either permanently or during a particular task (e.g. by curbing ILEs).

Panels

Methodologies for Tutoring in Procedural Domains

Carol Redfield (Co-chair), Mei Technology Corporation/St. Mary's University
Ben Bell (Co-chair), Columbia University
Patricia Y. Hsieh, Mei Technology Corporation
Joseph Lamos, University Corporation for Atmospheric Research
R. Bowen Loftin, NASA Johnson Space Center
David Palumbo, University of Houston

There are more and more computer-based training and tutoring systems each year. In this panel, we will consider device or procedure-oriented instruction such as how to operate a piece of equipment, as opposed to conceptually-oriented instruction such as pure mathematics. We will be identifying what methodologies exist for developing tutors in these domains, what authoring systems and environments seem to support procedural tasks, and what commonalities exist between procedural tutors. For example, evaluating procedural tasks is often very different from evaluating conceptual knowledge. In many cases, procedural performance may have extreme consequences that should be taken into account during the training situation. Teaching someone how to do something certainly requires a different set of interface requirements than those required to teach the conceptual aspects of a domain. Also, we expect that there are parallel questions and issues in the difference between "education" in the traditional sense and "training" with hands-on applications. We will address the following questions: How is device training distinct from other types of training? What is common about device trainers? Are device trainers really useful - how do they get fielded successfully? How does CBT/ITS training compare to on-the-job or full simulation training? Each person on the panel will speak and there will be questions posed to the panel.

ITS Technologies in Virtual Environments: Can We Harness the Synergy?

Carol Horwitz (Chair), Command Technologies, Inc./AFRL
Jeff Rickel, USC Information Sciences Institute
Allen Munro, USC Behavioral Technology Laboratories
Craig Hall, Air Force Research Laboratory
Randy Stiles, Lockheed Martin Advanced Technology Center
Helen Gigley, Office of Naval Research

This panel will discuss the development and effective delivery of instructional content in virtual environments (VE), based on their practical experience in this arena. Individually, panelists represent research in simulation-based training, ITS authoring tools, intelligent agents, virtual environments, pedagogical principles, and training effectiveness. For the past few years, these panelists have teamed to develop collaborative software components to achieve effective, maintainable, and affordable VE-based learning environments. The Air Force Research Laboratory (AFRL) has used this maturing technology to field two VE-based training systems. The Virtual Environment Safe-for-Maintenance Tutor (VEST) is used by the 363rd Training Squadron at Sheppard AFB for F15-E weapons systems familiarization and procedural training. Additionally, the Advanced Virtual Adaptive Tutor for Air traffic control Readiness (AVATAR) is providing low-cost part-task training at the 81st Training Wing of the 334th Training Squadron at Keesler AFB. Currently, under the Virtual Environments for Training (VET) initiative funded by the Office of Naval Research (ONR), this collaborative effort has focused on applications to team training, a challenge to ITS technologies in and of itself. Embodied intelligent agents can be assigned to act as a team member or tutor a specific student. Both students and agents can manipulate objects in the virtual world. Primary issues for discussion include: collaboration of software components -- functionally and practically, realizing the potential of VE-based training systems: who, why and where, what aspects of VE hamper learning, what are the issues for conventional ITS architectures and instructional strategies in this new medium, and can we build cost-effective ITS/VE systems today?

Semantics and Pedagogy in Authoring Educational Technology: Confronting the Mismatch Between Researchers' Expectations and Users'

Benjamin Bell (Chair), Teachers College, Columbia University
Alex Kass, The Institute for the Learning Sciences, Northwestern University
M. David Merrill, Department of Instructional Technology, Utah State University
Tom Murray, Computer Science Department, University of Massachusetts
Brenda M. Wenzel, Mei Technology Corporation

As technological approaches to instruction become more widely available (and expected), developers have turned to authoring tools as a solution to two classic problems: (1) how can software be produced more easily and rapidly; (2) how can teacher practitioners and instructional designers create sophisticated, technology-enhanced curriculum materials without relying on computer programmers and researchers? Research in educational technology has led to constructivist and situated-inspired paradigms such as Anchored Instruction and Goal-Based Scenarios, yet few authoring tools have emerged that would help a designer create examples of these paradigms. Recently, however, researchers have been engaged in creating authoring environments that adhere to explicit models of instruction and that assist/cajole/coerce users in adhering to those models. One early result from these experiences has been the variation in the degree to which tool users are willing to adhere to the suggestions of the authoring tool. As a consequence, users create artifacts that may lie beyond the expectations of the tools' creators. Some issues to explore in this regard are: How can the semantics of a tool be effectively expressed? What is a "Goal"? A "Scenario"? A "Project"? How can we scaffold tool users in creating materials that both fit their needs and are aligned with the instructional models and goals of the creators of the tool? What should a tool "know" about instruction? It's domain? How flexible should a special-purpose tool be? How "special-purpose" should we be aiming for? How can we encourage the change of culture that is required to use tools for advanced educational technology? This symposium will address these and related issues in the context of specific tools and experiences with users engaged in software design with these tools. Presenters will describe individual authoring environments and share results and case studies arising from empirical trials. We expect that this symposium will begin to articulate principles that will help make tools for authoring educational software more attuned to the needs of its users and better able to convey their underlying semantics and pedagogy.

The Use of 'War Stories' in Intelligent Learning Environments

Benjamin Bell (Co-chair), Teachers College, Columbia University
Jan Hawkins (Co-chair), Educational Development Corporation
R. Bowen Loftin, University of Houston
Tom Carey, University of Waterloo
Alex Kass, Northwestern University

Stories occupy a central role in training and instruction, and in many professional contexts is an intrinsic element in the enculturation and education of novice practitioners. "War stories" are valuable pieces of information that experienced mentors share with trainees, and when appropriately selected, can illustrate a concept when the learner is in a position to best understand and apply that concept. Stories hold promise for instructional applications because: *Stories are contextual:* a story encapsulates ideas and concepts within a rich set of contextual cues that can render the ideas and concepts immediately accessible to the learner. *Stories show utility:* a story can not only illustrate a skill or concept, but also a set of conditions under which that skill or concept is appropriate (or inappropriate) to apply. *Stories are real:* abstractions are often difficult to master whereas a story is a real-life instantiation of some abstract set of principles. *Stories are memorable:* Human memory is organized experientially; we are more adept at logging away specific episodes than at memorizing facts and axioms. A story is more readily retained because it associates a set of concepts with a corresponding sequence of events. *Stories are provocative:* Much of human conversation entails telling stories. As we hear a story we naturally draw inferences, explain, pose questions, and get reminded of similar stories. *Stories are believable:* Reading a decontextualized explanation of a phenomenon is not nearly as convincing as hearing a credible mentor discuss first-hand knowledge of that phenomenon. Researchers have been developing technological approaches that introduce a story-telling factor into the teaching equation, both as primary features of the learner's task environment and as secondary resources to enrich the learning experience. The issues faced in this area of research include how to index stories such that they are available to a learner under some appropriate set of conditions, how to use stories to the best pedagogical advantage, and which combinations of technologies and media offer promise for large scale distribution of story-based instruction. These issues are being addressed in different ways by the panelists. The role that stories play varies among the represented projects from short accounts of first-hand encounters to complete immersion in scenarios generated from stories. The role of the learner varies from a viewer of multiple linked stories to a participant in them. The relationships among the stories vary from thematically-linked stories about discrete, unrelated events to stories about a single organization over time. And the technologies vary in response to the properties of each project, but in a way that can inform future efforts at integrating stories within computer-based learning environments.

Lessons Learned from Large-Scale Implementation of Adaptive Tutoring Systems: The Fundamental Skills Training Project

Kurt Rowley (Chair), Command Technologies
Kurt Steuck, US Air Force Research Laboratories
D'Anne Redmon, MacArthur High School
Todd Miller, Mei Technology Corporation

The panel will present a large-scale ITS implementation project that spanned seven years. The emphasis of the research was on the measurement and evaluation of tutor effectiveness, and lessons learned related to the design of tutoring systems and their integration with 9th grade classroom instruction. Three aspects of evaluation of tutoring systems will be discussed including design issues, implementation issues, and effectiveness issues. An introductory overview and summary of overall lessons learned from research with three tutors will also be presented. The panel will be informal and time will be allocated for comments and questions from the audience in-between and after the presentations. References and short papers on the tutors will be available.

Workshop I - Intelligent Tutoring Systems on the Web

Beverly P. Woolf and Mia K. Stern

University of Massachusetts, Massachusetts, USA

Educational material has begun to proliferate on the World Wide Web. However, most of these applications are rather simple, providing little interaction or customization for students. A promising approach to Web-based education is the use of intelligent Web-based systems. In this workshop, we investigate the application of intelligent tutoring systems on the Web and bring together researchers who have had and can share their experiences in developing Web-based intelligent tutoring systems. Some of the questions we address concern the specific problems and advantages of the Web for intelligent tutoring systems. In particular, we address topics such as:

- How can we increase interactivity on the Web?
- How can we overcome delays due to downloading?
- Where will the intelligence be located? On the client? The server? A mix of both?
- What kind of intelligence can be used? Can we build systems as smart as our standalone systems?
- What type of connectivity and communication is possible between intelligent systems?

Contributions from researchers in the following areas are sought:

- user modeling on the WWW
- user modeling reused across different WWW-based adaptive systems
- communication among different adaptive systems on the WWW
- Web-based collaborative learning
- evaluation of web-based educational methods
- future trends and perspectives

Workshop II - Pedagogical Agents

Claude Frasson[1] and Guy Gouarderes[2]

[1]Université de Montréal, Canada
[2]Université de Pau, France

This workshop will bring together researchers having different conception of the notion of an agent. It will particularly focus on how these notions have growth to reach the needs of Intelligent Tutoring Systems in student modeling, multi-agents learning environments, collaborative learning, animated agents, multi modal interfaces, personality, emotions and animated characters, empirical evaluation of agents-based environments. It will focus on the following questions.

- How do pedagogical agents contribute to learning?
- What are the advantages of agent oriented environments?
- How can they improve student-machine interactions?
- What roles can personality, emotions, behaviour, play in pedagogical agents?

Workshop III - Efficient ITS Development

Allen Munro[1] and Wouter R. Van Joolingen[2]

[1]University of Southern California, California, USA
[2]University of Twente, the Netherlands

This workshop will address theoretical and applied issues in the efficient development of intelligent tutoring systems. Approaches to efficient ITS development that will be covered include:

- Specialized ITS authoring systems
- ITS development with reusable components
- Domain content analysis or encoding systems
- ... and others

A number of questions will be addressed, including the following:

- Are efficiencies possible in ITS development?
- How much development time or cost can be saved using efficient ITS development techniques?
- Do reusable ITS components exist? Or are any being built?
- What tradeoffs must be made to achieve efficiency?
  - How narrowly must the domain of ITS topics be circumscribed in order to achieve efficiencies using various techniques?
  - What options must the ITS developer forgo in order to achieve efficiencies?

Theorists, practitioners, teachers, and students with an interest in efficient ITS development will participate in this workshop.

Workshop IV - The Failure of Cognitive Science in the Courseware Marketplace: If We're So Damned Smart, Why Aren't We Rich?

J. Wesley Regian

Air Force Research Laboratory, Texas, USA

The Clinton administration has made great efforts to promote a next-generation learning industry in the United States, but the goal has been elusive. The most visible results so far are 1) a plethora of expensive reports that restate subsets of the published literature on learning technology and reflect primarily the perspective of the various authors, 2) a variety of interesting media exercises (Net Day, Cyber Ed, etc.), and 3) a variety of large scale hardware-dissemination exercises (Tech Corps, TIIAP, Goals 2000). With the exception of a measurably improving internet infrastructure, all this activity has not brought us markedly closer to a commercially viable and self perpetuating next-generation learning industry. Why not? I believe we are already in possession of an important component for such an industry - a workable engineering discipline for the principled implementation of consistently effective courseware. I don't argue that research on the optimization of courseware should stop. Further advances in this area are certain to occur as research proceeds. What I am claiming is that a documented approach already exists for engineering courseware that roughly doubles the effectiveness of today's best mainstream courseware. Research on cognitively based tutoring systems, often called Intelligent Tutoring Systems, has generated the new approach. Development methods for current-generation ITSs are sufficiently mature to support routine application. These methods are derived directly from cognitive science, but the mainstream courseware industry has failed to adopt the methods. One reason for the failure is that we have failed to package our methods in a straightforwardly applicable manner. This workshop will collectively outline the general methods of CISD (Cognitive Instructional Systems Design) and develop a first-generation CISD standard to be published in an appropriate forum.

Exhibits (as of May 1998)

A Prototype for an Intelligent Tutoring System for Situation Awareness Training in Complex, Dynamic Environments
Ellen J. Bass, Samuel T. Ernst-Fortin
Search Technology

SQL-Tutor: An ITS for SQL programming
Tanja Mitrovic
University of Canterbury

The HISIDE ITS Authoring Tool: USAF's AIDA + MITT Writer
Carol L. Redfield, Cathy Connolly
Mei Technology Corporation, Galaxy Scientific

The Disciple Learning Agent Shell and a Disciple Test Generation Agent
Gheorghe Tecuci, Harry Keeling, Tomasz Dybala, Kathryn Wright, David Webster
George Mason University

MAESTRO: The Web-Based Writing Process Tutor
Melinda Crevoisier, Kurt Rowley
Command Technologies, Inc.

Intelligent Tutoring Systems in Real World settings: Instruction in Scientific Inquiry Skills (ISIS)
Thomas Meyer, Todd Miller, Jenifer Wheeler, Keith Brown, James Johnson, Marcia Cromley, Chris Allen, Kurt Steuck
Mei Technology Corporation, Air Force Research Laboratory (AFRL)

Virtual Reality for Training: Evaluating Knowledge Retention
Craig R. Hall, Randy J. Stiles, Carol D. Horwitz
Air Force Research Laboratory (AFRL), Lockheed Martin, Command Technologies

Supporting Reflective Learning Interactions in Component-based Collaborative Learning Environments
Dan Suthers
Learning Research and Development Center, University of Pittsburgh

Calques 3D: a Microworld for Spatial Geometry Learning
Nicolas Van Labeke
LORIA, Universiti Henri Poincari - Nancy I

Author Index

628

Springer
and the
environment

At Springer we firmly believe that an international science publisher has a special obligation to the environment, and our corporate policies consistently reflect this conviction.

We also expect our business partners – paper mills, printers, packaging manufacturers, etc. – to commit themselves to using materials and production processes that do not harm the environment. The paper in this book is made from low- or no-chlorine pulp and is acid free, in conformance with international standards for paper permanency.

Lecture Notes in Computer Science

For information about Vols. 1–1371

please contact your bookseller or Springer-Verlag